Chapters in the History of Social Legislation in the United States to 1860

BY

HENRY W. FARNAM

EDITED BY

CLIVE DAY

With an Introductory Note by

VICTOR S. CLARK

THE LAWBOOK EXCHANGE, LTD.
UNION, NEW JERSEY
2000

ISBN-13: 978-1-58477-054-1
ISBN-10: 1-58477-054-6

Third printing 2007

Printed in the United States of America on acid-free paper

THE LAWBOOK EXCHANGE, LTD.
33 Terminal Avenue
Clark, New Jersey 07066-1321

Please see our website for a selection of our other publications and fine facsimile reprints of classic works of legal history:
www.lawbookexchange.com

Library of Congress Cataloging-in-Publication Data

Farnam, Henry W. (Henry Walcott), 1853-1933.
Chapters in the history of social legislation in the United States to 1860 / by HenryW. Farnam ; edited by Clive Day ; with an introductory note by Victor S. Clark.
p. cm.
Originally published: Washington : Carnegie Institution of Washington, 1938. (Carnegie Institution of Washington publication ; 488).
Includes bibliographical references and index.
ISBN 1-58477-054-6 (cloth : alk. paper)
1. Social legislation--United States--HIstory. 2. United States--Economic conditions--To 1865. 3. United States-- Social conditions--To 1865. I. Day, Clive, 1871-1951. II. Titile.

KF3300.F3 2000
344.73-dc21 99-049362

Chapters in the History of Social Legislation in the United States to 1860

BY

HENRY W. FARNAM

EDITED BY

CLIVE DAY

With an Introductory Note by

VICTOR S. CLARK

PUBLISHED BY CARNEGIE INSTITUTION OF WASHINGTON

WASHINGTON, 1938

Carnegie Institution of Washington
Publication No. 488

Waverly Press
Baltimore, Md.

"The law of a nation is not only the expression of its character, but a main factor in its greatness."

—*James Bryce, University and Historical Addresses*

INTRODUCTORY NOTE

When the last century drew to a close, academic economics in America was still a relatively cloistered branch of learning. Since the time of Alexander Hamilton we had had economists of the forum and the market place who had been a force in shaping public policy. They had received a wider hearing at home and abroad than our economists of the chair. Occasionally one more versatile than the others, like Francis Walker, synthesized the experience of practical life for class room use. But traditions of the library rather than of the counting room, and principles elaborated in an atmosphere unsullied by extramural contacts, still characterized most economic instruction in our colleges.

Nevertheless a movement to relate this discipline of the schools with current problems was gathering headway. Students returning from German universities brought home new notions of economics as a dynamic science coordinating historical and contemporary data as they appear in new relations with the ceaseless evolution of society. This conception called for resources and apparatus far greater than did the introvert economics of the past. To provide these was the first task of the generation then entering active life. Fact-finding specialists were in demand. The age of monographs began.

Meanwhile a new force was making itself felt in science as a whole. This was endowed research. An awakening of business minds to the dependence of industrial progress and profits upon the advance of physical science doubtless prompted some monied men to found research institutions, but most of these donors were moved by a broader purpose. The first and most important independent endowment of this kind was the Carnegie Institution of Washington, which was incorporated under its present charter in 1904 to administer funds donated by Andrew Carnegie two years earlier. Its general object was stated in its articles of incorporation to be "to encourage, in the broadest and most liberal manner, investigation, research, and discovery, and the application of knowledge to the improvement of mankind."

In April, 1902, a few months after the establishment of the fund and before the Institution assumed its final form, a committee consisting of Carroll D. Wright, Henry W. Farnam and John Bates Clark, appointed by the trustees to prepare a plan for economic research, made its report. The first in the group of subjects which this committee recommended for investigation was, "social legislation of the States, which should be critically examined with reference to its results." Widened to include colonial and federal as well as state legislation, this became Professor Farnam's special field in the long labor of economic and social inquiry then initiated.

Following the submission of this report the Carnegie Institution established a Department of Economics and Sociology to promote the kind of research which the development of these studies demanded. The Department chose for investigation historical rather than contemporary aspects of our economic life, partly to keep the early stages of its work clear of controversial entanglements, but mainly because the first need of scholars seemed to be an orderly presentation of the past economic experience of the nation. Therefore it was decided to prepare a series of contributions to American economic history. The present volume concludes this series.

During the third of a century since this work began the personnel and organization of the Department have changed. In 1916 it ceased to be part of the Carnegie Institution, though still assisted with funds originally donated by that body and publishing most of its contributions under the Institution's auspices. That year, for reasons explained later, the division heads of the Department reorganized as an independent Board of Research Associates in American Economic History. Professor Farnam, who had been the first secretary of the Department and after Carroll D. Wright's death in 1909 succeeded him as chairman, became chairman of the new Board and personally financed a major part of its activities.

For the twelve years that the original Department was a division of the Carnegie Institution it applied its funds largely to aiding the researches of advanced students in special fields of American economic history. Wholly or partly through this encouragement more than two hundred articles and monographs were prepared, about half of which eventually appeared in print. Indexes of economic materials in the documents of thirteen States were compiled and published. Finally, a *History of Domestic and Foreign Commerce of the United States* and the first volume of a *History of Manufactures in the United States* were completed and issued as publications of the Institution.

When the Board of Research Associates took up its task in 1917 it decided to concentrate its resources upon the preparation of major contributions like the two last mentioned. Therefore aid to student researchers largely ceased and the index of economic materials in State documents was discontinued. The resulting list of histories, including those wholly or partly written under the auspices of the old Department, stands at date as follows: *History of Domestic and Foreign Commerce of the United States*, by Emory R. Johnson and collaborators, in two volumes; *History of Manufactures in the United States*, by Victor S. Clark, in three volumes; *History of Transportation in the United States before 1860*, prepared under the direction of Balthasar H. Meyer; *History of Labour in the United States*, by John R. Commons and associates, in four volumes; *History of Agriculture in the Northern United States, 1620–1860*, by Percy W. Bidwell and John I. Falconer; *History of Agriculture in the Southern United States to 1860*, by Lewis C. Gray, in two volumes; and *Chapters in the History of Social Legislation in the United States to 1860*, by Henry W. Farnam, which constitutes the present volume.

While Professor Farnam thus appears as the author of only one of the fourteen volumes issued, he took a real and effective part as editorial adviser and critic in preparing most of the others. Indeed it was his devotion to this work that compelled him to leave his own contribution to the series unfinished; for he gave time and labor to these inconspicuous but indispensable duties comparable in the aggregate with that which the other authors gave to their histories. This service began when he became chairman of the original Department in 1909 and it was rendered without remission for the remaining twenty-five years of his life. Indeed the continuance after 1917 of the program recommended by the committee of which he was a member in 1902 was due to his personal labor as well as his financial aid. In a just sense he was the creator of the Contributions to American Economic History and they are a monument to him.

It is fitting therefore that this introduction—or valedictory—should contain a word about the man himself. He inherited an adequate but not onerous fortune, which in his case eased the way to scholarly attainment and which he administered throughout his life in the spirit of a public trust. Prior to entering Yale College he had spent four years at Heidelberg and Weimar and had acquired an intimate acquaintance with European life and languages. After graduating at Yale and taking one year of advanced courses at the same institution he again went abroad, studying at Berlin, Goettingen and Strassburg, and receiving his doctorate *magna cum laude* at the last of these institutions. Upon his return to America he taught Latin at Yale for two years. From 1880 until 1918, when he became emeritus, he was professor of political economy or professor of economics, as the titles changed, at Yale University. In 1881 he succeeded Francis A. Walker in the chair of economics at Sheffield Scientific School and for twenty-two years thereafter occupied this post as well as his university position. His association with German scholarship, to which he was introduced during its liberal era, continued during most of his active academic life. He published three monographs, including his thesis for the doctorate, in the language of Germany and he was at the point of beginning a course of lectures as Roosevelt Professor at the University of Berlin when the World War abruptly ended such intellectual exchanges between America and that country. He acquired from his student discipline abroad and from frequently renewed contacts with the best phases of academic thought in Europe, high standards of research and a breadth and depth of scholarly interest that made him an exacting editor and through him influenced the program of the Board he headed.

These contacts and antecedents explain in part the strong hold that social legislation took upon Professor Farnam's thought. He had resided in Germany during the period of the anti-Socialist law, when every avenue of organized self help was closed to the working people, and had followed with deep interest Bismarck's policy of counteracting their resistance to political repression by government measures to better their material condition. During the first years of his economic teaching at Yale, Germany established accident, invalidity and old age insurance, regulated the employment of women and children, and inaugurated the enlightened paternalism toward labor that characterized the remaining period of the empire. He admired the results, though he did not approve the method and purpose of this policy. It probably fortified in him the spirit of Yankee localism which can be read between the lines of the present volume. He was not a socialist, because he distrusted doctrinaire programs. In 1916, in his report as Chairman of the Department of Economics and Sociology to the Trustees of the Carnegie Institution, he wrote in this connection: "Any author who undertakes historical or scientific research under the bias of a philosophical theory can hardly fail to make such a presentation of facts that they will confirm his theory." A similar conviction made his attitude towards schemes for social betterment, practical and experimental. It was logical that he should have been a founder of the American Association for Labor Legislation and should have been its president during the first four years of its existence. Indeed civic duties of this kind occupied a large place in his life. He was an active member of many organizations to promote better government and better conditions for the forgotten and half-forgotten classes. In a word his interest in social legislation was not exclusively intellectual and scholarly, nor was it on the other hand strongly emotional; it was the well balanced expression of an enlightened and sympathetic social instinct.

A former pupil and a lifelong friend and academic associate, Professor Irving Fisher, wrote of him shortly after his death:

> "Primarily Henry Farnam was a philanthropist. One could scarcely mention an activity of his which was not fundamentally altruistic. It must have been largely his altruistic and conscientious spirit which led him to choose economics as a profession. Certain it is that his thorough training in economics fitted him to be an inspiring teacher, a wise giver, and a supremely effective participant in the discussion of all great public questions. I first knew him, over forty years ago, as a teacher in the theory and practice of taxation—the most interesting teacher I ever had in that supposedly dry subject. A little later I heard him speak at a political rally in 1892 in favor of a lower tariff. I remember his saying, 'People ask why we economists have gone over to the Democratic party. We have not. That party has come over to us!' In politics, as in every department of life, he was an independent. His only partisanship was based not on prejudice, tradition or class consciousness but on principle. He invariably stood for what seemed to him fundamentally right as representing his reasoned conclusions reached by careful study. Like Huxley's ideal scientist he had only one sort of fanaticism—fanaticism for the truth. He had a great and warm heart but he never allowed it to deceive his unusually clear head."

A man of this type, living in a university center and in a city and State where he was by inherited position and predilection very much a functioning part of the community, had numerous public and quasi-public calls upon his time and energy. The distraction of many useful things to do made impossible the continuous literary labor of the detached student. Professor Farnam did nevertheless accomplish a fairly large amount of writing as well as of executive literary work. He was for six years, in addition to other duties, president of a morning daily in New Haven, and for nine years he was editor of the *Yale Review*. His contributions to periodicals were scholarly and not infrequent. He published a book on *Shakespeare's Economics* and a collection of papers entitled *The Economic Utilization of History*.

The present volume, and several chapters of a second volume upon the history of social legislation in America between 1860 and the World War, were virtually completed when Professor Farnam died. One of his Yale colleagues, Professor Clive Day, has generously performed for this manuscript the many services of final preparation which he himself earlier bestowed upon previous contributions of the series.

Organized economic research has changed greatly in ideals and methods during the third of a century since the Carnegie Institution pioneered this kind of coöperative inquiry in America. When Andrew Carnegie gave then unprecedented sums to aid scientific investigation, the academic world welcomed the benefactions with a satisfaction tempered with some misgiving. Might not such endowments tend to specialize research in institutions separate from the universities and to limit the latter to routine pedagogic activities devoid of the stimulus and inspiration of exploring the unknown? The conception of universities as exclusively teaching institutions was still dominant in the public mind. Those who were struggling to make them nurseries of new knowledge as well as repositories of old knowledge were alarmed lest their labors receive a setback. They therefore urged that the Carnegie funds should be used to subsidize research by existing university agencies.

Carroll D. Wright, the first head of the Department of Economics and Sociology, was also a trustee of the Carnegie Institution. Although he was an administrative official without close academic ties and interests he believed it wise "to farm out research to those already in the business." Moreover the first Department of Labor at Washington, which he had directed since its inception in 1884 and which was one of the first research bureaus of the Federal Government, had little immediate contact with universities nor indeed was encouraged by the circumstances that surrounded it to cultivate an academic atmosphere; but its administrative precedents rather favored the dispersion of activities implied in subsidizing university workers. Meanwhile Professor Farnam, who was associated with Carroll D. Wright in organizing the Department of Economics and Sociology, had academic interests much at heart, and was familiar with the German professorial practice of conducting research with the aid of satellite students.

For these and other reasons the original Department of Economics and Sociology consisted of twelve divisions, each covering an important economic field, most of which were headed by university professors who received no personal remuneration and who were expected to direct their investigations from their study chairs, with the assistance of students and instructors whom they subsidized to gather and organize materials. This scheme did not prove successful, partly because American universities were not yet sufficiently research institutions. Their faculties were too heavily loaded with teaching and administrative duties to carry through promptly and efficiently projects like those proposed. Students were helped to write the theses and monographs already mentioned, but most of these lacked qualities befitting the products of a great research body. Eventually the Carnegie trustees, who had before them the example of better organized departments making notable contributions to scientific knowledge, became dissatisfied. They wished to give the Department a salaried staff like other important sections of the Institution and to place it in charge of a full-time director; and they desired Professor Farnam, who was then chairman of the Department, to accept the latter post.

When Professor Farnam decided that in justice to more imperative duties he could not assume this responsibility, it seemed for a time that the work might be dropped as an unsuccessful experiment in research organization. But for his resourcefulness and financial aid that probably would have happened. With the consent of the Carnegie trustees and the assent of the Department collaborators, however, he devised and carried through the reorganization that made it possible to complete much of the program outlined fifteen years before.

The new Board consisted of the division heads of the old Department, whose functions remained essentially unchanged. But it approved henceforth only well-matured major projects and financed them on a system of payment by results. The idea that research specialists should be remunerated for their work in the same way as teachers was not yet recognized in the case of economics although it was already accepted in the field of natural science. To that extent the Board was limited by its antecedents and resources to the practice of an older generation. Nevertheless an effort was made, as far as funds permitted, to apply the principle that the researcher is worthy of his hire and to get away from the assumption that original investigation is a pursuit so gratifying intellectually that it needs no material compensation.

Therefore this series of contributions represents a chapter in the history of research technique in America. Since it was begun, more amply endowed and more efficiently organized bureaus and institutions have taken up in a much larger way the tasks to which its planners addressed themselves thirty-three years ago. Nevertheless these have left a worthy record of their labors. And as in many such instances, whatever they have accomplished was made possible largely by the devotion and sacrifice of one man.

May, 1938 VICTOR S. CLARK

PREFACE

Professor Henry W. Farnam spent some twenty years of his life gathering the material for the *History of Social Legislation in the United States*. Before his illness prevented him from carrying his plan to completion, he had assembled most of the data, had prepared chapter outlines, and had written the major part of the history down to 1910. When the question of publishing the manuscript arose after his death in 1933, it was felt that the events leading up to and following the World War and the depression had so changed the concept and ideals of social legislation that it would be unwise to carry the history beyond 1860. The breadth of field even in the earlier period made it impossible to include all phases of social legislation, and the student will miss many subjects, such as poor relief, immigration, etc., to which Professor Farnam had given much thought, but which he had not had time to treat adequately in his manuscript. It was felt that a thorough treatment of these would delay the book indefinitely, and it has therefore been decided to publish the volume as it now stands, in the hope that future scholars will benefit by it and be inspired to continue and complete the study.

Among the materials used in the preparation of the manuscript should be included certain monographs written for this study under grants from the Carnegie Institution of Washington. Professor Farnam planned, supervised and edited these monographs, and they form the ground work of the history of social legislation as shaped in this volume. The following were published:

J. Lynn Barnard, *Factory Legislation in Pennsylvania; Its History and Administration.* Publications of the University of Pennsylvania, Series in Political Economy and Public Law, No. 19. Philadelphia, 1907.

E. H. Downey. *History of Labor Legislation in Iowa.* Iowa Economic History Series, State Historical Society of Iowa. Edited by Benjamin F. Shambaugh. Iowa City, 1910.

Lucile Eaves. *A History of California Labor Legislation,* with an Introductory Sketch of the San Francisco Labor Movement. University of California Publications in Economics, II. Berkeley, Calif., 1910.

Alba M. Edwards. *The Labor Legislation of Connecticut.* American Economic Association, 3d series, VIII, No. 3. New York, 1907.

Fred Rogers Fairchild. *The Factory Legislation of the State of New York.* American Economic Association, 3d series, VI, No. 4. New York, 1905.

Arthur Sargent Field. *The Child Labor Policy of New Jersey.* American Economic Association, 3d series, XI, No. 3. Cambridge, Mass., 1910.

George Gorham Groat. *Trade Unions and the Law in New York.* Columbia University Studies in History, Economics and Public Law, XIX, No. 3. New York, 1905.

Reuben McKitrick. *The Public Land System of Texas, 1823–1910.* Bulletin of the University of Texas, Economics and Political Science Series, IX, No. 1. Madison, Wis., 1918.

John Ker Towles. *Factory Legislation of Rhode Island.* American Economic Association, 3d series, IX, No. 3. Princeton, 1908.

A complete list is given here, for the information of those who may wish to consult them in the future, of the monographs which are still in manuscript form.

Charles B. Austin. The Labor Legislation of Indiana. 1909.
W. L. Bailey. Mechanics' Lien Laws of the United States. 1910.
F. Spencer Baldwin. Recent Labor Legislation in Massachusetts. 1909.
S. E. W. Bedford. The Labor Legislation of Kansas. 1909.
John L. Coulter. Educational Land Grants of North Dakota. 1909.

Thomas Crafer. Trade Unions and the Law in Wisconsin. 1909.
———. The Administration of Public Poor Relief in Wisconsin. 1908.
Clive Day. Social Legislation of the Colonies. 1909.
G. W. Dyer. The Origin of the Population of the South. 1908.
———. The Mountain Whites and Social Legislation. 1908.
Alba M. Edwards. Federal Legislation for the Protection of American Seamen. 1907.
———. The Marine Hospital Service of the United States. 1909.
James Edward Hagerty and Beatrice H. Sheets. The History of the Poor Law of Ohio. 1910.
Nathan T. Isaacs. The Mining Laws of Ohio, Indiana, and Illinois. 1908.
Carl E. Parry. The Labor Legislation of Michigan. 1909.
D. L. Peacock. The Mining Laws of the Southern States. 1909.
T. J. Riley. The Poor Law and Public Relief in Missouri. 1909.
J. H. Underwood. Homestead and Exemption Laws in the Northern States. 1909.

The following chapters of the present volume are under special obligations to these monographs: Chapters IV and V on Land Tenure are based on the monograph written by the editor; and Chapter VII on Fair Trade and Chapter VIII on The Public Food Supply are taken substantially unchanged from that work. The part of Chapter X on Land Policy which deals with the Spanish land laws is from the monograph *The Public Land System of Texas*, by Reuben McKitrick. Chapter XI, Laws Regulating the Relation of Debtor and Creditor, rests in part on the monograph by J. Harding Underwood. Chapters XVIII and XIX, dealing with The Insurance of Seamen Against Illness, and The Protection of Seamen, are based on the studies by Dr. Alba M. Edwards.

Frequent references have been made to the other published and unpublished monographs, but in the main, a great part of the material therein relates to the period after 1860. After the publication of the present volume, these monographs, together with the remainder of the unpublished material accumulated by Professor Farnam, will be deposited in the Sterling Memorial Library at Yale University, and thus be available for future research workers.

One of Professor Farnam's colleagues, Professor Emeritus Charles M. Andrews, generously gave his time twice to read the part dealing with the Colonial Period, and, from his specialized and scholarly knowledge of that period, made pertinent suggestions and corrections which as far as practicable were incorporated by Professor Farnam before his death. An extension of the study of this period, to cover the history of some of the colonies in greater detail, could not, unfortunately, be carried out.

Special acknowledgment is due Miss Vera A. Timm, who was Professor Farnam's secretarial assistant for many years and helped him to prepare for press previous volumes of this series. That experience plus her familiarity with the manuscript of the present book and its sources has made her assistance invaluable to the editor. She has compiled and verified the bibliography in accordance with precedents established for the earlier volumes, and drafted and tabulated the appendix on slave laws outlined by Professor Farnam when the text was written. Finally she has had charge of reference checking, styling and proof reading. All together, therefore, her contribution to this work has been most substantial.

While a graduate student in Yale University, Mr. Alexander Trachtenberg made an abstract of the slave laws of the States which has formed the basis of the more extended analysis made by Professor Farnam.

The editor wishes also to express his obligation to his student aid in Berkeley College,

Mr. L. C. Peters, for competent assistance, and to the librarians and staffs of the University Library and Law Library of Yale, and of the American Antiquarian Society at Worcester, who have been unfailing in their help.

Without the constant encouragement and scholarly advice of Dr. Victor S. Clark, Consultant in Economics of the Library of Congress, and now chairman of the Board of Research Associates in American Economic History, this volume could not have been published. As Professor Farnam had given himself to editing the other volumes in the series, so Dr. Clark, as a labor of love, stood by this volume throughout the period of its revision, and took the responsibility of presenting it to the Carnegie Institution of Washington.

May, 1938 CLIVE DAY, *Editor*

CONTENTS

PART I—THE COLONIAL PERIOD

Chapter XIX

Chapter XX

PART I

THE COLONIAL PERIOD

CHAPTER I

INTRODUCTION

ELEMENTS DETERMINING ECONOMIC HISTORY

The economic history of a nation is determined by the interactions of land, people, and institutions. The two former are commonly recognized as elements, but not always the latter. Yet we should leave out of account a very important factor, if we did not also consider the institutions which, though they may sometimes be treated as part of the human element, are yet something distinct. We might, for example, have two countries similar in climate, extent, and soil. They might both be inhabited by people of similar race, physique, and mental characteristics. Yet if for any reason one country adopted a system of large estates with slaves, while the other adopted a system of peasant proprietorship, we should see very great differences in their development.

Certain types of social organization are well understood, and certain contrasts are familiar. We distinguish between feudalism and capitalism; we distinguish between a labor system based on slavery, and one based on freedom. What we often fail to recognize is that in fact one system always shades into the other. Systems are never changed at a stroke. They are destroyed by a process of shredding, and many fibres are carried over from the past into the future, when the system, as a whole, is practically abolished. New systems likewise never spring fully armed from the head of an Olympian legislator. They come into being piecemeal. Thus at any given time, we have a mixture of different and even incongruous systems. Moreover, under a Federal form of government the changes may take place with differing rapidity in different sections, so that, while a country as a whole may have a certain system, individual parts may have very different ones. Germany before the World War was an empire, and yet it contained three republics. When the feudal system prevailed generally, the cities had an independent organization quite different from feudalism.

INFLUENCE OF INSTITUTIONS ON ECONOMIC LIFE

The relations of institutions to economic life are twofold:

The institutions themselves, when carried over from one country to another, or from an earlier period to a later, influence the economic life. Such transfers are not infrequently made as the result of colonization, because it is easier to borrow the laws of the mother country than to invent new ones. As a rule the ancient Roman colonies copied Roman institutions, the Spanish those of Spain, the English those of Britain. The Civil Code prevails to the present day in Louisiana, not because the climate or resources of that State are different from those of neighboring common-law States, but because it happened to be first colonized by the French.

Such survivals or transfers may be a help to progress, where they represent a higher stage of development, or they may serve as a drag, where they represent a lower stage. It was doubtless a help to the continental Europeans of the later Middle Ages to be able to adopt such a splendid monument of human reasoning as the Roman Law. It was as convenient as when a mining camp on the frontier can import a carload of ready-made clothes; they may not all fit exactly, but they serve the purpose, and are better than any that the camp itself could make. The republican traditions of the United States are a great help in founding new communities. There are certain fundamental principles which need no discussion. There are certain fundamental methods, such as the organization of meetings under parliamentary law, the appointment of committees, and so forth, which people adopt because they are accustomed to them, and which enable them to enter at once upon the real business of government without wasting time in discussing principles or methods. When, however, a system remains too long unchanged, it may hinder progress. This is most apt to be the case when a certain institution is carried over from a period in which it meets the demands of the time to one in which the economic or social environment is quite different and which it no longer serves. The rigid rules of the gild system, useful in the thirteenth century, hindered the development of industry in the eighteenth and nineteenth centuries, and the change in methods of manufacture did more than anything else to break up the system.

We are sometimes told that laws are a reflection of the needs of the people, and that you cannot force ideals upon them. In a general way this is true, but it should be qualified when it is used, as often happens, as an argument against reform. For progressive nations are constantly changing and generally improving their ideals, under the influence of those who are more far-sighted than the mass of the people. It is in this way that progress takes place. By the time the idea has permeated the mass of the people, they have, in most cases, forgotten its origin. This process is often very slow. Not infrequently some pioneer proposes a certain subject, or propounds a certain proposition, which, though accepted by a small troop of followers, is scorned or derided or misunderstood by the mass of the people. In the course of time, perhaps a generation, the idea is rediscovered or revivified, and the people now accept it with eagerness.[1]

INFLUENCE OF ECONOMIC CONDITIONS ON INSTITUTIONS

Economic conditions also react upon institutions. When carried down from one generation to another, or when carried over from one place to another, laws often undergo a great change. Thus the feudal system survived in theory and in name long after it had changed its character. Originally it was a scheme under which the control of land in large blocks was given as the condition of public service. Privilege was balanced by obligation. It had to be abolished when the method of performing the service had become so faulty as to be a farce, and privilege outlived the duties originally coupled with it.

Slavery may be advantageous under certain conditions, especially when coercion is the only stimulus to industry to which the mind of man responds. But it is the reverse, when there is a demand for skill and intensity of labor which coercion cannot produce, and which can be stimulated only by the hope of preferment. Hence, in a progressive

[1] On the general subject of the origin of law, see Wilson, "The Law and the Facts", in *American Political Science Review*, V, 1–11, Feb., 1911.

society, legal reforms are not an exceptional affair, but a permanent need. Economic change requires change in legal forms.

Changes are usually opposed by two elements. First, there are those whose economic or political interests are bound up with the existing state of things. Land owners in England naturally oppose reforms in taxation which increase their burdens. Protected manufacturers are usually hostile to a low tariff. Slave owners do not wish to have emancipation. But changes are also opposed by those who simply cannot think quickly enough to keep pace with a change of ideas. This drag upon progress is not always understood and is apt to be underestimated. Its operation may be seen in the history of civil service reform in our country. The economic interests are almost all in favor of the merit system. The mass of the people who are not in office have everything to gain by it. The office holders, themselves, as a class, are in favor of it, because it gives them greater certainty of tenure. The higher officials of the Government, who take any interest in their work, are in favor of it, and have been from the beginning, because it relieves them of the waste of time involved in distributing patronage. The only people who have anything to lose by it are a comparatively small group of petty politicians and office seekers. Yet it has taken years to convince people generally of its wisdom, and even now many who would be shocked if we were to restore the "spoils system" to fields from which it has been banished, have not sufficient mental alertness to favor the expulsion of the system from still other fields, though its evils are notorious and flagrant. On account of the time required to diffuse new ideas, change is almost always slow. The law may reflect the needs of the people but these needs are often those of years, if not decades, before the time at which the reform is accomplished, because the general realization of the need requires so long a time to leaven the social mind. Law is like an old house belonging to a slovenly owner; repairs are often deferred until they are almost hopeless, and nothing short of rebuilding will answer the purpose.

EFFECT OF MIGRATION

The bodily transfer of people usually mobilizes their minds as well as their persons. "Home-keeping youth have ever homely wits." We all find it difficult to alter ideas and institutions which are associated with a certain place as long as we stay in that place. The moment we move to another country, change becomes more easy. When Horace says, "Caelum non animum mutant qui trans mare currunt," he states the exact opposite of modern experience. Nothing helps a change of mind as much as a change of sky. Hence we generally find in colonial settlements a readiness to alter institutions in order to meet new needs, as well as great fecundity in the production of new social ideals and a great willingness to try new social institutions.

Bogart says that our economic history "is largely the story of the achievements of a people working under free competition, untrammeled by custom, tradition, or political limitations."[2] The view is not uncommon that our country has been free from any conscious legislative regulation of social conditions. Thirty years ago a German scholar wrote a book entitled (in the English translation) *The Breakdown of Industrial Freedom and the Victory of State Socialism in the United States,* in which he endeavored

[2] Bogart, *Economic History of the United States* (2d ed., 1913), Preface, vii.

to show how the night-watchman theory of government had generally prevailed in the United States, and that the state meant in America not much more than an insurance company, created to ward off danger to life and property, and maintained by regular premiums in the form of taxes.[3] As will be shown later, this was certainly not true in the colonial period, nor has it been true in any such degree in any period of our history. There is, it is true, an objection to arbitrary interference with the individual, and there is also an objection, based largely upon sad experience, to allowing the government to go into business. We are willing, however, to submit to a good deal of personal restriction for what the people are convinced is a public object, and even State enterprise has had many examples, as may be seen in the history of the First and Second United States Banks, and the building of railroads and canals by States.

The liquor laws of our States are a familiar instance of interference with individual liberty for the sake of a social ideal, and it would not be difficult for a historian bent on disproving the popular theory, to draw a contrast between the descendants of the Puritans advocating prohibition, and the descendants of the Germans opposing liquor legislation in the interest of personal liberty. All hasty generalizations are, however, dangerous, and it is the purpose of this study to examine the facts of history in order to find out how far our country has enacted social legislation, and what the evolution and operation of such laws have been.

SCOPE OF SOCIAL LEGISLATION

It is not easy to draw the line between social legislation and general economic legislation. The aim in the following pages is to treat only legislation intended to influence the social structure. Many laws enacted with a very different purpose may, of course, influence society, but to study them all would be far too difficult and ambitious a task. It has, therefore, been thought best to study only those laws which indicate a conscious social policy, or an intention to influence the social structure. This involves a still further definition and explanation, for what do we understand by the social structure in a country like the United States?

The fact that our country has never had a caste system like that of India, or an hereditary aristocracy, like that of Prussia, or a real theocracy, like that of the ancient Jews, has popularized the idea that there are no social classes in our country, and that the individual economic and moral forces have had full play, uninfluenced by legislation.

This view is not borne out by the facts of history. On the contrary, we find a constant effort to realize by legislation certain social ideals, and even though these ideals are in the main those of liberty rather than of constraint or subordination, the very realization of liberty often involves restraint upon those who would interfere with it.

It is not always easy to distinguish between the legislation that can be described as social and that which is general. Of the great body of the law of a people, the larger part affects at best indirectly and remotely its economic and social life. Of those laws which do affect wealth, many are designed to influence the wealth of the state as a whole rather than the distribution of wealth or the organization of production. This

[3] Herr, *Der Zusammenbruch der Wirtschaftsfreiheit* (1906), 2.

is true of such laws as deal with navigation, tariff, and currency. We are concerned mainly, therefore, with laws which affect the relation of the citizen to property and production, as distinguished, on the one hand, from those which affect the relations of one person to another, such as criminal law or family law, and, on the other hand, from those which relate mainly to wealth as a whole, such as those designed to increase the productivity of the soil, to stimulate commerce, or to regulate the currency. In individual cases it is not always easy to know just what laws to include in this class. Inasmuch as we generally refuse to recognize hereditary distinctions, most of the laws which come within our field relate to economic classes. Although we have no caste system, we have economic interests which often conflict. We have the interests of employers conflicting with those of wage earners; we have landlords and tenants, farmers and manufacturers, merchants and carriers. And it must be acknowledged that in spite of the general principles of equality which are embodied, not merely in the Declaration of Independence, but also in most of our constitutions, the existence of Negro slavery has, in fact, led to elaborate legislation, regulating the relations of races, and, therefore, involving precisely those hereditary distinctions which we are supposed to reject.

DIVISIONS OF THE SUBJECT

Inasmuch, however, as the bulk of social legislation affects economic interests, it naturally divides itself into two main groups: first, that relating to property and its distribution, including both land and capital; and second, that relating to labor, including not only the status of labor, but also the great mass of legislation which has come up since the middle of the nineteenth century under the general term labor legislation.

Chronologically, the whole subject naturally divides itself into two periods, the colonial and the constitutional. In one sense this may be thought to be an arbitrary division, inasmuch as the Revolutionary War made changes which were political rather than social, and two of the colonies, Connecticut and Rhode Island, carried over their royal charters practically untouched into the next century. Nevertheless, there did grow up with the adoption of written constitutions by the people themselves, a greater tendency to impose certain distinct ideals upon the social structure, and for that reason, the year 1776 is a convenient turning point.

Further, in the constitutional period, a definite break appears at the time of the Civil War. Changes which had begun before 1860 went on more rapidly during and after the conflict, created new conditions, and set new social problems. The present volume will cover the history of social legislation only to the decade beginning in 1860, leaving to other authors the treatment of the development since that time.

CHAPTER II

FACTORS INFLUENCING COLONIAL LAW

Nationality, 8. Period of Colonization, 8. English Common Law, 9. Dutch Influence, 11. Clerical Influence on Political Institutions, 13. Clerical Influence on Social Policy, 14. Economic Environment, 16.

The most important of the fundamental data to be considered here are: nationality, period, legal traditions, religious beliefs, and economic conditions.

NATIONALITY

The North American Colonies were the creation of members of the English nation, which, in the seventeenth century, was just beginning its struggle for the control of lands beyond the sea, both west and east. That struggle resulted, on the North American coast, in the rapid expulsion of the Spaniards, and in their practical elimination from influence upon the social policy of this country, until the annexation of Texas and the conquests of the Mexican War brought in by indirection a Spanish element. Similarly, in the French and Indian Wars, the French were shut out in Canada and the Southwest, and it was not until the Louisiana Purchase of 1803 that an element of French law came into the complex legal structure of the United States. The Dutch were not pushed out but absorbed, and their influence, though considerable, was not that of an alien race but of a first cousin. Now, one of the remarkable things in history is the prepotency of the first shoot. Just as a graft upon an apple tree, though merely a stick of wood a few inches in length, will determine the character of the fruit borne by whole branches, so the institutions of the first settlers of a country tend to perpetuate themselves, unless crushed by some very powerful force. In spite, therefore, of the large admixture of races now inhabiting the United States, it is fair to say that as far as social legislation is concerned, our ancestry was English. One hundred eighty thousand Italians entering the United States in one year have had less influence on our institutions than a handful of Pilgrims in the *Mayflower*.

PERIOD OF COLONIZATION

The period of history in which the early settlements took place exercised a profound influence on their law. The seventeenth century followed the revival of arts and letters which had set its stamp upon the sixteenth century, while it preceded the great progress made by science in the eighteenth and nineteenth. It was chiefly notable in England for its remarkable political activity. The changes in the government of England during the seventeenth century have no parallel in the history of that country at any other period, and are comparable only to the kaleidoscopic changes which took place in France from the Revolution of 1789 to the establishment of the Third Republic in 1870. At the beginning of the century, in 1603, the House of Stuart supplanted the House of Tudor. In 1649 there followed the execution of Charles I and the establishment of the Commonwealth. This in turn was set aside in 1660 by the restoration of the Stuarts, while they had to yield in 1688–1689 to the House of Orange. Three dynasties, one republic, and a civil war in the space of 85 years meant violent changes for a conservative country. But the seventeenth century also witnessed the enactment of the Habeas Corpus Act and the Bill of Rights. Thus the possibility of sudden changes in the organization of the government, as well as the adoption of legal and constitutional guarantees in consequence of these changes, lay in the very political atmosphere of the time. It was natural for the colonists, therefore, to adopt written instruments of government and to rely upon them to safeguard the interests and rights of the citizen.

The seventeenth century was remarkable also for religious activity and theological controversy. While the Thirty Years War led to the settlement of the religious question in Germany for many years to come, a religious ferment was in process in Great Britain, and profoundly influenced the thought and ideals of the time. This was the period of the definitive establishment of Protestantism in England under the peculiarly conservative form of the Church of England, which in turn forced those of more advanced views, whether in doctrine, form, or ethics, to separate themselves from the mother church. This meant great intellectual activity, much reading of the Bible, the formation of independent views, and a readiness to act on conviction rather than tradition.

ENGLISH COMMON LAW

The legal elements which were carried across the sea into the new settlements were mainly English. It is sometimes said that the common law of England went with the colonists to the new country. It is a question whether, even theoretically, this was strictly true. Practically only as much was brought across the ocean as was thought to be adapted to the needs or the wishes of the colonists.[1] From the start, the ideal of the social structure was obviously different from that of the mother-country, and colonial law "always retained the impress of the earlier originality, when new conditions brought forth new institutions and new legal ideas."[2] The Massachusetts Bay Colony was formed in the beginning as a trading company, with the government in the hands of the General Court in England. The decision, August 29, 1629, to move the General Court to America had the effect of making it virtually independent of the English law, and, though the common law was recognized in general in the absence of legislation to the contrary, the colonists did not consider themselves bound by it as a whole.[3]

The same point of view is seen in the Constitution of Connecticut of 1638, often spoken of as the first written constitution in the history of the world.[4] The preamble says:

"And well knowing where a people are gathered together the word of God requires that to mayntayne the peace and vnion of such a people there should be an orderly and decent Gouerment established according to God, to order and dispose of the affayres of

[1] See Morris, *Studies in the History of American Law* (1930), chap. i; and *American and English Encyclopaedia of Law* (2d ed., 1898), VI, 271.

[2] Reinsch, "The English Common Law in the Early American Colonies", in *Select Essays in Anglo-American Legal History* (1907), I, 367.

[3] See Hilkey, *Legal Development in Colonial Massachusetts, 1630–1686* (1910), in *Columbia University Studies*, XXXVII, 167.

[4] So recently in Channing, *A History of the United States* (1905 ff.), I, 404.

the people at all seasons as occation shall require; doe therefore assotiate and conioyne our selues to be as one Publike State or Cōmonwelth."[5]

The New Haven Colony is cited by Levermore as perhaps "the sole instance of the formation of an independent civil government by a general compact wherein all the parties to the agreement were legally required to be actual signers thereof."[6] At a time when "John Locke was in his seventh year, and Rousseau was a century away", the free planters formally met and, after a full discussion, adopted the so-called "Fundamentall Agreement" at a meeting held in Newman's barn, June 4, 1639. This was in the nature of six "Quaeries" which were put by the Rev. John Davenport, and it was ordered by all the free planters, "thatt all those thatt hereafter should be received as planters" should sign their names to this agreement.[7]

That the colonists themselves did not believe that the common law applied to them is clear from the arguments presented in the famous case involving the Winthrop will in Connecticut. "John Winthrop, a grandson of one Connecticut Governor and nephew of another, denying the validity of the intestate law, claimed all the real estate of his father who had died in 1717, and, ignoring the right which he had of appeal from the Court of Probate to the Court of Assistants, expressed his determination to appeal to the King in Council."[8] This led to a hearing before the King's Council, and involved the legality of the Connecticut law. The colonists asserted that, from the nature of the laws passed, the colonial government never considered the common law to be in force within its jurisdiction; and in reply to the argument that the colonial legislature was only given the power to pass laws not contrary to those of England, Governor Talcott asked, "And why should we be directed to make laws not contrary to the laws of England if they were our laws, for what propriety can there be in making that a directory to us in making a law which was our law before we made it."[9] The interpretation, therefore, was that the colony could make its own laws, provided they were not in contradiction to laws specifically made for the colony by the Parliament. The Connecticut law was annulled by an Order in Council, February 15, 1728. However, two cases involving similar questions were decided in favor of the colonies by the King in Council, that of Phillips *vs.* Savage, carried up from Massachusetts, and that of Clark *vs.* Tousey.[10]

Blackstone, writing in 1765 regarding the common law in the colonies, said that, the North American colonies being mainly acquired by conquest, "the common law of England, as such, has no allowance or authority there; they being no part of the mother-country, but distinct, though dependent, dominions. They are subject, however, to the control of the parliament."[11]

In some cases even in the eighteenth century, the inapplicability of the English law was clearly stated. A statute of South Carolina, passed in 1712, had in its preamble: "Many of the statute-laws of the kingdom of England or South Britain, by reason of the different way of agriculture, and the differing productions of the earth of this Prov-

[5] Thorpe, *American Charters, Constitutions and Organic Laws* (1909), I, 519.
[6] Levermore, *The Republic of New Haven* (1886), 24.
[7] *Ibid.*, 17–21.
[8] Andrews, "The Connecticut Intestacy Law", in *Yale Review*, III, 276, Nov. 1894.
[9] *Ibid.*, 283, quoting *Talcott Papers*, II, Appendix, "Instructions to Agents".
[10] *Ibid.*, 276, 293; Morris, *Studies in the History of American Law*, 104, 118–119.
[11] Blackstone, *Commentaries* (Cooley's ed., 1872–1873), I, 68 (Book I, 107–108).

ince from that of England, are altogether useless, and many others, which otherwise are very apt and good, either by reason of their limitation to particular places, or because in themselves they are only executive by such nominal officers as are not in nor suitable for the Constitution of this government, are hereby become impracticable here."[12] The same principle was recognized by implication in the New York Constitution of 1777 which, while expressly recognizing the common law, gave validity only to "such parts of the common law of England, and of the statute law of England and Great Britain, . . . as together did form the law of the said colony on the 19th day of April in the year of our Lord, one thousand seven hundred and seventy-five."[13]

We may say, therefore, that, while the legal traditions and the fundamental notions of law which the colonists carried with them were undoubtedly English, there was from the beginning a great deal of independence with regard to adopting and applying the specific provisions of the common law.

Not only in the details of the law, but in the general structure of society was there a marked contrast between the mother country and the colonies. The aristocratic character of English law is shown in the fact that Blackstone addressed his *Commentaries* especially to gentlemen of fortune, who, he thought, needed them in managing their estates, or when taking their seats in Parliament, as he thought many of them were ambitious of doing at some time.[14] In the early part of the seventeenth century England was still a feudal monarchy. The military burdens of feudalism had not yet been formally removed. The Parliament, while it included a House of Commons, represented really the gentry and aristocracy, and such a thing as the direct representation of the mass of the people was unknown. Yet the compact[15] signed in the cabin of the *Mayflower*, brief as it was, declared that a body politic was formed "for the general Good of the Colony", a phrase which already indicated the democratic ideal of promoting the welfare of all. And yet, no people can entirely break with the past, and it is significant that one of the early laws of Massachusetts which humanely limited to forty the stripes with which a man might be beaten, exempted from all whipping "any true gentleman", and also, "any man equall to a gentleman", "unles his crime be very shamefull, and his course of life vitious and profligate."[16] In New Haven the idea of a commonwealth established for the common good did not exclude the possibility of distinctions among the citizens. There was, from the beginning, a differentiation between the stockholders, or proprietors, who had rights in the common lands, and all others. Among these, in turn, there were slaves, indentured servants, and freeholders, while throughout society there ran the distinction between church members and non-church members. The former alone had in the beginning the right of suffrage.[17] Similar distinctions existed commonly.

DUTCH INFLUENCE

A second legal factor entering into the structure of legislation, at least in the northeastern part of the colonies, was the Dutch law. The theory that this was the principal

[12] Grimké, *The Public Laws of the State of South Carolina* (1790), 25.
[13] Thorpe, *American Charters, Constitutions and Organic Laws*, V, 2635.
[14] Blackstone, *Commentaries* (Cooley's ed.), I, 3–4 (Book I, 6–9).
[15] Thorpe, *American Charters, Constitutions and Organic Laws*, III, 1841.
[16] *Body of Liberties*, No. 43, in *Colonial Laws of Massachusetts* (Whitmore's ed. of 1889).
[17] Levermore, *The Republic of New Haven*, 18, 35.

element has been especially developed by Campbell.[18] In a book written in 1893, that author marshalled a great mass of evidence tending to show that most of the good elements in the legal institutions of the United States came from the Puritans, and that the best ideas of the Puritans came from the Dutch, while the less desirable elements were those which came from England.

It would carry us too far to discuss these views at length. The criticism has been made by some historians[19] that there is no direct proof that the Puritans deliberately copied Dutch institutions, and that Campbell can at most make out the priority of the Dutch institutions. This argument does not seem to be conclusive. English colonists, sailing under English patents, and knowing that by virtue of their independence in religious matters they were objects of suspicion at home, would naturally be very careful not to acknowledge in any of their official documents their indebtedness to a foreign country. If, therefore, they established certain institutions, which are known to have existed in Holland, and which they may be presumed to have been familiar with, but which did not exist elsewhere, it seems reasonable to suppose, even without documentary evidence, that they were influenced by what they had learned in that country. In some cases, however, there is good proof that the institution did exist elsewhere. Let us take as an example the equal division of lands in the case of intestacy, cited by Campbell. The Plymouth Colony in its Code of 1636 directly referred to inheritance according to the custom of East Greenwich. In other words, we have here a clear case wherein they avowedly used a survival of primitive times, which was, to be sure, at variance with feudalism, but which nevertheless was English, and not Dutch, in its origin. With regard to other institutions, however, there is no proof that they could have taken them from England. They must, therefore, either have borrowed them from Holland, or invented them independently. The latter theory does not seem to be impossible. We have in history numerous instances of the independent origin of similar institutions. Feudalism grew up in Japan without any traceable connection with Europe. And yet imitation is in general so much easier than invention, and we have so many cases in history of the copying, sometimes perhaps unconscious, of laws and of ideas, that it may be laid down as a fairly safe maxim that where imitation is possible, invention is highly improbable. Certain facts, moreover, are unquestioned. In the reigns of James I and Charles I, a great many English Puritans moved over to Holland on account of religious persecutions. Still other Englishmen went there to improve their fortunes or to study in the Dutch universities, or to serve as soldiers. Under the treaty of 1585, England was required to furnish six thousand troops for the Netherlands, and kept them there some thirteen years.[20] No small number of these Englishmen who had lived in Holland became subsequently men of importance in the colonies. Among them were such leaders as Miles Standish, Governor Dudley, John Mason of Connecticut, John Davenport of New Haven, Lion Gardiner of Gardiner's Island, and Hugh Peters.[21] Thus whether or not we attribute to Dutch institutions the importance given them by Campbell, we can hardly deny that they furnished one element in

[18] Campbell, *The Puritan in Holland, England, and America.*
[19] Bourne, in *Yale Review*, I, 434–443, Feb. 1893, reviewing Campbell, *The Puritan in Holland, England, and America.*
[20] Campbell, *The Puritan in Holland, England, and America* (3d ed., 1893), II, 376.
[21] *Ibid.*, II, 377, 387.

colonial polity. It is not conceivable that such associations with Holland could have had no influence whatever on the legal conceptions and polity of the early New Englanders.[22]

CLERICAL INFLUENCE ON POLITICAL INSTITUTIONS

The influence of the church counted for more in the New England colonies than in those established in the South. But inasmuch as many of the New England institutions were afterwards adopted by the nation, or served as models for national institutions, anything entering into them has more than local significance. The Plymouth colony was established by avowed Separatists, who set up a form of church government quite distinct from that of England. The other New England colonies, Massachusetts Bay, Connecticut, and New Haven, were established by Puritans, who considered themselves members of the Church of England. Many of their clergymen were regularly ordained clergymen of the Established Church, who had been inducted into office by the laying on of hands by a bishop. Almost as soon, however, as they reached the shores of America, in the very first congregation they organized, they adopted the Plymouth form and became avowedly congregational in their church government.[23] Now the chief characteristics of Congregationalism were, as stated by Walker, the use of a distinct covenant as the basis of the local church, and the election and ordination of its ministers by the local congregation.[24] What was meant by the covenant may be seen by examining that which was adopted in the Spring of 1629 by the Salem church, the first Puritan church and the second Congregational church, as Walker says, in New England. The covenant ran as follows: "We Covenant with the Lord and one with another; and doe bynd our selves in the presence of God, to walke together in all his waies, according as he is pleased to reveale himself unto us in his Blessed word of truth."[25] Thus the covenant was in the nature of a social contract, analogous to that to which the Pilgrims bound themselves in the cabin of the *Mayflower*, and the Congregational churches were all organized as republics. This meant that admission to church membership depended upon the voluntary act of the individual, combined with the action of the congregation. A candidate must first be willing to sign the covenant and then must be acceptable to those who were already in the church. This involved not only voluntary action but intelligent action, therefore education, on the part of those who were about to become members of the church. We thus see that the general principles of the democratic government, developed later in the colonies and in the United States, were really found in miniature in the Congregational churches of New England.

When a New England commonwealth is spoken of as a theocracy we must understand that this was something very different from a hierarchy. These communities were theocracies in the sense that they aimed to be governed by the word of God as revealed in the Scriptures, but they were governed by the word as interpreted by reason, not as imposed upon them by authority or tradition. Even in those colonies in which the

[22] Channing thought that until further research had been made, it was impossible to give a decisive answer to the question of Dutch influence. See *History of the United States*, I, 439.
[23] Walker, *History of Congregational Churches* (1894), 100.
[24] *Ibid.*, 102.
[25] *Ibid.*, 104.

suffrage was confined to church members, like New Haven and Massachusetts, in contradistinction to Plymouth and Connecticut, state and church were not connected, but were distinct. In England, membership in the state implied membership in the church. In Massachusetts and in New Haven, active membership in the state, in the sense of the right to vote, was confined to church members, but they exercised this right as members of the state, not as members of the church. This condition was imposed, because it was thought that those who were church members would have the character and responsibility required for the exercise of civic functions. The clergymen exercised an influence on public affairs on account of their learning and character, but did not, as clergymen, govern. As Walker says: "The minister was reverenced and consulted as perhaps in no other British territory; but a jealous public sentiment excluded him from political office, and kept the ultimate control of the churches and of the state in the hands of the General Court". The church itself was controlled by laymen. Between 1629 and 1639 some thirty-three churches were thus organized, and practically all on the same lines.[26] "They everywhere presented the conception of a church as a body of persons of religious experience bound together by a covenant, choosing its own officers, administering its own affairs, and independent of other ecclesiastical control. They stood everywhere, also, for a free, unliturgical form of worship, an educated ministry, and a strenuous moral discipline."[27]

CLERICAL INFLUENCE ON SOCIAL POLICY

Not only did the Congregational churches in New England set a model for the colonial states and later for the national government, but they also powerfully influenced social policy.

New England was settled mainly by people who came in order that they might worship God according to their own conscience. The leaders, whether laymen or clergymen, were strongly religious. They were familiar with the Bible and in the habit of reading it, learning it by heart, and discussing its doctrines. It was quite natural, therefore, that they should consider it the highest authority, not only in moral but also in political and social matters, and should naturally turn to it for guidance on vexing questions.

The framers of laws were in many instances clergymen who were peculiarly versed in the Scriptures, and not averse to applying their knowledge. We see this direct influence in many cases. Cotton Mather writing in his *Magnalia* of the adoption of the *Massachusetts Body of Liberties*, said: "It was then requested of Mr. *Cotton*, That he would, from the Laws wherewith God governed his ancient People, form an *Abstract* of such as were of a Moral and Lasting *Equity*: Which he performed as acceptably as judiciously."[28] This draft was, it is true, not adopted, but the one which was finally passed was likewise the work of a clergyman, Rev. Nathaniel Ward of Ipswich.[29]

In New Haven Colony clerical influence was equally strong. A debate arose early in

[26] *Ibid.*, 115, 116.
[27] *Ibid.*, 124.
[28] Mather, *Magnalia*, Bk. iii, chap. i, p. 21, §20 (original ed. of MDCCII); I, 243 (Andrus ed. of 1820); quoted in Low, *The American People* (1909), I, 146.
[29] *Colonial Laws of Massachusetts* (ed. of 1889), 18–19.

its history regarding the form of government which should be adopted. There was a difference of opinion between Mr. Davenport and Mr. Samuel Eaton, and the result was the composition of *A Discourse about Civil Government in a New Plantation whose design is Religion*. This has been attributed to John Cotton, but is now believed to have been the work of John Davenport.[30] This discourse is an elaborate treatise on government with special reference to the church. The author distinguished between the ecclesiastical administration and the civil administration. "Ecclesiastical Administrations, are a *Divine Order appointed to Believers for holy communion of holy things:* Civil Administrations are *An Humane Order appointed by God to men for Civil Fellowship of Humane things*."[31] He contended that these powers should not be confused.[32] He also distinguished between "a Common-wealth already setled, and a Common-wealth yet to be setled, and wherein men are free to chuse what form they shall judge best."[33] If a state was already settled, the people should be subject to whatever powers chanced to be over them, but if they were setting up a new state, they should rather choose for their judges members of the church. Davenport held that in a new plantation where all, or the most considerable part, of the free planters professed their purpose and desire of securing to themselves and to their posterity the peaceable enjoyment of Christ's Ordinances, such planters were bound, in laying the foundations of Church and Civil State, to take order "*that all the free Burgesses be such as are in fellowship of the Church or Churches which are, or may be gathered according to Christ; and that those free Burgesses have the only power of chusing from among themselves Civil Magistrates and men to be entrusted with transacting all publick Affairs of Importance, according to the rules and direction of Scripture*."[34] His elaborate argument in favor of this view was reenforced by ample reference to the Bible, especially to the Old Testament.

In the *Massachusetts Body of Liberties*, adopted in 1641, there were twelve capital crimes, the first eleven being based upon the Old Testament, and the twelfth being insurrection, rebellion, or attempting "the alteration and subversion of our frame of politie".[35] The Colony of Connecticut followed the example of Massachusetts and its capital code, adopted in 1642, contained likewise twelve crimes punishable by death, eleven of which were based on Scripture references.[36] This code seems drastic to modern minds but as compared with the English law of the period it was very humane. Dr. Bacon called attention to the fact that as against the twelve capital crimes of this code there were more than 150 crimes punishable by death in England.[37] As was well said by Stephen, "the number of capital offences on the statute book is no test of its severity. A few general enactments would be much more severe than a great number of special ones."[38] We can better compare the two systems of law by considering that all of the crimes in the Puritan code were crimes either against the state, against the person, against religion, or against nature. There was not a single crime against

[30] Bacon, *Historical Discourses* (1839), 19, 289.
[31] Davenport, *Discourse about Civil Government* (ed. of MDCLXIII), 6.
[32] *Ibid.*, 8.
[33] *Ibid.*, 9.
[34] *Ibid.*, 14.
[35] *Body of Liberties*, No. 94, in *Colonial Laws of Massachusetts* (ed. of 1889), 55.
[36] *The Public Records of the Colony of Connecticut* (ed. of 1850), I, 77.
[37] Bacon, *Historical Discourses*, 32.
[38] Stephen, *History of the Criminal Law of England* (1883), I, 470.

property, whereas towards the end of the seventeenth century in England, the penalty of death without benefit of clergy was imposed not only on high treason, petty treason, piracy, murder, and arson, but also on "burglary, housebreaking and putting in fear, highway robbery, horse stealing, stealing from the person above the value of a shilling, rape, and abduction with intent to marry. In the case of persons who could not read, all felonies, including manslaughter, every kind of theft above the value of a shilling, and all robbery were capital crimes".[39]

The very subject matter of the Bible, particularly of the Old Testament, must have made a strong appeal to the Puritans. The early history of the Jewish people was a history of wandering nomads. The Mosaic period was a period in which a new country was being settled by immigrants of a high degree of civilization and definite moral standards, just as the wilderness of New England was being settled by the Puritans. The simplicity of the Jewish life when the people dwelt in tents and were fed by manna, as well as the practical character of many of their ordinances, must have made the Bible seem much better adapted to New England conditions than the law of England, which implied the hierarchy of the feudal system with hereditary rights and duties, landed estates passing from father to son by the rule of primogeniture, and an elaborate social structure both in agriculture and in industry. It is also significant that the Old Testament contains a social code in which such remarkable institutions as the Year of Jubilee, the redemption of bondsmen, the general care of the poor, and many strictly sanitary regulations are enforced by religious sanction. Thus, while the Puritans laid more stress upon the moral side than the social side of life, it is evident that the Jewish polity, as explained in the Old Testament, influenced them profoundly. A good instance is the strict observance of the Sabbath, which was one of the most important social regulations of the decalogue and the value of which is being, as it were, rediscovered by the radical labor leaders of Europe in the twentieth century.

ECONOMIC ENVIRONMENT

The economic environment into which these legal and religious ideals were projected was that which is found in most new countries. Land and natural resources were abundant. Hence resulted the impossibility of making a privilege of land ownership, such as it had become in Europe. There was great lack of capital. Hence came the importance of encouraging permanent property, such as houses and ships. There was a scarcity of labor. The labor problem, therefore, became a pressing one from the start, though not in the modern sense. The problem was to get labor, not to protect its interests. Our task is to study the kind of social structure and social legislation which resulted from these conditions.

While the general economic conditions were those of a new country, they were not everywhere the same. New England was rocky, comparatively inhospitable, well wooded, and difficult to cultivate. The South was more fertile, the climate was milder, it was easier to raise produce from the soil, especially when its adaptability to tobacco was discovered. Hence, the general system of land tenure was different in the South from what it was in the North. But even in the North it was not uniform, and we find

[39] *Ibid.*, I, 467.

in a number of cases exceptions to the prevailing system of small holdings. These differences also made a great difference in the solution of the labor problem. In general, in a new country there is little differentiation of trades. Each man is more or less obliged to be a "jack of all trades", and unskilled labor is in great demand. But how that unskilled labor can be secured must in turn depend upon the conditions under which work is carried on, and, to some extent, also upon the social ideals. Hence in the case of labor we find even a sharper contrast between the North and the South than in the case of land tenure.

A peculiarity of the economic situation was that, although mineral resources such as gold, silver, copper, coal, iron, petroleum, and natural gas, proved to be very valuable in the nineteenth century, they were at first not discovered or were not utilized. Agriculture and forestry were the main extractive industries followed on the land, while the numerous rivers and harbors favored commerce, fishing and ship building. All of these occupations involved steady systematic labor, and most of them stable institutions. It must be considered fortunate for social development that the mineral resources were not exploited until the country had laid the foundations of its laws under conservative, if laborious, economic activities.

CHAPTER III

EARLY COLONIAL CODES

Stimson says that the English law has never been codified.[1] Yet before the middle of the seventeenth century, systematic bodies of laws had been enacted by the New England colonies of Plymouth, Massachusetts Bay, and Connecticut, as well as less formal codes adopted by the more southern colonies, and, as Reinsch says, codification is a general trait of early colonial law.[2] In the Connecticut code of 1642, the topics were even arranged alphabetically. We seem, therefore, to have in these cases a distinctly new departure in Anglo-Saxon law. Whether the colonists were inspired by the Ten Commandments of the Jews, or by the Corpus Juris of the Romans, or whether the more formal statement was their own invention, need not be discussed, and is indeed not important. It is significant that at so early a period they should have felt the need of laying down the legal principles under which their lives were to be regulated. The general character of these early codes may be shown by examples taken from three different sections of the country, New England, the middle colonies, and the South.

THE PLYMOUTH CODE, 1636

The legal organization of the Plymouth colony was peculiar. The Pilgrims who started from Leyden went under the management of an unincorporated joint stock company, the shares of which might be secured by the payment of £10 in cash, or by the enlistment of one person as a colonist, while a person going at his own expense received two shares. The organization was thus distinctly that of a business corporation. Moreover, the contract involved in the beginning a system of community of goods for seven years. Little provision was made for any form of government until just before landing, when a simple agreement was drawn up in the cabin of the *Mayflower* and signed by all of the men in the party excepting the seven servants, who were inclined to be mutinous. Very few laws were needed at first, and none seems to have been formally enacted until 1623. Two pages contain the entire legislation from 1623 to 1627. Most of these laws regulated economic conditions. The one exception is the first law, passed in 1623, which provided for trial by jury in criminal cases, as well as in matters of trespass and debt. Others prohibited the exportation of timber, in order to prevent a scarcity, forbade handicraftsmen to work for strangers without the consent of the governor and council, until "the necessity of the the colony be served", forbade the exportation of corn, beans, and peas, without government consent, and prohibited the use of straw and reed for thatching houses, requiring them to be covered either

[1] Stimson, *Popular Law-Making* (1910), 17.
[2] Reinsch, "The English Common Law in the Early American Colonies", in *Select Essays in Anglo-American Legal History*, I, 410.

with board or pale.[3] These laws all clearly indicate the purpose of restraining the individual in his economic actions for the sake of promoting abundance or preventing loss of wealth in the interest of the community. Of a more general nature were the laws passed in 1627, which provided for an equitable division of lands, but allowed all to get firewood while reserving the timber trees for the owners of the ground. These laws also provided that fowling, fishing, and hunting be free, that the old pathways be still allowed, and that every man be allowed a convenient way to the water.

In 1636 a general code was adopted covering about twenty-two pages of print. This code included public as well as private law and was first drafted by a committee instructed to examine the ordinances already in force "that so those that are still fitting might be established; those that time hath made unnecessary might be rejected; and others that were wanting might be prepared." The fundamental principle adopted in the very beginning and based upon the privileges of the free-born subjects of the state of England, was that no imposition, law, or ordinance should be imposed upon them, "but such as shall be made or imposed by consent according to the free liberties of the state and Kingdome of Engl. and no otherwise." The code then provided for the election of a governor and seven assistants, to be chosen for one year, and prescribed their duties. All laws were to be made only by the freemen and all taxations were to be "without partiality so as the freeman be not spared for his freedome, but the levy be equall." Some fundamental principles of personal liberty were enacted, such as the right to trial by jury. Capital offenses were eight, of which one was treason against the "King, State or Commonwealth, either of England or these Colonies", and another was "willfull or purposed burning of ships houses [*sic*]". A third was witchcraft, and the rest were sexual offenses. The great mass of the remainder related to economic interests. The Winchester standard of weights and measures was to be adopted; cattle brands were to be recorded; no man was to sell out of the colony any boards or timber growing in the swamps reserved for public use. All conveyances of land were to be publicly recorded. Inheritance was to go "according to the comendable custome of Engl. and hold of Est. Greenwich." In case of the death of a husband, the wife was to have a third of his lands during her life and one-third of his goods, "at her owne disposeinge".

An important general principle was laid down in the provision "That Whereas Lands are given & granted to persons upon supposall of their living upon them for the maintenance & strength of society; if it fall out that such persons shall not occupie any such lands, but dep^{t} from the same place such former graunt or grants to be of none effect but shall returne & be otherwise disposed of by the Govern^{t} in Generall or Towneship in particular as it shall fall out".

Provision was also made for the children who might be born in the colony, and might want lands. These were to be provided for ahead of any that came from England or elsewhere. Another provision in the public interest was "That no man keep more swine than he can ordinarily keepe about his owne place and that they be doubly wrung or at least sufficiently wrung that they roote not up & destroy the meadows". A penalty was put upon the neglect of this ordinance, one half the fine going to the informer, and one half to the township. Similar provisions were also made against

[3] See Brigham (ed.), *The Compact with the Charter and Laws of the Colony of New Plymouth* (1836), 28–47 for this and following references to the laws of New Plymouth.

damage done by other domestic animals. Only one section related to labor. That was, "That such servants as come out of their times and are by their Cov^{ts} to have lands to have onely five acres apeece at pr^{nt}. And that if they be found fit to occupie it for themselves in some convenient place." The perennial liquor problem was dealt with by a law which prohibited the selling of wine, strong water, and beer, "except in inns or victualling houses," while another provided for the punishment of drunkards, and forbade the entertainment of children and servants in public houses. The price of beer was limited to 2d. the Winchester quart.

THE MASSACHUSETTS BODY OF LIBERTIES, 1641

The Body of Liberties of Massachusetts, enacted in 1641, was intended at the time to be a kind of Magna Charta of the colony.[4] It not only contained certain general principles protecting the citizen against being despoiled of his property or deprived of his life and liberty but also forbade monopolies, limited the rate of interest, protected servants, and even provided against cruelty to animals. Prominent among the provisions protecting the rights of persons and property was number 5, which reads: "No man shall be compelled to any publique worke or service unlesse the presse be grounded upon some act of the generall Court, and have reasonable allowance therefore." Section 8 similarly provided that no man's cattle or goods should be taken for public use without warrant of some act of the General Court. Section 9 prohibited all monopolies "but of such new Inventions that are profitable to the Countrie, and that for a short time." Section 12 gave freedom to all inhabitants, whether free or not free, to come to any public court, council, or town meeting, and to present their petitions. The rate of interest was limited to 8 per cent. (sec. 23), and all lands and heritages were to be free from all fines upon alienation and other feudal burdens (sec. 10). The law of inheritance provided that in case of intestacy, the elder son should have a double portion of the whole estate, real and personal, unless the General Court should judge otherwise (sec. 81). The desire for democratic equality showed itself in section 63, which stated that no governor, deputy governor, assistant, associate, or grand juryman should bear his own charges at any court, thus making it as easy for the poor man as for the rich man to assume public office. The abuses of the legal profession were evidently intended to be checked by section 26, which provided that a man who found himself unfit to plead his own cause should have liberty to employ any man against whom the court did not object, "Provided he give him noe fee or reward for his paines".

A number of provisions testified to the humane character of the framers. Section 43 prohibited beating a man with more than forty stripes. Wives were protected against bodily correction by their husbands "unlesse it be in his owne defence upon her assalt" (sec. 80), while children were safeguarded against unnatural severity on the part of their parents (sec. 83). Servants who fled from the tyranny and cruelty of their masters were to be protected until proper action could be taken (sec. 85). They could not be turned over to any other person for a period of more than one year, unless by consent of the authorities (sec. 86), and if the master should "smite out the eye or tooth of his man-servant, or maid servant, or otherwise mayme or much disfigure him, unlesse

[4] *Colonial Laws of Massachusetts*, 16–18. This and the following quotations are taken from the Whitmore edition of 1889.

it be by meere casualtie, he shall let them goe free" (sec. 87). Servants who had served diligently and satisfactorily should not be sent away empty, when their time of service expired (sec. 88). Slavery in general was restricted to those lawful captives taken in war, and "such strangers as willingly selle themselves or are sold to us. And these shall have all the liberties and Christian usages which the law of god established in Israell concerning such persons doeth morally require" (sec. 91). Those who might be shipwrecked, "be it freind or enemy", were to suffer no wrong in person or goods (sec. 90). Even cattle were considered in this early law, and if they were being driven from one place to another, and were weary, or hungry, or sick, or lame, they might be rested and refreshed "in any open place that is not Corne, meadow, or inclosed for some peculiar use" (sec. 93), and "No man shall exercise any Tirranny or Crueltie towards any bruite Creature which are usuallie kept for man's use" (sec. 92).

The provisions of the Body of Liberties are quoted at some length, because they represented such an advanced type of legislation, and because they show that, even in the middle of the seventeenth century, the Puritans set up social ideals which were not generally realized or perhaps even recognized for many years by the rest of the world. Indeed, it may well be questioned whether the bit of international law which is found in the provision regarding the treatment of shipwrecked enemies may not indicate views in advance of the practice of the early part of the twentieth century.

THE VIRGINIA LAWS

Virginia was the first of the colonies to be planted by the English, and preceded Plymouth by nearly fourteen years, but this difference in time does not alone account for the contrast between its early laws and those of New England. It was settled more directly for economic purposes. The first twelve years after the establishment of Jamestown in 1607 were hard. According to the Charter of 1609, the boundaries, which at first had been confined to a tract 100 miles square, were extended to the Pacific; but this vast estate meant little without good laws. The colony was governed by a Council of Fifty, sitting in London. The Governor, Lord Delaware, had power "to rule, punish, pardon, govern", according to instructions from home or, in their absence, according to his discretion. This arbitrary rule was supplanted in 1611 by a Code of Laws, "divine, morral, martiall", brought over by Sir Thomas Dale, but these too were very severe. George Bancroft says of the first twelve years, "The Colony was ruled during that period by laws written in blood."[5] It was not until 1619 that Sir George Yeardley arrived, bringing a commission for the establishment of a Council and a General Assembly of Burgesses, chosen by the people. In the proceedings of this General Assembly, held in July, 1619, we have the Magna Charta of Virginia.

The program of the Assembly was divided into four heads: "namely, first, the great charter of orders, lawes, and priviledges: Secondly, which of the instructions given by the Counsel in England * * * might conveniently putt on the habite of lawes; Thirdly, what lawes might issue out of the private conceipte of any of the Burgesses, or any other of the Colony; and lastly, what petitions were fitt to be sente home for England."[6]

Under the second head, we have a code covering about four pages, with certain addi-

[5] "Introductory Note" to *Colonial Records of Virginia* (Senate Document, Extra, 1874), vi.
[6] *Ibid.*, 15.

tions under the third head covering as much more. These laws began with the prohibitions against idleness, gaming, and drunkenness. They also included a penalty on excess in apparel, according to which each man was "cessed in the churche for all publique contributions, if he be unmarried according to his owne apparrell, if he be married, according to his owne and his wives."[7] There were also laws against allowing too many Indians to settle among the whites, laws requiring the people to plant corn as well as other things, such as mulberry trees, flax, anise, and other seeds. Contracts made in England between the owners of land and the tenants and servants were to be duly performed, no one was to entice away the tenants or servants of another. A magazine or store-house was to "be preserved from wrong and sinister practices", and the Cape merchant was to accept tobacco at the rate of "three shillings the pounde the beste, and 18d the second sorte."[8]

The early Virginia statutes, in contrast to those of Massachusetts, contained many clauses relating to servants. Servants were punished for marrying without the consent of their masters. A penalty was imposed on hiring runaway servants. Runaway servants were punished by being required to serve double the time lost or even more at the end of their indenture, and might be branded with the letter R on the cheek for a second offense.[9] There was a penalty upon dealing with other men's servants, or apprentices.[10] All this points to a state of things in which hired servants played an important part and furnished most of the labor.

FUNDAMENTAL CONSTITUTIONS OF CAROLINA, 1669

Another type of government is found in the Fundamental Constitutions of Carolina. The original charter of 1663 granted to the eight proprietors named in the deed a tract of land on terms similar to those applied elsewhere. They were to hold the land in free and common socage, were to pay a yearly rental of 20 marks to the Crown, and were to have the right to grant the premises "in fee simple or fee tayle", or for a term of years, or for life, as they might elect.[11] The second charter, granted in 1665, enlarged the grant, but maintained essentially the same terms.

In 1669 a philosopher was called in to organize the ideal state, and the "Fundamental Constitutions of Carolina", framed by John Locke and amended by Anthony Ashley Cooper (Lord Shaftesbury), were adopted.[12] This constitution was never fully in operation and was abrogated by the Lords Proprietors in 1693. But, though it played so insignificant a part in the history of the colony it is of special interest to the student of institutions, who must analyze both failure and success in explaining the survival of laws. This constitution provided for an elaborate hierarchy beginning with the Palatine, who was the oldest of the Lords Proprietors, and who was to be succeeded on his death by the oldest surviving proprietor. The other seven chief offices were to be assigned by lot to the other proprietors. The whole territory was to be divided into counties, each containing eight signiories, eight baronies, and four precincts, each pre-

[7] *Ibid.*, 20.
[8] *Ibid.*, 22, 23.
[9] *Statutes at Large of Virginia* (ed. by Hening), I, 252–255.
[10] *Ibid.*, I, 274.
[11] Thorpe, *American Charters, Constitutions and Organic Laws*, V, 2743–2753, 2761–2771.
[12] *Ibid.*, V, 2772–2786.

cinct consisting of six colonies. Each of these signiories, baronies, and colonies was to consist of 12,000 acres. The eight signiories were to be the share of the eight proprietors; the eight baronies, of the nobility; while the other three-fifths should belong to the people. The aristocracy consisted of landgraves and caziques. The whole system involved hereditary political power, based upon land. It likewise connected the right to hold court with land, and made of this a source of revenue, inasmuch as money had to be paid for appeals. Lawyers, however, were discouraged, and it was declared "a base and vile thing to plead for money or reward", and no one but a near kinsman should plead for anyone unless he had taken oath that he did not plead for money.

Provision was, to be sure, made for a parliament in which the proprietors, or their deputies, the landgraves and caziques, as well as freeholders chosen from each precinct, had seats. But the right to be chosen was limited to those who had not less than 500 acres of freehold. Thus political power was connected with land ownership as well as with feudal office. Not only was there an hereditary system of nobility, but the commoner was excluded from rising, since it was provided that the children of leet-men should always be leet-men.

Slavery was recognized in section 110 which gave the freeman absolute power over his Negro slaves. At the same time the system of government was strongly centralized and the mayors of towns were chosen from among the aldermen by the Palatine's Court. Freeholds were not absolute but held in payment of one English penny or that amount of silver per acre.

It is easy to deride this constitution as theoretical, but it was a reflection of a system which had stood the test of centuries in England. It failed to work in America because its whole social system was so ill adapted to frontier conditions that it can hardly be said to have gone through even the form of a struggle for existence. In the first place, land was too plentiful to give it the value implied in a feudal hierarchy. Then, the large landholders rendered practically no service in return for their privileges. Finally, the people were gradually growing too enlightened to submit to mere authority, imposed from without.

THE FREEDOMS AND EXEMPTIONS OF NEW NETHERLAND

In the Dutch colony of New Netherland, we find still another type. In the "New Project of Freedom and Exemptions", probably issued between 1629 and 1635,[13] elaborate provision was made for the patroons, their rights and duties. Here we have a peculiar polity which did not prove to be lasting, but did involve an elaborate system of land tenure, feudal in its character.[14]

In this charter the term "freedom" is used in quite a different sense from the term liberty in the Massachusetts Body of Liberties. In the latter case, reference was made to the liberty of the people; in New Netherland, the expression "freedom" was coupled with exemption and referred to the freedom of the privileged class. This whole charter defined the position of the patroons and was in large part devoted to an explanation of their special rights and duties. In general, those were recognized as Lords and Patroons who would within six years undertake to plant in New Netherland a colony of

[13] The manuscript is not dated, but is filed in the archives in a bundle marked 1630–1635.
[14] *New York Documents Relative to Colonial History* (ed. by O'Callaghan, 1853 ff.), I, 96.

forty-eight souls, on pain of being deprived of their freedoms, privileges, and exemptions, in case of palpable neglect (sec. 4). As soon as the patroons had designated the places in which they wished to plant their colonies, they were to be preferred above all others in those lands. They might extend their limit six miles along the sea coast or on both sides of a navigable river, and so deep landward as they demanded, and no one could approach within seven or eight miles of them against their will (sec. 8). The rights of the patroons extended to all "the fruits, superficies, minerals, rivers, and fountains thereof, for them, their heirs or assigns, with high, middle and low jurisdiction, tenths, fishing, fowling, wind and [water] mills and all other privileges, preeminences and rights, to be holden as free, allodial and patrimonial property" (sec. 10). If they prospered sufficiently "to be able to found one or more towns or cities, they shall have the authority to appoint officers and magistrates therein; enact laws and police, and make use of the titles and arms of their Colonies, according to their will and pleasure" (sec. 11). On the other hand, they should "furnish proper instructions to their Colonies, in order that they may be ruled and appointed, both in police and justice, conformably to the mode of government observed here" (sec. 13). The patroons were empowered to send over in the company's ships all their people and property, paying for freight 5 per cent. cash on the cost of goods in the mother country, but cattle and agricultural implements were to be taken over free, one-fourth part of all ships being reserved therefor. Patroons were to provide everything necessary to the maintenance of the cattle (sec. 14). Ships should sail at least yearly for New Netherland (sec. 15). Patroons were also privileged to send their own ships which might attack and conquer offensively and defensively the enemies of the state (sec. 16). Furthermore, the patroons were given trading privileges extending from Florida to Newfoundland and including all the wild islands of the West Indies (sec. 17). They were given freedom from any customs, toll, excise, impost or other tax (sec. 21).

"No person shall be at liberty to take from the service of the Patroons any of their Colonists, whether man, woman, son, daughter, maid-servant, or man servant" (sec. 22). This, of course, applied to the term of years during which servants were bound to their service, "after the expiration of which time, the Patroons shall be at liberty to send back to this country the Colonists who leave their service, and then first discharge them; and if any Colonist run away to another Patroon, or resume his freedom contrary to his contract, other Patroons of New Netherlands shall be bound, and do promise their High Mightinesses to cause him, as far as lies in his power, to be surrendered into the hands of the Patroon or his Commissary" (sec. 22). "The Patroons discovering shores, bays, or places adapted to Fishing or the manufacture of Salt, may take possession of them . . . to the exclusion of all others" (sec. 23).

On the other hand, "if any Colonist belonging to a Patroon happen to discover minerals, precious stones, crystals, marbles, pearl fishery or such like, they shall remain the Patroon's property, provided he allow such discoverer, as a premium thereof, so much as the Patroon shall have stipulated for that purpose" (sec. 25), but the patroon was bound to purchase from the Lords Sachems in New Netherland the ground on which he proposed to settle (sec. 27). The patroons had the duty of providing for a clergyman, a schoolmaster, and a comforter of the sick (sec. 28). "Their High Mightinesses shall exert themselves to provide the Patroons with persons bound to service, who shall be obliged to serve out their bounden time, in all obedience, for their board and clothing only, which being done, on bringing to this country a certificate thereof from the Patroons, or their Commissaries, such persons shall be here restored to their former state and freedom" (sec. 30). The West India Company should also allot to each patroon twelve black men and women out of the prizes in which Negroes were found (sec. 31).

"All private and poor people (*onvermogen personen*) are excluded from these Exemptions Privileges and Freedoms, and are not allowed to purchase any lands or grounds from the Sachems or Indians in New Netherland, but must repair under the jurisdiction of the respective Lord Patroons" (sec. 33).

EXPERIMENTAL CHARACTER OF COLONIAL LAWS

This review of some of the early codes of the seventeenth century shows that definite ideals of social structure and of social policy were embodied in the constitutions of the colonies from the very beginning, but that these ideals differed considerably according to the interests or the prepossessions of the founders. In no case, not even in John Locke's Constitutions of Carolina, do we find an exact copy of the government of the mother country. The aim was rather to devise laws which would presumably fit the new and untried conditions of the American plantations. We have, therefore, here the beginning of that long line of experimental legislation which has continued to the present day. In the following chapters some topics of fundamental economic interest, particularly land and labor, will be considered.

CHAPTER IV

LAND TENURE IN NEW ENGLAND

The first problem facing the settlers in America, first not only in time but also in permanent importance, was that of securing a livelihood from the resources of the new country. From the very beginning the colonists were forced to realize the hopelessness of maintaining their traditional economic organization, and in search of the means of subsistence they followed with few exceptions the same course; they took to the land. At the opening of the national period, nine-tenths of the people of the United States were engaged in agriculture;[1] in the period before the Revolution the proportion of those dependent on extractive industries was certainly larger rather than less. A topic of primary importance, therefore, in the social policy of the colonies is the system of tenure by which the land was apportioned and held. The reader needs but to consider the contrast, for example, of the mediaeval and modern land systems, or of the cottier tenures of Ireland, the peasant holdings of France and Germany, the great estates of England, and the communal tenure of Russia, to realize the profound influence of a system of land tenure in determining social classification, and the welfare of a people.

TENURE OF FREE SOCAGE

The settling of new lands in the English colonies in the seventeenth century was frequently done by means of companies. In form, therefore, it was commercial rather than political, and the definition of the rights of these companies was of great importance. In the charter of the London Company, which became the charter of Virginia in 1606, the king distinctly said that the lands in question were "To Be Holden of Us, our Heires and Successors, as of our Manor of *East-Greenwich*, in the County of *Kent*, in free and common Soccage only, and not in Capite."[2] Almost exactly the same terms were used in the charter of the Plymouth Company and in many others.[3] The rent was usually the fifth part of the gold or silver which should be found in the territory. What was the meaning of free and common socage? Blackstone devoted six pages to the explanation of socage tenure. It was contrasted with tenure in chivalry in that it was held in return for a definite payment or service, while chivalry implied a precarious and uncertain service. A distinction was made between *free*-socage, where the services

[1] Estimate of Tench Coxe, quoted by Adams, Henry Carter, *Taxation in the United States, 1789–1816* (1884), in *Johns Hopkins University Studies*, II, 273.
[2] Thorpe, *American Charters, Constitutions and Organic Laws*, VII, 3789.
[3] *Ibid.*, III, 1834.

were not only certain but honorable, and *villein*-socage, where the services, though certain, were of a baser nature.[4] The very origin of the word was in doubt in the period when the colonies were established. Some derived it from *soca*, meaning a plow, and implying that the tenant was bound to perform labor for his lord; Blackstone preferred the derivation from *soc*, a Saxon word, meaning "liberty", or "privilege".[5] He explained that in the reigns of both Edward I and Charles II, it was thought to be of much value to the tenants to reduce their tenure by knight-service to tenure by socage. This tenure was thought to be a relic of Saxon liberty retained by such persons as had neither forfeited their lands to the king nor been obliged to exchange their tenure for knight-service. This was peculiarly the case in the tenure prevailing in Kent, and called gavelkind. Those who thus preserved their tenure through the Norman Conquest were said to hold "in free and common socage". This tenure might apply not only to farm lands but also to town lands for which a rent was paid. Some of the peculiarities of gavelkind were that the estate did not escheat in case of felony, and that the lands descended, not to the eldest or youngest son, but to all together, which, said Blackstone, "was indeed anciently the most usual course of descent all over England".[6] Yet socage tenure was distinctly a feudal tenure and subject to a number of feudal burdens. With the Restoration of 1660, the military tenure was abolished, and all lands "holden *by one universal tenure of free and common socage*".[7]

Thus before the formal abolition of military tenure in 1660, the colonists were given what was considered a very favorable title to their land, and were regarded legally as a part of the county of Kent, in which there had survived from Saxon times the custom of gavelkind, involving an equal partition of the estate among all of the sons. In these original grants, therefore, we have the kernel, not only of land ownership, but also of what afterwards became the common, though not the universal, rule of inheritance in the colonies.

CONTRAST OF NEW ENGLAND AND OTHER COLONIES

In discussing the subject of the land system it will be necessary to consider separately the New England colonies and those of the Middle and South. The two groups are distinguished by several important differences. New England, with its niggardly soil and harsh climate, offered to the farmer the means of self-subsistence, but yielded little more. The central and southern colonies were bountiful in comparison, and, in particular, furnished crops like tobacco, rice, and the cereals, for which there was an active demand in other regions. In social structure the New England colonies were homogeneous as compared with the South, where, from the beginning, the extremes of European class distinctions had been represented and where slavery found a field favorable to its growth. Finally, New England was politically almost self-contained, while the other colonies were subject to royal or proprietary control which seriously modified the course of their development. The elements of similarity were so great throughout

[4] Blackstone, *Commentaries* (Cooley's ed.), I, 377–379 (Bk. II, 78–81).
[5] Maitland, *Domesday Book and Beyond* (1897), 66, 80 *et seq.*, the best modern authority, derives the word from *sócn*, a seeking, meaning jurisdiction.
[6] Blackstone, *Commentaries* (Cooley's ed.), I, 382 (Bk II, 84).
[7] *Ibid.*, I, 385 (Bk. II, 89).

the colonial organization that the land tenures of North and of South showed a general agreement, more striking than any differences. These differences did exist, however, and may be summed up in the statement that the system of peasant freeholds, prevailing in New England, was modified in the other colonies by aristocratic influences which sought to build up a system of great estates. A further difference and a very typical one showed itself in the stiff resistance of the New Englanders to the quit rent system. This was implied in socage tenure and accepted in England and quite generally in the North American colonies with the exception of New England. But, as shown by a student of the subject, the attempts of the home government to introduce quit rent ended in failure on account of the unwillingness of the settlers to accept a tenure perpetuating anything feudal.[8]

Somewhat oddly, however, one colony experimented also with communism and while its experience was brief, it should not be omitted in an account of the social policy of American settlements. We have to distinguish, therefore, three competing types of land tenure: 1. the community of land; 2. the democratic system of peasant farms, found generally in New England; 3. the aristocratic system of plantations or manors, found mainly in the South. The land system of the middle colonies falls between the second and third of these divisions.

COMMUNISM IN EARLY PLYMOUTH

When the congregation of Separatists at Leyden decided to emigrate, they obtained a patent from the Virginia Company, granted June 9/19, 1619. This was taken out, not in their names, but in that of Mr. John Wincob (or Whincop). It is said, however, that this was not used. The following year, under the advice of Thomas Weston, a London merchant, articles of agreement were drawn up, under which there should be a common stock, the shares to be 10 pounds each, to be taken up either by a deposit of money, or of goods for the undertaking. This plan originally involved a seven years' partnership during which the labor of the colonists, except for two days in the week, was to be for the common benefit. At the end of the time, when the profits were divided, the houses and improved lands were to go to the planters. This agreement was, however, changed by Robert Cushman in order to please the "merchant adventurers", and the planters were to give all their time to the company, while at the end of the seven years, houses, lands, and goods were to be divided between the "merchant adventurers" and the planters.[9] Thus the extreme communism, under which all individual reward for labor was to be given up, was due, not to any social ideal, but to the pressure from the capitalists who wanted a larger share for themselves.

In November 1621, nearly a year after the landing of the settlers, a new patent was brought over by Cushman from the President and Council of New England, in the name of John Peirce and Associates, which was used for eight and one-half years.[10] But the system of communism worked so badly that it was modified in 1624. It was then decided to assign an acre of land to each head of a family for planting, until the division of profits with the London merchants could be effected.

[8] Bond, *The Quit-Rent System in the American Colonies* (1919), chap. ii,
[9] Dexter, F. B., "The Pilgrim Church and Plymouth Colony", chap. viii in Winsor's *Narrative and Critical History* (1884), III, 265, 266.
[10] *Ibid.*, 275.

The planters were becoming restless and returns were at first small. Many merchant adventurers withdrew, and the result was an agreement to terminate the partnership "in consideration of the payment of £1,800 in nine equal annual installments, beginning in 1628. This arrangement was effected in London in November, 1626, * * * and the resident adult males (except a few thought unworthy of confidence) were constituted stockholders, each one being allowed shares up to the number of his family."[11] This was followed by an allotment of land to each shareholder and the distribution of the cattle among groups of families. As the financial burden of buying out the stockholders was heavy, eight leading planters with the help of four London friends undertook to make the first six annual payments in return for a monopoly of the foreign trade. In this way, individual proprietorship took the place of communism.[12]

Some of the details of this apportionment are given in Bradford's *History of Plymouth Plantation.* Bradford said that as some government was necessary to preserve the unity of the plantation, it was agreed that all heads of families or single young men of ability, free and able to govern themselves, and be helpful to the commonwealth, must be taken into partnership. "Yet they resolved to keep shuch a mean in the distribution of lands, and other courses, as should not hinder their growth in others coming to them." In accordance with this principle it was agreed that the trade should be managed as before, and all heads of families and single young men as above described should be enrolled as purchasers; that single free men should have a single share; that the father of a family should be allowed to purchase a share for each member of his family; but that servants were to have no share except such as their masters might give them out of theirs, or as their merit should gain them from the company later.

"Thus all were to be cast into single shares * * *; and so every one was to pay his part according to his proportion towards the purchase, and all other debts, what the profite of the trade would not reach too."[13]

The cattle were divided as follows: "a cowe to .6. persons or shares, and .2. to goats the same, which were first equalised for age and goodnes, and then lotted for." The swine, though more (146) in number, were allotted by the same rule. It was also agreed that every person or share should have 20 acres of land besides the single acres which they had already, to be divided by lot. Certain persons were named to do this, and rules laid down "as that they should only lay out settable or tillable land, at least shuch of it as should butt on the water side, . . . and pass by the rest as refuse and commone."[14]

It was also agreed, in order to keep the people together, that those whose lots should fall next to the town, or nearest for convenience, should take a neighbor or two and have them plant corn with them for four years, and afterwards they might use as much of their neighbors' land, for as long a time. Every share of 20 acres must be laid out ".5. acres in breadth by the water side, and .4. acres in length." No meadows were to be laid out at first "because they were but streight of meadow grounds; and if they had bene now given out, it would have hindred all addition to them afterwards; but every season all were appoynted wher they should mowe, according to the proportion of

[11] *Ibid.*, 276.
[12] *Ibid.*, 276.
[13] *Bradford's History of Plymouth Plantation* (Ford's ed. of 1912), II, 8–9.
[14] *Ibid.*, II, 9.

catle they had." "Also they gave the Gove [rno]r and .4. or .5. of the spetiall men amongst them, the houses they lived in; the rest were valued and equalised at an indiferent rate, and so every man kept his owne, and he that had a better alowed some thing to him that had a worse, as the valuation wente."[15]

It is obvious from this that the plan was to divide the land as far as possible according to the ability to use it, and otherwise to make an equal division both of land and of cattle. It was not an easy matter to raise the money needed to buy out the proprietors, and the rights of Bradford and the other men who undertook the contract had to be very carefully defined. They were to have and freely enjoy the "pinass" which was last built and other boats and implements belonging to them in the store of the company, together with all of the stock of furs, beads, corn, wampum, hatchets, knives, etc., now in store or due to them. They were to have the monopoly of the trade for six years, and upon the expiration of that time the whole was to return to the colony as before.[16] This is, in brief, the story of communism in Plymouth, and of its displacement by a system of individual ownership.[17]

SYSTEM OF SMALL FREEHOLDS

In New England, as in other colonies to the south, large tracts of land, amounting in some cases to many thousands or even to millions of acres, were granted to individuals or to groups. No such serious attempt was made, however, as in the other colonies, to establish large landed estates; and the results were not considerable. The aims of the colonists accorded with the conditions of their environment in leading to the establishment almost everywhere of a system of small freeholds.

Proprietary rights over the lands in New England were exercised by the colonial governments, which through their charters acquired the title proceeding originally from the king. The colonial government, through its General Court, occasionally made grants of unsettled land to individuals, as a mark of favor or to reward services rendered; but the individual estates formed in this way were comparatively few in number and small in extent.[18] As a rule, the colony did not itself deal with individual settlers or promoters. It received a petition from a group of people, who purposed a new settlement, and if it approved their plan, it incorporated the group as a town, and assigned to it a definite area for settlement.[19] The disposal of the land then lay with the group, under the general provisions laid down by the General Court in the grant.

The principles governing the action of the town authorities, in allotting land at the time of the original settlement, have been described as follows: "first, that of preventing the engrossing of lands and their accumulation in the hands of a few, the dangers of which in England were familiar to the colonists; secondly, that of subserving the law

[15] *Ibid.*, II, 11, 12.

[16] *Ibid.*, II, 30.

[17] Johnson, E. A. J., *American Economic Thought in the Seventeenth Century* (1932), chap. xii, "The Condemnation of Communism", sketches the Plymouth experiment and discusses at greater length than is possible here colonial views on the subject of communal property.

[18] Egleston, *The Land System of the New England Colonies* (1886), in *Johns Hopkins University Studies*, IV, 568 *et seq.*; Hutchinson, *History of Massachusetts* (3d ed., 1795), II, 299 *et seq.*

[19] Akagi, *The Town Proprietors of the New England Colonies* (1924), 30 *et seq.*; Osgood, *The American Colonies in the Seventeenth Century* (1904), I, 429 *et seq.*; Mead, "Land System of the Connecticut Towns", in *Political Science Quarterly*, XXI, 61, March, 1906.

of equity by treating every man fairly, not only in giving him a share in conquered or purchased lands, but also in so allotting that share that he might be subject to all the advantages and drawbacks that bore upon his neighbors; and thirdly, that of hastening settlement and the improvement of land".[20]

With regard to the first of these points, it is apparent that not only was the town group of New England democratic in structure, but also that it followed consciously a policy designed to establish equality among its members.[21] The term "equality" must not be construed too strictly. Occasionally we find a case like that of Wenham, Massachusetts, in which the group, with only one dissenting voice, adopted the rule "that all commoners should stand equally, both as to quantity and quality;"[22] but such cases are exceptional. In most towns the land was originally allotted in some proportion to the investment which men could make in the town to aid its development, measured sometimes by the contributions toward the expense of settlement, sometimes by the personal property owned, largely live-stock, or by the number in the family.[23] It is significant, however, that even the poorest of the settlers was classed with the others, not set apart in a class beneath them; the largest share might be twice or four times the smallest,[24] but it would still be a peasant's holding, of the same order of magnitude as the rest.

CONDITIONS OF TENURE IN EARLY TOWNS

It was frequently the practice at the time of settlement to reserve lots of land for such objects of common interest as the church or the grist-mill.[25] In a later period shares in the town land were often reserved for the support of a minister, for a school, or for the benefit of Harvard College or of Yale College.[26] In New Hampshire, a farm of five hundred acres was reserved in each township as a perquisite for the governor of the time, and an equal amount was to be set aside for the Society for the Propagation of the Gospel.[27]

A considerable part of the land, further, was usually left undivided at the start of the settlement, to be used in common and portioned out as need for it arose. In the course of time a distinction grew up between the "proprietary", the group of successors to the original settlers, and the town itself, which included later immigrants with full political rights in town meeting, but lacking proprietary rights in the undivided land. When a new division was made of land hitherto held in common, the land was usually portioned in shares equal in number to the number of original proprietors, but subdivided into fractions according with the splitting up of the interests by inheritance, bequest, and purchase. Various devices were employed to attain justice in the division: assignment by drawing of lots, assignment of larger areas of the poorer land,

[20] Andrews, "The Connecticut Intestacy Law," in *Yale Review*, III, 263–264, Nov. 1894.
[21] Osgood, *The American Colonies in the Seventeenth Century* (1904), I, 425; Mead, "Land System of the Connecticut Towns", 73.
[22] Egleston, *The Land System of the New England Colonies*, 587.
[23] Osgood, *The American Colonies in the Seventeenth Century*, I, 446, 456 *et seq.*
[24] Egleston, *The Land System of the New England Colonies*, 589.
[25] Andrews, *The River Towns of Connecticut* (1889), in *Johns Hopkins University Studies*, VII, 45.
[26] Akagi, *The Town Proprietors of the New England Colonies*, 208, footnote.
[27] *New York Documents Relative to Colonial History* (ed. by O'Callaghan, 1853 ff.), VII, 937; VIII, 275, 335.

scattering of the lots so as to combine different qualities of land in each holding. In the eighteenth century, as will be noted immediately, the contrast between representatives of the proprietary and townspeople who did not share in its rights became of substantial importance, but in the earlier period the two groups were scarcely distinguishable, and some towns made a conscious effort to maintain the equality in landed property of their members.[28]

Restrictions upon alienation were common in New England. Frequently no one could sell without the consent of the community.[29] This was done for the protection of the common interest so that, although the individual held the title to his land in fee simple, he could not sell it in such a way as to injure his neighbors, which might be done either by allowing some large landowner to buy up a number of holdings, or by introducing elements that would be disturbing to the peace and good order of the community. The idea that land should be held by those who would use it properly, is seen in a section of the code of laws of Connecticut, passed May, 1650, which says:

"Home Lotts.

"Whereas there is creeping in, in severall Townes and plantations within this Jurissdiction, a great abuse of buying and purchasing Home Lotts and laying them together, by means whereof great depopulations are like to follow, It is ordered that all dwelling or mansion howses that are or shall bee allowed in any plantation or Towne within this Jurissdiction, shall be vpheld, repaired and meinteined sufficiently in a comely way: As allso, whosoeuer shall possess and inioye any homelotts within any such plantation or Towne, that is not yet built vppon, shall, within twelue months after the making of this order, erect and build a howse there, fitt for an inhabitant to dwell in, vnless the Courte, vpon knowledge of the case, finde cause to abate or giue longer time for building."[30] In time, of course, these restrictions came to be disregarded, and when land passed through several hands, they were plainly difficult to maintain.

DEVELOPMENT OF ABSENTEE TENURE AND SPECULATION IN LAND

Land was granted to a group of colonists by the colonial government on condition that a settlement be actually established there, with proper provision for the social and religious life of the community. Early towns, to further their own interests, welcomed newcomers, and treated them generously in the grant or sale of land. As the frontier was pushed forward, and settlement became more dense behind it, land began to acquire a scarcity value, if not in the immediate present, at least with a view to the future. Speculation in landed property became active in New England. There was at last a surplus of capital seeking investment, and the prospect of an "unearned increment" in growing communities was attractive. In America as in England the speculative spirit grew in force even among men of Puritan descent; land banks, land auctions, lotteries, evidenced its presence. Absentee ownership, both in old and in new towns, became common. Land agents traversed New England, New York, and

[28] Akagi, *The Town Proprietors of the New England Colonies*, 108.
[29] Cases quoted in Egleston, *The Land System of the New England Colonies*, 593–594.
[30] *The Public Records of the Colony of Connecticut* I. 562–563.

New Jersey, peddling rights to land. Ezra Stiles, a Connecticut minister, president of Yale College, bought numerous rights in Connecticut, Massachusetts, and New Hampshire. "While on his way to Boston, in 1761, he bought of a travelling salesman at Dedham a right in one of the lately created townships for two dollars;" nothing came of it, he regretfully recorded in his diary.[31] "Eastern men of property," to use Turner's phrase, were set off against the democratic pioneers of the frontier. In the older towns a marked cleft appeared between the group of successors to the original proprietors, and the other inhabitants. At various dates before and after 1700 the General Courts of the different New England colonies recognized the rights of the "proprietary" to dispose of unallotted lands, and established regular procedure for its activities. Protests of other taxpayers were fruitless. Jonathan Edwards, writing in the middle of the eighteenth century, described the people of Northampton as having been divided for fifty years over the land question, "somewhat like the court and country parties of England, if I may compare small things with great".[32] The proprietary system faded away as the stock of common, undivided land was exhausted, or when the whole body of taxpayers bought out the rights attached to the successors of the original proprietors. In its operation in the eighteenth century it certainly illustrates the evils rather than the benefits of a system of private property in land.[33]

The working of the proprietary system may be illustrated by the history of the town of New Haven, in which for years the management of the land was an important piece of business for the proprietors. First of all the town was laid out in the familiar nine squares, the central one being reserved for a market place and common.[34] Then a tract of land, about one mile from the town on all sides was set apart as the "Two-Mile Square" or "The Upland." Every planter received a part of the upland and of the meadow land around the town, "according to the proportion of estate which he hath given in, and the number of heads in his family".[35] Each subscriber of £100 received five acres of upland and of meadow, and in addition to this, two and one-half acres of upland and one-half acre of meadow were given for each head in the family. These were assigned in such a way as to make the farm land contiguous to the town plots, as far as possible. A large section to the northwest of the town was reserved for a common pasturage, the cow pasture on the hither side, and the ox pasture on the further side, of Beaver Pond. The cattle were to be driven to pasture with a keeper. The land on the neck (now Fair Haven) was tilled in common for a time.[36] Later in the year, a second and final division of the outland consisting of the upland outside of the two-mile square was made. This was done at the rate of twenty acres for each £100 and two and one-half acres per head.[37] No large grants were made to any individual.

[31] Akagi, *The Town Proprietors of the New England Colonies*, 216, quoting *Extracts from the Itineraries .... of Ezra Stiles* (ed. by F. B. Dexter, 1916), 99–100. See Akagi, *Ibid.*, pt. ii, "Land Speculation in New England in the Eighteenth Century", for a detailed account of this period.

[32] Quoted in Egleston, *The Land System of the New England Colonies*, 585. Akagi, *The Town Proprietors of the New England Colonies*, 124 *et seq.*, gives a full account of the controversies.

[33] The best account of the system will be found in Akagi, *The Town Proprietors of the New England Colonies*; see also Egleston, *The Land System of the New England Colonies*, and Mead, "The Land System of the Connecticut Towns."

[34] Levermore, *The Republic of New Haven*, 32.

[35] *Ibid.*, 81.

[36] *Ibid.*, 81.

[37] Levermore says that in fact only two acres per head were assigned, see *ibid.*, 82, footnote.

Even the leaders like John Davenport and Governor Eaton fared little better than the rest except in the matter of location.[38] As time went on, even though the bulk of the land had been distributed, there was a distinction between the commoners or representatives of the original proprietors and the non-commoners, a distinction not unlike that which exists in some of the Swiss villages between the simple residents or "Beisassen", who have no rights in the Allmende, and those who have. In New Haven a liberal policy prevented any serious rupture, and yet the local expressions "town-born" and "interlopers" still survive as a relic of the early distinction. The term "town-born" does not mean born in New Haven, but descended from one of the original proprietors. Some of the most distinguished citizens of New Haven, such as James Hillhouse and Roger Sherman, were technically "interlopers".[39]

PERSISTENCE OF THE PROPRIETARY TO THE PRESENT

The proprietary system itself still exists in form in New Haven though with attenuated functions, and the story of the changes which it underwent, after it had accomplished its purpose, is not without interest to the student of institutions. By the end of the eighteenth century the greater part of the valuable land had been distributed, but the flats on the harbor, the faces of East and West Rock, the Green, and some other tracts were still in the hands of the proprietors. Their meetings had become infrequent as the amount of business to be done grew less, but down to 1805 they were still called together occasionally, to act upon the alienation of the land. The last meeting was held December 30, 1805,[40] when a committee, appointed at a previous meeting, reported on the general subject of land sales. After enumerating the various pieces of land, mainly flats, owned by the proprietors, and also several applications to buy land, build roads, etc., they recorded as their findings, that:

"No further distribution among them as proprietors is intended. That the power of selling has been vested in a proprietors Committee who have sold from time to time, yielding the avails to the town treasury. As the power of compassing public objects is in the selectmen, they report as their opinion that by a proprietors' vote all the flats opposite the public streets should be established to be perpetually open for public use . . . and that in respect to all the other proprietory property they report as their opinion that a permanent board of five proprietors be appointed with power to supply vacancies in their number, occasioned by death or resignation; which board shall have full power to alienate the proprietory property by and with the advice of the selectmen, for the time being, as fully and absolutely as the same could now be alienated by vote of the proprietors. And all issues & profits shall go into the town treasury," unless otherwise determined by the selectmen. This was accepted and approved by the proprietors, and a committee of five was appointed to secure confirmation by the General Assembly.[41]

As some question came up regarding their right to take this action the General Assembly passed an act in October, 1810, confirming the proprietors' committee in their power to sell lands and to turn over the proceeds to the town. Thus with char-

[38] *Ibid.*, 83.
[39] *Ibid.*, 228–230.
[40] This account of the proprietors' committee is taken from the old book of records which goes back to 1771. The author was indebted to Messrs. Roger S. and Oliver S. White for allowing him to examine it.
[41] *Minute Book*, 38.

acteristic conservatism, the New Haven proprietary has never terminated formally its corporate existence, but it has turned over its functions to a self-perpetuating committee and its pecuniary interest to the town; and the proprietors' committee is still called upon to act, if any measures are to be taken regarding those parts of the original grant, especially the New Haven Green, which are still in their hands.

LACK OF LARGE ESTATES

The land system of the New England colonies, starting in the ill-fated experiments with common property at Plymouth, developed on the principle of attracting and rewarding the individual settler. Some elements in it which now would be called capitalistic, and which showed themselves prominently in the course of the eighteenth century, were not strong enough to affect the general result, which was the establishment of a democratic body of simple freeholders. The laws were not distinctly opposed to the growth of great landed properties. They were framed, however, with the peasant proprietor chiefly in mind and would have needed far more support than they secured from the physical and economic environment, to have led to an aristocratic system of tenures. The difficulty of building up in New England a system of large estates, settled with tenants, had been apparent from the earliest times. Governor Talcott wrote, in the early part of the eighteenth century, "in this poor country, if the landlord lives, the tenant starves: few estates here will let for little more than for maintaining fences and paying taxes".[42] "Of course we have no tenanted lands," wrote a Connecticut clergyman, describing his town about 1800.[43] An excellent observer twenty years later could make a statement nearly as broad of all New England. "In these countries," said Dwight, "lands are universally held in fee simple,"[44] and although in other places he noted instances in which men worked on the lands of others, he thought them too unimportant to modify his general statement.

PROPRIETARY SYSTEM IN NEW NETHERLAND

A system similar to that of the New England proprietaries grew up in the Dutch possessions on the Hudson River and in that neighborhood. In 1650, Van Tienhoven, the Dutch secretary under Stuyvesant, laid down, in information which he sent to Holland, the general principles under which the towns should be settled, advocating the selection of a suitable spot, the laying out of a village with good streets, and the fencing of the whole with a high palisade, closed with gates.[45] There is evidence that in a good many of these Dutch settlements a part of the land was held in common. The bulk of the land was, however, divided up among the share-holders by lot. Thus a patent to Gravesend was issued in 1645.[46] In 1650 the inhabitants agreed that they would fence in a certain quantity of land to contain 28 shares and these were to be divided by lot and everyone was "inioyned to build and inhabit in the towne by a daye agreed vppon, for the mutual strengthning of one another, for the peace with the Indians being new".[47] It was likewise ordered that none of the inhabitants should sell

[42] Quoted by Andrews, "Connecticut Intestacy Laws," 268.
[43] Goodrich, *Statistical Account of Ridgefield*, MS. in Connecticut Historical Society, f. 9.
[44] Dwight, *Travels in New England and New York* (New Haven ed., 1821), I, 17.
[45] Elting, *Dutch Village Communities on the Hudson River* (1886), in *Johns Hopkins University Studies*, IV, 23.
[46] *Ibid.*, 26.
[47] *Ibid.*, 27, quoting from *New York Documents Relative to Colonial History*, XIV, 128–129.

their lots, unless they had first offered them to the town in general. Then they could sell them to outsiders, unless the buyer were known to be "an infamous person or a disturber of the common peace."[48] In this Dutch institution we find a close parallel to the New England system in spite of the efforts of the West India Company to encourage manors.

LARGE ESTATES IN THE NARRAGANSETT COUNTRY

The only serious exception to the system of peasant holdings prevailing in New England was found in the southwestern part of Rhode Island.[49] Of the land in that district, part was very fertile, and much of the remainder was admirably suited to grazing; water boundaries supplied the need of fencing, elsewhere a considerable item of expense. This land was held in the eighteenth century in estates so large that they were reckoned in square miles and thousands of acres, and, in contrast to large holdings in northern New England, the estates were going concerns, manned by a large population of slaves. The natural conditions suited the large stock and dairy farms which were established here, and which yielded good profits to the owners, who exported horses, wool, and especially cheese and other dairy products. It seems probable, however, that even here the land would have been held in small estates but for influences which must be considered political in character, and which were peculiar to the district. This part of Rhode Island was claimed by two rival land companies, and was for half a century a debatable territory between Rhode Island and Connecticut. In the long conflict, the men of small means were weeded out from among the claimants, and the land fell prize finally to the few who had the political power and the economic resources to bring the struggle to a successful issue. It is noteworthy that one of the few districts in which Dwight later found a system of tenant holdings was in the neighboring part of Connecticut, where dairy farms were leased out to tenants who came, in large part, from Rhode Island.[50]

LAWS OF INHERITANCE

That it was the conscious policy of the New England colonies, in general, to further the system of peasant holdings rather than that of large estates is proved not only by the customs of land division, but also by the customs of inheritance and the laws of intestacy. By the English common law the eldest son of an intestate was the sole heir to real estate; this rule prevailed down to the passage of the Administration of Estates Act, 1925. Plymouth adopted early a rule "That Inheritances shall descend according to the comendable Custom tenure and hold of east greenwich",[51] and the Massachusetts Body of Liberties provided that "When parents dye intestate, the Elder sonne shall have a doble portion of his whole estate reall and personall, unlesse the Generall Court upon just cause alleadged shall Judge otherwise" (Liberty 81). Thus the English law seems to have been nullified by general agreement from early times,[52] and

[48] *Ibid.*, 27.
[49] Channing, *Narragansett Planters* (1886), in *Johns Hopkins University Studies*, IV, No. 3.
[50] Dwight, *Travels in New England and New York* (New Haven ed.), III, 24.
[51] *Records of the Colony of New Plymouth* (ed. by Shurtleff, 1855–1861), XI, 187; *cf.* Connecticut law of 1692, in *The Public Statute Laws of Connecticut* (ed. of 1808), I, 432.
[52] *Cf.* Andrews. "Connecticut Intestacy Law," 267–268.

before the close of the seventeenth century, it had been abrogated by specific provisions on the colonial statute books. The Massachusetts law of 1692/3 set forth in its preamble that "estates in these plantations do consist chiefly of lands which have been subdued and brought to improvement by the industry and labour of the proprietors, with the assistance of their children, the younger children generally having been longest and most serviceable unto their parents in that behalf, who have not personal estates to give out unto them in portions or otherwise to recompence their labour":[53] and then, while it recognized the right of individuals to dispose of lands by will, it provided that in case of intestacy the land was to go in equal shares to all the children except the eldest son, to whom a double portion was assigned. The same provision, which was that of the Mosaic law, and which probably commended itself to Puritan legislators on that account, was adopted by New Hampshire in 1693, and by Connecticut in 1699.[54]

The reasons for the colonial intestacy law were set forth as follows by Governor Talcott of Connecticut: "much of our lands remain unsubdued, and must continue so without the assistance of the younger sons, which in reason can't be expected if they have no part of the inheritance; . . . By this custom of dividing inheritances, all were supply'd with land to work upon, the land as well occupy'd as the number of hands would admit of, the people universally imploy'd in husbandry; . . . the younger brethren do not depart from us, but others are rather encouraged to settle among us, and it's manifest that New England does populate faster than the Colonies where the land descends according to the rules of the common law."[55]

The New Hampshire act was repealed by the Queen in Council, on the ground that it was contrary to English law and altered the descent of inheritances of persons living in England, "besides that it will be inconvenient to divide plantations";[56] and the Connecticut law also was annulled on the appeal of interested parties;[57] but the colonies persisted in their practice, and finally established it against the rather perfunctory opposition of the English authorities.

EXCEPTIONAL POSITION OF RHODE ISLAND

The colony of Rhode Island, which has already been noted for its departures from the system of land tenure prevailing in New England, takes again an exceptional position with regard to the customs and laws of inheritance. Apparently the English custom of primogeniture was originally practiced in this colony, for the preamble of the law of 1718 recited that "it hath been found by experience in this colony, to be very wrongful and injurious to the public good, as well as private interest, of the younger children of persons dying intestate, that the whole real estate of such persons dying intestate, should descend to the eldest son, and thereby the other children, whose labors have been very useful, and advantageous to their parents in reducing and improving such real estate, should be left destitute."[58]

[53] *Acts and Resolves of the Province of Massachusetts Bay*, I, 43.
[54] *Laws of New Hampshire* (ed. by Batchellor, 1904), I, 566; *The Public Records of the Colony of Connecticut*, IV, 307.
[55] Andrews, "Connecticut Intestacy Law," 268, quoting from *Talcott Papers*, I, 145–146.
[56] *Laws of New Hampshire* (ed. by Batchellor), I, 860, 861.
[57] Andrews, "Connecticut Intestacy Law," 276.
[58] *Acts and Laws of His Majesty's Colony of Rhode-Island* (Boston, 1179 [*sic*], facsimile reprint of original of 1719 by S. H. Rider, 1895), 95–96.

This law adopted what may be called the New England system; after providing for the dower rights of the widow it gave a double share to the eldest son, or, in case of his death, to his legal representatives, and one share to each of the other children. After a trial of ten years, however, it was repealed, as it was "by experience found very prejudicial in this Colony, by destroying Inheritances."[59] Rhode Island adopted in 1750 the English practice of dividing the personal property in equal shares among the children,[60] but did not abandon the principle of primogeniture as applied to real estate until 1770. The legislature had appointed a committee the year before to draft an act, of which the preamble is an extended statement of the justification of departure from the English system:

"As Reason and Equity plainly point out, that the Estate of a Parent, who dies Intestate, should be divided among all his Children, in an equitable Proportion, unless where some political Considerations may make a contrary Method more suitable to the Circumstances and Constitution of a Country: none of which Reasons do at present, nor can, for a long Time, exist in this Colony."[61] The new law followed the common custom of a division of the real estate equally among the children except for a double share to the eldest son. In 1790, after Rhode Island had become a State of the Union, the legislature returned to the subject and finally, in 1792, passed an act which provided for an absolutely equal division of the real estate of an intestate, without any preference of the eldest son.[62]

The departure of Rhode Island from the practices of other New England colonies may not have been so decided as one would suppose from a study merely of the laws. Channing thinks that their practical importance has been exaggerated, and that even the large estates were divided in more or less equitable fashion.[63] It is clear, at any rate, that the leaders who determined the legislation of Rhode Island were in spirit more aristocratic than their neighbors. The contrast appears again in the laws fixing the liability of a decedent debtor's land to levy and execution for debt. Massachusetts adopted, in 1692/3, the principle that lands held in fee simple were liable for debts; and it was said that to this provision, and to that providing for the equal distribution of intestate estates, "much of the populousness and of the commerce of the Massachusetts is owing."[64] In the unpublished manuscript of Chalmers, from which the quotation is made, attention was directed to the "dissimilar spirit" of the southern colonies, where, in fact, the English principle, requiring the creditor to look only to personal property for the satisfaction of his claims, was generally retained. In this respect, Pennsylvania, after several changes, ultimately followed the northern practice, treating land and personal property alike,[65] while Rhode Island again clung to the English rule, and did not make the real estate of a deceased person liable for his debts until 1769.[66]

[59] Act of Feb. 1728, in *Acts and Laws of His Majesty's Colony of Rhode-Island* (1730), 163, 182.

[60] *Records of the Colony of Rhode Island*, V, 289.

[61] *Ibid.*, VI, 597; VII, 24; Act of Feb. 1770, in *Acts and Laws of the English Colony of Rhode Island* (1772, facsimile reprint, 1893), 25.

[62] *Records of the Colony of Rhode Island*, X, 372, 476; *The Public Laws of the State of Rhode Island* (1798), 287.

[63] Channing, *Narragansett Planters*, 120.

[64] *Acts and Resolves of the Province of Massachusetts Bay*, I, 68, 107 *fn.*, quoting from Chalmers' unpublished MS., a continuation of his *Political Annals*, in library of Massachusetts Historical Society.

[65] *Charter to William Penn and Laws of the Province of Pennsylvania*, 100, 120, 180, 217, 231, 244; *Statutes at Large of Pennsylvania, 1682–1801* (compiled by Mitchell and Flanders, 1896–1911), II, 53.

[66] *Records of the Colony of Rhode Island*, VI, 605; *cf.* Channing, *Narragansett Planters*, 120.

Rhode Island showed a more liberal spirit in another part of the law akin to that of primogeniture, namely, the law of entail. The practice of entailing land was not unknown in New England, and even in Massachusetts the collection of *Acts and Resolves* contains frequent references, during the first half of the eighteenth century, to estates tail, though all the cases noted were of tail general, and therefore of no great social significance. When the legislature of Rhode Island found that the act of 1718, against the descent of real estate by primogeniture, was applied to entailed estates, "whereby an estate tail will be destroyed by dividing, and contrary to the intent of the first testator," it resisted for the moment, and determined that "all estates tail shall enure according to the laws of England."[67] Within a few years, however, the legislature provided the means for breaking entails which were commonly employed in England, and which, in the absence of family settlements, would lead to a democratic division of the land. The Rhode Island act of June, 1725,[68] complained in its preamble that it was the undoubted right of His Majesty's subjects living in England, if seized of estates tail, to dock and cut off the entail by a fine or common recovery, but subjects in the colony, from lack of proper officers, had been deprived of this benefit. The statute provided, therefore, that the General Assembly should appoint "a Cursitor, Prothonotary, Receiver of the King's Silver, Exemplification Office, Alienation Office, and all other Offices and Officers" needed for the purpose, and the title of an act passed in 1731, "for recording fines and common recoveries", shows that action was taken even if all the specified officers and offices were not established.[69]

REFORMS OF THE REVOLUTIONARY PERIOD

In all of the colonies the period at the close of the eighteenth century, marked as it was by the establishment of national independence and by the organization of new governments under the Constitution, was a time of active social legislation. It was then that economists and philosophers began first seriously to influence the course of policy, and the political self-consciousness induced by independence stimulated a rationalistic and critical examination of institutions carried on from the past. In land tenure, as in other fields of social policy, the new spirit prevailed.[70]

Colonies which had not already done so now took a stand against entails and similar features of the old régime, and the New England colonies departed finally from the characteristic provision which gave to the eldest son of an intestate a double share of his father's land. However much this provision may have recommended itself to the Puritans, by reason of Biblical authority, it answered no longer the ideas of natural justice which ruled the time, and gave way to the system of a perfectly equal division of land among the children.[71]

[67] *Records of the Colony of Rhode Island*, IV, 258; this was in the session of September, 1719.
[68] *Acts and Laws of His Majesty's Colony of Rhode-Island* (1730), 138.
[69] *Ibid.*, 138; *Records of the Colony of Rhode Island*, IV, 406.
[70] See Jameson, *The American Revolution considered as a Social Movement* (1926), especially chap. ii, "The Revolution and the Land."
[71] New Hampshire Act of 1789, in *The Perpetual Laws of the State of New Hampshire* (1789), 76; Massachusetts Act of 1789, in *The Perpetual Laws of the Commonwealth* (1789), 230; Rhode Island Act of 1792, in *Records of the Colony of Rhode Island*, X, 476, and *Public Laws of the State of Rhode Island* (1798), 287; Connecticut Act of 1792, in *The Public Statute Laws of Connecticut* (ed. of 1808), 271.

CHAPTER V

LAND TENURE IN THE MIDDLE AND SOUTHERN COLONIES

IMPORTANCE OF THE LARGE ESTATES

The peculiar features of the New England land system, the town group with its peasant holdings and its common lands, were present also to a less extent in New York and in some of the other colonies.[1] They became, however, less frequent and less characteristic as one went south. The peasant freeholds which were so nearly universal in New England were not lacking elsewhere, for they represented a type of subsistence farming which was natural in the colonial environment, and which could and did arise perfectly well apart from the system of the New England town. Along with these small holdings, however, often predominating over them in area and importance, were estates of which the majority were, perhaps, not over 1000 acres, but which ranged from that comparatively moderate size to great territories whose area was described in blocks of miles. Some of these large estates were cultivated as economic units by a dependent population. The influences—physical, economic, and social—which gave rise to the plantation system, have often been described. Most of the large estates, however, were cultivated only in part, and some not at all; they were legal rather than economic units, representing the rights of an owner to exclude other men from their enjoyment and use, but no inclination or ability on his own part to make them serviceable. The student of social policy asks, naturally, how such rights were acquired and maintained.

Without entering into the details, we may accept as natural the plantations on which were cultivated, by slave labor, the export products of the southern colonies.[2] We may assume that the hope of plantation profits explains the desire of individuals to acquire large estates. To understand, however, why so many of these estates were called into being and allowed to persist, when they offered to society so little in return for the rights which it conferred, we must understand the underlying political conditions, without which the land system would be unintelligible.

POLITICAL BASIS OF THE LARGE ESTATES

There is, in this aspect, a sharp distinction between the corporate colonies of New England, and the proprietary colonies of the Middle and South.[3] The New England

[1] *Cf.* Osgood, *The American Colonies in the Seventeenth Century*, II, 50; Elting, *Dutch Village Communities*, in *Johns Hopkins University Studies*, IV, 39, 47 *et seq.*; Holcomb, *Pennsylvania Boroughs* (1886), *Ibid.*, IV, 139, 148; Ingle, *Local Institutions of Virginia* (1885), *Ibid.*, III, 138.

[2] See Gray, *History of Agriculture in the Southern United States* (1933), chaps. xiv, xv; see also chap. xvii, "The Colonial Land System," for many details which are omitted from the present account.

[3] See Osgood, in *The American Colonies in the Seventeenth Century*, who has done most to explain the character and importance of this distinction.

colonies recognized a political superior in the English government, but were little troubled by its interference. They had secured from the Crown a title to their land which gave them the right to dispose of it almost without restriction. They exercised this right with a view to the practical conditions of the country, and in the light of their own social and political ideals; and established a land system which, on the whole, answered admirably to their requirements. The very name of proprietary colony suggests that the settlers in the Middle and South established themselves under different conditions. The land belonged to an overlord, who regarded it as a private estate, to be exploited for his profit; and even when the original proprietary rights were extinguished and the colony became a royal province, the King still clung to the established view, and treated the land of the province as a source of income.

At best, therefore, the proprietary colonies were subject to a European influence from which the corporate colonies were free, and would naturally show in their land system some elements at least, betraying mistaken efforts to realize European ideas in the new environment. These colonies suffered even more, however, from the weakness of the proprietary or royal system of government than they did from the strength of its influence. The proprietors and the Crown found it necessary to delegate much of their power, not only as rulers but as owners, to representatives in America, and the result was authority divided, with an ocean between. The colonial government under these circumstances found it too often easy and profitable to represent, not the interests of the people of the colony, nor even the interests of the proprietors or Crown, but only the interests of its own individual members. The worst features of colonial land policy were a result of the corruption or the negligence of the colonial administration.

If conditions had permitted, the proprietors would unquestionably have desired to treat the unsettled land as they would have treated one of their European estates, to be let out on terms which would have permitted them to resume the title and enjoy the growth in value. Such a practice was scarcely attempted. A single example will show its futility. A piece of swampy land of about seventy acres, which had been included in one of the extravagant grants in New York and then taken back, was henceforth to be granted for no longer period than the governor's term in office. It was a stagnant spot, a menace to the health of the neighboring town, but no one would take it unless he was given the fee simple for it, and only under those terms was it finally cleared and brought under cultivation.[4] The proprietor's problem was, actually, not how to keep the title from men who wanted it and would be encouraged by it to develop the land, but how to find such men, and bring them and the land together.

ATTEMPTS TO ESTABLISH A MANORIAL SYSTEM

An approach to this problem, characteristic especially of the proprietary colonies, was the attempt to use the social organization, as it existed in Europe, for a means of subduing the wild land of the new continent. The plan offered this attractive feature, that the proprietor or his agents need deal only with a few leaders, who were endowed with such social and quasi-political prerogatives as would enable them to gather a

[4] *New York Documents Relative to Colonial History*, V, 915, 962.

group of followers from the lower classes, and who would assume the responsibilities of an enterprise from which the profits were to be shared.

The South Carolina scheme, elaborated in the "Fundamental Constitutions", with its seigniories, baronies, and manors, is the classic example of this policy.[5] It was not, however, confined to any one colony or any one period. Even at the close of the eighteenth century, we find, in a settlement projected in the western part of New York, an excellent illustration of the survival of the same idea, viz.—the establishment of an American colony on the basis of the European social order.[6] The settlement, comprising 10,000 acres, was to be distributed as follows:

"For the ministry	100 acres
For the school, about	60
Ten gentlemen, 500 acres each	5,000
Ten farmers, 100 acres each	1,000
Forty farmers, 78 acres each	3,120
For the village, sixty lots of 12 acres each	720
	10,000 acres"

The most common and characteristic expression of this idea was the grant of manorial privileges to the leader of a group of settlers. The English manor at this period had, of course, declined from the important position which it once occupied, but it was still a regular feature of rural organization. It represented in form, if not in fact, the monarchical element in social grouping, and seemed to promise, ready at hand, a means of organizing settlement so as to relieve the government of the petty detail of dealing with the individual cultivators. The French counterpart of this institution was actually realized in Canada, and was an effective element in the colonial system there. In the English colonies, the attempt to establish the manorial system was an experiment, not without interest to the student of institutions, but of no serious practical importance.

The name of "manor" is found even in New England,[7] and is by no means uncommon in the more southern colonies.[8] Investigators have been rash, however, in supposing that corresponding to the name was a reality of practical significance. Even in New York, in which, of all the colonies, the most determined effort was made to establish the manorial system, the manorial influence on social policy is almost negligible.

MANORS IN NEW NETHERLAND AND NEW YORK

The Dutch succeeded ill in their early attempts to colonize New Netherland, and in 1629 decided to offer manorial privileges to leaders who would establish settlements there.[9] These leaders, dignified by the term patroons, were tempted by the offer of

[5] *Cf.* Smith, W. Roy, *South Carolina as a Royal Province* (1903), 26, 35.

[6] *Documentary History of the State of New York* (qto. ed. by O'Callaghan, 1853–1887), II, 672.

[7] *The Talcott Papers, Correspondence and Documents, 1724–1736* (Connecticut Historical Society, Collections, IV), I, 162; Hibbard, *History of the Town of Goshen, Connecticut* (1897), 187.

[8] *Cf.* "Charter for the Province of Pennsylvania, 1681," in Thorpe, *American Charters, Constitutions and Organic Laws*, V, 3042; Johnson, J. H., *Old Maryland Manors* (1883), in *Johns Hopkins University Studies*, I, No. 7; Wilhelm, *Local Institutions of Maryland* (1885), *Ibid.*, III, 315, 325, 335; Carroll, *Historical Collections of South Carolina* (1836), II, 366. The list of references could be considerably extended.

[9] Brodhead, *History of the State of New York* (ed. of 1872), I, 186 *et seq.*; *Van Rensselaer Bowier Manuscripts* (New York State Library History Bulletin, No. 7, ed. by Van Laer, 1908) contain a full collection of documents on the manors of New York to about 1650.

tracts of land almost unlimited in extent, "together with the fruits, rights, minerals, rivers and fountains thereof; as also the chief command and lower jurisdictions, fishing, fowling, and grinding, to the exclusion of all others, to be holden from the company as a perpetual inheritance".[10]

The list of privileges was printed and circulated in the United Provinces,[11] and was confirmed, with no important changes, in 1650.[12] The privileges were opposed, naturally, on the ground that they discouraged the settlement of simple freemen,[13] and even in 1655 the Dutch directors wrote to Governor Stuyvesant, that "as to establishing a colony under the same conditions as those of *Rensselaerswyck*, you know very well, that long ago we have considered the granting of such colonies unadvisable and injurious to the increase of population and that instead of it we have decided to accommodate private parties with as much land, as they are able to cultivate, without giving them any privileges; you will act accordingly."[14]

The only patroons who succeeded in getting any substantial advantage from their grants in the Dutch period were the Van Rensselaers, who built up a settlement near Albany.[15] Under the English rule the Van Rensselaer colony was converted into "an English manor, with its lords and stewards, its court-leet and court-baron";[16] and new manors were constituted: Livingston, Cortlandt, Fordham, Pelham, and others whose names have not even been preserved as the titles of railroad stations.[17]

The constitution (on paper) of one of these manors may be gathered from the grant which Governor Dongan made in 1686 to Robert Livingston to reward, so he said, the expense of purchase and settlement, and to encourage future settlement. The patent constituted "one Lordshipp or Mannor to all Intents and Purposes," with rights to hold a court leet and a court baron, and authority to "Destrain for the Rents Services," and to have all "Wasts, Estrayes, Wrecks, Deodands, Goods of felons," fines and advowsons.[18]

There is no evidence that any of these manors were of importance as units of agrarian organization. Even in the Old World, the manors in this aspect had lost their significance with the passing of villainage. We read, it is true, in an early lease on the Rensselaer manor, of a tenant bound to carrying services besides his payments in kind;[19] but accounts of this settlement agree in stating that it prospered chiefly as a staple of the Indian trade, and that the people on it were merchants rather than cultivators.

[10] O'Callaghan, *History of New Netherland* (1846), I, 114.

[11] Brodhead, *History of the State of New York*, I, 199.

[12] *New York Documents Relative to Colonial History*, I, 401 *et seq.*

[13] *Cf. New York Documents Relative to Colonial History*, I, 154; O'Callaghan, *History of New Netherland*, II, 69; Elting, *Dutch Village Communities*, 17.

[14] *New York Documents Relative to Colonial History*, XIV, 333.

[15] *Ibid.*, I, 181; *Documentary History of the State of New York* (qto. ed.), IV, 16.

[16] Lamb, "The Van Rensselaer Manor," in *Magazine of American History*, XI, 31 *et seq.*, Jan. 1884.

[17] Frequent references are made in the *Documents Relative to Colonial History*, and the *Documentary History of the State of New York*, to these manors, and others such as Phillips, St. George and Bentley; and even the local town records furnish similar examples. *Cf.* Huntington (N. Y.), *Town Records* (ed. by Street, 1887–1889), I, 419 *et seq.*, 451 *et seq.*

[18] *Documentary History of the State of New York* (qto. ed.), III, 375–376. Deodands were actually found in all the colonies, the offending animal or instrument being forfeited to the crown or proprietor. See Karraker, C. H., "Deodands in Colonial Virginia and Maryland," in *American Historical Review*, XXXVII, 712, July 1932.

[19] O'Callaghan, *History of New Netherland*, I, 475. The list of settlers in Rensselaerswyck, 1630–1658, in *Van Rensselaer Bowier Manuscripts*, 805 *et seq.*, shows that the manor was far from being a settled agrarian organization.

In 1700, the Governor of New York, in reporting on the condition of the manors in the province, showed how empty are the lordly terms which were used in the bestowal of privileges. "Mr Livingston has on his great grant of 16 miles long and 24 broad, but 4 or 5 cottagers as I am told, men that live in vassallage under him and work for him and are too poor to be farmers having not wherewithall to buy Cattle or to stock a farm, Collonel Courtland has also on his great grants 4 to 5 of those poor families."[20]

Rights of jurisdiction seem actually to have been exercised by the manorial lords. A Jesuit, describing Rensselaerswyck in 1644, when it comprised about one hundred persons, said that there was "a kind of bailiff here whom they call Sénéschal, who administers justice."[21] The patroon required members of the settlement to sign a paper, agreeing that they would not appeal to any higher court, and banished them at his pleasure.[22]

Soon after the English established their rule the Governor thought it necessary to withdraw from the proprietors of Rensselaerswyck and of Fordham Manor the rights of jurisdiction which they asserted.[23] It would be a mistake, however, to think that in this period a manorial grant was a necessary condition for the exercise of independent authority. Even in New England a town group would sometimes organize and carry on its government without any license from a superior authority; and, on the other hand, the Virginia Company recognized the necessity of giving the leaders of particular plantations the liberty of regulating the affairs of themselves and their subordinates.[24] The New York manors, therefore, were in this respect like other groups of the time, and though they differed in the explicit recognition of their independence, and though the grant of local authority to the representative of a single family was exceptional, these differences were short-lived and of no serious significance.

POLITICAL INFLUENCE OF GREAT LANDLORDS IN NEW YORK

More striking, and more serious in its results (as will appear in discussing the large land grants of New York), was the privilege enjoyed by some of the manors of sending a representative to the colonial legislature. In 1774 the Assembly of New York was composed of thirty-one members, of whom three were elected by the freeholders of the manors of Rensselaerswyck, Livingston, and Cortlandt, the remainder representing the large towns and the counties.[25] For forty years one of the Livingston family was elected member of the Assembly for the county in which the family interest lay,[26] and in 1775 the home government was informed that lords of the manors had an "exorbitant influence." In the region of Albany, representation was granted to each of two manors and a borough, besides two members for the city and county; and the freeholders in

[20] *New York Documents Relative to Colonial History*, IV, 822.

[21] Father Isaac Jogues' "Description of New Netherlands," in *Documentary History of the State of New York* (qto. ed.), IV, 16.

[22] *New York Documents Relative to Colonial History*, I, 423, 427. Further details in *Van Rensselaer Bowier MSS.*

[23] *New York Documents Relative to Colonial History*, II, 625, 627.

[24] *Cf.* Channing, *History of the United States*, I, 217, 385.

[25] Tryon's Report in *New York Documents Relative to Colonial History*, VIII, 444. The origin of these rights can be traced, *Ibid.*, IV, 823; VI, 28; and *Documentary History of the State of New York* (qto. ed.), III, 411 *et seq.*

[26] The passage follows almost verbally the text of Colden's letter, in *New York Documents Relative to Colonial History*, VIII, 61; it does not seem certain that Livingston represented the manor itself.

the borough and manors had become so numerous that, if they had chosen to vote in the county elections, they might have returned all five members.[27] The influence of the great landlords was opposed to that of the Crown, and on that account may have been exaggerated in the report. There is no evidence that the lords made use of any peculiar manorial privileges to increase their power. It seems certain, however, that they enjoyed advantages from the system of representation, above those of ordinary freeholders.

ATTEMPTS TO COLONIZE THE LARGE ESTATES

Judged by their practical results, the attempts to establish colonies on the basis of the European social ideas were failures which had no considerable influence on the organization or policy of the colonial period. Even at the time when manorial privileges were offered to tempt leaders of colonies, the proprietors were seeking themselves to attract the simple cultivators who were to do the hard work of colonization.

They gave land for the asking, and often added thereto a free passage, stock and implements, seed corn, etc. The expense of transporting and establishing a family in the New World was not small. An estimate of the early eighteenth century allowed three to four pounds sterling per capita for transportation, two for the supply of the necessary implements, and five for subsistence during the first year.[28] The proprietors were not long able to meet the demands upon their purse which the settlement of a considerable number of people involved, and sought assistance from intending colonists who had the means to pay their own way and that of others also. Their object was to people their possessions, in the hope of an ultimate return from rent and taxes. They were always ready to grant land to anyone who would superintend its settlement, while on the other hand promoters did not need to be tempted by the antiquated forms of manorial privilege, if they could see a chance for profits in the private arrangements of an economic kind that they could make with their followers.

GRANT OF LAND BY HEAD RIGHT IN THE SOUTH

In early Virginia and in some other colonies, the "head right" was the form under which land was most commonly acquired.[29] Anyone who transported an emigrant to the colony acquired thereby a claim to fifty acres. In Maryland the terms of the grant were more liberal, fifty acres being granted for the transportation even of a child, while an adventurer, under some circumstances, might secure four hundred acres for an adult male.[30] It would be a mistake, however, to emphasize any contrasts such as are suggested in the terms of these grants. In practice the letter of the law was systematically evaded. In Virginia two hundred acres were frequently obtained for one individual brought to the colony, and finally head rights were sold by the clerks of

[27] *New York Documents Relative to Colonial History*, VIII, 565.

[28] *Report of Board of Trade*, 1709, in *New York Documents Relative to Colonial History*, V, 87. *Cf.* Bruce, *Economic History of Virginia* (1907), I, 516.

[29] Bruce, *Economic History of Virginia*, I, 512 *et seq.*

[30] Mereness, *Maryland as a Proprietary Province* (1901), 50; Gould, *The Land System in Maryland, 1720–1765* (1913), in *Johns Hopkins University Studies*, XXXI, 9 *et seq.* See Gray, *History of Agriculture in the Southern United States*, 389–391, for head rights in the other southern colonies.

the administration without even the pretence that they were based on the transportation of immigrants.[31]

We touch here on the heart of the land question in the proprietary colonies. It mattered little what attitude the proprietors might adopt, or what rules they might lay down; they could and did influence the course of policy in its details, but they were helpless to determine it. When they attempted to check the spread of settlement, or to subject the settlers to restrictions, they could be told that it was "against the laws of God and nature that so much land should be idle while so many Christians wanted it to labour on and to raise their bread."[32]

FAILURE TO CONTROL THE GRANTS OF LAND

Outside the legal forms by which title could be acquired, the squatter everywhere asserted himself; even in Virginia the common men got their land on the frontier by "corn right," by "tomahawk right" and by "cabin right."[33] Any man of ordinary energy, who was personally free (*i.e.*, not a slave or an indentured servant), could in any colony secure for himself a peasant freehold. On the other hand, a man of determination and of some slight means could scarcely be prevented from securing for himself a great estate, far more than he could cultivate alone, and even much more than he could cultivate by all the laborers and tenants whom he could muster. The Governor of New York, writing just before the War of Independence, had to admit that the limit of one thousand acres set for new estates was transgressed, "frequently, and I believe generally." "But," he continued, "if this is an evil, it is hardly to be prevented. Men of property in a country where the soil is of little value, must have it in their power to purchase large Tracts, if they chuse this method to raise their families, tho' as the benefit seems, at present, remote, the temptation is not very strong."[34] The temptation was stronger in the South than in the North, for reasons to which reference has already been made; and in the South the opposing forces were much weaker than in the North, where the democratic structure of society and system of government offered effective obstacles to the growth of a system of large estates. A survey of the course of events in a few of the proprietary and royal colonies will suggest the contrast between them and the corporate colonies in respect to land tenure and land policy.

SOUTH CAROLINA

In South Carolina, where the tendency to the absorption of landed estates in a few hands was most marked, the proprietors had sought at the origin of the colony to impress on it an aristocratic structure.[35] They had made grants of immense tracts of land to the favored individuals who were to assume the position of magnates of the European order, and though the grants for a long time were a menace for the future rather than an expression of present facts, they were a source of trouble from the start. The patentees took up all the best land on the navigable rivers, skinned land

[31] Bruce, *Economic History of Virginia*, I, 522 *et seq.*
[32] Greene, *Provincial America* (1905), 233; the remark is attributed to the Scotch-Irish.
[33] Ingle, *Local Institutions of Virginia*, in *Johns Hopkins University Studies*, III, 141.
[34] Governor Tryon to the Earl of Dartmouth, 1773, in *New York Documents Relative to Colonial History*, VIII, 374.
[35] Smith, W. Roy, *South Carolina as a Royal Province*, 31–53.

of its timber only to abandon it for fresh forest, and held always their claims to more land in reserve. When the royal government took control of the province in the eighteenth century, much harm had been done, but there was still time to check the excesses of the inherited system. Most of the land was still untouched by proprietary claims, which were but vaguely asserted, and which were opposed to the principles of good law as well as to those of public policy. The claims were realized in the eighteenth century, only because the officers of the colonial government sacrificed the interests of the people below them and of the King above them to their private advantage. At the critical time when the validity of their claims was the question to be settled, the government of the province in all its branches was ruled by men who, in one way or another, had succeeded to the rights of the early patentees. They triumphed over the opposition of the people and of the honest officials of the province; they managed, in some way unknown to us, to nullify the recommendations of the Board of Trade and of the Treasury Board in England; and thus they secured the confirmation of the loose grants which had been made in the previous century. Abuses did not cease until all the best lands had been granted away.

VIRGINIA

In Virginia during the seventeenth century the grant of land was regulated chiefly by the rule of head rights, described above.[36] The rule was, however, subject to exceptions, and was at best so laxly administered that it had little practical effect in limiting grants. Even in the seventeenth century, estates appear which were reckoned by the tens of thousands of acres, and the large estates were sufficiently numerous to be put by Bruce in a class by themselves, with an average of five thousand acres.[37] These large holdings were ordinarily the result of the accumulation of a number of plantations, each issuing from a separate patent. At the close of the century a definite purchase price for the land was fixed, and during the eighteenth century very large grants became common. In theory, the title to land was perfected only by occupation and improvement. In fact, however, in Virginia as in other colonies, the administration of the land office was controlled by men who were or who meant to be large landholders, and who used their official position to advance their private interests. Spotswood, who was governor in the early years of the eighteenth century, granted to himself 86,000 acres; and one of the planters left at his death 179,440 acres of the best land in the colony.[38]

NEW YORK

The colony of New York presented in its social structure a transition between the colonies of the North and of the South. Shortly before the Revolution, Colden distinguished four different ranks in the province: proprietors of large tracts of land, over one hundred thousand acres; gentlemen of the law; merchants; and farmers and mechanics.[39] Though the fourth rank comprised, according to Colden's account, "the

[36] Bruce, *Economic History of Virginia*, I, 502 *et seq.*
[37] *Ibid.*, II, 252–253.
[38] Greene, *Provincial America*, 270–271.
[39] *New York Documents Relative to Colonial History*, VII, 795.

bulk of the People and in them consists the strength of the Province", it was far from being the ruling class, and we find the agrarian policy of the colony to have been determined by influences as aristocratic as any which appear in Virginia or South Carolina. About 1700 the Governor protested to the English authorities that "this whole Province is given away to about thirty persons in effect;" a dozen extravagant grants, as large as English counties, took in about three quarters of the land of the whole colony.[40] Most of the excessive grants were annulled, but they were followed by others in the course of the eighteenth century. Before the middle of the century the governor was asking for an increase of salary, since he could hope to make no fees from land grants, "there being now no vacant lands remaining."[41] Fresh land was secured by purchase from the Indians, and this was distributed as before, much of it in vast estates measured by hundreds of thousands of acres. Three tracts, according to the claims of their proprietors, contained over a million acres each, several others over two hundred thousand acres.[42] On the very eve of the Revolution the authorities were still acquiescent while this distribution of the spoils went on.[43]

The conditions of the early grants were so vague and indulgent that they had no influence in furthering the settlement of the province or the growth of revenue.[44] The English government in the eighteenth century adopted the principles that land patents should not exceed a thousand acres to an individual, that the land should be subject to a quit-rent of two shillings and sixpence per hundred acres, and that it should be settled in three years under pain of forfeiture.[45] The history of landed property in the colony would have been very different, if these principles had been observed. They were in fact, however, so riddled by exemptions and evasions that they had no practical influence. The large proprietors were frankly speculators. They would not themselves engage to undertake the expensive task of bringing the lands under cultivation; "they forsee perhaps that a few years may people the Province from Germany Ireland and other Parts of Europe and are preparing before hand to lay in for themselves an estate on easy Terms. . . ."[46]

Some cases we do find in which they transported settlers, provided them with necessaries, and maintained them in the trying years of the start;[47] but their sacrifices, however much they cost them as individuals, were in the aggregate of little service to society. The land of New York was cleared and cultivated by common people, working for themselves, and not for others. In the second half of the eighteenth century the colonial government adopted the plan of settling land in townships and it was under the township system that population spread and occupied the vacant lands of the State.[48]

[40] Bellomont to Lords of Trade, 1698–1699, in *New York Documents Relative to Colonial History*, IV, 397, 506. See Bellomont's correspondence in this volume, *passim*, and also *Report of Board of Trade, 1698*, p. 391.

[41] *New York Documents Relative to Colonial History*, VI, 246; *cf. Documentary History of the State of New York* (qto. ed.), I, 249 *et seq.*; *New York Documents Relative to Colonial History*, V, 171; VIII, 268.

[42] Colden to Lords of Trade, 1764, in *New York Documents Relative to Colonial History*, VII, 654.

[43] *Cf. New York Documents Relative to Colonial History*, VII, 902; VIII, 378–380, 392, 398, 567, 573.

[44] *Cf. Documentary History of the State of New York* (qto. ed.), I, 249; *New York Documents Relative to Colonial History*, IV, 384, 822.

[45] *New York Documents Relative to Colonial History*, IV, 396, 411, 425, 537, etc. The principles underwent considerable changes, which it seems unnecessary to trace here. *Cf.*, *e.g.*, V, 25.

[46] *New York Documents Relative to Colonial History*, VI, 60.

[47] *Cf.* Memorials of Skene, Campbell, and Moore, in *Ibid.*, VII, 615, 629, etc.; case of Sir William Johnson, in *Documentary History of the State of New York* (qto. ed.), IV, 222.

[48] *Documentary History of the State of New York* (qto. ed.), IV, 635.

POLITICAL CORRUPTION IN NEW YORK

The English government, in New York at least, was not a party to the practices by which the great estates were accumulated. The Lords of Trade spoke of the royal land system as "established in order to prevent the many evils and great discouragement to cultivation, which arose from persons obtaining extravagant Grants of Lands in order to make a Job of them, by fraudulent conveyances & other indirect practices."[49]

The governors ordinarily accepted the principles of the royal system, in their correspondence with the home government, and admitted that patents to land should be granted only for the purpose of peopling and planting the country.[50] An exception, single, so far as the documents show, appears in a letter of Governor Tryon written shortly before the Revolution. "I conceive it My Lord, good policy to lodge large Tracts of Land in the hands of Gentlemen of weight and consideration. They will naturally farm out their lands to Tenants; a method which will ever create subordination and counterpoise, in some measure, the general levelling spirit, that so much prevails in some of His Maj$^{ty's}$ Govern^{ts}."[51] The only excuse ordinarily offered for the grant of large tracts of land was the difficulty involved in purchasing lands of the Indian tribes; the expense of the tedious negotiations made it unprofitable to undertake them, unless the government would consent to ratify the transfer of considerable tracts by its letters patent.[52]

As a rule, the grants were made on grounds which officers of the colonial administration did not dare to justify. The Governor made them to oblige his friends, to win a following, or merely to make some money from bribes or from a share of the grant.[53] One of the men who was loudest in his denunciation of the extravagant grants, was open to the suspicion, when he attained office, of abusing his power in exactly the same way.[54] The corruption of land-jobbing infected also the judiciary and the legislature. The Chief Justice of the Colony, according to Governor Bellomont's account, had used his official position and the favor of a preceding governor to secure a great tract at the eastern end of Long Island, for which he forced the town of Southampton to receive a beggarly ten pounds.[55] Throughout the eighteenth century complaints were constant that it was hopeless to invoke the law in restraint of extravagant land grants. Sometimes the Chief Justice was himself a land-robber, like Smith, or a great landlord like Livingston, of whom it was said that "no cause of any consequence can come before him, in which, or in similar cases, he or the Livingstone family are not interested."[56] In general, it was asserted that "the Judges and principal Lawyers are proprietors of extravagant grants of land, or strongly connected with them in Interest, or family alliances," and the influence of great landed proprietors was pictured as one of the chief obstacles to the course of justice in the colony.[57] The same influence pervaded the

[49] *New York Documents Relative to Colonial History*, VII, 429.

[50] *Cf.* letter of Hunter, 1718, *Ibid.*, V, 511, in which there is a sketch of the process by which patents were acquired.

[51] Tryon to Hillsborough, 1772, *Ibid.*, VIII, 293.

[52] *Cf. Ibid.*, VII, 491; VIII, 374.

[53] *Cf.* charges against Gov. Fletcher, *Ibid.*, IV, 392, 422, 785; on the practices of later governors, see V, 953.

[54] Lieut. Gov. Colden, *Ibid.*, VII, 474, 491.

[55] 1699, *Ibid.*, IV, 535.

[56] Colden to Lords of Trade, 1765, *Ibid.*, VII, 703; *cf. Ibid.*, VII, 549, 906.

[57] *Ibid.*, VII, 677, 906.

governor's council,[58] and was a power even in the Assembly, where we should expect to find the interests of the common people represented. The act of 1699, which annulled some of the excessive land grants, "was carried thro' with Spirit of party in the assembly," leaving some of the extravagant grants untouched;[59] and even this half measure would have been repealed but for the disapproval of the Crown.[60] If we can believe the reports to the English government, the proprietors of the large land grants carried on a regular campaign to establish their influence and to further their interests in the Assembly, and succeeded so well that the governor and the officials representing the interests of the Crown could do little to reach them.[61] By means of their political influence they escaped payment, not only of quit-rents, but of all the other taxes that fell upon the ordinary landholder.[62] They passed an "Act for the more easy recovery of the possession of Lands,"[63] which proposed to extend to sixty years the term within which they might eject squatters, and which would have put settlers on their lands entirely within their power if it had not been rejected by the Governor. The provisions of this last act were particularly obnoxious in that the bounds of the great estates were very ill-defined. It was charged, indeed, that the proprietors preferred to leave them doubtful, to be extended at their pleasure.[64]

EFFECTS OF THE PREVALENCE OF LARGE ESTATES

Complaint was often made, in New York, as in other provinces, that the amassing of landed estates in the hands of a few, discouraged settlement and drove the inhabitants to districts where they could secure land on better terms.[65] Influences of this kind were felt, undoubtedly, but it is hard to measure them. The effects seem to have been less serious than is commonly supposed. The injustice of the system of large estates is apparent, but its importance, where conditions did not permit of the establishment of slave-plantations, remains to be proved. Transfers of land were simple and inexpensive.[66] The large proprietors were often land-poor and eager to realize on their holdings; and an effective combination, which would have enabled them to secure a monopoly price for their land was impracticable. It is true that the conditions made it difficult for the common people to secure information, or to move to the district when they could secure land at the least cost. Yet the terms on which they acquired land from private proprietors were certainly not oppressive. Rack-renting was unknown. Leases ran ordinarily for several lives or in perpetuity, and bound the

58 *Ibid.*, IV, 725; V, 578.

59 *Documentary History of the State of New York* (qto. ed.), I, 251; *cf. New York Documents Relative to Colonial History*, IV, 553; V, 479.

60 *New York Documents Relative to Colonial History*, V, 22 *et seq.*, 54.

61 *Ibid.*, V, 806; VII, 486, 654, 876. For a later attempt to influence the votes of tenants, see Wansey, *Journal of an Excursion to the United States of North America in the Summer of 1794* (1796), 242; he states that a lady wrote to her tenants in northern New York to vote for a certain candidate for State senator; the letter was published and was universally reprobated.

62 *New York Documents Relative to Colonial History*, V, 900; VII, 655.

63 *Ibid.*, VIII, 369–370.

64 *Documentary History of the State of New York* (qto. ed.), I, 251–252; *New York Documents Relative to Colonial History*, V, 808; VIII, 370.

65 *Cf. New York Documents Relative to Colonial History*, IV, 393, 397, 791; V, 459, 953; Kalm, *Travels into North America* (2d ed., in Pinkerton, *A General Collection . . . Voyages and Travels*, XIII, 1812), 463; *Documentary History of the State of New York* (qto. ed.), I, 252.

66 Morris, *Studies in the History of American Law*, 69 *et seq.*, describes the simplification of English practice in the colonies.

tenant to a payment which was little more than nominal, corresponding to the quit-rent demanded by the government of those who took up the public lands. Most of the large estates seem to have crumbled away without enriching their proprietors or impoverishing the cultivators who acquired the land of which they were composed. The remnants of the old system which gave rise to the anti-rent agitation in New York in the second quarter of the nineteenth century, became hateful to the people who rose against them, not because they entailed a serious economic burden, but because they promised to preserve indefinitely a distinction which was not justified by the economic conditions, and which was opposed to the social and political ideals of the nation.[67]

LAWS OF INTESTACY

The aristocratic tendency of the Middle and Southern colonies is shown, not only by the history of landed estates, but also by the laws which governed in them the course of descent of the property of a family. Unlike the New England colonies, they accepted, in general, the English practice of primogeniture; in case of intestacy the landed property passed to the eldest son, burdened only with certain dower rights, while the personal estate was divided in accordance with the English Statute of Distribution.[68]

Pennsylvania took, in this respect, an exceptional position. That colony is remarkable for a provision in its earliest Body of Laws[69] which imposed a certain distribution of his estate on the testator, unless it appeared that in some other way he had fulfilled the spirit of the law; the testator, namely, was to leave one-third of the estate to the widow, one-third to the children in equal shares, "and the other third as he pleaseth." This law was abrogated by the Crown in 1693, and was replaced by the usual provision granting freedom of disposal to the testator.[70] In legislation on intestacy, the colony showed a more determined spirit and prevailed finally against English opposition. It early accepted the rule prevailing in New England, by which the eldest son was distinguished only by a share double that of the other children and, after successive vetoes of acts in which this principle was embodied, provided finally for complete equality of distribution in an act which was never formally approved by the English government, but was allowed to become a law by lapse of time.[71]

The other colonies waited until after the Revolution to make similar modifications in the English law, which, as stated in the preamble of the Maryland statute, "originated with the feudal system and military tenures, is contrary to justice, and ought to be abolished."[72]

[67] *Cf.* Chaney, *The Anti-rent Agitation in the State of New York, 1839–1846* (1887), in *University of Pennsylvania Publications*, Political Economy and Public Law Series, No. 2.

[68] 1670, in *22 & 23 Charles II*, chap. x, in Great Britain, *Statutes at Large*, III, 357.

[69] 1683, in *Charter to William Penn and Laws of the Province of Pennsylvania*, 141.

[70] *Ibid.*, 231.

[71] *Ibid.*, 142, 174, 231, 265; *Statutes at Large of Pennsylvania* (compiled by Mitchell and Flanders), II, 32, 204.

[72] The dates of the statutes are as follows: New York, law of 1782, in *Laws of the State of New York* (ed. of 1886–1887), I, 502; Delaware, law of 1750, in *Laws of the State of Delaware* (ed. of 1797), I, 289 (double share to eldest); law of 1794, *Ibid.*, II, 1122 (equal share); Maryland, law of 1786, in *The Laws of Maryland* (ed. by Kilty, 1799–1800), chap. xlv; Virginia, law of 1785, in *Statutes at Large of Virginia* (ed. by Hening), XII, 138; Georgia, *Constitution of 1777*, interpreted in Act of 1785, in *Digest of the Laws of Georgia* (ed. by Watkins, 1800), 313. Morris, *Studies in the History of American Law*, 81, notes also North Carolina, law of 1784, and South Carolina, law of 1791.

LAWS OF ENTAIL

Throughout the colonial period the practice of entailing land was followed in various forms in the different colonies.[73] The printed records, in general, give but scant indication of the extent and importance of the practice; the statutes show merely that colonial legislators, especially in the eighteenth century, desired to simplify the process by which entails could be broken, and to facilitate conversion into fee simple.[74] Georgia suffered in its early period from the restriction of many tenures to tail-male, and in the State Constitutions of 1777 and 1789 adopted articles forbidding entails.[75]

Virginia appears to be, of all the colonies, that in which the entailing of land was most common, and certainly it strove, as did none of the other colonies, to maintain and extend the privilege of entail. While in England at this period entails could be barred by the collusive practice of fines and common recoveries, and while the other colonies aimed to simplify the cumbrous procedure for effecting this end, Virginia prohibited fines and recoveries early in the eighteenth century, and determined that estates tail could be barred only by act of the Assembly.[76] The legislature went even further in its attempt to encourage the maintenance of large family properties. An act described as "for the better settling and preservation of estates within this dominion" declared slaves "to be real estate and not chattels,"[77] and so enabled plantations, fully stocked, to be held intact for an indefinite period.

The act gave rise to some practical difficulties, and was amended after twenty years so as to secure more effectively the rights of creditors, but with the declaration, at the same time, that it "hath been found by experience very beneficial for the preservation and improvement of estates;" the act now expressly stated that anyone who devised land in tail could annex to it "slaves and their increase so long as any of them shall be living," and gave to the tenant in tail the same privilege of binding slaves to the soil.[78] Among the acts of the Assembly in this period appear many cases in which specific permission was asked and given for the sale or exchange of entailed lands. In 1748 a general concession was made to the tenants in tail of separate parcels of land worth not over two hundred pounds sterling, "as many poor people are seized in fee tail of small and inconsiderable parcels of land, often ignorantly or undesignedly by their ancestors devised in tail, and the docking such intails by easier methods will be a great relief to such persons, and their families, who otherwise must be confined to labour upon such small parcels of lands, when by selling them they might be enabled to purchase slaves, and other lands more improveable."[79] Aside from another and less important departure[80] from the general rule, the system was maintained until the

[73] See Morris, *Studies in the History of American Law*, 82–125, for a full discussion of the law of entail in the colonies in all its complications. The subject bristles with difficulties.

[74] New York, law of 1782, in *Laws of the State of New York* (ed. of 1886–1887), I, 501; Pennsylvania, law of 1705–1706, in *Statutes at Large of Pennsylvania* (compiled by Mitchell and Flanders), II, 208; law of 1710–1711, *Ibid.*, II, 351; law of 1749–1750, *Ibid.*, V, 100; Maryland, law of 1766, in *Laws of Maryland* (ed. by Kilty), chap. xxi; law of 1782, *Ibid.*, chap. xxiii; Delaware, law of 1751, in *Laws of the State of Delaware* (ed. of 1797–1837), I, 331; law of 1793, *Ibid.*, II, 1054.

[75] Talifer, *A True and Historical Narrative of the Colony of Georgia* (Force, *Tracts*, ed. of 1835, I, No. 4), 54, *et seq.*; *Digest of the Laws of Georgia* (ed. by Watkins), 15, 29.

[76] Law of 1705, in *Statutes at Large of Virginia* (ed. by Hening), III, 320; law of 1710, *Ibid.*, III, 517.

[77] Law of 1705, *Ibid.*, III, 333.

[78] Law of 1727, *Ibid.*, IV, 222–225.

[79] *Ibid.*, V, 414.

[80] *Ibid.*, VI, 57.

outbreak of the War of Independence. A statute of 1776 made a sweeping conversion of tenures in tail into fee simple, and later statutes confirmed this action.[81]

QUIT-RENTS

In closing this discussion of the land policy of the colonial period it is necessary to consider still one more topic, the system of quit-rents,[82] which had a bearing on social policy apart entirely from its importance as a source of revenue. The quit-rent was not a rent at all, in the modern economic sense. It had no relation to the "differential advantages" of tracts of land. It was a due, fixed, and payable in perpetuity, imposed on land when it was granted by a political superior, and expressing the subjection of the possessor of the land to this superior. Regarded even as a tax it was feudal rather than modern in character. In the corporate colonies of New England a system of quit-rents would have had little meaning, and in fact was never established.[83] In the provinces of the Middle and South, however, it was a natural expression of the proprietary superiority asserted by the lords proprietors or by the King, and was normally the condition on which lands were granted.

The quit-rent was sometimes purely nominal, as a peppercorn imposed on land set apart for a church glebe,[84] or a raccoon's skin, a lamb, or a fat buck, which represented the modest return demanded from the patentees of some of the great tracts, hundreds of thousands of acres in extent, granted in New York in the seventeenth century.[85] Commonly, however, the quit-rent was payable in money even when payment in kind was accepted, and was proportioned to the size of the grant. It varied much at different times in different colonies. The customary rate was, in New York, two shillings, six pence for 100 acres; in Pennsylvania a half-penny or a penny an acre;[86] in Virginia a shilling for 50 acres.[87] The sum seems small, measured from the standpoint of the individual cultivator; on the other hand, when multiplied so as to cover the occupied land of a province, it seems to have promised handsome returns to the political superior.

Actually, as is well known, the attempt to collect the quit-rents involved the colonial administrations in hopeless difficulties. Surveys and records were so imperfect that it was difficult to determine the amounts which were due from different individuals, and the colonists held on to their money with such tenacity that even an acknowledged debt was of but little value to the creditor.

In New York about 1700 the actual collections amounted to between £200 and £300, perhaps one tenth of the estimated return.[88] The Attorney General asserted in 1710

[81] *Ibid.*, IX, 226; XI, 271; XII, 156; (new series, ed. by Shepherd), I, 86.

[82] For details, see the exhaustive study by Bond, *The Quit-Rent System in the American Colonies.*

[83] *Cf.* Osgood, *American Colonies in the Seventeenth Century*, II, 5. Quit-rents seem to have been imposed on the western lands of New Hampshire; *cf. New York Documents Relative to Colonial History*, VII, 564–565, 598; VIII, 384, etc.; and sporadic examples can be found elsewhere.

[84] *Documentary History of the State of New York* (qto. ed.), III, 348.

[85] *New York Documents Relative to Colonial History*, III, 401; IV, 392; V, 11. *Documentary History of the State of New York* (qto. ed.), I, 251.

[86] Holcomb, *Pennsylvania Boroughs* (1886), in *Johns Hopkins University Studies*, IV, 141; *cf. New York Documents Relative to Colonial History*, VIII, 275.

[87] Ripley, *Financial History of Virginia, 1609–1776* (1893), in *Columbia University Studies*, IV, 46.

[88] *New York Documents Relative to Colonial History*, IV, 419.

that they were less than £100;[89] and the Governor in 1712–1713 said that there had been "for some years past a total cessation".[90] In 1720 they had risen to about £500,[91] while in 1767 an account shows the receipt of £1806, with arrears tenfold that sum uncollected.[92] The quit-rents had never been sufficient to pay the cost of collection. In other colonies the history of the quit-rents was much the same.[93] Everywhere the government secured but a small fraction of the amount due, and even this with such difficulty that it hardly paid for the trouble. The colonies evaded so effectually the payment of quit-rents that they scarcely needed to abolish them formally by statute, as some did after the outbreak of the Revolution.[94]

The quit-rents were important in their bearing on social policy, because it seems certain that, if they had been imposed and collected impartially, they would have broken up many or most of the large estates of land. They bore but lightly on the man who was using his land, and who got from its annual yield the means of paying the tax. Only he need fear them who was keeping large tracts of land from use, who was getting no income, because he was performing no service. The quit-rents, like any other tax, were universally unpopular. They were held up to general reprobation, because they promised to give the government a permanent source of revenue which was free from popular control. But it seems probable, though it still remains to be proved, that they owed their failure to the opposition of a small group of politicians, who wanted to keep their land, as they had obtained it, without sacrifice or service, and who were really furthering personal and selfish interests at the expense of the general welfare.[95]

This sketch of land tenure in the colonies shows that, owing mainly to the ideals or the interests of the patentees, different types of land tenure were established in different parts of the colonies. Some of these were democratic, others were feudal. It gradually became evident that the feudal systems, as seen in the Dutch patroonships, the Maryland manors, and the baronies of Carolina were ill adapted to the conditions of frontier life. They nevertheless left their impression upon the size of estates, as well as upon the social life of some of the colonies. The systems which survived did so because they proved to be well adapted to those parts of the country in which they were established, and thus the large plantation became typical of the South, the small farm of the North.

89 *Ibid.*, V, 162.
90 *Ibid.*, V, 357.
91 *Ibid.*, V, 552.
92 *Ibid.*, VII, 901.
93 *Cf.* Bond, *The Quit-Rent System in the American Colonies, passim*; Channing, *History of the United States*, I, 526; II, 320, 359; Smith, W. Roy, *South Carolina as a Royal Province*, 28–31, sec. i, chap. iii; Raper, *North Carolina, a Study in English Colonial Government* (1904), 57, 118–124.
94 *Cf.* Law of 1779, in *Laws of the Commonwealth of Pennsylvania* (ed. of 1810), I, 481; law of 1779, in *Statutes at Large of Virginia* (ed. by Hening), X, 64.
95 The social service which quit-rents could render by putting land in the hands of people who would use it was frequently recognized. *Cf.* Hunter's *Report to Lords of Trade*, in *New York Documents Relative to Colonial History*, V, 180; Colden's *Report on Lands*, in *Documentary History of the State of New York* (qto. ed.), I, 253 *et seq.*; Tryon's letter to Dartmouth, in *New York Documents Relative to Colonial History*, VIII, 383, 385, 398.

CHAPTER VI

THE LABOR POLICY OF THE COLONIES

Prohibition of Idleness, 55. Child Labor, 56. Unfree Labor, 56. Regulation of Free Labor, 57. Failure of Attempts to Regulate Wages, 59. White Servitude, 60. Sources of Indentured Servants, 61. Regulation of Immigration, 63. Status of Indentured Servants, 64. Slavery, 64. Slavery in New England, 65. Slavery in New Jersey, 66. Slavery in Virginia, 67. Slavery in North Carolina, 68.

PROHIBITION OF IDLENESS

The land was here when the patents were issued. It was a comparatively simple matter to divide it. The real problem was to get labor, and this involved the twofold task of importing laborers, and of securing their activity after importation. It is easy to raise a laugh by speaking of the efforts of our ancestors to punish idleness, but the problem was a serious one in the seventeenth century, and has by no means disappeared at the present day. Even in the eighteenth century Blackstone wrote: "Idleness in any person whatsoever is also a high offense against the public economy. In China it is a maxim, that if there be a man who does not work, or a woman that is idle, in the empire, somebody must suffer cold or hunger: the produce of the lands not being more than sufficient, with culture, to maintain the inhabitants: and therefore, though the idle person may shift off the want from himself, yet it must in the end fall somewhere."[1] The American colonies were in very much this same position in the early days. They not only required laborers, but they could not endure idlers. They needed, therefore, to supplement the policy of importing labor with the policy of making laborers work. Whether the fault lay in the education and in the general treatment of human beings by those in authority, or whether it lay in the still imperfectly developed *mores* of the population, the seventeenth century evidently thought that it could not secure sufficient labor by simply holding out the reward of good wages. Nor can we of the twentieth. For in the midst of a labor famine, we may have an army of tramps who do nothing to remedy it. Perhaps science will discover other agents of laziness than the hookworm, but thus far it has not done so, and we still resort, as did our ancestors, to moral suasion and, when that fails, to force.

Regulations with regard to idleness were not uncommon. An act passed in Massachusetts in 1633 fixed the wages of sundry artisans, and ordered "that noe pson, howse houlder or oth^r, shall spend his time idlely or vnpffitably, vnder paine of such punishm^t as the Court shall thinke meete to inflict," and "the constable of eũy place shall vse spetiall care & deligence to take knowledge of offenders in this kinde, espetially of cōmon coasters, vnpfittable fowlers, & tobacco takers, & to psent the same to the 2 nexte Assistants."[2]

[1] Blackstone, *Commentaries* (Cooley's ed.), II, 399–400 (Bk. IV, 169).
[2] *Records of Massachusetts Bay* (1853), I, 109.

CHILD LABOR

The movement against idleness on the part of adults naturally extended to children, and it was thought that the colonies would be one means of giving employment and habits of industry to the surplus child population of England. As early as 1583, Sir George Peckham in his discourse on "Westerne Planting" showed how the colonies would furnish employment not only for unemployed men but also for children of 12 or 14 and for women. Captain John Smith, Sir Edwin Sandys, and other pioneers emphasized this idea.[3] It was stated in a letter from England that 1,400 or 1,500 children went to Virginia in 1627.[4] Special premiums were put by the colonies upon the importation of children. In 1698, South Carolina offered 13 pounds for white male servants, "Irish only excepted," above 16 years and under 40 who had not less than 4 years to serve, and 12 pounds for boys with not less than 7 years to serve.[5] Massachusetts in 1708/1709 offered a premium of 40 shillings for the importation of English male servants between the ages of 8 and 25.[6]

The Dutch pursued a similar policy. It was proposed at The Hague to take from the almshouses and orphan asylums 300 or 400 boys and girls who were to be bound for not longer than 6 or 7 years. In 1654, the burgomaster of Amsterdam wrote to Director Stuyvesant that he had decided to do the company a service by sending some of the almshouse people to New Netherland, and accordingly shipped 28 boys and girls. Four years later the vice-director wrote of the safe arrival of these children and asked that more be sent, but preferably not under 15 years of age "and somewhat strong, as little profit is to be expected here without labor."[7] The children were obviously of little value unless apprenticed, that is, unless brought under strict discipline and trained to habits of industry. A Massachusetts act of 1642 complained of "the great neglect in many parents and masters in training up their children in learning and labor, and other employments which may be profitable to the Commonwealth."[8] The combination of "learning and labor" is significant, as showing that the general care for education, although often based upon religious grounds, also aimed to promote efficiency in the colonists.[9]

UNFREE LABOR

Laws against idleness, however, did not attract labor, and the cost of transportation was so great that even the prospect of good wages would not always ensure a supply Hence, we find that, of the three kinds of labor used in the colonies, two were unfree. Besides the free laborer who was brought over by his employer or who came at his own expense and hired out for wages, we find indentured servants, or white persons who were

[3] Quoted by Otey, *The Beginnings of Child Labor Legislation* (*Report on Condition of Woman and Child Wage Earners in the United States*, VI, Sen. Doc., 61 Cong., 2 Sess., No. 645, 1910), 10.

[4] Abbott, *Women in Industry* (1910), 333, cites contemporary sources but the figures must be exaggerated.

[5] *Statutes at Large of South Carolina* (1836–1841), II, 154.

[6] *Acts and Resolves of the Province of Massachusetts Bay*, I, 634.

[7] Otey, *The Beginnings of Child Labor Legislation*, 13, quoting from *New York Documents Relative to Colonial History*, II, 52.

[8] *Ibid.*, 15.

[9] For colonial laws on education, see quotations in Otey, *The Beginnings of Child Labor Legislation*, 16, and Jernegan, *Laboring and Dependent Classes in Colonial America, 1607–1783* (1931), pts. ii, iii.

under a temporary servitude, and black persons or redskins, who were under a lifelong servitude. Slavery and white servitude were recognized in New England as well as in the South. The Articles of Confederation, drawn up by the New England colonies in 1643, distinctly stipulated for dividing up proportionally among the confederates, "the whole advantage of the warr (if it please God to bless their Endeavours), whether it be in lands, goods or persons."[10] In 1638, Emanuel Downing told Governor Winthrop that labor was so scarce that slaves would be necessary to improve the country.[11] Nevertheless these three classes of labor were found in different proportions in the several colonies, the climate, the economic conditions, and the motives which led to settlement combining to make slavery especially prevalent in the South.

REGULATION OF FREE LABOR

Free labor[12] received much less attention from the legislators than indentured labor or slavery. The people who worked for wages were not numerous enough to constitute an important class, and the ease with which land could be obtained, as well as the great difficulty of obtaining labor in a new country, made them independent. Winthrop tells us that his man Richard, after completing his service, earned so much that in a little over a year "he had scraped together about £25, and then returned with his prey to England."[13] As a consequence of the scarcity of labor Winthrop, writing in 1660, advised Englishmen to bring their own servants.[14] In view of these economic conditions the early settlers felt it more important to keep wages down than to try to better the condition of the wage receivers. This legislation was in accordance with the English tradition running back as far as the Statute of Laborers of 1349. Such laws as were passed appear to have been a mixture of class legislation and of an honest attempt to establish equitable prices both for labor and for commodities. Massachusetts made a number of attempts to meet this situation. As early as 1630, the General Court passed an order limiting the pay of carpenters, joiners, brick-layers, sawyers and thatchers to 2s. a day and imposing a fine of 10s. upon the taker and the giver of more. The same order determined the rate that could be charged for sawing boards by the hundred.[15] The next month another order was issued fixing the wages for certain master mechanics at 16d. a day, including meat and drink, while "the second sort" were to receive not above 12d. a day, with the same fine.[16] But March 22, 1631, these orders were repealed and it was voted that wages "shall nowe be lefte free & att libertie as men shall

[10] Steiner, *History of Slavery in Connecticut* (1893), in *Johns Hopkins University Studies*, XI, 379.

[11] Weeden, *Economic and Social History of New England* (1890), I, 103. Donnan, *Documents Illustrative of the History of the Slave Trade to America* (1930–1935), III, 8, reprints a letter from Downing to Winthrop (1645) in which he says, "for I doe not see how wee can thrive untill wee get into a stock of slaves sufficient to doe all our buisiness, for our children's children will hardly see this great Continent filled with people, soe that our servants will still desire freedome to plant for them-selves, and not stay but for verie great wages. And I suppose you know verie well how wee shall mayneteyne 20 Moores cheaper than one English servant."

[12] *Cf.* Von Waltershausen, *Die Arbeits-Verfassung der Englischen Kolonien in Nordamerika* (1894), chap. viii.

[13] Quoted in Weeden, *Economic and Social History of New England*, I, 180.

[14] *Ibid.*, I, 204.

[15] *Records of Massachusetts Bay*, I, 74. See Johnson, E. A. J., *American Economic Thought in the Seventeenth Century* (1932), 206 *et seq.*, for a discussion of the ideas underlying all this legislation.

[16] *Records of Massachusetts Bay*, I, 76.

reasonably agree."[17] In 1633 a further effort was made to fix the wages of workmen,[18] and the following year, September 3, 1634, the fine for giving wages above the legal rate was repealed, while the penalty on accepting them was retained. At the same time provision was made for arbitration, in case a person had bargained for the performance of any work and the bargain should prove not equal on his part.[19] The court showed, however, a good deal of vacillation in its policy, occasioned doubtless by the difficulty of the situation. In September 1635, it repealed the law which "prohibited takeing above iiij[d] in the shilling pffitt for comodities, & that w[ch] restrained workemens wages to a certainety."[20] In the same month, however, we learn that "Whereas two former lawes, the one concerneing the wages of workemen, the other concerneing the prizes of comodyties, were for dyvers good consideracons repealed this psent Court, nowe, for avoydeing such mischeifes as may followe therevpon by such ill disposed psons as may take liberty to oppresse & wronge their neighb[rs], by takeing excessiue wages for worke, or vnreasonable prizes for such necessary merchandizes or oth[r] comodyties as shall passe from man to man, it is therefore nowe ordered, y[t] if any man shall offend in any of the said cases against the true intent of this lawe, hee shalbe punished by ffine or imprisonm[t], according to the quallity of the offence."[21] The following year, a vote passed October 28, 1636, ordered the freemen of every town to agree among themselves on the rate of wages to be paid "workmen, laborers, & servants."[22]

In 1641, when the people were feeling severely the cessation of immigration with its demand for their produce, they complained that it was impossible, on account of the scarcity of money and the lower prices of cattle and corn, to pay such high wages as formerly, and, as stated in the statute, many preferred to give up business. The General Court threatened that it would punish the laborers, if they did not abate their demands.[23] In some cases a special vote was passed to compensate people for the fall in the price of the corn which they had taken in payment.[24] Later in the same year a new law determined that workmen's wages might be paid in corn, but that if the parties could not agree upon the price, it should be valued by two indifferent freemen, chosen, one by the master, the other by the servant, and in case of disagreement between these, a third man was to be chosen by the nearest magistrate or constable.[25]

During the harvest time the labor famine was likely to be especially acute; the General Court accordingly provided in 1646 that the mechanics might be required in each town to help in mowing, reaping, and other harvest operations.[26] In this case the interest of the community was placed above the claims of individual liberty, and field work was treated as a public service, like military or jury duty. There was a good English precedent for this in the statute of Richard II, passed in 1388, requiring craftsmen to help with the harvest.[27]

[17] *Ibid.*, I, 84. See also Weeden, *Economic and Social History of New England*, I, 99
[18] *Records of Massachusetts Bay*, I, 109.
[19] *Ibid.*, I, 127; *cf.* Weeden, *Economic and Social History of New England*, I, 104.
[20] *Records of Massachusetts Bay*, I, 159.
[21] *Ibid.*, I, 160.
[22] *Ibid.*, I, 183.
[23] *Ibid.*, I, 326.
[24] *Ibid.*, I, 330, 338.
[25] *Ibid.*, I, 340.
[26] *Ibid.*, II, 180–181.
[27] Stimson, *Popular Law-Making*, 75–76.

In the Massachusetts code of 1649 the colony returned to the principle of the law of 1636, leaving the freemen of each town to settle the rate of wages, and expressed this policy of local regulation by a clause empowering the selectmen of Boston and Charlestown to regulate the wages of porters, "who many times do require and exact more than is just and righteous for their labours."[28]

In 1655 a committee on trade was directed to consider some way to regulate workmen's wages, "if any way may be found," and in 1672, in an act forbidding the giving of liquor for wages, the Court noted that in spite of its endeavors to redress oppressions, complaints of excessive wages continued and increased.[29]

FAILURE OF ATTEMPTS TO REGULATE WAGES

On the surface these laws regulating wages show a distinct bias against the laborer. The reader cannot fail to have been impressed by the preponderance of laws to keep wages down, and the lack of laws to raise them. The period covered was, to be sure, one of falling prices, but if that argument is advanced to justify the legislation, the apologist may be challenged to find in the later history of Massachusetts, when currency changes brought rising prices, a similar series of laws designed to raise the wages of labor. The repeal of the laws against giving high wages, when the penalty for taking them was retained, seems conclusive evidence that the legislators had the interests of the employer primarily in mind. There was as yet, of course, no labor class. The men who worked for wages were, in most cases, on their way to become employers themselves. Obstacles to their rise merely lengthened the period of their dependence and did not make it permanent.

If the legislators lie open to the charge of serving their class interests, there is something to be said in their defence which might not occur to a reader of the present day. The medieval ideal of a static society, in which each individual had and kept his place, persisted long after the period in question. Society in its new environment was exposed to sweeping changes, but it was the most natural thing in the world for organized society, as represented in the government, to resist these changes, and at the least to attempt to moderate them. The legislators held to the functional theory of society, that the man in any occupation owed his services to the group, which in turn owed him a living; the concept of a competition which would further some at the expense of others was foreign to them, the abuse of a competitive advantage was hateful.

For nearly half a century the colonial legislature of Massachusetts experimented with general laws seeking to regulate wages. In 1675, as will be shown in the next chapter, on the regulation of prices, the attempt was abandoned, and matter both of wages and prices was left to the control of local authorities. The fluctuations to which the early colony was exposed had by then subsided, and the legislature was doubtless glad to rid itself of a problem to the solution of which it had contributed so little. A law passed in 1741/2 with regard to porters in Boston, which provided for licensing them, required them to wear a badge, and instructed the selectmen to fix their wages,[30] was, like the Pennsylvania law of March 14, 1761, regulating wagoners, carters, draymen,

[28] *Colonial Laws of Massachusetts* (Whitmore's ed. of 1889), 174, 185:
[29] *Records of Massachusetts Bay*, IV, pt. i, 247; IV, pt. ii, 510.
[30] *Acts and Resolves of the Province of Massachusetts Bay*, II, 1067.

and porters within the city of Philadelphia,[31] in line with the modern regulation of the charges made by operators of taxicabs and delivery services, who are permitted to use the streets to ply a public trade, and such laws do not imply any definite labor policy. It was not until the outbreak of the Revolutionary War and the disturbance of prices caused by paper money that the legislature, now of the State and not of the colony, passed on January 25, 1777, a somewhat drastic law to prevent monopoly and oppression. This law fixed the price of farming labor in summer at not over "3 shillings by the day, and found, as usual, and so in usual proportion at other seasons of the year; and the labour of mechanics and tradesmen, and other labour beside what is herein hereafter especially enumerated, in proportion thereunto according to the usages and customs which have heretofore been adopted and practiced in this State, when compared with farming labor."[32] The same act, however, also fixed in detail the maximum prices of some 15 articles, including salt, rum, molasses, and shoes. All of these were to apply to Boston, and in other towns the selectmen were to adjust the rates to local differences, as well as to fix the prices of commodities not enumerated. Massachusetts seems in this new emergency to have repeated its experience of the seventeenth century, for a few months later, May 10, 1777, the act was amended so as to authorize the selectmen of the several towns to fix the prices of farm labor as well as of commodities.[33] Thus the arbitrary determination of wages and prices by general law was again found objectionable.

WHITE SERVITUDE

The first suggestion of what developed into the institution of indentured servants seems to have come from Sir George Peckham, a partner with Sir Humphrey Gilbert in his colonization schemes. Writing in 1582, he stated in a tract on the "Advantages of Colonization," "there are at this day great numbers (God he knoweth) which liue in such penurie & want, as they could be contented to hazard their liues, and to serue one yeere for meat, drinke and apparell only, without wages, in hope thereby to amend their estates."[34]

That there was great poverty in England and much complaint of high prices, appears in William Stafford's "Briefe Conceipt of English Pollicy," which was published in 1581, and which referred to the difficulty of getting employment. The enactment of the Elizabethan poor laws also indicated the prevalence of distress. On the other hand, there was a great demand for labor in the new country. The difficulty lay in the cost of transportation, which stood between the supply and the demand. This gap could be bridged over most successfully by the system of indentured service, by which those who could not afford to pay their passage could cross the ocean and be given an opportunity to work off their indebtedness in the new country.

In the early days of the colony of Virginia, most of the hard labor was performed by indentured servants. In 1625, there were about 464 white servants in the colony, and

[31] *Statutes at Large of Pennsylvania* (compiled by Mitchell and Flanders), VI, 65.

[32] *Acts and Resolves of the Province of Massachusetts Bay*, V, 584.

[33] *Ibid.*, V, 642.

[34] Quoted by Geiser, *Redemptioners and Indentured Servants in Pennsylvania* (1901), 5, from Hart, *American History told by Contemporaries* (1897 *ff.*), I, 157.

only 22 Negroes. Although the Negroes ultimately increased more rapidly than the white servants, as late as 1671 the whites outnumbered the blacks three to one, as there were then counted 6,000 white servants and only 2,000 slaves.[35]

Though white servitude was especially important in Virginia, Maryland, and Pennsylvania, it also existed in New England, the Carolinas, and Georgia.[36] Indeed, in Virginia the planters themselves were from 1606 to 1617 almost in a condition of servitude, as they were obliged to work for the Company, and were dependent upon the council in England for everything.[37] The situation was much the same during the early days of Plymouth Colony. The system of indenture was, however, formally established by law in Virginia in 1619.[38] As the bulk of the servants brought over were sold for tobacco, the principal month for importing them was September; they then reached their destination at the time when the crop was in shape for shipment.[39] Indentured servants were never an important feature in the history of North Carolina,[40] though their condition was regulated by law and some of the "poor white trash" of a later generation were descended from the less thrifty among them.[41] They seem to have been recognized in the Massachusetts *Body of Liberties*, which in Liberties 85 and 87 protected servants from the tyranny and cruelty of their masters.

SOURCES OF INDENTURED SERVANTS

The system of indentured servants depended for its success upon the existence of a poverty-stricken class in Europe on the one hand and a demand for labor in America on the other. Only those who were living on a low plane abroad would voluntarily subject themselves to the hardships of life as temporary slaves in a new country. Nor would the planters have taken such people if there had been a supply of men able to pay their passage. There were several channels, however, through which they entered this condition.

Very commonly, indentured servants were those who, before embarking, signed an indenture agreeing with the master of the vessel to serve him or his assigns for a period of years in return for their passage. This may be considered the normal and legitimate method. It was, in form, simply a device by which the immigrant could work out his passage after landing in the new country. The master of the vessel owned the servant, until he sold him to some purchaser, usually the highest bidder in one of the colonies.

Another class, commonly called redemptioners, were those who, without any formal indenture, agreed with the master of the vessel to be shipped and, on landing, were

[35] Bruce, *Economic History of Virginia*, I, 572.

[36] Ballagh, *White Servitude in the Colony of Virginia* (1895), in *Johns Hopkins University Studies*, XIII, 267, 268. The aggregate number of indentured servants in the course of the colonial period is estimated at more than a quarter of a million. Jernegan, *Laboring and Dependent Classes in Colonial America*, 45, 223. Beard and Beard, *The Rise of American Civilization* (1927), I, 103, hazard the guess that half the immigrants to the colonies, certainly if New England be excluded, were indentured servants or Negro slaves.

[37] Ballagh, *White Servitude in the Colony of Virginia*, 283, 284.

[38] *Ibid.*, 289.

[39] Bruce, *Economic History of Virginia*, I, 620–622.

[40] Bassett, *Slavery and Servitude in the Colony of North Carolina* (1896), in *Johns Hopkins University Studies*, XIV, 183.

[41] *Ibid.*, 253.

given a short time in which to find relatives or friends to pay their passage. If none could be found, the captain might sell them to the highest bidder, and their status became that of indentured servants.[42]

In still other cases, voluntary immigrants started with the intention of paying for their passage, but unexpected expenses or mishaps used up their money and, being unable to meet the demands of the captain on landing, they were sold for cash. Sometimes persons, especially young people, were actually kidnapped in England, put on a vessel, shipped to the colony, and then sold without any legal justification whatever. Boys and girls under age were often indentured as apprentices. Their legal status was like that of the servants. The main difference was that the master was obliged to teach them a trade.

Some indentured servants began their service as convicts, and the transition, when they were indentured, was very slight. Indeed, it meant an improvement in their condition. The Virginia colonists strongly objected to having the country filled up with this class, and before 1670, at least, the number so imported seems to have been small.[43] Many of those, however, who were legally felons, were, in fact, merely political offenders. Many of them possessed good qualities as pioneers and, far from representing a degenerate element of the population, were really taken from the sturdy yeoman class. It is said that 610 Scotch prisoners were sent to Virginia after the battle of Worcester in 1651. Two years later 100 Irish Tories were sent over.[44] The General Court of Virginia prohibited the further transportation of felons after 1671, and this law was confirmed in England, but in 1717 Parliament passed a law which virtually made America the dumping ground for felons.[45] Altogether nine of the colonies are known to have received felons as servants, and the total number imported is estimated roughly at 50,000.[46]

The importation of indentured servants played a particularly important and interesting part in the settlement of Pennsylvania, on account of the fact that shortly after the charter had been granted circumstances arose in Germany which powerfully stimulated the desire to emigrate. The harrying of the Palatinate by Louis XIV, in 1685, the invasion of 1693, and the War of the Spanish Succession from 1701 to 1714 produced fearful misery and poverty in the German provinces on the Rhine. The result was that large numbers of German peasants sought to escape from these conditions and many tracts were issued in order to turn the tide of German migration towards Pennsylvania. A letter from William Penn, published in 1683, was translated into Dutch, German, and French the following year, and this was followed by pamphlets written by Dutch and German people, painting conditions in the colony in glowing colors.[47] The policy of religious toleration adopted by Penn attracted others who went in order to escape religious persecution at home. Not only Quakers, but also Mennonites from Germany, Labadists from Friesland, Pietists, Dunkards, Moravians, and others flocked to the land of freedom. Many of these people came as redemptioners and were sold

[42] Geiser, *Redemptioners and Indentured Servants in Pennsylvania*, 6.
[43] Bruce, *Economic History of Virginia*, I, 599–600, 610.
[44] Ballagh, *White Servitude in the Colony of Virginia*, 293.
[45] *Ibid.*, 294–295.
[46] Jernegan, *Laboring and Dependent Classes in Colonial America*, 48, 223.
[47] Geiser, *Redemptioners and Indentured Servants in Pennsylvania*, 9–18.

to the highest bidder on landing. The hardships of the journey were very great, especially for the Germans.[48] They had to travel down the Rhine to some port of Holland, Rotterdam or Amsterdam. They were often detained here before they could get ship to England. In England they were again obliged to land, go through the customs house, and wait for another ship. Their baggage was often sent on a separate vessel, and as their provisions for the voyage were not uncommonly packed with their goods, the result was great sickness and an incredible death rate from disease or starvation. Of 400 Palatinates, who sailed for New York in 1709, 20 per cent. are said to have died on the voyage. The deaths in 15 vessels in 1738 are estimated at some 1,600 to 2,000.[49]

REGULATION OF IMMIGRATION

The consequence of these conditions and of another evil, the transportation from England of convicts and other undesirable elements, was a series of laws passed during the eighteenth century in Pennsylvania to regulate immigration. One such law, passed in 1700, prohibited the landing of passengers with a contagious disease.[50] Laws were also passed against importing convicts and lunatics. Such a law, passed in 1729, required all masters of vessels who imported passengers to declare their names before the Collector of the Customs within 24 hours after the arrival of the vessel. Only those passengers were allowed to land who were deemed worthy of becoming citizens, and a duty of five pounds was put on each convict imported. This was in direct conflict with the law of England enjoining the transportation of convicts.[51]

A petition of the people of Philadelphia called attention to the evils of overcrowding in 1749 and led to an act providing that no ship should import a greater number of passengers than could be suitably provided for, while each passenger of 14 years or upwards was to have a berth at least 6 feet in length and 1 foot, 6 inches in breadth. If the passengers were under 14, two were to occupy this same space.[52] A similar law with practically the same provisions was passed by Massachusetts, February 6, 1750/1, in order to check the sickness and death caused by the fact that "Germans and other persons" were overcrowded on the ships.[53] Moderate as these restrictions were, they were evaded by taking advantage of the failure to specify the third dimension. Inasmuch as nothing was said about the height, the berths were so constructed as to reduce the former height, and give no greater number of cubic feet than before.[54] This and other abuses led to the formation in 1764 of the "German Society of Pennsylvania." They secured the passage of a law in 1765 protecting the passenger against abuses, requiring a surgeon for the free use of the passengers, and providing that the room allowed each passenger by the previous act should be at least 3 feet, 9 inches in height in the fore part of the ship, and 2 feet, 9 inches in the cabin and steerage.[55] There is a striking parallel between the regulation of immigration in Pennsylvania and Massa-

[48] *Ibid.*, chap. v.
[49] *Ibid.*, 46–50. Jernegan, *Laboring and Dependent Classes in Colonial America*, 50–51, gives vivid details illustrating the horrors of the passage.
[50] *Statutes at Large of Pennsylvania* (compiled by Mitchell and Flanders), II, 80.
[51] Geiser, *Redemptioners and Indentured Servants in Pennsylvania*, 62–63.
[52] *Ibid.*, 63–64.
[53] *Acts and Resolves of the Province of Massachusetts Bay*, III, 536.
[54] Geiser, *Redemptioners and Indentured Servants in Pennsylvania*, 64.
[55] *Ibid.*, 64–66.

chusetts in the eighteenth century and that which took place in the next century under the acts of the Federal Government.

STATUS OF INDENTURED SERVANTS

In spite of cruelties and abuses the status of indentured servants was pretty well established. They enjoyed the right of trial by jury.[56] They were entitled to certain customary gifts on acquiring their freedom, such as suits of clothes, farming tools, or money. They often received land. In the beginning Pennsylvania promised them 50 acres of land.[57] On the other hand, there were some laws against running away, against attacking masters, and so forth; and the period of servitude was often extended as a penalty for misconduct.[58]

SLAVERY

In the seventeenth century, white slavery had disappeared from civilized states, but the enslavement of Indians and Negroes was recognized as a device which might legitimately be used to aid colonization. In fact, colonization and slavery went hand in hand, and it is safe to say that without the demand for labor in the newly discovered parts of the earth, a demand directly created by the large amount of unoccupied land, Negro slavery, with all of its social and political results, would not have persisted. It was therefore quite in accordance with the spirit of the age which created the East India Company and the Hudson's Bay Company to produce also the Royal African Company.[59] This company, which received a charter from Charles II in 1662 and was rechartered in 1672, had as its governor the Duke of York, while the committee of management of which he was chairman frequently met in his apartments at Whitehall. The business of the company was to import into England gold dust from the Guinea coast and to supply the West India planters with slaves. Thus the royal sanction was given to the slave trade which had been for many years practiced in the interests of, and to a certain extent by, the American colonies. The first cargo of African slaves is said to have been imported into Virginia in 1619,[60] but Virginia was not the only colony to profit by this traffic. Negro slaves had their price regularly quoted in the Boston market, and throughout the eighteenth century the slave trade was carried on quite actively in Rhode Island, where Newport was the principal port of entry.[61] In February 1707/8 Rhode Island laid a tax of £3 on each Negro imported.[62] By 1729 this amounted to enough to justify a division of its proceeds, one half being devoted to pav-

[56] McCormac, *White Servitude in Maryland* (1904), in *Johns Hopkins University Studies*, XXII, 173.
[57] Geiser, *Redemptioners and Indentured Servants in Pennsylvania*, 72.
[58] McCormac, *White Servitude in Maryland*, 163 *et seq.*
[59] Scott, *The Constitution and Finance of . . . Joint Stock Companies* (1910), II, 17 *et seq.*; Macpherson, *Annals of Commerce* (1805), II, 508.
[60] The Virginia statement of 1619 records a "Dutch man of Warre that sold us twenty negars;" Russell, *The Free Negro in Virginia* (1913), in *Johns Hopkins University Studies*, XXXI, 398, thinks that the Negroes were bound only to a limited period of servitude.
[61] Donnan, *Documents Illustrative of the History of the Slave Trade to America*, has treated the subject of importation so exhaustively, especially for Rhode Island and Massachusetts, that it is not necessary to do more than outline the subject here. See also Weeden, *Economic and Social History of New England*, II, 453.
[62] Donnan, *Documents Illustrative of the History of the Slave Trade*, III, 109; *Rhode Island Colonial Records*, IV, 34.

ing the streets of Newport, and the other half to building "the great bridges on the main."[63] The tax was repealed in 1732.[64]

SLAVERY IN NEW ENGLAND

Though slavery was recognized legally in all of the colonies down to the end of the eighteenth century, there were considerable differences among them in the regulation of the status of slaves, and in the definition of their rights. These differences tended to grow as the number of slaves increased, and laid the foundation for the acute antagonisms of the nineteenth century. The tendencies may be illustrated by examples taken from New England, from the Middle Colonies, and from the South.

The Massachusetts Body of Liberties of 1641 established at least a moral presumption against slavery in the provision: "That here shall never be any bond slaverie, villinage, or Captivitie amongst us unles it be lawfull Captives taken in just warres, and such strangers as willingly selle themselves or are sold to us. And these shall have all the liberties and Christian usages which the law of god established in Israell concerning such persons doeth morally require." Similarly, the Connecticut statutes of 1642, following the law in Exodus, enacted "If any man stealeth a man or mankind, he shall be put to death."[65] Though this clause was probably intended to apply to white persons, a literal application of it would have made impossible the method by which Africans were usually reduced to slavery. These provisions represent a pious wish of the founders rather than a legal enactment dealing with practical matters, but by the end of the century, Connecticut introduced laws dealing more fully with some of the problems which the presence of Negro slaves brought in. In 1690, the legislature decreed that any Negro, mulatto, or Indian servant found outside of his town without a ticket or pass from an assistant or justice of the peace, or his owner, should be considered a runaway, and might be seized and returned to the owner by any one finding him.[66] To protect the public against the burden of supporting dependent freedmen, a law was passed in 1702 and reinforced in 1711 requiring that slaves who became dependent after having been manumitted must be relieved by the former owners or by their representatives.[67]

According to a law of 1708, a penalty was imposed upon buying or receiving property from slaves without an order from their master. Slaves detected in theft were to be whipped with not over 30 stripes and the same penalty was imposed upon a Negro disturbing the peace or offering to strike a white person.[68] The act of 1730 provided that a slave speaking words which would be actionable in a free person should be whipped with not over 40 stripes, and sold for the costs, unless the master were willing to pay them.[69] Yet the law also provided that the slave might make the same pleas and offer the same evidence as a free person, and other laws show that the slaves in Connecticut had well recognized rights. If a master killed his slave, he was liable to

[63] Weeden, *Economic and Social History of New England*, II, 455.
[64] See Donnan, *Documents Illustrative of the History of the Slave Trade*, III, 122–123, where the act of repeal is reprinted.
[65] See Steiner, *History of Slavery in Connecticut*, 381.
[66] *Ibid.*, 382; *Public Records of Connecticut, August 1689-May 1706*, p. 40.
[67] Steiner, *History of Slavery in Connecticut*, 375–376, 408; *Acts and Laws* (1715 ed.), 164–165.
[68] *Ibid.*, 383.
[69] *Ibid.*, 385.

the same punishment as if he killed a freeman. He was also liable to be sued by the slave in an action for beating, wounding, or immoderate punishment, as he would have been for thus treating an apprentice. A slave was capable of holding property in the character of a legatee. In general, slaves had the same right of life and property as apprentices.[70] In the remarkable trial of the mulatto slave Abda, in 1703, damages were given in the lower court against the claimant for detaining Abda in his services as a bondsman for a year, Abda's principal claim to his freedom being that he had white blood.[71] This decision was, to be sure, overruled on appeal in 1704.

In the second half of the eighteenth century many people in the colony began to have conscientious scruples with regard to slavery, and began to free their slaves; and in 1774 a law was passed absolutely prohibiting the importation of Indian, Negro, or mulatto slaves.[72] Slavery was thus still legal in Connecticut, when the colonies declared their independence, but before the Federal Constitution had been adopted, a law had been passed, introducing gradual emancipation. This act of 1784 provided that no Negro or mulatto born after March 1, 1784, should be held as a slave after his twenty-fifth year.[73] The result was that Connecticut signed the Constitution as a State committed to freedom, and when the complete abolition of slavery was carried in 1848, it affected only a handful of people over 64 years of age.[74]

SLAVERY IN NEW JERSEY

In New Jersey, slavery was recognized at the very beginning in the "Concessions" of the Lords Proprietors, issued in 1664, which offered 75 acres of land for each slave brought in during the first year, and 30 acres for every one in the third. Thus a special premium was put on early importation.[75] The slaves seem to have increased quite rapidly under this stimulus. In 1737, there were enumerated 3,981; in 1790, 11,433; in 1800, 12,422.[76]

New Jersey resorted to the usual measures necessary to protect property, whether in slaves or against slaves. In 1675, a penalty was put upon harboring runaway slaves.[77] In 1682, all traffic with slaves was forbidden. In 1694, the carrying of guns by slaves was prohibited.[78] During the proprietary period (1664–1702), the criminal laws seem to have been the same for bond and for free, but in 1695, special courts were created for the trial of slaves, and special punishments introduced. It was not until 1768 that the special courts were discontinued, and not until 1788 that the special punishments disappeared.[79] Yet the interests of slaves were recognized to a certain extent. In 1682, a law required masters to give the slaves sufficient food and clothing, and in 1798,

[70] *Ibid.*, 387, quoting Judge Reeves, *Law of Baron and Femme*, 340–341.
[71] *Ibid.*, 388.
[72] *Ibid.*, 386. Donnan, *Documents Illustrative of the History of the Slave Trade*, III, 3, states that legislation in 1769 forbade further importation into the colony, as the increase in slaves was injurious to the poor.
[73] Steiner, *History of Slavery in Connecticut*, 400; *Statutes of Connecticut* (1808), I, 623.
[74] *Ibid.*, 405; *Public Acts, 1848*, p. 70.
[75] Cooley, *A Study of Slavery in New Jersey* (1896), in *Johns Hopkins University Studies*, XIV, 419.
[76] *Ibid.*, 441.
[77] *Ibid.*, 442.
[78] *Ibid.*, 446.
[79] *Ibid.*, 447–448; *Revised Laws* (1821), p. 377.

after the Revolutionary War, slaves and colored servants born after November 26, 1788, were required to be taught to read and write.[80]

SLAVERY IN VIRGINIA

Virginia was the first colony to introduce Negroes, but it was not until 1661 that slavery was formally recognized by statute in that colony.[81] In the early days, the blacks were servants rather than slaves, although servants for life, and "although the conditions surrounding a negro or Indian in possession could easily make him a *de facto* slave, the colonist seems to have preferred to retain him only as a servant."[82] Indian slavery did not prove to be successful in any of the colonies, but as the African slaves increased in numbers, there was a steady tendency to intensify the incidents of their state of unfreedom. First of all certain sentimental misgivings about holding Christians as slaves were removed by law. The act of 1667 provided that baptizing blacks did not change their legal condition.[83] A law passed in 1670 provided that all non-Christian servants imported into Virginia by shipping were to be servants for life, while those who came by land were to serve, if boys or girls, until thirty years of age, and if adults for twelve years only. This implied a presumption in favor of liberty for those who were Christians. Therefore, twelve years later the act was repealed, because it was found to prevent the importation of Christianized slaves.[84]

Emancipation seems to have been common in the early days, and freedmen not only frequently held property but might enjoy the right of suffrage. In 1699, an act was passed requiring the exportation of every manumitted African slave within six months after his emancipation.[85] In 1723, no slave was to be emancipated except for meritorious services and then only with the permission of the governor and council.[86] At the same time, it was specifically provided that no free Negro, mulatto, or Indian should enjoy the rights of suffrage.[87]

The various disabilities of slaves seem to have increased with time. It was but a measure of self-protection to prohibit the carrying of weapons by slaves, as was done in 1680.[88] The same was true of the provision that no slave should leave his master's plantation without a certificate,[89] but in 1692 a special tribunal was created for slaves in order to secure their "speedy prosecution" and their right of trial by jury was done away with.[90] Not only did the slave lose the protection which the law gave the white man, in case he was charged with crime, but he was also put in a position of disadvantage in case of a wrong suffered by him. An act passed in 1705 provided that, if a

[80] Cooley, *A History of Slavery in New Jersey*, 460, 461; *Revised Laws* (1821), p. 372.
[81] Ballagh, *History of Slavery in Virginia* (1902), in *Johns Hopkins University Studies*, extra volume XXIV, 34. See Donnan, *Documents Illustrative of the History of the Slave Trade*, IV, 2–7, 49–234, for history and documents relative to the slave trade of Virginia.
[82] *Ibid.*, 31; Russell, *The Free Negro in Virginia*, 370 *et seq.*
[83] *Statutes at Large of Virginia* (ed. by Hening), II, 260.
[84] *Ibid.*, II, 283, 491.
[85] *Ibid.*, III, 87.
[86] *Ibid.*, IV, 132.
[87] *Ibid.*, IV, 133, 134.
[88] *Ibid.*, II, 481, 482.
[89] *Ibid.*, II, 481, 493.
[90] *Ibid.*, III, 102.

slave resisted correction and happened to be killed, the master was free from all prosecution or punishment.[91] In 1723, the provision was reenacted, exempting the master from prosecution unless it could be proved that the slave was killed "wilfully, maliciously, or designedly."[92] It was not until 1788, when a particularly flagrant case came up for trial, that this law was repealed,[93] so that thereafter "the killing and maming of a slave were punishable as if he were a free white man." This, however, still left the slave without any protection against beating which did not result in death or maiming, though, as Ballagh points out, "a person who cruelly beat a horse or other beast was subject to a fine of $50."[94] These various acts indicate an unmistakable tendency, at least down to the end of the eighteenth century, to make the position of the slave more and more helpless and hopeless.

SLAVERY IN NORTH CAROLINA

This tendency was perhaps even more marked in North Carolina. The provision of section 110 of The Fundamental Constitutions of 1669 that "every freeman of Carolina shall have absolute power and authority over his negro slaves, of what opinion or religion soever"[95] is more interesting as an indication of policy than as a sample of statutory law, since this constitution was soon superseded. But before long, legislation with regard to slaves became active. In 1715, an attempt was made to prevent the running away of slaves by imposing a penalty upon anyone who should harbor a runaway for more than one night, and by providing that anyone who should kill a runaway, "that hath lyen out two months," while apprehending him, was not to be held accountable, if he could swear that he had committed the act in self-defence.[96] In 1741, a fine was imposed upon anyone who tempted a slave to run away, and special provisions were made for finding the owner. If he could not be discovered, the slave might be hired out to some person approved by the county court or by two justices of the peace, but to distinguish him from others he was to have an iron collar placed about his neck bearing the letters "P G" signifying "public gaol."[97] Such laws, as well as laws prohibiting a slave from travelling without a certificate, or being found in the kitchens of white people at night, or hunting, or having commercial dealings with people, were measures of self-protection in view of the common tendency of persons who themselves are property to amalgamate with other forms of property. But in some cases the laws indicated a severity which could not be explained in this way. The act of 1741, which dealt both with servants and with slaves, required masters to provide "wholesome and competent diet, cloathing and lodging" for their Christian servants,[98] but had no such provisions in the interest of slaves. The nearest approach to protection in North Carolina was a law passed in 1753, providing that, if a slave who was not properly

[91] *Ibid.*, III, 459.
[92] *Ibid.*, IV, 133.
[93] *Ibid.*, XII, 681.
[94] Ballagh, *History of Slavery in Virginia*, 81.
[95] Thorpe, *American Charters, Constitutions and Organic Laws*, V, 2785; also quoted in Bassett, *Slavery and Servitude in the Colony of North Carolina*, 195.
[96] Bassett, *Slavery and Servitude in the Colony of North Carolina*, 200–201.
[97] *Ibid.*, 203; *Laws of the State of North Carolina* (ed. of 1821), I, 159, 162.
[98] *Laws of the State of North Carolina* (ed. of 1821), I, 153.

clothed and fed stole from another than his master, the man who was wronged might recover from the owner.[99]

The right of the slave to an impartial administration of justice was also more and more curtailed with time. By the law of 1715 special courts were provided for the slave, and he could not be tried in the court open to free men. In the case of a serious offence, he had to be taken before a court composed of any three justices of the peace and three additional freeholders, who were also slave holders.[100] Thus the court was naturally not prejudiced in favor of the slave. In 1741, the laws were slightly changed, and the jurisdiction of the court broadened. It was a not unnatural rule in the South that a slave could not testify against a white person in the courts, and this was formally recognized in a case tried in 1719. But it received a considerable extension in 1746, when a law of North Carolina declared that "all negroes, mulattoes, bond and free, to the third generation, and Indian servants and slaves, shall be deemed to be taken as persons incapable in law to be witnesses in any case whatsoever, excepting against each other."[101] This continued down to the abolition of slavery.

The lack of protection against cruelty was brought into relief by the efforts of the British government to introduce more humane treatment. Burrington, the first royal governor, was instructed to get a law passed in order to restrain inhuman severity towards slaves, without result. The same instructions were given to Governor Dobbs in 1754, but his bill was defeated in the council after passing the house. In 1773 another bill was rejected, and it was not until 1774 that one was passed. Even this was not very effective, inasmuch as it simply provided that, if anyone should "wilfully and maliciously" kill a slave he should be imprisoned twelve months for the first offense, and suffer death for the second offense.[102] The teeth were drawn from this law, however, by an additional provision, that it should not apply to outlaws, nor to slaves who should die under moderate correction, nor to those who were killed while resisting their master. The law, therefore, implied that correction issuing in death might be considered moderate. Moreover, inasmuch as one can hardly imagine even a Negro slave allowing himself to be killed without making some resistance, and inasmuch as after the death of a Negro there would be as a rule no one to testify against his master, it is clear that the whole law was rendered nugatory by these provisions.

The policy of the different colonies was undoubtedly influenced, as has been pointed out by Von Waltershausen, by the extent to which slavery prevailed in them. Those which had a large proportion of slaves in their population were naturally more afraid of insurrection and therefore more severe in their criminal laws, than those which had fewer, while their pecuniary interests made them more opposed to emancipation.[103] But in the New England States and in Pennsylvania, which abolished slavery, either at once or gradually, towards the end of the eighteenth century, the impulse was due mainly to ethical or religious ideals. The Quakers were particularly active in pleading for freedom. They began by prohibiting the ownership of slaves in their own

[99] Bassett, *Slavery and Servitude in the Colony of North Carolina*, 210.
[100] *Ibid.*, 195–196.
[101] *Ibid.*, 196, 197.
[102] *Ibid.*, 211–212.
[103] Von Waltershausen, *Die Arbeits-Verfassung der Englischen Kolonien*, 163–164.

community, and carried this through as early as 1774 in Pennsylvania, 1782 in New England, 1784 in New York, and 1787 in the Southern States.[104] The ideals of freedom and equality which came in with the doctrine of natural rights and were embodied in the Declaration of Independence also supplemented this ethical impulse,[105] and created, even in some of the Southern States, a certain presumption in favor of emancipation. The conflict between these newer ideals and the profits of slave-holding grew into the political controversies which in the next century racked and well nigh split the Republic.

[104] Jorns, *Studien über die Sozialpolitik der Quäker* (1912), 133.
[105] Von Waltershausen, *Die Arbeits-Verfassung der Englischen Kolonien*, 164.

CHAPTER VII

FAIR TRADE

Meager as is the social policy of the colonies with respect to labor, it is extraordinarily rich in other lines of activity, to which we are now unused. Apart entirely from the relations of the employing and laboring classes, the law-makers found a field in which they could express the modern ideals of fair treatment and of equality of opportunity. This field embraced, not the relations of dependent producers to their superiors, but the relation of the community of consumers to the producers, and particularly to the merchants who served the public needs.

REGULATION OF PRICES

The Boston ordinance of 1635, which empowered a committee to set the rate of wages, instructed it also to set prices upon all cattle, commodities, and victuals. It is not probable that the committee arranged a schedule such as that which determined in detail the wages of laborers. Laws of this period, fixing the prices of commodities, applied generally to only a few specific wares, often to corn alone. Acts or orders, fixing the price of grain, were common in the early history of New England[1] and the Middle Colonies;[2] and in Virginia in the early decades the prices of provisions were often set by proclamations of the Governor and Council.[3] An act of 1623/4, passed shortly after Virginia had attained some share of legislative power, provided that, "For the encouragement of men to plant store of corne, the prise shall not be stinted, but it shall be free for every man to sell it as deere as he can." The provision was repeated in 1631/2 with the remark that it was contrary to the precedent of other countries, and that it was justified by the fact that all had land enough, and could have as much corn as they would plant. But in 1647, a year of want, the price of corn was fixed in tobacco, and again from time to time in the later years, 1666, 1682, and 1755.[4] Attempts were made, sporadically, to fix the prices of products throughout the colonial period, as the memory of former failures faded; in the period of the Revolution, with the depreciation of the paper money, they were widespread. We know the futility of the later laws; it is hard to believe that even the earliest laws were of any use.

[1] Examples in *Records of Massachusetts Bay*, I, 142; *The Public Records of the Colony of Connecticut*, I, 13, 18.
[2] *Cf. Laws and Ordinances of New Netherland, 1638–1674* (ed. by O'Callaghan, 1868), 120, 150; Huntington (N. Y.), *Town Records* (ed. by Street), I, 115, footnote.
[3] Bruce, *Economic History of Virginia*, II, 205.
[4] *Statutes of Virginia, 1619–1630* (ed. by Hening), I, 125, 173, 197, 347; *1660–1682*, II, 233, 506; VI, 553. *Cf.* Bruce, *Economic History of Virginia*, I, 380.

Their justification must be sought in the industrial organization of the colonies where they were passed. In a community where production for self-consumption is the rule, where exchange is rare, and is limited to the equalization of the accidental surpluses and deficits that arise in one household or another, a set rate for this exchange, even a very rough one, may be an advantage. But the colonies, even in the earliest period, had passed beyond this stage of organization; with the specialization of occupations that afterwards disappeared, and with the constant arrival of new immigrants, exchange was really more active than in a later period. Bradford said in 1626 that when the people found their surplus corn to be a commodity which would bring them a price of 6s. a bushel they were very diligent in planting.[5] They were producing for exchange, for a certain rate of exchange; and any attempt to limit the rate by law would defeat its object, in so far as it was effective, by causing stock to be withheld from sale and by checking production. The laws probably did no great harm, but the objects which they had in view were attained by other means. The institution of markets eliminated, as far as possible, the personal elements that would block the way to a fair bargain. The supply of corn to the poor was undertaken by distributions from the public treasury, and by the regulation of the grain trade, without attempting to interfere directly with the prices at which grain passed; and individual cases of extortion were prevented by the action of the courts.

LIMITATION OF PROFITS

Another series of regulations aimed to set the prices of imported articles, not by fixing absolute rates at which they must pass, but by limiting the profits of the merchants. European wares were of special importance to the colonists in the early period, before they had learned to supply their own needs or to do without; they grudged the commodities which went out in payment for these wares, and endeavored to shift the hardship by legislation.

Peculiar justification for such a course can be found in a colony like Virginia. The account given by Bruce[6] of the early trade between that colony and England is an absolute contrast to trade relations in modern times. Cargoes were provided by subscription or by lottery in England, were put in charge of a Cape Merchant, and were doled out by him at rates fixed in England if the colonists could pay them, if not, for what they could give. The Company assumed the responsibility of supporting the colonists, and demanded, properly enough, a monopoly of the trade, to get what gains it could. It allowed private traders, under certain circumstances, to sell in Virginia, if they did not take advantage of the necessities of the inhabitants to sell *above* the Company's rates. The Company set a limit of 25 per cent. on its profits in trade, and set rates on commodities in Virginia.[7]

A somewhat similar scheme was proposed for Massachusetts in 1629, by which a joint stock association was to supply the colony with commodities at a fixed profit of 25 to 30 per cent., taking beaver in pay at a fixed valuation.[8] The northern colonies did not pass through the long period of tutelage that marked the beginning of Virginia, but

[5] Bradford, *History of Plymouth Plantation* (Ford ed. of 1912), I, 447.
[6] Bruce, *Economic History of Virginia,* II, 260 *et seq.*
[7] *Ibid.*, 286.
[8] Young, *Chronicles of Massachusetts Bay* (1846), 114 *et seq.*, 146.

they did experience a time when their existence depended in large part on the charity as well as the business interests of those who were able to extend help, in the Old World and the New; and the ideas formed under these conditions became ideals which they endeavored to realize in legislation.

An act passed in Massachusetts in November 1633 recited the fact that wages had been set, and affirmed that it was only just to the laborer to set the prices of his necessaries, that he might not be wronged or discouraged. Accordingly, no commodities were to be sold for an advance of more than 4d. in the shilling above their cost in England, except such as were exposed to the danger of spoiling or leakage, which might be sold at such rates as buyer and seller could agree upon, provided that these were moderate.[9] This law was repealed in less than two years; and a similar law in New Haven was allowed to remain in force an even shorter time.[10] In Virginia, after the repeal of the set rates for the exchange of European goods and tobacco, an act was in force for a time which forbade more than 50 per cent. gain in merchandise, though this was also repealed 1654/5. The Council of New Netherland prohibited in 1653 the sale of goods, except in the Indian trade, at more than 100 (temporarily 120) per cent. advance above the invoice value.[11]

It is evident that laws limiting the profit on imported commodities must have been from the beginning even more futile than those which designed to set the rate of exchange for domestic products. In the case of the latter, it is conceivable that individuals, who had produced primarily for their own consumption, would be willing to exchange a surplus at the legal rate, with the feeling that at another time conditions might be reversed, and they would have the other end of the bargain. Foreign trade, however, represented the highest economic development with which the colonists came in contact; it would be most sensitive to any interference with its profits, and would punish such interference most quickly by withholding its supplies. The legislators had to seek other means to facilitate the distribution of imported wares through the population, and the measure which they adopted, was a restriction on speculation in laws against forestalling at the ports.

PUNISHMENT OF EXTORTION

When the impracticability of determining wages and prices by general laws was finally recognized in Massachusetts, the government still took cognizance of individual cases of exchange in which it appeared that injustice had been wrought, and punished the offenders. In 1635, as noted in the preceding chapter, the laws setting wages and prices had been "for dyvers good consideracons" repealed, and it was ordered, to prevent ill-disposed persons from oppressing and wronging their neighbors, that if any man should offend against the true intent of this law he should be punished by fine or imprisonment. What the "true intent" of the law may have been, we can guess only from the general terms quoted; but under it a man was fined for selling knives and

[9] *Records of Massachusetts Bay*, I, 111.

[10] *Ibid.*, I, 159; *Records of the Colony and Plantation of New Haven, 1638–1649* (ed. by Hoadley), I, 35, 61.

[11] Bruce, *Economic History of Virginia*, II, 289, 336 footnote; *Statutes at Large of Virginia* (ed. by Hen ing), I, 413; *Laws and Ordinances of New Netherland* (ed. by O'Callaghan), 149, 150, 151.

scythes for more than 4d. in the shilling profit.[12] Two years later there were still complaints of oppression in wages and prices; a committee was appointed to report a remedy, but appears to have taken no action.[13]

As finally settled by the act of 1675,[14] any person judging himself oppressed by mechanics or laborers was to appeal to the selectmen of the town for redress. In case of oppression by merchants or shopkeepers he could complain to the grand jurors or to the county court, and if the court found an injury done, it was to fine the offender, and require him to return double the amount of the overcharge. Somewhat similar provisions are found in the Connecticut act against oppression, "a mischievous evil the nature of man is prone unto." If any person had complaint to make of a merchant or trader, or of any handicraftsman or laborer, he could require an official to call together two or three of the same trade or occupation, to give their judgment on the price under oath, and this judgment was to be the ground for legal conviction.[15]

As it will be necessary, in later pages, to consider the case of certain artisans who were said to abuse their power by charging extortionate rates for their services, the discussion may here be limited to the oppressions said to have been exercised in trade.[16] We must remember that the people of the colonial period were on a standard of living below the level to which even the poorer classes have attained today; most of them had few luxuries or comforts, and no superfluity of necessaries. Extortion, then, the act of a shopkeeper in securing from the ignorance or the necessities of a customer a greater price than that which he would be willing to take from other customers, had more serious social results. On the other side, the opportunities for extortion must have been vastly greater than they are today. As retail trade was carried on chiefly by barter, the comparison of prices required skill and knowledge, and gave to the professional dealer a superiority to his customer greater than that to which we are now used. The fact that exchange rested largely on credit undoubtedly magnified the chances of mischief. There can have been little competition between stores, especially in the early period, and the automatic punishment for sharp dealing now provided by the withdrawal of custom was impracticable.

A final judgment on the colonial extortion laws would have to be based on a study of the cases tried under them in the courts. Only a few scattered examples can be cited from the early period. Winthrop, under date of 1640, said that the evil of extortion was notorious, but the example that he cited in that place is hardly a good one; a man on the voyage to America sold the milk of his cow at 2d. a quart, and being afterward at a sermon where oppression was complained of, fell distracted.[17] The price was certainly not dear under the circumstances, as Winthrop admits; milk brought a penny a quart on land, in early Massachusetts. A better example is the case of Robert Keaine,[18] who kept a shop in Boston, and was complained of for extortion beyond the

[12] *Records of Massachusetts Bay*, I, 160; Weeden, *Economic and Social History of New England*, I, 119.
[13] *Records of Massachusetts Bay*, I, 223.
[14] *Ibid.*, V, 62–63.
[15] This act does not appear in *Public Records of the Colony of Connecticut, 1665–1678*. The preamble and first clause are printed in *The Laws of Connecticut*, of 1673 (Brinley reprint of 1865), 55; and are repeated with the addition of the rule of procedure in *Acts and Laws of His Majesty's Colony of Connecticut* (ed. of 1702, re-issued in 1901), 91.
[16] With the discussion of extortion in the text compare Johnson, E. A. J., *American Economic Thought in the Seventeenth Century*, chap. vii, "The Morality of the Market Place."
[17] Winthrop, *History of New England* (ed. by Savage, 1825–1826), II, 21–22.
[18] *Ibid.*, I, 313–316.

other tradesmen, because he was wealthy and sold dearer than most of the others. He was charged with excessive profit, over 100 per cent. in the case of some small wares, and was fined the large sum of £100. His fine was afterwards remitted in part, but Savage thinks that the case must have been a flagrant one, as Keaine was ordered by the Court to restore to a woman "her necessary clothes." Savage has seen the original affidavit in another case in which Keaine figured, in which the plaintiff swore that he had done work at Keaine's house for which 38s. were due him; that Keaine gave him in payment a piece of cloth which he pretended was Spanish broadcloth, at the rate of 17s. a yard; while four persons swore that it was clothrash, worth 9 to 10s. at most.[19]

These cases of Keaine are the ones that bring out most clearly the grounds of defense of the extortion laws. When a public body complained of an overcharge, as in the case of a man who was fined for extortion in the price which he demanded for building the Boston stocks, one suspects the misuse of political power.[20] Personal animosity had a part in the charge of extortion brought in Maine, in 1640, against a trader who had the only store in a considerable neighborhood, and who kept the price of beaver down and the price of powder and shot up.[21] The case of Captain Turner, involving alleged overcharges, against Mrs. Stolion in New Haven, in 1645, seems to have been a contest between equals, not the exploitation of a weaker party by a stronger.[22]

It is very possible that the laws were misused in the colonies where they were passed, that they did not reach the cases where their application would seem justifiable, and that they were a means of persecution rather than of protection. No laws could eliminate the personal element from the retail trade of the colonial period, or secure the protection which competition now affords. The merchant must have been tempted to many gains which would now be regarded as dishonorable, and which would certainly be bad policy for any man who had an opportunity to extend his market. No such positive and practical proof was possible then as now, that a moderate profit is the best policy.

THEORIES OF JUST PRICE

Keaine's extortion case evoked an interesting discussion, preserved by Winthrop.[23] He said that most of the magistrates were inclined to moderation in the matter, because there was then no law in force limiting the profit of trade, and "it is the common practice, in all countries, for men to make use of advantages for raising the prices of their commodities," because many men in the country were guilty of similar excesses in the sale of their cattle, corn, or labor, and "Because a certain rule could not be found out for an equal rate between buyer and seller, though much labour had been bestowed on it, and divers laws had been made, which, upon experience, were repealed, as being neither safe nor equal." The magistrates, furthermore, were moved especially by the fact that the law of God appointed no other punishment than double restitution.

Cotton treated the subject in one of his lectures, which was reported by Winthrop. The principle that a man may sell as dear as he can and may buy as cheap as he can

[19] *Ibid.*, II, 71 footnote.
[20] Hutchinson, *The History of Massachusetts* (3d ed., 1795), I, 385.
[21] Maine Historical Society, *Collections* (1831), I, 34.
[22] *Records of the Colony and Plantation of New Haven* (ed. by Hoadley), I, 174–176.
[23] Winthrop, *History of New England* (ed. by Savage), I, 316 *et seq.*

was false, he said. The true principle was, "A man may not sell above the current price, i.e., such a price as is usual in the time and place, and as another (who knows the worth of the commodity) would give for it, if he had occasion to use it." If a man paid too dear for a commodity he must not try to make up for his want of skill by keeping up the price. If he lost some of his commodities by accident, as by shipwreck, it was a loss cast on him by Providence which he might not try to shift to another, "for so a man should seem to provide against all providences &c. that he should never lose; but where there is a scarcity of the commodity, there men may raise their price, for now it is a hand of God upon the commodity and not the person." Other false principles were that a man could ask more than his selling price, and that "as a man may take advantage of his own skill or ability, so he may of another's ignorance or necessity."

The preamble to a Massachusetts law of 1641 noted the inconvenience of differences of method in the appraisal of cattle in the country. The true rule was stated as follows by the Court: "it is not to bee iudged the m^r^kett or true price wch some are forced by vrgent necessity to sell a beast for, but what benefit may arise by the milke & increase of a cowe, or labo^r^ of an oxe, charges of hay, &c considered; & it is desired that all men will indevor to frame their comerce according to this rule."[24] Although the candidates for masters' degrees at Harvard in 1725 agreed that prices could be regulated by law, and that it was not always lawful to give and take the market price,[25] the frequent changes made in the law showed what practical difficulties this kind of legislation encounters.

GOVERNMENT TRADING

When attempts to fix the prices of wares by legislation proved fruitless, the law makers tried other means to protect the community from exploitation. Sometimes the government took the trade into its own hands. Massachusetts, in a year of scarcity (1636), bought a cargo of provisions for the general stock, and distributed among the towns according to their needs; Winthrop says that the colony saved £200 by this procedure.[26] A few years later the same colony proposed to undertake a reversed form of this trade, freighting a ship with wheat contributed by the towns, to be sent off in exchange for foreign commodities.[27] Similar examples could be cited from other colonies, and government undertakings in the form of municipal trading became later of considerable importance, as will be shown. Ordinarily, however, the government preferred to leave the risks of trade to private individuals, and contented itself with such control as promised to preserve the interests of its subjects. In pursuing this object, it endeavored to put in force the principles which for centuries had been embodied in the market regulations of Europe.[28]

[24] *Records of Massachusetts Bay*, I, 331.

[25] Weeden, *Economic and Social History of New England*, II, 524.

[26] Winthrop, *History of New England* (ed. by Savage), I, 185 *et seq.*, 388; Young, *Chronicles of Massachusetts Bay*, 351–353.

[27] *Records of Massachusetts Bay*, I, 337.

[28] A discussion of the market regulations as applied to foreign trade is omitted here. See Bruce, *Economic History of Virginia*, II, 353 *et seq. Cf. Proceedings and Acts of Maryland, 1637/8–1754* (1883–1933), 161; *Laws of Maryland* (ed. by Bacon, 1765), chap. xlviii; etc. Massachusetts experimented with a variety of port regulations designed to protect the interests of consumers.

ESTABLISHMENT OF MARKETS

The occasion for the establishment of a market is best shown by the preamble to the New Netherland ordinance of 1656,[29] establishing a market on the beach at New Amsterdam, which follows in full, in modern spelling: "Whereas divers articles, such as Beef, Pork, Butter, Cheese, Turnips, Carrots, Cabbages and other Country produce are brought to this City, now and again by Farmers to be sold here, with which being come hither, they are obliged to remain a long time at the Beach with their produce, frequently to their serious loss, because the Commonalty, or at least a majority thereof, who live at a distance from the Beach, are not aware that such articles are brought for sale, which tends not only to the inconvenience of the Burgher, but also to the serious damage of the industrious Farmer, who oftentimes loses more by his absence from home than he has gained on his produce," a Saturday market was established. So in a description of Boston, 1794,[30] the writer gives a long list of articles made by families in the vicinity, and brought into town for sale by country women. The women had to hawk their wares about until they were forced by fatigue to part with them, if not at a loss yet at a price that discouraged their industry. They were forced to barter their wares for gewgaws, and were deprived of the means of purchasing materials with which to continue their trade. There ought to be a cloth *market*, said the writer, where buyer and seller could meet; the sellers would then get ready money and the buyers could buy what they wanted at first hand. The competition would improve the manufactures, as they would be viewed together.

The grants of markets were attempts to secure coincidence in the colonial organization, bring buyers and sellers of wares together, encourage each to produce for the other, enable each to satisfy his wants to the best advantage by the comparison and selection of wares, and by the protection from extortionate prices that the competition of a number of dealers assured him. The colonists were accustomed to markets and fairs as institutions of exchange, and missed them in America. Higginson wrote to intending settlers, in the Fall of 1629, to bring with them everything that they might need; there were no shops in America, "here are yet neither markets nor fairs to buy what you want."[31] Most of the colonists, even in a much later period, lived isolated and self-dependent to such an extent that, without some means to bring them together, a man with wares to sell might waste his life seeking a purchaser. When an extraordinary sale was to be made, it was necessary to take extraordinary means to appraise the people of it and to collect customers; notices were posted in various prominent places, and announcements were made with the beat of a drum. So in an account which Kingsbury gives of a cattle-trading expedition into New York State, the trader, Bishop, was preceded by a man in antiquated clothes, riding on the axle-tree of a cart without the body and with two wheels of different size, driving mismated cattle and pretending to be in search of Bishop to make a trade in them.[32] Such means were necessary to break through the intercellular partitions which divided the industrial organism. In granting a market, the colony took on itself the same function as the town of Boston in 1642,

[29] *Laws and Ordinances of New Netherland* (ed. by O'Callaghan), 251.
[30] [Pemberton], "A Topographical and Historical Description of Boston," in Massachusetts Historical Society, *Collections for the Year 1794*, 1st series (reprint of 1810), III, 283.
[31] Young, *Chronicles of Massachusetts Bay*, 264.
[32] New Haven Historical Society, *Papers*, III, 72.

when it announced that people who desired to buy milk should repair to Richard Fayrebankes, who had promised to deal with such as had milk to sell, and would direct the people so that they might be provided.[33] The market was an attempt to further exchange and to increase its benefits, by organizing it, and by giving public notice of opportunities to trade. Beyond this formal announcement of a conventional time and place where buyer and seller could meet, most of the market grants did not go.

ATTEMPTS TO ORGANIZE MARKETS IN VIRGINIA

In the establishment of markets, as in many other respects, the legislation of Virginia is a contrast with that of the other colonies. In spite of an industrial organization differing absolutely from that of England, an attempt was made to impose on the colony an elaborate system of industrial legislation, founded on the English. It is inconceivable that the people introduced and attempted to maintain this system of their own initiative, and Bruce shows that in fact it was due to English influence.[34] The legislation had no serious practical results, but deserves such illustration as may be given by quotations from various statutes.[35]

In 1631/2, it was ordered that the laws of England against forestalling and engrossing should be published and executed. In 1649, a market was granted to James City, to be held twice a week. Bonds made on any bargain in the market, and attested by the clerk, were to have the force of a judgment, and any commissioner of the quorum could issue executions on them. The act fixed the bounds of the market, the salary of the clerk, and other details.

In 1654/5, a law enacted that in every county there should be appointed one or two places, ten miles apart, where the trade of the county must be concentrated. Merchants could sell only in the market, and could transport goods from one market to another only under the control of a certificate. This act was repealed the next year, with the remark that it was likely to prove inconvenient; it was said, at the same time, that any county or individual settling a place where merchants would willingly come for the sale of goods would be regarded as a public benefactor.

The act of cohabitation, June, 1680,[36] repeated the attempt to establish a town in each county, to which the entire trade of the county was to be confined. Only certain country produce could be sold outside the towns. This act was suspended by the King in the following year. An account of Virginia, said to have been written between 1696 and 1698, criticized these laws in the light of the real conditions—the sparsity of population, and the inconsiderable development of manufactures and internal trade—and showed their impracticability. The writer said that the law confining trade in imported goods to towns was "a great force upon trade," and would have made everyone very uneasy if it had actually been executed; he believed that Virginia tried to establish too many towns.[37]

The climax of extravagance is reached in the act for establishing ports and towns,

[33] Boston, *Town Records, 1634–1660* (2d ed., 1881), 68. The series is printed in *Reports of the Record Commissioners of the City of Boston.*
[34] Bruce, *Economic History of Virginia,* II, 539, 555, etc.
[35] *Statutes at Large of Virginia* (ed. by Hening), I, 172, 362, 397, 412, 476.
[36] *Ibid.,* II, 471 *et seq.*
[37] Massachusetts Historical Society, *Collections,* 1st series, V, 128 *et seq.*

made in accordance with royal suggestion in 1705, and repealed by proclamation in 1710.[38] It named a number of towns and established them as free burghs; it provided that no provisions were to be sold within five miles of them, if on the same side of the river as that on which they stood, that no imported goods, with certain exceptions, were to be sold within the same distance, and that no inns were to be established within ten miles. Town inhabitants were freed from three-fourths of the duties laid on trade, and were given other privileges. Each town was to have a market at least twice a week, and a fair once a year; was to have "a merchant guild and community with all customs and libertys belonging to a free burgh;" if it counted thirty families exclusive of innkeepers, it was to have eight "benchers of the guild hall;" and so forth. All this was to apply to a country where, even toward the close of the century, one-half of the forty-four towns recognized by the Assembly had not more than five houses, and the other half were with few exceptions inconsiderable villages.[39] In view of the character of all this legislation, it is impossible to attach much significance to the later grants of market privileges, in which the clerk of the market was given assize of bread, beer, wine, and wood, and other functions of the office as it was known in England.

SLIGHT IMPORTANCE OF MARKETS AND FAIRS

Aside from the provision markets in the large towns, which will be the subject of discussion later, the market appears in few cases to have had an importance comparable to that of its European prototype. So far as appears the only approach to an attempt to confine trade to the market, in the northern colonies, was in Bristol, Rhode Island (1693),[40] where the sale of produce on any other than the market day was forbidden, unless the transaction took place at a remote farm house; and it seems scarcely possible that this regulation was enforced. New Amsterdam, in its early years, maintained for its inhabitants a monopoly of trading against outsiders, and admitted strangers to trade only on market days. In most cases, however, the market had little control over the trade of the early towns. It may have been an impulse to the starting and to the regularity of exchange, but it was certainly not an important factor in the regulation of trade. Towns that were granted a market made nothing of the grant, showing precisely the same organization as towns that had no grant; neither class of towns had any apparatus for the control of its trade. "Market-places" did not imply institutions for the regulation of trade. It is common enough to find clerks of the market chosen where there was no legal market, and not chosen where there was one; their chief duty seems to have been the sealing of weights and measures, and they were chosen only spasmodically, even when their election was enjoined by a colonial statute.

From the standpoint of social policy, the fairs of the colonial period were as unimportant as the markets of the small towns. Grants of fairs, including often such characteristic features as a court of pie powder, freedom from tolls and dues, and exemptions from arrest, were nearly as common as were the market grants. Often, however, the fairs which they authorized were never established; few attained to any considerable

[38] *Statutes at Large of Virginia* (ed. by Hening), III, 404 *et seq.*

[39] Burnaby, *Travels throughout the Middle Settlements in North America in the Years 1759 and 1760* (3d ed., 1798), 16; (Wilson's reprint of 3d ed., 1904), 45.

[40] Weeden, *Economic and Social History of New England*, I, 406.

importance, and these only as cattle markets.[41] The volume of internal commerce was so small that it could not support even such an institution as the fair, which thrives only in the early stages of trade.

The colonial laws which established markets and fairs were an attempt to organize trade in a general way, so as to assure to all the people a fair chance to satisfy their needs. This general attempt at organization did not, as shown above, solve the problem of fair trade. Exchanges remained still individual and isolated, and complaints continued, as they were certain to do in lack of the protection afforded by a market. The legislators, therefore, were forced to descend from the general to the particular. They singled out those occupations in which apparent abuses led to common complaint, and regulated them in detail. Illustrations of this policy appear in the legislation on the quality of wares and on peddling.

PUBLIC INSPECTION TO REGULATE THE QUALITY OF WARES

The colonial statute books and town records are filled with provisions regulating by public authority the technical processes in the manufacture of wares, and providing for public certification of their quantity and quality. The fact that so few of these laws have maintained themselves must be ascribed to the growth of an industrial and commercial competition which has rendered them superfluous, by giving opportunity for the elimination of inferior processes and products without the interference of the state.

Following a convenient summary, which obviates the necessity of going into the endless details of the legislation, in Massachusetts as late as 1856,[42] State statutes regulated the public inspection of leather, fish, lumber, shingles and clapboards, hoops and staves, beef and pork, wood, bark, and charcoal; and wherever trade in these articles was carried on, there must be public officers to determine the quality or quantity. Inspectors of hay and lime could be appointed by the towns, but their appointment was not obligatory. They generally received no salary, and were not elected with regularity, but they appear in greater or less number in all the towns, and it is safe to assume that their functions in the trade of the time were regarded as normal and necessary. Most of these regulations applied to articles designed for export. In internal trade, the determination of quality by public officers was customary in the case of staples so commonly used for payment that the need of a certain standard was felt; tobacco in the South and corn and pork in the North present familiar examples. In the exchange of most articles, however, people determined for themselves the quality, and applied to public officers only for a certification of the quantity of wares not readily measured. Complaints were common of frauds in the sale of wood, hay, lime, lumber products, and so forth, and laws were passed that individuals could apply to officials who had the technical knowledge and appliances to measure these wares and assure the purchaser that he was getting what he paid for.

Especial importance was attached to the inspection of wares designed for export, and in reference to them the laws show a somewhat different purpose; they aimed not only to ascertain the quantity and quality, but also to exclude entirely from trade all

[41] This summary of the colonial fairs is based on the study of a considerable amount of detailed material, to which it seems unnecessary to give references.

[42] Kingsbury, *Massachusetts Townsman* (1856), 343–371.

wares below a certain standard of quality. Before the export business had assumed such proportions that the foreign customer knew the exporter through many dealings, wares were known, not by the man who shipped them but by the colony from which they came. This fact, that the wares of one locality were classed together abroad, led the people of that locality to class their export wares together in their laws; they set a certain standard under the belief that the community lost more than the individual gained by a trade in wares of an inferior quality. So in Massachusetts, about the middle of the eighteenth century, Hutchinson wrote that the potash manufacture promised well, and should be encouraged. "The least that can be done by every government where it is manufactured, is a law to compel every person to set his name, and the name of the town where he lives, upon the cask in which he packs his pot-ash. This will go a great way towards preventing fraud."[43] Beyond this attempt to make the manufacturer identify himself with his ware, however, it was the usual practice for the government itself to vouch for the quality and quantity of a ware by official inspection and branding. So, *e.g.*, in Virginia, "as sound policy requires that our flour trade should be put upon a respectable footing, which can only be done by establishing such regulations as will prevent the manufacturer from bringing to market any flour that will not pass the public inspections with credit, or entitle the merchant to preference in every foreign market," previous regulations were strengthened by detailed provisions, regulating not only the quality of the ware, and the quantity in each package, but also the mode of packing.[44]

REGULATION OF THE PROCESSES OF PRODUCTION

While most of the inspection laws applied to wares in the course of exchange, the government interfered also in the processes of production. The time when brick clay was to be dug and turned over, and the character and size of the molds, were determined by law.[45] The Massachusetts Assembly directed the inhabitants how to wash wool and ordered them to keep out dirt, by statute;[46] the Connecticut Assembly regulated by law the time when bayberries were to be picked.[47] In New England the government interfered especially in the manufacture of leather, a ware which took a position of peculiar importance in the colonial economy, as it was used largely for clothing, by reason of the cost of textile fabrics. The conditions of transportation forbade the growth of a tanning business on a large scale, and put the industry in the hands of petty tanners, scattered through all the small communities, and following their trade only as a by-employment. The village tanner was often unskilled, and worked necessarily under unfavorable technical conditions, but he had a practical monopoly. Farmers had to apply to the local tanner for their leather, unless they were willing to establish vats of their own; and if they suffered from poor work they could not transfer their custom. Instead, they applied to the courts, with the feeling, apparently, that any man who exercised functions so important to the community as those of the tanner

[43] Hutchinson, *The History of Massachusetts* (3d ed., 1795), II, 401.
[44] *Statutes at Large of Virginia* (ed. by Hening), X, 496.
[45] *Public Records of the Colony of Connecticut*, III, 192.
[46] *Records of Massachusetts Bay*, II, 180; IV, pt. i, 121; V, 212.
[47] Thorpe, *North Haven Annals* (1892), 114.

was a public person, and should be subjected to public control. The New Haven Court gave notice that Goodman Osborne had spoiled divers hides in tanning, because of want of experience in the tan of the country, but that he promised to make good in the future what hides he spoiled, and was to be held responsible for them.[48] To obviate complaints, the courts put in the form of laws what they believed were the proper processes to be pursued, and imposed their ideas of technique on the trade. Such laws were common throughout the colonial period, and were enforced to some extent, as is shown by notices in the records of fines and confiscations for infractions of them. It is possible that they disseminated some useful information, and helped to raise the standard of the country workmen. In general, however, it is apparent that they were impracticable, and were simply a helpless reaction against the natural difficulties of the situation. The recurring complaints of poor leather betray their failure.

APPROACHES TO GILD ORGANIZATION

It was in connection with the attempt of the government to regulate the quality of wares that the nearest approach to the gild organization was reached in colonial times. The Virginia law of 1705, establishing a gild merchant in each town, was a bit of English legislation which could have no result in the colony to which it was applied. The practice of restricting retail trade to the inhabitants of the town, as found in Boston and New Amsterdam, led to no distinct organization in the town comparable to the gild merchant, though cited by Weeden[49] as showing its survival. The germ of a gild merchant might be found, if anywhere, among the Indian traders, who went out in parties of considerable size, and who must have had some organization.[50]

There were a few cases, however, in the early history of Massachusetts, in which the government, apparently discouraged by the difficulty of regulating trades by public officers, took steps which marked at least the beginning in the establishment of craft gilds. An act of 1642,[51] passed to prevent the inconvenience of ill-tanned leather, introduced in the leather manufacture the separation of trades so characteristic of the gild system; each workman was to be something of a specialist, responsible for the results of his work before the ware passed to the next process. No butcher, currier, or shoemaker was to use the "mystery" of a tanner, and conversely; only tanners were to buy rough hides in the hair, and no currier was to curry any leather, unless it was well tanned. Another approach to the gild organization appears in 1644, when, for the better building of ships, it was ordered[52] that there should be a company of the trade after the manner of other places, with power to regulate ship-building and to make orders for the conduct of the members of the company; this act was rather an invitation to the shipbuilders to organize, than mandatory, for it was made conditional on their cooperation, and failing that it seems to have come to nothing. The next year coopers living outside of Boston were informed that such as desired to join with the coopers of Boston

[48] *Records of the Colony and Plantation of New Haven* (ed. by Hoadley), I, 86.
[49] *Economic and Social History of New England*, I, 80.
[50] *Cf. New York Documents Relative to Colonial History*, III, 436.
[51] *Records of Massachusetts Bay*, II, 18; *cf. Public Records of the Colony of Connecticut*, IV, 74.
[52] *Records of Massachusetts Bay*, II, 69.

in a company, invested with power to regulate the trade, should come to the next session of the Court, and give their opinions and advice.[53]

In October 1648, coopers and shoemakers were incorporated in separate companies, by commissions which were practically identical.[54] Upon petition of the shoemakers of Boston, it was said, and upon consideration of the complaints of the damage sustained by the country because of bad wares made by some of that trade, the Court empowered four men named, and other shoemakers of Boston, to meet and elect a master and two wardens, with four or six associates, a clerk, a sealer, a searcher, and a beadle, with such other officers as were found necessary. The assembled shoemakers were to have power to make orders for the government of their company, in all the affairs of their trade, and could impose reasonable penalties; but no order or amendment was to be in force until it had been allowed by the County Court or the Court of Assistants. The master and either warden, with any three of the associates, could hear cases of transgression of the orders, and could assess fines up to forty shillings, which were to go to the company, subject to an appeal to the County Court. On complaint by the company of any person exercising any part of the trade of a shoemaker, who was not approved by the officers as a sufficient workman, the County Court was empowered to summon such person and suppress him. The Court reserved the right to establish other companies. It was provided that the shoemakers' company should make no unlawful combination to enhance the prices of boots, shoes, or wages, whereby either natives or strangers could suffer; and no shoemaker was to refuse to make shoes for inhabitants, of their own leather, for the use of themselves and families only, at reasonable rates.

The incorporation of the coopers was in the same terms; it was granted on petition of the coopers inhabiting Boston and Charlestown, and in consideration of the many complaints of damages sustained from defective and insufficient casks. These acts were to be in force for three years, and at the expiration of that time they were not continued. The only reference to them which has been noted is in *Johnson's Wonder Working Providence*,[55] where the author speaks of the incorporation of the coopers and shoemakers, and singles out members of those trades as "inriching themselves by their trades very much." Their materials were cheap and they sold dear. As to tanners and shoemakers, "between them both they have kept men to their stander hitherto," charging almost double English prices.

In 1664, a man petitioned the General Court for authority to set up as a cooper in Boston; the petition was allowed, provided that he was found sufficient in his art, on trial by four skilful men in the trade, two to be chosen by the Boston selectmen, two by the petitioner, and any three of these to determine the case.[56] At the same time the Boston town government and not the coopers determined matters connected with the exercise of the trade; in 1661, a man was ordered by the town to cease employing a Negro as a cooper; in 1667, on complaint of the coopers, the selectmen forbade a man to employ his son as a cooper before he had served his seven year apprenticeship.[57]

[53] *Ibid.*, II, 98–99.
[54] *Ibid.*, II, 249–251; III, 132–133.
[55] *Johnson's Wonder Working Providence, 1628–1651* (ed. by Jameson, 1910), 247–248.
[56] *Records of Massachusetts Bay*, IV, pt. ii, 107.
[57] Boston, *Town Records, 1660–1701*, pp. 5, 39.

Members of the different crafts continued active in pressing their interests, but they did so as individuals, and the regulation of the craft continued to be exercised by the town or colony government. In 1668, the coopers of Boston and Charlestown petitioned the General Court for redress of certain evils, not named; a committee was appointed to confer with them. In 1677, in answer to a petition of the shoemakers, coopers, tailors, and joiners of Boston, the Court appointed a committee to draw up regulations for the trades, but no report is on record.[58]

Boston required a seven year apprenticeship of anyone who wanted to open a shop or exercise a manufacture in the town,[59] and the colonial governments required in certain callings proof of capacity on the part of those who desired to exercise them. It was said in the New Netherland ordinance of 1656[60] that frauds might occur in tapping or baking, "for the concealment whereof excuses may be set up and invented, because no Guild or association is hitherto known;" and it was ordered that no one should be a baker or tapster, unless he got a license from the court in his jurisdiction, to be renewed quarterly. So in early New York, no one was to undertake the brewing of beer for sale, except "such as are known to have Sufficient Skill and knowledge in the art and Mistery of a Brewer."[61] In Connecticut, in 1692, because of the insufficiency of previous orders to prevent unskilful tanning, an act was passed [62] that no one was to tan unless he had manifested his skill to the County Court and obtained liberty to set up the trade. A memorandum in the account book of the first tanner in Goshen shows that he obtained a license at the County Court in Hartford, in 1748, paying 10/6 old tenor in fees.[63] Apparently he had learned his trade by experience, and had served no regular apprenticeship.

Licenses were not required of physicians, and though they could be obtained by application to the courts, many practiced without them. A number of physicians in New London County in 1774 petitioned the General Assembly for a better regulation of the practice of medicine,[64] but medical associations were not incorporated in Connecticut until after the Revolution. The present Massachusetts Medical Society was established in 1781,[65] with the power to examine and license candidates for practice. Smith said that quacks abounded in New York, and thought it a shame that there was no regulation;[66] an early law had restricted practice to methods that were approved by custom,[67] but an examination and license were not required of candidates for practice in New York City until 1760.[68] An act of 1772 regulated the practice of physic and surgery in New Jersey.[69]

The most real example in America of the gild idea would probably be found in the

[58] *Records of Massachusetts Bay*, IV, pt. ii, 377; V, 143.
[59] Boston, *Town Records, 1634–1660*, p. 156.
[60] *Laws and Ordinances of New Netherland* (ed. by O'Callaghan), 262.
[61] *East-Hampton Book of Laws, June ye 24th, 1665* (New York Historical Society, *Collections for the Year 1809*, I), 324.
[62] *Public Records of the Colony of Connecticut*, IV, 82–83.
[63] Hibbard, *History of Goshen, Connecticut*, 370.
[64] Caulkins, *History of Norwich* [Connecticut] (1874), 359.
[65] Burrage, *A History of the Massachusetts Medical Society, 1781–1922* (1923). p. 1.
[66] Smith, William, *History of New-York* (1814), 326.
[67] *East-Hampton Book of Laws*, 335.
[68] *The Colonial Laws of New York* (1894), IV, 455.
[69] *Acts of the Province of New Jersey, 1702–1776* (ed. by Allinson, 1776), 376.

incorporated medical associations. The craft gilds showed no vitality, as has been seen; the incorporation later of a Master Taylors' Society in South Carolina,[70] and similar examples, had reference merely to benefit organizations.

REGULATION OF PEDDLERS

With a scattered agricultural population, such as that of the colonial period, peddling had an importance that it has lost today. Many of the farmers lived at such a distance from stores as to make a visit to them inconvenient; they had many minor wants, not great enough to bring them to a point of supply, but which they were glad to satisfy if the wares were brought to their doors. So with a growth of stores in the places where there was a tendency to a concentration of the population—near the meeting house, the mill, the village smithy or the river landing—there grew up a peddling trade in the thinly settled districts. In Connecticut, as early as 1650, "David the Jew" was fined for going into houses and trading with children, when the heads of the family were absent;[71] and the peddlers continued the activity, begun thus early, well into the nineteenth century.

The peddlers carried small articles, generally petty luxuries, which would awaken a desire when seen, but the need of which would not be felt so strongly as to bring the farmers of their own initiative to the store.[72] They attended markets and fairs, and on court days, or whenever there was a concourse of people, they competed with the local shop keepers; but they found their real field in the country districts. The South Carolina law of 1738 described peddlers who "have travelled from town to town, and from one plantation to another, both by land and water, exposing to sale rum, sugar and other goods, wares and merchandizes, and taken in payment therefor from negroes and other slaves, hogs, fowls, rice, corn, and other produce."[73] The agency of the peddler in marketing the manufactures of the households and shops of New England is well known.

Laws to regulate and restrict peddling were common throughout the colonial period. The colonial governments, inclined always to interfere freely in the processes of exchange, disliked an itinerant trader, who removed himself from observation and could readily escape from jurisdiction. The peddler could keep his place only by a clear proof of his services to the community. The fact that the peddler dealt so largely in luxuries made this proof difficult, and it was employed by an influential class of competitors, the store keepers, to secure legislation which put the peddler at a disadvantage, and sometimes prohibited his activities entirely. Some extracts from the preambles of laws on peddling will illustrate the reasoning of the legislators. In a law enacted by Andros and his council in 1687,[74] complaint was made that many persons had lately become peddlers, "passing from town to town vending sundry wares, and that which is unserviceable, at excessive rates, to the great detriment of the settled trade of this country," and all persons except merchants from beyond the seas were forbidden to

[70] *Statutes at Large of South Carolina* (ed. by Cooper and McCord, 1836–1841), IV, 702; VIII, 132; etc.
[71] Trumbull, *Memorial History of Hartford County* (1886), I, 321.
[72] For details of the peddlers' trade, *cf.* Kingsbury, "Old Connecticut," in New Haven Historical Society, *Papers*, III, 77; Dwight, *Travels in New England and New York*, II, 53–55; Lambert, *History of The Colony of New Haven* (1838), 203; Wright, *Hawkers and Walkers in Early America* (1927), 17–96.
[73] *Statutes at Large of South Carolina*, III, 487.
[74] *Public Records of the Colony of Connecticut*, III, 435–436.

expose goods for sale outside the town or farm where they lived. In Massachusetts, in 1713/4,[75] complaint was made of great harm done to trade, and its decay, due to hawkers who peddled through the country, goods of which many had probably been stolen at the time of the late fire in Boston, "and by frequent robberies and thefts since committed;" all peddling, therefore, was prohibited. The act was temporary, but the prohibition was continued later, and an act, copied in great part verbally from it, was passed in New Hampshire in 1718.[76] The reason alleged for the New Jersey act of 1730,[77] which restricted peddling to inhabitants of the province who had been recommended as honest by a justice of the peace and had paid for a license, was that many idle and vagrant persons, under pretence of being hawkers, had greatly imposed on people in the sale of goods, and had entered houses, using trade as a mere pretext, and had committed misdemeanors. What was stated in this law as a fact seemed sufficiently dangerous as a possibility to warrant similar restrictions in Pennsylvania in 1784;[78] idle and vagrant persons might enter the State as peddlers, might impose on people in respect to the price and quality of wares, and might commit felonies. In the Rhode Island act of 1698,[79] complaint was made that peddlers secured a quantity of goods from merchants in Boston, sold them in Rhode Island, and then ran away without paying the merchants what was due them. The act of 1738[80] in Virginia complained that peddlers exported skins and furs without payment of duty, and the act of 1752 repeated this complaint, with the additional charge that they committed many frauds and abuses "in exchanging with the inhabitants of this colony for their valuable commodities, wares of little or no use."

Incidental reference has been made in the acts cited to the hurt that established traders felt in the competition of peddlers. This competition, deemed unfair because the peddlers paid no local taxes, was made the chief motive for the passage of many laws. License fees were imposed in South Carolina, in New Jersey, and in New York, with the express statement that they were designed to offset the taxes which settled traders had to pay. Sometimes the reasoning was distinctly mercantilist in character. So the Rhode Island statute of 1698 charged that peddlers departed from the colony, "gathering up quantities of ready money and carrying it off, and who pay little or no acknowledgment to the government, or scot or lote, nor are at those charges the freemen and inhabitants that trade are at, who also trust the inhabitants, and yearly take off considerable quantities of the produce of the Collony in part of pay, which the other transient traders do not; but carry off the ready money, to the damage not only of the traders but of the government and inhabitants in generall."[81] In New York, likewise, peddlers were said to injure the trade of the province by "carrying a great deal of money out of it with them."[82] In comment on these charges it may be said that even peddlers granted credit, as we know from a petition from one of them who had debts

[75] *Acts and Resolves of the Province of Massachusetts Bay*, I, 720.
[76] *Laws of New Hampshire* (ed. by Batchellor), II, 255.
[77] *Acts of the Province of New Jersey* (ed. by Allinson), 89.
[78] *Laws of the Commonwealth of Pennsylvania*, (ed. of 1810), II, 99.
[79] *Records of the Colony of Rhode Island*, III, 358.
[80] *Statutes at Large of Virginia* (ed. by Hening), V, 54; VI, 245.
[81] *Records of the Colony of Rhode Island*, III, 358.
[82] *New York Documents Relative to Colonial History*, VI, 161.

owing to him in most of the counties of Connecticut,[83] but they undoubtedly did take money in exchange whenever they could get it, on account of the difficulty of transporting country produce.

INTERESTS INVOLVED IN THE REGULATION OF PEDDLERS

It is difficult to estimate the justice of the preceding complaints, as information on the peddling trade is scanty outside the laws themselves. It seems probable that the peddlers did practice what would have been called extortion or fraud by the courts of the time. Their customer was not protected in his bargain by any market. Some peddlers seem to have confined their trade to a particular route; apparently this must have been the case when they granted credit. At best, however, they saw their customers only at considerable intervals, and were checked even less than the ordinary storekeeper in driving a bargain, by fear of future loss of trade. Dwight's ideas on the subject are worthy of attention.[84] He thought that bargaining for small wares made men sharpers, and that the consequences of peddling and of all similar employments were malignant. Every gainful bargain was considered good, and this led the peddler to fraud. "Often employed in disputes he becomes noisy, pertinacious, and impudent." Berlin, Connecticut, he thought, had suffered not a little from the peddling by which its tin wares were marketed; if its manufactures were sold in the same way as other merchandise, less profit would be made, "but the corruption of a considerable number of human beings would be prevented." The traditions of the Yankee peddler that have come down to us do seem to show that his trade nurtured certain qualities that no moralist would consider amiable, and that no economist would consider useful or necessary in a settled society. He was to a certain extent different from other traders in his standard of dealings, and in so far as the law was forced to take cognizance of him and classify him, it would, in this respect, classify him as bad. His position in the eyes of the legislators was not helped by the fact that he supplied the population in large part with "unnecessaries;" the laws distinguished between peddlers of different kinds of wares.

Neither of these points, however, was the real basis for the adverse legislation. There is nothing to show that the peddlers' customers were the moving force in restricting or abolishing the trade. They wanted to buy just what the peddler brought to them, and if they had been cheated, they forgot about it before the peddler came again. More weight might be allowed to the social rather than the economic dangers of the peddler's wandering life; he was undoubtedly more apt than other people to commit misdemeanors, to steal or to pass stolen goods, because he was less likely to be found and punished. Outside the charges made against the peddlers in the laws, however, there appears only one statement on this point, that merchandise obtained by unlawful intercourse with the British, in Norwich 1781/2, was not dealt in by honorable traders, but sold covertly, "or distributed by peddlers."[85]

The main reason for the restrictive legislation was undoubtedly the influence of the shopkeepers, who hoped to secure the entire trade for themselves. They demanded

[83] Trumbull, *Memorial History of Hartford County*, I, 321, footnote 2.
[84] Dwight, *Travels in New England and New York*, I, 306; II, 53–55.
[85] Caulkins, *History of Norwich* [Connecticut], 397.

that the peddlers should be taxed, and this the government granted readily; they made the most of the evils of peddling, and secured its entire prohibition in a number of the colonies. So Governor Hunter of New York wrote to the Board of Trade in 1714, of an act for licensing peddlers, that "the chief intent of this Act is the encouragement of the City and shop keepers, and at the same time if it does not lessen the number of pedlars, oblige them to pay something towards the uses of the Government."[86] A memorial against peddlers from 24 citizens of Stonington, in 1727, extracted by Swift from the Connecticut archives, is probably a sample of many similar.[87] It referred to the restrictions on peddling imposed in the other colonies and in England, and contained a great variety of charges against peddlers, imputing to them, among other things, the spread of disloyalty (why did they leave their native land?), and the spread of disease (for could they not buy wares cheaper in places where disease was prevalent?). Further, they hurt the domestic storekeepers, who "not only make it their whole Imploy, But p^r^haps many of them are in no other way to maintain and support their famelys. Men through much paines and fatigue Do keep by them all Sourtes of necessarys to supply their neighbours with on reasonable terms, and are taxed yearly for their s^d^ Privelidge and faculty, which they not only readily but Gladly Pay, While those Strangers and foreigners Carry off yE profitt."

Many different measures were employed to protect the community against the alleged abuses of peddlers. Commonly the peddlers were required to take out a license, for which they had sometimes to pay a fee as high as £20. They were restricted often to dealings in domestic products. Sometimes, particularly in periods of epidemic disease, they were prohibited entirely. The legislation was, on the whole, much more strict in the North than in the South, where stores were less common, and the services of the peddlers were more highly prized.

REGULATION OF USURY

While the laws against peddling dealt with a branch of trade which is now so insignificant that it rouses little attention, some likeness to modern policy appears in a survey of the usury laws of the colonial period.[88] It is proper to remark, however, that the credit relations which were of the greatest social importance in the colonies were chiefly those arising in retail trade, and that these were too private and individual in character to be influenced by usury legislation. Most of the colonists never reached the stage of "money-economy." Dealings were commonly expressed, it is true, in terms of money, but money as a medium of exchange was little used in the country districts. Exchange transactions were ordinarily effected by barter, and partly on that account, were generally on a credit basis.[89] The difficulty of securing coincidence under a barter system made it generally impossible to close a transaction on the spot. The farmer wanted goods at the store when the season offered him no products to pay for them, and entered into the merchant's books for what he needed. He engaged the

[86] *New York Documents Relative to Colonial History*, V, 379.
[87] Trumbull, *Memorial History of Hartford County*, I, 321.
[88] On the subject of usury, see also Johnson, E. A. J., *American Economic Thought in the Seventeenth Century*, 213 *et seq.*
[89] On this subject compare Gould, *Money and Transportation in Maryland, 1720–1765* (1915), in *Johns Hopkins University Studies*, XXXIII, 9–176.

services of a shoemaker or a smith, and paid for them by doing odd jobs and supplying farm products throughout the year. In these barter transactions among the colonists accounts were allowed to stand open for years before they were balanced.

Usury laws, therefore, can have had but a limited application in everyday affairs. The general character of their provisions is set forth in the accompanying table, giving the legal rates of interest in different times and places,[90] and in the paragraphs following.

Colony	Date	Legal Rate of Interest per cent.
New Hampshire	1696	6
Massachusetts	1641	8
	1693	6
Rhode Island	1767	6
New York	1717	6
	1718	8
	1737	7
West Jersey	1694	8
New Jersey	1719	8
	1738/9	7 (chap. 593, 6% disallowed)
Delaware	Not specified	6
Pennsylvania	1682	8
	1722/3	6
Maryland	1704	6, in money 8, in wares or tobacco
Virginia	1730	6
	1734	5
North Carolina	1741	6
South Carolina	1719	10
	1748	8
	1777	7
Georgia	1755	10
	1759	8

In England, the legal rate was reduced from 10 per cent. to 8 per cent. in 1624; was made 6 per cent. in 1652 and 1660; and 5 per cent. in 1714.

Infraction of the laws was commonly punished by forfeiture of the loan, sometimes by forfeiture of double or treble the value. Brokers' fees for making or renewing a loan were often fixed at rates varying from 1 to 5 per cent. A large part of the later acts was taken up with regulations designed to prevent evasions, and determining procedure in case of infractions.

The Massachusetts act of 1693 stated expressly that it did not apply to the letting of cattle or to like usages among farmers, and on the other hand it did not apply to "maritime contracts among merchants, as bottommary, or course of exchange as hath been heretofore accustomed."[91] The same exceptions are expressed in the New Hampshire law, and though they appear in the laws of none of the other colonies, they may have

[90] *Acts and Laws of the Province of New Hampshire*, 265; *Records of Massachusetts Bay*, II, 48; *Acts and Resolves of the Province of Massachusetts Bay*, I, 113; Arnold, *History of Rhode Island* (1894), II, 274; *The Colonial Laws of New York*, I, 909, 1004; II, 980; *The Grants, Concessions and Original Constitutions of the Province of New Jersey* (ed. by Leaming and Spicer, 1752), 532; *Acts of the Province of New Jersey* (ed. by Allinson), 61, 110; *Laws of New Castle, Kent and Sussex upon Delaware* (1752), 63; *Charter to William Penn and Laws of the Province of Pennsylvania*, 180; *Laws of the Commonwealth of Pennsylvania* (ed. of 1810), I, 156; *Laws of Maryland* (ed. by Bacon), chap. lxix; *Statutes at Large of Virginia* (ed. by Hening), IV, 294, 395; *State Records of North Carolina*, xxiii, 168; *Statutes at Large of South Carolina*, III, 104, 709; IV, 363; *Digest of Laws of Georgia* (ed. by Watkins), 44, 58.

[91] *Acts and Resolves of the Province of Massachusetts Bay*, I, 113.

been recognized in practice. The law was meant, apparently, for cases in which it could practically be applied, and in which the absence of competition seemed to render an application necessary. The language used in the laws of some of the southern colonies makes it seem probable that loans on land were chiefly had in mind; but most of the laws are so general in their terms that it is impossible to determine from them the character of the transactions.

One of the laws proposed by Cotton in 1641,[92] based like the others on scriptural texts, was a prohibition to take any increase on what was lent to a poor brother. Winthrop, in his "Modell of Christian Charity,"[93] was more moderate in the rule that he laid down for lending. If your brother has neither present nor probable nor possible means of repaying, you must give, not lend, to him; "if he hath present means of repaying thee, thou art to look at him not as an act of mercy, but by way of Commerce, wherein thou arte to walk by the rule of justice; but if his means of repaying thee be only probable or possible, then is he an object of thy mercy, thou must lend him, though there be danger of losing it." As to the rule to be used in forgiving, when the debt was due, "Whether thou didst lend by way of commerce or in mercy, if he hath nothing to pay thee, must forgive (except in cause where thou hast a surety or a lawfull pleadge)".

It is probable that ideas like these lasted on in sermons throughout the colonial period, but they do not appear in the laws. In them, interest was always recognized as justifiable, and the only question was as to the rate. The complaint in the New Hampshire act of 1769, that "the usurer makes as much profit by his money only, as the fair dealer, the honest husband-man, and ingenious artificer, can by their money, time and labor," is exceptional. A fair sample of the motives as set forth in the laws appeared in the preamble of the Massachusetts act of 1693, lowering the legal rate to 6 per cent., "as the abatement of interest has always been found beneficial to the advancement of trade and improvement of lands by good husbandry; and whereas the taking of eight in the hundred tends to the great discouragement of ingenuity and industry in the husbandry, trade and commerce of this province."[94] The colonists sorely needed capital to make the most of their new country, and passed laws that they should have what they wanted; that seems to be the gist of colonial usury laws.

Discouragement of industry, trade and commerce, obstruction to settlement—phrases in which these results of high interest were adduced as reasons for lowering the rates—occur so commonly in the laws, and in terms so nearly identical, that the idea of mere coincidence is impossible. The colonial legislators were borrowing ideas from each other, and following each other in lowering the rates. In the New Jersey act of 1738/9 it was expressly affirmed that one reason for lowering the rate was that legal interest in New Jersey was above that established in any of the neighboring colonies. The South Carolina act of 1748, fixing the rate at 8 per cent., recited English acts against usury, and then stated that the rate in most of the colonies had been reduced below 10 per cent. "after the example of our mother country," and should be reduced in South Carolina.

[92] Hutchinson, *Collection of Original Papers Relative to the History of the Colony of Massachusetts-Bay* (1769), 171.
[93] Massachusetts Historical Society, *Collections*, series 3, VII, 37.
[94] *Acts and Resolves of the Province of Massachusetts Bay*, I, 113.

The colonial usury laws were framed, apparently, to lower the rate of interest rather than to prevent individual cases of extortion, and they diverged so far from whatever market rate there may have been as to make their application spasmodic and harmful. Only in the case of New York, where there was an attempt to establish a rate of 6 per cent. in 1717 and then the government returned to the old rate of 8 per cent. in 1718, because the former act had not "attained the ends designed," does there appear recognition of the principle of regulating the law by the rate rather than the reverse. A solitary example of an attempt to lower the rate by encouraging the lender appeared in the South Carolina act of 1784, which sought foreign capital for the development of the colony by empowering the subjects of other States to collect their debts even in time of war.

The laws can scarcely have been enforced, in view of the ease of evasion. When Peter Stuyvesant brought suit in 1653 for payment of 450 florins, with interest according to the bond and the penal sum of 900 florins stipulated thereon, the 900 florins may easily have been usurious interest.[95] Legitimate bottomry bills were used in the colonial period but the bottomry bonds on which suit was brought in New Amsterdam could have been fabricated to cover usury.[96] Burnaby said that protested bills of exchange on which interest was double the common rate, were used in Virginia for usurious purposes;[97] and the South Carolina law of 1721 stated that lenders had taken 25 per cent. more by requiring the borrower to sign a bond, payable within a year, for a much greater amount than he received.

[95] *The Records of New Amsterdam, 1653–1674* (ed. by Fernow, 1897), I, 132.
[96] *Ibid.*, I, 106, 384; *cf.* Massachusetts Historical Society, *Collections*, series 3, VII, 202.
[97] Burnaby, *Travels* (ed. of 1798), 26, footnote; (reprint, 1904), 55, footnote.

CHAPTER VIII

THE PUBLIC FOOD SUPPLY

In many of the colonies, the difficulty of exchange and the meager economic resources of the people led to the formulation of a policy which aimed to make the group self-sufficient. Prohibitions to export wood cut on the common lands were usual in New England towns and colonies, and could be readily justified as a protection of common property against a waste which would benefit only individuals.[1] Restrictions on the export of fish and shell-fish could be viewed in the same light.[2] Attempts to retain in the colony the raw material of clothing, especially skins and hides, were common in the seventeenth century; these were based on reasons of a broader character, and many examples, both from northern and from southern colonies, could be given. Like the attempts to stimulate local industries by protective import duties, of which there was an abundance, they sought to quicken the circulation of wares inside the colony, and to develop its industrial organization. These restrictions were felt to be burdensome, however, and in most cases were soon repealed; they occurred only sporadically in the eighteenth century.

REASONS FOR THE REGULATION OF THE PROVISION TRADE

Restrictions on export such as those noted in the preceding paragraph are of interest as parts of colonial economic policy, but they had little social significance. The regulation of the exchange of food-stuffs, which was wide-spread and long maintained, had a more serious importance as a part of a system of social policy. It represented a settled determination on the part of the state to interfere with exchange in behalf of the weaker members of the community, that all might be assured a provision of the necessaries of life. It was not merely in the first years of settlement that the lack of provisions was so generally felt as to assume public importance and to call for public action. Throughout the colonial period a short crop in any section could raise prices far above the normal. It has been said[3] that the lack of opportunity to market products made the necessaries of life very abundant in the northern colonies, even though the luxuries were wanting. Such a statement is incomplete. In fact, the farmers designed to plant enough land to provide a safety fund against mishap, and often had a considerable surplus; but in really bad years they lacked a comfortable supply. There was always

[1] Common in the seventeenth century, these restrictions disappeared in the eighteenth century except in Connecticut. *Cf. Public Records of the Colony of Connecticut*, V, 434; IX, 286.

[2] *Records of the Town of Brookhaven . . . New York* (1888), II, 148, etc.; Orcutt and Beardsley, *History of the Old Town of Derby, Connecticut, 1642–1880* (1880), 246; *The Ancient Records of Norwalk, Connecticut* (ed. by Hall, 1847), 110–111.

[3] Von Waltershausen, *Arbeits-Verfassung der Englischen Kolonien in Nordamerika*, 48.

the danger of a fluctuation such as that in early Virginia: in 1634, a surplus of 10,000 bushels of corn was shipped thence to New England, while two years later corn was so scarce there as to bring 20s. a bushel, and the poor were forced to live on garden vegetables.[4] Even in a seaport town like Boston, in 1696, maize and wheat rose to double their usual price,[5] and the rise of prices in years of scarcity was worse in the interior, where grain could be carried only over bad roads. In 1813, frost killed most of the corn in Northwood, New Hampshire, and "The year following, many poor families, for several weeks together, had not a single loaf of bread."[6]

EMBARGOES

The ordinary method of dealing with a threatened or actual shortage of food supplies was an embargo, which sealed the outlet of supplies from the colony, and rendered them all available to the domestic consumer. Embargoes were laid for periods varying from one or two months to a year or more; very often a period was set terminating with the next harvest. The right to lay an embargo was sometimes expressly conferred on the governor,[7] and seems sometimes to have been exercised by him without a special warrant; so the statutes of the colonial period, laying specific embargoes, present a list which is by no means complete. So far as the statutes show, however, embargoes were uncommon in the middle colonies after the earliest period and before the Revolution; examples appear in New York, 1709; New Jersey, 1713/14, 1754; Pennsylvania, 1755, 1756. Virginia and Maryland did not make common use of the embargoes except in the earliest period, North Carolina had but two, while South Carolina had many, perhaps ten, and Georgia, four. In Massachusetts embargoes appear in the statutes of the seventeenth century, in 1630, 1648, 1653, 1662, 1675, and 1697, but after that the power to lay them seems to have been exercised by the governor. Rhode Island laid embargoes in 1676, 1713, and 1724, and Connecticut, with a list of more than a dozen, seems to have been the colony which exercised most frequently its right to prohibit the export of provisions. The history of embargoes in Connecticut may be used to illustrate the policy.[8]

During the early years of the colony the government provided first for a public supply of corn to the people, and then for a disposal by government agency of the surplus corn raised; but after 1650 the government steadily followed the policy of letting individuals seek their own market for the sale of grain, except in times of scarcity or war, when they were not allowed to sell outside the colony. So, on account of scarcity, a prohibition to export provisions, valid until the next court, was passed in 1652, and another in 1662. In October, 1675, the time of King Philip's War, the export of grain from the colony was allowed only under special license; the next month the Council prohibited the export of provisions from New London County for two months, the only case observed in which lines were drawn inside a colony. At a Council meeting in

[4] Bruce, *Economic History of Virginia*, I, 310, 312; *cf.* Winthrop, *History of New England* (ed. by Savage), I, 191.
[5] Weeden, *Economic and Social History of New England*, I, 400.
[6] New Hampshire Historical Society, *Collections*, III, 72.
[7] *Statutes at Large of Virginia* (ed. by Hening), IV, 221; *Acts and Laws of the English Colony of Rhode Island* (1767), 89; *Public Records of the Colony of Connecticut*, VIII, 376.
[8] All references are to the statutes in *Public Records of the Colony of Connecticut.*

January, 1675/6, Massachusetts petitioned that provisions might be exported from Connecticut. The government replied that the army could have what it needed, but that it did not venture to open the doors wide, as corn was scarce, and the war might prevent the colony from sowing and planting. "You cannot judge it to our interest to withhold what we can spare; having noe other market." In April Massachusetts complained that the export of corn which its inhabitants had bought and paid for was stopped. In May corn could be exported, if the shipper gave security that he would provide an equal amount for the people of Connecticut within three months. In 1681 the General Court approved the action of the Governor and Council in laying an embargo on grain, but thought it no longer necessary, and removed it. In 1690 a three months embargo was put on provisions, because of the uncertainty of war; and the danger from pirates in the transportation to Boston. Embargoes were laid in 1695 and 1710. In December, 1713, letters were laid before the Council showing a great scarcity of grain in Massachusetts and Rhode Island. There was a good supply in Connecticut, but several vessels were designing to load for Madeira, and those who had grain held it at such a high price that the poor were in danger of suffering want. It was ordered that no grain should be exported except by special license, and then to be carried only to Massachusetts or Rhode Island. In March 1714, in consideration of a good supply in Massachusetts and Rhode Island, the embargo was removed. In May, 1737, in answer to complaints from the people of the scarcity of grain, an embargo was laid to hold until June, and the Governor was given power to extend the period. In 1741 the Governor and Council were given general power to lay an embargo on grain until the next session of the General Assembly, and exercised this power at intervals down to the Revolution.

Before the passage of early embargo acts a survey was sometimes made of the stock of provisions in the country, as in Massachusetts, 1648 and 1662,[9] but more commonly and apparently always in the later period, the embargo was not based on any such accurate knowledge of the food supply, and was merely the conventional answer to popular complaints of scarcity. The embargo sometimes prohibited entirely the export of provisions, and sometimes merely restricted it by export duties.[10] The statute provided sometimes for automatic action, the restriction coming in force only when the price of grain rose above a certain point;[11] and was sometimes balanced by an arrangement for the vent of surplus stock in time of plenty.[12] The one instance observed of a town group levying an embargo on food stuffs is that of Nantucket[13] and is to be explained, of course, by the town's insular position.

PUBLIC IMPORTANCE OF THE GRIST MILL

Colonial legislation aimed not only to provide the raw materials of food, but also to assure to the people an opportunity to procure at a fair price their meal or flour. Indian

[9] *Records of Massachusetts Bay*, II, 240; IV, pt. ii, 43; *cf. Records of the Colony of Rhode Island*, II, 536; *New York Documents Relative to Colonial History*, XIV, 205.

[10] *Statutes at Large of Virginia* (ed. by Hening), II, 21; *Acts of the Province of New Jersey* (ed. by Allinson), 32.

[11] *Proceedings and Acts of Maryland, 1637/8–1754*, p. 96; *Statutes at Large of Virginia* (ed. by Hening), I, 227.

[12] *Public Records of the Colony of Connecticut*, I, 116–117, 119, 131.

[13] Bliss, *Quaint Nantucket* (1896), 35.

corn remained the staple article of food throughout the colonial period, with all the differences of detail there might be in various localities. The meal was at first obtained by pounding the grain in a samp mortar or grinding it in a hand mill, or quarn, by a laborious process. Bradford said that the Pilgrims were forced to pound their corn in mortars for many years before they could get a mill[14] and this was characteristic in general of the early years of settlement. The grist mill, however, offered such advantages that journeys of considerable length were made to avoid the hardship of grinding at home. In early New England, journeys were mainly confined to two objects, "to mill and to meeting,"[15] and corn was taken to the mill to be ground even if it had to be carried on the back, as between Bridgewater and Concord, for thirteen miles.[16] A town felt so keenly the need of a grist mill that it managed, ordinarily, to secure one within a few years after its settlement. Conditions sometimes forced the use of wind for motive power, but a water mill was the preferred and ordinary form. "Mill stream" is the common name by which Dwight, in his travels, designated a small stream of water.

The erection of a water mill, involving the transportation of the mill stones and shaft, and the building of a dam, was an enterprise which in the early period often surpassed the capacity of individuals, and required the common action of the local group. In most cases, at this time, the grist mill was "a public institution, established like the school and the church, by the legal authorities of the settlement."[17] Colonial legislation furthered the building of mills, especially by laws facilitating the acquisition of mill sites by men who would put them to good use. Even on the entailed lands of Virginia, guarded in general so jealously, the builder of a mill could acquire an acre in fee simple for the site of his enterprise.[18] The laws ranked millers with state officials, college professors, ministers, and physicians in exemption from jury duty or military training.[19]

PRIVATE MILLS AFFECTED WITH A PUBLIC INTEREST

The mill was given public privileges because of the importance of its functions, which made it an institution of the first necessity to any community. On the same account it was made subject to public control. The Supreme Court of the United States, in its famous decision in Munn *vs.* Illinois,[20] which subjected a private grain elevator to public control and paved the way for the present regulation of the rates of public utilities, found a precedent in the colonial legislation regulating the weight and quantity of bread. A mill took in the colonial economy a public position fully as important as that which a grain elevator or a railroad takes in a modern American community, and was removed as summarily from the arbitrary control of its proprietor, even when he had borne all the costs of its establishment. So in the North Carolina act of 1758, "every Water Grist-Mill already built, or which shall hereafter be built, that hath, or shall at any Time grind for Toll, shall be held and deemed, and is hereby declared to be a Public Mill;" it was subject to the usual regulations as to service and rates of toll,

[14] Bradford, *History of Plymouth Plantation* (Ford ed. of 1912), I, 373.
[15] Thorpe, *North Haven Annals*, 17.
[16] New Hampshire Historical Society, *Collections*, III, 191.
[17] Orcutt and Beardsley, *History of the Old Town of Derby, Connecticut*, 76.
[18] *Statutes at Large of Virginia* (ed. by Hening), VI, 57.
[19] *Acts and Resolves of the Province of Massachusetts Bay*, I, 130; *Public Records of the Colony of Connecticut*, I, 205, 333; Orcutt and Beardsley, *History of the Old Town of Derby, Connecticut*, 54–55,
[20] 94 *United States*, IV, 125.

and could be built only by order of the County Court.[21] It is not probable that a man who proposed to build a mill on his own land always sought the consent of the community. Local records show that he did this in some cases. So at a town meeting in Suffield, 1747, a man who owned a mill right said that some inhabitants were in favor of his building a mill, but the town had not formally requested him to do it; and he asked if the town wanted him to build, and where it wanted the mill placed.[22] Whether a man made or did not make formal application for leave to build a mill is of little importance. The important fact is that the mill; built from a man's private resources and placed on his own land, became, whether he willed it or not, a public institution, as soon as it was opened to public use.

TERMS OF SERVICE OF THE MILL

The mill was commonly built according to a contract between the town community and an·individual who was to take the position of town miller. According to the articles of agreement between Heminway and the inhabitants of East Haven, Connecticut, in 1681,[23] the town offered to grant the dam of an old iron furnace and a number of acres of land, allowed the timber and stones necessary to build and repair the mill, and agreed to set it up, freed it from town taxes, and engaged to bring corn to it to be ground. Heminway engaged to set up a sufficient grist mill and warehouse for corn, and keep them in repair, engaged to attend the mill one day a fortnight and to grind all the corn brought on that day, to take no more toll than the law allowed, and if he let the mill to another he promised that it should be to one of whom the village approved.[24] There was great variety in the terms of the contracts. The cost of erecting the mill was borne sometimes by the individual, sometimes by the town, and was sometimes shared between the two. The feature common to almost all the agreements was the condition that the miller should be allowed to exercise his functions only so long as he gave good service at a certain rate of toll.

In New Netherland patroons were granted a monopoly of grinding by the Freedoms and Exemptions of 1629; this monopoly was recognized in a grant to Johan van Rensselaer and was repeated in the Freedoms of 1650.[25] A similar condition existed in Canada, and it has been suggested that the French-Canadian *censitaire* was really benefited by the obligation to grind his corn at the seignior's mill.[26] It was not the obligation but the opportunity to grind which was an advantage; and though the two went together in the earliest period of all the settlements, free as well as manorial, the patroons would have been unable to preserve their monopoly long, if they had used it to exploit their tenants. No complaint of it appears in the references to the New York manors; and private mills are said to have existed from an early period on the Van Rensselaer manor.

[21] *State Records of North Carolina*, XXIII, 483.

[22] *Documentary History of Suffield ... Massachusetts Bay* (ed. by Sheldon, 1880), 303; *cf.* Chapin, *Glastenbury for Two Hundred Years* (1853), 129–132.

[23] Dodd, *East-Haven Register* (revised by Sarah E. Hughes, 1908), 121 *et seq.*

[24] In the nineteenth century the title to land has sometimes been contested (in Providence, R. I., and in Waterbury, Conn.) on the ground that it was granted only on condition of a mill being maintained on it forever; the millers' heirs kept the land in the two cases noted.

[25] *New York Documents Relative to Colonial History*, I, 383, 402. Documents in the *Van Rensselaer Bowier Manuscripts* (ed. by Van Laer) show that mills on the Van Rensselaer estates were often leased.

[26] Munro, *The Signiorial System in Canada* (1907), 125. Bourinot, *Local Government in Canada* (1887), in *Johns Hopkins University Studies*, V, 190.

In the early years of settlement the community was ready to undertake a great deal to obtain a mill. To secure the cooperation of individual capital, the promise was often made that the miller should enjoy a monopoly as long as he kept to the conditions. So in Boston, 1643, one of the articles of agreement provided that "The town will not allow any other common mill to be erected, except the necessary occasion of the town require it."[27] In New London, 1650, the inhabitants voted to cooperate with John Winthrop in establishing a grist mill, and promised that no other should be set up in town, as long as he and his heirs maintained one to grind the town corn. From the records of a town meeting in 1709, however, it appears that the town had suffered from bad service; the heirs of Winthrop claimed the privilege of supplying the town with what grist mills were necessary, but took no care of their mill, and it was likely to be useless soon. Petition for leave to set up a second mill was granted.[28] In a petition to the Governor and Council of New York, 1657, the idea appears again, that a miller should have a certain legal as well as natural monopoly of the custom of the surrounding territory. The petitioner said that he did not want to harm Mr. Coe's mill, but that it was already overworked, and the country could well afford to employ two mills; he asked, therefore, for a mill right at Middleborough, and an order that none should erect a mill near enough to his to be a prejudice to it.[29] In Stratford, 1795, the town attempted to revoke an exclusive mill privilege, and was prevented by the miller, who appealed to the legislature;[30] but ordinarily the town was not deterred by formal obstacles from enlarging the number of mills, or threatening to do so, if it thought it could thereby obtain better service.

In the later period, when the erection of at least one mill had satisfied the first necessities of the townsmen, and the building of others was regarded as a means of private profit as much as of public benefit, the town assumed no obligations, but set forth the duties of the miller in detail. In Norwalk, 1709, for example, the mill must be built within a certain time, must be kept in proper repair, and be well tended, the miller was to charge only lawful toll, and was to allow no strangers to grind unless convenient for the town.[31] Brookhaven grants of 1803 and 1820 showed similar conditions.[32]

RATES OF TOLL

The early grants usually fixed the toll in each case. Plymouth, in granting leave in 1636 to erect a mill, established the miller's toll at a pottle (half-gallon) of corn on the bushel for the first two years, thereafter a quart a bushel, but a pottle if the miller fetched the grain himself.[33] In 1638, the toll of the Scituate miller was fixed at one-sixteenth.[34] In Windsor, Connecticut, 1658/9, the town voted that the miller should take single toll (one-sixteenth) for wheat, and toll and a half for corn.[35]

[27] Snow, *History of Boston* (1825), 124–125; *cf. Records of the Colony and Plantation of New Haven* (ed. by Hoadley), I, 76.
[28] Caulkins, *History of New London, Connecticut* (2d ed., 1860), 66–67, 403.
[29] *New York Documents Relative to Colonial History*, XIV, 378.
[30] Orcutt, *History of the Old Town of Stratford . . . Connecticut* (1886), I, 406–407.
[31] *The Ancient Records of Norwalk, Connecticut* (ed. by Hall), 103.
[32] *Records of the Town of Brookhaven . . . New York*, II, 69–70, 232.
[33] *Records of the Colony of New Plymouth* (ed. by Shurtleff), XI, 26.
[34] *Ibid.*, XI, 30.
[35] Stiles, *The History of Ancient Windsor, Connecticut* (1859), 148.

The matter became a subject of general colonial legislation, and the towns either stipulated legal toll or accepted that toll as a matter of course; certain exceptions will be noted later. The following table presents a summary of the colonial statutes on the toll of grist mills.[36]

Colony	Date	Toll
New Hampshire	1718	1/12 Indian (maize); 1/16 all other grain
Massachusetts	1635/6 1728/9 1763	1/16 all 1/16 all 1/16 all
Rhode Island		1/16 all. Special contracts allowed
Connecticut	1662/3	1/12 Indian; 1/16 all other. Special contracts allowed
New York		No general law
West Jersey	1696	1/10 all
Delaware	1752	1/10 all, in Newcastle County; 1/10 wheat and malt, 1/8 other, in Kent and Sussex Counties*
Maryland	1704	1/6 Indian, 1/8 wheat
Virginia	1645 1671 1748	1/6 all 1/6 Indian; 1/8 wheat 1/8 all
North Carolina	1772 in force. Date not specified	1/6 Indian; 1/8 wheat
South Carolina	1785	1/8 for any quantity under 10 bushels; 1/10 for larger quantity
Georgia	1786	1/8 all

* An earlier law, 12 George II, was not printed in any collection to which the author had access.

Some attempt was evidently made in the acts to adjust the rate to the conditions of different times and places, though no reasons are given in any act for the specific rate imposed. The amount of the rate, within reasonable limits, appears to have been of less importance than the fact that there was an established rate at which the work should be done. Nothing has been found to show whether rates were lowered by competition, when the mills in a town multiplied. Apparently rates were maintained in Boston, to judge from the complaints made there in the eighteenth century. The early mills were operated only a day or two a week, and, reasoning in a modern way, we should say that they could have afforded to grind cheaper when the community had increased so as to give them more constant employment. The records give the impression, however, that mills multiplied on the basis of the old rates, dividing the business and each getting enough to keep running only a small part of the time.

It is evident that the rate set for an entire colony could not answer the individual circumstances of every town; and in Connecticut and Rhode Island departures from the established rates were expressly permitted.

[36] *Acts and Laws of the Province of New Hampshire*, 72; *Records of Massachusetts Bay*, I, 168; *Acts and Laws of the English Colony of Rhode Island* (1767), 193; *Public Records of the Colony of Connecticut*, I, 393; *The Grants, Concessions and Original Constitutions of the Province of New Jersey* (ed. by Leaming and Spicer), 547; *Laws of the State of Delaware* (ed. of 1797), I, 326; *Laws of Maryland* (ed. by Bacon), chap. xvi; *Statutes at Large of Virginia* (ed. by Hening), I, 301; II, 286; VI, 58; *The State Records of North Carolina*, XXIII, 487; *Statutes at Large of South Carolina*, IV, 652; *Digest of the Laws of Georgia* (ed. by Watkins), 321.

DIFFICULTY OF ENFORCING REGULATIONS

To arrive at a fair knowledge of the working of the laws regulating toll, a study would have to be made of the judicial cases decided under them. In Massachusetts, 1639, a miller was fined £3 for taking excessive toll, sometimes double what was due him; and the miller of Concord was fined the same sum for gross abuse in overtolling.[37] There were probably many cases of the kind. In the later period, in Boston, 1725/6, the town voted that the selectmen should prepare a bill to prevent the abuses of millers in regard to tolls.[38] The Massachusetts act of 1728/9[39] notes great complaint from the inhabitants of Boston and Charlestown that the millers did not grind their corn seasonably, and demanded unreasonable tolls; measures were passed to prevent the abuses. In 1763, it was said that in spite of all the laws great complaints were made of the injustices of millers, especially in Boston, Roxbury, and Charlestown; it was ordered that the millers in those towns should provide themselves with suitable mill stones, fans, and screens, keep them in good order, use them only for wheat, and grind according to the regulations.[40] Conditions were the same in the other colonies. In Virginia, 1666, the millers refused to grind according to turn for legal toll.[41] In Brooklyn, 1668, the miller refused to grind for some of the people, "on very frivolous pretences," the town could not constrain him, and the Governor himself had to interfere.[42] In Connecticut complaint was made of the miller at New London, and the General Court passed orders to remedy the evil.[43] It is apparent that there were infractions of the regulations, and that there was a struggle to maintain them.

Just as the modern world, in attempts to deal with the railroad problem, has had to give up the old idea of the efficacy of free competition as a regulating force, and has been compelled to choose between the alternatives of state control and state ownership, and has found satisfaction nowhere; so the colonials, hundreds of years ago, experimented with a problem which the conditions of the time made insoluble. A review of the history of the grist mill in a few particular towns will illustrate the point. In Plymouth, 1671, the owners of the corn mill were warned that unless they provided a good storehouse for grain, kept the mill in repair, and had a good man there constantly, so that persons should not be wronged as they had been, the town would have another mill erected. In 1681 a committee was appointed to treat for the purchase of the corn mill by the town; in case the owners refused to sell, they were to be told that the town proposed to build another mill, and the committee was authorized to make the necessary preparations for its erection. The committee was appointed again the next year, but apparently the town contented itself still with the regulation of the old mill, and did not build one of its own. In 1718 several people complained that they had suffered wrong from the ill grinding of their corn by "a child"; a committee was appointed to inform the man who held the privilege of the stream that it would not suffer a lad to be the town's miller, and that he must keep to the conditions, or the town would find some

37 *Records of Massachusetts Bay*, I, 267.
38 Boston, *Town Records, 1700–1728*, 197.
39 *Acts and Resolves of Massachusetts Bay*, II, 497.
40 *Ibid.*, IV, 608.
41 *Statutes at Large of Virginia* (ed. by Hening), II, 242.
42 *New York Documents Relative to Colonial History*, XIV, 610.
43 *Public Records of the Colony of Connecticut*, II, 29.

other method to have the work done. The next year the town voted that, if the owners of the grist mill did not put it in good condition for work, the town would give liberty to others to set up a mill to do the town work. As far as the records show. complaints ceased thereafter.[44]

PUBLIC MILLS

Public administration of the mill, so often threatened in Plymouth, was carried into effect in some of the Connecticut towns. In Hartford a mill had been built in 1639 by Matthew Allen, but the community was dissatisfied with its service, and appointed a committee to make arrangements for building a town mill. Apparently it was not built at this time; the town voted in 1643 to settle by arbitration all the differences with Allen about his mill. In 1655/6 the town voted £100 toward building a mill for its own proper right and use, and £200 more in each of the two following years; committees were appointed to execute the work. An old mill was purchased, but apparently only for its site, as a new building was constructed. During the three years, 1658 to 1660, committees were chosen to order the affairs of the town mill, but none appear after that time; the town mill had been sold to private purchasers before 1663.[45] A similar municipal undertaking had a much longer and more successful career in Guilford, where the town owned and operated the mill from 1646 down to the time when Steiner wrote, 1897. Under an early arrangement the miller received half the toll. In 1667 the town chose a committee of three to manage the mill in its interest; in 1705/6, it leased the mill for fifteen years at an annual rent of £8; it then returned to the former system of management, though it voted again in 1809 to lease the mill for five years. In the eighteenth century the mill became involved in quarrels between different parts of the town, and rebates on toll were granted to inhabitants of the Old Parish, in whose control it was. The town voted sometimes for, sometimes against, the legal rates of toll; and at the rates set, the town mill returned a considerable surplus, with which a bolting mill and church bells were purchased. Private grist mills were allowed at times, especially in remote parts of the town.[46]

Each stage of the organization presents its own characteristic problems. The people of the early colonies fought long to secure fair service and fair rates in the grinding of their grain, and had at best but indifferent success, so long as the small size of the social group gave to the single miller a practical monopoly. The troubles which had fretted them grew less, if they did not entirely disappear, when the group grew so large that effective competition between mills became possible. Even if rates were maintained, as they appear to have been, the mills must have competed in the service which they offered. Yet the larger group, again, had difficulties of its own, which now demand consideration.

PROBLEM OF THE SUPPLY OF PROVISIONS IN LARGE TOWNS

The largest towns of the colonial period seem absurdly small in comparison with modern urban centers. Small as they were, however, they marked a great advance

[44] *Records of the Town of Plymouth* (1889–1903), I, 123, 167, 171; II, 192, 198–199.

[45] Hartford, *Town Votes, 1635–1716* (Connecticut Historical Society, *Collections*, 1897, VI), I, 7, 14, 30–31, 64, 106–110, 114, 120–122, 140.

[46] Steiner, *History of the Plantation of Menunkatuck and of the Original Town of Guilford, Connecticut* (1897), 227 *et seq.*

beyond the agricultural villages of the seventeenth century. The population of Boston[47] increased from 12,000 in 1722 to 20,000 in 1760; Newport[48] had a population of 6,000 or 7,000 in 1760 and over 9,000 before the Revolution; New York[49] was estimated at 12,000 and Philadelphia at 40,000 when Morse wrote in 1784; Baltimore[50] had nearly 7,000 before the Revolution and double that number in 1790. Other places of considerable size grew up along the coast, their importance depending mainly on their foreign trade. In the South, Charleston[51] was the only urban center; while the largest town in the interior, Lancaster, Pennsylvania,[52] had in 1786 a population of about 700 families.

These places retained some of their rural characteristics for a considerable time, but the larger part of their food supply had necessarily to be imported from outside the town limits. Complaints of the increasing prices of the necessaries of life, and of abuses in the trade in them, became common; and attempts were made by a vigorous application of commercial regulations to remedy the evil, and to enable consumers to free themselves from dependence on the middlemen. The market, which had been a mere shadow of organization in the small village, assumed a position of practical importance in the large town.

Thanks to the full records which have been preserved of the Boston[53] town government, it is possible to trace the history of the market in that town with some fullness of detail, and the annals of the Boston market will serve to illustrate the rise and operation of the system of regulation. A market was established at Boston in 1633/4, but it remained probably for a long time merely a name for a common meeting place, with little or no regulation. In 1681/2, however, complaint was made in town meeting against hucksters who forestalled the market by going out on the highway to Boston to buy up provisions that were being brought to town, in order to sell the same again at the very dear rates. The selectmen were directed to make some order to prevent the practice. It was undoubtedly in answer to complaints like this that the legislature passed the act of 1696, "for the settlement and well ordering of a publick market and fairs, within the town of Boston."[54] The preamble set forth that, by long experience in England, fairs and markets had been found of general advantage, and that great inconveniences attended the inhabitants of Boston and of the surrounding country for want of a public market. The act was passed "to the intent that forestalling, regrating and ingrossing of victuals and other commodities may the better be prevented." Those who offered goods for sale before the opening of the market, who bought or contracted to buy goods of any kind on their way to market, or who made "any motion, by word,

[47] *The Memorial History of Boston* (ed. by Winsor, 1880–1881), II, 439; Burnaby, *Travels through the Middle Settlements* (Wilson's reprint of 1904), 132.

[48] Burnaby, *Travels through the Middle Settlements* (Wilson's reprint of 1904), 90.

[49] Morse, *Geography Made Easy* (no date, preface dated Oct., 1784), 45, 50; Adam Seybert, *Statistical Annals* (1818), 47, cites figures from the first national census giving New York, including the county, 33,000, and Philadelphia, excluding the suburbs, 28,000.

[50] Thomas, *City Government of Baltimore* (1896), in *Johns Hopkins University Studies*, XIV, 51, 56.

[51] Greene, *Provincial America*, 243.

[52] Bishop, *History of American Manufactures* (1864), I, 415.

[53] Boston, *Town Records* and *Records of Boston Selectmen*. Detailed references are omitted to these authorities, on which the following studies of the social policy of Boston are based; the date in the text, supplemented by the excellent indexes of the *Records*, will make the verification easy.

[54] *Acts and Resolves of Massachusetts Bay*, I, 237.

letter or otherwise to any person for the enhancing of the price or dearer selling any commodity in the said market" were forestallers.[55] "In regard that the market is principally intended for the benefit of housekeepers, who buy for their own use and behoof . . . (to the intent that the housekeepers may provide themselves in the morning of every day at the first hand, and pay moderate rates for their provisions)" retailers and hucksters were not to buy before the afternoon, on pain of being proceeded against as regraters or ingrossers. The penalty for infraction was a fine of 20s.; justices of the peace were empowered to try cases summarily, "without being obliged to follow the strict rules of ordinary process." No person bringing any commodity to Boston for sale was to sell it in any other place than the market on penalty of forfeiture, a general rule which must have been practically nullified by a list of exceptions which seems to have included nearly all forms of country produce. No toll was to be paid for goods brought to market, or for the use of stands; goods left unsold could be freely sold at another time. The market was to be held on Tuesday, Thursday, and Saturday, from six, seven, or nine, according to the season, to four or six. At a meeting of the justices and selectmen in June 1696, it was agreed that the market should be held in and about the Town House, and that it should be opened in August.

The act expired in 1697, and apparently no attempt was made to secure its renewal: it seems doubtful whether it was ever really enforced, and it was certainly soon forgotten. Uring, a traveller who visited Boston in 1709, wrote that the town, although it was so populous, could never be brought to establish a market, notwithstanding the fact that several governors had tried to convince the inhabitants of the benefits which would follow.[56]

From 1697, until the re-establishment of the market in 1733, no general market regulations were in force; but the town meeting from time to time passed orders, to be executed by the selectmen, against what seemed to it abuses. In 1701, it was ordered that no inhabitant should bargain for any provisions (grain, butter, meats, etc.), while they were being brought to market, between Roxbury gate and the houses of the town, before two in the afternoon; a special regulation forbade butchers to buy meat being brought to market, to sell it again. In 1711, similar regulations were passed to prevent the forestalling by hucksters: no one was to buy any provisions with the intent to sell them again, inside or outside the town, before 3 P.M. In the years following, the selectmen appointed persons to prosecute those who broke the regulations against hucksters. In 1714 the selectmen were desired by the town to make enforcement of the regulation effectual; they were directed to prepare a penal order against those who sold to hucksters, and to allow a reward to informers. In March, 1714/15, the town appointed a committee to consider the abuses of hucksters and, if necessary, to consult some person learned in the law about them. The committee reported, a year later, that the best way to prevent the abuse was to set up a public market, and was directed to present its ideas on the subject. The project of establishing a market was continued from meeting to meeting, a copy of it was posted in the Town House where all the people could study it, and finally, in March, 1717/8, it was voted down. The question

[55] *Cf.* the long definition of forestallers, designed to cover all possible infractions, in *Statutes at Large of Virginia* (ed. by Hening), I, 194; IX, 382; regrator and engrosser are defined, *Ibid.*, IX, 382, 385.
[56] New Hampshire Historical Society, *Collections*, III, 143.

remained alive, however; Dr. Benjamin Coleman published in 1719 a pamphlet representing the advantages of establishing a market house.[57]

In 1723 Roxbury passed a by-law, undoubtedly influenced thereto by Boston, prohibiting any persons from buying provisions which were being taken to the Boston market, unless it was for their personal use.[58] In Boston the abuses of hucksters continued to be the topic of frequent discussion; in 1728 a committee was appointed to consider them, and, in accordance with its report, the order of 1711 against hucksters was enacted again. It was thought that Indian and Negro servants enhanced the price of provisions; they were forbidden to buy, but could direct the country people to their masters. After 1730 petitions in large number were presented, for and against a market, and in 1732 the town finally voted that a market under proper regulation would be of service, and chose a committee to consider the details.

The regulations adopted in 1733, as amended after conference with the Suffolk County Court, were in their general features the same as those established in 1696, but somewhat more detailed. Three markets, instead of one, were established, and market was to be held every day except on days appointed for religious service, closing at 1 P.M. The general regulation was repeated, that no provisions should be sold in Boston outside of the market, but it was subject, as before, to a bewildering variety of exceptions; it did not apply to meat sold in butchers' shops, to provisions imported by sea, to grain, meal, all sorts of roots, fruit, and herbs, to "bread, milk, cider, live swine and wild pigeons." Fish brought by water could be sold at the usual wharves; fresh-water fish brought by land must be sold in the market, with the exception of frost-fish and smelts. It is hard to see the reasons for these distinctions, and to determine the articles in which the market did have a monopoly. Evidently no attempt was made to concentrate the whole provision trade of the city in the market; trade at the shops continued as before, and not even all those who had hawked their wares around the streets were drawn inside the market. Whatever the facts may have been in this regard, everything could be sold in the market, and—the real gist of the legislation—no one but consumers could buy there. To assure direct trade between producer and consumer, retailers and hucksters were forbidden to buy in the market, with the intention of selling again. The legislation included a number of sanitary and police regulations, and established a salaried clerk for each market, to enforce the rules. The markets were to begin on June 4, 1734.

The *Boston News Letter*,[59] in its account of the opening, said that the markets were well attended, and that an abundance of provisions was brought for sale. The articles which were good and cheap went off quickly, those that were poor or dear, more slowly. The writer thought that the market would be of benefit in inducing the country people to bring a good quality of provisions to town. On June 25, 1734, a petition was read in town meeting, asking that the town butchers be prevented from selling their meat in the public markets. Evidently the butchers were leaving their shops to compete with the country people for the market custom. They were forbidden to do this, but were promised stalls to be built by the town at a suitable distance. At the town meeting of

[57] Drake, *History and Antiquities of Boston* (1856), 556, footnote.
[58] *The Memorial History of Boston* (ed. by Winsor), II, 355.
[59] Snow, *History of Boston*, 226.

March 10, 1734/5, a petition of sundry inhabitants that the market houses might be appropriated to some other use was rejected by a vote of 377 to 275; but in March of the next year the town voted to discontinue the three clerks of the markets, and the ringing of bells at their opening. This meant abandonment of the strict system of market regulation. A motion to reconsider passed, 138 to 135, but the matter was then adjourned to the afternoon, when 398 voted against continuing the clerks, 278 in favor of so doing. It is apparent that there was bitter feeling in the matter.

For a knowledge of the lines on which parties divided on this question of the markets in Boston, the chief source of information is a description of Boston written in 1794.[60] The author says that before the erection of markets, trading was done at butchers' and hucksters' shops, and market men used to hawk meat and vegetables about the streets. Some people preferred to purchase of these hawkers at their own doors; they "urged the probability that in this way provisions would be prevented from being dearer, the market men having no place of shelter in inclement weather," and complained of loss of time in going to the market houses. The town butchers, "deprived in great measure of their family customers", were opposed, of course, to the market system. The party in favor of the markets must have been composed of those consumers who thought the better opportunity for selection, and the lower prices due to a concentration of the supply, made up for personal inconvenience. The *Boston News Letter*, in the article quoted, says that the interest of the country people, as well as that of the townsmen, had been aimed at in the market act; they would benefit from the improvement of their wares which would ensue. As a matter of fact, the country people in general were opposed to the establishment of markets in the town. Uring said, in 1709, "the reason they give for it is, if market days were appointed, all the country people coming in at the same time would glut it, and the town's people would buy their provisions for what they pleased, so rather choose to send them as they think fit; and sometimes a tall fellow brings a turkey or goose to sell, and will travel through the whole town to see who will give most for it, and it is at last sold for 3s. 6d. or 4s. and if he had stayed at home, he could have earned a crown by his labour."[61]

The date is not quite clear (1736/7, it is said), but the fact is certain, that the town butchers and the consumers who sympathized with them assembled in the night disguised as clergymen, and totally demolished the central market house. The other two houses were damaged and were no longer occupied as markets. In 1737, the town voted, on recommendation of the selectmen, that the southern market should be let out for shops, and the northern market torn down; a man who charged the selectmen with agreeing with the mob was censured by the moderator and by the meeting. Until the completion of Faneuil market in 1742, the town remained without a public market.

In 1740, a petition of 340 inhabitants was read in town meeting, setting forth the fact that the old market had given satisfaction to a great number of inhabitants, but had been demolished for several years, and that the inhabitants, having no certain meeting

[60] [Pemberton], "A Topographical and Historical Description of Boston, 1794," in Massachusetts Historical Society, *Collections*, 1st series (reprint of 1810), III, 255.
[61] New Hampshire Historical Society, *Collections*, III, 143.

place for buyer and seller, were forced to go out on Boston Neck, and spend a great part of the day providing necessaries for their families, to the great hindrance of business. They asked that Peter Faneuil's offer to build a market should be accepted, but that the market people should still be free to carry their marketing wherever they pleased about the town. The vote on the question was close, and there was evidently again deep party feeling; a proposal that every person should write his name on his vote was negatived, and Faneuil's offer was finally accepted, 367 to 360.

The regulations adopted on the acceptance of the market by the town, in September 1742, were, with unimportant variations, like those of 1733; the order against hucksters' purchasing before the close of the market was repeated. It was said that the main object of the market was to encourage country people to bring provisions to town, for the supply of the inhabitants at first hand, and therefore butchers and other persons buying to sell again were not to bring any provisions to the market place for sale, and were excluded from the stalls.

In January, 1742/3, it was represented that the indulgence allowed people of staying after market hours had been attended with inconvenience, and thereafter the market was to be cleared at one o'clock. The town voted, after long debate, that the market should be open only three days a week, and refused to consider petitions for the opening of the northern and southern markets. Petitions were presented in 1746, asking that Faneuil market should be closed, and the town voted in April 1747, to close the market until September. At that time the opening was deferred until the next year, but the town voted in April 1748, to keep the market open every day. Drake[62] thinks that the market was closed because so few people resorted to it, and the vote, when the market was closed again in 1752, was certainly so light (129 to 102) as to show that the people had lost interest in the question. A petition, presented in 1751, that the town should regulate the market for hay and sand, a sample of many similar petitions, was refused by the town meeting. After the closing of the market in 1752, a petition against the extravagant price of provisions, especially meat, was signed by over 300 persons; and it was proposed to ask the selectmen to set the prices of the necessaries of life at their weekly meetings. The town voted that the signers of the petition should be asked not to purchase any provisions at or near Dock Square, where the market building was. In this period the people thought, apparently, that the market *raised* the price of provisions.

The market was opened in 1753, with the intention, according to Drake, of securing income from the lease of stalls; it was closed and again opened in 1759. A committee reported that the principal cause why the market raised the price of provisions was that it continued too long. If the market were shut at eleven instead of at one, it would be better both for those who bought at the market, and for those who depended on being supplied at their homes, as the sellers would sooner take up with the prices offered by the former, and disperse sooner to supply the latter. A by-law was passed, to be in force on trial for four months, closing the market at eleven, and making it a penal offence to buy in Dock Square out of market hours.

[62] Drake, *History and Antiquities of Boston*, 611, footnote.

Faneuil market was burned, by accident, in 1761, was rebuilt and again occupied in 1764.[63] In the interval, various petitioners complained of forestalling, and the town clerk was ordered to publish in all the newspapers the law against forestalling by hucksters. A committee reported in 1763 that the town could do no more to remedy the evil; its deputies must secure a law from the General Court. The legislature accordingly passed a law in June 1764,[64] fining traders who encumbered Dock Square with their carts. Forestalling in this period consisted not so much in purchases made outside of the town, as in purchases made by hucksters in the streets near the market. Quincy[65] says that before he carried his reforms, in 1823, the space around the market was small, and the approaches to it were narrow and crooked. On high market days they were often completely blocked. Farmers had to take their stand far from the market building, and, because of this exclusion from their customers, "were often obliged to sell their goods to forestallers greatly to their loss and discontent. Forestalling became, consequently, not only a lucrative but an acknowledged employment." Juries would seldom convict offenders, because the inadequacy of the market seemed to make fair competition impossible, and forestalling necessary, both to farmer and townsman. The market rules adopted in 1783 aimed especially to prevent this forestalling in the streets. They contained a number of police regulations that were felt as grievances in the neighboring towns; in 1784, Muddy River and Weston appointed committees to confer with committees from other towns, in the endeavor to secure amendment of the rules.[66]

In 1793 and 1794, persons were convicted of forestalling, and were excluded from the market. The by-laws of 1801[67] contained regulations aimed "to discourage, as far as may be, the injurious practice, too frequent among butchers and others of forestalling the market, by buying up in the country and on the road to town, poultry and other provisions, in order to sell and utter them again at advanced prices." Offenders were never to be permitted to hold a stand in the market place, "and all persons having the least regard to justice and to the poor inhabitants of this town, are requested to give information" against them. In 1809, a man was fined £5 for forestalling, but, as he was then charged with being an idler and was sent to the almshouse, the application of the law cannot be considered normal.[68]

In the early part of the nineteenth century new markets were built in various parts of the town.[69] The city ordinance of 1833,[70] regulating Faneuil market, is composed mainly of police provisions against obstruction, uncleanliness, and disturbances. In the case of Quincy market, finished in 1827, charges of forestalling and monopolizing have often been made by discontented persons, but investigations (1865, 1870) by committees of the City Council have proved them to be groundless.[71]

Provision markets were established in many large towns of the colonial period; in

[63] *The Memorial History of Boston* (ed. by Winsor), II, 266.
[64] *Acts and Resolves of Massachusetts Bay*, IV, 724.
[65] *Municipal History of Boston* (ed. by Quincy, 1852), 75–76.
[66] *Muddy River and Brookline Records* (1875), 336; Weston, *Records*, 362.
[67] *The By-Laws and Orders of the Town of Boston* (1801), 29.
[68] Savage, *Police Records and Recollections; or, Boston by Daylight and Gaslight* (1873), 53.
[69] Snow, *History of Boston*, 332.
[70] *The Charter and Ordinances of the City of Boston* (ed. by Wetmore and Prescott, 1834), 222–225.
[71] *The Memorial History of Boston* (ed. by Winsor), III, 229, footnote 2.

New York,[72] Philadelphia,[73] Charleston,[74] and other places[75] of somewhat smaller population. They were often provided by the legislature with a very complete administrative apparatus. It is dangerous, however, to assume that the market regulations, which make such a brave show on paper, were carried into effect; and it is apparent that in many cases they remained a dead letter. For the student of social policy the market regulations have at least the significance of an ideal which the legislators endeavored to realize. Whether they had a more serious influence on social and economic development remains to be proved.

THE ASSIZE OF BREAD

Similar in their spirit to the market regulations of the towns, and subject in their interpretation to the same difficulties, were the many attempts to protect people from the abuses of bakers, by the assize of bread.

In 1640 a law[76] was passed in Massachusetts, designed to set a maximum price of bread; the attempt was not repeated. The assize of bread was established by an act of 1646.[77] In 1681 the colony put the matter in the hands of the towns.[78] Boston made full use of the power to regulate the price of bread from 1682 to 1801. No other town in Massachusetts, so far as appears, made any systematic attempt to apply the assize. The selectmen of Roxbury in 1779 assured the Boston selectmen of their readiness to cooperate in the assize; weighers of bread, instructed to govern themselves by the Boston standard, were chosen in Muddy River, 1787/9; the town of Worcester voted in 1784 that the selectmen should fix the weight of bread according to law; surveyors of bread were elected in Weston in 1793 and following years.[79]

In New Hampshire an act of 1766[80] authorized the towns to establish an assize, and their powers were extended by the act of 1769, both acts lasting but a few years.

The town of Portsmouth, Rhode Island,[81] established an assize in 1638. The colony passed a law in 1707[82] that all towns should annually choose officers to regulate bakers, but the law was incomplete and seems to have had no effect. An act of 1763 stated that bakers in the colony were not confined to any regular standard in setting the assize of bread, and town officers were empowered, but not required, to set the assize.

No regulation by colonial authority of the price or weight of bread appears in Connecticut. The third monthly court held in New Haven licensed a public baker and

[72] See, in general, DeVoe, *The Market Book* (1862). Dwight speaks of the New York markets as well regulated, in his *Travels in New England and New York*, III, 465; and the New York City *By-laws and Ordinances* (1839) show that old ideas about forestalling, etc., were still maintained, at that time.

[73] The Philadelphia market seems to have been less strictly regulated; the restriction against forestalling appeared first in the act of 1779, see *Laws of the Commonwealth of Pennsylvania* (ed. by Dallas, 1793), I, 798; repealed in 1801.

[74] *Statutes at Large of South Carolina*, II, 351; IV, 540, 692–697.

[75] For Savannah, *cf. Digest of the Laws of Georgia* (ed. by Watkins), 44, 52, 61, 104; for New Haven, Levermore, *Republic of New Haven*, 237; Dwight, *Travels in New England and New York*, I, 194.

[76] *Records of Massachusetts Bay*, I, 296.

[77] *Ibid.*, II, 181.

[78] *Ibid.*, V, 322.

[79] Boston, *Town Records, 1778–1783*, pp. 56–57; *Muddy River and Brookline Records, 1643–1838*, pp. 355, 360; Worcester, *Town Records* (Worcester Society for Antiquities, *Collections*, 1890, VIII), 13; Weston, *Records* (1893).

[80] *Acts and Laws of the Province of New Hampshire*, 22, 36.

[81] *The Records of the Colony of Rhode Island*, I, 61; *Acts and Laws of the English Colony of Rhode Island* (1767), 23.

[82] *Records of the Colony of Rhode Island*, IV, 11.

established an assize on the English model; the law then enacted was among those published in 1656, supported by Biblical references. The historian of the town, however, has found no record of officers chosen to administer the law in New Haven.[83] The *Middlesex Gazette*, of Middletown, Connecticut, published an assize about every fortnight from February to July 1789; examination of the files as far as December 1791 fails to show continuance of the regulation.

In New Netherland the weight of bread was regulated in 1649, and the court was authorized to set prices according to the price of grain.[84] A New Amsterdam city ordinance of 1661 established prices, marks, and other details of the assize.[85] Laws of 1649, 1651, 1656, and 1658 show that the assize was enforced in the colony; Robert Livingston, in his contract to supply provisions for the Palatine immigrants in 1710, was to furnish bread of the weight and fineness specified in the New York assize of the time. Complaint was made, in the law of 1773, of bread made of bad flour, contrary to the assize.[86] In the New York (City) By-Laws of 1839 bread was to be made of wholesome flour, and was to be sold by avoirdupois weight; the attempt to regulate the price had been given up.[87]

On account of the abuses of the bakers a law was passed in West Jersey,[88] 1696, setting the assize of bread. In 1740 and 1742, justices of the Court of Quarter Sessions in the counties of New Castle, Dover and Lewes, Delaware, were instructed to set the assize.[89]

A law with the usual provisions setting the assize was passed in Pennsylvania[90] in 1682, and was repeated, so far as is shown in the title, in 1693, 1700, 1752, 1761, 1772, and 1773. Complaint was made in 1779 that there were great abuses in Philadelphia[91] in the assize of bread, and justices of the peace were empowered to set the assize there and in any of the counties. In the act incorporating Philadelphia, 1789, the mayor was authorized to appoint clerks of the market, who were to have the assize of bread, wine, beer, and wood, with other duties. The act setting the assize was suspended in 1793 for two years, with the remark that doubts had arisen whether it did not "infringe the equality of rights established by the constitution of this commonwealth;" it was again suspended in 1795 and repealed in 1797, leaving in force merely the restriction that bread should be sold by avoirdupois weight, and that every baker should keep weights and scales therefor.

In Virginia there appears to have been no colonial law setting the assize of bread, but the power of regulation was sometimes granted to local authorities. An act with the usual table, setting the assize according to the price of flour in Charleston, was passed in South Carolina, 1749, and was made perpetual in 1783.[92] In 1805, in answer to a

[83] Levermore, *The Republic of New Haven*, 69–70, 148; *Records of the Colony and Plantation of New Haven* (ed. by Hoadley), II, 574; VIII, 84.

[84] *Laws and Ordinances of New Netherland* (ed. by O'Callaghan), 113.

[85] *The Records of New Amsterdam* (ed. by Fernow), I, 46–47.

[86] *Documentary History of the State of New York* (qto. ed.), III, 391; *The Colonial Laws of New York*, V, 544.

[87] New York City, *By-Laws and Ordinances* (1839), 281.

[88] *The Grants, Concessions and Original Constitutions of the Province of New Jersey* (ed. by Leaming and Spicer), 546.

[89] *Laws of the State of Delaware* (ed. of 1797), I, 184, 251.

[90] *Charter to William Penn and Laws of the Province of Pennsylvania*, 135, 230.

[91] For 1793 *et seq.*, see *Laws of the Commonwealth of Pennsylvania* (ed. by Dallas), I, 800; III, 447, 702; for 1810, see *Laws of the Commonwealth of Pennsylvania* (ed. of 1810), I, 425; II, 473; III, 294.

[92] *Statutes at Large of South Carolina*, III, 715; IV, 540.

petition from the town of Beaufort, the town council was authorized to regulate the price and assize of bread, showing, apparently, that the previous act was confined in its operation to Charleston. Georgia passed laws regulating the assize of bread in 1758 and 1763.[93] A law of 1768, the first that is printed in full in the collection of the statutes, seems to have applied only to Savannah.[94]

APPLICATION OF THE LAWS OF ASSIZE OF BREAD

The laws, of which a summary is presented above, furnish inadequate material for a study of the question of the extent to which the practice of regulating the price of bread was carried. In many, perhaps in most cases, the laws were inoperative. Many of the early laws must have been mere reminiscences of European customs. In Portsmouth, Rhode Island,[95] there were only nineteen freemen in the town, when one of the number was appointed to bake bread for it according to the assize, and the population of the early towns of Rhode Island, it is said, was even more scattered than was customary in New England. It is hard to believe that baking was a distinct occupation in the ordinary farming town, although to some extent bread may have been sold from one house to another. Mrs. Earle, who usually gives full information on matters of domestic economy, has no evidence but the laws to support her statement that New England housewives did little baking at home in the early days.[96] The frequent references to bakers in the Boston Selectmen's *Records*, and the number of licenses granted to bake different kinds of bread, show that the baker's trade was actively pursued in that town; but the Massachusetts act of 1681, giving the towns authority to regulate the assize, referred evidently to Boston only, although it was general in its terms. Ellis says that in early Massachusetts the governor's wife baked her own bread.[97] He means to emphasize, probably, the housewives' independence of domestic servants; but it was characteristic of the separate households also, to be independent.

The baker probably became a prominent figure, and the question of regulating bakers' charges first became of practical importance, when the large mercantile towns, with a considerable population of poor, grew up. The question of baking at home or buying the bread may have been determined in many towns by the presence or absence therein of a professional baker. Rogers, who settled in New London about 1660, was a baker on a large scale, contracting for the supply of biscuit to seamen and troops;[98] men like him may have supplied the population of the seaport towns where they plied their trade. Weeden refers to a petition of President Dunster of Harvard College, that a woman of Cambridge be encouraged in her calling of baking bread by being allowed also to brew and sell beer, without which she could not continue to exist.[99] Baking was not a widespread trade, and only where it was pursued as a trade could the laws of the assize have been of any practical effect.

[93] *Digest of the Laws of Georgia* (ed. by Watkins), 56, 86, 146.

[94] For persistence of the assize in southern towns in a later period see "Notice of Assize of Bread, Charleston, 1825", reprinted from Charleston, *City Gazette*, March 4, 1825, in Commons, *Documentary History of American Industrial Society*, II, 343; "An Assize of Bread in Mobile, Alabama", in *Quarterly Journal of Economics*, XXI, 330, Feb. 1907.

[95] *Records of the Colony of Rhode Island*, I, 52.

[96] Earle, *Customs and Fashions in Old New England* (1893), 150.

[97] *The Memorial History of Boston* (ed. by Winsor), I, 161.

[98] Caulkins, *History of New London*, 201.

[99] *Economic and Social History of New England*, I, 195.

The Massachusetts act of 1646[100] may be taken as a sample of the form of regulation. A published table fixed the weight of the penny loaf of three different kinds of bread—white, wheaten, and household, according to the variations in price of wheat. This table had a range from 3s. to 6s. 6d. per bushel for wheat, at intervals of sixpence. Like the European assize, therefore, this was not a regulation of the price of bread, but a regulation of the piece wage of bakers; it determined that the price of a loaf should be made up of the fixed remuneration of the baker and the fluctuating price of the grain, or, in later laws, of the flour. So in the act of 1720/1[101] the Massachusetts selectmen were directed to set the assize according to the price of grain, meal, or flour in the town, "making reasonable allowance to the bakers for their charges, pains and livelyhood." The act of 1685[102] allowed the baker 4s. for each quarter of wheat, while the act of 1720/1 left the matter, as said, to the selectmen, whose charges, as found in the Boston Selectmen's *Records*, varied greatly with the fluctuations in the currency: 3s. per bushel in 1729, 2s. in 1743, 4d. in 1750. Such an elaborate analysis of the items of the baker's charge as is to be found in some of the European regulations was not attempted.

Each baker was to brand his bread with a special mark, and was to sell it only in loaves of the specified weight. If he broke the assize, or refused to bake, he was subject to a penalty, usually a fine. In New Amsterdam, according to the ordinance of 1651, he was forbidden thereafter to carry on his trade for a year and six weeks.

The reasons for the acts can be given by quoting the preamble of the New Hampshire act of 1766 (in modern spelling): "Whereas a just proportion between the price of flour and the weight and price of bread, is now a matter of importance, as many people purchase the greatest part of their bread of bakers, and without such regulation they were left to judge for themselves, where their impartiality will be much questioned, and as it is reasonable they should be allowed a suitable profit in their business, to encourage their industry and their fidelity in vending wholesome, well made bread, it is necessary a just medium should be established," and the usual regulations followed. In nearly all the acts in which a motive is stated, it is said to be the protection of the poor against extortion. In South Carolina there was no assize of bread before 1749, "and covetous and evil-disposed persons, taking advantage thereof, have, for their own gain and lucre, deceived and oppressed his Majesty's subjects, and more especially the poorer sort of people." In Georgia, 1768, the assize of bread was thought to be absolutely necessary to prevent deception and oppression, particularly of the poor.

An examination of the course of legislation in Massachusetts and in Boston[103] will show the difficulties against which the officers executing the assize had to contend. In 1652 complaint was made that bakers pretended that they had no bread except for their own use, when the clerks of the market came to weigh it, but afterward sold bread of light weight; the legislature ordered that all people who usually sold bread should bake all bread, including that for their own use, according to the assize. In 1679 four Boston bakers petitioned for a committee to examine and report whether the assize was such as they could live by; they secured the committee, but its report does not

[100] *Acts and Resolves of Massachusetts Bay*, II, 181.
[101] *Ibid.*, II, 166.
[102] *Records of Massachusetts Bay*, V, 499.
[103] *Ibid.*, III, 266; IV, pt. i, 79; V, 222, 272, 317, 322–323, 499; *Acts and Resolves of Massachusetts Bay*, I, 252; II, 166. References to Boston, *Town Records* and *Records of Boston Selectmen* can be found under dates given.

appear upon the records. Two years later the Boston bakers remonstrated again, and in answer to their petition the act was passed which reorganized the administration of the assize under the town governments. Stale bread was not to be forfeited, unless it lacked one-sixteenth of the proper weight. The Boston town meeting chose three men in 1682 to inquire into the middle price of wheat when sold in quantities, and to publish the same to the bakers and the clerks of the market, according to the act of 1681. The General Court appointed a committee in 1685 to consider complaints of the bakers, and to report on what might be amiss in the assize; meanwhile, better terms were to be allowed the bakers. In 1696 another general act was passed, regulating the assize. References to the seizure of bread in Boston would seem to show that it was enforced there, but another act of the colony, 1720/1, said that it had been found ineffectual, that there was little or no observance of it, and that people were oppressed, especially the poorer sort. The new act attempted to remedy the evil by detailed provisions of an administrative nature. The Boston town meeting in 1727 instructed the selectmen to be vigilant in the execution of the law; and individuals called attention to infractions, from time to time. In 1743 complaint was made that the bakers refused to bake wheaten bread, and the assize was lowered to favor them; they appeared at the next meeting of the selectmen, complaining still of the assize, but received no further consideration. The fact that prices were set for the different kinds of bread led the bakers, evidently, to make the kind which was most profitable, to the exclusion of the others. Similarly, in New Netherland, 1651,[104] bakers refused to bake rye bread, so that poor people suffered for lack of bread, and farmers could not sell their rye. The government ordered the bakers to bake all kinds of bread, according to the assize, on penalty of fine and exclusion from business, but did not succeed in abolishing the evil, as was shown by the recurrence of complaints. The Boston bakers petitioned again in September, 1745, that the assize might be altered; they asserted that they had to give 19s. 6d., old tenor, for wheat, which the August assize had put at 18s., and secured the change of the assize to 20s. Similar complaints and changes occurred from time to time. As new kinds of bread came into use, the selectmen arranged special terms for them: so for French bread in 1743 and for a new kind of brown bread in 1757. The selectmen received complaints in 1762 that the bakers resisted search and seizure, and voted that they should be prosecuted; again, in 1782, they engaged counsel to assist the clerks of the market in their suits against the bakers. A petition presented to a town meeting in 1782, that measures be taken to prevent the alarming effects of a combination of the bakers, formed to compel the inhabitants to receive bread on their own terms, was laid on the table after some discussion, then taken up again, "and after much debate and altercation with the Bakers" was finally dropped. The assize continues in the Selectmen's *Records*, until an act of the State Legislature, in 1801,[105] repealed all laws regulating the assize of bread, and provided only that bread should be sold in Boston in loaves of specified weights, marked with the weight and the maker's name. This act was still in force in 1834.

It is hardly credible that the persistence with which the Boston town government endeavored to regulate bakers' charges was rewarded by any advantages commensurate

[104] *Laws and Ordinances of New Netherland* (ed. by O'Callaghan), 120, 261, 321.
[105] *Charter and Ordinances of Boston* (ed. by Wetmore and Prescott), 52.

with the efforts put forth. There can be no question that the legislation sometimes worked positive evil, harming the very class which it was supposed to help. But Boston was a large town, grain prices were high, as bread stuffs had to be imported, and there was a large and restless element of poor in the population. The policy of a public grain supply, forced on the town by this turbulent part of the people, will be described immediately. The assize of bread must be considered a concession to their ignorance or prejudice. It was maintained for over a century, not because it made bread cheaper, but because enough people believed that it made bread cheaper to require the municipal government to adopt it as part of the town policy.

PUBLIC SUPPLY OF PROVISIONS

The colonial governments not only regulated the trade in grain, the manufacture of flour, and the baking of bread, in behalf of their subjects, but also, on occasions, became themselves participants in trade, and provided food supplies on the public account. The government of Massachusetts, in the early period, often assisted the people to secure the necessary food supplies; Connecticut, in 1637/8, and Rhode Island, in 1724, dealt in grain on the public account; and the southern colonies show similar activities in the second half of the eighteenth century, Virginia in 1759, South Carolina in 1753 and 1766, and Georgia in 1766.[106]

The colonial government preferred ordinarily to leave the responsibility for such functions to the local groups. Virginia attempted to impose on them the duty of accumulating reserves of grain, as security against famine;[107] and Cotton proposed a law in Massachusetts, 1641, requiring each town to maintain a magazine of grain, for the relief of such poor as were not members of the church, for the maintenance of officers, and chiefly, "for the preserving of the livelihood of each towne within itselfe."[108] These measures, looking to the establishment of local centers of public grain supply, on a system which was much later practiced in Russia,[109] seem never to have been carried into effect. Many instances could doubtless be found, like those of Hartford and Braintree, in which towns provided grain from the public treasury in time of especial need.[110]

HISTORY OF PUBLIC GRAIN SUPPLY IN BOSTON

Boston took in this regard a position apart, for that town accepted the idea of public grain supply, not as an extraordinary but as an ordinary municipal function. It reverted to the practice which had long been common in Europe, and made the collection and distribution of grain a regular feature of its administration.

In the early years of the eighteenth century, the Boston selectmen made frequent appeals to the colonial authorities to lay an embargo as a remedy for the scarcity of

[106] *Records of Massachusetts Bay*, III, 153; *Public Records of the Colony of Connecticut*, I, 11; Trumbull, B., *History of Connecticut* (1898), I, 69; *Colonial Records of Rhode Island*, IV, 351; *Statutes of Virginia* (ed. by Hening), VII, 312; *Statutes at Large of South Carolina*, IV, 237; *Digest of the Laws of Georgia* (ed. by Watkins), 136.

[107] Bruce, *Economic History of Virginia*, I, 236, 274, 380, 466.

[108] Hutchinson, *Collection of Original Papers Relative to the History of the Colony of Massachusetts-Bay* (1769), 166.

[109] *Cf.* Kablukow, "Die Russische Gesetzgebung betr. die Versorgung des Volkes bei Missernten," in Braun's *Archiv für Soziale Gesetzgebung und Statistik* (1891), IV, 290–314.

[110] Hartford, *Town Votes* (Connecticut Historical Society, *Collections*, VI), I, 242–243; *Records of the Town of Braintree* [Massachusetts] (ed. by Bates, 1886), 495.

provisions.[111] As their petitions were without effect, they were forced to take independent action, and in 1710 they voted that the representatives of the town should move the General Assembly for an act to enable any town to levy on the inhabitants, in the same way as for other town rates, such sums as were necessary to purchase a stock of provisions for the town's use. No record appears of any action following this vote, and the matter might have been allowed to drop but for a bread riot, May 20, 1713, which seems to have frightened the town authorities to a decision.[112] Two hundred people or more, provoked by a large shipment of grain to Curaçao in a time of scarcity, broke down a warehouse on the Common, thinking to find grain there; the riot was committed at night, and the mob wounded the lieutenant-governor and another person. There was a large element of disorder in the population of Boston throughout the colonial period, and, as instanced in the burning of the Ursuline convent, well into the nineteenth century. Boston mobs played a prominent part in the period just before the Revolution, and to a considerable extent they dictated the town policy in the eighteenth century. Mention has been made of the destruction of the market house by a mob. A few days before that event, a mob had demolished a house of ill fame, with the countenance of some of the magistrates,[113] and mobs were common on Guy Fawkes Day and similar occasions. The character of the town as a seaport may account to some extent for the rough element; Caulkins[114] ascribes to such a cause the turbulence and disorder of the people of New London, who at times could hardly be kept in check. Whatever may be the explanation of the riotous element in Boston, there can be little question that the system of public grain supply was a result of fear of the mob. The authorities preferred to sell grain cheap, rather than have people fight for it.

In November, 1713, pursuant to a proclamation of the governor, the selectmen ordered that the master of any vessel bringing grain to Boston should supply, to every family which applied, an amount not to exceed one to two and one-half bushels, according to the size of the cargo (500 to 1500 bushels), and of flour one barrel to each family. The "present moderate customary prices" were stated, wheat 7 to 8s. a bushel, and so on; these prices may have been published merely for the information of the people, as there was no statement that sales must be in accordance with them.

In March, 1714, the town voted to lay in a stock of grain, and directed the selectmen to purchase 5,000 bushels of Indian corn, at a price not over 3s. 6d. per bushel, which was considerably below the moderate customary price of the previous November, 5s. About this time (1709/10), it was computed that the town consumed 70,000 bushels of grain yearly, so the 5,000 bushels would form an important quota. The selectmen were empowered to borrow at interest to purchase the corn, and were directed to dispose of it as they saw fit; items of expenditure for an attendant and rent, in the selectmen's record for 1715, show that the town vote was carried into effect.

From this time on, the purchase of grain by the town and its distribution by the

[111] For 1701, see *Records of Boston Selectmen, 1701–1715*, p. 5; for 1709–1710, *Ibid.*, 94–95, 101–102, 106; for 1711, Boston, *Town Records, 1700–1728*, p. 84; for 1713, *Records of Boston Selectmen, 1701–1715*, pp. 194–195. References to these records are omitted hereafter.

[112] *The Memorial History of Boston* (ed. by Winsor), II, 460, footnote.

[113] Drake, *History and Antiquities of Boston*, 597 footnote.

[114] Caulkins, *History of New London, Connecticut* (2d ed.), 148–149, 179, 246 *et seq.*

selectmen formed a regular feature of municipal activity. In 1714/5 the selectmen were directed to procure 3,000 bushels of corn, 500 of wheat and 500 of rye; and in June 1715, the money coming from the sale of the Blue Hill lands was appropriated to the purchase of provisions. It was voted that whatever loss occurred on the sale of the grain should be made good by the town from time to time, so that the stock should not become exhausted; and the selectmen were allowed to loan at interest the money appropriated, so far as it was not used. In the next year permission was given the selectmen to increase the stock to 5,000 bushels; and thereafter routine references to the town grain show that the system was maintained in regular operation. The grain appears to have been obtained mostly from "the westward," from Connecticut; and the method of disposing of it seems in this period to have been left entirely to the selectmen. In October, 1718, the selectmen voted that if any considerable quantity of Indian corn should be imported and exposed for sale before winter, any four of the selectmen could open the town granary and order the sale of corn at 4s. 6d. per bushel, to check the exorbitant demands of sellers. How such a policy might affect the inclination of merchants to seek Boston as a market for their grain we are not, of course, informed. In December 1718, the selectmen contracted for 10,000 pounds of bread, under apprehension of scarcity; they were directed by the town meeting to suspend for a month the disposal of it in large quantities, and meanwhile to sell it to the inhabitants in small quantities. The granaries at this period were kept open two days a week, notice being given by a crier; and grain was sold at fixed prices (in 1724, *e.g.*, maize at 5s. a bushel, rye at 6s.), the amount being restricted sometimes to 1 or 2 bushels to a family, and more often no limit being stated. In 1725/6, the town voted to entrust the management of the town grain to a committee of three, who were empowered to set the terms of sale.

In 1727/8, the town voted for a granary to be built on the Common, near the almshouse, at a cost of £1,000; this was described in 1794 as a long wooden building, with a capacity of 12,000 bushels.[115] In 1733, a similar granary was voted for the North End, to cost not over £100; but no regular attendant was maintained at this granary. The large granary had a salaried overseer, who received from the committee of three directions as to the amount to be sold, and the prices. In 1736, he was ordered to deliver to no person more than half a bushel of grain or meal of the same sort at one time. No general statement appears in the records as to the system followed in fixing prices; the author of the description of Boston in 1794 says that grain was sold at not more than 10 per cent. for charges. The town records contain an account of the stock in the granary at the close of each year. In March, 1738, for example, it had 1316 bushels of maize, 25 bushels of rice, and some £266 in bills of credit; in other years, rye and flour were mentioned in the stock.

The elections of committees of management, and the accounts of stock, show the granary to have been in active operation until 1774, when a committee was appointed to inquire into its condition, and report as to whether it would be expedient for the town to continue to maintain it. The committee reported that from 1769 to 1774, 5836 bushels of corn and rye had been purchased, and that the expenses of measuring, cart-

[115] [Pemberton], "A Topographical and Historical Description of Boston, 1794", in Massachusetts Historical Society, *Collections,* 1st series (reprint of 1810), III, 255.

ing, and the keeper's allowance amounted to £238. A stock of £380, on hand in 1752, had increased to £486 in 1762, but had since then diminished year by year, and amounted at the time to but £150. The committee, after a strict inquiry, could assign no reasons for this. Only 605 bushels of grain had been sold during the previous year, while the expenses were heavy. The committee was of the opinion that it would not be for the interest of the town to keep the granary open during the remainder of the year; and the town voted to lend the stock to the keeper.

At the March meeting, 1775, and in later years, a committee of three purchasers of grain was chosen with the usual directions, but apparently the old system had been abandoned. When there was a scarcity of breadstuffs in 1779, the committee recommended that the town should purchase a quantity of grain and flour by subscription, not by taxation, and this course was followed. In 1786, the selectmen voted to let the granary; and in 1794, it was used for the office of the inspector of potash.

Boston experimented on occasion in other lines of municipal trading. It assumed control of the provision trade in 1747, when Faneuil market was closed, raised money on a loan, and arranged with the town butchers to act as its agents in the purchase and sale of meat; but abandoned this function when the market was again opened in 1749. On one occasion, in 1741, it appropriated money for the purchase of 400 cords of fire wood, to supply the inhabitants; but though complaints of the scarcity of fuel continued common, the town seems thereafter to have restricted itself to a regulation of the private trade. In 1779/80, the town attempted to better the supply of vegetables to the inhabitants, by enclosing and leasing out waste land in West Boston.

PART II

THE CONSTITUTIONAL PERIOD

CHAPTER IX

SOCIAL IDEALS IN THE FUNDAMENTAL LAW OF THE REPUBLIC

PLACE OF THE AMERICAN REVOLUTION IN EUROPEAN HISTORY

The independence of the colonies was brought about by an armed revolution, whose objects were in the main political while its motives were largely economic. The colonies objected to the government of George III, particularly to its taxation, and, therefore, wished to govern themselves. They did not contemplate any change in institutions or in social conditions. Social differences did not create the principal lines of cleavage, though they did appear to this extent, that the friends of England were found mainly among the wealthy classes, which generally favor conservatism. But though the attainment of independence did not in itself produce any marked change in social conditions or in social legislation, it fixes the date at which certain ideals were first formally expressed in law. If Europe in the seventeenth century had been noted for its political and religious changes, it was distinguished in the eighteenth for its social, economic, and philosophic changes. It was in this century that political economy became a recognized science under the leadership of the French Physiocrats and of Adam Smith. It was in this century that the ax was laid at the roots both of the gild system and of the system of serfdom, though neither fully disappeared until the next century. It was in this century that the power of the French aristocracy was broken, and that the middle class became strong and almost dominant in England. While, therefore, it was an accident that the Declaration of Independence was adopted in the same year in which Adam Smith's "*Wealth of Nations*" was published, and in which Turgot issued his six reform edicts; while it was also an accident that the inauguration of the Constitution of the United States occurred in the year of the outbreak of the French Revolution: all of these events belonged together in the latter part of the eighteenth century, and were all significant of the spirit of the times. Indeed in his edict of February 1776, abolishing the privileges of the gilds, Turgot referred to the revolt of the American colonies as making the time especially favorable for a more liberal policy. He thought that the injury which this revolution would bring to English industry might lead English artisans to move over to France and bring their processes and inventions with them.[1]

THE SOCIAL COMPACT AND STATE CONSTITUTIONS

Of the social and political theories which were characteristic of the second half of the eighteenth century, few, if any, exercised a greater influence than the doctrine of the

[1] Farnam, *Die innere Französische Gewerbepolitik von Colbert bis Turgot* (1878), 52.

social compact, which was popularized by Rousseau in his *Contrat Social,* published in 1762. The idea that all government arises from a social contract, under which each individual surrenders for the benefit of society as a whole a part of his natural rights, was not original with Rousseau. John Locke, in his *Treatise on Civil Government* in 1690, had expressed similar views, and as early as 1651, Hobbes, in his *Leviathan,* had said essentially the same thing. But the doctrine harmonized well with the principles of natural law prevalent in the eighteenth century and appeared to find a remarkable historical confirmation in the experience of some of the colonies. The Pilgrims on the *Mayflower,* the early settlers of New Haven, and other groups had in fact formed voluntary agreements as the basis of civil government. This does not prove the historical truth of Rousseau's theory, for these colonists did not emerge from a state of nature. They were members of a civilized country which had for centuries enjoyed the blessings, as well as the burdens, of government. They were simply separated physically from the source of sovereignty in the mother country, and thus put in a position in which they could voluntarily create, *de novo,* the machinery for carrying out ideas which were already familiar to them. Yet this experience naturally predisposed the Americans to look favorably upon the theory of the social compact. Indeed, many people at the time held that the Revolution threw the colonists back to a state of nature,[2] so that they had to begin over again with a new compact, and the general craving for some guiding principles was seen in the prompt adoption of constitutions by all but two of the several States, even before the adoption of the Articles of Confederation in 1781. And although Connecticut and Rhode Island found their royal charters liberal enough to serve their purposes until the next century, Connecticut yielded sufficiently to the *Zeitgeist* to adopt a preamble, and all of the other States except Rhode Island framed constitutions within a very few years. Of the original thirteen colonies, Maryland, New Hampshire, New Jersey, North Carolina, Pennsylvania, South Carolina, Virginia, and Delaware, eight in all, took this step in 1776, and were followed by Georgia and New York in 1777. In the same year Vermont, which was not admitted to the Union till 1791, also voted itself a constitution. Massachusetts adopted in 1780 a constitution, the first draft having been rejected at the polls in 1778, and New Hampshire adopted a second constitution in 1784. Thus we have twelve States, in all, which adopted constitutions between 1776 and 1780, and these may be taken to represent fairly the authoritative opinion of the day on social and political questions.

DOCTRINES OF FREEDOM AND EQUALITY

Of these constitutions, eight stated directly or implied the social compact theory of government. Maryland, Massachusetts, New Hampshire, New Jersey, New York, North Carolina, Pennsylvania, and Virginia were in this list. The fact that these States are scattered over the different parts of the seaboard shows how general the notion was, and justifies the assumption that, where it was omitted, the cause was presumably accidental. Another feature which was not quite so common was the doctrine of the natural freedom of man. Six of the States, Massachusetts, New Hampshire, New York,

[2] Cushing, *History of the Transition from Provincial to Commonwealth Government in Massachusetts* (1896), in *Columbia University Studies,* VII, 7.

Pennsylvania, Virginia and Vermont, had some reference to this, using such phrases as "free and equal," or "equal," or "free and independent." Five of these six States also referred to the theory of the social compact, and all but one of the five were in the North. Stimson mentions the use of a similar expression as far back as the time of Henry VIII. "In 1514 the king manumitted two villeins with the significant words, 'Whereas God created all men free.'"[3] Another curious reference to the same idea is found in a primer of penmanship published in 1570. The very first page contained the sentence:

> "All men are by nature equal, made all by one workman
> of like myre, & howesoeuer we deceaue our selues as
> dere unto God is the poorest begger as the moste pom
> pous Prince liuing in the worlde."

This sentence is attributed to Plato. But whoever may have been the author, many boys learning to write during the latter part of the sixteenth century must, by virtue of copying this sentiment, have become familiar with it.[4] The idea of the original equality of men can be traced still further back. At the time of the Peasants' War in the fourteenth century, John Ball is said to have used the couplet,

> "When Adam delved and Eve span
> Who was then the gentleman."

While, therefore, the idea of a natural state of freedom and equality was not the invention of Thomas Jefferson or of his contemporaries, it was due to them and to their part in bringing about the independence of the United States that this doctrine was formally incorporated in written constitutions.

The doctrine of the natural freedom and equality of men, if taken literally, would have banned slavery. Vermont was the one State which apparently did not hesitate to draw this logical conclusion, for after stating in its constitution "that all men are born equally free and independent,"[5] it continued, in a passage quoted later in the text,[6] with an explicit prohibition of slavery in the State.

The doctrine of the equality and freedom of mankind did not necessarily imply anything with regard to the right to take part in government, and "a majority of the states placed direct property qualifications on the voters, and the other states eliminated practically all who were not taxpayers."[7] As this statement refers only to the original thirteen States, Vermont is not included. The Green Mountain State, which was radical on the subject of slavery, was quite consistent in giving the right of suffrage to every man of the age of twenty-one who had resided in the State for one year, who was "of a quiet and peaceable behaviour," and who would take the required oath.[8]

[3] *Popular Law-Making*, 107.

[4] The only copy of this book, by John de Beauchesne and John Baildon, which is known to exist, is in the collection of Mr. George A. Plimpton of New York, who kindly allowed the writer to examine it. See Farnam, *Shakespeare's Economics* (1931), 136, for photostatic copy of the sentence quoted.

[5] Constitution of 1777, chap. i, art. 1.

[6] See page 212.

[7] Beard, *An Economic Interpretation of the Constitution of the United States* (1913), 71.

[8] *Constitution of 1777*, chap. ii, sect. 6, in Thorpe, *American Charters, Constitutions and Organic Laws*, VI, 3742.

Thus, though the States generally retained in practice certain class distinctions which they had inherited from the mother country, and though in most of them the qualifications which were required for the suffrage put political power into the hands of the property owners, many of them adopted at the outset of their independent political life certain general principles which were destined in time to lead to a more democratic policy.

SOCIAL IDEALS IN THE DECLARATION OF INDEPENDENCE

The Declaration of Independence summarized on behalf of the people of the States as a whole some of the social ideals which were the common property of all, and which, though expressed in only some of the constitutions, were doubtless generally accepted. The Declaration was not an instrument of government. It had not the force of law. It was a political manifesto, comparable to the platform of a political party. But its literary form, as well as the fact that it was the first general statement of the political principles of the United States, gives it a position of recognized authority. It began with the familiar statement "that all men are created equal, that they are endowed by their Creator with certain unalienable Rights, that among these are Life, Liberty and the pursuit of Happiness. That to secure these rights, Governments are instituted among Men, deriving their just powers from the consent of the governed, That whenever any Form of Government becomes destructive of these ends, it is the Right of the People to alter or to abolish it. . . ."[9] Here the compact theory of the state, based upon the assumption of the original equality of men in a state of nature, was set forth as a justification for armed rebellion, and was given to the world in deference to "a decent respect to the opinions of mankind."[10] Thus political necessity forced the declaration of a certain theory of government, which in turn implied a certain theory of society. It will be noticed that the expression of the Declaration, "that all men are created equal," was more general and indefinite than the expression even of the Virginia constitution which said, "that all men are by nature equally free and independent." The latter can hardly be reconciled with the practice of slavery, whereas the former may be taken to refer to a prehistoric or to an ideal state, whose maxims need not necessarily be applied in practice. Nevertheless, it is believed that this general statement created a presumption in favor of freedom, and it is well known that both Jefferson, the author of the Declaration of Independence, and Washington, though slave holders, were strong supporters of the emancipation of slaves. Jefferson's views, indeed, went further than the Declaration of Independence in its final form. The first draft contained a passage declaring the slave trade "piratical warfare against human nature itself." This was stricken out to please South Carolina and Georgia, which did not object to the importation of slaves, and wished to continue it.[11]

The Declaration of Independence was a political document, and the charges which it brought against the King of Great Britain were mainly of a political nature. Yet two of them referred to economic and social conditions, for we are told that, "He has

[9] *Ibid.*, I, 3–4.
[10] *Ibid.*, I, 3.
[11] Frothingham, *Rise of the Republic of the United States* (ed. of 1881), 539, quoting Jefferson's *Memoirs*, I, 15.

endeavoured to prevent the population of these States; for that purpose obstructing the Laws for Naturalization of Foreigners; refusing to pass others to encourage their migration hither, and raising the conditions of new Appropriations of Lands."[12] In this one paragraph we have the labor question and the land question coupled together.

The Articles of Confederation, though not adopted until 1781, were drafted in 1777, in the early part of the war, when the important object was to get the States to act together, and military success took precedence of all other considerations. There was, therefore, no place for social problems, and the form of government under the Articles was so loose as not to be well adapted even to the prosecution of a war by the common action of the States. It was inevitable, therefore, that the Articles should be superseded, and that in the new instrument of government more attention should be paid to economic and social problems.

Landon enumerates, "four causes which more powerfully than any others disclosed the utter weakness of the confederacy, which, after several years of distress, finally led to the formation of a new and stronger Constitution. First, the want of power to regulate commerce; second, the want of power to raise money to pay the national debts and to support the national government both at home and abroad; third, the want of power to provide a uniform and good currency; fourth, the want of power to forbid a state to pass laws impairing the obligation of contracts."[13]

These functions all related to economic matters. There was also trouble with regard to the western lands, and finally came the outbreak of Shays's Rebellion in western Massachusetts, in 1786. Shays's Rebellion was a revolt of debtors against creditors, and, therefore, involved economic and social questions. It may thus be fairly said that it was mainly to solve economic problems that the Constitution was adopted.

ECONOMIC AND SOCIAL FEATURES OF THE CONSTITUTION

It has been remarked that the Declaration of Independence did not include the word property, and only implied it under the general term "pursuit of happiness."[14] This defect, if it was one, was made good in the Constitution, some of the most important sections of which related to property or to matters connected with it. Section 8, of article i, which enumerated the powers of Congress, was devoted mainly to creating uniformity in certain important economic fields. Among these were the powers to tax, to borrow money, to regulate commerce, to regulate naturalization and bankruptcy, to coin money, to fix the standard of weights and measures, to punish counterfeiting, to establish postoffices, to provide for patents and copyrights. The only other powers enumerated in this section related to the tribunals, to the punishment of crime, to the exercise of the war power through the army and navy, and to the government of the District of Columbia. Two passages touched directly upon a burning question of social politics. One was the paragraph of section 9 which prohibited Congress from enjoining the slave trade before the year 1808; the other was section 2, of article iv, which authorized Congress to pass laws regarding fugitive slaves. The exclusion of titles of nobility was significant but not novel, under the conditions then existing.

[12] Thorpe, *American Charters, Constitutions and Organic Laws*, I, 5.
[13] Landon, *The Constitutional History and Government of the United States* (1889), 58.
[14] Stimson, *Popular Law Making*, 127.

Most of our federal social legislation, *i.e.*, legislation aiming directly at defining or regulating the interests of different social classes, has been developed under powers which in the beginning did not apparently contemplate this purpose at all. Thus the taxing power has been used to limit or even destroy certain industries or institutions, as in the case of the tax upon State bank notes. The power to establish postoffices has been used to establish postal savings banks as an institution for the encouragement of thrift, as well as to punish promoters of fraudulent investment and stock jobbing schemes, and purveyors of obscene literature. The power to declare war and carry it on through the army and navy, led to the most important social act ever undertaken by the Federal Government, when the slaves in the States that had seceded were freed by executive proclamation. The power to make treaties has involved the acquisition of land by treaty; and the power "to dispose of and make all needful Rules and Regulations respecting the Territory" of the United States (art. iv, section 3) involved legislating on the subject of slavery and has enabled Congress to frame and carry out an elaborate land policy, a public school policy, a policy for higher education in agriculture and the mechanic arts, and a conservation policy. The power of exclusive jurisdiction over the District of Columbia makes it possible for the Government, on a limited scale, to carry out almost any sociological experiment that it desires, using the District as a kind of laboratory in which to develop ideal conditions regarding labor, sanitation, tenements, and city planning. One of the most prolific of all the powers in this field has been the power to regulate commerce between the States and with foreign nations, which has been the basis of the regulation of railroads, the limitation of monopolies, and the control of immigration, and which probably also should be taken to justify the introduction of a system of compulsory insurance against illness for seamen in the merchant marine.

BILLS OF RIGHTS

The Constitution followed the Articles in not including a bill of rights. This, however, had become so common a feature of State constitutions, that in the very first year of the establishment of the Government ten amendments were passed, of which the first eight were a bill of rights, securing the individual rights of person and property against governmental infringement. The idea of a constitutional guarantee of personal and social rights in the modern sense of the word may be said to be a Puritan gift to the world, since it was first embodied in the constitution of John Lilburne submitted to the House of Commons in 1647 but never adopted. This had, to be sure, its predecessors in the Magna Charta and in the coronation oath, both of which guaranteed certain rights to the individual. The Magna Charta, however, implied feudalism; the coronation oath implied a monarchy. The peculiarity of the guarantees in John Lilburne's constitution, as well as in the constitutions of the United States and of the several States, was that they were a self-limitation of the people, a formal act by which the people as a whole limited their own authority to interfere with the rights of the individual, and could thus insure certain social ideals.

The general presumption of the bills of rights in the early constitutions and in the first eight amendments to the Federal Constitution was in favor of the liberty of the individual, and the protection of his property rights against arbitrary power on the part of the government. This in turn created a presumption in favor of personal freedom against the subordination of human rights to property rights. It also created a presumption in favor of equality of opportunity. The tendency in the State constitutions has also been to make increasingly elaborate provisions for the establishment of principles of social legislation. These will be considered in connection with the several topics to which they refer in later chapters.

COMPROMISES OF THE CONSTITUTION

When the Constitution was adopted, it was necessarily a compromise on account of the different ideals prevailing in different parts of the country, and, as Beard has pointed out, the mercantile and urban classes in the North and the slave holders in the South made mutual concessions to each other. The consequence was that the North received the regulation of commerce which it desired, while the South secured the recognition of slavery. As Hamilton said in regard to the clause which allowed the representation in Congress of three-fifths of the Negroes: "Much has been said of the impropriety of representing men who have no will of their own. . . . The regulation complained of was one result of the spirit of accommodation which governed the convention; and without this indulgence no Union could possibly have been formed."[15] In the constitutional convention, General Pinckney said plainly that, if the committee should fail to insert some security to the Southern States against the emancipation of their slaves, he would vote against the report,[16] and in another session he expressed the wish that some provision might be inserted in favor of property in slaves.[17] Without such concessions the Constitution itself would probably never have been adopted, and there is good reason for holding with Beard that the Constitution was proposed by people whose property interests were expected to be served by it, and that it was carried by the same element. Even at the time, the opponents of the Constitution often spoke of it as aristocratic. It should be remembered, however, that the word aristocratic, applied under these conditions, had a purely relative significance. The constitutional party was aristocratic, if that expression can be applied to the more substantial property owning classes of the country. It was not aristocratic in the European sense of the word. It did not represent the wishes or the interests of an hereditary class. It represented what would be called in Europe the upper middle classes, and there can be no doubt that in those days the interests of these classes were synonymous with the business interests of the country as a whole. It was only by doing away with paper money, by securing the rights of property, and by preventing the repudiation of debt that any expansion of business operations, whether mercantile, manufacturing, or agricultural, was possible.

Although the Constitution does not contain many paragraphs which would be classed as social legislation at the present day, it is nevertheless the most important piece of social legislation enacted in the United States during the eighteenth century, because it

[15] Speech on the "Compromises of the Constitution," made in the Convention of New York, June 20, 1788, printed in *The Works of Alexander Hamilton* (ed. by John C. Hamilton, 1850), II, 434.

[16] Madison, *Journal of the Federal Convention* (ed. by E. H. Scott, 1893), 418; Farrand, *Records of the Federal Convention* (1911), II, 95.

[17] Madison, *Journal of the Federal Convention*, 623; Farrand, *Records of the Federal Convention*, II, 443.

made later legislation possible. Let us imagine, for the moment, that the Articles of Confederation had never been superseded, and that the United States had continued to live under them down to the present day. The great accessions of territory would have been impossible, because the United States would have had neither the money to buy territory nor the military force to conquer it. The Louisiana Purchase, the Mexican cession, the purchase of Alaska, would all have been out of the question. Each State would have managed its own land and its own labor problems. The general inauguration of the homestead system for disposing of the public land would have been impossible. The general abolition of slavery would have required independent action by each separate State, which means that slavery would probably still exist south of Mason and Dixon's line. The uniformity of the currency and of weights and measures, the absence of tariff barriers between the States, the prohibition of discrimination on the part of one State against other States, the introduction of a uniform postal system, of uniform patent laws, and of uniform rules of naturalization, were all essential to the broadening of the market which brought the different parts of the country together, and which, while it has created many new problems, has also made possible national movements of reform. Not only has the Constitution enabled the United States, through its Congress, to carry out many important social measures, but it has also brought about a certain unity of sentiment and of action which, even in the spheres within which each State legislature is supreme, has tended to produce similarity, if not uniformity, in the legislation of the several States.

The effect of having differing ideals represented in States united under one Constitution was to bring institutions into competition. During the colonial period, each little colony was connected with the others mainly by a commerce which involved a territorial division of labor and the exchange of products of different latitudes. There was comparatively little competition among them. The Southerner might exchange his tobacco and his cotton for the manufactures and lumber of the North, but there was no way by which the relative efficiency of large and small estates, of slave and free labor could be tested, because they were not applied to the same products, nor could any one colony aspire to influence the general policy of the mother country. When, however, thirteen and more States were united under the same legislature, there naturally arose a rivalry between the different parts of the country to impose their ideals on that government. This competition of standards lies at the basis of most of our political controversies, and was especially evident during the prolonged and often bitter discussions which preceded the Civil War. The following pages are intended to trace the steps by which competing ideals have affected the solution of our social problems. With the growth of population and of wealth, with the acquisition of new land, with the introduction of new processes of production, and new forms of business organization, new problems have arisen, while the solution has been in many cases retarded by conflicting economic interests, and conflicting standards of public policy. Whatever progress has been made, has been due to the survival of those ideals which were best able to impose themselves upon the policy of the country.

CHAPTER X

LAND POLICY, 1784–1862

When the American continent was settled by Europeans, the first question to decide was, on what terms and under what system should the land be distributed. This problem was solved differently in different parts of the country. With the achievement of political independence, the same question presented itself under new conditions. The greater part of the accessible land of the thirteen revolting colonies was pretty well settled; it was at any rate explored, and each colony had adopted a definite system of its own. But seven of the colonies claimed, under their charters, land which was remote from the settled area on the seaboard, and the boundaries of which were uncertain. In many cases these grants were limited only by the ignorance of the grantors. The extent of the continent was unknown and the simplest definition was to run the boundaries on lines of latitude from ocean to ocean. The seven colonies which were thus provided were Massachusetts, Connecticut, New York, Virginia, North Carolina, South Carolina, and Georgia.

DEVELOPMENT OF THE FEDERAL DOMAIN

In order to carry on the war, Congress offered in 1776 and later bounties in land to the soldiers. Commissioned officers were to have from 150 to 500 acres, while the non-commissioned officers were to have 100 acres and a bounty of $20.[1] But inasmuch as Congress possessed no public lands, it could not meet its obligations unless it obtained what was needed by cession or purchase. The States which had no lands objected to purchase, inasmuch as they would have to share in the taxes to be raised for the purpose. Maryland was particularly firm in this attitude, and as a consequence long withheld its ratification of the Articles of Confederation. The effect of this was to bring pressure to bear upon the other States to make cessions. New York, Virginia, and Connecticut offered to do so, and Maryland's delegates signed the Articles, March 1, 1781.[2]

These promises were gradually made good. New York made its cession March 1, 1781, turning over 315.91 square miles. The other States followed, though North Carolina and Georgia did not make their cessions until after the adoption of the Constitution, the former in 1790, the latter in 1802. The result was that the Federal Government, first under the Articles of Confederation, and then under the Constitu-

[1] Sato, *History of the Land Question in the United States* (1886), in *Johns Hopkins University Studies*, IV, 285.

[2] *Ibid.*, 293.

tion, acquired some 404,955 square miles or over 259,000,000 acres.[3] This was the beginning of the domain of the United States, subsequently enlarged by the Louisiana Purchase in 1803, by the acquisition of Florida in 1819, by the Mexican cession after the war with Mexico in 1848, by the Gadsden Purchase of 45,535 square miles of Mexico in 1853, and by the purchase of Alaska in 1867. Though the annexation of Texas added enormously to the area of the United States, it did not add so much to its domain, inasmuch as Texas retained all of its public lands. It was not until 1850, after the Mexican War, that a part of the original territory of 376,123 square miles was purchased of Texas by the United States, and that in this way 101,767 square miles were added to the public domain.[4]

The possession of these vast areas of unoccupied land, though due to a number of entirely different causes, partly political, partly military, and partly diplomatic, led the United States to legislate upon four different subjects of social policy: 1. The distribution of real estate; 2. Slavery; 3. Education; 4. The conservation of natural resources. Another important result followed from the transfer of the western lands to the national government. The land question became primarily a national question. If each State had retained its own lands, each could have pursued such a policy as it pleased, without much reference to the others. As soon as the domain became national, there arose a competition among the ideals prevailing in different parts of the country, each one pressing for recognition in national legislation. In this way questions of policy were debated more vigorously and decided more consciously. At the same time they inevitably became the subjects of national controversy and affected the alignment of parties.

The federal land policy divides itself quite naturally into five periods. The first extends from the creation of the national domain to 1820, during which time the credit system prevailed.[5] From 1820 to 1841 there was an era of controversy which ended in the adoption of the preemption system. From 1841 to 1862 the movement towards liberalizing the land laws progressed, until it resulted in the passage of the Homestead Act. The homestead system has prevailed ever since that time, but the abuses which had grown up in the administration of our public lands gradually led to a new movement which we may call the conservation movement, and which may be dated from about 1891.

ORDINANCES FOR GOVERNMENT OF THE NORTHWEST TERRITORY

The first laws in any new department of government are of great importance, as establishing a precedent which it is difficult to change. The first laws regarding the domain of the United States turned out to be peculiarly important, because they established a system, not only for the territory in question, but also for vastly greater territories, the acquisition of which was hardly dreamed of in those days. The area ceded by the States was under 405,000 square miles; the total area acquired down to and inclusive of the Alaskan purchase was 2,894,235.91 square miles, or seven times as

[3] *Ibid.*, 293–298.
[4] *Ibid.*, 318, 334.
[5] See Treat, *The National Land System, 1785–1820* (1910).

great.[6] Yet many of the features which were adopted for the smaller area have, in spite of changes in general policy, been retained for the great national domain. Our first land law was the Ordinance of 1784 for the Northwest Territory. No settlement of the territory was made under this law, and it therefore had no practical effects. And yet it possesses considerable interest on account of the fact that in the original draft, which was made by Jefferson, slavery was to be prohibited after the year 1800. This was lost by a single vote,[7] for though six States voted in favor, and three against, the votes of seven States were necessary to carry any measure, and the plurality therefore did not count. Three of the States were not represented, and the vote of North Carolina, whose representative, Mr. Spaight, had made the motion, was divided. Virginia voted with Maryland and South Carolina against the clause.

Before the next general ordinance was passed in 1787, it was necessary to make some provision for the surveying of the public lands, and this was done in the Ordinance of May 20, 1785.[8] Two systems were at this time in competition for the favor of Congress. One was the New England system of township planting. According to this, each township was laid out first and subdivided into tracts by the colony, the town, or the proprietors. The survey was made before the land was settled. In the eighteenth century groups of townships were sometimes laid out in tiers. The common area of a township was 6 miles square. Another peculiarity of the New England system was that land was often reserved for educational and religious purposes,[9] and the propagation across the country of the New England ideal of community settlement can be traced in the history of the towns settled by New Englanders.[10]

The southern plan was quite different. Though the land was supposed to be surveyed, this was carelessly done. The records were poorly kept. A person could select whatever land suited him without reference to others, under the so-called system of "indiscriminate location." It was an individualistic, rather than a community system. Though the committee to which this question was referred contained a majority of southern members (three out of five), it reported, under Jefferson's leadership, in favor of the New England system, including a rectangular survey, and townships of the uniform size of 6 miles square, divided into 36 sections of 1 mile square each.

The Ordinance of 1785 specified the details of sale to go into effect as soon as preliminary surveys had been completed. After provision had been made to supply the Secretary of War with land to satisfy the claims of soldiers for bounties, the remainder was to be divided by lot among the thirteen States in proportion to the number of soldiers which they had furnished to the Continental Army. The land was to be offered for sale in the separate States under a compromise plan designed to combine the methods of land settlement practised in different parts of the country. The method was to sell Township No. 1 in the First Range entire; No. 2 in sections and so on alternately. In the Second Range, No. 1 was sold by sections and Township No. 2

[6] Sato, *History of the Land Question in the United States*, 334.
[7] *Ibid.*, 342.
[8] *Ibid.*, 391.
[9] Treat, *The National Land System*, 23–25.
[10] For a vivid picture of this process, see Mathews, *Expansion of New England* (1909).

entire.[11] By this alternating method they satisfied the New Englander who preferred settlement by township, and the southerner who preferred individual settlement. The minimum price was to be $1 per acre, not including the cost of surveying.[12]

ORDINANCE OF 1787

The Ordinance of 1787, which superseded that of 1784, dealt with the entire government of the territory. It is not necessary to speak here of its political features, excepting to say that in the beginning the region was to be under a governor and secretary appointed by Congress, who, together with three judges also appointed by Congress, were to exercise temporary legislative power until the organization of the general assembly. A number of provisions were distinctly social in their aim. The estates of persons dying intestate were to be divided equally among their heirs, according to the New England plan. The conveyance of estates was made very simple, and conveyances were to be recorded by registers within one year. The Ordinance also contained a bill of rights in six sections, securing civil and religious liberty, the right of *habeas corpus*, and the protection of property and contracts. It required that due regard should be paid to the property and rights of the Indians. Equality of taxation for both resident and non-resident proprietors was secured. Article III demanded that "schools and the means of education shall forever be encouraged." The last article said, "There shall be neither slavery nor involuntary servitude in the said territory, otherwise than in the punishment of crimes, whereof the party shall have been duly convicted." Provision was, however, made for the surrender of fugitive slaves.[13]

It is a curious fact that, though this Ordinance is by common consent one of the most noteworthy laws in the early history of the United States, its constitutionality is open to serious question. Madison, speaking in the *Federalist* of the action of Congress, says: "All this has been done; and done without the least colour of constitutional authority. Yet no blame has been whispered; no alarm has been sounded."[14]

For a long time there was a question as to who deserved the chief credit for the Ordinance of 1787. The original inoperative Ordinance of 1784 was due mainly to Jefferson. The chief merit for the one of 1787 has been claimed by Daniel Webster and others for Nathan Dane of Massachusetts, who doubtless had a great deal to do with drafting it. Indeed, he himself pointed out that the section forbidding slavery was in his own handwriting.[15] On the other hand, there is also good reason for believing that the chief credit for the Ordinance belongs to Rev. Manasseh Cutler. Dr. Cutler was born in Killingly, Connecticut, graduated from Yale College in 1765, studied law, afterwards entered the ministry, and served as a chaplain in the Revolutionary War. In 1786, he became associated with a company which was afterwards known as the Ohio Company, and which was made up to a large extent of Revolutionary officers. This company desired to purchase a large tract of land, and Dr. Cutler visited New York as its

[11] Sato, *History of the Land Question in the United States*, 394; Hibbard, *A History of the Public Land Policies* (1924), 39. The reader will find a brief but clear description of the technique and nomenclature of the survey in Kirkland, *History of American Economic Life* (1932), 143.

[12] Treat, *The National Land System*, 34–37.

[13] MacDonald, *Select Documents Illustrative of the History of the United States, 1776–1861* (1898), 21–28.

[14] *The Federalist*, No. xxxviii (ed. of 1802), I, 252.

[15] Sato, *History of the Land Question in the United States*, 364.

agent in June 1787, while the Ordinance was still under discussion. The draft was put into his hands for examination, and there is reason to believe that he exercised a considerable influence upon its provisions.[16] Whatever may be the relative merits of Dane and Cutler in securing the passage of the Ordinance, it is certainly true that its provisions embodied, on the whole, New England principles. The fact that New England stockholders wished to buy a large tract of land, and that the Government was anxious, for financial reasons, to make the sale, led to the incorporation of the New England ideas of free labor and provision for education in the Ordinance.[17]

FISCAL MOTIVE OF EARLY LAND LAWS

In the beginning, there were but two methods of disposing of the public lands which were seriously considered by Congress; one was to give them in satisfaction of military bounties, the other was to sell them. In both cases it may be said that the purpose was financial, since the bounties had been offered to soldiers as a means of carrying on the war and as a substitute for taxation. It is not necessary to describe the details of the bounty system.[18] The idea of giving lands to soldiers is very old. It was used by the Romans to colonize their conquests in central Europe. In the Middle Ages it formed the basis of the feudal system. The policy of the Government of the United States underwent a certain development quite typical of modern commercial life. It was expected in the beginning that the recipients of the land bounties would form settlements on the frontiers, which would keep back the Indians and at one stroke both settle and protect the land. In 1788, however, the bounty warrants were made transferable. Thus the idea of a military reserve disappeared, and the purely financial point of view was emphasized.

The bulk of the land was intended to be sold, and the main problem was to fix the terms of sale. The emphasis on the financial point of view is seen in the fact that in the beginning the minimum amount which could be bought was a section of 640 acres.[19] At almost the very time when in France the democratic revolution was taking land from the privileged classes and offering it to the people, the American Government followed a course which put its great reserve of public land at the disposal of the speculator rather than of the common man. The Rev. Manasseh Cutler and others organized the Ohio Company, ostensibly to assist the settlement of veterans on the land, but with attractive promises of profit to the promoters; and by some shrewd political manipulation the organizers obtained a grant of 1,500,000 acres, to be purchased on terms amounting to a price of only eight or nine cents an acre. The company met with difficulties in carrying out the terms of the contract, and actually obtained patents to less than a million acres, but another company, organized by John C. Symmes, brought the total alienated in these large blocks to over one million acres, while the government sold in small parcels by auction less than 100,000 acres. In dealing directly with would-be

[16] *Ibid.*, 369.

[17] For a discussion of the claims of Dane and Cutler, see Sato, *History of the Land Question in the United States*, 362–375; Avery, *A History of the United States and its People* (1904–1910), VI, 407–408; the biographies of Cutler by C. M. Fuess, and of Dane by H. W. H. Knott, in *Dictionary of American Biography*, V, 13, 63.

[18] For full account, see Treat, *The National Land System*, 230–262.

[19] Ordinance of 1785, Sato, *History of the Land Question in the United States*, 395. An attempt to reduce the minimum to 320 acres failed. Hibbard, *A History of the Public Land Policies*, 39.

settlers, the government was in competition not only with the speculative companies which it had recognized, but also with some of the States, which now offered their vacant land for sale on terms more liberal than the Congress of the Confederation was willing to grant.[20]

The land was also made to serve another financial purpose. By act of March 3, 1795 (sec. 8), the net profits of the public lands were to be turned over to the sinking fund.[21] In the beginning, no credit was given to purchasers, but this was allowed after 1787, with results which were far from favorable.[22]

The stress laid upon fiscal considerations came from the fact that the Government was young and poor, and that it had incurred obligations which, it believed, could be settled only by the sale of land. Therefore, in the reference to the matter which was made by President Washington in his annual address of October 25, 1791, he said : "A provision for the sale of vacant lands of the United States is particularly urged, among other reasons, by the important considerations that they are pledged as a fund for reimbursing the public debt. . . ."[23] Similarly, President Jefferson, in his message of December 8, 1801, said: "The success which has attended the late sales of the public lands shews that with attention they may be made an important source of receipt."[24] Other aspects of the public land policy were debated in the early Congresses, meeting in 1789 and the following years; there was general agreement that the plan followed under the Confederation was unsatisfactory; but there was no agreement on a plan which would meet the insistent need for revenue, and which would at the same time be adapted to the actual conditions of the frontier. Migration westward had increased rapidly, and was outrunning the surveys of the government; the new settlers in thousands of cases were squatters, without regular title to the land on which they were living. The plan to establish a land office in the West, near to the frontier, and to offer land there for sale in small tracts at low prices was rejected as likely to reduce the receipts of the treasury. Hamilton, in a report made in 1790, recognized the needs of the actual settler by proposing that lots of 100 acres or less be available for purchase, but made the sale of land in large blocks, 500 acres and more or whole townships, the central feature of his project.[25]

Congress finally acted in 1796, providing for sale of the land in sections of 640 acres and in quarter-townships, at a minimum price of $2 an acre. In the four years following, less than 50,000 acres were sold. Settlers bought at better terms from the private companies, or established themselves on the public domain without the formality of purchase. An act passed in 1800, at the insistence of representatives from the western territory, marked a real advance in several respects of primary importance. Four land offices were to be established in the Northwest Territory. Land was to be surveyed and sold in half-sections, of 320 acres; Congress defeated proposals either to increase or to reduce this normal minimum, but four years later halved it again, to 160 acres.

[20] Hibbard, *A History of the Public Land Policies*, 41 *et seq.*
[21] United States, *Statutes at Large*, I, 435.
[22] Treat, *The National Land System*, 44.
[23] Richardson, *A Compilation of the Messages and Papers of the Presidents, 1789–1897* (1896), I, 108.
[24] *Ibid.*, I, 329.
[25] Hibbard, *A History of the Public Land Policies*, 59 *et seq.*; Treat, *The National Land System*, 70 *et seq.*

Finally, in place of the provision of the earlier act which had required completion of payment within a year, credit was allowed up to two and four years for parts of the payment.[26]

The minimum auction price remained unchanged, at $2 an acre, until 1820. This price was set mainly for fiscal reasons, but was defended also as a bar to speculation, and as a defence against depreciation of land values in the older parts of the country. Low as this price may seem today, it was in fact beyond the means of many or most settlers on the frontier. They found it desperately hard to accumulate that amount of cash, over and above the expense of moving a family and making a start on fresh land. The $2 minimum was to some extent nominal, for a provision that payment might be made in government evidences of debt reduced it to $1.50, and discounts were offered for cash. When all allowance was made, however, the price was beyond the capacity of so many that the extension of credit was inevitable, and even then the payment of debt was impracticable. In its refusal to recognize the facts of the situation, the Government followed a most unhappy and unwholesome course, insisting on the terms of the debt and then by special act forgiving the debtor.[27]

Beginning with 1809, extension of time, suspension of the forfeiture of lands on which payments were still due, and other concessions were made in successive acts. The credit system was finally abolished by act of April 24, 1820.[28] But this did not abolish the accumulation of evils, and many acts were passed after that time to provide relief. From 1809 to 1832 inclusive, no less than twenty-three relief acts were passed, or about one a year.[29]

If the Government held stubbornly in this period to its asking price for the land, it did at least make purchase easier by reducing the minimum acreage of the lots which it stood ready to sell. The size, set at a quarter-section in 1804, was halved in 1817–1820, and was halved again in 1832. It is instructive to review the descending series of the minimum: 1785–1796, 640 acres; 1800, 320 acres; 1804, 160 acres; 1817–1820, 80 acres; 1832, 40 acres.[30]

CHANGE IN CONDITIONS AFTER 1820

The period 1820–1841 was important, not so much for what it actually accomplished, as for the forces which began to operate, though they did not make themselves fully felt until later. In the first thirty years of the Republic, the United States was almost exclusively an agricultural community. There were few large cities and comparatively few non-agricultural industries. There were no modern means of transportation. As the market was restricted, each community was to a large extent self-sufficing. Towards the end of the period, however, a number of things occurred to change the situation. The Embargo Act, the Non-Intercourse Act, and the War of 1812 which followed, had the natural effect of stimulating manufactures, and although there was a large importation of foreign goods in the years following the war, the stimulus did not lose

[26] Hibbard, *A History of the Public Land Policies*, 67–81; Treat, *The National Land System*, 85–95.
[27] Hibbard, *A History of the Public Land Policies*, 75 *et seq.*
[28] Treat, *The National Land System*, 140–141; United States, *Statutes at Large*, III, 566, chap. li.
[29] Sato, *History of the Land Question in the United States*, 407.
[30] Hibbard, *History of the Public Land Policies*, 75.

its influence, and other circumstances, such as inventions and the growth of capital, came in to increase the manufacturing population. In 1800, there were eight small cotton factories in the country, consuming altogether only a few hundred bales of imported cotton. In the decade ending in 1815, the annual consumption of cotton was supposed to have risen from 500 to 90,000 bales of 300 pounds each; and the cotton factories in the latter year were estimated to employ 100,000 operatives. The growth continued thereafter, as may be gathered from the estimate that the number of spindles in the country quadrupled between 1820 and 1831, and the number of factory looms increased tenfold.[31] The increase in cotton manufacturing was typical of manufacturing in general. Figures of the Census, admitted to be imperfect, but representing the only statistical information available, made the total value of the manufactured product under $53,000,000 in 1820, over $483,000,000 in 1840.[32] With less exaggeration the Census of Occupations shows an increase in the percentage of working population engaged in manufacturing and mechanical pursuits from 12.1 in 1820 to 14.6 in 1840.[33]

With the increase in manufactures came an increase in immigration. No statistics of immigration were kept before 1820, but it is estimated that from 1783 to 1820, a period of 37 years, about 250,000 persons entered the country.[34] In the single decade following, 1820–1830, over 150,000 entered, and in the decade 1830–1840, nearly 600,000.[35] Immigration naturally increased the general demand for land, more than internal migration, since the latter always involved a diminution of the pressure in the East as fast as the pressure grew upon the West. But immigration also had the effect of adding to the factory population of the industrial centers, and of introducing radical ideas which were not found among the land-owning farmer class, from whose families most of the factory population had hitherto been drawn.

Together with the demand for western lands went a demand for additional means of transportation to give access to them. Important facts of this period were the growth of shipping on the Great Lakes and the construction of the Erie Canal, finished in 1825. Somewhat later the first railroads were built, and although their mileage was still very small at the close of the period, and the roads comparatively short, yet they all contributed towards expanding the market and therefore making possible a greater territorial division of labor. This in turn made the investment of capital in industrial enterprises more profitable and led to the differentiation of the capitalist class from the wage-earning class. It was in the early part of this period, therefore, that the beginnings of the modern labor movement are found, and it is significant that many of its demands related to land.

CONFLICTING VIEWS ON LAND POLICY

On October 25, 1828, the *Mechanics' Free Press* published a memorial which was to be presented to Congress, and which demanded that public lands should be given to

[31] Clark, *History of Manufactures in the United States* (1929), I, 535, 538, 544.

[32] United States Census, 1900, *Manufactures*, VII, l, li, lii, Tables B and D, printing tables compiled by the Treasury in 1855.

[33] Whelpton, "Occupational Groups in the United States, 1820–1920," in *Journal of the American Statistical Association*, XXI, 340, Sept. 1926.

[34] Hall, *Immigration and its Effects upon the United States* (2d ed., 1913), 4, quoting Bureau of Statistics, *Quarterly Report*, No. 2, p. 7, series 1892–1893.

[35] Immigration Commission, "Statistical Review of Immigration, 1820–1910," in *Abstract of Reports* (*Senate Document*, 61 Cong., 3 sess., No. 747, 1911), 1, 57.

settlers without payment. The plan was to give to each settler a perpetual lease free from rent, but the land was to revert to the government when the lessee or his heirs failed to cultivate it or occupy it in person.[36] This petition went further than any legislation that has since been passed. If it could have been carried out, it would have made land speculation, as well as absentee land owning, impossible. No one could have realized the unearned increment from land without remaining upon it, and cultivating it. In 1833, George Henry Evans advocated a similar reform. In his journal, *The Man*, published in 1835, he said, regarding a strike of German boot-makers in Newark, "We wish all these useful mechanics success in their object, knowing as we do that they deserve it, but we tell them again, as we have often told them before, that they must look to something more radical than turn-outs to give them a just remuneration for their labor. They must look to a removal of the cause which creates a surplus of laborers in each mechanical branch, the Monopoly of the Land by speculators." As the solution, therefore, of the labor problem, Evans proposed that the lands should "no longer be sold, but that any man, unpossessed of land, should be allowed to take possession of a certain portion of the unappropriated domain for the purpose of cultivation, and, to prevent speculation, that no one should be allowed to hold more than a certain portion."[37] We have, therefore, in these radical labor movements the germ of the later land policy of the United States, as embodied in the homestead principle.

During the greater part of this period, however, the financial consideration was still the prevailing one among those who were in control of the government. John Quincy Adams, in his message of December 6, 1825, said: "Under the system of sales, matured as it has been by experience, and adapted to the exigencies of the times, the lands will continue as they have become, an abundant source of revenue; and when the pledge of them to the public creditor shall have been redeemed by the entire discharge of the national debt, the swelling tide of wealth with which they replenish the common Treasury may be made to reflow in unfailing streams of improvement from the Atlantic to the Pacific Ocean."[38]

The same point of view was repeated in his messages of December 4, 1827, and December 2, 1828, though in both cases he advocated leniency to debtors. In Congress, too, the social point of view was not yet strongly emphasized, though the land question was the storm center of debate, and came to involve a large number of other political and constitutional questions. This is the period in which two aspects of the land system, preemption and graduation, came more and more to be subjects of discussion. The right of preemption would have granted to a squatter on the public lands the privilege of purchasing his holding at the minimum price, free from the interference of speculators who might outbid him. The principle of graduation would have reduced the price of the poorer lands, after they had been in the market for some time without sale, and so would have facilitated settlement by people of straitened means.[39] In the South, there was a reaction against the control of the public lands by the Federal Government and a demand on the part of some of the southern politicians, like Calhoun, to have the Government retrocede the land to the States. This revived the old, indeed the peren-

[36] Commons *et al.*, *A Documentary History of American Industrial Society* (1910), V, 45.
[37] *Ibid.*, V, 46–47.
[38] Richardson, *A Compilation of the Messages and Papers of the Presidents*, II, 305.
[39] Hibbard, *A History of the Public Land Policies*, chap. xv, "Graduation of the Price of Land".

nial, controversy of American politics, between the advocates of States' rights and those of nationalization, and Webster's famous speech against Hayne arose out of a comparatively harmless resolution of Mr. Foot, instructing the committee on public lands to inquire into the expediency of limiting for a time the sale of lands. In this debate, which took place in January 1830, Senator Hayne of South Carolina stated quite plainly that he did not intend to confine himself to the merits of the resolution, but proposed to discuss the whole public land policy.[40] Among other things Hayne charged that the purpose of the Foot resolution was to prevent emigration to the West, and thus keep in the East a low and degraded population to work in the factories. He thus stood for free access to the public lands, but repudiated the idea of dividing them up among the States. Webster retorted by defending the New England States and dwelt at length upon the wisdom of the Ordinance of 1787, which prohibited slavery in the territory of the Northwest, and which he attributed to Nathan Dane of Massachusetts. This in turn led Hayne into a defense of the South and an attack upon New England, which involved a discussion not only of the land policy, but also of internal improvements, slavery (including its effect upon wealth and the character of the whites), the tariff, the War of 1812, the Hartford Convention, and State sovereignty. Thus the land question became entangled with almost all of the important social problems which interested the country down to the era of the Civil War.[41] Hayne favored on the whole a liberal policy, under which the lands would be open to settlement, while Webster laid more stress upon the importance of using the land to obtain an income. Webster, however, repudiated the idea of treating the public lands simply as a financial resource, and asserted that it was an important social consideration to get them settled.

Andrew Jackson represented the point of view of the Westerners, who wanted free access to the lands, rather than that of the labor reformers of the factory centers, who counted on the lands to solve the labor problem. With his election, we find the frontier recognized as a factor in politics. In his message of December 4, 1832, President Jackson ranked the public lands next to the public debt in importance. He stated that the western lands of the States had been ceded to the United States to meet the expenses of war and to secure harmony. These purposes having been accomplished "it is in the discretion of Congress to dispose of them in such way as best to conduce to the quiet, harmony, and the general interest of the American people." "It seems to me," he continued, "to be our true policy that the public lands shall cease as soon as practicable to be a source of revenue, and that they be sold to settlers in limited parcels at a price barely sufficient to reimburse to the United States the expense of the present system and the cost arising under our Indian compacts."

While Jackson thus brought out the point of view of social harmony, the sectional point of view also influenced him, for he said in the same message: "The adventurous and hardy population of the West, besides contributing their equal share of taxation under our impost system, have in the progress of our Government, for the lands they occupy, paid into the Treasury a large proportion of $40,000,000, and of the revenue received therefrom but a small part has been expended amongst them." It was "to afford to every American citizen of enterprise the opportunity of securing an independ-

[40] Gales and Seaton, *Register of Debates*, VI, pt. i, 31 *et seq.*

[41] For a full discussion of the political controversies connected with the public lands, see Wellington, *Political and Sectional Influence of Public Lands, 1828–1842* (1914).

ent freehold" that the President advocated abandoning the idea of securing a revenue from the public lands.[42]

The same idea was expressed by Martin Van Buren in his message of December 5, 1837, when he said: "A policy which should be limited to the mere object of selling the lands for the greatest possible sum of money, without regard to higher considerations, finds but few advocates." He thought that, while the policy should always be a prudent one, "yet its leading object ought to be the early settlement and cultivation of the lands sold, and that it should discountenance, if it can not prevent, the accumulation of large tracts in the same hands, which must necessarily retard the growth of the new States or entail upon them a dependent tenantry and its attendant evils."[43] President Van Buren enlarged upon the details of the plan which he had proposed in the same message, and among other things advocated a graduation of the price so as to make it proportional to the value of the lands, instead of having all the lands, good and bad, put in at one price. He pointed out the difficulties that had arisen from the fact that people had settled upon lands without any legal right, and showed that Congress had been obliged to make special laws providing for them. "This course of legislation tends to impair public respect for the laws of the country. Either the laws to prevent intrusion upon the public lands should be executed, or, if that should be impracticable or inexpedient, they should be modified or repealed."[44] He accordingly recommended a general preemption law for the benefit of those who had occupied public lands since the last preemption law, together with the preparatory steps towards the graduation of the price of the public lands. These recommendations were repeated in the message of December 3, 1838, and again, December 2, 1839.[45]

ESTABLISHMENT OF THE PRINCIPLE OF PREEMPTION

After many years of discussion, in which bills were vetoed by the President or rejected by one of the Houses, Clay's distribution bill became law, September 4, 1841. This provided that, after deducting 10 per cent of the net proceeds of the sales of public lands within eight of the western States, all the net proceeds, subsequent to December 31, 1841, should be divided, *pro rata*, among the twenty-six States and three Territories, and the District of Columbia, according to population. At the same time, "State-selections" to the amount of 500,000 acres were granted for internal improvements to each new State that should be admitted.[46] This was a political rather than a social measure. More important from the point of view of this study was the incorporation in the same act of the preemption principle. This was not a new idea, and, indeed, had already been under discussion many times in Congress.[47] Eighteen acts involving the principle of preemption were passed in all, but generally of limited application, either applying to individual settlers or to particular States or Territories. A general act was passed May 29, 1830, but only for a year.[48] The general provisions of the preemption

[42] Richardson, *A Compilation of the Messages and Papers of the Presidents*, II, 600.
[43] *Ibid.*, III, 384–385.
[44] *Ibid.*, III, 388–389.
[45] *Ibid.*, III, 496, 536.
[46] United States, *Statutes at Large*, V, 453–458.
[47] Hibbard, *A History of the Public Land Policies*, 144 *et seq.*; Sato, *History of the Land Question in the United States*, 418.
[48] United States, *Statutes at Large*, IV, 420–421, chap. ccvii; Sato, *History of the Land Question in the United States*, 419.

act of September 4, 1841, were as follows: Any head of a family, widow, or single person over the age of twenty-one who was a citizen or had declared his or her intention of becoming one, and who was not the owner of 320 acres, could enter the public lands on condition of actual residence and improvement. The maximum area that he could take was 160 acres, and he was allowed for final proof and payment a period of twelve months.[49] The land was to be had at the minimum price, but later, when the transcontinental railroads were built, the price was doubled for the land lying within the ribbon granted to them. Preemption did not thus imply a free gift but it did imply more liberal terms than the earlier acts, and it implied actual residence and improvement.

LAND POLICY AND PARTY POLITICS, 1841–1862

The agitation of the land question was active during the twenty years following the passage of the Preemption Act, but it was involved with, and to a certain extent eclipsed by the slavery question, which dominated political controversy during this period. The provision of the Ordinance of the Northwest Territory of 1787, which prohibited slavery, did not apply to the newer acquisitions of the United States. Although this provision was supported in the eighteenth century by people from both the North and the South, the increase in the slave power prevented it sixty years later from gaining the support of Congress. The Wilmot Proviso, which was brought up in 1846, and aimed at prohibiting slavery in the territory to be acquired from Mexico, though passed by the House, reached the Senate too late to be acted upon, and the same provision also failed, when an attempt was made to apply it to Oregon.[50] The question as to the mode in which the public lands should be disposed of had to give way before the greater question, whether slavery should be permitted upon these lands. Thus the land question through its connection with slavery was brought into the field of party politics, and the Free Soil Democracy was formed in 1848. Its motto was "Free Soil, Free Speech, Free Labor, and Free Men" and it declared in section 14 of its platform: "That the free grant to actual settlers * * * * of reasonable portions of the public lands, under suitable limitations, is a wise and just measure of public policy, which will promote in various ways the interests of all the States of this Union."[51] It nominated as its candidates for the Presidency and Vice-Presidency Martin Van Buren and Charles Francis Adams. The movement for free grants had actually begun in Congress the year before, Mr. Thomasson of Kentucky having introduced in 1845 a bill granting 40 acres free to settlers who were heads of families. A number of other bills were introduced during the next Congress, but they received no consideration.[52] Among these bills was one introduced by Horace Greeley which would have given 40 acres to a single person, or 80 acres to the head of a family, on condition of settlement and occupancy during seven years.[53]

[49] United States, *Statutes at Large*, V, 455–458, secs. 10, 15.
[50] Johnston, *A History of American Politics* (ed. of 1910), 151–152.
[51] Houghton, *Conspectus of the History of Political Parties* (1880), 41–42.
[52] Sanborn, "Some Political Aspects of Homestead Legislation," in *American Historical Review*, VI, 27–28, Oct. 1900.
[53] Greeley, "The First Homestead Bill", in *Magazine of American History*, XVII, 164–165, Jan. 1887.

In 1852, the Free Soil party went so far as to lay down the proposition "That all men have a natural right to a portion of the soil; and that as the use of the soil is indispensable to life, the right of all men to the soil is as sacred as their right to life itself." It accordingly demanded, "that the public lands of the United States should not be sold to individuals nor granted to corporations, but should be held as a sacred trust for the benefit of the people, and should be granted in limited quantities, free of cost, to landless settlers."[54] Its candidates were John P. Hale and George F. Julian. This party was not yet strong enough to carry a national election. But it was rapidly gaining in strength and finally evolved into the Republican party which set up as its candidates in 1856 John C. Fremont and William L. Dayton. The contest in Kansas so occupied the minds of the people, that it apparently crowded out the question of land policy in the platform of that year. But the land question was not forgotten in Congress. For a series of years preceding 1854, a homestead bill had annually passed the House, only to be defeated in the Senate. Early in the session which began in 1857, the subject was introduced in the Senate but postponed after a short discussion. In the next session of the same Congress another homestead bill passed the House by a vote of 120 to 76, but on February 17, 1859, the Senate, which was evenly divided, was committed to postponing the matter through the casting vote of the Vice-President, Breckenridge.[55]

A compromise bill finally passed both houses, but was vetoed by President Buchanan, June 22, 1860, partly on constitutional grounds, partly on grounds of partiality. He asserted that if the newcomers could acquire land for nothing, or at an insignificant price, they would lower the price of real estate already held. He thought the bill also to be unjust to the older States, because it would deprive them of their just proportion of the public revenue. Buchanan further objected that it would open the way to speculation; and that it would not offer the same privileges both to native and naturalized citizens; that the government would be deprived of a source of revenue.[56]

Buchanan and his party were, however, doomed to defeat, and the Republican party carried the election in 1860, with a platform which demanded "the passage by Congress of the complete and satisfactory homestead measure which has already passed the House."[57] The election of Lincoln in that year meant, not only the outbreak of Civil War, but also an important step in our land policy. A new homestead bill was introduced into the House, July 8, 1861, was passed by both houses, and was signed by the President May 20, 1862. At last the actual settler was given free of charge the land on which to found a home.

INDEPENDENT CONTROL OF PUBLIC LANDS BY TEXAS

The cession to the United States of the western lands which some of the original States had carried over from the colonial period, and the subsequent acquisition of vast additional areas, made the Federal Government the principal owner of unsettled tracts, and, therefore, the chief authority in determining on what terms, if at all, Government land should pass into private ownership. The bulk of the land which has been taken up by individual proprietors during the past century and a quarter has thus been

[54] Houghton, *Conspectus of the History of Political Parties*, 44.
[55] Sanborn, "Some Political Aspects of Homestead Legislation", 31–33.
[56] Richardson, *A Compilation of the Messages and Papers of the Presidents*, V, 608–614.
[57] Houghton, *Conspectus of the History of Political Parties*, sec. 13, p. 50.

taken from the domain of the United States. Nevertheless, there is an important exception to this general statement. The State of Texas, covering an area larger than that of some first class European powers, has from the beginning been the owner of the public lands within its boundaries, and has, therefore, determined its own policy with regard to them.

SPANISH POLICY IN TEXAS

The history of the land policy of Texas[58] is especially instructive on account of the fact that in some respects it anticipated, and may have served as a model for, the land policy of the United States. Texas is also interesting in that it forms the most notable exception to the general rule that the institutions of the United States are of English origin. Just as the legal foundations of Louisiana are French, so those of Texas are Spanish. From the beginning, liberal donations of land and large outlays from the royal treasury[59] were made by the Spanish government in order to encourage the colonization and settlement of its American possessions in Texas. Elaborate laws were proclaimed which prescribed the mode of government for the new colonies, and which set forth in minute detail the plans whereby meritorious citizens were to be given large quantities of land and were to be protected in the enjoyment of their property rights. An offer was made to distribute houses, lots, and lands to all those who would settle on new land.[60] According to this law, a distinction was made between gentlemen (*escuderos*) and laborers (*poenes*) or those of inferior merit, and the size of the grants was graduated according to the qualifications and services of the grantees. Settlers were required to build on their lots, to live in their houses, to clear and cultivate the arable lands and to stock the parts designated as pasture lands. After these obligations had been fulfilled and the settlers had lived on their land four years, they were authorized to dispose of their grants freely as their own property. Again in 1776 a new decree was issued by the king according to which he placed special officers in charge of these settlements, directed them to encourage the settlers to sow, raise and prepare flax and hemp, and authorized them to make a distribution of his lands, if they should deem it necessary, in order to accomplish this important object.[61]

The Spanish government endeavored to establish permanent settlements in Texas because it sincerely hoped to Christianize the Indians and establish the Catholic religion in America. In addition to this it hoped to derive a revenue from the use of its public lands. These two purposes, religious and financial, were the incentives for all its colonizing activity.[62]

The most important form of settlement was the mission, which was composed principally of a small group of priests and a number of Indians, who were gathered within its walls to receive instruction in the forms of the Catholic religion, and in agriculture and the commonest arts and industries. Other forms of settlement, often closely allied

[58] This account of Texas land policy is based upon a monograph, *The Public Land System of Texas, 1823–1910*, written for the Carnegie Institution of Washington by Reuben McKitrick, and published in University of Wisconsin *Bulletin* No. 905, Economics and Political Science Series, IX, 1–172. Considerable passages are reproduced verbally.
[59] Garrison, *Texas, a Contest of Civilizations* (1903), 87–88.
[60] McKitrick, *The Public Land System of Texas*, 26; Sayles, *Early Laws of Texas* (1888), I, 17–19.
[61] Sayles, *Early Laws of Texas*, I, 37–41.
[62] See Garrison, *Texas*, 53-66; and Sayles, *Early Laws of Texas*, I, 30, 37–41.

with the mission, were the *presidio* or the military post and the *pueblo* or civil community.

Spanish efforts to build up permanent settlements in Texas were a failure. In all, twenty-five missions and presidios were established; but when the Anglo-Americans began to enter Texas early in the nineteenth century, only three remained.[63] The reason for this failure is found in the fact that the efforts of the government were directed toward establishing, supporting and protecting missions instead of developing civil communities capable of supporting and protecting themselves. Spain sent missionaries, explorers, and soldiers to Texas, but never succeeded, in spite of the large inducements that were offered, in enlisting the services of the actual settler. The failure of Spanish colonization has been explained in the significant statement that Spain neither took care of the colonists nor taught them how to take care of themselves.[64]

The history of Texas, like that of many of the other Spanish possessions, was a turbulent one during the first part of the nineteenth century. The period of unrest led to the independence of Mexico (including what is now the State of Texas) in 1821, though it was not until 1824 that a permanent government in Mexico was organized. In 1836, Texas declared its independence of Mexico, adopting a constitution of its own, and joined the American Union in 1845. Thus all of its legislation down to that time was passed independently of the authority of the United States. It was not, however, independent of the people of the United States, for many adventurers settled in the territory, and the legislation that was enacted was, therefore, influenced in part by the Spanish tradition, in part by the ideas of those who migrated from the United States. This migration began in 1821 when Moses Austin, formerly a citizen of the United States, obtained a contract from the Spanish government which authorized him to establish a colony of 300 settlers in Texas, to grant lands to them, and to receive a grant of premium lands for himself as a payment for his services.[65] Before the formalities of making the contract had been completed, Moses Austin died, but the work which he had begun was taken up by his son, Stephen Fuller Austin. The Spanish governor of Texas asked the latter to prepare a plan for the distribution of lands to the colonists, and the plan which he presented in writing virtually became the principle of the later Mexican colonization laws. Austin encountered a great deal of difficulty, however, in the unsettled conditions of the government which followed the overthrow of Spanish authority in Mexico. He was compelled to visit the City of Mexico and to remain there and work his contract through all the successive changes in government outlined in the preceding paragraph until he finally secured its approval by the recognized authorities of the republic in 1824.

MEXICAN COLONIZATION LAWS

The members of Austin's colony finally received their lands in accordance with the colonization law of 1823.[66] But since the same decree, which made this law applicable

[63] Yoakum, *History of Texas* (1856), I, 53–64; Garrison, *Texas*, 65.

[64] Garrison, *Texas*, 99.

[65] For full account of Austin's negotiations in obtaining his contract, see White, *A New Collection of Laws, Charters, and Local Ordinances . . . Laws of Mexico and Texas* (1839), I, 559–586, and various laws and decrees of Spain, Mexico, and the State of Coahuila and Texas immediately following.

[66] An English translation of this law may be found, *Ibid.*, I, 588; Sayles, *Early Laws of Texas*, I, 42; Gammel, *Laws of Texas* (1898), I, 27.

to Austin's colony, suspended it with reference to all other colonies, the new Congress passed another general colonization law which merely adapted the principles of the former one to the new form of government.[67] The act of August 18, 1824, expressed the purpose of the government to colonize the territories of the republic, and applied to all those lands of the nation which were not the property of individuals, corporations, or towns. It extended an invitation to foreigners to settle in the State and promised security for their persons and property, if they would subject themselves to the law of the country. In addition to this, it offered free lands to the settlers and guaranteed the contracts which *empresarios*, contractors, might make with families so far as they were not contrary to law. Furthermore, the imposition of any tax whatsoever upon the foreigners was prohibited for a period of four years after their entrance. The duty of making such additional laws and regulations as might be necessary to accomplish this purpose was imposed upon the various State legislatures.

Pursuant to the foregoing act, the State of Coahuila and Texas enacted a colonization law which became effective March 24, 1825.[68] The State also invited foreigners to immigrate to Texas and guaranteed security to all who should do so. As a special inducement to such immigration, lands were freely offered on condition that the immigrant should present a certificate of good character, take an oath of allegiance to the Mexican government, promise to observe the Roman Catholic religion, agree to live on the land and cultivate it for a period of six years, and at the end of the six-year period pay the State a small nominal sum proportional to the class and quantity of the land received, as an acknowledgment of the grant. The land was classified in two general grades, arable and grazing. To those families whose occupation was the cultivation of the soil, one *labor* (177 acres) would be given; and to those who intended to raise stock, enough grazing land would be added to complete a *sitio* or *league* (4,428 acres). If the raising of stock were the exclusive occupation of the family, the quantity was limited to 24,000,000 square *varas* (4,251 acres). Single men were entitled to receive one fourth of the quantity allotted to a family. When they were married, their quantity would be augmented to that of a family; and if they married natives, they would receive one fourth more. The State executive was authorized to increase the quantities thus specified in the law in proportion to the family, industry, and activity of the colonists. Freedom from state taxation during a period of ten years for any purpose whatsoever, except to prevent or repel a foreign invasion, was also held out as a special inducement to colonists.

THE EMPRESARIO SYSTEM

The empresario system was a method of colonization whereby the government entered into a contract with the immigration agent to the effect that, if he would establish a colony of not less than a given number of persons within a definitely described territory and within a given time, it would furnish the land for these settlers on easy terms and pay him for his services in premium lands. In Mexico, this system had its legal basis

[67] White, *A New Collection of Laws, Charters and Local Ordinances*, I, 601; Sayles, *Early Laws of Texas*, I, 51; Gammel, *Laws of Texas*, I, 38.

[68] White, *A New Collection of Laws, Charters and Local Ordinances*, I, 602; Sayles, *Early Laws of Texas*, I, 64: Gammel, *Laws of Texas*, I, 40.

in the colonization laws of 1823 and 1825. The plan was suggested by Austin's contract, and the occasion for its adoption grew out of the economic conditions of the time. Mexico was abundantly rich in lands which had little value, either from an individual or a national point of view, unless they were occupied and used. The government could offer large inducements to foreigners to settle upon and develop its public lands, but it had no means of publishing its offers in foreign countries or of seeking out those who might emigrate and become desirable citizens.

Consequently, the law of 1825 specified that a grant of lands in the nature of a premium would be given to any man who should agree to introduce one hundred or more families at his and their own expense. The empresario or contractor was authorized to offer to all whom he might induce to immigrate the quantities of land that had been specified for other colonists. For these services the empresario would be given five sitios or leagues of grazing land and five labors of land (of which one-half should be non-irrigable) for each one hundred families, up to the limit of eight hundred in all, that he introduced and established within the State. No land whatever would be given to the empresario if he failed to introduce the minimum of one hundred families. The empresario thus became the advertising agent for the State. He went to foreign countries, particularly to the United States and to Germany, sought those individuals who he thought would make good settlers, and in a personal way presented the advantages and conditions of settlement which the Mexican nation had to offer. He did for the State what he otherwise might have done if it had seemed more economical to the Mexican Congress to employ him merely as an agent and to pay him in cash directly out of the public treasury. The empresario system, however, was a much more efficient method of colonization than this, for it made the success or failure of the colony a question of financial success or failure for the empresario. The return which he received for his efforts depended not only upon the number of colonists he introduced but also upon their character as well, because the value of the land which he received was directly affected by their stability and industry.

SPECIAL FEATURES OF THE MEXICAN COLONIZATION LAWS

Many modifications were made in the original colonization laws as outlined above, but these were only matters of detail. So far as the general principle is concerned, it remained unchanged and it was used later by the Republic of Texas. It is important to notice, however, the special provisions worked out in these laws which were intended to preserve an equitable distribution of property. The general law of 1824 prohibited anyone from acquiring more than one league of land suitable for irrigation, four leagues of arable land without facilities of irrigation, and six leagues of grazing land; eleven leagues (48,700 acres) altogether. Empresarios might acquire more than eleven leagues as premium land, but they were required to sell all the excess within a period of twelve years, otherwise the political authorities of the State were authorized to sell such excess at auction and pay the receipts, deducting the costs of the sale, to the former owner. Land could not be transferred in mortmain.

One other law relating to this subject of colonization which is of special significance was the Homestead Exemption Law of 1829.[69] This is probably the first law of its

[69] White, *A New Collection of Laws, Charters and Local Ordinances*, I, 527; Sayles, *Early Laws of Texas*, I, 77; Gammel, *Laws of Texas*, I, 220.

kind of which we have any record. It made the land of colonists and empresarios wholly exempt from seizure for the collection of debts contracted previously to the acquisition of the land, regardless of the source from which said debts may have originated. Neither could a colonist or an empresario be sued or discommoded in any way on account of such debts for a period of twelve years. After twelve years they might be sued, but they could not be obliged to pay in lands, implements, or tools. Fruits of the land or money were, then, the only things which could be seized for debt. The same principle was reenacted in the laws of the Republic of Texas in 1840,[70] and has been firmly fixed in Texas jurisprudence ever since.

The empresario system offered the solution of the problem of Mexican colonization. Two large grants were made in less than a month after the law was passed and one author in writing on this subject says that within seven years the whole map of Texas was plastered over, from the Sabine to the Nueses, with the claims of empresarios.[71] Of course, a large number of the empresarios failed to complete their contracts, but others were eminently successful. An estimate, said to be probably near the truth, gives the population of Texas in 1827 as 10,000 and another in 1830 made the number 20,000 which is five times as large as the one estimated for 1821. These figures are exclusive of Indians.[72]

The Mexican colonization laws opened the doors to the outside world and encouraged actual settlers to go to Texas. The laws also afforded an opportunity for the growth on Texas soil of a civilization which was wholly different from that of Mexico, and which was soon to wrest Texas from the Mexican nation. Though many of the settlers came from Europe, particularly Germany, most of them came from the United States. They were men of a rugged, hardy type, full of hope and determination; and though not adventurers for the mere sake of adventure, they were by no means lacking in courage. Pioneers in the true sense, they had gone to Texas not for speculation, but to establish homes, to share in the hardships as well as the benefits of this undertaking. Thus Texas was rapidly becoming the home of aggressive and industrious groups of men generally accustomed to having a voice in all matters which concerned their immediate well-being, and very much given to having their own way in the isolated Texas communities where they had been a law unto themselves during the previous decade. It was this type of citizenship with which the Mexican government came in contact when it tried more vigorously to assert its authority over the northern frontier early in the thirties. A revolution ensued, the essential cause of which was "the conflict between two inharmonious varieties of civilization, independently of any accident of Mexican policy."[73]

As the liberal land policy of Texas led indirectly to revolution and independence, the new constitution naturally dealt with the land question. There had been great abuses connected with the lavish grants of the public domain, no less than 4,870,800 acres having been granted to John T. Mason of New York, and other foreigners. For a time, therefore, the land system was suspended; but it was very important to build up the

[70] Gammel, *Laws of Texas*, II, 347.
[71] See map of Spanish Texas in 1835, which shows the location of the different empresario contracts, published in Sayles, *Early Laws of Texas*, I, *Pocket Appendix*.
[72] Garrison, *Texas*, 155–156.
[73] *Ibid.*, 108.

country, and as Texas had to compete with the cheap public lands of the United States it was forced to continue a liberal policy.

The constitution of 1836, accordingly, first defined citizenship by providing that all persons who were living in Texas on March 2, 1836, should be citizens of the Republic, with the exception of Negroes and Indians. It also gave the privileges of citizenship to free white persons who would move into Texas, and live there for six months, provided they would swear that they intended to reside there permanently, and that they would be true to the Republic. Those who had left the country to avoid taking part in the struggle for independence were, however, excluded.

TERMS OF LAND GRANTS

The constitution then specified that every citizen living in Texas who was the head of a family should be entitled to one league and one labor of land (4,605 acres) and that every single man over seventeen years of age should be entitled to one-third of a league. Those citizens who, previous to the adoption of the constitution, had received only one league according to Mexican laws, or, as single men, only one-fourth of a league, were also entitled to such additional quantities as would make for them, respectively, one league and one labor, and one-third of a league. After having thus defined the qualifications of citizenship and having thus specified the quantities of land to which each citizen was entitled, the constitution was very explicit in stating that: "The citizens of the Republic shall not be compelled to reside on the land, but shall have these lines plainly marked."[74] Aliens were prohibited from holding land in the Republic except by titles emanating directly from the government. Those aliens, however, who should acquire land by direct inheritance were guaranteed a reasonable time in which to take possession of and to dispose of such land. Actual settlers and occupants of the soil were given the right in locating their land to include their improvements in preference to all other claimants.

A special law was passed in 1836 to establish a general land office and to provide for liberal "conditional grants", which were practically equivalent to homestead rights. Any free white person who was the head of a family and who arrived in the Republic of Texas within the time specified in the law was entitled to a "conditional grant" of 1,280 acres. If the immigrant was a single man, he was entitled to 640 acres on the same terms. The conditions were that the grantee should remain and permanently reside within the Republic and do and perform all the duties required of other like citizens for a period of three years. The Board of Land Commissioners was directed to issue to this class of claimants a certificate for their claims as soon as proof was offered which would show the amount of land located and the time of arrival within the Republic. Subsequent laws were passed which enabled all immigrants who arrived within the Republic before January 1, 1842, to acquire land in accordance with this method, except that the size of the tracts was reduced to 640 and 320 acres. The last of these acts modified the conditions of the grant to the extent that the claimant must reside on the land three years and cultivate at least ten acres, but even this clause was repealed February 4, 1842.[75]

[74] Thorpe, *Charters, Constitutions and Organic Laws*, VI, 3540.
[75] Sayles, *Early Laws of Texas*, I, 512.

In spite of the inducements offered to settlers in the shape of free lands, the population of Texas was still small in proportion to its area, and for a few years it attempted to draw immigrants by means of the contract system. Under the act of 1841, the President was authorized to contract with W. S. Peters and associates for the importation of immigrants, and similar measures were adopted in 1842, but in 1844 Congress repealed all of these acts, and this particular method, which was not unlike the empresario system of stimulating settlement, failed. A further step was taken when Texas introduced the preemption system in the act of 1845.

PREEMPTION AND HOMESTEAD LEGISLATION IN TEXAS

Preemption never had the historical setting in Texas that it had in the United States. It was a fully developed principle of land legislation when it was first enacted in the land laws of the Republic and of the new Commonwealth. In fact, the principle was probably borrowed directly from the United States; since the first preemption law of any importance in Texas was passed within four years after such a law had been incorporated into the general land system of the Federal Government. The enactment of such legislation was the result of a general sentiment prevailing in Texas at that time, to the effect that a law which would prevent any mode of acquiring a right to lands other than by occupancy would be a strong inducement to those who wished to obtain lands to settle upon them, and thereby give to the frontiers a most needed additional strength.[76]

The payment of a purchase price was not such an important consideration in the preemption system of Texas as in the United States. For the most part, lands could be be acquired for fifty cents an acre. Settlement and cultivation were the essential features. The adoption of the preemption and homestead principles of land settlement marked the relaxation of the government from those aggressive methods of direct colonization embodied in the laws authorizing headright grants and immigration contracts, and indicated the assumption of a more passive attitude toward this subject.

Within thirty days after a settler had moved upon a piece of land, he was required to file with the surveyor of the county or district in which the land was situated a sworn written application which would designate the land he wished to claim. The application also stated that he claimed the land for himself in good faith; that he did not own 160 acres of land in the State; that he had no other residence on land of his own; that he had actually settled upon the land which he claimed; and that he believed it to be "vacant and unappropriated" public domain. Failure to make this application within the time prescribed would forfeit all rights to claim the land. This application served as a notice to the surveyor to survey the land and keep a record of the claim. Usually a preemptor could not claim more than 160 acres, though under the law of 1845 he might claim 320. The privilege of preemption, together with the improvements on the land, could be sold to another actual settler and occupant. As soon as the assignee had completed the requirements of the law, he was entitled to the patent just as the original claimant would have been. When the preemptor or his assignee had completed a residence of three years on the land, he was required to present an affidavit to that

[76] House Committee on Public Lands, *Report*, published in *Houston Telegraph and Texas Register*, 1839.

effect from two respectable witnesses and pay such dues and fees as were specified by the law, whereupon a patent would be issued to him. Details of the law were changed from time to time, but the principle remained unaffected. With the exception of four years intervening between February 13, 1854, and February 10, 1858, land could be acquired in Texas by right of preemption from 1845 till 1889. At the last mentioned date all preemption laws were repealed.[77]

As in the United States, so in Texas, the final stage in the development of a system for settling lands was represented by the homestead system, but in this, as in the system of homestead exemptions, Texas anticipated the United States, for what was practically its first homestead law was enacted in 1836, as a part of the act to establish a General Land Office. The liberal provisions of this act are given above.

[77] For a brief review of the preemption laws of Texas and citations to separate acts, see Sayles, *A Treatise on the Laws of Texas relating to Real Estate* (1890–1892), I, 288–301.

CHAPTER XI

LAWS REGULATING THE RELATION OF DEBTOR AND CREDITOR

HOMESTEAD EXEMPTION[1]

The possession of large domains by the Federal Government necessitated some policy with regard to the distribution of land, and this ultimately resulted in the establishment of the homestead system. The same general motives which brought about the establishment of the homestead system also led to the establishment of the homestead exemption system. It is not enough to carve the public domain up into small farms. The small owner must also be protected against conditions which may result in his dispossession. The history of the world shows that this is a real danger. The disturbed condition of Europe in the early Middle Ages led the small holder to surrender his land to the military leader for the sake of protection. It was mainly through the power of capital that the wealthier classes of Rome got possession of large tracts of land, far larger than were allowed by law, and dispossessed the small owners. It was to correct this abuse that Tiberius Gracchus proposed and carried his agrarian law of 133 B.C.

On the other hand, the history of the world also has examples of prophylactic legislation, intended to prevent these evils from arising. The most familiar case is the elaborate system of the early Jewish polity, providing specifically that the land was not to be held permanently in absolute ownership. "The land shall not be sold for ever; for the land is Mine," is the phrase used in the Bible.[2] The Year of Jubilee in which "ye shall return every man unto his possession, and ye shall return every man unto his family" was one of the means of carrying this into effect.[3] Another provision was the right of redeeming a dwelling house in a walled city within a year after it had been sold.[4]

The homestead exemption laws of the States are to be distinguished from the homestead laws of the Federal Government and of Texas mentioned later. Indeed, in spite of the similarity of names, and of general purpose, they were quite different in their immediate operation. The homestead right under the Federal law of 1862 was intended to make it easy for a man to obtain land; the homestead exemption was intended to make it difficult for him to lose it. Thus homestead exemption was a device for the protection of debtors, and for securing the means of livelihood to their families. The American system seems, however, to represent a reaction against the hardships

[1] This account of the Homestead Exemption Laws is based upon an unpublished monograph written for the Carnegie Institution by J. Harding Underwood.

[2] *Leviticus*, XXV, 23.

[3] *Leviticus*, XXV, 10.

[4] *Leviticus*, XXV, 29. For a full discussion of the social polity of the Jews, see Ruhland, *System der Politischen Oekonomie* (1903), I, 218 *et seq.*

which had grown up under the English law rather than a conscious attempt to copy the institutions of the Jews or of other nations of antiquity.

ENGLISH LAW OF DEBT

In the Middle Ages the English policy in this regard was much more liberal than it became during the eighteenth and nineteenth centuries. Under feudalism, the economic and military importance of fixed tenantry was too great to allow the possibility of the land being taken from the lord by execution against the lesser holder. On the other hand, the personal service of the vassal to the lord forbade the possibility that this service should be diminished by imprisonment for debt. But with the decline of feudalism, the increasing economic independence of the subject and the detachment of persons from fixed relations to the land made execution against the person possible, without serious impairment of the rights of the lord. The increasing importance of the commercial classes gradually brought about greater strictness in the execution for debt, first against the person, and later against the land, and thus operated a modification of the common law to the detriment of the debtor. Thus imprisonment for debt came to be a common fate of impecunious debtors. Similarly, by a series of statutes, the power of the creditor over the land of the debtor increased. The Statute Merchant (1285) provided that the debtor in the course of trade might enter into a recognizance before the mayor of London or before the church warden of another city. Upon default, the body and goods of the debtor were subject to execution. The plaintiff might take all of his land and hold it until the debts were cancelled from the profits. The Statute Staple (1354) permitted such recognizance to be made before the chief magistrate of any staple mart. Later (1532), the same provisions were extended to all of the subjects of the kingdom. Thus private property triumphed over feudal incidents, and in the height of a commercial régime the person was frequently punished more for debt than for crime. It was not, however, until 1833 that the interests in land of a decedent became assets for the payment of his debts. The creditor was permitted to make sale of the lands of the debtor in order to satisfy his debts by 1 and 2 Victoria, c.110.[5]

SPANISH LAW AS APPLIED IN TEXAS

Historically, the homestead exemption system of the United States had its origin in the new State of Texas. Its roots lie, therefore, more in Spanish than in English law, though in a principle of Spanish law which was not unlike the early mediaeval principle of English law. The Spanish law exempted a large list of articles from execution, among them, things designated for divine worship, implements and beasts of husbandry, tools of artificers, wearing apparel and things necessary for daily use; also the houses, arms, and horses of knights and noblemen, except for a debt to the Crown.[6] The point of view, however, of most of these exemptions was that of maintaining the existing status of society, and the means of livelihood of the people, while the homestead exemption law was at first a device for encouraging immigration. As already explained in

[5] For other details of the progress of English law, see Folz, "Exemption Laws and Public Policy", in *The American Law Register*, LIII (O. S.), XLIV (N.S.), 722–737, Dec. 1905.
[6] *Institutions of the Civil Law of Spain* (prefixed to White, *A New Collection of Laws, Charters and Local Ordinances*, I, 322), Bk. III, title x, §6.

Chapter X,[7] Texas adopted the empresario system of settling the country even before it broke away from Mexico. After its independence it provided in 1829 that, in order to attract immigrants, lands acquired under the colonization law should not be subject to the payment of debts contracted previous to the acquisition of these lands, and that for twelve years the colonists could not be incommoded by the judges on account of such debts. The law of 1839 went a step further, and exempted a specific amount of land not merely from the payment of debts contracted previous to settlement, but from all debts. This law limited the exemption to 50 acres of land or one town lot, including the homestead, and improvements not exceeding $500 in value, also household furniture up to $200; implements of husbandry up to $50; tools, apparatus, and books belonging to the trade or profession of a citizen; a certain amount of livestock; and one year's provisions.[8]

EXEMPTION LAWS OF THE STATES

From this beginning exemptions went on increasing in importance, and received the sanction of the Constitution of 1845 (art. vii, sec. 22), which gave the legislature the right "to protect, by law, from forced sale a certain portion of the property of all heads of families." It then specified that, "The homestead of a family, not to exceed two hundred acres of land, (not included in a town or city, or any town or city lot or lots), in value not to exceed two thousand dollars, shall not be subject to forced sale for any debts hereafter contracted; nor shall the owner, if a married man, be at liberty to alienate the same, unless by the consent of the wife."[9] The dates at which the other States followed the example of Texas, and the main facts with regard to the amount exempted are shown in a table on page 151, in which, for the convenience of the student, the survey is extended to cover the period after 1860.

The chronology of legislation shows that the homestead exemption principle spread to the States of the Union before Texas had been admitted, so that, although the system originated in Texas, Mississippi, whose law goes back to 1841, was the first State in the Union to adopt the system of homestead exemptions. The next States to follow were also southern States, Alabama having passed a law in 1843, and Florida in 1845. Connecticut followed in 1847 with a law which was repealed after a year's trial. The movement now spread to the West, Wisconsin and Michigan taking up the matter in 1848, while two New England States, Maine and Vermont, followed in 1849. If we summarize the progress of the homestead exemption principle down to the Civil War, we find that eighteen States in the North (not counting Connecticut) had adopted it, as against eight States in the South. If we look at the progress with regard to time, it appears that, of the twenty-six States involved: two adopted the system between 1839 and 1842; twenty adopted the system between 1843 and 1852; four adopted the system between 1853 and 1860. Thus the decade 1843 to 1852 was the period in which the bulk of the States first introduced the exemption principle.

The movement, therefore, came to a head in the period in which many other movements for equalizing conditions were active. It represented in a modified form the

[7] See p. 142.
[8] Gammel, *Laws of Texas*, II, 126.
[9] Thorpe, *American Charters, Constitutions and Organic Laws*, VI, 3561–3562.

TABLE I
Exemption Laws of the States

	Year	Amount	Year	Amount	Year	Amount
I. Northern States						
Connecticut (repealed)	1847	$500	1860	$700	1885	$1000
Wisconsin	1848	40 acres	1901	value limit $5000		
Michigan	1848	1500				
Maine	1849	500				
Vermont	1849	500				
Pennsylvania	1849	300				
Ohio	1849	500	1869	1000		
Iowa	1849	500				
New York	1850	1000				
New Hampshire	1851	500				
California	1851	5000				
Massachusetts	1851	500	1855	800		
Illinois	1851	1000				
Indiana	1852	300	1879	600		
New Jersey	1852	1000				
Kansas	1855	750	1859	1000	1868	160 acres
Nebraska	1855	500	1867	160 acres	1879	$2000 limit
Minnesota	1858	{80 acres {$1000	1866	$1500		
Washington	1860	500	1881	1000	1895	$2000
II. Southern States:						
Texas	1839	500	1845	2000	1870	5000
Mississippi	1841	1500	1865	4000	1882	3000
Georgia	1845	50 acres	1868	1600		
Alabama	1843	400	1877	2000		
Florida	1845	200	1866	1000		
Louisiana	1852	1000	1865	2000		
Tennessee	1852	500	1868	1000		
Arkansas	1852	160 acres	1871	5000		
West Virginia			1864	500	1872	1000
Kentucky			1865	1000		
Virginia			1867	2000		
North Carolina			1868	1500		
South Carolina			1868	1000		
III. The later laws:						
North Dakota	1862	80 acres	1877	160 acres or one in town		
			1891	160 acres or two in town, $5000 limit		
South Dakota	1862	80 acres	1877	160 acres or one in town		
			1890	$5000		
Idaho			1864	3000	1874	$5000
Arizona			1864	5000	1901	2500
Montana			1864	3000	1869	2500
Nevada			1865	5000		
Colorado			1868	2000		
Oregon			1868	1000	1893	1500
Wyoming			1869	1500		
Utah			1870	$1000 and $250 for each other member of the family		
			1896	$1500 and $500 for wife and $250 for each child		
New Mexico			1875	1000		
Oklahoma			Ind. Ter. laws, $2500		1907	$5000

principle already expressed by George Henry Evans as the motto of the *Working Man's Advocate*, in 1829, when he said, "All children are entitled to equal education; all adults to equal property; and all mankind to equal privileges."[10] The crisis of 1837 and the losses through wild-cat banking and speculation in western lands doubtless reinforced the humanitarian movement and the tendency towards greater democracy, in bringing about the enactment of these laws for the benefit of the debtor. But the immediate occasion for the exemption laws naturally differed from time to time and place to place. In Texas, the main point of view in the beginning was to secure the settlement of the country. In the decade in which the system spread through the North and West, the immediate motive was to protect the debtor class and prevent families from sinking into hopeless poverty.

LAW OF MECHANICS' LIEN[11]

Labor protection in the United States really begins with mechanics' lien laws, but the labor problem at the time in which these laws were introduced was very different from the labor problem of the second half of the nineteenth century. At the end of the eighteenth century there were comparatively few capitalistic enterprises. The skilled mechanic passed easily from the position of a wage receiver to that of a small capitalist, owning manager, or contractor, who might still work with his own hands, and who was not separated by any great gulf from his journeymen. The same law, therefore, was made to cover both the journeyman and the contractor, and the principle of mechanics' liens, like the principle of homestead exemptions, was introduced, not so much for the benefit of the "proletarian" as for representatives of the great middle class.

A mechanics' lien is, in general, the right of a mechanic, or of someone who has furnished labor or materials, in the object produced by his aid. It may apply either to real property or to personal. It is what the Roman jurists called a *jus in re*, as distinguished from a *jus in personam*. In other words, it gives the claimant not only the right to sue for what is owing him, but the right to hold the property itself as security for the debt. This is a system which has developed in the United States independently of, and in contrast to, the English common law. The common law, being based upon the feudal system, naturally emphasized the rights of the landowner as against those of other persons. The American system has in this respect much greater resemblance to the Roman law. The latter recognized the lien upon the building of one who had loaned money to repair a house as a right which arose without any special contract. It also recognized a special *privilegium*, or preference, arising out of *versio in rem*, which related particularly to the advances made in order to acquire, maintain, or repair ships or houses.[12] Whether our mechanics' liens have any direct connection with the Roman law or not is questionable. It is barely possible that such a connection can be traced through Thomas Jefferson, who was a member of the committee which recommended the first mechanics' lien law in the United States, and who was more or less familiar

[10] Commons, *Documentary History of American Industrial Society*, VII, 30.

[11] The author is indebted for most of the facts in this part of the chapter to an unpublished monograph by Professor W. L. Bailey of Grinnell College.

[12] Windscheid, *Lehrbuch des Pandektenrechts* (5th ed., 1882), I, 740, 798.

with Roman law concepts in French institutions. But even if some suggestions as to methods may have come from Rome, the application of the principle undoubtedly grew out of the economic conditions of our country. "The American mechanics' and laborers' lien is as characteristic of our condition and need as that of the common law is of its place and time."[13] The common law lien was mainly upon personal property, and limited to the rights of such classes as inn-keepers, and others who had to serve the general public, though it was also extended to small tradesmen and artisans of almost every class. The mechanics' lien applied mainly to the improvement of real property, and was intended to secure the rights of those whose services or goods were needed to improve this property.

It is thus quite comparable to the homestead exemption right, although apparently opposed to it. The homestead exemption right secured the right to land and house as against claimants; the mechanics' lien secured the right of a certain class of claimants against land and house. One favored the debtor, the other the creditor. Yet both were elements in the building up of the country. The homestead right put a premium upon the acquisition and improvement of land; the mechanics' lien offered an inducement to those who were engaged to do the necessary work for the owner. Inasmuch, however, as one involved a claim on the land, the other a privilege of the landowner, the two have naturally come into conflict, and it has been necessary to decide how far the homestead exemption right is a bar to the mechanics' lien. This question has not been answered uniformly in the different States. If, however, we consider the rights of three classes, namely, the mechanic, the landowner, and the capitalist creditor, the tendency of the two principles has been to give the mechanic a certain claim upon the landowner, and the landowner a certain exemption against the capitalist creditor, so that, although the mechanic and the owner of a homestead might come into conflict, the two laws together have favored the man of moderate means as against the capitalist.

ACT OF 1791 RELATING TO THE CITY OF WASHINGTON

The history of the mechanics' lien bears out the idea that it arose out of our economic conditions, and was a part of the policy of developing the country. The first law to be passed was purely local, and applied to the still unbuilt city of Washington. It was felt to be important to have the city constructed quickly. The commissioners appointed for this purpose held a meeting, September 8, 1791, and adopted a memorial urging the Assembly of Maryland to pass an act creating a lien "in favor of the builder of any house within the City, contracted for by the peice [*sic*] or gross for his just Claim on the house and ground on which it may stand." Thomas Jefferson and James Madison were both members of this commission, and were present when the memorial was adopted. The reason for it was clearly stated in the document itself, which said: "Your memorialists also conceive . . . that it would encourage master builders to contract for the erecting and finishing houses for certain prices, agreed on, if a lien was created by law for their just Claim on the house erected and the lot of ground on which it stood."[14]

[13] Bailey, in the monograph cited above.

[14] *Proceedings of the Commissioners, 1791–95*, pp. 28, 29. The writer was indebted to Mr. A. P. C. Griffin of the Library of Congress for this transcription from the original manuscript preserved in the office of Public Buildings and Grounds under control of the District Commissioners.

In consequence of this suggestion, the legislature of Maryland, which still had jurisdiction over the area ceded to the United States for the seat of the government, included in a general act "concerning the territory of Columbia and the city of Washington," passed December 19, 1791, the following provision:

"Sec. X. AND, for the encouragement of master-builders to undertake the building and finishing houses within the said city, by securing to them a just and effectual remedy for their advances and earnings,

"BE IT ENACTED, That for all sums due and owing, on written contracts, for the building any house in the said city, or the brick work, or carpenters or joiners work thereon, the undertaker, or workmen, employed by the person for whose use the house shall be built, shall have a lien on the house and the ground on which the same is erected, as well as for the materials found by him; provided the said written contract shall have been acknowledged before one of the commissioners, a justice of the peace, or an alderman of the corporation of George-town, and recorded in the office of the clerk for recording deeds herein created, within six calendar months from the time of acknowledgement as aforesaid; and if, within two years after the last of the work is done, he proceeds in equity, he shall have remedy as upon a mortgage, or if he proceeds at law within the same time, he may have execution against the house and land, in whose hands soever the same may be; but this remedy shall be considered as additional only, nor shall, as to the land, take place of any legal incumbrance made prior to the commencement of such a claim."[15]

This act was typical in several respects. It related to the building of dwelling houses in a city, and it was of local application. The tendency, as will be seen, has been to extend the right from dwelling houses, first to other buildings, and then to other structures, and then to extend it from specifically named towns to whole States.

PENNSYLVANIA ACT OF 1803

The next act was passed by Pennsylvania in 1803. This applied only to dwelling houses and other buildings in Philadelphia, in the district of Southwark, and the township of the Northern Liberties, and it subjected these buildings to the payment of debts contracted by the owner or owners thereof for any work done or materials provided by any brickmaker, bricklayer, stone-cutter, mason, and other mechanics or material men specified at length. No mention was made in this law of the contractor as such, and it was provided that, in case the house should not sell for enough to pay the claims, they should be averaged.[16] The act was limited in its operation to three years, and the lien was to be effective for two years. This act had a precedent in a Pennsylvania act of March 27, 1784,[17] amended by act of February 9, 1793,[18] which gave to mechanics who had furnished labor or materials a lien on ships and boats built or rebuilt in the State. The Pennsylvania law became a model followed by a number of States, while the New

[15] Copy transcribed from a contemporary pamphlet in the Congressional Library, entitled *Acts passed by the General Assembly of Maryland, concerning the Territory of Columbia and the City of Washington*, 60–61; also reprinted in *The Laws of Maryland* (ed. by Kilty, 1800), II, chap. xlv, of Acts of 1791.

[16] *Acts of the General Assembly of the Commonwealth of Pennsylvania* (Thompson ed., 1803), V, 591–592.

[17] *Statutes at Large of Pennsylvania* (compiled by Mitchell and Flanders), XI, 289–291.

[18] *Ibid.*, XIV, 333.

York law, passed in 1830, emphasizing the position of the general contractor as against subcontractors and actual laborers, created another type followed by other groups of States.

DEVELOPMENT OF THE LAW OF MECHANICS' LIEN

The geographical spread of the law of mechanics' lien from its original locus presents an interesting problem to the student of the history of law. In Pennsylvania, from the first law passed in 1803 down to 1860, over thirty statutes were passed extending bit by bit the territory subject to the principle, adding every few years a county or a group of counties; the process was similar but more rapid in New York. It would be interesting to discover how close was the connection between the legislation and a ripening of the economic conditions in the territory affected.

Over the larger territory of the nation there was a similar piecemeal extension. Beginning in the Middle East, and in connection with specific cities, the mechanics' lien was adopted by the States one after another, spreading first, on the whole, towards the southwest, then to New England, and somewhat later to New York (1830)[19] and Virginia (1843).[20] It soon came to be commonly accepted in the western frontier States as a fundamental principle.

While the mechanics' lien had its origin in the desire to build up the country and to induce contractors to assist in this process, it owed its extension, at least in part, to the desire of labor leaders to improve the condition of wage receivers. Commons says on this subject: "One of the first results of the Working Men's Party was a lien law in New York good for the journeyman and laborer as well as the contractor; and this was the crude beginning of another revolution which today requires the employer to pay his laborers regularly, and in cash or equivalent, before all other creditors.[21] At a meeting of nearly three thousand mechanics and other workingmen held December 29, 1829, a series of resolutions was adopted, one of which demanded "a well constructed lien law, which would secure to thousands of our fellow-citizens that just recompense their services entitle them to, and prevent innumerable frauds being practised on the producing classes."[22] At the Lowell Convention, March 1845, it was "RESOLVED, that the present Lien Law of Massachusetts is a disgrace to the statute book, . . . enriching at the expense of honest labor, the designing and unscrupulous."[23] At the Fall River Convention, September 1845, Mr. Babcock of Boston spoke of the way in which mechanics were treated by the State Legislature when that body was petitioned from many parts of the State for a lien law, "for the protection of Mechanics against dishonest soulless contractors."[24]

The principle of the mechanics' lien, starting with a local and limited enactment, has been subject to gradual extension in respect to the area affected, the persons protected, and the structures to which it applied. The earliest laws were limited to spe-

[19] *Laws of the State of New York, 1830*, chap. 330, pp. 412–414.
[20] *Acts of the General Assembly of Virginia, 1843*, chap. 76, pp. 52–54.
[21] *Documentary History of American Industrial Society*, V, 28, 29.
[22] *Ibid.*, V, 161.
[23] *Ibid.*, VIII, 100.
[24] *Ibid.*, VIII, 123.

cific cities and their neighborhood. Then the principle spread from town to country. Rhode Island, in 1834,[25] was the first State to make the application State-wide; in many of the southern States this extension was not made until after the Civil War. The extension has affected not only those who did the work but also those with different interests in the property. Starting at first with owners in fee simple, the law has bound those with a legal or equitable title of any extent in the property.[26] In Pennsylvania, as early as 1836, in the case of *Anshutz vs. McClelland*,[27] the principle was extended to bind a lessee. Applied originally to dwelling houses, the law was made to include buildings and structures of the most varied kind. Designed originally to apply only to new construction, it was soon extended to improvements and repairs. Complaint was made in Maine that the lumbermen would cut logs and float them down to the mill without sufficient means for carrying on the business. When the logs reached their market, their value was absorbed by other claims, and the laborers discharged unpaid. The Maine law of 1848[28] accordingly gave these persons a lien on the product which was subsequently extended to analogous cases in other States.

[25] *Public Laws of the State of Rhode Island. . . . passed since the Session of the General Assembly in January 1833*, p. 829.
[26] Phillips, Samuel L., *A Treatise on the Law of Mechanics' Liens* (1874), 11.
[27] *V Watts Pennsylvania Reports*, 487.
[28] *Acts and Resolves passed by the Twenty-eighth Legislature, 1848*, chap. 72, p. 60.

CHAPTER XII

EDUCATIONAL POLICY

THE NEW ENGLAND PRECEDENT

The Ordinance of the Northwest Territory was the starting point both of the land policy and of the educational policy of the United States. It has been shown that the former had its roots in New England custom and the same is true of the latter. In a sense, the New England policy of land grants had its roots in old England. For, after the destruction of the monasteries in the sixteenth century, the schools, which had declined, were in many cases endowed with portions of the sequestrated church lands. Later, when individuals wished to endow schools, they gave them land.[1]

In New England the importance of education was recognized at the very beginning and great sacrifices were made by the early colonists to provide instruction for their children. In New Haven as early as 1641, only a little over three years after the first settlement, the General Court voted, "thatt a free schoole be set up in this towne," and the purpose was stated in 1644 to be, "for the better trayning upp of youth in this towne, that, through God's blessing they may be fitted for publique service hereafter, either in church or commonweale."[2] This phrase is almost the same as that which was used nearly sixty years later in the charter of Yale College.

The Massachusetts act of 1642 required the selectmen of every town, under penalty of a fine, to take account of the training of the children in "learning and labor," more especially "of their ability to read and understand the principles of religion and the capital lawes of the country," and an act of the same colony in 1647 made the establishment of elementary schools compulsory for towns of fifty or more householders. By 1671 all of New England except Rhode Island had made elementary education compulsory; school attendance was not required, even to the end of the colonial period, but parents or masters must undertake to supply instruction if it was not received at school.[3]

In the beginning the schools were generally supported by taxation, but before long a certain amount of land was sometimes appropriated for their support. In 1641, according to the records of Boston, Deer Island was to be improved for the maintenance of a free school for the town. In 1639 Dorchester appropriated Thompson's Island for the use of the schools.[4] As the seacoast settlements began to spread west-

[1] Schafer, *Land Grants for Education* (1902), in University of Wisconsin, *Bulletin* No. 63, Historical Series, I, 9, 10.

[2] Steiner, *The History of Education in Connecticut* (1893), in Bureau of Education, *Circular of Information* No. 2, p. 16, quoting *Records of the Colony and Plantation of New Haven*, I, 62, 210.

[3] Jernegan, *Laboring and Dependent Classes in Colonial America*, pt. ii, gives a detailed account of the colonial development.

[4] Schafer, *Land Grants for Education*, 12.

ward by the establishment of new towns, it became customary to set aside a certain tract of land for school purposes. Sometimes these grants were made by the colony as a whole. Thus in 1672, the General Court of Connecticut granted to Fairfield and New London 600 acres of land apiece "to be taken up where it may not prejudice any former grant," to be used for the benefit of a grammar school in these county towns.[5] Similar grants were made to New Haven and Hartford.

A still further development was the setting aside of special reservations in new townships. Thus, in the grant of the town of Sutton, Massachusetts, the charter provided that the grantees should settle thirty families and a minister within seven years after the end of the war with the Indians, and that they should reserve 300 acres for the first minister, 400 for the ministry, and 200 for the use of the school.[6] When Litchfield County, Connecticut, was settled, a bill was passed by the General Assembly in May 1733, setting aside seven towns in that county and providing that the money paid for this land should be used for the support of the schools in those towns that were settled. A few years later, in 1737, when arrangements were made for selling some of these towns, one fifty-third of each town was reserved for school land.[7]

While the idea of endowing schools by a grant of land was not new, the conditions under which the grants were made in New England were very different from those under which the early English grammar schools were established. In old England, the government simply gave to schools already settled land which it had confiscated. In New England, the assembly provided in advance of settlement for the endowment of schools to be created in the future, thus showing an amount of foresight in the domain of education rarely, if ever, found in the previous history of the world. Another difference is that the schools thus endowed were distinctly schools for all the people, involving in some cases, as in New Haven, gratuitous as well as public education.[8] In other words, they foreshadowed the principle of an educated democracy. This recognition of the importance of schools for the people grew out of the needs and ideals of the Congregational Church, and had its roots in Calvinism.[9] The conception of the church as a self-governing religious body, made up of persons who had voluntarily taken its covenant, and who selected their own minister, necessarily involved the education of the mass of the people. The school was as much an integral part of the New England town as was, in the early days, the church. Both were necessary to the community life, and a detailed study of individual towns shows how this New England social unit moved across the continent by a series of offshoots as the frontier was pushed westward, part of the people migrating from one New England town to establish one farther west, and each new town being in turn the mother of other towns.[10]

The New England idea was often carried out by settlements from New England in the other colonies. Thus Connecticut colonists who settled Wyoming Valley, Pennsylvania, decided in 1768 that every township should reserve 960 acres of land for the

[5] *Ibid.*, 23.
[6] *Ibid.*, 26.
[7] Steiner, *History of Education in Connecticut*, 31.
[8] Dexter, E. G., *A History of Education in the United States* (1904), 45.
[9] Carlton, *Economic Influence upon Educational Progress in the United States* (1908), in University of Wisconsin, *Bulletin* No. 221, Economics and Political Science Series, IV, 11, 18.
[10] For an interesting study of this process, see Mathews, *Expansion of New England*.

support of "the gospel ministry and the schools," and this continued until 1834, when a State school system was established.[11] Some of the other States carried out a similar idea. In 1786, the State of New York passed a law setting aside in each township one section of the unappropriated lands for the support of "gospel and schools," and one "for promoting literature," and in 1805 ordered that 500,000 acres of vacant lands should be devoted to the establishment of a permanent fund for the support of common schools.[12] In 1772, Delaware began its system of land grants for education by giving to New Castle a lot of land for a school.[13] In the South the mode of settlement made it more difficult to maintain schools and also diminished the sense of their necessity. The plantations were so far apart that it was not easy to send the children to a common school house, while, on the other hand, the plantation owners were able to arrange private instruction for their own children. Virginia made a serious attempt to provide for the education of certain classes of children—orphans, illegitimate, children of the poor—but south of Virginia there were no schools until the eighteenth century.[14]

PROVISIONS FOR EDUCATION BY THE CONFEDERATION

When the United States, still operating under the Articles of Confederation, found themselves in possession of a large domain, the idea of providing in advance of settlement for schools forced itself upon the members of Congress and was advocated by representatives of the South, as well as of New England. It was a New Englander, Timothy Pickering of Massachusetts, who suggested the plan for the proposed State to be organized in the Ohio country, and recommended that, after satisfying the just demands of the Revolutionary soldiers, the surplus lands should be disposed of for the common good, "as for laying out roads, building bridges, erecting buildings, establishing schools and academies."[15] Pickering objected to the first bill reported by Jefferson in May 1784, on the ground that there was "no provision made for ministers of the Gospel, nor even for schools or academies." A new ordinance was then drawn up providing that "There shall be reserved the central section of every township for the maintenance of public schools, and the section immediately adjoining for the support of religion."[16] The part regarding religion was stricken out, but that regarding education was left, and the same principle was embodied in the later and more famous Ordinance of 1787. This ordinance contained certain articles formally adopted as articles of compact "between the original States and the people of the States in said territory" which were to "forever remain unalterable unless by common consent" (sec. 14). In this solemn compact, Article III said that "religion, morality and knowledge, being necessary to good government and the happiness of mankind, schools and the means of education shall forever be encouraged." In pursuance of this principle the instructions of Congress to the Board of the Treasury concerning the sales of land in

[11] Dexter, E. G., *A History of Education in the United States*, 61, 62.
[12] *Ibid.*, 77; Sowers, *Financial History of New York* (1914), in Columbia University, *Studies in History, Economics and Public Law*, LVII, 263.
[13] Dexter, E. G., *A History of Education in the United States*, 58–59.
[14] Carlton, *Economic Influence upon Educational Progress*, 16; Jernegan, *Laboring and Dependent Classes in Colonial America*, pt. iii; Dexter, E.G., *A History of Education in the United States*, 67.
[15] Knight, *History and Management of Land Grants for Education* (1885), in American Historical Association, *Papers*, I, No. 3, pp. 80–81.
[16] Schafer, *Land Grants for Education*, 39.

the Northwest authorized the grant of section sixteen for education and section twenty-nine for religion in each township, as well as the grant of two whole townships for a university.[17] The provision for religion was soon dropped, having been made in only two cases[18] and even land grants for education did not become a part of our settled policy for many years. For while school reservations were made in the purchases of the Ohio Company and of John Cleve Symmes, no such provision was made for the rest of the Northwest, and none was made in the bill which passed the House of the newly organized Congress in 1791. Even as late as 1800, Congress passed an act for the sale of lands without the educational proviso. But the act of April 30, 1802, which provided for the admission of the State of Ohio, restored the educational land grants,[19] and ever since that time the Federal Government has consistently maintained and even extended the practice.

LAND GRANTS FOR THE SUPPORT OF COMMON SCHOOLS

The earlier rule was to set aside the sixteenth section of each township for the maintenance of common schools. When the Oregon Territory was organized in 1848, this reservation was doubled, so that every State admitted since that time has received the sixteenth and thirty-sixth sections for school purposes.[20] Inasmuch as Texas had from the first richly endowed its schools out of its own domain, the matter may be summarized in the statement that in all of the States west of the Alleghanies with the exception of West Virginia (which was carved out of Virginia after the Civil War), Kentucky, and Tennessee, the schools have been endowed by grants of land.[21]

Out of the public land system of the United States has grown a typical and important feature of our State educational systems. When Connecticut ceded its western lands to the Government, it reserved a certain tract which became afterwards known as the Western Reserve, and it passed an act in 1795 providing that lands be sold for education and that the "Proceeds of this sale are to be made into a perpetual fund, from which shall be, and hereby is, appropriated to the support of the schools in the several societies constituted by law, according to the list of polls and ratable estates."[22] This was the origin of the school fund of Connecticut, which has since been maintained as a permanent endowment of the public school system, and which has found its counterpart in the school funds of most of the other States.

Whether the generosity of Congress has in all cases been well placed need not be discussed here. Bryce thought that the effect of the permanent school fund, in some of the States in which it was largest, had been to lower the efficiency of the schools and the interest of the people in them.[23] There is no doubt that education went through a period of depression in the first third of the nineteenth century, and that the existence of a school fund weakened initiative in some of the towns. Nor can it be claimed that the States have always shown prudence or skill in managing their funds. Even

17 Treat, *The National Land System*, 266.
18 See United States Bureau of Education, *Report of the Commissioner for 1868*, p. 68.
19 Treat, *The National Land System*, 266–268.
20 Buffum, *Federal and State Aid to Education in Iowa* (1907), 7.
21 Dutton and Snedden, *Administration of Public Education in the United States* (1908), 29.
22 Steiner, *History of Education in Connecticut*, 39.
23 Bryce, *The American Commonwealth* (ed. of 1888), I, 585, footnote 4.

Ohio, which was the first of the new States to profit by the generosity of Congress, waited until 1825 before establishing a compulsory common school system.[24] To examine critically the actual administration of school funds in the States would carry us far beyond the scope of this study, and involve investigation of details such as has thus far only been undertaken in a few cases. The significant thing is that in spite of lapses and shortcomings in administration the endowment of the common schools was recognized as an integral part of our public land policy.

PROVISIONS FOR HIGHER EDUCATION

It is probably in the field of higher education that Congress has displayed the most originality. In the provision for common schools, it has done little more than to give subsidies in the form of land grants, leaving the determination of school policy to the States. In the matter of higher education, it has created distinctly new institutions which have materially influenced the educational policy of the whole country, and have led to great scientific and economic advances. The colleges established by the colonies were in the main the creation of private initiative. They were, it is true, chartered by the legislatures and in some cases they received grants of money, but their management was in the hands of the people who were interested in education or in religion for its own sake, and who founded colleges as feeders to the ministry or to public service. The interest of the Federal Government in higher education is contemporaneous with its interest in the common schools. For the contract of October 27, 1787, which authorized the reservation in the grant of the Ohio Company of section sixteen in each township for public schools, also authorized the reservation of two townships to be used for a university,[25] and this policy was "followed, to a greater or less degree, and with some variations, in every State admitted to the Union and in every Territory organized since the adoption of the Federal Constitution."[26]

Not only was higher education provided for in the new territory, but there was a movement which began in the Constitutional Convention to establish a national university in Washington, and although this object has not yet been realized, the matter has been brought forward by successive Presidents with remarkable persistency. The original resolution to incorporate a plan for a national university in the Constitution of the United States was introduced by Madison of Virginia and Pinckney of South Carolina. It is remarkable that this proposal to extend the powers of the Federal Government should have been made by two men from the South. No less remarkable is the fact that it was omitted from the Constitution on the ground brought forward by Morris and others that it was included within the power of Congress to govern the District of Columbia.[27]

George Washington in his first annual message, January 8, 1790, spoke of the importance of knowledge as being "in every country the surest basis of public happiness." Among the many advantages to be obtained from it, he specified, "to distinguish be-

[24] Mathews, *Expansion of New England*, 189.
[25] Treat, *The National Land System*, 51, 278; Cutler's *Diary* gives July 27 as the date of the passage of the Ordinance by Congress (*Life, Journals and Correspondence* (1888), I, 305); and October 27 as the date of signing the contract (*Ibid.*, I, 326).
[26] Buffum, *Federal and State Aid to Education in Iowa*, 10.
[27] Farrand, *The Records of the Federal Convention of 1787*, II, 616.

tween oppression and the necessary exercise of lawful authority; between burthens proceeding from a disregard to their convenience and those resulting from the inevitable exigencies of society," and he concluded by saying: "Whether this desirable object will be best promoted by affording aids to seminaries of learning already established, by the institution of a national university, or by any other expedients will be well worthy of a place in the deliberations of the Legislature."[28] Again, in his message of December 7, 1796, Washington brought up the same matter in emphatically recommending both a national university and a military academy.[29]

Jefferson, though representing the States' Rights Party, also favored "a national establishment for education," not for the purpose of taking education out of the hands of individuals, but rather because he thought that a public institution alone could supply those sciences which contribute to the improvement of the country and to its preservation. He held, however, that an amendment to the Constitution would be necessary to carry this into effect.[30] Madison, in his message of December 5, 1810, recommended a "seminary of learning instituted by the National Legislature,"[31] and Monroe, in his message of December 2, 1817, proposed an amendment to the Constitution giving Congress the power to establish institutions of learning throughout the United States.[32] Many later Presidents[33] have recommended the establishment of a national university, but without result. Congress has, however, through its control of the public lands, furnished the means for the endowment of universities in practically all of the western States, and thus created a distinct type among our higher institutions of learning.

PROVISIONS FOR STATE UNIVERSITIES

As already stated, provision was made for a university in the contract with the Ohio Company as early as 1787. In 1804 Congress established three land districts in the Northwest Territory. In each of these one township was set apart for a seminary of learning, and subsequently Indiana, Illinois, and Michigan each received one of these seminary townships.[34] The exact terms of land grants on the admission of States differed in different cases. In Illinois, for example, which was admitted in 1818, school sections and the saline lands were granted on the same terms as in Ohio, but instead of giving 5 per cent. of the sale of public lands for roads, the Government gave 2 per cent. for roads, and 3 per cent. for the encouragement of learning. Of this one-sixth was to be used for a college or university.[35] Iowa received seven grants besides the sixteenth section grant. One of these was the five hundred thousand acre grant made in 1841 for internal improvements, such as railroads, canals, and the like, but Iowa decided to use it for schools.[36] In 1840, two townships were granted for the university in the

[28] Richardson, *A Compilation of the Messages and Papers of the Presidents*, I, 66.
[29] *Ibid.*, I, 202.
[30] "Message of Dec. 2, 1806", *Ibid.*, I, 409–410.
[31] *Ibid.*, I, 485.
[32] *Ibid.*, II, 18.
[33] See Germann, *National Legislation Concerning Education* (1899), 23–30.
[34] Knight, *History and Management of Land Grants for Education* (1899), 90.
[35] *Ibid.*, 108.
[36] Buffum, *Federal and State Aid to Education in Iowa*, 26–27.

Territory of Iowa.[37] Thus grants of public lands for State universities became an almost universal feature of our educational system in the western and southern States, where thirty institutions of learning have had land given them for this purpose with tracts ranging from 46,080 to 246,080 acres.[38]

The first grants of public lands to State universities came at a period in which there was a growing distrust of the colleges organized as close corporations.[39] These grants thus became a means of stimulating the movement towards higher institutions of learning which should bear a closer relation to the common school system of popular education. Though often mismanaged and subjected to political influences, these universities have gradually improved in character and achievement, until they have come to be regarded no longer as an experiment but as the normal expression of the national will and interest in matters of higher education.[40]

PROVISIONS OF STATE CONSTITUTIONS REGARDING EDUCATION

Although the Federal Government showed its interest in education even under the Articles of Confederation by making land grants, the general management of this subject was left, under our Constitution, to the States and their subdivisions, and it is, therefore, to State legislation and State administration that we must look for changes in methods and spirit. That education was held to be important for the welfare of the State in the earliest days of the Republic is seen from the fact that so many of the constitutions referred to this subject, even at a time when these fundamental instruments were still comparatively brief and did not deal with details of policy. The three New England States which adopted constitutions before 1800 all had in them some reference to education; and Connecticut and Rhode Island followed the same plan when they substituted constitutions for royal charters in 1818 and 1842 respectively. The Massachusetts Constitution of 1780 said with regard to the subject: "Wisdom and knowledge, as well as virtue, diffused generally among the body of the people, being necessary for the preservation of their rights and liberties; and as these depend on spreading the opportunities and advantages of education in the various parts of the country, and among the different orders of the people, it shall be the duty of legislatures and magistrates, in all future periods of this commonwealth, to cherish the interests of literature and the sciences, and all seminaries of them; especially the university at Cambridge, public schools, and grammar schools in the towns."[41] New Hampshire in its Constitution of 1784[42] followed, in the main, the wording of the constitution of Massachusetts, and Vermont in its Constitution of 1777 provided more specifically: "A school or schools shall be established in each town by the legislature, for the convenient instruction of youth, with such salaries [*sic*] to the masters, paid by each town; making proper use of school lands in each town, thereby to enable them to instruct youth at low prices."[43]

[37] *Ibid.*, 36–37.
[38] *Ibid.*, 142–143.
[39] Brown, E. E., *Origin of American State Universities*, in University of California, *Publications, Education*, III, No. 1, p. 17, April 10, 1913.
[40] Wheeler, *Unterricht und Demokratie in Amerika* (1910), 160.
[41] Thorpe, *American Charters, Constitutions and Organic Laws*, III, 1907.
[42] *Ibid.*, IV, 2467.
[43] *Ibid.*, VI, 3748.

To turn to other parts of the country, Pennsylvania[44] and North Carolina[45] in their constitutions of 1776 provided for schools in order to give instruction at low prices, while the Georgia[46] constitution of 1798 had a general provision for the education of the people. Of the twenty-four States which had joined the Union down to the end of the first third of the century, sixteen had by 1834 made some provision for education in their constitutions. Those which made no such provision were Maryland, South Carolina, Virginia, Louisiana, and Kentucky in the South, and New Jersey, Illinois, and Rhode Island in the North.

DECLINE OF POPULAR EDUCATION

In spite of the principles laid down in the fundamental laws, popular education in the first part of the nineteenth century was at a low ebb. The early religious impulse had lost its force, the people had scattered over a large area, the country was still poor and was seeking wealth with less regard for higher things. The district school was the common instrument of instruction; it lacked effective supervision and was not supported by any public institutions for the training of teachers. The State of Massachusetts, in 1837, was paying only $2.73 per pupil for the education of its children.[47] Connecticut, in 1821, repealed the provision imposing a penalty on parents and employers who neglected the education of children subject to them.[48] That State, in 1813, had imposed upon the proprietors of manufacturing establishments the duty of teaching children employed in factories to read, write, and cipher, but this law, according to Dr. Barnard in 1840, was "a dead letter in nearly, if not every town in the State." A law of 1842, which forbade the employment of children under fifteen years of age in factories unless they had been to school for at least three months of the year preceding, was designed to remedy this condition; but Connecticut did not finally pass a general compulsory education act until 1872, and Massachusetts was in fact the only State which, by its act of 1852, gave effective expression to this principle before the Civil War.[49]

THE HUMANITARIAN MOVEMENT

There were two movements towards the end of the first third and the opening of the second third of the century which were beginning to create a change for the better. One was what may be called, for lack of a better term, the humanitarian movement. In the field of religion, it showed itself partly in the liberalizing ferment of Unitarianism, partly in a greater sense of social service and in an impulse to carry Christianity to distant parts of the earth. The earliest foreign missionary society was the American Board of Commissioners for Foreign Missions, established in 1810. This was followed by a remarkable expansion of religious effort. "In 1816 the American Bible Society, previously a local organization, was expanded into a national society. In 1824 came

[44] *Ibid.*, V, 3091.
[45] *Ibid.*, V, 2794.
[46] *Ibid.*, II, 801.
[47] Dexter, E.G., *History of Education in the United States*, 98.
[48] "Connecticut", in United States Bureau of Education, *Report of Commissioner, 1888–1889*, I, 486–487.
[49] *Ibid.*, I, 472.

the Sunday School Union; in 1825 the American Tract Society; 1826 saw the organization of the Home Missionary Society, and of the American Temperance Society. . . . By 1830 this national religious movement was in full swing, though later years were to witness a marvelous expansion."[50] In literature, this spirit produced the American transcendentalists, Emerson, Thoreau, Ripley, Olcott, and Channing. Socially, this was the period of Owenism, Fourierism, and of a multitude of similar reforms.[51] Brook Farm, whose short experience during the years 1841 to 1847 has played a larger part in literary than in economic history, represents the union of the intellectual and the social phases of this movement, which had its chief center in New England. In its earlier phases, humanitarianism was essentially educational. The very effort to carry the gospel to distant parts, to bring higher ideals to the frontier communities, as was done by the Iowa Band in 1843,[52] to introduce more rational modes of living in the older communities, inevitably involved teaching as a means to the end.

THE LABOR MOVEMENT

The other influence was the labor movement, which was as yet in its infancy, but which had already developed some active leaders and radical thinkers. While, in the early days of the Republic, education had been thought of as essential to citizenship, with the development of factories and the differentiation of classes it began to appear important as a means of raising the economic condition of the wage receivers. Hence free education became a common demand of the labor organizations. In an address to the workingmen of the District of Columbia issued December 1835, we are told: "Let the ten-hour system be established, and we have obtained one step to improve our condition—this will give us time for study and useful reflections, and by a few hours, thus afforded, we can gain much useful knowledge, and be better able to perform our allotted labor, more to our employers' advantage and our own. . . . We ask for a universal system of education."[53]

Nevertheless, it is probably an overstatement to say as A. M. Simons does regarding the labor movement, "there is no escape from the conclusion that to this movement, more than to any other single cause, if not more than to all other causes combined, is due the common school system of the United States."[54] A study of the facts seems to show that the labor movement was only one of several causes which helped to make education more democratic by making it both gratuitous and compulsory. It contributed a new argument for extending a system which began in the early days of the settlement of New England, which extended to other colonies and States, and which was implied in the whole system of Federal grants to education. In the early Puritan days, education was emphasized as an essential of citizenship in a free state; the labor movement laid stress upon the economic importance of education and showed that it was necessary in order to secure better remuneration and a greater equality of opportunity. It must also be remembered that during the early period of the labor move-

[50] Adams, E. D., *The Power of Ideals in American History* (1913), 103.
[51] See Commons' graphic description in *Documentary History of American Industrial Society,* VII, 19–20.
[52] See Adams, E. D., *The Power of Ideals in American History,* 110 *et seq.*
[53] Commons, *Documentary History of American Industrial Society,* VI, 119.
[54] Simons, *Social Forces in American History* (1912), 183.

ment, its leaders had comparatively little political influence, and the real initiative in improving educational methods was taken by men who represented rather the humanitarian point of view.

THE EDUCATIONAL REVIVAL

One of the most noted among these active reformers was Horace Mann, who became secretary of the Massachusetts State Board of Education when it was organized in 1837. He was a leader in furthering the changes which transformed the educational system towards the middle of the century: effective supervision and adequate support of the elementary schools, the establishment of normal schools for the training of teachers, a longer school year, decent buildings, and better text-books.[55] Massachusetts took an important step in the efficient enforcement of these reforms when it authorized, in 1854, city and town superintendents of education.

In the West, the communities differed. In those that were settled from New England by farmers, provision was made at an early day for a public school system. In Ohio, as early as 1788, Manasseh Cutler sent out $200 to pay for a school master and minister in the new settlement at Marietta,[56] and in 1821, Ohio passed its first public school law.[57] This, to be sure, was purely permissive, but it was made mandatory in 1825, and the beginning of a serious public school system in Ohio dates really from that law. In Indiana, a general public school law was passed in 1824.[58] A similar law, passed in Illinois in 1825,[59] was, however, so far in advance of public sentiment that it was practically repealed in 1827 by a proviso that no person should be taxed for schools without his consent.[60] In the States between the Mississippi and the Pacific, provision was made at an early day for public schools, those States having before them the example of the public school system of the East, so that, although in the mining communities there was at first little interest in education, this was a stage of civilization that was soon outgrown, and the western States at a comparatively early period of their existence as States made liberal provision for free common schools.

The South was on the whole backward in its educational policy, and yet even here there is evidence that the ideal of an educated citizenship was not lacking. In addition to the States of North Carolina and Georgia, already mentioned, Texas recognized in its Constitution of 1827 the need of an adequate number of common schools. Alabama in its Constitution of 1819 provided for the encouragement of schools by a fund. Mississippi provided for the encouragement of schools in its Constitutions of 1817 and 1832. Kentucky in 1850 decreed that the common school fund should be inviolate. The existence of slavery, however, checked any impulse to realize in fact the ideals of the constitutions, and the South had to wait until after the Civil War for a general spread of elementary popular education.

[55] Dexter, E. G., *A History of Education in the United States*, 98–101.
[56] *Ibid.*, 104.
[57] *Ibid.*, 105.
[58] *Ibid.*, 107.
[59] *Ibid.*, 109.
[60] *Ibid.*, 110.

CHAPTER XIII

SLAVERY DOWN TO THE CIVIL WAR

IMPORTANCE OF SLAVERY IN THE HISTORY OF THE UNITED STATES

It can be said without exaggeration that no single topic, either domestic or international, has played a greater part in the history of the United States than slavery. For decades it divided parties. It was involved in the vital questions of territorial expansion which came up in connection with Texas and the Mexican War; it has influenced our land policy, our railroad policy, our tariff policy, our territorial policy, the interpretation of the Federal Constitution, and the admission of States to the Union. It split for a time and almost destroyed the Union. To attempt to write the history of slavery would not only expand a few chapters into several volumes, but it would involve the repetition of many familiar facts of general history. And yet to omit all reference to the subject would be to leave out the key to a large number of other topics treated in this volume. Even if the slavery problem had been less important in itself, even if it had not raised vital questions of social policy, it would still have to be considered as an element affecting other forms of legislative activity. A scholar who should try to familiarize himself with all other phases of social legislation and maintain a complete ignorance of the subject of slavery, would as inevitably be led to suspect its existence, as the astronomers were led to discover the planet Neptune by observing the otherwise inexplicable aberrations in the solar system. If slavery, while it existed, affected directly our national policy in many fields, its abolition has led to a great mass of laws affecting the race question directly, while it has indirectly influenced our homestead exemption and our mechanics' lien legislation, and our liquor policy, and has helped to create the peculiar conditions surrounding the mountain whites. Its most important by-product is probably the fourteenth amendment to the Federal Constitution, which in turn has had a far-reaching and unforeseen influence upon the judicial interpretation of labor laws and many other types of legislation. It goes without saying that the abolition of slavery created what we call the Negro problem, with its own many ramifications.

ELEMENTS IN THE QUESTION OF SLAVERY

To treat the differences of opinion regarding slavery as resting solely on rational economic considerations or antagonistic interests is to take a partial, not to say superficial, view. It is true that the economic advantage of slavery was felt in the South more than in the North, but people are always guided, not so much by their interests as by what they believe to be their interests. The opinion that slavery was absolutely essential to the economic life of the South, though widespread, was not based on any real test, since the South had had no means of experimenting with an educated, free, black, laboring population; it was an opinion influenced in part by prejudice or inertia. It is natural and almost universal for people who find themselves prosperous under a certain system to desire the continuance of that system, simply because they do not wish to take the risk and undergo the mental labor of changing it. The history of social legislation is full of reforms which have been declared in advance to be ruinous to certain interests, but which have been found by subsequent experience to be innocuous. The abolition of slavery is one of them. But unfortunately the controversy did not merely turn upon whether slave labor was or was not economical and efficient. The question became a political one, that is to say, was made the subject of controversy between different parties, on account of its being connected with other questions. For, besides the purely economic elements, four others entered in to embitter and complicate the controversy.

1. The clash of changing ideals. The progress of the world has been, broadly speaking, from bondage to freedom. Economists generally agree that when captives taken in war were put to work instead of being put to death, this represented a great step forward. It made the accumulation of capital possible. It trained people to habits of industry. But it is equally clear that, when the system of contract superseded that of force, a still greater advance was made. The stimulus of wages made labor more efficient, more industrious, and more responsible. This change had been going on throughout the centuries, when the possession by Europeans of large tracts of land in a warm climate and the peculiar needs of the tobacco crop created a strong demand for labor, which could be best met, in the opinion of the time, by the importation of black slaves from Africa. This new situation produced a reaction towards a more primitive form of labor, just as the frontier life of new communities produces for the time being a reaction towards ruder methods of work and modes of life. In the meantime, those who were not under the influence of this peculiar situation continued to raise their social ideals, and to demand not only greater liberty, but also greater humanity and greater equality. People, therefore, who in the beginning were fairly homogeneous, became more and more unlike as some of them adopted these higher ideals and others did not.

2. Sectional feeling. Slavery being especially profitable in the warmer sections, the differences of opinion became local. People who are neighbors, even when they differ decidedly in opinion, have an opportunity for compromise and mutual concession which does not exist when they are widely separated. The mere distance tends to intensify feeling.

3. Race antagonism. A white servile population may be absorbed in a few generations, and there will be no outward index of its previous condition. But the very color of the skin, the kink of the hair, stamp for generations, even when there is a large admixture of white blood, those who are descended from black slaves. Hence it was inevitable that even if slavery could be abolished the Negro question would persist.

4. Constitutional controversy. When the Federal Government was forced to legislate for the Territories and for States carved out of the newly acquired western land, its authority to deal with slavery was challenged, not only on grounds of expediency, but on grounds of constitutional right.

Partly in consequence of the facts just mentioned, and in contrast to the history of most other pieces of social legislation in our country, Federal and State authorities competed, and at times conflicted, in attempting to deal with slavery. Moreover, the tendencies of State legislation in the North and the South diverged widely. The result has been that each section tried to influence Federal legislation, and when the long conflict ended in emancipation, this consummation was imposed by that part of the country which had no slaves upon that part which had. Those whose interests were most directly affected were thus subjected to a policy which they did not want and indeed bitterly opposed.

In the following pages an attempt will be made to show: some of the influences that were making for and against emancipation; the tendencies of legislation in the South; the tendencies of legislation in the North; the tendencies of Federal legislation ending in emancipation by constitutional amendment.

EARLY ADVOCATES OF EMANCIPATION IN THE SOUTH

At the time of the adoption of the Constitution there was no such marked sectional difference of opinion on the subject as showed itself in the middle of the nineteenth century. Slavery was less profitable and less prevalent in the North than in the South. But in both parts of the country there was a growing feeling that it was a wrong system, and many people, south and north, began to oppose it on principle.

George Washington, though a large slave owner, favored the gradual emancipation of slaves and, when he died, directed that all of his slaves should be freed on the death of his wife.[1] Washington believed that the existence of slavery would sooner or later imperil the Union.[2] Jefferson was a lifelong and pronounced advocate of gradual emancipation. In his first draft of the Declaration of Independence, he added a clause which inveighed against the slave trade, referring to the fact that King George III had forbidden the attempts "to prohibit or restrain this execrable commerce."[3] He proposed the prohibition of slavery in the Ordinance of the Northwest Territory. In his "Answers to Questions Propounded by M. de Meusnier, January 24, 1786," he used the following expression:

"I conjecture there are 650,000 negroes in the five Southernmost states, and not 50,000 in the rest. In most of these latter, effectual measures have been taken for their future emancipation. In the former, nothing is done towards that. The disposition to emancipate them is strongest in Virginia. Those who desire it, form, as yet, the minority of the whole state, but it bears a respectable portion to the whole in numbers & weight of character, & it is continually recruiting by the addition of nearly the whole of the young men as fast as they come into public life. I flatter myself it will take place there at some period of time not very distant. In Maryland & N. Carolina a very few are disposed to emancipate. In S. Carolina & Georgia not the smallest symptoms of it, but, on the contrary, these two states, & N. Carolina continue importations of negroes. These have long been prohibited in all the other States."[4]

[1] Lodge, *George Washington* (1889), I, 105.
[2] *Ibid.*, II, 340.
[3] Von Holst, *The Constitutional and Political History of the United States* (1876 *ff.*), I, 282.
[4] Jefferson, *Writings* (Ford ed., 1892–1899), IV, 145–146; (Washington ed., 1854), IX, 290.

In a letter written September 8, 1823, to William Short, he spoke of slavery as a blot which was becoming less offensive by the improvement in the condition of the race, but added:

"Still it is a hideous blot, as well from the heteromorph peculiarities of the race, as that, with them, physical compulsion to action must be substituted for the moral necessity which constrains the free laborers to work equally hard. We feel and deplore it morally and politically."[5] As late as the Convention of 1831 to 1832, Thomas Jefferson Randolph, a grandson of Jefferson, moved to appoint a committee to consider gradual emancipation.[6]

JUDGE TUCKER'S DISSERTATION ON SLAVERY

An elaborate argument against slavery from the point of view of a Virginian was presented in the dissertation of Judge Tucker on slavery, which was printed in 1796.[7] At the very beginning of this essay, Judge Tucker called attention to the inconsistency of the people of the United States in fighting for their liberties, and at the same time, keeping people in a state of slavery. "Whilst we adjured the God of Hosts," he said, "to witness our resolution to live free, or die, and imprecated curses on their heads who refused to unite with us in establishing the empire of freedom; we were imposing upon our fellow men, who differ in complexion from us, a *slavery*, ten thousand times more cruel than the utmost extremity of those grievances and oppressions, of which we complained."[8] Judge Tucker based his opposition to slavery not only upon its well known social and moral evils, but also upon its inconsistency with the fundamental principles of the constitution of Virginia, and said: "our bill of rights declares, 'that all men are by nature *equally free* and independent, and have certain rights of which they cannot deprive or divest their posterity, namely, the enjoyment of life and *liberty*, with the means of *acquiring* and *possessing* property.' This is indeed no more than a recognition of the first principles of the law of nature, which teaches us this equality, and enjoins every man, whatever advantages he may possess over another, as to the various qualities or endowments of body or mind, to practice the precepts of the law of nature to those who are in these respects his *inferiors*, no less than it enjoins his *inferiors* to practice them towards *him*."[9]

Judge Tucker traced the history of the institution in the United States and the English colonies, asserting that it was really forced upon the colonies by the mother country, but that in time laws regarding it had become very severe. Regarding the discrimination against slaves in matters of law, he said: "We have found actions, innocent or indifferent, punishable with a rigour scarcely due to any, but the most atrocious offences against civil society; justice distributed by an unequal measure to the master and the slave; and even the hand of mercy arrested, where mercy might have been extended to the wretched culprit, had his complexion been the same with that of his

[5] *Ibid.* (Washington ed., 1854), VII, 310.
[6] Von Holst, *The Constitutional and Political History of the United States*, II, 91.
[7] Tucker, *A Dissertation on Slavery with a Proposal for the Gradual Abolition of it in the State of Virginia* (1796, reprinted in 1861).
[8] *Ibid.*, 8.
[9] *Ibid.*, 48.

judges."[10] Judge Tucker had a perfectly definite and simple proposal for gradually abolishing slavery. It was that every female born after the adoption of the plan should be free and should transmit freedom to all of her descendants. But as a compensation to those persons in whose families such females, or their descendants, might be born, they should serve until the age of twenty-eight years, then receive $20 in money, two suits of clothes, a hat, a pair of shoes, and two blankets. Thus, little by little, the Negroes would become free, without depriving their owners of any property right in any person then living.[11]

This plan of Judge Tucker's, though not unlike that actually carried out in Pennsylvania in 1789 and in Connecticut under the law of 1784, was in advance of the general sentiment of the South. Thus although the Ordinance of the Northwest Territory prohibited slavery, North Carolina made its cession of land in 1790 only on condition that nothing should be done by Congress to emancipate the slaves. Likewise, when Georgia ceded its territory, April 2, 1802, it stipulated that the Ordinance of the Northwest Territory should apply excepting the part prohibiting slavery.[12] And yet the attachment to slavery was not strong enough to defeat the Ordinance itself, and the prominence and influence of the advocates of emancipation in the South gave good reason for thinking in the eighteenth century that that section would gradually free its slaves. Even as late as the early part of the nineteenth century anti-slavery societies were formed in some of the southern States, as in Tennessee in 1814, in North Carolina in 1816, in Maryland in 1817, and in Virginia in 1823, and the delegates of these States attended national meetings with delegates from northern societies.[13]

DEVELOPMENT OF AN ANTI-SLAVERY MOVEMENT

In the North, the Quakers were the first people to oppose slavery as a religious body and it was in the Quaker community of Pennsylvania that the first society for the suppression of slavery was organized in 1775.[14] But not a few of the New England clergy were among the intellectual pioneers of the movement for emancipation. Foremost among them was Jonathan Edwards, whose treatise on the *Nature of True Virtue* may be considered as the philosophical basis of the anti-slavery feeling of the generation following him. "He asserted that the elemental principle in virtue is benevolence, or love to intelligent being in proportion to the amount of being which each personality possesses."[15] "It was no accident that classed Samuel Hopkins, sternest of the pupils of Edwards, or Jonathan Edwards the younger, clearest-minded expounder of the Edwardean system, among the earliest New England opponents of negro slavery, or drew the earliest missionaries of the American Board from Edwardean ranks."[16] Hopkins was the first of the New England clergy to denounce slavery from his pulpit. This he began to do as early as 1770 or 1771, regardless of the fact that he was preaching in Newport, Rhode Island, where fortunes were made by the slave trade, and to a congre-

[10] *Ibid.*, 64.
[11] *Ibid.*, 89.
[12] Von Holst, *The Constitutional and Political History of the United States*, I, 309.
[13] Hart, *Slavery and Abolition* (1906), 158–161.
[14] See Jorns, *Studien über die Sozialpolitik der Quäker.*
[15] Walker, *Ten New England Leaders* (1901), 255.
[16] *Ibid.*, 256.

gation in which were many persons interested in the trade. Hopkins endeavored, partly by personal contributions, to secure the freedom of a number of slaves owned by his Newport neighbors, and in 1773 joined with Rev. Ezra Stiles, later president of Yale College, in an appeal for means to train colored missionaries for labor in Africa. In 1776, Hopkins published *A Dialogue concerning the Slavery of the Africans; showing it to be the Duty and Interest of the American States to emancipate all their African Slaves.*[17]

During the nineteenth century when some of the business interests of New England were allied with slavery and not a few of the clergy supported the institution, there was at the same time a strong movement among clergymen against it. Dr. Leonard Bacon was one of the earliest to express himself vigorously on this subject. He had found the anti-slavery feeling strong at Andover, where he studied theology. The topic was frequently debated before the "Society of Inquiry" in the Seminary, and a report which Dr. Bacon made to that society condemned slavery in most positive terms. As a clergyman in New Haven, Dr. Bacon gave as his oration on the Fourth of July, 1825, "A Plea for Africa;" and a year later he declared that: "Public opinion throughout the free States must hold a different course on the subject of slavery from that which it now holds. Instead of exhausting itself fruitlessly and worse than fruitlessly upon the *operation* of the system, it must be directed towards the *principle* on which the system rests."[18] This was five years before the founding of the *Liberator* by William Lloyd Garrison. Dr. Bacon, though strongly opposed to slavery, did not believe in the extreme doctrine of the radical abolitionists. He was a warm advocate, however, of emancipation in spite of much opposition from his friends, and a small volume which he published in 1846 reached the table of Abraham Lincoln, and had no little effect in shaping the opinions of the future President on this subject. Dr. Bacon himself refers modestly to the event in the following words: "Less than four years ago, not knowing that he had ever heard of me, I had the privilege of an interview with him; and his first word, after our introduction to each other, was a reference to that volume, with a frank approval of its principles. Since then I have heard of his mentioning the same book to a friend of mine in terms which showed that it made an impression on his earnest and thoughtful soul."[19]

CHANGE IN THE STATUS OF SLAVERY AFTER INTRODUCTION OF WHITNEY'S COTTON GIN

The reason that the early efforts to abolish slavery, which found such eminent support all over the country, were of no avail is familiar to all students of American history and constitutes one of the most striking illustrations which history gives of the resistance to social and economic progress offered by a capitalized economic interest. The institution of slavery became entangled in a very profitable cotton growing industry. Although some varieties of cotton were indigenous in this country and others were introduced early in our colonial history, the cultivation of the plant had not been established on any important scale at the beginning of our national existence. Most of the cotton used and exported came from the West Indies. Just about the beginning of

[17] *Ibid.*, 349–351.
[18] Walker, *Ten New England Leaders*, 446, quoting Bacon, *Irenics and Polemics*, 184, 185.
[19] *Commemorative Volume*, 96, quoted in Walker, *Ten New England Leaders*, 450.

the national period, the cultivation of the Sea Island variety, with a long staple from which the seeds were readily separated, was domiciled on the eastern coast, but the growth of the upland variety, to which vast areas of the interior were adapted, was hindered by the difficulty of detaching the short staple from the seeds. The invention of the saw gin by Eli Whitney, in 1793, worked a revolution. Even when we discount Whitney's claim that the gin enabled one man to do what had before required the labor of a thousand,[20] we have evidence, in the rapid spread of cotton cultivation in the interior, of the importance of his contribution. The soil and climate were peculiarly adapted to the crop. The labor of Negro slaves, while by no means necessary, could at least be profitably utilized. The distribution of the various tasks through the year and the opportunity to work the slaves in gangs made possible the application of slave labor in spite of its inherent faults. The new textile industry, based on machinery, and manufacturing for a constantly broadening market, had an apparently insatiable demand for its raw material. To meet this demand the planters required more slaves, and were willing to pay a price which accorded with their profits; the rise of a cent a pound in cotton added $100 to the value of a prime field hand. Thus the profits of slavery were capitalized both for those who employed slave labor in raising cotton and also for those slave owners in the border States who sold their surplus stock to the cotton growers. The situation was made dramatic by two facts. One was that the invention which perpetuated slavery in the South was made by a citizen of a northern State which had already abolished slavery. The other was that the demand for raw cotton which created so profitable a market for the cotton planters was caused by the improvements in manufacturing machinery and organization which ushered in the so-called industrial revolution. Thus progress in certain parts of the world favored reaction in others and created a certain community of interest between the manufacturing capitalists and the slave owners, although they differed widely in some of their ideals of civilization. On account of this peculiar interrelation, the early anti-slavery movement of the end of the eighteenth century had, in the course of forty years, lost its momentum, and had ceased to produce much effect on legislation.

A new force was projected into the controversy when William Lloyd Garrison began his abolition crusade and founded the *Liberator* which he edited from 1831 to 1865.[21] This movement, carried on with fanatical zeal by Garrison and his associates, and reinforced by such books as Mrs. Harriet Beecher Stowe's *Uncle Tom's Cabin*, published in 1852, is a familiar episode both in the political and in the literary history of the country, and is a part of the humanitarian movement of the period referred to elsewhere in this work.

THE QUESTION OF SLAVERY IN CONGRESS

The violence of the abolitionists led to a corresponding resistance on the part of the Southerners in Congress, and in 1836 the so-called "gag resolution" was adopted, providing that petitions relating in any way to the subject of slavery, "shall, without being either printed or referred, be laid upon the table and that no further action what-

[20] Whitney's "Memorial" of 1812 in *American State Papers, Miscellaneous*, II, 183. Other estimates in Von Holst, *The Constitutional and Political History of the United States*, I, 351; and in Rhodes, *History of the United States* (ed. of 1920), I, 25.

[21] Hart, *Slavery and Abolition*, 180–181.

ever shall be had thereon."[22] Instead of defending slavery on economic grounds as a necessary evil or as a transitional institution leading to something better, many of the Southerners now went so far as to claim that the institution was in itself a good thing. Senator Calhoun in his speech in the Senate "On the Reception of Abolition Petitions", February 6, 1837, said: "But let me not be understood as admitting even by implication that the existing relation between the two races in the slave-holding States is an evil:—far otherwise; I hold it to be a good, as it has thus far proved to be to both, and will continue to prove so if not disturbed by the fell spirit of abolition." Quite consistently, Calhoun treated the institution of forced labor as an essential element in all civilized societies. "I hold then," he said, "that there never has yet existed a wealthy and civilized society in which one portion of the community did not, in point of fact, live on the labor of the other." He said that, "it would not be difficult to trace the various devices by which the wealth of all civilized communities has been so unequally divided, and to show by what means so small a share has been allotted to those by whose labor it was produced, and so large a share given to the non-producing classes. The devices are almost innumerable, from the brute force and gross superstition of ancient times, to the subtle and artful fiscal contrivances of modern. I might well challenge a comparison between them and the more direct, simple, and patriarchal mode by which the labor of the African race is, among us, commanded by the European." He justified slavery not only on social grounds but also on political. He said, "I fearlessly assert that the existing relation between the two races in the South, against which these blind fanatics are waging war, forms the most solid and durable foundation on which to rear free and stable political institutions."[23] Hart says, regarding this view: "the author has under his hand between fifty and a hundred citations to the same effect."[24]

DIFFERENCES OF OPINION IN THE PUBLIC

The ideals of those who believed in a society based on equality and of those who believed in a subordinated labor class kept getting further apart, until the Southerners in their advocacy of slavery repudiated Jefferson and the Declaration of Independence, while the abolitionists of the North, in some extreme cases, went so far in their defense of freedom as to attack the Constitution. A compromise between the two extremes was offered by the policy of colonization, under which the blacks were to be taken back to Africa and settled in a free commonwealth of their own; but this was soon found to be open to too many difficulties to be seriously thought of as a solution of the problem, and though it led to the creation of Liberia, it played little part in the history of our social legislation.

Public opinion was not unanimous in the North, and even in the South there were some dissenters from the prevailing pro-slavery doctrine. In contrast to the fanatical abolitionists and the large group of more moderate idealists, philosophers, poets, Oberlin and Andover students, and others whose influence has been so well sketched by E. D. Adams,[25] there were many conservative business men who deprecated any agitation

[22] *Ibid.*, 259, quoting *Niles' Register*, L, 241–248.
[23] Calhoun, *Works* (1851–67), I, 630–632.
[24] *Slavery and Abolition*, 151, footnote.
[25] *The Power of Ideals in American History*, chap. ii.

of a subject which might endanger the Union; there were also many clergymen who opposed the preaching of abolition for fear it might disrupt the church; and there was the mob which dragged Garrison through the streets of Boston with a halter around his neck. In the political world, the Democratic party, whose leaders were Southerners, was naturally opposed to the agitation, and even some of the German Socialists took the same attitude.[26]

HELPER'S ANALYSIS OF SLAVERY

While a great deal of the controversy with regard to slavery turned upon humanitarian or constitutional considerations, there were not lacking people who, even before the Civil War, called attention to the marked economic contrast between the slave States and the free States. This difference appeared in the many books of travel which were written at the time, not only by Europeans who visited our country, but also by such American authors as Frederick Law Olmsted, who traveled through the South. A more definite attempt to show the difference statistically was made by Hinton Rowan Helper in his *Impending Crisis of the South*, published in 1857. Helper represented the point of view of the poor whites in the South, his ancestors having lived there, as he says, for more than a century.[27] He not only gave utterance to the resentment of the poor whites towards the slave-holding oligarchy which had controlled politics in the South from the beginning, but showed by such statistics as were then available that the South was economically far behind the North. This was true in manufactures, in foreign commerce, in wealth, in growth of population, in literature, and in its command of the luxuries of life. Even in agriculture, in which the South specialized, the production of food stuffs was behind that of the North. In his enumeration, recapitulating the principal crops, such as wheat, oats, Indian corn, and potatoes, he showed that in 1850 the production of the free States was valued at over $351,000,000, while the slave States turned out but about $306,000,000.[28] Even the great export crops of cotton, tobacco, and rice, with hay and sundry other products of the slave States added, were worth only some $138,000,000 as against a hay crop in the free States of $142,000,000.[29]

Helper's book had a wide circulation, furthered by the violent attacks made on it by Southerners in the House of Representatives. It helped to confirm the views of abolitionists. The figures were as trustworthy as any statistics of the kind could be, and to many seemed convincing. They were obviously open to criticism in that they compared the products of the two sections without proper allowance for differences in population, climate, and resources, and they threw no light on the difficult question, how far the backwardness of the South was due to slavery, how far to the fact that its labor force was composed so largely of Negroes.

From the southern side, the book was answered by another, Kettell's *Southern Wealth and Northern Profits*,[30] which sought to show that the southern staples, making up by far the largest part of the total exports of the country, really supported the trade and

[26] Schlüter, *Lincoln, Labor, and Slavery* (1913), 74.
[27] Helper, *Impending Crisis*, Preface, vi.
[28] *Ibid.*, 39.
[29] *Ibid.*, 53.
[30] Kettell, *Southern Wealth and Northern Profits* (1860). Kettell had been editor of the *Democratic Review.*

manufactures of the North, that without cotton to pay our debts and buy our goods abroad the North would be bankrupt.

COMPROMISES REGARDING SLAVERY

For reasons already given, the diverging views of the North and the South soon made any consistent policy on the part of the Federal Government impossible, and our history from the early part of the nineteenth century down to the Civil War is punctuated by one compromise after another on this vital question. The Missouri Compromise was brought about in 1820, upon the application of that State to come into the Union. Missouri was admitted as a slave State, and Maine as a free State, but slavery was to be forever prohibited in other parts of the Louisiana Purchase lying north of 36°30′. This established a line of demarcation following a parallel of latitude. An equally important development was the Compromise of 1850. This contained a series of measures supposed to offset each other. California was admitted without restriction regarding slavery, but as it had an anti-slave constitution, this meant a gain for the free States. On the other hand, a more stringent fugitive slave law was passed. A distinct advance was the prohibition of trading in slaves brought to the District of Columbia for sale. During all these years, it may be stated that practically no progress was made in the direction of either the extension or the limitation of slavery. Both sections insisted on their views, and simply pushed the dividing line along the same parallel further into the West, until the introduction of the Kansas-Nebraska bill in 1854.

The act authorizing the organization of the territories of Kansas and Nebraska on the principle of squatter sovereignty, leaving each to determine for itself whether it would recognize slavery or nor, had the ultimate effect of forcing the United States to commit itself to one policy or the other, because it repealed the Missouri Compromise, and thus reopened the rivalry between antagonistic policies which had been kept dormant. That rivalry took the form of civil war in Kansas when the "Border Ruffians" from Missouri and the New England settlers of the Emigrant Aid Societies in turn tried to determine the future policy of the territory.[31] It was paradoxically stimulated by a decision of the Supreme Court, the very body which was supposed to be entirely removed from the danger of political influence. This was the Dred Scott decision,[32] rendered by the Supreme Court of the United States in 1857. Scott was a slave belonging to Dr. Emerson, a surgeon in the United States Army. In 1834, Emerson went to the military post of Rock Island, Illinois, and in 1836, to Fort Snelling on the west bank of the Mississippi, where he held Scott as a slave until 1838. In 1838, Emerson removed Scott and his wife to Missouri, and later sold him to Sandford. Scott sued for his freedom on the ground that residence in a free territory had made him free. The decision, rendered in 1857, held among other things that a Negro of the African race whose ancestors were brought to this country and sold as slaves was not a citizen within the meaning of the Constitution, inasmuch as when this was adopted, they were not regarded in any of the States as members of the community. This meant, therefore, the establishment of an hereditary caste system. But the court went further, and

[31] Smith, T. C., *Parties and Slavery, 1850–1859* (1906), 150 *et seq.*
[32] *Scott vs. Sandford*, 19 How., 393.

held that Congress had no right to prohibit citizens of any State from taking up their homes in any other State; or to give privileges to one class of citizens which it refused to another. Every citizen had the right to take with him into the Territories any object which the Constitution regarded as property. This meant that the Missouri Compromise, which had already been repealed by the Kansas-Nebraska bill of 1854, was unconstitutional. The significant point of this decision was that slavery was upheld in the interest of property rights, just as, in March 1911, the Workmen's Compensation Act of New York was declared unconstitutional as a violation of property rights. The old controversy between persons and property simply assumed a special form in the Dred Scott decision. Thus, it may be said, that, while most of the Federal legislation during this period was in the nature of compromise, the law as a whole, if we include State law and court decisions, was in the direction of confirming slavery and extending the power of the slave owners, and not in the direction of repealing or even limiting the institution. Yet during this period, the tendency of public sentiment was more and more humanitarian, while the leaders of the still young labor movement were working in the direction of greater equality of opportunity and a more equal distribution of the advantages of civilization.[33]

SUMMARY REGARDING SLAVERY

Viewed in its broadest economic and social aspects, the slavery question involved a contest between the ideals of a static and those of a dynamic society. Slavery was not incompatible with culture, refinement, kindliness, and religion on the part of individual slave owners, and the Southerners could quote good authority in the writings of the Greek philosophers for thinking that a free commonwealth should be based on slavery. But, disregarding entirely the abuses of slavery, and considering it only at its best, it is clear that it is inconsistent with economic progress, certainly with the kind of economic progress which has characterized the nineteenth century. That progress implies a constant increase in wealth by means of the application of science, of mechanical appliances, and of improved business organization to the processes of production. This, however, implies a skilled, intelligent, responsible, and, above all, an adaptable laboring class. Slavery doubtless possessed mobility in the territorial sense and this has been claimed as one of its advantages.[34] But it had little functional mobility and did not meet modern conditions. The laboring class must be in a position to adjust itself to new processes. Its mental outfit, whether the result of natural endowment or of education, must be such that it can easily and quickly turn from one method to another. Such progress involves competition. A system which is based upon status, not only keeps the laboring man inefficient, by denying him the right to rise, but deprives the property-owning classes of the stimulus which comes from the rivalry of new men coming into the control of affairs.

An illustration of the indirect effect which slavery produced upon the progress of the South is seen in the life of Joseph E. Sheffield. He was a northern man who went south after the War of 1812, and engaged successfully in business in Mobile, Alabama. He was unwilling to have his children brought up in a slave-holding community, and

[33] See Schlüter, *Lincoln, Labor, and Slavery*.
[34] Phillips, Ulrich B., *American Negro Slavery* (1918), 401.

accordingly moved North in 1835, taking up his residence in New Haven, Connecticut. Mr. Sheffield subsequently engaged in important railroad enterprises, and founded the Sheffield Scientific School of Yale University. It is fair to say that the institution of slavery cost the South whatever contributions Mr. Sheffield made to the wealth and educational advantages of the North.[35] Yet Mr. Sheffield had no sympathy with the northern abolitionists, but advocated a policy of gradual emancipation, which, if the South could have been persuaded to adopt it, might have prevented the Civil War.

As has happened in so many similar cases, facts and figures produced little effect upon those who had committed themselves to the defense of slavery as an ideal, and it is hard to say how, under the circumstances, anything short of the argument of arms could have convinced the ruling class of the South that slavery was on the whole a bad economic system. In 1860, the fourteen southern States had a population of about 12,396,505 (7,946,000 whites and 4,177,000 Negroes), as against 19,248,000 in the twenty northern States. In spite of this disparity in population, the South seemed not an uneven match for the North at the opening of the Civil War. It had statesmen of ability; it had military leaders of training and talent. It was not lacking in courage or in a devotion to what it believed to be a righteous cause. But it could not stand the economic strain. Its reliance upon the cotton monopoly to produce intervention on the part of European powers proved to be vain. There is no doubt that in the beginning the sentiment of most of the leading men in England was entirely with the South. They felt that they had much more in common with the aristocratic plantation owners, the gentlemen of leisure, the patrons of manly sports of the slave States, than with the hard-working farmers and business men of the North. But in the long run this could not be counted upon. As has been shown in a special study of the period by Charles Francis Adams, a factor of no little importance in the situation was the willingness of the working class of England to endure the hardship and privation which resulted from the cotton famine rather than support even indirectly the institution of slavery. Adams says: "A proclamation ending human slavery was promulgated; a moral issue presented itself. The parliamentary majority sustaining the veteran's [*i.e.* Palmerston] Government was narrow, and he did not wish to face a division which could equally well be avoided. If let alone, the thing was pretty sure satisfactorily to settle itself; then why provoke an unnecessary home contest? Why rouse a sleeping dog?—the dog in question chancing in this case to be the British conscience."[36] In the absence of foreign aid, the rough ordeal of civil war brought out the weak points of the system in its general effect on society. For even if the South had increased in property and capital as rapidly as the North, which it did not do, and even if its population had increased as rapidly, it is clear that slaves can not be forced or even safely allowed to fight. To arm them and train them would make them conscious of their numerical strength, and encourage insurrection. Not only, therefore, is the fighting power of a slave-owning state impaired, but its power to support an army is lessened on account of the difficulty of maintaining discipline and intelligent direction when the slave owners are in the field.

War proved in the end the weakness of a social system based on slavery. But even

[35] Farnam, "Joseph Earl Sheffield", in The New Haven Colony Historical Society, *Papers*, VII, 75, 1908.

[36] Adams, Charles Francis, *Trans-Atlantic Historical Solidarity* (1913), 114; see also Schlüter, *Lincoln, Labor, and Slavery*, chap. v.

before this proof was complete, or accepted as convincing by the slave States, on September 22, 1862, Lincoln issued his proclamation, freeing on January 1, 1863, the slaves who belonged to persons in a state of rebellion. This was merely a war measure, and although it affected the greater part of the slaves, the abolition was not complete until the passage and ratification of the Thirteenth Amendment to the Constitution in 1865. This was the boldest and most radical piece of social legislation thus far enacted in our country. But it is the fatal mark of legislation passed under stress of war to be undiscriminating and careless of details. Therefore, while solving the one predominant problem of the United States which had been the subject of more controversy than any other since the formation of the Government, this proclamation raised a host of minor problems to be solved by future generations. The cutting of the Gordian knot inevitably leaves a good many loose ends.

CHAPTER XIV

SOUTHERN LEGISLATION REGARDING SLAVERY

PROVISIONS IN STATE CONSTITUTIONS REGARDING EMANCIPATION

To consider first the policy of the South, we can tell by a study of the constitutions what features seemed sufficiently important to be embodied in the fundamental law. Almost all of the southern States had some constitutional enactments regarding the Negroes.[1] A common provision prohibited compulsory emancipation. The Georgia Constitution of 1798, though forbidding the importation of slaves, said: "The legislature shall have no power to pass laws for the emancipation of slaves without the consent of each of their respective owners, previous to such emancipation" (art. iv, sec. 11). Similar provisions are found in the Alabama Constitution of 1819 (*Slaves*, sec. 1), in that of Florida of 1838 (art. xvi, sec. 1), in that of Kentucky of 1792 (art. ix, sec. 1), repeated in 1799 (art. vii), and again in 1850 (art. x). Mississippi had a similar clause in its Constitution of 1817 (*Slaves*, sec. 1), repeated in 1832 (*Slaves*, sec. 1), Missouri in its Constitution of 1820 (art. iii, sec. 26) and Arkansas in its Constitution of 1836 (art. vii, *Emancipation of Slaves*, sec. 1). South Carolina, in its Constitution of 1776, specified among its grievances against Great Britain that governors and others bearing the royal commission had proclaimed freedom to servants and slaves.

Texas, as a province of Mexico, in 1827 provided that "In this State no person shall be born a slave, after this Constitution is published in the capital of each District, and six months thereafter neither will the introduction of slaves be permitted under any pretext" (*Preliminary Disposition*, sec. 13). On acquiring independence in 1836, it reversed its policy and not only prohibited the Congress from emancipating slaves, but prohibited any slave holder from emancipating his or her own slaves without the consent of Congress, "unless he or she shall send his or her slave or slaves without the limits of the republic." And it added: "No free person of African descent, either in whole or in part, shall be permitted to reside permanently in the republic without the consent of congress" (*General Provisions*, sec. 9). In 1845 Texas repeated the prohibition already quoted according to which the legislature could not emancipate slaves without the consent of their owners (art. viii, sec. 1).

Kentucky went so far in 1850 as to declare that "The right of property is before and higher than any constitutional sanction; and the right of the owner of a slave to such slave, and its increase, is the same, and as inviolable as the right of the owner of any

[1] The specific volume and pages of Thorpe, *American Charters, Constitutions and Organic Laws* are not given for these references to the constitutions of the various States, here and in the following pages, as they are arranged in that work alphabetically by States and chronologically under each State.

property whatever" (Constitution of 1850, art. xiii, sec. 3). Virginia in its Constitution of 1850 put a penalty upon emancipation by providing that slaves thereafter emancipated should forfeit their freedom by remaining more than 12 months in the State, and allowed the General Assembly to impose restrictions on the power of slave owners to emancipate their slaves (art. iv, secs. 19 and 20). It nevertheless retained in this constitution the same preamble which it had adopted in 1776, in which it recited among the misdeeds of George the Third, that "by an inhuman use of his negative, he had refused us permission to exclude by law" the Negroes. This preamble stands as a landmark to show how far in 1850 Virginia had drifted from the principles of 1776 as enunciated by Jefferson. Voluntary emancipation was discouraged by Kentucky, which specifically provided in 1850 (art. x, sec. 2) for the punishment of free Negroes or mulattoes immigrating from other States and of those who, having been freed in the State, refused to leave. Maryland, while not absolutely prohibiting the general abolition of slavery, required in an amendment to its Constitution of 1776, ratified in 1837 (sec. 26), that any law for general emancipation should have the unanimous consent of two succeeding legislatures.

The only southern States whose constitutions make any provision seeming to favor voluntary emancipation were Missouri and Texas. The latter in 1845 provided (art. viii, sec. 1) that the legislature might permit the freeing of slaves by the owner, but this concession was made only on condition that the rights of creditors should be safeguarded and that the slaves so freed should not become a public charge. The Missouri Constitution of 1820 (art. iii, sec. 26) contained similar provisions.

Thus nine southern States besides Maryland had constitutional provisions discouraging either statutory or voluntary emancipation or both.

REGULATION OF IMPORTATION

The importation of slaves was regulated constitutionally by only a few of the southern States before the Civil War. Kentucky in 1792 (art. ix), Georgia in 1798 (art. iv, sec. 11), and Florida in 1838 (art. xvi, sec. 2) prohibited the legislature from forbidding immigrants to bring their slaves with them; but Kentucky in 1792 (art. ix), Mississippi in 1817 (art. vi, *Slaves*, sec. 1), Alabama in 1819 (art. vi, Slaves, sec. 1), Missouri in 1820 (art. iii, sec. 26), Arkansas in 1836 (art. iv, sec. 25), and Texas in 1845 (art. viii, sec. 1) gave the legislature the power to prohibit the importation of slaves as merchandise or for speculation. Arkansas in 1836 (art. iv, sec. 23) also forbade the importation of slaves who had committed "any high crime" in any other State or Territory. The Kentucky provisions were retained in the revisions of 1799 (art. vii, sec. 1) and 1850 (art. x, sec. 1), while Mississippi in its Constitution of 1832 (art. vii, *Slaves*, sec. 1), definitely forbade importation of slaves as merchandise after May 1833. The importation of slaves from Africa or from outside of the United States was prohibited "after the first day of October next" in the constitution of Georgia in 1798 (art. iv, sec. 11), and in the Congressional Act for the temporary government of the Territories of Louisiana and Orleans passed in 1804 (sec. 7).

Thus there were eight States which in one way or another restricted the slave trade or authorized its restrictions.

PROTECTION OF SLAVES IN THE CONSTITUTIONS

Humane treatment of slaves by their masters was provided in six States[2] and some States safeguarded their rights when accused of crime.[3] Certain of the States required that a person who deprived a slave of his life should receive the same punishment as if he had committed the same offense against a white person.[4] It is to be noted, however, that the States that required the same punishment for killing a slave as for killing a white person excepted the death of a slave in insurrection, while Georgia also excepted the case of a slave dying under "moderate correction", and Mississippi, which had the requirement of jury trial in its Constitution of 1817, omitted it from that of 1832.

There were few references to free Negroes in the constitutions. Florida in 1838 provided that the Assembly should have power to prevent their immigration (art. xvi, sec. 3) and Kentucky in 1850 specifically authorized the punishment of those who might immigrate from other States or refuse to leave the State after having been emancipated (art. x, sec. 2).

THE BLACK CODES[5]

While the constitutions laid down the general policy of the southern States with regard to slavery, the application of these principles was embodied in a voluminous mass of legislation known as the Black Codes. These codes covered a wide range of topics which may be classified under the following heads:

I. The slave as the object of property rights.
II. Criminal law.
III. Runaway slaves and insurrection.
IV. Protection of slaves.
V. General disabilities, including teaching and preaching, miscegenation.
VI. Importation and immigration or regulation of the slave trade.
VII. Emancipation.
VIII. Free Negroes.
IX. Premonitions of Civil War.

Among the questions which naturally arise in the light of later developments are the following. Did the law tend to make manumission easier or more difficult in course of time, or did it recognize the possibility of gradual emancipation as anticipated by Jefferson? Did the law work in the direction of limiting the disabilities and increasing the protection of slaves, or in the opposite direction? Did it tend to better the position of the freedmen? Did it prepare the Negroes for freedom? In short, was the general

[2] The following States authorized the legislature to provide for the humane treatment of slaves: Kentucky in 1792 (art. ix), 1799 (art. vii, sec. 1), and 1850 (art. x, sec. 1); Mississippi in 1817 (art. vi, *Slaves*, sec. 1) and 1832 (art. vii, Slaves, sec. 1); Alabama in 1819 (art. vi, *Slaves*, sec. 1); Missouri in 1820 (art. iii, sec. 26); Arkansas in 1836 (art. iv, sec. 25); Texas in 1845 (art. viii, sec. 1).

[3] The legislatures were forbidden to deprive slaves of an impartial jury trial in Kentucky in 1799 (art. vii, sec. 2) and 1850 (art. x, sec. 3); in Mississippi in 1817 (art. vi, *Slaves*, sec. 2); in Missouri in 1820 (art. iii, sec. 26); in Alabama in 1819 (art. vi, *Slaves*, sec. 2); and in Arkansas in 1836 (art. iv, sec. 25).

[4] Georgia in 1798 (art. iv, sec. 12); Alabama in 1819 (art. vi, *Slaves*, sec. 3); Missouri in 1820 (art. iii, sec. 28); and Texas in 1845 (art. viii, sec. 3).

[5] The reader is referred to the Tables of Slave Codes, pages 323–474, for specific references to the laws quoted in the following pages.

trend towards putting an end to slavery or towards perpetuating it? The legislation of the States south of Mason and Dixon's Line, which became known as Slave States in 1861, did not begin at the same period. Thus Alabama was not organized as a State until 1819, and before that time the laws of the Mississippi Territory applied. Louisiana was not admitted as a State until 1812, and the earlier laws, including the important code of 1806, were those of the Territory of Orleans. The same was true of Missouri until 1812 when it became the Territory of Missouri. Arkansas was part of the Territory of Louisiana until 1812, and from 1812 to 1819 part of the Territory of Missouri. Florida was under Spanish law until ceded in 1819. Texas passed through several stages, being first one of the States of Mexico, and then (1836) an independent republic before joining the United States in 1845.

The legislation of the older States, moreover, had its roots in laws passed by the same commonwealths as colonies, and these in turn were sometimes modelled after legislation in the West India Islands,[6] or neighboring colonies. The purpose of this chapter is not to give a complete digest of Negro legislation at any one period but to trace its tendencies during the period from the adoption of the Federal Constitution down to the Civil War, and thereby to attempt to answer the questions stated above.

I. THE SLAVE AS AN OBJECT OF PROPERTY RIGHTS

To say that the slave is property raises at once the question: What kind of property, real or personal? Inasmuch as the slave, like other mammalia, is capable of locomotion, it would seem abnormal to classify him with the immobilia, as real estate, and we find in fact that the earlier laws generally treated him as personal property. This was the case in Virginia before 1705,[7] and was legally enacted by the Territory of Orleans (Louisiana and Missouri) in 1804, Mississippi in 1822, Florida in 1828, Arkansas in 1838, Kentucky in 1851. But in not a few cases, as in Virginia in 1705, Kentucky in 1798, Louisiana in 1806, the slave was declared by law to be real estate. The purpose of this change was to make it easier to settle estates and "to protect orphans, widows and reversioners in their rights by saving widow's dowers, and preventing a defeat of reversionary interests by a widow or widow's husband selling dower slaves out of the colony."[8] It was in the interest of property, not of the slaves, and did not prevent the sale of slaves individually, or even the breaking up of families. It did not constitute like the *adscriptio glebae* of the Middle Ages a step towards freedom or a mitigation of the hardships of slavery. The change was, however, not without its difficulties and an attempt was made by the colony of Virginia in 1748 to return to the doctrine of personalty. This was frustrated by the veto of the king[9] and it was not until after the independence of the colonies that Virginia passed a law (1792/3) making slaves personal property.[10]

At one time in Virginia slaves were made legal tender in money judgments not exceeding £20 and in land judgments of not over £100,[11] and under the act of 1792 a creditor, if other property was not available, "might seize even emancipated slaves though they

[6] Phillips, U. B., *American Negro Slavery*, 490–493.
[7] See Ballagh, *History of Slavery in Virginia*, 63.
[8] *Ibid.*, 63.
[9] *Ibid.*, 67.
[10] *Ibid.*, 70.
[11] 1782 and 1783, see *Ibid.*, 69.

had enjoyed their freedom for many years if the debt was contracted before emancipation." This was done to prevent emancipation for the purpose of evading creditors. Thus the proper classification of slaves as property was a problem which may be said never to have received a satisfactory solution in southern legislation. The different States did not pursue a uniform policy nor were the individual States consistent with themselves.

But whatever the classification from the point of view of the slave holder might be, there was no doubt what slavery meant to the slave. It was nothing less than the complete denial of his own will. This was expressed in the Texas Penal Code of 1856 in the words: "The right of the master to the obedience and submission of his slave, in all lawful things, is perfect; and the power belongs to the master to inflict any punishment upon the slave not affecting life or limb, and not coming within the definition of cruel treatment, or unreasonable abuse, which he may consider necessary for the purpose of keeping him in such submission, and enforcing such submission to his commands; and if, in the exercise of this right, with or without cause, the slave resists and kills his master, it is murder."[12]

II. CRIMINAL LAW

All of the southern States had special laws relating to crimes committed by the Negroes and differing more or less from the laws applying to free men. The reasons for a special criminal code are obvious. There were certain crimes, such as evasion by flight, insurrection, and the like, to which the slaves were tempted, and for which there would be no motive among free men. Then the punishments must, in the nature of things, be different. To be imprisoned or even to work at forced labor was a relatively light penalty to one whose whole life was one of involuntary toil. Imprisonment, moreover, really penalized not so much the slave as his owner. It was, therefore, almost universal to punish slaves by personal chastisement in preference to imprisonment. Flogging was the most common penalty, varied, however, by the pillory, by cutting off the ears and, in extreme cases, by hanging. If the master's property rights were safeguarded by the substitution of flogging for imprisonment, so in the case of the execution of a slave, it was not uncommon to provide that the owner should be compensated for this loss.

There were a few cases in which States endeavored to establish a parity between the blacks and the whites with regard to punishment. Thus Mississippi in 1833 provided that the laws in force for the trial of free white persons for capital offenses should be applied in the trial of slaves charged with such offenses, and Maryland, in 1846, provided that slaves convicted of the crime of murder in the second degree, rape, arson, burglary, and offences of similar gravity, should be punished in the same manner as other persons for the same offense.

In many cases, however, crimes committed by Negroes were punished more severely than the same crimes committed by whites. The list of capital crimes in particular was very much longer in the case of Negroes. Thus the death penalty was applied to committing an assault, poisoning, or shooting at any free white person, with intent to

[12] *The Penal Code of the State of Texas* (1857), pt. iii, title i, art. 802, sec. 1, p. 159.

kill, by Kentucky in 1811, by Louisiana in 1806, 1814, 1816, and 1857, by the Territory of Florida in 1828, by Virginia in 1843, by Tennessee in 1836 and 1852 (poisoning), and by Texas in 1837 and 1856. In Mississippi, administering poison to any person or assaulting a white person "with intent to kill," was punishable by death in 1822. The Mississippi law was modified in 1829 by providing that if the killing did not actually occur, the proof of malice aforethought expressed in connection with assault should subject the guilty one to capital punishment, but in lack of such proof the slave should merely be whipped.

A few States specifically prohibited the sale of poisonous drugs to slaves, as Alabama in 1835, Florida and Missouri in 1843; while Tennessee, possibly with the fear of the abuse of drugs in view, in 1831 prohibited slaves from practicing medicine.

Burning buildings or grain, barrels of pitch, tar, or any commodities, stealing goods or chattels, or enticing slaves to run away, involved the death penalty in Georgia in 1806. Destroying stacks of rice or corn, produce or grains, houses or buildings, involved the same penalty in Louisiana in 1806 and 1855, while it was likewise applied to arson by Mississippi in 1814 and 1822, Florida in 1828, Texas in 1837, 1856 and 1858, Kentucky in 1842, and Louisiana in 1857. Attempted rape on a white person was commonly made a capital crime, as in Georgia in 1806, Louisiana in 1806 and 1857, Kentucky in 1811, Mississippi in 1814 and 1822, North Carolina and Virginia in 1823, Florida in 1828, Tennessee in 1833 and 1850, Texas in 1837 and 1856, and South Carolina in 1843. Louisiana punished with death wounding a white person in 1806, striking a master or mistress or their children so as to cause bleeding in 1806, 1814, and 1857. In a few cases burglary was punished by death, as in Texas in 1837, 1856 and 1858, and Louisiana in 1857. Likewise burglary or robbery was punished by Florida in 1828 either by the death penalty or by the penalty of having the ears nailed to the post for an hour and receiving thirty-nine lashes.

Under the Texas law of 1856, resistance of a slave to correction, resulting in homicide, rendered him guilty of murder.[13] The same law provided that: "If a slave by insolence, provokes chastisement, and then slay the person chastising him, it will be murder."[14]

There seems to be little change from period to period with regard to these penalties. The early laws as well as the later ones contain examples of them, and one of the most comprehensive and severe was the Louisiana Code of 1806. Virginia provided in 1792 for the emasculation of a slave convicted of an attempt to ravish a white woman, and decreed that a slave giving false testimony should "without further trial" have first one and then the other ear nailed to the pillory for an hour and then have both ears cut off, and receive thirty-nine lashes. Mississippi imposed the same penalty on false testimony in 1807. In the general codification of its criminal law issued by Virginia in 1848, the death penalty was imposed upon a slave guilty of any crime for which a white person would suffer death or be imprisoned three years.

III. LAWS REGARDING RUNAWAY SLAVES

Wherever there is forced labor, there is the ever present danger that the workers will try to escape, or engage in insurrection or rebellion. Hence, all of the slave-holding

[13] *Penal Code of the State of Texas*, pt. iii, title i, sec. 3.
[14] *Ibid.*, pt. iii, title ii, sec. 8.

States enacted, many of them at an early date, laws with regard to these matters. In order to make escape more difficult, a great many States provided that slaves should not absent themselves from their home plantation, and if absent a certain time, should be considered runaways. The punishment was usually whipping. Thus the law of Orleans, including the Territories of Missouri and Arkansas, in 1804 provided that slaves found without permission on the plantation of strangers should receive ten lashes from the owner of the plantation. In 1825 Arkansas allowed these to be given by the captain of the patrol, or else the slave might be punished by the magistrate up to thirty-nine lashes. Louisiana in 1806 made it lawful to fire on runaway slaves who were armed or those who refused to surrender when pursued. The value of the slave so killed was to be paid to the owner from the proceeds of the tax on slaves. This suggests the provision under which now in some States the owners of sheep killed by dogs are to be compensated out of the proceeds of the dog tax.

In some cases it was provided that slaves put in jail for running away and not claimed within a certain time should be sold at auction. Maryland passed such a law in 1803 (amended in 1810 to require a runaway slave to be brought before a Justice to ascertain whether a runaway or not), Alabama in 1809, North Carolina in 1818, Mississippi in 1822, Tennessee in 1825, Florida in 1828, Georgia in 1832, Texas in 1841. Virginia in 1822 provided that runaway slaves should not be sold except upon an order of the court. It will be noticed that all of these laws, with the exception of that of Texas, date from the first third of the century.

Any one who helped a slave to run away or gave him asylum after he had escaped was guilty of one of the most serious offenses against property rights. Hence we find almost all of the States putting heavy penalties upon such conduct. In the case of the Alabama laws of 1824 and 1841 the law applied only to aid given to slaves guilty of capital offenses; in some cases, the law was general and applied to aid given by anyone to a runaway slave; in other cases, the law applied specifically to masters of vessels or those in control of ferries, toll bridges, or railroads. Louisiana in 1807 put a penalty upon concealing slaves amounting to two dollars for each day, or imprisonment of from fifteen days to three months, but this was raised in 1809 to a fine of from one hundred to three hundred dollars. Similar laws, though with varying punishments, were passed by Alabama in 1819; by Florida in 1831, 1832, 1851, and 1855; by Georgia in 1816 and 1833; North Carolina in 1821, 1832, and 1852; South Carolina in 1821, Kentucky in 1830 and 1845; Maryland in 1819, 1828 and 1850; Mississippi in 1822, 1823, 1839 and 1852; Missouri in 1843; Arkansas in 1843 and 1858; Tennessee in 1799, 1806, 1836; Texas in 1839 and 1858; Virginia in 1798, 1824, 1829, 1834 and 1848. Of these fourteen States all but five had passed laws by 1830, and all but three by 1833.

Special laws were also passed applicable to vessels and in later years to railroads. Thus North Carolina in 1792 imposed the death penalty upon masters of vessels allowing slaves on board with the intent to escape, and this penalty was reenacted in 1825. Georgia in 1826 put a fine on captains of vessels carrying Negroes without a certificate of freedom, and in 1850 provided that conductors were not to allow slaves on trains without a permit, and that the owners might recover from the railroads if a slave had escaped on a car or on the locomotive. Kentucky in 1820, 1827, and 1831 put a special penalty upon ferrymen carrying slaves across the Ohio River without a permit. Mississippi in 1822 provided that keepers of ferries and toll bridges were not to allow slaves to cross without permission of the owners. Maryland in 1839 made railroads and steamboats carrying slaves without permission of owners liable to the owners for damages. Tennessee in 1833 fined state contractors and masters of vessels who carried slaves or freemen without obtaining permission from their owners or certificates of freedom. Virginia in 1776 and 1802 passed laws prohibiting masters of vessels from taking slaves. In 1837 that State prohibited railroads from carrying slaves without permission, and in 1839 imposed a special penalty upon keepers of ferries who allowed slaves to cross rivers separating Virginia from other States. In 1841 Virginia required the inspection of vessels previous to departure in order to prevent their carrying away slaves, and passed other laws on the same subject in 1848 and 1856. Alabama in 1841 and 1843 imposed a penalty of ten years imprisonment upon any one who should entice a slave away or enable him to reach some other State in which he might enjoy freedom.

The stealing of slaves was a particularly heinous offense, and was made punishable by the death penalty in Virginia in 1792, and in Mississippi in 1822. Florida imposed the death penalty upon stealing slaves in 1822 and 1829. In 1831 that State punished the stealing of a slave by a white person with fine, or whipping, or imprisonment; in 1832 it added the pillory or branding. In 1851 it imposed the death penalty upon a Negro guilty of the same offense.

PENALTIES FOR INSURRECTION

Rebellion on the part of slaves endangered the very institution of slavery and was made subject to the death penalty in Virginia in 1792, North Carolina in 1802, Missouri Territory (including Arkansas) in 1804; Alabama in 1805 and 1841; Louisiana in 1806 and 1843; Kentucky in 1811; Mississippi in 1822; Florida in 1828; and Texas in 1853 and 1858. Tennessee in 1831 punished insurrection by death or whipping and standing in the pillory "at discretion of the court", and stated that the leaders who refused to surrender "may lawfully be killed." The North Carolina law of 1802 provided that, if a sufficient example had been made by executing some of the conspirators, the death penalty might be commuted for others, and the culprits transported outside of the limits of the United States. Of these eleven States imposing the death penalty all but one had passed laws before Nat Turner's insurrection of 1831.[15] Kentucky in 1798 inflicted thirty lashes on a Negro or slave for lifting his hands against a white person.

To incite rebellion was in many cases as serious an offense as to rebel, and was likewise often subject to the death penalty. The distribution of seditious literature was in some cases punished in the same way. Thus Virginia, as early as 1798 and again in 1817, punished with death free persons inciting rebellion, and in 1832 prohibited the circulation of literature by free Negroes or slaves advising rebellion, under penalty of flogging for a first offense and death for a second. Under the law of 1836 the offenders were to be transported outside of the United States. Alabama in 1812 imposed the death penalty on free persons inciting insurrection, and applied the same penalty in 1832 to the publishing or distributing of literature tending to arouse insurrection.

[15] Hart, *Slavery and Abolition*, 218.

Similar laws imposing the death penalty upon the incitement to rebellion were passed by Georgia in 1804, and, as regards literature, in 1829; by Louisiana in 1806, 1830[16] and again in the Black Code of 1855; by Maryland in 1810; by Kentucky in 1811, by Mississippi and South Carolina in 1822; by Florida in 1828; by North Carolina in 1830 on a second conviction for circulating seditious literature, and for a first offense in 1861; by Texas in 1837; by Tennessee in 1858, though the law of 1836 had imposed only a maximum of twenty years imprisonment for a second offense; by Arkansas in 1861. South Carolina in 1820 fined whites for circulating literature aiming to disturb the peace, and fined free Negroes for the first offense but punished them by corporal punishment and banishment for the second offense. If they returned to the State they were to suffer death. Mississippi in 1830 punished white persons who circulated literature tending to produce disaffection among Negroes by fine and imprisonment. For the same offense slaves and free Negroes were to suffer death, and no Negro was to be employed on printing presses.

Thus thirteen States imposed the death penalty upon inciting rebellion, and of these nine had passed laws by 1830, while in three cases only do the laws fall within the period of agitation immediately preceding the Civil War. Missouri in 1837 punished the third offence with life imprisonment, and less severe punishments, involving minimum terms of imprisonment of five or ten years, were imposed by Kentucky in 1846, Mississippi in 1839 and 1861, and Texas in 1858. Arkansas punished in 1850 by fine and imprisonment free persons circulating literature against the right to own slaves, or inciting insurrection.

How far were laws against insurrection the direct result of agitation for freedom either on the part of the blacks or of white abolitionists? Phillips, who gives a very full history of the different attempts at insurrection from 1792 down to the Civil War, says that the result of Nat Turner's insurrection, the most serious of the series, was "a plentitude of public discussion and of repressive legislation"[17] and adds regarding the revolts in general, that "net effect of this was to restrain that progress of liberalism which the consideration of economic interests, the doctrines of human rights and the spirit of kindliness all tended to promote."[18] It is true that in some cases repressive legislation followed specific revolts. Thus the North Carolina law of 1802 followed some scattering outbreaks in that year; Georgia passed the law of 1804 after some slight disturbances in that year; the Virginia law of 1817 followed the Boxley plot of 1816; the South Carolina law of 1822 followed the Vesey plot of that year, and Virginia passed laws in 1832 following the Nat Turner insurrection of 1831. But Virginia had imposed the death penalty on insurrection in 1792 and nine States had imposed the death penalty on inciting insurrection before 1831. While in some cases the outbreaks may have occasioned the passage of a law at a particular time, these laws had their real justification in the institution of slavery itself and were practically universal.

IV. PROTECTION OF SLAVES

A few States, while punishing severely crimes committed by Negroes, tried to protect them against unfair treatment when accused of crime. In fact, the North Carolina

[16] Or life imprisonment, at the discretion of the court.
[17] Phillips, U. B., *American Negro Slavery*, 483.
[18] *Ibid.*, 488.

law of 1791 laid down broad principles of humanity. Its preamble stated that under the Act of 1774 "the killing of a slave, however wanton, cruel and deliberate, is only punishable in the first instance by imprisonment and paying the value thereof to the owner; which distinction of criminality between the murder of a white person and of one who is equally an human creature, but merely of a different complexion, is disgraceful to humanity and degrading in the highest degree to the laws and principles of a free, Christian and enlightened country." It then provided that any person wilfully and maliciously killing a slave should be guilty of murder, and suffer the same penalty as if he had killed a white man.[19] The practical value of this protection was somewhat impaired by the further provision (also found in other States) that the killing of a slave "dying under moderate correction," should not be punished as murder. But the humane purpose was further shown in the North Carolina law of 1793 which provided for counsel and trial by jury for slaves in cases involving life or limb, and in the law of 1816 which required that such trials should be conducted in the same manner as trials of freemen. Georgia also provided in 1811 for a jury trial of slaves in capital cases, and enacted in 1816 that a slave committing a crime not punishable by death or life imprisonment under the coercion of his owner or overseer should not be adjudged guilty, but that the person who instigated the crime should be prosecuted. Tennessee required in 1815 for the criminal trial of slaves three justices and nine freeholders as jury, but in 1825 required trial by a jury of slave owners. The Florida penal code of 1822 provided that for capital offenses slaves should be fined and punished as whites. Texas in 1837 required a jury of twelve to try slaves for non-capital offenses, and in 1853 provided for a jury of twelve for capital offenses and excluded a person interested in the slave from serving on the jury. In most States no provision was made for a regular jury, but in some cases, a smaller jury was provided. Thus in Louisiana in 1825, the trial must be conducted by a parish judge and six freeholders in case a slave was accused of a non-capital crime, and in 1843 it was provided that the six freeholders constituting the jury must be unanimous in order to convict. Unanimity was also required when, in 1846, the jury in capital crimes was increased to two justices of the peace and ten owners of slaves. Mississippi provided in 1823 that when a slave was accused of a capital crime the court should employ counsel for him if the owner did not.

In addition to giving slaves a certain protection against injustice in the courts, some of the southern States provided for the economic and physical welfare of the Negroes by requiring humane treatment on the part of their masters. The earliest as well as the most thorough and comprehensive example of this kind of protection is found in the general Black Code enacted for the Territory of Orleans in 1806. This provided that slaves with the exception of domestic servants were not to be worked on Sunday and if worked should be paid; it specified in detail the rations to which they were entitled; it required certain articles of clothing for those who did not have a lot of ground on the owner's land to cultivate; it required the maintenance of sick and disabled slaves and the provision of "all kinds of temporal or spiritual assistance;" it allowed a half hour for breakfast and from one and a half to two hours for dinner, according to the season, the shorter time being from May to November. It provided that disabled slaves were not to be sold at public sales without their children against their will, and that children

[19] *Laws of North Carolina* (ed. of 1821), 654.

below ten were not to be sold without their mothers. Finally, any person might lodge a complaint before a justice on behalf of an abused slave, and justices of the peace were authorized to keep themselves informed regarding the treatment of slaves in their districts and to enforce the act. The fine, which was $20 in the original act, was raised in 1855 to from $50 to $200.

Nothing so complete as this code was enacted in any of the States, though some of its provisions are found elsewhere. Thus North Carolina required in 1798 that owners of slaves should provide proper maintenance for such as had become incapable of service. Georgia in 1816, 1833 and 1851 imposed fine and imprisonment at the discretion of the court for cruel treatment of slaves, for denying them sufficient food and clothing and for beating them excessively. Cruel punishments were forbidden by Mississippi in 1822. Labor on the Sabbath was prohibited in Florida Territory in 1828 under a fine of $2.00, and cruel punishments were forbidden by the same act. The Alabama Constitution of 1819 authorized the legislature to pass laws requiring proper food and clothing for slaves but no such law was passed until 1832, and that was repealed the same year. It was not until 1848 that the provision again appeared upon the statute books. It was followed up in 1852 by the provision that in addition to proper food and clothing the owner should supply medical care in case of illness and support in old age. At the same time no child under five was to be separated from its mother in case of sale under execution, nor could a child under ten be so separated, though this was coupled with the ominous qualification, "unless the parties in interest, or one of them makes affidavit .... that he believes his interest will be materially prejudiced by selling the slaves together." The right of property in this case prevailed over the rights of the child. Phillips says that this protection was copied from the Louisiana Code and that Alabama was the only State to adopt such a provision.[20] Cruel and unusual punishments on the part of those in charge of slaves were forbidden by Alabama in 1841.

Texas in 1840 imposed a fine of from $250 to $2,000 upon anyone treating a slave unreasonably or cruelly. It reduced this in 1848 to from $20 to $500, and increased it again in 1858 to from $100 to $2,000. South Carolina in 1858 imposed imprisonment and a fine upon cruelty in punishing slaves, but with the proviso that owners "could inflict such punishment as may be necessary for the good government of the same." Laws designed to protect free Negroes from being reduced to slavery have been detailed in the following chapter.

It is difficult to trace any definite line of progress in this legislation. Ten States legislated to protect slaves against ill-treatment on the part of their owners, but the most comprehensive law was passed as early as 1806. In all but two the laws fall within the first third of the century, and there is little evidence that the humanitarian sentiment which led to the protection of the labor of children in the industrial states of the world in the second quarter of the century produced any appreciable influence upon legislation for the slaves. In only six States (Alabama, Florida, Georgia, Kentucky, Louisiana, and North Carolina) was provision made for suitable food and clothing.

[20] Phillips, U. B., *American Negro Slavery*, 494.

V. SPECIAL DISABILITIES OF THE SLAVE

The general status of the slave was well defined by Louisiana in its extensive code of 1806, which read: "The condition of a slave being merely a passive one, his subordination to his master and to all who represent him is not susceptible to any modification or restriction. . . . . He owes his master and family a respect without bounds, and absolute obedience, and is to execute all orders."[21] The general denial of free initiative which this definition implies was not thought sufficient and not a few laws were passed in the slave-holding States forbidding to the slave, sometimes without, sometimes with his master's consent, certain activities conceded to the free man. Among these were the right to trade, the right to own and cultivate property, the right to appear as a witness, the right to carry arms, the right to travel, and the right to read.

Every slave-holding State put some restriction upon the right of the slave to buy or sell property. There were both general laws restricting buying and selling, and specific laws applying to liquors and poisonous drugs. The former appeared at a very early date, and were a necessary concomitant of slavery, since anything sold by a slave is presumably pilfered. Thus Virginia in 1785 provided that no slave could trade without his owner's consent, and similar laws were enacted by Kentucky in 1792, South Carolina in 1796 (reenacted with increased penalties in 1817 and 1857), Tennessee in 1799 and 1803, Alabama in 1805, North Carolina in 1819, Mississippi and Missouri in 1822, Florida in 1822 and 1828, Georgia in 1833, and Texas in 1850. South Carolina in 1834 forbade the employment of Negroes as salesmen or clerks. In other cases a penalty was put upon persons dealing with slaves, as in Missouri Territory in 1804, and Georgia in 1803.

More specific restrictions were put upon the buying or selling of liquor and poisonous drugs. These laws were not, however, so universal, nor do they appear at so early a date, and some of them prohibited the sale of liquor to slaves, others the sale by slaves. Georgia in 1808, 1833, and 1859 prohibited the sale of liquor to slaves. Kentucky in 1834 provided that those holding licenses to keep taverns should not be allowed to sell to slaves without the consent of the owner, and that no license should be given to Negroes. In Mississippi in 1822 no spirits could be sold to slaves without permission.

Similar laws were passed by Tennessee in 1813, 1830, and 1832, Louisiana and Virginia in 1832, South Carolina in 1834, Texas in 1840, Florida in 1847 and 1853 and Alabama in 1850. The selling of liquor by slaves was forbidden by Maryland in 1828 (near camp meetings), by Virginia (near any public assembly) in 1832, and by Alabama in 1850.

A common restriction forbade owners to allow slaves to hire out their own time, and such laws appeared in many of the States at an early date, as in Virginia in 1782, in Maryland in 1787 (subsequently extended by other acts), in North Carolina in 1794, and in Kentucky in 1798, where the owner forfeited his property right in a slave by allowing him to hire his time. Similar laws, though not always so severe, were passed by Kentucky in 1802, Louisiana in 1806, Tennessee in 1813, Mississippi and South Carolina in 1822, Florida in 1822 and 1856, Missouri in 1841, Texas in 1846, and Ala-

[21] *Acts of the Territory of Louisiana, 1806*, p. 150.

bama in 1848. Georgia in 1803 fined the owners who permitted their slaves to work for themselves but excepted the towns of Savannah, Augusta and Sunbury, while Alabama imposed a similar fine in 1805.

There were several reasons for these laws. One was that as slaves were often thus hired to engage in mechanical pursuits in the cities, they came into competition with white mechanics. Another was that they became too independent. A third, and perhaps the principal one, was that hiring time tended to pave the way to manumission. It is certainly true that to forbid the hiring of his time to the slave deprived him of the one available means of purchasing his liberty and thus tended to perpetuate slavery. These laws were, however, difficult to enforce as the master could often make money out of a slave by letting him work for himself.[22]

Laws restricting general property rights were common, but by no means uniform. In some States, as in Louisiana in 1806 and in Alabama in 1852, there were laws prohibiting the holding of any property by slaves without the owner's consent, and Louisiana in 1825, provided that slaves could make no contracts except for their own emancipation. In other States, slaves were forbidden to own or raise certain specific kinds of property, particularly live stock, such as horses, sheep, hogs, and cattle. Such laws are found in North Carolina in 1779, Mississippi, including Alabama, in 1805, and Florida in 1828. Mississippi in 1822 specifically forbade any slave to cultivate cotton for his own use, as well as to possess stock.

It was common to prohibit slaves from being witnesses against white people, though most of the laws relating to this matter provided that they might give testimony in court against slaves or free Negroes. Restrictive laws of this kind were passed by North Carolina and Virginia in 1777, Tennessee in 1794, Kentucky in 1798, Maryland in 1796, 1801, 1808 and 1847, Alabama in 1805 and 1852, Louisiana in 1806, Mississippi in 1822, Florida in 1828, and Texas in 1846.

For obvious reasons, slaves were generally prohibited from carrying fire arms. This prohibition was enacted at an early date in many States, as by Virginia in 1785, Kentucky in 1798, the Districts of Louisiana and Orleans, covering the States of Louisiana, Arkansas and Missouri, in 1804, Alabama in 1805, Louisiana in 1806, Maryland in 1807, South Carolina in 1819, Mississippi in 1822, Florida in 1828 and 1833, and Texas in 1840, 1850, and 1856. North Carolina in 1831 repealed the law of 1741 which allowed the granting of certificates to slaves to carry guns. In Kentucky, an exception was made in the law of 1798 in favor of free Negroes on the frontier, who were allowed one gun, while all Negroes could keep arms under a license from a justice of peace. The Tennessee Constitution of 1834 (art. i, sec. 26) gave the right to bear arms to free white men, which by implication excluded all Negroes.

The enforcement of the black codes was often entrusted to patrols. Laws creating or recognizing patrols were passed by Virginia in 1784, 1792, and 1839; by Georgia in 1757,[23] 1792, 1806, 1830, 1845, and 1854; by North Carolina in 1794; by South Carolina in 1800, 1819, and 1839; by Territory of Louisiana (covering Missouri and Arkansas) in 1804; by Tennessee in 1806; by Mississippi in 1812, 1819, and 1822; by Alabama in

[22] See Phillips, U. B., *American Negro Slavery*, 411–414.

[23] Amended and continued by acts of 1759, 1765, 1768, 1770, 1773, 1777, and "made perpetual" by act of 1784.

1819 and 1836; by Florida in 1825, 1832, 1833, 1834 (repealed in 1836, and law of 1833 revived); and by Arkansas in 1825 and 1838. The methods of appointment differed in different States, as did the powers entrusted to the patrols. The patrol law of Mississippi, as amended in 1812, required every military captain or commanding officer of a company to make a complete list of male persons in his district liable for patrol duty, and imposed a fine on those failing to attend meetings or send a substitute. Similar laws were passed in 1819, and in 1822 with more detailed instructions to patrols. In 1794, North Carolina provided that patrollers should be appointed for one year and as compensation should be exempt from jury duty, work on the roads, and certain taxes, while also enjoying a percentage of the penalties. In Tennessee patrols were formed under an act of 1806 by appointment on the part of captains of militia. In a number of States they were authorized to execute the laws, and inflict corporal punishment for violations.

To prevent running away and insurrection, restrictions to which reference has already been made, were put upon the movements of slaves. It was not uncommon to provide either that they should not leave the plantation, or travel without permission, as in Virginia, 1782, in Alabama, 1805, in Mississippi, 1822, in Florida, 1828, or that they should not be carried by mail, stages, coaches, boat or railroad cars, as in Tennessee in 1833, in Kentucky in 1838, Missouri in 1841, North Carolina in 1841. Assemblies of Negroes, particularly with white people, were also forbidden in a number of States, as in Virginia in 1792, in Tennessee in 1803 and 1806, and Florida in 1828. In 1804 Virginia declared all night-meetings of slaves illegal. Games, particularly with white people, and in some cases betting, were prohibited by North Carolina in 1830–1831, Virginia in 1852, and Florida in 1855. Hunting with fire was prohibited by South Carolina in 1789, and by Florida in 1828. In some States white overseers were required. Thus in South Carolina in 1800 a white overseer was required on every plantation having ten slaves. Alabama in 1856 required a white agent for those having six slaves, but in 1861 provided that in Shelby County not more than one slave should be without a white agent.

Teaching may easily awaken independent ideas in the mind of the pupil. Hence a good many States thought to protect themselves against rebellion and conspiracy by keeping the Negroes in ignorance, and laws intended to prevent their instruction are found in about half of the southern States. It is to be noted that most of these laws were passed after 1830. Thus Virginia, which in 1805 had provided for the teaching of reading, writing and arithmetic to black or mulatto orphans who might be bound out, in 1831 put the penalty of corporal punishment on free Negroes, and of fine and imprisonment upon white persons, who should teach slaves to read and write. This was clearly the consequence of Turner's Rebellion. Similar laws were passed against the education of Negroes, both slave and free, by Georgia in 1829, by Louisiana in 1830, by North Carolina in 1831, by South Carolina in 1834, and by Missouri in 1847. The North Carolina act read: "Whereas the teaching of slaves to read and write has a tendency to excite dissatisfaction in their minds and to produce insurrection and rebellion to the manifest injury of the citizens of this State," any white person who should teach slaves to read and write, or the use of figures, or who should give them books, should pay a fine of from $100 to $200, or be imprisoned; and if a free colored person should teach them he should be fined, imprisoned and whipped with not less than twenty or more than thirty-nine lashes; while slaves teaching others should receive thirty-nine lashes. Georgia in 1829 forbade the employment of slaves in printing offices on account of the danger that they might thereby learn to read, and in 1833 forbade teaching them to read or write.

In addition to the prohibition of teaching Negroes, several States limited preaching by Negroes. Thus Georgia in 1792 provided that no congregation or company of Negroes should under the pretense of divine worship assemble contrary to the act regulating patrols, and in 1833 put restrictions upon preaching by persons of color. North Carolina in 1831–1832 and Virginia in 1832 prohibited free Negroes or slaves from preaching before slaves or free Negroes.

Miscegenation was not as commonly prohibited as we should expect in view of the racial antagonisms of the South. Virginia tried to discourage intercourse between whites and Negroes by adopting in 1662 the maxim *partus sequitur ventrem* and special disabilities were put upon the class of mulattoes.[24] But the law "unwittingly set a premium upon immorality, as the fall of the female mulatto not only added an additional term to her period of service, but her offspring was by a law of 1723 in turn forced to serve the master until the age of thirty-one years."[25]

While North Carolina in 1787 prohibited marriage between a free Negro or mulatto and a slave without the consent of the master, it was not until 1830 that a law (reenacted in 1838–1839) prohibited marriage of whites and free Negroes. Such marriages were to be considered null and void and whoever performed the marriage ceremony was to be imprisoned. The same law repeated the prohibition of the marriage of free Negroes and slaves. Tennessee in 1822 and Florida in 1832 prohibited the intermarriage of white and colored persons. Texas passed a similar law in 1837 and in 1858 provided specifically that a white person who married a Negro or a person of mixed blood to the third generation, or, having married such a person out of the State, should continue cohabitation, should be imprisoned for from two to five years. Georgia did not prohibit the intermarriage of races but provided merely in 1852 that a white man living in adultery with a colored woman should be subject to fine and imprisonment; in 1861 the penalty of imprisonment was put upon a white woman cohabiting with a slave or free Negro, while the slave or free Negro was to be imprisoned for a week, and receive during the week thirty-nine lashes on three different days. Laws against miscegenation are recorded in only five out of the fourteen slave States, possibly because the colonial laws still held and did not have to be reenacted.

[24] Ballagh, *A History of Slavery in Virginia*, 57–58.
[25] *Ibid.*, 59.

CHAPTER XV

SOUTHERN LEGISLATION REGARDING SLAVERY (Continued)

VI. REGULATION OF THE SLAVE TRADE[1]

While laws were made for the protection of slaves, there were none which aimed at the institution of slavery, and such laws as restricted the importation of slaves into a State were intended to check the abuses and dangers of the traffic, rather than to diminish the number of slaves.

Laws limiting or forbidding the importation of slaves into the States were very common even before Congress acted upon the provision of the Constitution which allowed it to forbid the importation of slaves after 1808. The laws, however, were not altogether uniform on this subject. They represented varying motives and the policy of some States was quite vacillating. Most of the absolute prohibitions occurred early in the history. Thus Virginia provided in 1778 that slaves should not be imported and that those imported should be set free, but this was not to apply to importation by immigrants. The law was, however, relaxed in later years. A statute passed in 1811 provided that citizens of the State might bring in slaves to which they were entitled by marriage or inheritance, and an act of 1812 allowed citizens or intending residents to import into Virginia slaves born in the United States, provided they exported an equal number of female slaves between the ages of 10 and 30. An act of 1819 allowed importation subject only to the restrictions that the slaves must have been born in the United States, and must not have been convicted of crime.

North Carolina, in 1786, prohibited the importation of slaves from abroad, and in 1816 provided that those brought in contrary to the act of Congress should be sold for the profit of the State. South Carolina, in 1788, in a rider attached to a law regulating the settlement of debts, forbade the importation of slaves after January 1, 1793, excepting those who were the property of citizens of the country and who were in the United States when the act was passed. Later acts prohibited the importation of slaves from abroad; and an act of 1816 prohibited absolutely the importation of slaves or the immigration of free Negroes, but this act was repealed in 1818.

In many cases the States were anxious to restrict the slave trade, and therefore provided either that no slaves should be imported for sale or for hire, or that slaves might be imported only by persons immigrating into the State, or by residents bringing their own slaves with them; and in some cases, the selling of the slave within a certain number of years was prohibited. Laws of this general purport were authorized in the Alabama Constitution of 1819, and a law was passed to this effect in Alabama in 1827.

[1] The reader is referred to Miss Donnan's *Documents Illustrative of the History of the Slave Trade to America* for fuller information.

The legislature seems, however, to have been somewhat vacillating on this subject, for it repealed the law in 1829 only to reenact it in 1832, and again repeal it the same year. A similar change of policy showed itself in other States. Tennessee put prohibitions upon the importation of slaves as merchandise in 1812 and 1826, but repealed the latter act in 1855. In Texas, the importation of Negroes except from the United States was prohibited in the Constitution of 1836, and such importation was declared to be piracy, though the State could not prevent immigrants from bringing in their own slaves. Georgia prohibited the importation of slaves with intent to sell in 1816, and in 1817 provided that citizens and immigrants could bring in slaves for their own use, registering them with the court, but repealed all acts of this kind in 1842, while the repealing act was itself repealed in 1843. In 1849, laws prohibiting or restricting the importation of slaves from slave-holding States were again repealed and municipalities were authorized to regulate the slave-trade. This act was repealed in 1852 but was revived again in 1856. Mississippi allowed in 1822 the importation of slaves born in the United States, but prohibited the importation of those born elsewhere or convicted of crime, and required a certificate from the place of importation. In 1833, a tax of 2½ per cent. was imposed upon the value of each slave imported for sale. In the same year an act was passed authorizing an amendment to the constitution which would give the legislature power to regulate or prohibit the importation of slaves, and this was followed in 1837 by an act prohibiting the importation of slaves as merchandise under penalty of $500 fine and imprisonment for six months, while notes given for slaves were declared void. This act was, however, repealed in 1846, and the provisions of the act of 1822 were to be enforced. Kentucky limited, in 1815, the importation of slaves to those brought by persons who immigrated in order to settle, or to those of citizens passing through, or to those bought by residents for their own use. The operation of this law was extended in 1833 and in 1849, but in 1860 all laws restricting the importation of slaves were repealed except as regards those convicted of felony. Louisiana prohibited the importation of slaves with intent to sell or hire in 1826, but repealed the law in 1828. In 1831, Louisiana provided that immigrants might bring their slaves for their own use, but excepted those coming from Alabama, Mississippi, Arkansas and Florida. Slaves imported were not to be sold within five years. The penalty for violation was fine and emancipation, but the slave so freed was to be sent out of the State. This was repealed in 1834. In 1842 Louisiana provided that no slave was to be brought into the State who was entitled to freedom at a future time, and also that slaves were not to be taken out of the State by their owners to any other State or country where slavery was not allowed. Maryland prohibited in 1796 the bringing in of slaves for sale or to reside, with exceptions in favor of those coming into the State to settle, and provided that those brought in contrary to this law should be entitled to their freedom. A similar law was passed in 1832 with the proviso that slaves imported in violation of this act should leave the State or be removed to Liberia. Missouri in 1855 fined those who brought in slaves not belonging to residents, but repealed the act in 1859.

It was common to provide against the importation of slaves who had been guilty of crimes in other States. Thus the Territory of Mississippi, including Alabama, had such a provision in 1808, Florida in 1828, Louisiana in 1810 and 1817, while in 1829, Louisiana specifically prohibited the importation of slaves accused of conspiracy or insurrection in other States. Mississippi likewise excluded in 1822 slaves convicted of crime, and Virginia allowed in 1819 the importation only of slaves not convicted of crime.

This review shows that while nearly all the southern States passed laws restricting or forbidding importation, this legislation was not altogether consistent and was peculiarly subject to change. In general, it reflected a desire to exclude criminals, and to restrict the evils of the slave market, and of the overseas slave trade, while not discouraging the immigration of slave holders. Yet laws restricting the importation of slaves were in many cases repealed, particularly towards the latter part of the period, *e.g.*, in Alabama (1832), Georgia (1842), Kentucky (1860), Mississippi (1846), Missouri (1859), South Carolina (1818), Tennessee (1855), and in general the more stringent laws are found in the eighteenth century.

VII. EMANCIPATION OF SLAVES

Legislation with regard to emancipation is particularly significant as showing the trend of policy in the South and answering the question whether the trend of law was towards freedom or away from it and therefore whether slavery would ultimately have been abolished by the South if it had been left to itself.

Two States, Virginia and Kentucky, passed laws in the eighteenth century which seemed to limit slavery. The Virginia act of 1778 prohibited importation and provided that those brought in should be declared free. The act of 1785 provided that no persons should be held as slaves except such as were slaves at the beginning of the session and their descendants, and added that those who had been introduced into the State and who had lived there a year should be considered free.[2] The Kentucky act of 1798 provided that those only should be slaves who were such in 1785 and the descendants of females of this class. These are apparently the only laws in the list which seem to set limitations upon the institution of slavery and it will be observed that all three belong to the eighteenth century. There were a number of States, however, which in their earlier legislation recognized, and in some cases possibly facilitated, the manumission of slaves by their owners.

Maryland in 1796 allowed manumission by will, but only of slaves under forty-five, able to maintain themselves and not needed to satisfy creditors. Healthy slaves under forty-five might also be freed by deed. North Carolina in 1777 and 1796 and the Territory of Mississippi (which then included Alabama) in 1805 allowed slaves to be manumitted but only for meritorious service; the latter required the owner to give a bond that slaves so freed would not become a public charge, and provided also that they should be liable to be taken in satisfaction of a debt contracted before their emancipation. A similar law was passed in Louisiana Territory (covering Missouri and Arkansas) in 1804, providing that the owner was to care for minors and those over forty-five years of age. Kentucky in 1794 provided that the owners might emancipate their slaves by application to the court or by will, though the court was to demand security for the support of aged or infirm freedmen, and in 1825 Negroes not claimed as slaves and proving to be free were to be given a certificate of freedom. Kentucky as late as 1842 like-

[2] Ballagh, *A History of Slavery in Virginia*, 55, 56.

wise provided for the issuing of a certificate of emancipation on application to the courts. Georgia in 1801 required owners who would emancipate their slaves to apply to the legislature.

Louisiana in 1806 distinctly provided for manumission as a reward for slaves disclosing any plot to commit rebellion or murder, and while in the following year this was limited by a provision that no slave under thirty was to be emancipated, unless he had maintained an honest conduct for four years previous, these conditions were waived in the case of a slave who had saved his master or any member of his family, and in 1813 the State provided compensation for owners of three slaves who were set free for disclosing plots threatening the tranquility of the State. Louisiana was particularly solicitous in behalf of slaves in its civil code of 1825, for it allowed slaves who had acquired the right to be set free at a future time to receive property by gift, and the child of a woman who had acquired this right was to obtain his freedom at the time specified, even if the mother should have previously died. As late as 1830, while Louisiana required owners emancipating their slaves to give security that they would leave the State, it made an exception in the case of slaves who had rendered meritorious service to the State or the owner, or who had preserved the life of the owner.

Maryland in 1810 provided that owners manumitting their slaves at a future period might provide that their children should be considered free before actual manumission. The slave so manumitted was not to be sold outside of the State.

Missouri in 1824 allowed persons held in slavery to sue for their freedom. South Carolina in 1800 provided for emancipation by deed upon examination by magistrate and freeholders of the slave's character and ability to support himself. Tennessee in 1801 simply provided that persons desiring to emancipate their slaves must petition the court, and that the latter should demand security against the slave becoming a public charge. Tennessee actually protected the persons held in slavery by providing in 1817 that in suits for freedom the defendant should give security against his running off with the plaintiff, and in 1829 provided that when a slave had been freed by will, the administrator should petition the court to recognize this, and if he failed, the slave might petition.

Texas, as one of the Mexican States, provided in 1827 that slaves of owners who died without heirs should become free, and that in case of a change of owners by succession one-tenth of the slaves should be emancipated.

Thus on all of the territory subsequently covered by the southern States, with the exception of Florida, provision was made by law for voluntary manumission, and although in some cases the law was restrictive, manumission was not prohibited. A Florida law of 1829 is the one act of this period which positively forbade manumission by the owner.

TENDENCY TO GREATER SEVERITY

In the course of time restrictions became more severe and prohibitions more common. The change of sentiment may be illustrated by the history of such a State as North Carolina. At the beginning of the Revolutionary War, North Carolina was evidently afraid of the unrest that might come from emancipation. An act passed in 1777 required that no slave should be freed except for meritorious services and gave as a reason,

"Whereas the evil and pernicious practice of freeing slaves in this State ought at this alarming and critical time to be guarded." At this period it was evidently still common to free slaves, and the law simply took the usual precautions against vagabondage or pauperism, when in 1795 it required bonds for the good behavior of the freedman and in 1801 required persons manumitting their slaves to give bonds against their becoming a public charge. The act of 1818, however, provided that the power of emancipation should rest exclusively with the superior courts, and in 1830–1831 the law provided that persons desiring to emancipate their slaves must give security that they would leave the State in 90 days, the only exception being made in the case of slaves over fifty years of age, freed for meritorious service. But even in this case security must be given that the slaves would not become a public charge.

Georgia in 1818 reenacted with a higher fine the law of 1801, requiring the consent of the legislature to make a manumission valid, and declared all private instruments of manumission void; and in 1859 declared all post mortem deeds of emancipation void. South Carolina required as early as 1820 that no emancipation should take place except by an act of the legislature, and in 1841 it made any bequest for the emancipation of slaves after the death of the owner void, while gifts and bequests to slaves were also void. Mississippi provided in 1822 that persons claiming to be wrongly enslaved might appeal to the courts, but that anyone aiding in a suit for freedom and failing to establish the same should be subject to a fine, while no member of an emancipation society was to sit as juror. Emancipation was to be allowed only by will, and upon proof to the court that the slave had done meritorious service. In 1842 the same State provided that no person was to devise slaves or remove them from the State for purposes of emancipation. Florida in 1829 prohibited the emancipation of slaves brought in after the passage of the act. Tennessee followed in 1831 the common plan of requiring that a manumitted slave should be removed from the State, though a law of 1833 exempted those slaves who contracted for their freedom before the passage of the act; and in 1854 the State even required emancipated slaves to be transported to the west coast of Africa.

Alabama provided in 1834 that the county court was to free slaves only for meritorious service and that emancipated slaves were to leave the State within twelve months. In 1860 it declared void all wills manumitting slaves, and repealed all laws authorizing manumission by the courts. Maryland, as said above, provided in 1837 that the relation of master and slave should not be abolished, unless by a unanimous vote of both houses in two successive legislatures, or without full compensation. In 1858 Maryland required as a condition of manumission that the freedman should leave the State, and in 1860 prohibited manumission by deed or by will.

Texas, which as one of the Mexican States had provided in its Constitution of 1827 that no one should be born a slave and that no slaves should be imported, completely reversed itself in the next decade. In its Constitution of 1836, as an independent State, it provided that owners should not emancipate their slaves without the consent of Congress unless they sent them outside of the State; and in its Constitution of 1845, as a State of the Union, it prohibited the emancipation of slaves without the consent of their owners.

Louisiana, which had in its earlier codes been considerate of the interests of the Negroes, provided in 1846 that no slave was to be given his freedom under pretense that he or she had been in a State or country in which slavery did not exist. In 1852 emancipation of slaves was permitted only on condition that they would be sent out of the country, and in 1857 no further emancipation was to be allowed. Virginia as a border State was one of the first to prohibit emancipated slaves from staying in the State. As early as 1806 it provided that a freedman remaining in the State twelve months should forfeit his freedom and be sold for the benefit of the poor. This act was repealed in 1827, but in 1831 a free Negro convicted of remaining in the State contrary to law was required to be sold. In 1837 a law provided that an emancipated slave might apply to the court instead of the legislature for permission to stay in a county of the State, but the two counties of Accomac and Northampton were exempted on account of their peculiar position on the peninsula. The Constitution of 1850, however, provided that all emancipated slaves should forfeit their freedom by remaining more than twelve months in the State. Kentucky provided in 1851 that an emancipated slave, failing to leave the State within three months, should be imprisoned, and in 1860 decreed that no slave was to be considered emancipated unless bonds had been deposited for his removal from the State. Arkansas in 1858 forbade further emancipation.

Thus thirteen of the southern States (*viz.* Alabama, Arkansas, Florida, Georgia, Kentucky, Louisiana, Maryland, Mississippi, North Carolina, South Carolina, Tennessee, Texas, and Virginia) had made emancipation legally difficult; in seven of them (Alabama, Kentucky, Louisiana, Maryland, North Carolina, Tennessee, and Virginia) emancipated slaves were not allowed to remain in the State and in all of them the immigration of freedmen was prohibited. The tendency was steadily away from manumission. No laws encouraging it were passed except early in the period, and with the exception of Missouri, all of the ten States enumerated as either countenancing or mildly favoring freedom, passed laws at a later period restricting it.

VIII. FREE NEGROES

In any country in which Negro slavery prevails, the free Negro constitutes a real problem. His status is anomalous and difficult, unless the legislature pursues a policy of gradual emancipation under which freedom is the ultimate goal. In this case he is simply a forerunner of what ultimately all Negroes are expected to be. Where slavery is regarded as permanent, the free Negro is liable to be a constant source of irritation. On the one hand, he may become a charge on the public, unless carefully trained to self support, and on the other hand, he is under suspicion as the possible cause of discontent and even the instigator of revolt among the slaves. Hence legislation with regard to free Negroes was universal in the slave-holding States, and certain topics of legislation recurred frequently. Particularly prominent were laws relating to the immigration of free Negroes; laws prohibiting meetings and association with slaves without the consent of the owner; laws limiting the liquor trade among them, either by prohibiting the sale of liquor to them, or by prohibiting them from selling liquor; and finally laws creating such disabilities as to put them almost on a level with slaves in respect to the criminal law or other matters.

Restriction of immigration was the topic which recurred most frequently in connection with the free Negro. Such legislation began as early as 1793 in Virginia, and spread later to all the other southern States. Even Louisiana, which was relatively liberal regarding free Negroes, and in which they constituted a large and respectable class, noted in some districts for "their intelligence, industry, and habits of good order,"[3] passed a law as early as 1807 prohibiting their immigration. Other States which enacted such legislation at an early date were Maryland in 1807, Kentucky in 1808, Georgia in 1818, South Carolina in 1820, Mississippi in 1822, North Carolina in 1826, Florida in 1826, Tennessee in 1831, and Alabama in 1832. All these States prohibited immigration within the first third of the century, and were followed by Texas in 1840, Arkansas and Missouri in 1843.

Thus all the southern States ultimately had such laws. No one of them repealed or relaxed these laws, but not a few increased their stringency as time went on. Georgia illustrated this tendency very clearly. Although the act of 1807 recognized "the great injury and inconvenience" of the presence of free Negroes, and therefore put them under police regulations, their immigration was still permitted in 1810 upon payment of a tax of $20 and upon registration on arrival, but by 1818 their immigration was prohibited, and those coming into the State were liable to be sold as slaves. In 1829, Georgia provided that ships arriving with free Negroes should undergo quarantine for forty days, that no colored person of the State should go on board or have communication with those on the ship, and that Negroes from the ship having communication with Negroes of the State were to be imprisoned until the time of the departure of the vessel. A further step was taken in 1835 when a law provided that a free Negro leaving the State forfeited his right to return, while in 1859 another law was passed, providing that no free Negro should be imported under penalty of being sold into slavery.

Florida went through a similar course. The prohibition of the immigration of free Negroes in 1826, 1828 and 1832 was followed in 1842 by a law providing that if any free Negro came into the State after 1832 he should be sent away, and if he should return he was to be sold into slavery for ninety-nine years. This act was, however, repealed in 1843, and the former laws revived. Kentucky provided in 1851 that free Negroes were to be registered, and if one of them removed from the State and returned he was to be imprisoned for a term ranging from two to five years. Louisiana, which prohibited the immigration of free Negroes in its code of 1807, under a penalty of $20 for every week of stay after the first fortnight, in 1830 increased the penalty to deportation, or to a year in jail. The law was somewhat modified in 1831 by the provision that free Negroes who exercised a trade might be allowed to return, unless they went to the West India Islands. But in 1842, a law provided that free Negroes returning after exportation should be imprisoned for five years, and for a second offense, for life.

Maryland absolutely prohibited the immigration of free Negroes in 1807, and provided that those who were unable to pay a fine of $10 for each week spent in the State should be sold for a time sufficient to pay the fine; and that persons hiring immigrant free Negroes were to be fined $5 a day. The fine was increased to $20 in 1832, and a free Negro staying out of the State for 30 days was to be considered an alien, with the exception of wagoners, and servants, and those engaged in navigation. In Missouri the immigration of free Negroes was prohibited in 1843 with a penalty of five years imprisonment for returning after being sent back, and with ten years for a second

[3] See Hurd, *The Law of Freedom and Bondage in the United States* (1862), II, 164, quoting *The State vs. Levy*.

offense, though natives of Missouri could go back and forth provided they did not establish a domicile in a free State. Free Negroes residing in Missouri had to procure a license to remain in the State, and in 1847 they were required to give a bond on going from one county to another. In 1857, those going into a free State or territory, and returning, were subject to a fine of not less than $500, or imprisonment for one year, or both.

North Carolina in 1826 imposed a penalty of $500 or servitude for not over ten years upon free Negro immigrants. South Carolina in 1820 prohibited their immigration, and provided that they should be sold for not over five years if they violated this provision. However, free Negroes who were natives might return after two years absence. In 1823 corporal punishment was imposed by South Carolina upon those who returned and refused to leave. Any persons bringing in free Negroes were to be fined $100 for the first offense, and $1000 for the second.

Tennessee passed a great many laws regarding the movement of free Negroes. In 1806 they had to be registered, and could not travel outside of their county without danger of being imprisoned. In 1831 they were not allowed to immigrate at all. The law was relaxed in 1842 by allowing free Negroes who were in the State prior to 1836 to petition the county court for permission to reside in a county, but this act was repealed in 1849, and the act of 1831, which imposed a fine or imprisonment upon the immigration of free Negroes, was revived.

Texas began by providing in 1837 that free Negroes who were in the State at the time of the declaration of independence in 1836 might remain; but in 1840 all immigration was prohibited, and two years were allowed for all free Negroes to leave the State, a period extended in 1842 by President Houston for a further period of two years. In 1856 the act of 1840 was amended, and a heavy fine was imposed on masters of vessels importing free Negroes into the State.

Virginia, possibly on account of its proximity to the free States of the North, was one of the first States to prohibit the immigration of free Negroes, under an act passed in 1793. That act provided that those violating the law should be removed to their place of origin. In 1831 this was made more stringent, and those remaining in the State contrary to law were to be sold. Virginia even made special appropriations to get rid of its free Negroes. In 1832 an act applying only to Northampton County allowed the county to raise funds by taxation to remove free Negroes from the State, and in 1833, an annual appropriation of $18,000 was made for five years to help the counties transport free Negroes. Twenty years later the act of 1853 created a Colonization Board for this purpose, and provided $30,000 annually for five years for the purpose of removing free Negroes to Africa. A tax of one dollar was to be levied for this purpose on all male free Negroes between the ages of 21 and 55.

SPECIAL DISABILITIES OF FREE NEGROES

The association of free Negroes with slaves was often restricted in order to make disorder and insurrection more difficult. In some cases, meetings at which the two groups were present were prohibited. In other cases, the law was more specific and aimed directly at insurrection or disturbance. Some of the laws which prohibited the presence of free Negroes at unlawful meetings of slaves were passed at an early date. North

Carolina in 1787 forbade free Negroes entertaining slaves on the Sabbath or at night, and in 1794 prohibited meetings for drinking or dancing. Kentucky adopted such a law in 1798, Missouri Territory (including Arkansas) in 1804, Alabama and Maryland in 1832. South Carolina in 1800 forbade secret meetings of free Negroes and slaves.

A ban was often put upon gambling. Thus whites gambling with Negroes were liable to imprisonment from one to three years under a Georgia law of 1837. Louisiana, in 1852, punished by fine and imprisonment any white person guilty of gambling or betting with free Negroes or slaves, and Kentucky in 1856 subjected to fine or imprisonment a free Negro who was found gaming with slaves or with whites, while in 1858 white persons who offended were subjected to the additional disqualification of exclusion from public office.

The fear of insurrection explains the occasional prohibition or restriction of religious services. Thus Mississippi in 1831 prohibited slaves and free Negroes from preaching, and Florida, in 1832, prohibited them from assembling for worship; the patrols were authorized to break up such meetings, and, for refusal to disperse, they might inflict corporal punishment up to 39 stripes. Georgia in 1833 prohibited free Negroes from preaching to more than seven of their own color without a certificate from three ordained ministers of their own order, and a license from the chief officer of the town. However, they might attend religious services, if whites were present.

In other cases the law aimed specifically at instigations to running away or revolting. Georgia in 1816 prohibited a free Negro from enticing a slave from his master's service under penalty of hard labor for one year and being sold into slavery for life. Mississippi in 1822 imposed the death penalty upon free Negroes who helped slaves to revolt. Louisiana in 1830 imposed a fine of $1000 or imprisonment at hard labor for from three to five years upon a free Negro who incited insurrection. Georgia in 1835 put a penalty upon free Negroes who harbored slaves and in 1837 Texas provided that a free Negro enticing a slave to escape should be fined the value of the slave, or be sold for life. Kentucky provided in 1834 that free Negroes keeping disorderly houses or harboring runaway slaves should be tried by the mayor and the trustees of the town, and might be hired out for not more than three months. In 1860 for the same offense free Negroes might be sold for periods running from two to ten years. In 1840 a law had provided that free Negroes enticing or aiding slaves to run away, or harboring them, might be punished by thirty-nine lashes and were liable for damage to the owners.

The same considerations which have brought about in recent years the general prohibition of liquor by the legislatures of the southern States undoubtedly influenced the enactment of laws regarding the sale of liquor and poisonous drugs by or to Negroes during the era of slavery. Nearly all of the States of the South had some laws on this subject passed at one time or another. Thus, Mississippi, including Alabama, prohibited the sale of liquor by freedmen in 1816, and to this was added the prohibition of gaming by Alabama in 1858. In Florida, free Negroes were in 1828 prohibited from selling liquor to slaves under a penalty of ten dollars fine and thirty-nine lashes, and in 1843 persons selling poisonous drugs to slaves or free Negroes without permission of their owners were subject to fine and imprisonment. Tennessee in 1836 prohibited slaves from keeping groceries or tippling shops. In North Carolina, 1844–1845, free Negroes were not to sell ardent spirits under fine and imprisonment but in 1858–1859 an exception was made in the case of sales for medicinal purposes or on the order of a physician. Arkansas prohibited the sale of liquor by free Negroes to slaves in 1853, and also forbade slaves to work in groceries, dram shops, or any place where liquor was sold. Virginia in 1832 prohibited the sale of liquor by slaves or free Negroes near any public assembly, and in 1858 provided that no liquor was to be sold to free Negroes without a certificate of good character from three or more justices of the peace. Georgia enacted in 1833 a law prohibiting the sale of liquor to slaves and free Negroes, and in 1835 put a similar prohibition on poisonous drugs. Kentucky in 1846 prohibited the sale or manufacture of liquor by free Negroes unless under white management, and in 1856 prohibited its sale to free Negroes excepting as medicine. Persons selling liquor were not allowed to employ slaves or free Negroes. Maryland coupled gunpowder with liquor in 1832 in its prohibition. South Carolina prohibited the distilling or selling of liquor by free Negroes in 1831. Alabama prohibited in 1850 the employment of slaves or other persons of color to sell liquor, and in 1852 prohibited selling to free Negroes. Thus, there were eleven of the southern States which put more or less restriction upon the sale of liquor and drugs to or by free Negroes. The laws were pretty well distributed in time but most of them occurred after the first third of the century.

GENERAL STATUS OF FREE NEGROES

Many general disabilities were imposed upon free Negroes in the southern States. One of the most common and most justifiable related to carrying firearms. Sometimes the prohibition was absolute, sometimes a license was required. Such laws were passed in 1806 and again in 1811 by Virginia, in 1807 by Maryland, in 1822 by Mississippi, in 1833 by Georgia, in 1833 and 1861 by North Carolina. Virginia in 1832 prohibited all weapons to free Negroes.

A number of sporadic disabilities were enacted in single States but were not found in others. South Carolina in 1820 prohibited the circulation among slaves of literature aiming to disturb the peace. The penalty was a fine not exceeding $1000 both for whites and for free Negroes, but the latter were subjected to an additional penalty of corporal punishment and banishment from the State for a second offense, while those returning from such banishment were to suffer death. A Georgia law of 1829 forbade the employment of slaves or of free persons of color as typesetters in printing offices. Peddling was forbidden to free Negroes by Virginia in 1798 and by Tennessee in 1856, while Virginia in 1843 forbade them in two counties to sell agricultural produce without certificates of two white persons.

Even when free from bondage the Negro was often made to feel that he was in an inferior social position. Thus Louisiana in 1806 provided that "Free people of color ought never to insult or strike white people, nor presume to conceive themselves equal to the white, but on the contrary that they ought to yield to them in every occasion, and never speak or answer to them, but with respect." The Territory of Missouri in 1804 imposed a penalty of up to thirty lashes upon any free Negro who raised his hand against a white person. Mississippi in 1822 imposed a penalty of thirty-nine lashes for using abusive language to or assaulting a white person, except when the assault was committed in self defense.

In not a few cases they were subjected like slaves to special penalties when convicted of crime. Virginia provided in 1823 that free Negroes or mulattoes convicted of offenses punishable by imprisonment for more than two years should be punished by stripes at the discretion of the jury, and be sold as slaves and transported without the limits of the United States. Petty larceny committed by free Negroes was, according to the Virginia law of 1825, subject to the same punishment as if committed by other free persons, but in the case of grand larceny the criminal was subject to corporal punishment and banishment from the State, and in case of return after banishment, he was to suffer death. In 1832 the rule of 1825 with regard to petty larceny was repealed, and for this offense free Negroes were to be punished in the same manner as slaves. Virginia provided in 1860 that for any penitentiary offense a free Negro might be sold into absolute slavery. Attempted rape on a free white female was made subject to the death penalty by Georgia in 1816, by Virginia in 1825, and by Texas in 1853. Georgia coupled free Negroes with slaves in its special capital code of 1821, as well as in the law of 1821 which imposed the death penalty upon burning of houses, and Alabama passed a similar law in 1836. Kentucky in 1798 imposed thirty lashes upon Negroes or slaves lifting their hands against any white person. South Carolina in 1821 punished white persons guilty of concealing runaway slaves by fine or imprisonment, but inflicted corporal punishment for the same offense upon free Negroes. In 1833 the same State abolished the penalty of branding, and instead provided in general that for non-capital offenses free Negroes and slaves should be punished by whipping, by confinement in stocks, by the treadmill, or should be fined. In Florida, under the law of 1828, free Negroes or slaves using abusive language or assaulting a white person were liable to a penalty of thirty-nine lashes, unless acting in self defense. For giving false testimony they were to have their ears nailed to a post for an hour and suffer thirty-nine lashes. For burning minor buildings, other than dwellings, colored persons, whether free or slave, were to receive thirty-nine lashes, and were to stand in the pillory for one hour; while for burning any public buildings, a free Negro was liable to receive one hundred stripes and have his ears nailed to the pillory for half a hour. In 1851 Florida provided that for stealing a free Negro a white person should be subject to fine, corporal punishment, or imprisonment for one year, whereas a Negro should suffer death. Maryland provided in 1858 that for simple larceny a free Negro might be sold into slavery for a period of from two to five years, and if guilty of robbery might be imprisoned or sold for ten years. A free Negro, if unable to pay a fine, was to be hired out to those who would pay it for him, according to a North Carolina law of 1831–1832. Just before the Civil War special penalties were placed by several States upon damaging railroads. Thus, Tennessee in 1860 imposed the death penalty upon Negroes for obstructing railroads. Georgia in 1861 put the same penalty upon destroying railroads.

A number of States refused to admit the testimony of free Negroes in courts of law except against each other, and often slaves and free Negroes were grouped together in one enactment. Maryland in 1796 provided that slaves manumitted after passage of the act should not be elected to any office of profit or trust, or be competent to give evidence against any white person, or in favor of the manumission of any slave petitioning for freedom. Laws excluding the testimony of free Negroes against whites were passed by Virginia and North Carolina in 1777, Tennessee in 1794, Kentucky in 1798, Maryland in 1847, Florida in 1828, Texas in 1846, and Alabama in 1852.

Thus in all of the southern States there were laws which to a greater or less degree imposed upon free Negroes special penalties more severe than those imposed on white people for the same offense, and which in many cases classed them with slaves.

The free Negro was regarded as an irresponsible person who could not be trusted very far, and not a few States provided by law for putting him under guardianship. Some of these laws were passed at an early date. Maryland in 1819 provided that the judges might bind out the children of free Negroes to learn a trade, on condition that they be taught to read and write, and Kentucky passed a similar law in 1825. The latter law was, however, modified in 1843 by the repeal of the educational requirements. Virginia in 1820 provided for hiring free Negroes out for payment of taxes. South Carolina in 1822 provided that free Negroes over fifteen years of age should have guardians appointed over them. North Carolina in 1826 required that those spending their time in idleness should be bound over to the court, which should demand security for their good behavior, and if they could not give a bond, should hire them out; the children of free Negroes might be bound out if it seemed "expedient" to the court. A similar law, passed by Maryland in the same year, required those to leave the State who failed to conform. Other guardianship laws were passed by Georgia in 1808, 1826, 1829, and 1833; by Florida in 1842, and for those over twelve years of age in 1848; by Alabama for those under twenty-one in 1852; and by Tennessee for children of indigent free Negroes in 1852. The Alabama law was modified in 1853 to 1854 by allowing free Negroes over fourteen to choose their guardians and allowing judges to appoint guardians for those under fourteen. Six of these nine States had passed guardianship laws by 1833.

Several States prohibited free Negroes from owning slaves. Laws to that effect were enacted by Georgia in 1818, Kentucky in 1851, and North Carolina in 1861. Virginia had a similar prohibition in its statutes of 1832 and 1858, but excepted from its operation the husband or wife and children of the free Negro, and also cases in which the ownership was acquired by inheritance. Georgia also prohibited them from holding real estate in 1818, but in 1839 made an exception in favor of the free Negroes of Darien and provided in 1845 that they should not be employed to repair buildings. Maryland forbade them to join secret societies in 1843, and provided that for a second offense they should be sold, though in 1846 this was so amended as to permit them to form charitable societies under permission of the mayor of Baltimore on payment of a tax of $5 each. Missouri in 1833 prohibited them from disturbing religious services. There were two States which enacted laws relating to military service, South Carolina, which in 1794 required free Negroes to serve in the militia, and North Carolina, which in 1812 prohibited their enlisting except as musicians.

Near the end of this period several States passed laws allowing free Negroes to choose their own masters and go back to slavery. Such laws were passed by Virginia in 1856, Tennessee and Texas in 1858, Louisiana and Florida in 1859, Alabama, Kentucky and Maryland in 1860.

PROTECTION OF FREE NEGROES

In contrast to the laws just enumerated, there were some cases in which the free Negroes were protected, especially against being reduced to slavery. Georgia provided in 1816 that for non-capital offenses the punishment of free Negroes should not extend to life or limb. Kentucky in 1823 imposed fine or imprisonment upon selling or removing out of the State a colored person entitled to freedom, without the permission of the county court, and repeated this in substance in 1840. Missouri Territory in 1804 imposed the death penalty on stealing and selling free persons as slaves. In 1829 Tennessee imposed imprisonment of from five to fifteen years upon any person who should steal a free Negro, and sell him as a slave. Louisiana imposed in 1830 a fine of $1000 for holding a free Negro as a slave. Texas in 1854 for a similar offense imposed the penalty of imprisonment at hard labor of from one to ten years. Alabama provided in 1841 that free Negroes unable to employ counsel might have attorneys supplied by the State at its expense. Arkansas in 1837 allowed persons held in slavery to sue as poor persons to establish their right to freedom. South Carolina in 1837 imposed a penalty of $1000 or imprisonment for a year for fraudulently abducting a free Negro with intent to deprive him of his liberty, while persons selling such free Negroes into slavery were also to receive thirty-nine lashes. Virginia in 1788 made the stealing or selling of a free person as a slave a felony without benefit of clergy. But in 1795, the "tedious and unfounded law suits" caused by voluntary associations of individuals acting "under cover of effecting that justice towards persons unwarrantably held in slavery which the sovereignty and duty of society alone ought to afford,"[4] led to the imposition of a penalty on any person aiding in the prosecution of a claim to freedom, if the claim should not be established. Mississippi adopted similar legislation in 1822. North Carolina extended in 1810 to all free persons of color the rights granted insolvent debtors. Tennessee in 1833 and Kentucky in 1856 provided pecuniary aid for colonizing free Negroes. Tennessee appropriated $10 for each Negro so transported but not more than $500 a year, and Kentucky voted $5000 annually to the Colonization Society.

It is difficult to generalize regarding these laws designed to safeguard the interests of free Negroes. There is no evidence of any progression. Of eleven laws quoted eight aimed to protect them against being reduced to slavery, but in two cases (Virginia and Mississippi) even the processes of the law were made difficult by imposing a penalty on the activity of anti-slavery societies, and both of these laws were passed long before the intensive agitation of the abolitionists had begun.

RELATIVE INCREASE OF FREE NEGROES AND OF SLAVES

The census figures give us a fair means of judging how far these laws regarding free Negroes produced the intended effect. The important facts may be shown in the following table[5] in which the figures for the fourteen southern States are combined.

	1800	1830	1860
Free Negroes	52,190	160,063	230,958
Slaves	847,698	1,996,064	3,948,713

This table shows that, in spite of the laws, free Negroes increased very considerably during the first sixty years of the century, but it also shows a marked change after 1830 in their rate of increase as compared with that of slaves. Thus in the first thirty years

[4] Hurd, *Law of Freedom and Bondage*, II, 5–6; *Virginia Statutes* (ed. by Shepherd), I, 363–365.

[5] Figures compiled from United States Census, 1860, *Population*, 598–604. In each case the date of the census is given without regard to the particular date of enumeration. Rates of increase are given in rounded integers, and two mistakes in the census computation are corrected.

free Negroes increased by 206 per cent. and slaves by 135 per cent. In the next thirty years, the positions were reversed and free Negroes increased by 44 per cent. while slaves increased by 97 per cent. To put the matter in a different way, the ratio of free Negroes to slaves which was 1:16.2 in 1800 rose to 1:12.4 in 1830 only to fall to 1:17 in 1860. This contrast is affected slightly but not materially by the fact that the six States which were not in the enumeration of 1800, but joined the Union subsequently, happened to be States in which the slaves generally increased more rapidly than the free Negroes.

The operation of the law is more striking if we study individual States, such as Virginia. The rate of increase of free Negroes there was 52 per cent. in the decade ending in 1810. In 1806 a statute required emancipated slaves to leave the State within twelve months, under penalty of being sold back into slavery. The rate of increase in the next decade, ending in 1820, fell to 21 per cent. In 1827 freedmen were allowed to remain in the State if they obtained special permission, but a statute of 1831 emphasized the penalty of a return to slavery for those who remained contrary to law. In the decade ending in 1830 the rate of increase had been 28 per cent., but in three following decades, ending in 1860, it fell to 5, 9, and 7 per cent. Thus the rate of increase in these last three decades was but about one-fifth of that of the preceding three decades.

The figures for other States tell a similar story. North Carolina in 1830 required slaves who had been freed to leave the State, and the rate of increase of free Negroes fell from 34 per cent. in the decade 1820 to 1830 to 16 per cent. in the following decade. Tennessee passed a similar law in 1831 and the rate fell from 67 per cent. to 21 per cent. Alabama passed such a law in 1834 and the rate fell from 175 per cent. to 30 per cent. On the other hand, the rate of the increase remained high in Missouri and Mississippi, which did not require the emigration of freedmen, though the total number in those States was so slight as not to affect materially the general totals, which showed a decided slowing up of the rate of increase of freedmen after 1830. Thus while the laws were not strictly enforced, they did have the effect of retarding the increase of free Negroes in the slave States.

The law was, however, not the only factor influencing the proportion of freedmen to slaves. As stated above, seven of the southern States required slaves who had been freed to leave the State. If these laws had been carried out we should expect to find less freedmen proportionately in these States than in the others. Yet, if we compare the free Negroes to the slaves in this group of States we find that they numbered in 1860 a little over 10 per cent., while in the other States they were but a little over 1 per cent., and even if we eliminate the State of Maryland, which did not require freedmen to leave the State until 1858, there is still a decided difference between the two groups.

The paradox is explained if we group the States according to geographical location. We then find that most of the States with a low percentage of freedmen were in the southerly tier, and these were also the States in which the blacks formed a relatively large fraction of the total population. The conclusion to be drawn from these figures is that the tendency to manumission was strongest in the northerly tier of States where slavery was least profitable, and that laws were made in those States to arrest this tendency.[6] The laws were less strict in the southern tier of States, where the abolition sentiment was weak. Yet in the decade preceding the Civil War manumissions were

[6] See Fox, *The American Colonization Society, 1817–1840* (1919), 29.

fairly numerous and were apparently increasing. The *Census Report* of 1860 says that there were 3,000 in the census year alone, and that they were double what they had been in 1850. The rate which in 1850 had been one manumission to 2,161 slaves had risen to one in 1,309 in 1860.[7]

The subject of southern policy regarding freedmen may be summarized as follows. Manumission was, as a rule, an act of generosity on the part of the slave owner. This was clearly the case, if he gave freedom to a slave outright. It was so to a less degree if he freed him by will, or if he allowed him to earn money enough to buy his freedom. As Phillips has pointed out,[8] this liberality was stimulated by the social doctrines of the revolutionary period, and this accounts for the very large increase in the number of freedmen in the decades 1800–1830. But as the profitableness of cotton increased, the plantation system became more and more identified with the prosperity of the South, hence the gradual weakening of the sentiment for emancipation and the erection of a legal wall intended to perpetuate slavery and discourage individual manumission. As this study has shown, excepting for the very early years of the republic, there is no evidence of any desire to create a favorable legal status for the free Negro or to fit him to assume the responsibilities of a free man. Even with the increased rate of 3,000 manumissions a year in 1860, assuming a stationary population, it would have taken 1,333 years to liberate the 4,000,000 slaves then in the United States. Thus in the absence of any State laws requiring emancipation, it is hard to see how slavery could have been abolished without external pressure.

IX. PREMONITIONS OF CIVIL WAR

As the slavery controversy grew in intensity, the legislatures went beyond the field of domestic legislation and passed resolutions aimed at other States, thus foreshadowing the conflict of arms which was ultimately to decide the whole question.

Virginia in 1836, and Missouri in 1839 passed a resolution condemning the attempts of certain groups to undermine the institution of slavery, and claiming the right of the State alone to deal with the question. The resolution said, "the institution of domestic slavery, as it now exists in many of the States of this confederacy, whether or not a moral or political evil, was entailed on us by our ancestors and recognized by the Constitution of the United States." In 1840 the same State passed a resolution condemning as a violation of the Constitution a law of New York which required masters claiming runaway slaves to establish the ownership of such slaves by a jury trial. A remarkable resolution was adopted by the Virginia legislature in 1840. It covered fourteen printed pages, and contained a long discussion upon slavery, States' rights, and other topics. It was adopted with reference to the demand of the executive of Virginia upon the executive of New York, calling for the surrender of three slaves, fugitives from justice, who were attached to a schooner, and had stolen a slave. The Governor of New York asserted that it was not an offense to steal a slave, because one man could not be the property of another. The resolution declared the action of the Governor of New York "a palpable and dangerous violation of the Constitution and Laws of the United States."

[7] United States Census, 1860, *Population*, xii.
[8] Phillips, U. B., *American Negro Slavery*, 425.

Georgia, in 1842, resolved "that Negroes, or persons of color are not citizens, under the Constitution of the United States; and that Georgia will never recognize such citizenship." This resolution was passed in reply to a resolution of Massachusetts against the imprisonment of free Negroes. The legislature took the ground that "Georgia has never rebuked Massachusetts for fraternizing with Negroes, nor held her up to the reprobation of the States of this Union, for her violations of the Charter of Confederacy, by proclaiming those citizens, who were not so at the time of the adoption of the Federal Constitution; thereby attempting to add to that sacred instrument, and thus violating the letter and spirit of that compact."[9]

Virginia again entered the lists in 1844 in passing a resolution condemning the proposition of the Massachusetts legislature to amend the Constitution by providing for the apportionment of representatives and taxes according to the number of free persons. The same State passed in 1849 concerning the Wilmot Proviso a resolution denying the right of the United States Government to control slavery. A resolution relating to legislation in regard to fugitive slaves was passed by the same State in 1850. Maryland passed in 1844 a resolution claiming the right of the State alone to deal with slavery, and in 1850 condemned the attempt of Congress to abolish slavery in the District of Columbia as a "violation of the implied conditions of the cession, a just cause of alarm to the slave-holding States," and as having "a direct and inevitable tendency to disturb and endanger the Union." In the same year, Maryland condemned the resolution of Vermont against slavery which was considered liable "to provoke a dissolution of the Union." In 1860 Maryland requested its representatives in Congress to work for a treaty with Great Britain with regard to slaves escaping from the southern States to Canada. Resolutions were passed by Texas in 1848 and by Florida in 1849 against the interference by Congress with the institution of slavery, Florida opposing the prohibition of slavery in the District of Columbia, and Texas protesting in particular against the attempt of Congress to prevent citizens of slave-holding States from emigrating with their property and settling in the territories which might be acquired from Mexico. This was stigmatized as "an insult to the southern people, and an outrage upon the sacred rights and privileges, which it is the object of all good governments to protect." Texas passed other resolutions regarding the matter in 1850, 1855 and 1858. The last resolution endorsed the proposed convention of representatives of slave-holding States to consider the question of slavery.

[9] *Acts of Georgia, 1842*, pp. 181–182.

CHAPTER XVI

NEGRO POLICY OF THE NORTHERN STATES

In 1790 there were slaves in all of the northern States except Massachusetts and Maine, then a part of Massachusetts. There were, as in the South, more slaves than free Negroes, the former numbering in the nine northern States (including Vermont which was admitted the following year) 49,257, while the latter numbered 31,008. The North, therefore, had its Negro problem. But it was much less intense than in the South. The seven southern States and territories (including Kentucky and Tennessee) had, in 1790, 32,357 free Negroes or only a few more than the North, but they had 657,527 slaves; and the colored element formed about 36 per cent. of the total population as against 3.9 per cent. in the North. Therefore, while in both sections the same forces, for and against slavery, were at work, they varied widely in relative strength, and the economic resistance to any movement towards emancipation was much greater in the South than in the North. This condition reflected itself in legislation. In the early years, the northern States dealt with much the same topics as the southern States, but the trend towards emancipation was so strong that very soon northern Negro legislation omitted slaves almost entirely and dealt predominantly with free Negroes.

This legislation will be considered under the following heads: I. emancipation, II. crime, III. disabilities, including miscegenation, IV. protection, V. migration, VI. the suffrage, VII. education, VIII. fugitive slaves.

I. EMANCIPATION: DECISION IN SOME STATES THAT SLAVERY WAS INCONSISTENT WITH THEIR INSTITUTIONS

The opinion of Judge Tucker of Virginia that slavery was inconsistent with the doctrine of the natural equality of men was independently applied in Massachusetts by the Supreme Court in one of the first cases brought before it. This case was quoted in Winchendon *vs.* Hatfield, decided in 1808, by Chief Justice Parsons, who said, "in the first action, involving the right of master, which came before the Supreme Judicial Court, after the establishment of the Constitution, the judges declared that by virtue of the first article of the Declaration of Rights, slavery in this State was no more."[1] But no contemporaneous report of the decision in question appears to be extant.[2]

[1] Hurd, *Law of Freedom and Bondage*, II, 29–30, footnote.

[2] *Ibid.*, II, 29. For a full account of the cases in which the provision of the Massachusetts Constitution declaring that "all men are born free and equal" was construed to prohibit slavery, see letter of Dr. Belknap to Judge Tucker of Virginia in Massachusetts Historical Society, *Collections, 1795* (reprint of 1810), 1st series, IV, 191–211. See also "Extinction of Slavery in Massachusetts," by Hon. Emory Washburn, in Massachusetts Historical Society, *Proceedings, 1855–58*, III, 188–203.

New Hampshire had in its constitutions of 1784 and 1792 a declaration similar to, but more comprehensive than that of Massachusetts. It held that "All men are born equally free and independent" and that they "have certain natural, essential, and inherent rights; among which are—the enjoying and defending life and liberty."[3] These provisions were held to exclude slavery, without specific legislation, as did the declaration in the constitution of Massachusetts.[4] Nevertheless, the census of 1790 enumerated 158 slaves in New Hampshire, while none were enumerated in Massachusetts.

Vermont in 1777 was more specific than either Massachusetts or New Hampshire in considering slavery inconsistent with natural rights. After stating that "all men are born equally free and independent," its constitution went on to say: "Therefore, no male person, born in this country, or brought from over sea, ought to be holden by law, to serve any person, as a servant, slave or apprentice, after he arrives to the age of twenty-one years, nor female, in like manner, after she arrives to the age of eighteen years, unless they are bound by their own consent, after they arrive to such age or bound by law, for payment of debts, damages, fines, costs, or the like."[5] Vermont contributed seventeen slaves to the census of 1790.

Maine, having been originally a part of Massachusetts, came into the Union in 1820 as a free State for the same reasons which held in Massachusetts and, like the mother State, had no slaves in 1790. Thus four of the original northern States, all in New England, based their prohibition of slavery upon natural rights as guaranteed by their constitutions.

PROVISION IN SOME STATES FOR GRADUAL EMANCIPATION

Another group of States, five in number, adopted the policy of gradual emancipation by law. Pennsylvania provided in 1780 that children born of slaves within the State after the passage of this act should not be considered slaves. Persons who would have been owners of the children of their slaves, if the act had not been passed, were authorized to claim the service of the children until they reached the age of 28, their status being that of servants bound by indenture. This principle of gradual emancipation was also adopted by Connecticut and Rhode Island in 1784, New York in 1799, and New Jersey (which had in 1786 and 1798 specifically provided the procedure for emancipating slaves) in 1804. New York had as early as 1781 encouraged manumission of slaves to recruit the army and in 1786 provided for the emancipation of slaves becoming the property of the State through the conviction of their owners. The New Jersey law of 1804, after having been amended in 1806, 1809, and 1811, was reenacted in 1820. While, therefore, in these States emancipation did not result immediately from the principle of natural rights, nevertheless, it was the outcome of the same sentiment which inspired the bills of rights of the constitutions and it was so recognized. Thus Pennsylvania had already declared in its Constitution of 1776 "That all men are born

[3] Constitution of 1784, arts. i and ii, in Thorpe, *American Charters, Constitutions and Organic Laws*, IV, 2453; Constitution of 1792, *Ibid.*, 2471.

[4] Hurd, *Law of Freedom and Bondage*, II, 35.

[5] Constitution of Vermont, 1777, chap. i, sec. 1, in Thorpe, *American Charters, Constitutions and Organic Laws*, VI, 3739–3740.

equally free and independent,"[6] and the preamble of the act of 1780, after referring to the emancipation of the United States from the tyranny of Great Britain says: "We esteem it a peculiar blessing granted to us, that we are enabled this day to add one more step to universal civilization by removing as much as possible the sorrows of those who have lived in undeserved bondage." Similarly, Rhode Island declared in the preamble of the law of 1784 that slavery was repugnant to the principle that "all men are entitled to life, liberty, and the pursuit of happiness."[7]

Delaware yielded to the spirit of the times sufficiently to declare in its Constitution of 1776 that "No person hereafter imported into this State from Africa ought to be held in slavery,"[8] but it never adopted in its later constitutions any general declaration regarding equality of rights and it never abolished slavery by enactment. From time to time laws were passed similar to the laws of the southern States, recognizing slavery and providing for its perpetuation. Thus in 1837 a fine was imposed on helping a slave to escape. In 1857 a penalty was imposed upon the captain of a ship or the conductor of a train who should carry a slave out of the State. As late as March 18, 1863, the State imposed the penalty of fine, or in case of default, of whipping, upon a slave who was out after ten o'clock at night without the permission of his master.[9] With the exception of Delaware, all of the original thirteen States north of Maryland, as well as Vermont, had by 1804 provided for the abolition of slavery, either by formal constitutional prohibition, by constitutional interpretation, or by statute.

Some of the States which provided for gradual emancipation took a more radical stand at a later date. Connecticut followed up the law of 1784 by providing in 1788 for the registration of Negro children entitled to their freedom at the age of 25; and in 1797 passed a further law providing that after August of that year no Negro children born in the State should be held in servitude after reaching their twenty-first year. Finally, in 1848, Connecticut closed the door to all possible doubt by providing that "no person shall hereafter be holden in slavery in this State." It also provided that the masters were to support those former slaves who were unable to support themselves. New York provided in 1817 that every Negro or mulatto or mustee born before July 4, 1799, should be free after July 4, 1827. This was followed in 1828 by a general act declaring that all persons born in the State and all persons brought into the State as slaves should be free. Rhode Island, having enacted gradual emancipation in 1784, provided in its Constitution of 1842 that "Slavery will not be permitted in this state."[10] New Jersey in 1846 prohibited slavery and declared all persons held as slaves to be free, while making provision for those unable to support themselves. Vermont passed a special act in 1858 declaring that no person within the State should be considered as property. Delaware, although it never abolished slavery, did in some instances provide for individual emancipation. Thus in 1787 it provided that a slave brought into the State contrary to law should be freed. In 1795 it repealed the colonial law of 1721

[6] "Declaration of Rights," art. i, in Thorpe, *American Charters, Constitutions and Organic Laws*, V, 3082.

[7] Hurd, *Law of Freedom and Bondage*, II, 48–49; *Statutes at Large of Pennsylvania, 1682–1801*, X, 67–73.

[8] Art. xxvi, in Thorpe, *American Charters, Constitutions and Organic Laws*, I, 567.

[9] *Laws of Delaware, 1863*, p. 333.

[10] Art. i. sec. 4 in Thorpe, *American Charters, Constitutions and Organic Laws*, VI, 3223.

making the child of a white woman by a Negro or mulatto father liable to servitude for 31 years. In 1797 it provided for emancipation as a penalty upon an attempt to export a slave, and allowed emancipation by will.

PROVISIONS REGARDING SLAVERY IN THE NEW STATES

With the settlement of the Northwest Territory there began early in the nineteenth century the organization of new States. Most of these were carved out of the territory in which slavery had been abolished by the Ordinance of 1787. Iowa was originally a part of Louisiana and slavery had been abolished within the area covered by it by act of Congress of March 6, 1820. Without exception these States came into the Union with a provision against slavery in their constitutions. These prohibitions began in 1802 with Ohio (art. viii, sec. 2) which was followed by Indiana in 1816 (art. xi, sec. 7), Illinois in 1818 (art. vi, sec. 1), Michigan in 1835 (art. xi), Iowa in 1846 (art. i, sec. 23), Wisconsin in 1848 (art. i, sec. 2), California in 1849 (art. i, sec. 18), Oregon in 1857 (art. i, sec. 35), Minnesota in 1857 (art. i, sec. 2) and Kansas in 1859 (Bill of Rights, sec. 6).[11] On account of the bitter controversy raging over the slavery issue in Kansas, the constitution of that State did not go into effect until 1861. In the meantime an act for abolition of slavery was passed over the governor's veto in 1860, and the State may therefore be set down as a free State in 1861, whatever doubt may have existed in 1859. Likewise the Territory of Nebraska in 1861 passed an emancipation act over the governor's veto. Therefore, with the single exception of Delaware, slavery had been made illegal by 1861 in every State north of Mason and Dixon's line, and in most of the older States steps had been taken to end it by the early part of the nineteenth century. Nearly all of their legislation, therefore, after 1804, related to free Negroes rather than to slaves. And yet there were peculiar exceptions in Illinois, which, in spite of its constitution, recognized the institution of slavery by implication in laws passed in 1819 and 1827, to which reference will be made later.

A peculiar situation existed, however, in the territories acquired from Mexico after the Mexican War. The law of New Mexico during the decade preceding the Civil War is doubtful. Hurd states[12] that, slavery having been abolished by the Republic of Mexico, there could be no slaves among those living in the territory at the time of its acquisition by the United States, which was consummated by its formal cession in 1853. But this law would hold only so far as not modified by the law of the new sovereignty, that is either by Federal law or territorial law. Both authorities acted, but in opposite directions. The territorial Legislature passed an act February 3, 1859, which contained the typical provisions of the black codes of the southern States. But a bill to declare null and void all laws of New Mexico legalizing slavery passed the national House of Representatives May 10, 1860.[13] The same general considerations apply to Utah except that, as Hurd says, "the laws of Mexico have never been taken to have had territorial extent therein."[14] The constitution of the State of Deseret, adopted in 1849, created at least a presumption against slavery in the vague state-

[11] See Thorpe, *American Charters, Constitutions and Organic Laws*, under the various States.
[12] *Law of Freedom and Bondage*, II, 204–208.
[13] *Ibid.*, II, 211, footnote 1.
[14] *Ibid.*, II, 211.

ment: "In republican governments all men should be born equally free and independent." This presumption did not of itself establish freedom and its indefiniteness was reflected in the act of 1852, which, without using the word slave, declared that persons bringing into the Territory "servants justly bound to them, arising from special contract or otherwise" should be entitled to the labor of their servants by filing satisfactory evidence of the obligation with the probate court.[15]

II. SPECIAL CRIMINAL LAWS REGARDING NEGROES

Before, and even after the abolition of slavery not a few States passed special criminal laws relating to the blacks. New York provided in 1790 that slaves convicted of crimes might be transported from the State with permission of the court, which might also inflict other punishment. New Jersey in 1796 empowered the courts to impose corporal punishment, not extending to life and limb, upon slaves for offenses not punishable with death. The same State in 1798 fined owners who permitted their slaves to go about begging, and in 1799 provided that the justices might send disobedient and disorderly slaves to the workhouse on complaint of their masters, who were to pay for their food and working material. In 1820 it provided that slaves convicted of arson, burglary and certain other crimes could be either punished as provided by law or sent out of the United States. Delaware provided in 1807 and again in 1811 that free Negroes, convicted of larceny, might be sold, and it imposed in 1767 and 1797 the penalty of whipping upon slaves convicted of beating a slave or a free Negro. But Delaware also required in 1789 that slaves in capital cases should be tried by a jury and in 1826 that they should be tried as free men. Michigan Territory in 1816 authorized the courts to inflict corporal punishment on slaves in lieu of other penalties, except in capital cases. Illinois provided in 1819 that in all cases in which free persons were punished by fines, servants were to be punished by receiving twenty lashes for every $8, unless they could find someone to pay for them, but that no servant should receive more than forty lashes at one time. The same code provided that slaves and servants found ten miles from home without permission from their masters, were to receive corporal punishment and, following the principles of slave-holding States, punished riots and seditions on the part of slaves with not more than thirty-nine lashes. It also imposed a fine upon persons permitting slaves or servants to assemble to the number of three or more. Kansas Territory in 1855 reflected the intensity of the controversy regarding slavery by imposing a penalty of not less than five years' imprisonment upon persons writing, printing, or circulating literature calculated to produce dissatisfaction among slaves, while the death penalty was imposed upon slaves engaging in rebellion and upon persons advocating rebellion. A Negro guilty of rape upon a white woman was subject to castration, while a white man guilty of the same crime was to suffer imprisonment for not less than five years.

The Territory of New Mexico provided, in the act of February 3, 1859, for the protection of property in slaves, and made the unlawful killing of a slave an offense equal to the killing of a white person. The same act provided corporal punishment not exceeding thirty-nine lashes for slaves guilty of disorderly conduct against white

[15] *Ibid.*, II, 212–214. See also Utah, *Acts, Resolutions and Memorials* (1855), 54, 160.

persons, punished by imprisonment and fine the forging of papers of freedom, provided that fines imposed upon slaves might be commuted to stripes or branding, and imposed the death penalty upon a slave committing rape upon a white woman.

III. DISABILITIES OF NEGROES

Negroes were often considered incompetent to act as witnesses in court. Most of the laws provided in the North, as in the South, that the testimony of a Negro should not be taken excepting against Negroes, or that it should not be taken in actions to which a white man was a party. Such laws were passed by Delaware in 1787, by New York in 1788, by New Jersey in 1798, by Ohio in 1807, by Indiana in 1817 and 1853, by Illinois in 1819, by Iowa in 1851, by California in 1851 and 1854, by Oregon Territory in 1855, by the Territory of Nebraska in 1857, by New Mexico in 1859. Pennsylvania, which passed in 1780 a law against accepting the testimony of Negroes, repealed it in 1847, and Ohio repealed its law in 1849. These laws were, however, not universal in the North and it will be noticed that no New England State is in the list. Delaware modified its law in 1799 by allowing free blacks to testify in criminal cases when no white was present, but not in charges of bastardy against a white man, and it retained this legislation in its revised code of 1852.

Other disabilities were occasionally imposed. New Jersey prohibited the enlistment of slaves in the Continental Army in 1781, and New Hampshire in 1792 excluded blacks from the militia, as did Illinois in 1818 and Indiana in its Constitution of 1851. New Jersey in 1798 prohibited trading by slaves without the consent of their masters. New York in 1788 prohibited trading with slaves and selling them liquor, while Illinois in its code of 1819 prohibited trading with slaves and in 1827 forbade selling them liquor. The code of 1819 also forbade Negroes, mulattoes, or Indians to purchase a servant other than of their own complexion, required resident Negroes to register, and prohibited the employment of blacks without certificates. Ohio in 1795 penalized the selling of strong liquor to any bond servant or slave. In Delaware, the meeting of blacks after ten o'clock in the evening was prohibited in 1832, as was also preaching by non-resident blacks; while in 1855 both political and camp meetings were barred. Delaware authorized in 1849 the hiring out of idle and vagabond free Negroes to compulsory service, and made in 1841 a distinction between white and black insolvents in their liability to imprisonment. New Mexico in 1859 prohibited trading, as well as gaming with slaves, and fined owners who permitted slaves to hire their time.

The fear of conspiracy and insurrection which inspired so much of the legislation of the South was naturally lacking in the free States. Hence laws against sedition and unlawful assemblies were comparatively rare. Yet they existed. New Jersey provided for the dispersion of disorderly assemblages of slaves in 1798. Illinois had provisions similar to those of the southern States in its black code of 1819. Kansas also passed them and in 1855 imposed the death penalty upon advocating rebellion by speech or the circulation of literature, while less severe penalties were imposed by New Mexico in 1859.

Intermarriage between Negroes and whites was specifically prohibited by Massachusetts in 1786, Delaware in 1807, Indiana in 1817 and 1852, Maine in 1821, Illinois in 1829, Iowa in 1840 (but was omitted from the marriage law in the Code of 1851),

Rhode Island in 1844, Michigan in 1846, California in 1850, Kansas Territory in 1855, Washington Territory in 1855, New Mexico in 1859. Massachusetts repealed, in 1834, its law of 1786, except the part which prohibited anyone from officiating at the marriage of a white person to a Negro, Indian or mulatto, but repealed this section in 1843. All sexual intercourse between masters or mistresses and their servants "of the African race" was prohibited by Utah in 1852. New York provided in 1809 that marriage contracts in which one or more parties were slaves were valid, and the children issuing from such marriages were legitimate.

IV. PROTECTION OF NEGROES

In some cases special provisions were made for safeguarding the rights of Negroes. Pennsylvania provided in 1780 that free Negroes or slaves should be tried and punished like other inhabitants of the State, except that a slave should not be admitted to bear witness against a free man. New York provided in 1785 that Negroes and slaves should have a jury trial in capital offenses, and in 1809 allowed manumitted slaves to hold real and personal property and recover the same in the courts, as if they were free born.

Laws against kidnapping Negroes for the purpose of enslaving them were quite common. Such laws were passed by Connecticut in 1788 and 1821; by Pennsylvania in 1788, 1820, 1826, 1847, and 1860; by Delaware in 1793; by New York in 1808 and 1813; by Maine in 1838; by the Territory of Michigan in 1816, 1827, 1855, and 1859; by Indiana in 1810; by Illinois in 1819, 1845, and 1855; by Ohio in 1819, 1831, and 1857; by California in 1850; by Nebraska Territory in 1858. Special penalties were imposed upon kidnapping by Wisconsin Territory in 1839, by Vermont and Connecticut in 1854, and by New York in 1840. Illinois in 1855 provided that the governor should appoint agents to reclaim persons who had been kidnapped and sold into slavery in another State. Indiana, in 1831, declared that the act of removing a person without establishing a claim upon his services was kidnapping, and provided as penalty a fine of from $100 to $5,000 and imprisonment of two to fourteen years. Kansas Territory, in 1855, also punished the kidnapping of persons for the purpose of selling them as slaves, and provided for the right of slaves to petition the courts to establish their right to freedom. Maine in 1857 declared that slaves brought in by their masters should become free, and it punished by fine or imprisonment the effort to exercise authority over them. Utah passed a special act in 1852 for the relief of Indian slaves and prisoners, stating in the preamble that Mexican traders were engaged in this traffic, and that the Indians gambled away their own women and children. It provided that masters who were guilty of cruelty or abuse in punishing their servants should forfeit their rights.

In 1797 Connecticut repealed the provisions of colonial days providing regulations with regard to the travel of free Negroes and slaves, as well as part of the act of 1708 imposing the penalty of whipping upon slaves guilty of defamation. Some States passed laws against the abuse or maltreatment of slaves. Pennsylvania prohibited in 1788 the separation of parents from children and one parent from another for more than ten miles. New Jersey in 1798 authorized the grand jury to indict persons guilty of abusing their slaves. Illinois in 1819 required that servants be provided with wholesome food, clothing, and lodging. New Mexico, in 1859, required a bond of those owners who failed to provide food, clothing, and shelter, and this Territory also punished owners for "inhuman treatment," and imposed a prison sentence upon holding a free Negro as a slave, though the same law imposed a penalty upon stealing slaves from their owners and helping them to escape. The Illinois code of 1819 provided that servants lawfully acquiring property during their term of service should enjoy full ownership of the same, and that they should receive a certificate of freedom on termination of their service. The same code, however, also provided for their corporal punishment in cases of laziness and misbehavior, and declared void contracts between them and their masters during their term of service. New Hampshire passed in 1857 an act declaring that "descent near or remote from a person of African blood" should not deprive such a person of the full rights of citizenship, and that persons holding in slavery persons of any color should be considered guilty of a felony.

This summary shows that while in the early part of the nineteenth century, before the laws for gradual emancipation had effected the complete abolition of slavery, a few laws were passed against maltreatment of slaves and free Negroes, most of the protective laws were aimed at the attempt to carry Negroes into slave-holding States for the purpose of reducing them to slavery. Laws of this kind will receive consideration again, later in the text, when the treatment of fugitive slaves is reviewed.

V. MIGRATION OF NEGROES

The importation of Negroes was generally discouraged. Connecticut had, as early as 1774, prohibited the importation of slaves on the ground that their increase was "injurious to the poor and inconvenient," a prohibition renewed in 1784. After the abolition of slavery, Connecticut provided in 1788 that its inhabitants should not be encouraged in the slave trade, and that a fine should be imposed for each slave taken on board a vessel and for each vessel engaged in the traffic. The slave trade was prohibited by Pennsylvania in 1788, and slaves brought into the State were to be set free. In the same year Massachusetts prohibited the importation of slaves from Africa; declared that insurance upon vessels engaged in the slave trade should be deemed void; and provided in its vagrancy law of 1788 that Negroes, other than citizens of the United States or subjects of Morocco, should not remain in the State more than two months. In the case of refusal to depart, they were to be placed in a house of correction at hard labor, and might, if still refusing to leave, contrary to the orders of a justice of the peace, be whipped with not exceeding ten stripes.

Rhode Island passed in 1787 an act to prevent the slave trade and in 1798 prohibited the importation of Negroes under penalty of emancipation upon their arrival, while a fine of $300 was also imposed for each slave imported. An exception was, however, made in favor of travellers with servants. In the same year transporting a slave out of the State without his consent was prohibited.

New Jersey passed an act to prohibit the importation of slaves in 1786, and again in 1798, excepting those immigrating or those passing through the State with their slaves. In 1798 free Negroes from other States could not travel or work without a certificate of freedom. In the same year the fitting out of vessels for the slave trade was prohibited, and provision was made for the removal of slaves from the State by their owners, though in 1812 this was repealed, and only the removal of slaves without their consent was prohibited. In 1820, New Jersey prohibited the exportation of slaves under a penalty of $1,000 to $2,000 fine, or imprisonment at hard labor for from two to four years, and provided that the slaves so exported should be free and that vessels equipped for exporting them should be forfeited. Persons residing in the State for five years and removing permanently could take their slaves with them if the slaves consented.

New York provided in 1788 that persons buying or receiving slaves to remove them from the State into another, to sell them there, should be subject to a fine, and that the slaves should be declared free, while in 1801 no slaves were to be imported, unless the person importing them came with the intention to reside permanently, and also unless he had owned them for at least a year. This was repealed in 1841. In 1807, however, persons residing in the State ten years were allowed to take their slaves into another State with them, provided they had owned the slaves for ten years. New York provided in 1817 that slaves born after 1799 and brought into the State as slaves should remain servants, if males, until twenty-eight years of age, if females, until twenty-five years, such servants to be taught by the owners. The time was, however, changed to twenty-one years in 1829 for those brought in after passage of the act, and the law was repealed in 1841. Travellers might, under the law of 1817, bring their slaves with them but might not remain over nine months. This, too, was repealed in 1841. The exportation of slaves from the State was made subject to heavy fine and imprisonment by New York in 1819.

Although Delaware did not abolish slavery it showed the same reluctance as the other States north of Mason and Dixon's line to allow the slave trade, and in 1787 forbade the exportation of slaves, while in 1789 it declared the forfeiture of vessels equipped for the African slave trade. But the same act allowed the introduction of slaves devised or inherited, and permitted slaves of citizens of other States to be attached for debt in Delaware. In 1807 it forbade the immigration of free Negroes, unless they could bring a testimonial of good character, and reenacted this provision in 1811. Both the importation and the exportation of slaves were prohibited in 1827, though the courts were authorized in 1829 to grant licenses for this trade. In 1851 free Negroes were prohibited from emigrating except to Maryland, on penalty of being sold, and in 1855 a fine was imposed on bringing in free Negroes. Thus the State of Delaware evidently did not want to have slaves or free Negroes migrate either outwards or inwards.

Illinois seems to have been peculiarly fearful of the Negro element. It provided in 1819 that no Negroes or mulattoes could settle in the State without first presenting a certificate of freedom and registering with the clerk's office, and colored persons not presenting such a certificate were to be deemed runaway slaves. Resident Negroes were also required to register. Slaves could not be brought into the State to be emancipated, unless bonds were furnished against their becoming public charges. In 1829 free Negroes could not come into the State to reside without giving a bond of $1,000 as security against their becoming public charges, and in 1831 a fine of $100 was imposed upon persons bringing in slaves to set them free. In 1848 the exclusion of Negroes was even embodied in the constitution, which required the Assembly to pass at its first session such laws as would prohibit free persons of color from immigrating into the State, and would also prevent the owners of slaves from bringing them into the State for the purpose of setting them free. In 1853 Illinois fined those who should bring slaves into the State, whether they were to be set free or not, and also imposed imprisonment for not more than one year. Negroes or mulattoes, bond or free, coming into the State and remaining more than ten days with the intention of residing, were to be deemed guilty of high misdemeanor. Persons of one-quarter Negro blood were to be deemed mulattoes.

Indiana Territory in 1807 allowed slave owners to bring in their slaves, upon making a record of the same, but limited the period of service for those under fifteen, to the age of thirty-five years in the case of males and thirty-two in the case of females. The act was repealed in 1810, but in the same year a penalty was put on removing Negroes from the State without a certificate from the court. Indiana likewise provided in 1831, that Negro immigrants should give bonds in the sum of $500 and those failing to give bonds should be either hired out or removed from the State. The Indiana Constitution of 1851 prohibited entirely the immigration of Negroes or mulattoes and provided that contracts made contrary to this section were to be void,[16] but this was held by the courts of the State to be repugnant to the Constitution of the United States.[17] In order to get rid of the Negroes, Indiana provided in 1852 for a colonization fund of $5,000, to which fines imposed under the above clause were to go, and further provisions were made in 1853 and 1855.

It was a common thing in the new communities of the West to require that Negroes desiring to settle should bring a certificate of freedom from some court and give bonds to insure their good behavior and self support. In addition to the Illinois and Indiana laws already quoted, such laws were passed by Ohio in 1804 and 1807, Michigan Territory in 1827, and Iowa Territory in 1839. The restrictions became more severe later. Free Negroes were excluded from settling by Iowa in 1851, and by Oregon in its Constitution of 1857.[18] Oregon Territory had, in 1849, prohibited the importation of Negroes on account of the danger of instilling in the minds of the Indians hostility to the white race. This was repealed in 1854. Ohio declared in 1857 that people bringing in slaves were guilty of false imprisonment and that the slaves so imported should be freed, but this was repealed the following year.

VI. THE SUFFRAGE

Voting was specifically confined to whites either by constitution or law in Delaware in 1792, 1831, 1852; Illinois in 1818; New Jersey in 1820 and 1844; Michigan in 1835; Pennsylvania in 1838; Iowa in 1846; Oregon in 1848 and 1857; California and Utah in 1849; Indiana in 1851; Ohio and Kansas in 1859. In Wisconsin Territory the suffrage was confined to whites by act of Congress in 1836, but the State Constitution of 1848 extended it to Indians who were citizens of the United States, and in 1849 the legislature submitted to the people an act including Negroes, which was ratified the same year.

Of the States which made no discrimination, Massachusetts led off in 1780; followed by New York in 1811 and 1821; Maine in 1819, Rhode Island in 1842; New Hampshire in 1843, 1847, and 1857. Connecticut, which had given Negroes the suffrage in 1802,

[16] Art. xiii, secs. 1 and 2, in Thorpe, *American Charters, Constitutions and Organic Laws*, II, 1089.
[17] *Ibid.*, II, 1090, 1095.
[18] Art. i, sec. 36, *Ibid.*, V, 3000.

withdrew it in 1814, and the Constitution of 1818 limited the suffrage to white male citizens. It will be noticed that the States giving the suffrage, with the exception of Wisconsin, were in the East; those denying it, with the exception of New Jersey and Connecticut, were in the West. New York required in its Constitution of 1821 a special property qualification of $250 for Negro voters not required of whites. This was retained in the Constitution of 1846.

VII. EDUCATION

The evils of ignorance in the colored population were realized by some of the northern States at an early day. A New Jersey law of 1798 required the owners, under a penalty of $30, to teach reading to their Negro slaves and servants who were born after 1788. In New York provision was made in 1810 that persons entitled to the services of a child born of a slave mother were to teach it to read, so that it could read the Holy Scriptures by the time it was twenty-one years of age; and a similar law was passed in 1817 by the same State, providing that children of slaves should be taught to read before they were eighteen years of age. In 1845 the Mayor and Council of Brooklyn authorized the laying out of school districts for colored children. Ohio provided in 1849 that in case colored children were not admitted to the common schools, separate schools should be established. Illinois passed in 1855 a law of doubtful merit, requiring the Board of Education in townships in which colored persons resided to allow such portions of the school fund to be used for their education as equalled the taxes collected from the colored people for school purposes.

Connecticut, which had been progressive in its opposition to slavery, took a reactionary step in 1833. In consequence of the excitement caused by the opening of Prudence Crandall's School in Canterbury, for "young ladies and little misses of color," a law was passed in that year prohibiting the establishment of schools for colored persons not inhabitants of the State, on the ground that such literary institutions "would tend to the great increase of the colored population of the State and thereby to the injury of the people."[19] But the reaction was short-lived and the act was repealed in 1838. Utah provided in 1852 that servants should be sent to school. No laws against educating Negroes are found in the northern States, and the fact that so few laws specifically provided for their education indicates that they shared in the benefits of the public school system.

VIII. FUGITIVE SLAVES

Legislation regarding fugitive slaves in the North was, in the nature of things, the converse of that which prevailed in the South. In the South, the object of the law was to prevent the escape of slaves. In the North, the law dealt only with those who had escaped, and regulated their treatment. This kind of legislation went through two distinct phases. In the earlier part of the period laws were passed facilitating their recovery. After the slavery question had become acute, especially after 1840, many States reversed their policy and passed laws designed to make the recapture of slaves difficult.

[19] Steiner, *History of Slavery in Connecticut*, 45–52.

Examples of the former policy occur at an early date. New York in 1788 made persons employing or harboring slaves without the consent of their owners liable to a fine. Rhode Island in 1776 to 1798 punished the concealing or assisting of slaves to escape. New Jersey in 1798 provided for the arrest of slaves coming into the State without a license, and punished those concealing or employing slaves without the consent of their masters. Ohio in 1804 prohibited the harboring of slaves and others, and provided a procedure in claiming runaways, amending it in 1839 and repealing it in 1843. Pennsylvania specified in 1780 and in 1826 the procedure for reclaiming fugitive slaves, as did Delaware in 1816 and 1826. In 1827 Pennsylvania declared null and void all sales of fugitive slaves made after the passage of the act, and punished the removal of a fugitive slave from the State by a fine. New Jersey, in 1826, and by a supplementary act in 1837, provided for the procedure in the case of claims upon fugitive slaves by their owners, and persons seizing fugitive slaves without due process were to be subject to fine or imprisonment. Indiana passed in 1816 an act "to prevent man-stealing", and provided the procedure for claiming fugitive slaves and for punishing the removal of Negroes without a certificate from the proper authorities. A similar act passed by the State in 1824 was declared to be unconstitutional on the authority of Prigg's case in 1850.[20] The Illinois code of 1819 provided that persons harboring slaves belonging to others were to be punished as receivers of stolen goods, and it also punished those carrying out of the State free Negroes or slaves belonging to others, similar provisions being reenacted in 1827, 1845, and 1853. Michigan Territory imposed in 1827 a fine upon those who should conceal the slaves of others.

Connecticut provided in 1838 for a formal procedure to be followed in apprehending and trying fugitive slaves from other States, and specified that the right of trial by jury might be granted on the request of either party, while in order to safeguard the interests of claimants against the bias of an abolitionist juryman, it excluded from the jury anyone "who believes there is not, constitutionally or legally, a slave in the land." This law represented the sentiment of a transition period, for while it protected the rights of the slave owner, it also established so elaborate a procedure as to make the enforcement of a claim difficult. In 1840, New York also required a jury trial for such cases.[21]

Iowa Territory provided for the return of fugitive slaves in 1839. California in 1852 fixed the procedure to be followed in reclaiming fugitive slaves, but prohibited the claimants from holding them in servitude in the State of California, and by an amendment in 1854 limited the continuance of this act to 1855. Kansas, reflecting the domination of the slave interests in the early period of its history, after determining the procedure for reclaiming fugitive slaves, went so far in 1855 as to impose the death penalty or imprisonment upon persons carrying away or assisting the escape of slaves with the intent to procure their freedom.

These laws were the last survivors of vanishing policy. More than a decade earlier, a change had begun to show itself in some of the eastern States, as in the Connecticut law of 1838 already quoted. The change was influenced in no small degree by a decision which the Supreme Court of the United States rendered in 1842, in the case of Prigg *vs.* Pennsylvania. Prigg had gone from Maryland into Pennsylvania to recover a fugitive

[20] Hurd, *Law of Freedom and Bondage*, II, 129, footnote 1.
[21] Steiner, *History of Slavery in Connecticut*, 33–34.

slave belonging to a citizen of Maryland. He had been arrested under the Pennsylvania law of 1826. The case involved, therefore, both the interpretation of article iv, section 2 of the Federal Constitution relating to fugitive slaves, and the constitutionality of the Pennsylvania act of 1826. In its decision the Supreme Court held that "The legislation of Congress, if constitutional, must supersede all State legislation on the same subject, and by necessary implication prohibit it." It declared the Pennsylvania act of 1826 void.[22]

The effect of this decision was to serve notice on the States to leave the execution of the Fugitive Slave Law of 1793 to the Federal authorities, and they were not slow to act upon it. The Massachusetts act of 1843 provided that no judge or justice of the peace should take cognizance of any case arising under the act of Congress of February 12, 1793, relating to fugitive slaves, and that no sheriff or other officer should arrest any person asserted to be a fugitive slave, under penalty of fine and imprisonment. Vermont passed a similar act in the same year and repealed the act of 1840 which specified the procedure for reclaiming slaves. Connecticut followed in 1844 with an act which repealed the act of 1838, and prohibited State officials from participating in the arrest of fugitive slaves, the preamble stating as a reason a decision of the Supreme Court declaring "that both the duty and the power of legislation on that subject pertain exclusively to the national government." Ohio in 1843 repealed the act of 1839 which provided for the return of fugitive slaves. Pennsylvania in 1847 punished the unlawful seizing of fugitives from labor, and provided that the jails should not be used for the detention of such fugitives, unless ordered by the judge. Rhode Island in 1848 prohibited its judges and sheriffs from taking cognizance of the Federal Fugitive Slave Act of 1793, and in 1854 extended the same provision to the Fugitive Slave Act of 1850.

LEGISLATION PRECEDING THE CIVIL WAR

In the decade preceding the Civil War State legislation was strongly influenced by the well known Fugitive Slave Act, passed by Congress in 1850, and by the Dred Scott decision rendered by the Supreme Court in 1857. The former, as part of the Compromise of 1850, was intended as a concession to slavery. The latter, which held that no Negro could be a citizen of the United States, was a distinct blow to abolition. Hence we find the northern States more and more striving by legislation to prevent the encroachment of the slave power upon free territory.

Vermont in 1850 gave circuit judges the right to grant writs of *habeas corpus* to persons claimed as fugitive slaves, and required the state attorneys to aid such fugitives. A more stringent personal liberty bill was passed by Connecticut in 1854, imposing a fine of $5,000 and imprisonment for five years upon any one who should falsely or maliciously pretend a free man to be a slave, with the intention of removing him from the State. In 1855, Maine and Massachusetts passed similar laws, providing that the judges should not take cognizance of claims arising under the Fugitive Slave Act of Congress of 1850, though part of the Massachusetts act was repealed in 1858. Michigan went so far, in 1855, as to provide for the protection of persons arrested as fugitive slaves and for their defense by the county prosecuting attorneys, requiring that they

[22] 16 *Peters*, 539.

should enjoy the rights of *habeas corpus* and trial by jury and that sheriffs should not detain those claimed as fugitive slaves. Maine, in 1857, provided that county attorneys should offer their legal assistance to persons arrested as fugitive slaves. Ohio passed in 1857 an act prohibiting the imprisonment of fugitive slaves. This act was repealed the following year, and the act of 1859 authorized jailers to receive prisoners by authority of United States officials. Wisconsin followed Michigan in 1858 in giving fugitive slaves the assistance of district attorneys in their defense. In the same year Nebraska Territory punished as kidnapping the act of carrying any person into another State without having established a claim under the laws of the United States. The whole trend of legislation in the North was towards safeguarding the rights of northern Negroes and preventing injustice under the Fugitive Slave Act.

In addition to formal acts the northern States passed a number of resolutions relating to the slavery question, which were the antitheses of those passed by the southern States on the same subject. The two sets were like the two sides of a long-range debate, carried on by the legislatures. Massachusetts was early in this field, as in most others, and passed in 1820 a resolution calling upon Congress to prevent the extension of so great a moral and political evil as slavery. This was naturally suggested by the Missouri Compromise. This was followed in 1837 by a resolution condemning the congressional resolution of 1837 which required all petitions relating to slavery to be laid upon the table. The following year Massachusetts called upon Congress to abolish slavery in the District of Columbia and not to admit any new State whose constitution permitted slavery. In 1839 Massachusetts requested Congress to enforce the law against the slave trade, and in 1847 protested against the extension of slavery in the United States by the acquisition of new territory or otherwise. It also condemned the annexation of Texas as aimed at the extension of slavery in the United States. In 1849 Massachusetts called upon Congress not to permit slavery in the Territories of New Mexico and California, and to abolish the slave trade and slavery in the District of Columbia. In 1855 Massachusetts declared the Fugitive Slave Act to be unconstitutional, and called for its repeal. Similar anti-slavery resolutions occasioned by the controversial incidents of different periods were passed by Maine in 1849, 1855, 1856, 1857, and 1859; by New Hampshire in 1847, 1848, 1849, 1855, 1856, 1857, 1858, and 1859; by New Jersey in 1847 and 1849; by New York in 1840, 1842, 1847, 1848, 1857, and 1859; by Pennsylvania in 1819 and 1829; by Rhode Island in 1848, 1849, and 1850; by Vermont in 1825, 1836, 1837, 1838, 1839, 1841, 1842, 1843, 1846, 1847, 1848, 1849, 1850, 1851, 1855, 1858, and 1861.

CHAPTER XVII

LABOR LEGISLATION IN THE NINETEENTH CENTURY

In its broadest sense, labor legislation means legislation relating to labor. It therefore might include legislation to suppress labor as well as legislation to help labor, and legislation to enforce labor, like the Statute of Laborers of 1349, as well as legislation to prevent excessive labor. It might apply to legislation relating to labor under any industrial system, including slavery, serfdom, and the gild system. As commonly understood, however, labor legislation is that which is enacted in the interest of those who labor, and it refers more specifically to labor done under the conditions of production on a large scale, which have developed with especial vigor during the nineteenth century.

The principal influences which have determined the character of this legislation in our country are summarized in the pages which follow.

THE PHYSICAL ENVIRONMENT

Of particular importance in the natural physical environment are the Atlantic Ocean and the long, indented seacoast, which have made their influence felt continuously since the first settlement of the country. The bare fact that the migration to America had to take place across the water instead of by land, as had been the case with regard to the movement of races from Asia and across Europe a thousand and more years before, meant that navigation employed from the beginning a large amount of labor. The ocean also encouraged fishing, and was the principal means of communication between the thirteen original States. It is, therefore, no mere accident that the first important labor legislation of the Federal government related to the protection of seamen. The ocean also helped to create the immigration problem, and led to laws for the protection of immigrants. Indeed the ocean may be said to have directly encouraged immigration, when once men had learned to navigate it effectively, since it was from the beginning and is still, cheaper to undertake a journey of 3000 miles by sea than overland, and it was also much quicker before the days of railroads.

The physiography of the country has also affected the character of labor legislation. The Appalachian wall for a time discouraged western settlements, and to that extent forced people to get their living near the sea. When once the inventions and discoveries of the nineteenth century, especially railroads and the use of steam for manufacturing, made it possible to utilize the coal, metals, and forests of these mountain ranges, the mountains themselves furnished in rails, railroad ties, steel, and coal the instruments of their own subjugation. They also gave rise to new labor problems, connected with mining, with transportation, and with the factory system. Closely connected with the physiography is the geology of the country, and much of the labor legislation relating to coal mining has depended upon the thickness, depth, and dip of the coal deposits. Finally, the climate is another natural feature which has had a bearing upon labor legislation. The climate was an important factor in inducing the importation of African slaves into the colonies, and has had an influence in determining the course of internal migration.

THE ARTIFICIAL ENVIRONMENT

The artificial environment of the laborer, which has been created through the ingenuity and the industry of man, also has had an influence in determining the labor problems for which legislation is enacted as a remedy. The features of this artificial environment are so familiar that it is not necessary to do more than call attention to them. Particularly noticeable were the improvements in transportation, including railroads and steamships, and the improvements in the machinery of manufacturing, which have created a demand for the labor of women and children, and at the same time have made the work of production more intense and exacting. Less striking, but still important, are the advances in engineering science, which have created at once the skyscraper and the tunnel, but with them the caisson disease. The broadening of the market, accompanied by the spread of a complex network of credit relations, has made all production, that of the farmer as well as that of the manufacturer, essentially speculative. Cycles of activity and of depression, all of the same general type but each marked by its own distinctive features, have been accompanied by increasing irregularity of employment. Finally, changes in business organization, the growth of capital, the encouragement of the corporate form of business enterprise, all stimulating to the creation of large-scale business operations, have tended to separate the worker from the employer and have helped to introduce many problems, especially those connected with labor organization.

In addition to the growth of capitalism and production on a large scale, which we share with modern Europe, there have been other economic changes peculiar to the United States, such as the gradual conquest of the frontier, the settlement of once vacant land, and the increasing stream of immigration. These economic conditions themselves have in turn been influenced in part by political situations and legal enactment. Political persecution in Europe, political freedom in the United States, have drawn immigrants to our country. On the other hand, the stimulation of the factory system by the protective tariff, by liberality in granting patents, by laws which made the incorporation of joint stock companies easy, has aided the growth of capitalism, and helped to turn a community made up largely of farmers operating on a small scale into a mercantile and manufacturing commonwealth, with the extreme division of labor which such a state of things implies.

SOCIAL AND ETHICAL IDEALS

There has been a steady change in the direction of greater consideration for those who are required to do the hard work of the world, a greater altruism, a greater sense of human solidarity. This humanitarianism was potent in the movement against slavery. It has also led to legislation for the protection of women and children. Internationally, it has shown itself in the peace movement, in the Red Cross Society, and in help given to distant countries suffering from flood, famine, war, and other disasters.

POLITICAL IDEALS; CLASS INTERESTS

The growth of democracy, which in turn has been partly the creation of the frontier, partly a reflection of European political movements, has powerfully influenced our social and industrial legislation, and has led to a broadening of the suffrage, and the introduction of greater political equality. Since the Civil War we have also had a strong tendency towards centralization, which has influenced the form and source of our social legislation, if it has not determined its substance.

Much is said at the present time regarding class consciousness. Not a little of what we hear on this subject is given out by those who have a direct interest in stimulating class consciousness, and who naturally like to claim as much for it as possible. We find this tendency not only on the part of Marxian socialists, of whose creed class consciousness forms a part, but also on the part of trade unionists of the anti-socialist wing. It can not be denied that trade unions and other organizations of wage receivers have been active, especially since the last quarter of the nineteenth century, in promoting labor legislation, but it should also be remembered that a great deal of this legislation began before these organizations were strong enough to exercise any real influence, and that many parts of labor legislation have, by the very nature of the case, not been influenced by those whose interests were directly concerned, and could not be so influenced. This was true of legislation for the benefit of slaves, who were incapable of helping themselves. This is also true of child labor laws, since children nowhere have the right to vote, or the power or knowledge to exercise an influence on their own behalf. It is also true of legislation for the protection of immigrants who, *ex vi termini*, are not even residents, still less citizens, of the country which passes such laws. It is also true that very much of the legislation enacted for the benefit of those classes which are organized and have the vote has been initiated by others, and could hardly have been carried through without their help. Yet the self interest of wage workers is normally a force to be reckoned with, and has found its expression in the labor movement.

WRITTEN CONSTITUTIONS; LEGAL TRADITION

Our constitutions not infrequently lay down certain principles which the legislature is required to carry into effect, and in that way they may stimulate social legislation. But this is mainly true of the newer constitutions. The older constitutions, on the other hand, which represented the ideals of an earlier generation, often exercised a retarding effect, and in recent years this influence has been so active as to excite no little criticism. The number of laws overthrown on constitutional grounds has been so great that no one takes an important law seriously until it has run the gauntlet of the courts. While this is true of general legislation, it is perhaps more particularly true of social legislation, and it is evident that the social ideals of a past generation, as expressed in the Constitution and interpreted by the courts, have acted as an impediment to change. According to the point of view of the observer, this check may appear as an advantage, or a disadvantage. There can be little doubt, however, of its existence.

Our constitutions are interpreted by the courts. The judges are men trained in the law and almost universally in the traditions of the common law. Even where the common law does not apply, therefore, its traditions strongly influence the judicial mind, and its general effect is antagonistic to any radical social legislation.

COMPETING INTERESTS

In tracing any one line of legislation, we must not overlook the influence of other lines. No one social problem can be solved entirely independently of others. They are all colored by the same *Zeitgeist,* and experiences in one field often stimulate action in another. Thus in its early phases the labor movement was closely connected with changes in our land policy. The movement for conserving our material resources has stimulated the movement for conserving human life, and creating improved conditions of labor. In other cases, however, the expenditure of energy in one field may withdraw activity from other lines of effort. This is particularly the case when a question becomes an absorbing and burning national issue. It can hardly be doubted that the intensity of feeling regarding slavery made people for the time being oblivious of other social problems, as it certainly did make them indifferent to certain political evils, which could not be attacked until after the Civil War.

PERIODS OF DEVELOPMENT IN THE NINETEENTH CENTURY

Labor legislation in the United States, with the exception of that relating to seamen and to immigration, has down to very recent times been in the main State legislation. It is consequently difficult to divide it into periods which will apply to all parts of the country. Each State has gone through its own process of development. The States, therefore, vary much in their rate of progress and in the time at which they first enter upon a movement. As a gust of wind sweeping over a wheat field depresses the grain in a series of waves, until by the time it has reached the further edge of the field, the wheat has already righted itself on the side first touched, so an impulse to social legislation, beginning in one State, may be passed on to others, and by the time it has reached the most backward State the one in which it began may be already dealing with different problems. While, therefore, the different phases of a movement tend to succeed each other in a certain order, their beginning may differ widely in time in the several States. And yet with all these differences in tempo we can recognize the dominance of certain powerful influences in different stages of our history, and we may, therefore, roughly divide the general growth of labor legislation in the nineteenth century into four periods:

1. From 1789 to about 1836. This was a period of inaction. The general economic conditions had not created much demand for labor legislation, excepting for seamen, nor had the doctrines of the early leaders of the labor movement produced much effect in our country.
2. From 1836 to the Civil War. During this period, we note the beginnings of labor

legislation applying to limited fields, and to a few States, and influenced largely by educational ideals.

3. From the Civil War to about 1890. The Civil War was an important mile-stone in this as in other parts of our economic history. This was partly because the settlement of the slavery question left the country free to take up other matters, partly also because the rapid expansion of industry and trade, the extension of the railroad system, and the great increase of immigration which followed the reestablishment of the Union, created new problems to be solved. It was during this period that trade unions came prominently upon the scene, and that the protection first given to women and children was extended to men.

4. After about 1890, new forces came into play, new problems pressed for solution, and new areas, particularly in the South, were reached. It cannot be said that there was any change of direction, but it seems, nevertheless, proper to emphasize the change in the volume and scope of labor legislation, which began in the last decade of the nineteenth century, and which indicated a decided change in the point of view of the public and of the courts.

PRINCIPAL TYPES OF LABOR LEGISLATION

Topically, labor legislation may be divided into three general divisions:

1. Laws regulating the conditions under which labor can be carried on. Most of these laws are prohibitory. They say that certain things shall not be done. They are intended to protect labor against certain dangers. The great bulk of our legislation falls under this head. In it are included not only laws prohibiting or restricting child labor, limiting the hours of employment of women and men, prohibiting unsanitary conditions in factories, but also laws affecting the elements of competition under which people work, more particularly laws checking or controlling immigration in the interest of the other workers, as well as laws providing for the safety of immigrants.

2. Laws regulating self-help, particularly the militant measures of labor organizations. These are in general permissive in character. They state what may be done. They do not require people to do anything. They assume that there is an impulse to improve conditions on the part of those interested, which may lead to abuses and which nevertheless is in itself salutary. Such laws have tended to become on the whole more and more liberal, but they may be divided into two classes, those which try to restrict the abuses of self-help, and those which give a certain privilege or power to organized labor, as distinguished from the unorganized individual. Our constitutions and laws have on the whole been favorable to voluntary organizations. But the principles which showed themselves in the prohibitory and restrictive laws of England down to the second quarter of the nineteenth century made themselves felt in the United States during the same period, through the application of the principles of the common law by the courts.

3. Laws regulating the risks of industry, and affecting the distribution of the burden in case of accident, industrial disease, or death. Laws of this kind represent in general the latest type to be developed, and in most countries laws regulating the conditions of labor have preceded by many years laws regulating its risks. And yet the first labor

laws enacted by the Federal Government really fall in this third class, though applying to a very limited group of people; and in the early laws for the care of seamen in sickness we have not only the beginnings of labor legislation in our country, but also an anticipation of the more general provision for social insurance, which did not become a feature of labor legislation in the United States until within comparatively few years.

It will not be possible in the treatment of the subject of labor legislation always to distinguish sharply between the three types just enumerated, because it often happens that one and the same law covers more than one of these topics. This is especially the case with regard to the laws relating to seamen, the exceptional character of whose work has led to elaborate provisions treating of the various disadvantages which affect them as a class. As these laws were the first in this field to be passed by the Federal Government, they will be the first ones to be treated.

CHAPTER XVIII

THE INSURANCE OF SEAMEN AGAINST ILLNESS[1]

Modern labor legislation, as defined in the last chapter, is enacted for the benefit of the wage receiver, and implies the separation from the capitalist employer of the man who works with his hands. Most of this legislation, therefore, dates from the introduction of the factory system, and of the joint stock company. There was, however, early in our history, a class of workers who were pretty sharply distinguished from the employers, and comparatively few of whom had any opportunities of becoming even small capitalists. These were the seamen; and it was in legislation for seamen that modern labor legislation in the United States began. It was doubtless not thought of at that time as involving any definite social policy, and the very phrase social politics was still unfamiliar. But, from the beginning of our history, navigation was an important industry and the life of the sailor was peculiarly hard. Hence it was that, in spite of the fact that the Constitution had granted no power over labor conditions to the Federal Government, within nine years of the inauguration of Washington, Congress had introduced what was virtually compulsory sick insurance for seamen. It thus anticipated in a limited field the adoption of German compulsory insurance by some 87 years, and set an example which the States themselves did not begin to follow until more than a century later. A curious feature of the law is that the question of its constitutionality seems hardly to have arisen and has never been passed upon by the Supreme Court. The whole system is, therefore, extremely interesting from the point of view of constitutional law. It is no less so, if we look at its history,[2] which can be traced back quite definitely to the destruction of the Spanish Armada in 1588. In other words, the event which established the supremacy of England upon the high seas, and thus led to her predominance as a colonizing nation, also led to the adoption of an important piece of social policy by the greatest of her children.

ENGLISH ORIGINS

After the destruction of the Spanish ships, there was a general demand that something be done for the sailors of the English fleet, and a royal hospital was established at Greenwich, for the care of those seamen of the royal navy who needed it through injury, sickness, or old age. It was supported by a deduction of 6 pence per month out of their wages. Another institution, known as the Chatham Chest, was established

[1] The author is indebted for the greater part of the material on which this chapter is based to an unpublished monograph written for the Carnegie Institution of Washington by Dr. Alba M. Edwards.

[2] For a history of the service, see Banks, "A Sketch of the English Prototype, and the Development of a Marine Hospital Service for Seamen in the United States," in United States Marine Hospital Service, *Annual Report of the Supervising Surgeon-General, 1899*, pp. 266–274; Appleton, *Annual Cyclopaedia*, new series, IV, 778–794, 1879.

at the Chatham dockyards. After these had been in existence for about a century, a demand arose for similar provision for the seamen of the merchant marine, and by an act of William III, passed in 1696, it was provided that seamen who should register themselves for His Majesty's service, and become disabled by virtue of age, wounds, or accident, should be provided for at the royal hospital at Greenwich. This relief was also extended to the widows and children of disabled seamen, and of those who should lose their lives in the service; and for the support of this institution a tax of 6 pence per month was deducted from the seaman's wages. The purpose of this act was the "Increase and encouragement of Seamen."[3] The provisions of these acts were extended by subsequent legislation. In 1729 the tax of 6 pence per month for the hospital at Greenwich was extended to vessels belonging to subjects living in the Channel Islands, the Isle of Man, and America,[4] and in 1761 this was made perpetual.[5]

EARLY ACTION BY THE STATES

After the Declaration of Independence, Virginia and North Carolina, and possibly other States, maintained the English system. Thus under the act of October 1780, Virginia required that 9 pence per month should be collected as hospital money from the pay of all seamen and marines in the State,[6] and in 1782, this amount was raised to a shilling.[7] In 1787, December 20,[8] a law was passed establishing a marine hospital and authorizing the selection of a site in the town of Washington, County of Norfolk, Virginia. North Carolina passed a law in 1789[9] providing for the creation of a hospital fund, and in the following year, an act required the commissioners of the poor at the different ports to act as collectors. This tax was a capitation tax, graded according to rank, captains arriving from a foreign voyage being required to pay 5 shillings, mates 2 shillings 6 pence, and seamen 1 shilling 6 pence.[10] Thus the idea of treating seamen as a class by themselves, requiring especial care, was familiar to the statesmen of the eighteenth century.

FEDERAL ACT OF 1798

Action which may be permissible and proper in one of the States may be beyond the scope of the Federal Government. The Constitution was a grant of powers, and such powers as were given were in many cases carefully defined. Congress could exercise only powers which were granted. Direct taxation had to be apportioned according to population. There is not a word in the Constitution regarding either workmen's insurance or hospitals, or the care of sailors. Nevertheless, in the very first Congress, which met March 4, 1789, it was ordered, under resolution of July 20, "That a committee be appointed to bring in a bill or bills, providing for the establishment of hospitals for sick and disabled seamen . . . ."[11] This did not at once result in any law creating the

[3] Great Britain, *Statutes at Large, 1 James I—10 William III*, vol. III, chap. xxi, 608.
[4] *Ibid., 1 George I—3 George II*, vol. V, chap. vii, 676.
[5] *Ibid., 30 George II—2 George III*, vol. VIII, chap. xxxi, 662–663.
[6] *Statutes at Large of Virginia* (ed. by Hening), X, 385.
[7] *Ibid.*, XI, 161.
[8] *Ibid.*, XII, 494–495.
[9] Haywood, *Manual of the Laws of North Carolina* (1801), 350; *Annals of Congress*, 2 Cong., 1791–1793, p. 695, Nov. 19, 1792.
[10] *Laws of the State of North-Carolina* (published by Iredell, 1791), 704.
[11] *Annals of Congress*, 1 Cong., 1789–1790, I, 685, July 20, 1789.

service, but at least five different bills were brought up from time to time, and a law was finally passed, July 16, 1798.[12] This law was in line with the English and Virginian precedents. It provided for the temporary maintenance of sick or disabled seamen in hospitals or other institutions established in the ports of the United States, and arranged for the levying of a tax of 20 cents a month for this purpose, to be deducted from the wages of each seaman and applied to his support when sick. It involved two distinct activities on the part of the Government, the collection of a direct tax, and the establishment of hospitals or other agencies for the care of sick seamen. The constitutionality of this measure does not seem to have been seriously questioned at the time of its adoption. The *Annals of Congress* contain no account of any debate on the subject in the Senate, and only a few pages are devoted to the debate in the House. A number of persons took part in this debate, among them Mr. Sewall of Massachusetts, Mr. Pinckney of South Carolina, Mr. Livingston of New York. Most of the discussion seems to have turned upon the question of fairness to the seamen in obliging them to pay for care which would ordinarily be considered a charge upon public charity. Somewhat oddly, the chief opponent of the measure seems to have been Mr. Sewall of Massachusetts, although, as the bulk of the seamen were from New England, it was thought that they would profit most from a general tax which would care for them, if they fell ill in the South, while the people of the Northeast would be relieved of certain demands upon their charity. The constitutionality of the measure seems to have been questioned only by Mr. Varnum, who said, regarding the measure, that he did not know how he would reconcile it with that clause of the Constitution which says "that no capitation or other direct tax, shall be laid, unless in proportion to the census or enumeration directed to be taken."[13] This objection, however, did not seem to make much impression, nor did it prevent the bill from being passed. In 1849, more than 50 years after the first act, the justification of the act was thus stated in a report of a Congressional commission: "This is almost the only direct tax laid by government. The power to lay it has always been granted on account of the highly charitable object had in view. From the income of a proverbially improvident class in the community a specific deduction has been made—and government becomes self-constituted guardian and trustee. . . . As the questionable legality of the taxation is laid aside by common consent, it is only asked that, while it is continued, it may be rendered distinct in all its operations."[14]

Its practical justification, apart from the question of its constitutionality, lay, as stated above, in the fact that sailors are improvident and irresponsible and that their vocation is peculiarly dangerous. It takes them away from home, few of them have families who can care for them in illness, and even if they have, they are liable to be sick at a distance from their regular homes. The fact that their work is performed without access to the ordinary diversions of the landsman makes them especially lavish in paying for amusement when they have a few days on shore, so that they seldom save money, and if they are desirous of saving, they have no safe place in which to deposit their funds. Hence they are liable to become the prey of swindlers and robbers. They

[12] United States, *Statutes at Large*, I, 605–606, chap. lxxvii.
[13] *Annals of Congress*, 5 Cong., 1797–1799, II, 1386, 1391, April 10, 1798.
[14] Loring and Edwards, "Report upon the Subject of Marine Hospitals" (1849), in *Senate Executive Documents*, 31 Cong., 2 sess., 1850–1851, III, No. 14, p. 24.

have not even a pauper settlement, if taken sick away from home, and as a rule pay no direct State taxes. The consequence is that the Government has not only made this provision for those that are sick, but has also enacted elaborate laws to protect them against imposition and abuses.

There was another reason for the interest of the Government in sailors. It seemed very important to build up a strong merchant marine in order to provide a supply of seamen for the men-of-war in case of hostilities with other nations. The law was, therefore, not simply a piece of social politics, but also of naval politics, a combination of humanity and national defense which is by no means unusual in the history of labor legislation. The first child labor law of Prussia was inspired by the observation that the recruits for the army in the textile districts were deteriorating in size and strength, and similar considerations have been used in England as an argument for improved labor laws.

The law of 1798[15] imposed a tax of 20 cents per month on the wages of each seaman who was employed on vessels of the United States engaged in the foreign and coasting trades. The tax was to be paid, however, by the masters of vessels, under a penalty of $100 for false accounting, and was to be deducted from the wages due. Out of the funds thus raised the President was authorized to furnish temporary relief in hospitals or other institutions in the ports of the United States to sick and disabled seamen. The money was to be expended in the districts in which it was collected. Unexpended money might be invested in stocks of the United States and used, when sufficient, to build marine hospitals. The President was also authorized to appoint directors of these hospitals. The law did not apply to men engaged in the fisheries, as they were supposed to have homes.

EXTENSIONS OF THE ACT

By an amendment, passed in 1799,[16] the provisions of the act were extended to the officers, seamen, and marines of the navy, and the limitation on expenditures was liberalized so as to make it possible to expend the funds within the State or the next adjoining State, with the exception of what should be collected in the New England States of New Hampshire, Massachusetts, Rhode Island, and Connecticut. Under an amending act of May 3, 1802,[17] all of the money was turned into a general fund, and the limitation removed.

Louisiana was not acquired until 1803, and yet many American seamen had occasion to stop at New Orleans, and were liable to be taken ill there. The advantages of the marine hospital service were accordingly extended by the act of 1802[18] so as to apply to persons employed on boats belonging to citizens of the United States and descending the Mississippi with the intention of going to New Orleans. The masters of such boats were required to report to the collector at Fort Adams, and pay over the tax of 20 cents per month to him. The same act permitted the admission of sick and disabled foreign seamen into the marine hospitals of the United States at a charge of 75 cents per day, to be paid by the masters of the vessels. The act also required collectors to pay into the

[15] United States, *Statutes at Large*, I, 605–606, chap. lxxvii.
[16] *Ibid.*, I, 729, chap. xxxvi.
[17] *Ibid.*, II, 192–193, chap. li.
[18] *Ibid.*, II, 192, chap. 1.

United States Treasury all money collected by them under the act, and allowed them the same commission as on other money collected, while the directors of marine hospitals were made accountable to the Treasury and allowed a commission of 1 per cent. on all sums expended. In 1811, by act of February 26,[19] separate hospitals were established for the navy. This was done on account of the inadequate relief and the poor service of the marine hospitals.[20] In 1843, by act of March 1,[21] the provisions of the act of 1798 were extended to the masters, owners, and seamen of registered vessels employed in carrying on the coasting trade. It seems that for some reason, the provisions of section 2 of the act of 1798, applying to coasting vessels, had been suspended by construction since the year 1831, and the act of 1843 simply revived this part of the original act.[22] These acts constitute the substantial part of the legislation relating to marine hospitals down to the Civil War.

INADEQUATE EXECUTION OF THE LAWS

In accordance with the provisions quoted above the Government began early in the nineteenth century to establish marine hospitals. The first one, located at Norfolk, Virginia, was purchased in 1800. In 1802 and 1803 a hospital for the port of Boston was built at Charlestown. There seems to have been a hospital at Newport, Rhode Island, since the Secretary of the Treasury mentions in his report for 1802 that it was discontinued. No others were established until 1834, when one was located at Charleston, South Carolina. During the first 45 years after the passage of the act, there were never more than three marine hospitals in operation at any one time. This was due partly to lack of funds, partly to lack of organization of the service, and partly to the lack of any popular demand for the establishment of such hospitals.

A change in public sentiment seems to have taken place after about 1830, and for twenty years strong pressure was brought to bear upon Congress by State legislatures and cities of the interior, asking for the establishment of marine hospitals along the Mississippi and Ohio rivers and on the Great Lakes. These petitions became so frequent that they could not be denied. The traffic on the rivers had increased, until in 1836 it was estimated that 40,000 hands were employed in navigating the steamboats and flatboats on the Mississippi and its tributaries, while 3,000 were employed on the boats of the lakes and canals. They thus equalled about two-thirds of the 63,000 who were employed in 1832 in the foreign and coasting trades of the United States.[23]

REPORT OF 1837

In 1837 a medical board, appointed in pursuance of the act of March 3, 1837 to select sites for marine hospitals, estimated that on the Mississippi and Ohio rivers there were 638 steamboats, employing over 15,950 officers and men, and 6,000 other boats, employing 30,000 officers and men, a total of over 45,950 persons. On Lake Erie,

[19] *Ibid.*, II, 650, chap. xxvi.
[20] United States, Secretary of the Navy, *Annual Report, 1882*, I, 392.
[21] United States, *Statutes at Large*, V, 602, chap. xlix.
[22] Loring and Edwards, "Report upon the Subject of Marine Hospitals," 3.
[23] Drake, "Report on Western Commercial Hospitals," in *House Executive Documents*, 24 Cong., 1 sess., 1835–1836, IV, No. 195.

it was estimated that there were 300 ships, brigs, schooners, and sloops, employing 2,100 officers and men; 42 steamboats, employing 1,260 officers and men; and 256 canal boats, employing 1,792 officers and men—a total on Lake Erie of 598 ships, and 5,152 men. Thus, taking Lake Erie and the Mississippi and Ohio rivers, there was a total of 7,236 craft and over 51,000 officers and men.[24] It was felt that these people needed relief quite as much as the seamen. The men who left the North in their flatboats often sickened and died when they reached the lower part of the river, with its warm, moist climate. One of the reports stated: "Nothing is more common, than for two out of the five hands, who generally manage one of these boats, to die; and it has even happened, that the whole have perished, and the boat with its cargo been left deserted, to be lost."[25] The boatmen had no claim for relief on the towns along their route, few of which were provided with hospitals.

The tax itself was collected in a careless manner. Only a small fraction of the boatmen paid it, and where there was a pretense of giving relief, it was given only to these few. The act providing for the collection of the tax at Fort Adams on boats descending the Mississippi was not deemed to be in force after May 3, 1807. Figures which were printed in 1836 giving money collected and expended from the passage of the law to December 31, 1834, showed that, while the United States as a whole paid out more than it took in, in six of the western and southwestern States the reverse was true, and nearly twice as much was collected as was paid out. This is shown in the following table:[26]

State	Collected	Expended
Tennessee	$407.41	$16.16
Kentucky		659.00
Missouri	83.16	
Mississippi	2,364.73	133.69
Ohio	2,096.63	1,672.42
Michigan	430.69	271.21
Total	$5,382.62	$2,752.48
United States	$1,729,045.81	$2,029,375.49

INCREASE IN ACTIVITY THEREAFTER

The result of this showing was that the Government, which in the beginning only built hospitals on the seaboard in order to provide for seamen in the merchant marine, now began to build them on the great interior waterways, and under authority of an act of March 3, 1837,[27] selected three sites on the Mississippi, three on the Ohio, and one on Lake Erie, while two other hospitals, one at New Orleans and one at Mobile, were provided for by the same act. For about twenty years there was a period of great activity in building hospitals. Under acts passed March 3, 1837, August 29, 1842, June 15, 1844, March 3, 1845, and August 4, 1854, further provision was made for the establishment of hospitals, and twenty-seven of them were erected down to the year 1861. The hospital at Galena, Illinois, was established in that year. Of the twenty-seven hospitals which had their origin in this period of active promotion, all but three

[24] "Report of Medical Board," in *Senate Documents*, 25 Cong., 2 sess., 1838, I, No. 1, p. 196.
[25] Drake, "Report on Western Commercial Hospitals," 2.
[26] "Report of Committee on Commerce," in *Senate Executive Documents*, 24 Cong., 1 sess., 1836, IV, No. 332, p. 4.
[27] United States, *Statutes at Large*, V, 189.

were in the South or West, and about half were in the interior, either on rivers or lakes. This activity reflected little credit upon the intelligence of the Government. Many of the hospitals were located in places where they were not needed, and on unhealthy sites; many were very badly constructed, with little reference to sanitation or to hospital needs, were poorly ventilated, improperly drained, devoid of toilet facilities, and with no adequate water supply. The system of construction by contract was expensive and defective.

REACTION AFTER 1855

Partly in consequence of these blunders, partly in consequence of the fact that the need of government hospitals was lessened by the erection of municipal hospitals, partly on account of the high per capita cost of relief in the government hospitals, which often had numerous attendants and few patients, public sentiment after 1855 turned against this policy. It was now discovered that it would be more advantageous for the Government to encourage the erection of private hospitals, by agreeing to pay a fair price for the treatment of sailors, or even to contract with private boarding houses for their care, rather than to build hospitals of its own.[28] This view was taken by the Secretary of the Treasury, James Guthrie, in December 1854, and Secretary Chase, in his report of 1860 to 1861, recommended that "no new structures be undertaken except in cases of the clearest expediency or necessity."[29] In the following year,[30] he was authorized to rent any of the marine hospitals to the authorities of the cities, towns, or counties in which they were located, and contract with such authorities for the relief of sick or disabled seamen.

MEDICAL SERVICE OF THE MARINE HOSPITALS

Table I, p. 238, shows that in spite of bad management, a considerable number of persons in the aggregate received relief. There were no reports before 1818, but the figures for the years after 1818 vary from a minimum of 2,692 patients in 1828 to a maximum of 13,640 in 1855, the number showing on the whole a steady increase.

The tax paid by the seamen proportioned to the number of persons receiving aid, gives the following averages: 1818, $13.03; 1836, $12.83; 1850, $10.92; 1858, $15.33. But in none of these years did the tax collected equal the cost of the service. The result was that the Government was obliged to supplement in almost every year the amount received from the sailors by a special appropriation, and even then many seamen failed to get relief. Table II, p. 238, based in part on estimates, shows approximately the relative importance of the different agencies employed at five dates.

FAULTS OF THE SERVICE

While the number of relief stations increased rapidly during the period covered by this table, the quality of the relief was open to much criticism. This was true even in the government hospitals, and as the proportion of those relieved in private families

[28] Gouge, "Report on Marine Hospitals," in *Senate Executive Documents*, 34 Cong., 1 and 2 sess., 1855–1856, V, No. 53, pp. 244–247.

[29] United States Marine Hospital Service, *Annual Report of the Supervising Surgeon, 1873*, p. 19.

[30] United States, *Statutes at Large*, XII, 348, chap. xxxiv.

TABLE I*

Sick and Disabled Seamen Relieved by the Marine Hospital Service

Year	Number	Year	Number
1818	Approximately 3,600†	1845	9,605
1820	Approximately 4,000‡	1848	9,655
1823	Approximately 3,000§	1849	9,770
1828	2,692	1850	9,748
1831	3,681	1851	9,399
1833	4,770	1852	9,262
1834	4,599	1853	9,916
1836	5,297	1854	9,153
1837	5,445	1855	13,640
1841	6,696	1856	10,223
1842	6,510	1857	10,006
1844	7,000	1858	10,703

† Estimated that there were 3,181 exclusive of those relieved at the United States Marine Hospital at Norfolk, and those at the Hospital at Charleston. See *State Papers, House Documents*, 16 Cong., 1 sess., III, No. 48.

‡ Estimated that there were 3,652 exclusive of those at Wiscasset, Norfolk, and Charleston. See *State Papers, House Documents*, 17 Cong., 1 sess., IV, No. 48.

§ Estimated that there were 2,206 exclusive of those at Savannah, Baltimore, Norfolk, and Charleston. See *House Documents*, 18 Cong., 2 sess., No. 66.

TABLE II

Relief by United States Marine Hospital Service

	1818	1823	1836	1850	1858
Number of relief stations in the United States†	26	37	70	85	95
United States Marine Hospitals, furnishing relief	2	2	3	7	16‡
City and private hospitals, furnishing relief	5	6	19	16	20
Almshouses, poorhouses, etc., furnishing relief	3	2	7	2	....
Private families and boarding houses, etc., furnishing relief	16	27	41	60	59
Total number of seamen relieved	3600§	3000§	5297	9748	10703
Relieved in U. S. marine hospitals	712§	567§	870	3437	3897
Relieved in city and private hospitals	1774§	1820§	3352	3862	2762
Relieved in almshouses and poorhouses	294	204§	199	46	....
Relieved in private families and boarding houses, etc.	820	409	876	2403	4044
Approximate average cost of relief per week per person (board and nursing):					
In U. S. marine hospitals	....	....	$3.21	$3.00	....
In city and private hospitals	$3.50	$3.25	2.75	2.75	$3.50
In almshouses and poorhouses	3.75	4.00	....	2.75	....
In private families and boarding houses	2.75	2.75	2.75	2.50	3.00

† In 1802, relief was given at thirteen places in the United States.

‡ The United States Hospitals at Cleveland, Ohio, Paducah, Kentucky, Vicksburg, Mississippi, and Burlington, Iowa, not reported as giving relief in 1858. See "Statement of Expenditures and Receipts, Marine Hospital Fund," in *Finance Report*, 132–143, *House Executive Documents*, 35 Cong., 2 sess., I, No. 3.

§ Approximately.

* This table, as well as others in this chapter, was compiled by Dr. Edwards from various reports of the Treasury Department, and is based on estimates in a few cases in which the original documents were defective.

and boarding houses increased rapidly until in 1858 it amounted to over 37 per cent. of the total, an increasing fraction of the sailors was cared for under conditions which were particularly subject to abuses. The faulty care administered in private houses and boarding houses was due to the low prices paid. In 1841 a circular issued by Secretary Ewing prescribed rates of payment as follows for seamen in ports where no hospitals existed: "$2.50 per week for boarding, lodging and nursing, in all ports north of Newbern; and $3 per week in all ports south of that city. The rates by which medical services are to be paid are also adjusted by the same circular, viz.: 20 cents per diem for a time less than 25 days, and $5 for every patient when the number does not exceed ten; $2.50 for every patient above that number. In ports south of the Potomac, 25 per cent. in addition to the above rates will be allowed for professional services."[31] But even in the government hospitals the conditions were very bad, and "outbreaks of erysipelas, gangrene, and pyæmia were frequent prior to the reorganization of the Service in 1871 and for some time thereafter."[32]

The law of 1798 provided only for temporary relief, but in some ports persons suffering from incurable diseases, the insane, and the superannuated came to be cared for indefinitely. As a result the Secretary of the Treasury in 1821 directed that all maniacs and incurables be discharged, and the collectors of ports were instructed to limit the annual expenditures for hospital relief to amounts collected in their ports during the same period.[33] As this often proved inadequate, some of the collectors consented to receive only those who had sailed from their port and paid money there. The result was that many deserving sailors were turned away, while in other cases impostors were relieved.[34]

FINANCIAL AND ADMINISTRATIVE DIFFICULTIES

A general survey of the finances of the marine hospital fund is given in Table III, p. 240, taken from the Annual Report of the Supervising Surgeon for 1873.

The figures of the table show that in the early years the amount spent was often less than the amount available, and with the exception of the year 1804, no regular appropriation was made by Congress to supplement the fund until 1813. For three years, 1813–1815, $20,000 were voted annually. From 1820 to 1840, eight appropriations were made. From 1841 on they occurred each year, excepting 1846 and 1854, in amounts which on the whole show a heavy increase, especially from 1851 on, when the amounts varied from $100,000 to $275,000 per annum. It will thus be seen that the expectations of the founders of the service that the assessments would pay for the services were not realized, though they contributed in the aggregate $4,500,000 out of a total of $7,000,000.

The difficulties seem, however, to have been difficulties of administration rather than of principle. The collectors were careless; the selection of sites was unwise; the construction of buildings was lavish, if not corrupt. There was more or less doubt with

[31] Loring and Edwards, "Report upon the Subject of Marine Hospitals," 27.

[32] United States Marine Hospital Service, *Annual Report of the Supervising Surgeon-General, 1893*, I, 48.

[33] See letters of Treasury Department in *American State Papers, House Documents*, 17 Cong., 1 sess., II, No. 13, pp. 7–19.

[34] See *Ibid.*, 5.

TABLE III*

Year	Collections	Appropriations	Available	Expenditures
1798	$141,690.25[a]	....	$141,699.25	$74,636.51[b]
1801	47,635.09[c]	....	47,635.09	38,500.74
1802	33,766.47	....	33,766.47	250.00
1803	54,933.21	....	54,933.21	31,087.36
1804	58,210.98	$1,000.00	59,210.98	84,027.50[d, e]
1805	57,928.20	....	57,928.20	59,828.41
1806	66,820.01	....	66,820.01	53,281.98[f]
1807	61,474.47	....	61,474.47	65,571.51
1808	36,515.44	....	36,515.44	60,383.16
1809	74,192.42[g]	....	74,192.42	70,901.75
1810	53,715.20	....	53,715.20	36,793.60
1811	54,586.34	....	54,586.34	57,109.08
1812	42,421.46	....	42,421.46	57,723.11[h]
1813	21,789.58	20,000.00	41,789.58	53,376.87
1814	10,191.97	20,000.00	30,191.97	45,226.50
1815	28,374.74	20,000.00	48,374.74	43,651.55
1816	43,864.21	....	43,864.21	82,555.68[i]
1817	48,081.88	....	48,081.88	81,749.28[j]
1818	46,911.27	....	46,911.27	87,230.62
1819	50,405.84	....	50,405.84	84,097.61
1820	48,765.01	81,319.34	130,084.35	87,217.39
1821	48,569.99	50,000.00	98,569.99	66,845.48
1822	51,923.72	30,000.00	81,923.72	44,324.61
1823	53,062.91	....	53,062.91	44,761.13
1824	51,877.52	12,875.00[k]	64,752.52	47,861.77
1825	56,992.39	....	56,992.39	54,938.51[l]
1826	58,133.10	....	58,133.10	51,236.98
1827	58,233.67	....	58,233.67	89,137.42[m]
1828	56,217.27	....	56,217.27	69,259.61
1829	58,361.34	....	58,361.34	63,562.28
1830	57,447.13	....	57,447.13	68,996.96
1831	59,182.17	....	59,182.17	65,563.98
1832	58,942.56	....	58,942.56	76,877.87
1833	62,901.15	15,750.00	78,651.15	68,948.73
1834	64,532.98	....	64,532.98	74,668.96
1835	66,621.77	25,000.00	91,621.77	86,268.43
1836	67,961.02	15,000.00	82,961.02	89,370.70
1837	27,021.24	175,000.00	202,021.24	97,935.75
1838	35,234.52	....	35,234.52	109,229.59
1839	66,311.83	....	66,311.83	121,653.31
1840	71,675.91	....	71,675.91	130,561.07
1841	72,760.20	97,000.00	1,169,760.20	109,758.82
1842	72,429.36	46,500.00	118,929.36	100,112.57
1843 half year	37,417.18	58,500.00	95,917.18	49,430.86
1844	85,864.42	25,000.00	110,864.42	62,148.67
1845	88,074.34	25,000.00	113,074.34	168,016.20
1846	90,675.68	....	90,675.68	68,678.70

[a] Includes $15,635.33 for hospital-money received from the Navy Department.
[b] Includes $6,185.33, for purchase of Norfolk hospital.
[c] Includes $2,500 hospital-money received from the Navy Department.
[d] Includes $14,842.34, cost of Charlestown hospital, at the port of Boston.
[e] Includes $157.66 carried to surplus fund.
[f] Includes $379.66 carried to surplus fund.
[g] Includes $38,513.96 hospital-fund received from the Navy Department.
[h] Includes 1 cent carried to surplus fund.
[i] Includes $6,500 expended for repairs of Norfolk hospital.
[j] Includes $5,500, cost of site of Charleston (S.C.) hospital.
[k] Received from sale of hospital at Charlestown, Mass.
[l] Includes $4,068, cost of site, etc., for marine hospital at Chelsea, Mass.
[m] Includes $27,603.39, cost of Chelsea hospital.

* Table taken from United States Marine Hospital Service, *Annual Report of Supervising Surgeon, 1873*, pp. 28–29.

TABLE III—*Concluded*

Year	Collections	Appropriations	Available	Expenditures
1847	95,216.73	25,000.00	120,216.73	123,257.42
1848	97,989.26	12,000.00	109,989.26	140,995.50
1849	103,496.38	12,000.00	115,496.38	103,167.65
1850	106,437.49	15,000.00	121,437.49	162,379.67
1851	133,447.07	200.000.00	333,447.07	139,220.43
1852	134,393.26	200,000.00	334,393.26	203,115.23
1853	133,718.08	100,000.00	233,718.08	280,750.10
1854	146,576.31	....	146,576.31	292,825.69
1855	148,733.43	200,000.00	348,733.43	345,987.46
1856	155,068.14	150,000.00	305,068.14	368,520.86
1857	167,325.29	250,000.00	417,325.29	354,053.90
1858	164,161.82	150,000.00	314,161.82	379,214.86
1859	178,195.59	150,000.00	328,195.59	349,890.36
1860	173,073.09	275,000.00	448.073.09	455,592.10
Total.........	$4,598,531.35	$2,456,944.34	$7,055,475.69	$7,034,321.40

regard to the meaning of the phrase "coasting trade". Did it include the trade of the interior lakes and rivers? Secretary Gallatin, in 1801, and his predecessor, Secretary Wolcott, held that the tax should not be collected in the lake districts, while in 1805 and in 1830, instructions were given for collecting it in these districts.[35] In 1836, however, Secretary Woodbury went back to the earlier view and held that the law did not require the money to be paid excepting in the case of registered vessels from abroad and coasting vessels, and that it did not apply to flatboats, rafts, and the like, on the Mississippi.[36] The acts of Congress were not altogether consistent, and, strange as it may seem, the act of 1798 seems never to have been construed directly by the Federal courts. In the case of two States, New York and California, the opinion of the courts favored the inclusion of trade upon the lakes and rivers in the coasting trade.[37] But these decisions were not binding upon the Federal officials.

Lack of organization was a chronic defect of the hospital service down past 1860. There was no general professional head. Though the President was authorized by the act of 1798 to appoint directors of marine hospitals, the act provided no salaries for them, and their function thus fell upon the collectors of customs, who had practically complete control of the relief given. The President reserved to himself the appointment of physicians, but the other employees were appointed by the collector. Both physicians and surgeons were often political appointees and quite unfit for their office. The tax due was often inefficiently collected as well as extravagantly and injudiciously expended, and there was no uniformity in the relief given. A congressional commission said regarding the service in 1849: "The fact that the whole system of marine hospitals has been hitherto almost without form, and void, has rendered all satisfactory accuracy of investigation extremely difficult, and in many cases utterly impossible."[38]

[35] Letters from the Secretary of the Treasury, in *State Papers, House Documents*, 21 Cong., 1 sess., III, 1830, No. 68, pp. 2, 27.
[36] *Senate Documents*, 24 Cong., 1 sess., IV, No. 297, p. 1.
[37] *Steamboat Co. vs. Livingston*, in 3 *Cowen's New York Reports* (1825), 747; and *San Francisco vs. Steam Navigation Company*, 10 *California* (1858), 507.
[38] Loring and Edwards, "Report upon the Subject of Marine Hospitals," 2.

CHAPTER XIX

THE PROTECTION OF SEAMEN[1]

THE SAILOR'S LIFE

The same general circumstances which led to the establishment of the marine hospital service have led to other pieces of special legislation aimed at improving the conditions of life at sea. The mental peculiarities of the sailor lie at the bottom of, and form in part the justification of, this whole mass of legislation. These are so pronounced, that he has been treated in law almost as a special variety of man. Indeed no less an authority than Dr. Jewell finds sailors to be "a distinct and peculiar species of the *genus homo* —a kind of floating gypsy."[2] There are, however, endless gradations among sailors. In contrast to those referred to in Stevenson's refrain: "Drink and the Devil had done for the rest," many leave the sea to take some employment on shore and are indistinguishable from the rest of mankind excepting by a greater handiness and the ability to tie knots that will hold. The abuses which have grown up are similar to abuses in other occupations, though intensified by the abnormal conditions of the seaman's work. Chief among these are its dangers and hardships, and the fact that it is generally performed on the high seas or on the Great Lakes, and therefore, if not outside of the jurisdiction of any State, at least at a distance from courts, officials of the law, and the restraining influences of public opinion.

Under such conditions the captain must needs be an autocrat with power to promote or degrade at will, to demand implicit obedience, and to punish for infractions of discipline. Otherwise there would be anarchy on shipboard. But such power, while necessary, is always liable to be abused by men of bad temper or intemperate habits. A trustworthy picture of the hardships under which sailors worked in the thirties is given in Dana's *Two Years Before the Mast.* The ships on which he made the voyage around the Horn to California and back belonged to Boston capitalists who supplied "an abundance of stores of the best kind that are given to seamen." The owners had so good a reputation for fair dealing that, in the words of the author, "when it was known that they had the *Alert* fitting out for a long voyage, and that hands were to be shipped at a certain time,—a half hour before the time, as one of the crew told me, sailors were steering down the wharf, hopping over the barrels, like a drove of sheep." Yet the captain had one of the sailors "seized up" to the shrouds and brutally flogged him with a rope. He then meted out the same punishment to another sailor, merely because he had asked why the first one was flogged. When the ship was in port, the

[1] A part of this chapter is based upon an unpublished study by Dr. Alba M. Edwards, "Federal Legislation for the Protection of American Seamen", made for the Carnegie Institution of Washington.
[2] Jewell, *Among Our Sailors* (1874), 14.

men were obliged to do the hardest kind of work on shore in loading hides, some carrying them on their heads down to the beach, exposed to the dust and dirt, while others who loaded them into the boats were constantly wet.

The ship in which Dana returned was undermanned. Indeed, he said: "Our merchant ships are always undermanned." It was insufficiently supplied with medicine, the forecastle was "so wet and dark and cheerless, and so lumbered up with chests and wet clothes, that sitting up is worse than lying in the berth." There was no stove, although they rounded the Horn in midwinter and were so drenched for weeks with snow and rain that they had to put on the clothes that were least wet, "as sailors have no other way of drying them than by the sun." Although Dana was known to have shipped for his health and the owners had given instructions to have him return to Boston in the *Alert*, the captain arbitrarily tried to send him back to work on the *Pilgrim* on the California coast, "condemning me to a punishment worse than a Botany Bay exile, and to a fate which might alter the whole current of my future life." When the long journey was over and the vessel signalled her arrival in Boston Harbor, "the landlords, runners, and sharks in Ann Street learned that there was a rich prize for them down in the bay,—a ship from round the Horn, with a crew to be paid off with two years' wages," and the impositions of land succeeded the dangers and hardships of the sea.[3]

ACT OF 1790

The need of some restraint on sailors, as well as on captains and owners, was so obvious that the very first Congress of the United States passed "An Act for the government and regulation of Seamen in the merchants service." This law, which was dated July 20, 1790,[4] provided that the master of each vessel bound from a port in the United States to any foreign port, or of any ship of 50 tons or more bound from a port in any State to a port in any other than an adjoining State, should execute an agreement with each seaman before starting on a voyage, declaring the terms under which the seaman shipped. If a master proceeded without such an agreement, he could be required to pay to every such mariner the highest wages paid at the port of starting for a similar voyage within the three months next preceding the time of shipment, and should forfeit 20 dollars for each seaman. A seaman who had not signed the contract was not bound by the regulations, nor subject to the penalties prescribed in the act. The agreement was to state the time at which the voyage was to begin, and the seaman was to be punished for delay in reporting (sec. 2). Provision was made for an investigation of unseaworthiness on the part of the ship. If a chief mate and a majority of the crew thought the vessel "too leaky" or unfit in respect to tackle, provisions, or stores, the master was required to stop at the nearest port for an investigation (sec. 3). The payment of wages was secured by section 6, which required the captain to pay one-third of the wages due at every port at which the ship should discharge her cargo, and the balance at the end of the voyage. Every ship was to carry a medicine chest (sec. 8), and a certain minimum of supplies, such as, for a ship crossing the Atlantic, 60 gallons of water, 100 pounds of "salted flesh meat," and 100 pounds of wholesome ship bread

[3] Dana, *Two Years Before the Mast* (ed. of 1869), 112–117, 305, 315, 361–362, 368, 376, 411, 425.
[4] United States, *Statutes at Large*, I, 131–135, chap. xxix.

for each person on board. In case of a short allowance the master was to pay each one of the crew one day's wages for every day of short rations (sec. 9).

On the other hand, penalties were put upon the seaman for absenting himself from his duty and for desertion. If he failed to render himself on board at the hour and on the day set in his contract, he forfeited one day's pay for each hour of tardiness (sec. 2). If he absented himself from the ship without leave, and returned within 48 hours, he forfeited 3 days' wages for each day of absence, but if after 48 hours, he forfeited all wages due him, and all of his property which might be on shipboard (sec. 5). If he deserted at any port, a justice of the peace might issue a warrant and bring him to justice, and on conviction he might be committed to a house of correction or common jail, until the vessel was ready to sail, or until the master required his discharge; and the costs might be deducted from his wages (sec. 7).

These provisions constituted what was later called "involuntary servitude" for the sailor, but it should be remembered that until the repeal of the Statute of Apprentices in 1813 and 1814[5] this was in law the status of the ordinary wage workers in England, and that even in the United States mechanics could be indicted for a combination to raise their wages.[6] Therefore, as compared with the prevailing law of the day, the act of 1790 represented progress, inasmuch as it provided at least some standards for the treatment of sailors and for their protection from abuse.

LATER COURSE OF LEGISLATION

It will be noticed that this act, which was the beginning of our legislation regarding sailors, covered a number of different topics, particularly the shipping contract and the conditions of life at sea. In the course of time other incidents of the sailor's life were subjected to regulation, such as his duties and rights in foreign ports, his status in case of shipwreck, and his protection from imposition when ashore. Later, special laws were made regarding the river boatman. As a rule these different topics were not dealt with separately but were combined in more or less comprehensive laws, though special laws have occasionally been passed to correct individual evils, such as shanghaiing. On the whole, the progress that was made down to the Civil War was slow and the legislation was not very extensive. Its tendencies can best be seen by tracing the changes under a few leading topics.

SHIPPING THE SAILOR

The act of 1790 laid stress upon the shipping contract which was the basis of its provisions. Without such a contract neither captain nor crew could be held to their obligations. The enactment had, in fact, very little effect, as it was often evaded or ignored, and the signing of an agreement was rarely complied with. When such a contract was to be made, it was customary in the early part of the nineteenth century for the captain to hoist his pennant at the mainmast as a signal that men were

[5] Webb, *The History of Trade Unionism* (ed. of 1902), 53–55.

[6] United States Commissioner of Labor, *Third Annual Report, Strikes and Lockouts, 1887*, p. 1112; Commons and Andrews, *Principles of Labor Legislation* (1920), 94. See also "Conspiracy Cases", in Commons, *Documentary History of American Industrial Society*, III and IV.

wanted. When the sailors came aboard they made their own agreements with him, and signed the articles lying on the capstan. "A minute was made by the captain of the place where each man boarded; and when the crew was wanted, the owner's clerk went from his counting room, informed them of the fact, and saw them on ship board."[7] Thus the masters really saw and chose their own men, and the men saw and chose their ships. By 1820, however, this method had changed. A class of shipping masters had arisen who organized crews, paid out advance wages, often from their own funds, and were reimbursed by the owner after the vessel had gone to sea. This custom of advancing wages, though it led to many evils, had a normal origin in the fact that the sailors often needed money to buy clothing for the voyage, to pay their bills, and to provide for their families, if any, when they were away. But what began as a convenience soon turned into an abuse.[8] The people who carried on this business were often keepers of boarding houses, and forced their services upon captains and sailors, no longer looking to the ship owners for their pay, but collecting it from the sailors. The contract had ceased to be one voluntarily entered into by both parties. The captain did not select his crew, nor the crew their ship. Outrageous abuses thus grew up, crews often being sent on board in a state of intoxication, after the boarding house keepers had robbed them of their money. The evil effects of advancing wages did not end with the sailing of the ship. When the sailor sobered up at sea, and found that he was paying with his labor for "a dead horse", he was much more likely to desert at the first opportunity, and this was often a great loss to the master. Worse still, "shanghaiing" was often resorted to.[9] The verb "to shanghai" is said to have originated in San Francisco in the early days of the gold fever. It was merely a euphemism for kidnapping. Persons who had no knowledge of the sea, and no intention of going to sea, were seized, sometimes knocked down, and forcibly shipped. Cases were known in which, when the crew were ordered to help make sail, some were found to be dead.[10] But little was done by Federal law to correct these abuses until after the Civil War, the whole matter being left to State or local regulation. Thus San Francisco passed in 1853 an ordinance requiring shipping offices to be licensed.[11]

Though these evils attracted attention as early as 1829 and 1830, as may be seen by articles published in the *Sailors' Magazine*, it was not until 1857 that a general movement for abolishing the system was started. In that year 107 firms of ship owners in New York made an agreement that they would not advance wages. But the boarding house keepers and agents entered into a combination to check this movement and would not let the men go to sea without the advance. At one time it was said that 50 ships lay at the wharf or in the stream unable to leave for lack of crews, and the boarding house keepers finally won their point.[12]

[7] *The Sailors' Magazine and Seamen's Friend*, LIII, 99–100, April 1881.
[8] Jewell, *Among Our Sailors*, 66 *et seq.*
[9] "Shanghaed and Robbed", from *Belfast (Me.) Journal*, in *Sailors' Magazine and Seamen's Friend*, XLIX, 19, Jan. 1877; Eaves, *A History of California Labor Legislation* (1910), in University of California, *Publications in Economics*, II, 336.
[10] *New York Times*, May 17, 1882, p. 8; *Boston Herald*, Jan. 24, 1883.
[11] Eaves, *A History of California Labor Legislation*, 336.
[12] *Sailors' Magazine and Seamen's Friend*, XXIX, 349, July 1857; 382–383, Aug. 1857; United States Marine Hospital Service, *Annual Report of Supervising Surgeon-General, 1881*, p. 16.

THE SAILOR AFLOAT

The act of 1790 provided that, if the mate and a majority of the crew found a vessel "too leaky" or unfit for the voyage, they could complain and require an investigation. But it is obvious that under the circumstances in which they generally found themselves, this was of little use. In 1840,[13] an act was passed allowing them to demand of consuls that their ships be examined in foreign ports under similar conditions. The complaint was to be in writing and signed by an officer and a majority of the crew. If the ship was unseaworthy, the consul might discharge the crew and require the payment of three months' extra wages to each seaman, a requirement which might be waived, if the consul was satisfied that the contract had expired or that the voyage had been protracted by circumstances beyond the control of the master (sec. 9). Similar provisions were contained in the act of 1850,[14] which required such a request to be signed either by the first or by the second and third officers and by a majority of the crew before it could be considered (sec. 6). The law was obviously of little use, as the officers would not as a rule wish to make complaints contrary to the interest of the owners. No steps were taken to regulate by law the quarters of the sailor in the forecastle until after the Civil War, but the requirement regarding medicines was improved by the act of 1805, and that regarding provisions by the act of 1840.

THE SAILOR IN FOREIGN PORTS

The discharge of sailors in foreign ports might be a great hardship to the men in the early days when there were no steamships and the voyages were long. Hence the act of 1792[15] provided that when a vessel belonging to citizens of the United States was sold in a foreign port, the master, unless the crew were liable by contract or consent to be discharged there, should send them back to the State in which they went on board or furnish them with sufficient means to return. By the subsequent act of 1803,[16] masters discharging their men in foreign ports were required to pay to the consul three months' wages over and above the sum due. Of this sum two-thirds were to be paid to the seamen and the remaining one-third put into a fund to provide for paying the passage of destitute seamen or citizens of the United States who desired to return to the United States, and for the maintenance of destitute American seamen in the foreign port. This provision was intended not only to protect seamen against the unemployment resulting from being discharged in a foreign port, but also to prevent the masters from discharging their crews abroad in order to hire cheaper ones. In the course of the next forty years, however, conditions changed. It was no longer as difficult as formerly for seamen to find employment in foreign ports. Sometimes they desired to change, and in order to evade the law requiring the payment of three months' wages, they deserted with the connivance of the masters. Hence the act of 1840[17] allowed consuls to dispense with the payment of three months' wages required by the act of 1803.

[13] United States, *Statutes at Large*, V, 396, chap. xlviii, secs. 9, 12, 13, 14.
[14] *Ibid.*, IX, 441, chap. xxvii, sec. 6.
[15] *Ibid.*, I, 256, chap. xxiv, sec. 8.
[16] *Ibid.*, II, 203, chap. ix, sec. 3.
[17] *Ibid.*, V, 395, chap. xlviii, sec. 5.

The following table gives for four years the figures relating to the relief of American seamen at foreign consulates.

	1840	1841	1842	1843
Number of seamen relieved	2,024	1,744	1,847	2,253
Amounts disbursed at consulates in addition to the extra wages received	$39,613	$46,604	$52,267	$61,432
Amounts received at consulates as extra wages	$9,912	$8,025	$6,804	$7,369
Number of passages paid at $10 each	329	383	565	644
Total seamen relieved and passages paid	2,353	2,127	2,412	2,897

It was estimated that in the 42 years following 1801 Congress appropriated for the relief and protection of American seamen in foreign countries, $1,406,500, a yearly average of $33,448.[18]

The provisions regarding discharge underwent a number of changes, the main purpose being to prevent the arbitrary discharge of the seamen, but at the same time to permit them to be discharged in their own interest, if they consented. The act of 1840 developed in practice the fault that it trusted too much to the discretion of each consular officer. There was, consequently, a lack of uniformity in practice. In some cases, the consuls ceased to collect the extra wages. In short, "the inconveniences and expenses resulting from this change of policy, as it had prevailed from the year 1803, were so many and great that, in 1856, the act of 1840 was repealed, and the discretion exercised by consuls under that statute, as to the discharge of seamen, was revoked."[19] This new act of 1856[20] provided that in the case of wrecked or stranded ships, or vessels condemned as unfit for service, no payment of extra wages should be required. The consuls were obliged to keep detailed lists of all seamen shipped and discharged by them, and of the payments, if any, made on account of each seaman discharged (sec. 27).

Special hardships arise in case of shipwreck, sickness, or captivity, and the act of 1792[21] required United States consuls in such cases to provide for the sailors at the expense of the United States an allowance not exceeding 12 cents per man per day. Moreover, all masters of vessels belonging to citizens of the United States were required under that act to transport such seamen to the United States without charge, provided that they need not take more than two men per 100 tons. In return, these men were required, if able, to work their passage. Changes were made in the details of this law in subsequent years. By the act of 1803,[22] vessels were allowed to charge not more than $10 for the transportation of such seamen, which sum remained the legal rate for 81 years until it was raised to $20 in 1884.[23]

THE SAILOR ASHORE

When released from the hard discipline and privations of the sea, the sailor naturally longs for relaxation and, inasmuch as an economic demand usually calls forth a supply, he finds many persons ready to minister to his wants and his weaknesses. Thus have

[18] *Senate Miscellaneous Document*, 33 Cong., 2 sess., Feb. 16, 1855, No. 16, p. 130.
[19] Jewell, *Among Our Sailors*, 82.
[20] United States, *Statutes at Large*, XI, 62, chap. cxxvii, sec. 26.
[21] *Ibid.*, I, 256, chap. xxiv, sec. 7.
[22] *Ibid.*, II, 204, chap. ix.
[23] *Ibid.*, XXIII, 55, chap. cxxi, sec. 9.

arisen the "land-sharks", who rob and cheat the sailor, often before he has actually set foot on shore. Many of these people appear as the proprietors of so-called boarding houses, which are usually of the lowest type. In 1837, it was said that of over 100 boarding houses for seamen in the city of New York, all but eight had licenses to sell rum. Most of them were resorts of the lowest class of people.[24] The owners of these boarding houses had their "runners" who went out to meet a ship often before she had docked, and being generous in the distribution of tobacco and liquor, gained the friendship of the sailors, and induced them to go to their houses. Once there, the sailor was usually brought into a state of intoxication in which all kinds of frauds might be practiced upon him. The end of the experience was often that the money in his pocket passed into the pocket of the boarding house keeper, and he was sent off to sea again, not only penniless, but ignorant of the port to which he was going, and of the conditions under which he had shipped, inasmuch as the contract was made when he was drunk.[25] It is not necessary to give details, which have been repeatedly described in books and magazines.

This subject has always been a difficult one to deal with by legislation on account of the violent and tricky character of the delinquents, and of the readiness with which their victims fall into their clutches. For while the evils are notorious, those who try to prevent them get little help from the weak characters of those on whose behalf efforts are made. In order to protect mariners and ship owners from imposition, Massachusetts passed an act in 1857 which prohibited the boarding without permission of vessels arriving in Boston and certain other harbors, and which forbade enticing the crew to leave.[26] It was not until after the Civil War, however, that other maritime States such as New York and Maine took action, and that the Federal Government undertook a more effective regulation. The mariner was dependent in the main for his protection against abuse and fraud upon philanthropic societies such as the Seamen's Friend Societies, which were established in a number of seaports.

THE SHIPWRECKED SAILOR

The law of shipwreck has for centuries been a harsh law. It had its origin at a time when navigation was much more hazardous than it is now, and when all travel was beset with peculiar danger. When the ships were small and propelled only by the wind; when the coasts were without lighthouses or life-saving stations; when science had done little to record the currents, the winds, and the deflections of the compass; and when, in addition to all of these natural dangers, pirates abounded; the person who invested in the shipping business needed the *aes triplex circum pectus* almost as much as in the time of Horace. At any rate, he demanded large speculative earnings to compensate him for the risk. Not all could boast with Antonio, "My ventures are not in one bottom trusted nor to one place." There were no great companies owning numerous vessels, operating on different routes, and able, therefore, in a sense to insure themselves. It was in those days that the maxim grew up, "freight is the mother of wages." If for

[24] *Sailors' Magazine and Seamen's Journal*, I, 3–4, 11, 19, 20, Sept. 1828; 37, 38, Oct. 1828; IX, 156, Jan. 1837; 238, April 1837.

[25] United States Marine Hospital Service, *Report of the Supervising Surgeon-General, 1873*, pp. 133–135; McFarland, "The Sailors' Law", in *Old and New*, IX, 363–364.

[26] *Acts and Resolves of Massachusetts*, 1857, p. 487, chap. 139.

any reason no freight could be earned, there was obviously no money out of which wages could be paid,[27] and in the case of a wreck the seaman's wages stopped automatically with the loss of the vessel.

A fundamental question in the law of shipwreck is what constitutes a wreck. This was settled in England by the first Statute of Westminster in 1275. A definition was necessary, because, under the common law, wrecks belonged to the crown until reclaimed by the owner, which claim had to be made within a year and a day from the discovery of the wreck.[28] Some of our States have similarly provided that wrecks belong to the State. It is clear that mishaps to ships may occur in numberless gradations, running from the case where the vessel grounds on a sand bar and is floated at the next tide, to the case where she is completely broken up or sinks in mid-ocean. While it was generally admitted that the ship was wrecked when all hands were lost, Parliament, in order to safeguard the rights of the owner as against the Crown, established the rule that "nothing shall be considered a wreck out of which a cat or a dog escapes alive; and from that time until the present day no vessel coasts about England without carrying a cat or a dog."[29]

In the United States, until after the Civil War, little was done to modify the harsh principles of the English law. The law of 1825 gave some protection to the ship owner as against robbers and pirates, by making it a felony to despoil or steal from a wreck,[30] but, according to the act of March 3, 1851, even as against shippers, the liability of the owners of the vessel was restricted to their interest in the vessel and her freight pending.[31] The act was advocated in the Senate on the ground that we ought to give our mercantile marine the same advantages as those enjoyed by Great Britain.[32]

THE CREW AND ITS DISCIPLINE

As one of the chief causes of the War of 1812 had been the impressment of American seamen by the British, Congress tried by law to encourage the employment by each nation of its own citizens. Hence the law of 1813 provided "That from and after the termination of the war in which the United States are now engaged with Great Britain, it shall not be lawful to employ on board any of the public or private vessels of the United States any person or persons except citizens of the United States or persons of colour, natives of the United States," but allowed a deficiency of seamen to be made up in a foreign port by the employment of foreigners.[33] Without repealing this act another act, passed in 1817, recognized the impossibility of enforcing it, by refusing bounties to fishing vessels unless three-fourths of the crew were American citizens, and by remitting tonnage duties on vessels entering from a foreign port only if officers and two-thirds of the crew were American.[34] It was, however, difficult to find American seamen to man the ships, and the law was frequently evaded by false oaths and false

[27] See *Cyclopedia of Law and Procedure*, XXXV, 1207, 1910.
[28] *Ibid.*, XXXVI, 427.
[29] Stimson, *Popular Law-Making*, 50; Halsbury, *The Laws of England*, XXVI, 548, 1914.
[30] United States, *Statutes at Large*, IV, 116, chap. lxv, sec. 9.
[31] *Ibid.*, IX, 635, chap. xliii; see *Cyclopedia of Law and Procedure*, XXXVI, 281.
[32] See speeches of Senators Hamlin, Foote, and others, in *Congressional Globe*, XXIII, 713–720.
[33] United States, *Statutes at Large*, II, 809, chap. xliii.
[34] *Ibid.*, III, 351–352, chap. xxxi, secs. 3, 5, 6, 7.

lists.[35] These laws, therefore, were a dead letter for many years before their repeal in 1864[36] when the only requirement retained was that the officers should be citizens of the United States.

That a certain power of punishment or at least arrest must be given to the officers of vessels lies in the nature of the case, and provision was made for discipline in the act of 1790,[37] as well as in subsequent acts. But it also became necessary to prevent the abuse of this power on the part of officers, and the act of 1835[38] penalized by fine not exceeding $1000, or by imprisonment not exceeding five years, or by both, the beating, wounding, or imprisoning of a member of the crew "from malice, hatred, or revenge and without justifiable cause", as well as the withholding of food and the infliction of cruel and unusual punishments. The difficulty, however, of proving "malice, hatred, or revenge" on the part of officers made it very difficult to secure convictions. The same act mitigated the punishment of sailors in case of mutiny by abolishing the death penalty and substituting a fine not exceeding $2000 and imprisonment for not over ten years. Attempted mutiny might be punished by half of these penalties.[39] In 1850 flogging was forbidden by law in the Navy and aboard vessels of commerce.[40] This law reflected the growing humanitarian sentiment of the day rather than the actual practice of the sea. "The effect of the Act," we are told, "instead of abolishing corporal punishment, was merely to change its character from the specific to the general: it prohibited the cat, and by implication, authorized the use of the belaying-pin and handspike."[41]

Minor enactments regarding seamen were: the act of 1803,[42] requiring masters of vessels bound on foreign voyages to deliver to the collectors of customs lists of their ship's companies, and the act of 1840,[43] requiring that the duplicate of the crew list should "be a fair copy in one uniform handwriting, without erasure or interlineation."

INADEQUACY OF LEGISLATION

What has been said shows that, although legislation for the benefit of sailors began with the first Congress, it did not advance rapidly during the seven decades which elapsed down to the Civil War. Our progress was slower than that of Great Britain during the same period. It is not difficult to detect in the general conditions which prevailed during that period at least some of the causes of this backwardness. The mind of the country was preoccupied during the latter half of the period with the slavery question. The party in power during most of the time was opposed on principle to extending the functions of the Federal Government. The labor movement had not as yet gone beyond weak and spasmodic beginnings. The spirit of the times was strongly individualistic. The lack of legislation was certainly not due to absence of abuses.

[35] Forbes, "Protection to American Seamen", in *Sailors' Magazine and Seamen's Friend*, XXXII, 195, March 1860; Codman, "Conditions and Requirements of the American Mercantile Marine", *Ibid.*, 263, May 1860; Jewell, *Among Our Sailors*, 49.

[36] United States, *Statutes at Large*, XIII, 201, chap. clxx.

[37] *Ibid.*, I, 113–114, chap. ix, sec. 8.

[38] *Ibid.*, IV, 776–777, chap. xl, sec. 3.

[39] *Ibid.*, IV, 776, chap. xl, sec. 1.

[40] *Ibid.*, IX, 515, chap. lxxx.

[41] MacArthur, "The American Seaman Under the Law," in *The Forum*, XXVI, 727, Feb. 1899.

[42] United States, *Statutes at Large*, II, 203, chap. ix, secs. 1, 2.

[43] *Ibid.*, V, 394, chap. xlviii.

Cases of cruelty at sea like those recorded by Richard H. Dana[44] and Dr. Jewell[45] and described in the files of the *Sailors' Magazine* were revolting in the extreme, while the maltreatment and robbery of Jack Tar on the land seem to have increased with better organization among the "land sharks."

PHILANTHROPIC EFFORT

These abuses and the hardships of life at sea aroused the same humanitarian spirit which had shown itself in the missionary movement, and, as in other fields of religious and social activity, this manifested itself first of all in the organization of philanthropic societies designed to improve conditions by voluntary effort.[46] The most important of these associations was the American Seamen's Friend Society, organized in 1828, and incorporated under the laws of New York in April 1833. This society can trace its genesis directly back to the missionary movement of the early part of the century, for it grew out of the New York Port Society, formed June 5, 1818, which in turn had its origin in prayer meetings held in the lower part of New York by members of the Brick Presbyterian Church as early as 1816.[47] It had its forerunner in the Boston Society for the Religious and Moral Improvement of Seamen, organized in 1812.[48] Hence in its very first year it opened negotiations with the American Board of Commissioners for Foreign Missions in Boston, and in consequence of this affiliation, it soon sent as chaplain to Canton, China, Rev. David Abeel, who began work there in 1830. Gradually, similar stations were opened in Honolulu, in Havre, in Havana, in Calcutta, in Singapore, in Cronstadt, in Sydney, in Sweden, in Valparaiso, as well as in some of the southern ports of the United States, in San Francisco, and on the Great Lakes.[49]

In addition to its strictly missionary work, the Society established a Seamen's Savings Bank in 1829 and a Sailors' Home in 1841; it began sending out sailors' libraries in 1837, and gave relief to destitute seamen.[50] The files of the *Sailors' Magazine*, published since 1829, record its activities. In 1860 to 1861, the Society boarded 2,711 sailors at the Home, relieved 187 men and boys, handled $12,183.00 of sailors' savings which were deposited in savings banks or sent to friends, and sent out 113 loan libraries.[51]

Massachusetts incorporated the Boston Seamen's Friend Society in 1829;[52] the Seamen's Widow and Orphan Association in 1844;[53] the Seamen's Aid Society in 1845;[54] the Sailors' Snug Harbor of Boston in 1852.[55] New York incorporated the Mariners'

[44] Dana, *Two Years Before the Mast* (ed. of 1869), 112 *et seq.*
[45] Jewell, *Among Our Sailors*, chaps. vii and viii, and *passim.*
[46] On humanitarianism in general, see Parmelee, "The Rise of Modern Humanitarianism," in *American Journal of Sociology*, XXI, 345–359, Nov. 1915.
[47] American Seamen's Friend Society, *Notes of Fifty Years of Efforts* (1878), 6, *et seq.;* see also Hall, "A Brief Historical Sketch," in American Seamen's Friend Society, *Fiftieth Annual Report with the Semi-Centenary Papers* (1878), 67–73.
[48] American Seamen's Friend Society, *Notes of Fifty Years Efforts*, 5.
[49] *Ibid.*, 23, 26, 28, 33, 36, 37, 44.
[50] *Ibid.*, 13, 33, 36–37.
[51] *Ibid.*, 63.
[52] *Laws of the Commonwealth of Massachusetts*, XI, 119, chap. lxxxi.
[53] *Acts and Resolves of the General Court of Massachusetts, 1843–1845*, p. 203, chap. 99.
[54] *Ibid., 1843–1845*, p. 417, chap. 51.
[55] *Acts and Resolves of the Commonwealth of Massachusetts, 1852*, p. 188, chap. 271.

Benevolent Association of the city of Troy in 1830[56] for the purpose of affording mutual relief to its members. Similar societies, many of them bearing the name Seamen's Friend Society, were established in other ports.

These societies worked for the individual. They aimed to influence the character and to minister to the material wants of the sailor rather than to improve the conditions under which he worked, or remove the economic causes of his troubles. They paved the way, however, for legislation which was enacted at a later period, when the conflict over slavery and disunion had been settled, and when public opinion recognized that fundamental abuses could not be removed by sedatives, but required the coercion of law.

[56] *Laws of the State of New York, 1830*, p. 382, chap. 317.

CHAPTER XX

PROTECTION OF LABOR IN GENERAL

INDUSTRY AND EDUCATION

The ideals which prevailed with reference to labor in the early part of the nineteenth century were still those of the colonial period, and may be summed up in the two words "industry" and "education". Industry was an economic necessity, as has already been pointed out, and was promoted by law. Education was desired in order to make the workers skillful and efficient. This did not necessarily mean that the colonists were indifferent to suffering and distress. That some of them had the interest of future generations at heart is seen in the reference of Nathaniel Morton to the condition of the children of the community of Pilgrims when living in Holland before the migration to Plymouth. He said: "Many of their children, through the extreme necessity that was upon them, although of the best dispositions and graciously inclined, and willing to bear part of their parents' burdens, were oftentimes so oppressed with their heavy labors, that although their spirits were free and willing, yet their bodies bowed under the weight of the same and became decrepit in their early youth, and the vigor of nature was consumed in the very bud."[1] But sympathy was not inconsistent with an appreciation of the importance of work, and throughout the eighteenth century efforts were made to introduce such manufactures as might give employment to women and children.

EMPLOYMENT OF CHILDREN IN THE COLONIAL PERIOD

In 1718 some Irish Protestant weavers arrived in New England and this gave an impetus to the spinning trade in Boston. At a town meeting two years later a committee was chosen to consider promoting a spinning school or schools for the instruction of the town in spinning.[2] At about this time the Governor of Pennsylvania recommended that the House of Representatives interest the people in silk culture, as it was "a Work of which the poorest & feeblest are capable, & children who can be of little other Service, may here find an Employment suitable to their Years."[3]

In 1751 a Boston "Society for Encouraging Industry and Employing the Poor" was

[1] Morton, *New England's Memorial* (1669, reprint of 1855), 11.

[2] Otey, *The Beginnings of Child Labor Legislation*, 20. Miss Otey's admirable monograph has furnished much of the material used in the first part of this chapter.

[3] *Ibid.*, 20, referring to Pennsylvania, *Colonial Records*, III, 392.

organized "to employ our own women and children who are now in a great measure idle."[4] About this time "Manufactory House" was built in Boston, with the support of public funds, by a society of whose members it was said: "They turned their attention to employ the Female Youth from eight years upwards whom where the Parents has [*sic*] numbers, Instead of being a Burthen to their Parents or the Town might not only support themselves but even help to support them and who at the same time might Preserve the Morrals of their Children, by fixing an early Habit of Industry in our Youth, the very Foundation of good Morrals and the most lasting Remembrance of the value of the Honest Produce of their own Labour." In the spinning school which a member of the society started in 1769, the founder stated that he had "learned at least 300 children and women to spin" in the first season.[5] A notice in the *Boston News Letter* of 1770 said that "the laudable practice of spinning" was "universally in vogue among the female children of the town."[6] From New York, too, Governor Moore reported to the Lords of Trade in 1767, that "every house swarms with children, who are set to work as soon as they are able to Spin and Card."[7]

The machinery used then was still primitive. Washington wrote of the Boston duck manufactory that, "They have 28 looms at work and 14 Girls spinning with Both hands (the flax being tied to their waists). Children (girls) turn the wheels for them, and with this assistance each spinner can turn out 14 lbs. of Thread p^{r} day when they stick to it." At the Haverhill duck manufactory he found a more ingenious scheme where "one small person turns a wheel which employs eight spinners, each acting independently of the other, so as to occasion no interruption to the rest if any one of them is stopped—whereas at the Boston manufactory of this article, each spinner has a small girl to turn the wheel."[8]

With the achievement of national independence and the establishment of constitutional government, the ideal of work assumed a new importance. It was now urged, not simply on general economic and ethical grounds, but as a matter of patriotism, and the protective tariff was advocated as a means at once of employing the people and of making the country industrially independent. Any thought of limiting the labor of women and children was, therefore, more than ever out of the question, and there is no doubt that Hamilton reflected the popular view when he said in his argument in favor of a protective tariff: "It is worthy of particular remark, that, in general, women and children are rendered more useful, and the latter more early useful, by manufacturing establishments, than they would otherwise be. Of the number of persons employed in the cotton manufactories of Great Britain, it is computed that four-sevenths, nearly, are women and children; of whom the greatest proportion are children, and many of them of a tender age."[9]

[4] Towles, *Factory Legislation of Rhode Island* (1908), in *American Economic Association Quarterly*, 3d series, IX, No. 3, p. 450.

[5] *Ibid.*, 22. See also Clark, *History of Manufactures in the United States* (1929), I, 189–190.

[6] Otey, *The Beginnings of Child Labor Legislation*, 22.

[7] *Ibid.*, 22, quoting from *The Documentary History of the State of New York* (qto. ed.), I, 498.

[8] Washington, *Diary* (ed. by Lossing, 1861), 33, 42.

[9] Hamilton, *Report on Manufactures, 1791*, in Secretary of the Treasury, *Reports on Finances, 1790–1814* (reprint of 1837), I, 87.

CONFLICT OF INDUSTRY AND EDUCATION

Education was likewise, from the first, one of the cardinal points of public policy in New England, as pointed out in an earlier chapter, and in the Massachusetts law of 1642, "learning and labor" were coupled together in a single phrase. The Puritan ideals persisted into the first part of the nineteenth century and were expressed in laws such as that enacted in Connecticut in 1813,[10] which provided that the proprietors of all manufacturing establishments "shall cause that the children employed in such factory or establishment, whether bound by indenture, by parol agreement or in any other manner, be taught to read and write, and also that they be instructed in the first four rules of arithmetic (provided the term of their service shall be of so long duration that such instruction can be given,) and that due attention be paid to the preservation of their morals; and that they be required by their masters or employers regularly to attend public worship, as is by law provided with regard to the other citizens of this state." Likewise in Vermont, at a somewhat later date but in the same primitive period of industrial development, a law[11] required that "it shall be the duty of the selectmen and overseers of the poor within their respective towns in this state, to examine into the treatment and condition of any minors employed in any manufacturing establishment in their respective towns; and, if in their opinion the education, morals, health, food or clothing of such minor is unreasonably neglected, or that such minor is treated with improper severity or abuse, or is compelled to labor at unseasonable hours or times, or in any unreasonable manner" the authorities were instructed to "admonish" the offender, and could, with the knowledge and consent of a justice of the peace, remove the child and bind him or her out to some trade in which, presumably, the conditions would be better. In the course of time, the excessive attention given to industry was found to militate against education and it was the desire to improve education which led to the first child labor laws. But this conflict was not generally appreciated in the early years of the nineteenth century. Moreover agriculture was so predominantly the principal occupation of the country that such evils as were connected with the infant factory system affected but a small percentage of the population. As late as 1820 agriculture still claimed 84 per cent. of those enumerated as engaged in gainful occupations, and by 1840 the percentage was still 77.5.[12]

A few of the most advanced thinkers were already looking ahead. One of the first was Governor Caleb Strong, of Massachusetts, who in his message of January 10, 1816, called attention to the employment of children in manufacturing establishments before they had received a school education.[13] Governor Levi Lincoln referred to the same matter in 1825.[14]

The impulse which led to legislation was, as foreshadowed in the message of Governor Strong, the importance of education. The ideal of bringing up a younger generation worthy to succeed was found to be impeded by the ideal of work, carried to an extreme under the factory system. Thus we have, beginning in New England, and extending

[10] *Public Acts of the State of Connecticut, 1813*, chap. ii.
[11] *Acts of Vermont, 1837*, No. 24, pp. 15–16.
[12] United States Census, 1900, *Occupations at the Twelfth Census* (Special Report, 1904), xxx.
[13] *Resolves of the General Court of Massachusetts, 1816*, p. 84.
[14] Persons, et al., *Labor Laws and Their Enforcement* (1911), 5; quoting from *Massachusetts Yeoman*, April 1825.

somewhat slowly to the other States, a strong movement in favor of protecting the labor of children, with special reference to education. This impulse was strengthened by the increase in the humanitarian feeling which had taken effect in the formation of numerous communities, often inspired by Fourier or Owen, or by the advanced thinkers of Europe. It also showed itself in the beginnings of the anti-slavery movement.

EARLY DISCUSSIONS OF THE PROBLEM OF CHILD LABOR

The matter of child labor in Massachusetts was referred significantly to the Committee on Education, and to it were also referred the returns made to the Secretary's office, under a resolve passed February 26, 1825, with reference to children in factories. The governor had expressed the sentiment, already embodied in the Constitution, that "wisdom & learning as well as virtue, diffused generally among the people, are necessary to the preservations of their rights and liberties."[15] The committee endorsed heartily this sentiment, but took the ground that the provisions already made for primary schools, academies, colleges, and universities showed that the movement was not being neglected, and they did not think it necessary for the legislature to take any steps, though they did deem it important that existing laws should be respected and enforced. With regard to the special case of factory children, "The Committee are happy to coincide with his Excellency that an 'American sentiment' prevails throughout the country, to which these establishments are not exceptions, & which prevents them from being dangerous 'to the moral habits & chaste manners' of the people."[16] This subject they thought "always deserving the parental care of a vigilant government." Though the committee did not advocate any steps they did collect elaborate statistics showing that the hours of work per day excepting on the Sabbath were generally twelve to thirteen, which, as they remarked, left little opportunity for daily instruction. And they thought that some further legislative provisions might become necessary "that the children who are at a future day to become proprietors of these establishments, or at least, greatly to influence their affairs, may not be subjected to too great devotion to pecuniary interest at the risk of more than an equivalent injury in the neglect of intellectual improvement."[17]

The interesting features of this report are: the optimistic confidence in the American sentiment as a means of correcting the evils of child labor; the assumption that factory children might at some day become proprietors, or at least influential in the management of the factories; and the emphasis laid on their intellectual development, rather than upon the social distribution of wealth. The fear in the minds of the committee was, apparently, not that whole masses of the population would be degraded and pauperized, but that the boys who began as millhands would become mere money makers later in life, and neglect intellectual advancement.

The evils of child labor were noticed also in Pennsylvania, which had investigated the subject in 1824. A few years later a communication to the *Philadelphia Mechanics' Free Press* of August 21, 1830, said, "It is a well known fact that the principal part of the helps in cotton factories consist of boys and girls, we may safely say from six to

[15] Massachusetts, "Report on Returns of Children Employed in Factories" (*Massachusetts Legislative Files*, 1825, Senate No. 8074, reprinted in Commons, *Documentary History of American Industrial Society*, V), 57–59.

[16] *Ibid.*, V, 57.

[17] *Ibid.*, V, 57–61.

seventeen years of age, and are confined to steady employment during the longest days in the year, from daylight until dark, allowing, at the outside, one hour and a half per day. In consequence of this close confinement, it renders it entirely impossible for the parents of such children to obtain for them any education or knowledge, save that of working that machine which they are compelled to work . . . ." The communication referred to the observation of a "Pawtucket friend," who thought that the children were brought up "as ignorant as Arabs of the Desert; for we are confident that not more than one-sixth of the boys and girls employed in such factories are capable of reading or writing their own name." This was signed "Many Operatives."[18] Conditions persisting in Rhode Island even to 1853 may be judged from the statute of that year[19] which forbade the employment in factories of children under 15 before 5 a.m., and of minors under 18 after 7.30 p.m. In Paterson, New Jersey, in 1835, the hours of labor of children were stated to be from sunrise to sunset, from March 1 to October 1.[20]

AGITATION FOR THE PROTECTION OF CHILDREN BY THE LABOR PARTY

The labor party, which was then in its beginning, also took under consideration the matter of child labor. The New England Association of Farmers, Mechanics, and Other Workingmen held a convention in Boston in 1832. A resolution from the committee on education, which was accepted, stated that, the "great and original cause of the present comparative degradation" of mechanics and others was due to lack of education, and "that the diffusion of knowledge was the most direct means of bettering their condition." The committee on education of children in manufacturing districts reported that two-fifths of the operatives in cotton mills were under sixteen years of age, that they worked thirteen and one-half to fourteen hours a day, and that the children could not be taken from the mill and sent to school for any length of time, without loss of employment.[21]

Seth Luther, a Rhode Island mechanic and labor agitator, in the summer of the same year spoke of the incompatibility of education and of thirteen hours' daily labor in an address at the convention of the New England Association of Farmers, Mechanics, and Other Workingmen.[22] Though he did not propose abolishing child labor, he did criticize Henry Clay's ideal of the "clockwork regularity of a large cotton manufactory," under which human beings were considered merely as instruments of production.[23] At the convention of the General Trades Union, held at New York in 1834, education was emphasized, and the long day of labor in cotton and woolen manufactories on the part of children condemned. The convention recommended "that lawful security should be exacted from the proprietors of manufactories for the education of every child employed by them therein."[24]

[18] *Ibid.*, V, 61–63.
[19] *Acts and Resolves of Rhode Island, January, 1853*, p. 246.
[20] See statement in *Paterson Courier* (reprinted in Commons, *Documentary History of American Industrial Society*, V), 64.
[21] Otey, *The Beginnings of Child Labor Legislation*, 34, quoting from *Free Enquirer*, New York, June 14, 1832. Report of committee, also in *Boston Transcript*, March 24, 1832.
[22] *Ibid.*, 35, quoting from "An Address to the Workingmen of New England on the State of Education", etc., Boston, 1832.
[23] *Ibid.*, 35, quoting from "Speech in Defense of the American System against the British Colonial System", 1852, p. 22.
[24] *Ibid.*, 36, quoting from *The Man*, August 30, 1834.

The change in conditions and the growth of public interest initiated a new period of legislation in which the broad and vague admonitions expressing the Puritan ideals gave place to specific provisions aiming to secure at least a minimum of schooling to every child employed in factory work.

LEGISLATION FOR THE EDUCATION OF CHILDREN IN FACTORIES

The Committee on Education of the Massachusetts Legislature considered the matter again in 1836, and this time the point of view had changed. It was estimated that a very large proportion of those engaged in industry were "of young and tender years." The reasons which led to the over-employment of children were those which have since become familiar. First of all, the high price of labor induced the employers to make use of women and children rather than men. Then a good many of the families who had been unsuccessful or unfortunate came to the mills with the intention of employing their young people. Consequently, "there is a strong interest and an urgent motive to seek constant employment for their children, at a very early age, if the wages obtained can aid them even but little in bearing the burden of their support." Otey states: "The school returns of 4 large manufacturing towns with a population of less than 20,000 showed that 1895 children between 4 and 16 years of age, with very slight deduction for those attending private schools, did not attend the common schools any part of the year."[25]

This report led to the passage of the Massachusetts statute of 1836, entitled "An Act for the better Instruction of Youth employed in Manufacturing Establishments," the first of a series of measures designed to reconcile the demand of the factories for labor with the requirements of education. According to this law children under fourteen were not to be employed in a factory in any year unless they had attended school at least three months in the year preceding.[26] After the law had gone into effect, Horace Mann, who was secretary of the Board of Education, stated that four hundred children in one manufacturing town went to school who had never gone before.[27]

A few years afterward, in 1840, Rhode Island passed a similar law, requiring attendance at school for three months in the year preceding any year of employment, but applied the provision only to children under twelve years of age.[28] Connecticut followed in 1842 with an act[29] which forbade the employment of children under fifteen in any manufacturing establishment "or other business" unless they had attended school three months out of the twelve in the year immediately preceding the year of their employment. The scope of these laws was extended by New Hampshire in a statute of 1846[30] which had similar provisions for children under fifteen years of age, and further required that no child under twelve should be employed in a manufacturing establishment unless he or she had attended school for six months in the previous year.

[25] *Ibid.*, 76.
[26] Otey, *The Beginnings of Child Labor Legislation*, 76–77; Whittelsey, *Massachusetts Labor Legislation* (1901), 10.
[27] Otey, *The Beginnings of Child Labor Legislation*, referring to *First Annual Report of the Secretary of the Board of Education, 1838*, p. 67.
[28] Towles, *Factory Legislation of Rhode Island*, 458–461.
[29] *Public Acts of the State of Connecticut, May Session, 1842*, chap. xxviii, 40.
[30] *New Hampshire Laws, 1846*, chap. 318, p. 298.

Maine copied this last provision in a statute passed in 1847.[31] All the laws of this series required schooling in the year before employment, but said nothing about school work while the child was actually employed. The penalty of non-employment in the succeeding year, if the child had not continued his schooling, may have been regarded as sufficient. Rhode Island was the first State to forbid the employment in factories of children (in this case under fifteen years of age) for more than nine months in any year, as well as to require a preliminary period of schooling.[32]

RESTRICTION OF WORKING AGE AND HOURS OF CHILDREN

Following this first series of laws, restricting the labor of children to provide for their education, came another series which forbade absolutely the employment of children below a minimum age, and set limits to the working day of young persons. Only four States covered both these subjects by legislation before the Civil War; five more restricted the working time without setting a definite age limit below which a child might not be employed.

As a result of the ten-hour movement in Massachusetts, that Commonwealth, in 1842,[33] forbade the employment in factories of children under twelve for more than ten hours a day, and in various ways tried to enforce a certain amount of educational preparation, but left entirely untouched the age at which a child might be set to factory work.[34] Connecticut, in the same year, limited the hours of work of children under fourteen, employed in cotton and woolen manufacturing establishments, to ten hours in any day, and much later forbade entirely the employment in factories of young children. An act of 1855 set the age limit at nine years, and this was raised in 1856 to ten years.[35] Pennsylvania, in 1848, prohibited the employment of children under twelve, but made the act applicable only to textile factories; New Jersey, in 1851, and Rhode Island, in 1853, made the prohibition general, and set the age limit at ten and twelve years respectively.[36]

These laws protecting young children contained also provisions limiting the hours of work of minors who might be employed, and other States (Maine, New Hampshire, Ohio), which set no age limit on employment, adopted likewise regulations restricting the hours of work of minors. Georgia, in 1853, fixed the limits at sunrise and sunset.

INEFFECTIVE ADMINISTRATION OF THE FACTORY ACTS

It would be unprofitable to describe and compare all the various provisions. It is highly probable that in New York and in other States which enacted no legislation on the subject, conditions were little different from those in States which had laws on the

[31] *Acts and Resolves of Maine, Public Laws, 1847,* chap. xxix, 25.

[32] *Acts and Resolves of Rhode Island, January Session, 1854,* p. 262.

[33] *Acts and Resolves of Massachusetts, Winter Session, 1842,* chap. 60, p. 517.

[34] The first proposal to forbid entirely the employment of young children came in 1860, when a bill prohibiting the employment in factories of children under twelve during the school session was introduced but not passed. See Otey, *The Beginnings of Child Labor Legislation,* 85.

[35] *Public Acts of the State of Connecticut, 1855,* chap. xlv, 49; *1856,* chap. xxxix, 38. These acts also reduced the permissible hours of labor for young persons under 18.

[36] *Laws of Pennsylvania, 1848,* chap. 227, p. 278; *Acts of New Jersey, 1851,* approved March 18, p. 322; *Acts and Resolves of Rhode Island, January 1853,* p. 245.

statute book. The experience of England had shown, what the Americans of this period had still to realize, that administration was nine-tenths of the law in factory acts. The Pennsylvania act of 1848, in the section limiting the hours of labor, seemingly asked to be ignored; it imposed no penalty, and was not to be construed to prevent minors above the age of fourteen being employed over ten hours a day "if the same be done by special contract with their parents or guardians." The penalty for infraction in the Connecticut act of 1842 was $7; this was raised later to $20, which was an amount commonly adopted as a fine. The legislature chose some agents already appointed for other purposes to enforce its acts, school visitors or school committees or the town constable; or neglected altogether to impose the duty of administration but encouraged informers by promising them half of the fine collected. Some of the statutes imposed their penalties on employers who "knowingly" transgressed them; all that the employer had to do, obviously, was to assert that he had been deceived as to the age by the child or its parents. No definite proof of age was required by any statute of the period. The best means of enforcement seems to have been the educational requirement, which could be administered by exacting a certificate from a teacher, and in which the school system was interested as the fines were often promised in whole or in part to support the schools. Even here, however, to judge from the experience of Rhode Island, conditions were lax; the School Commission of that State reported in 1856 that the enrollment of children of school age was only 69 per cent., and the attendance only 48⅔ per cent. of the proper number.[37] Not all the children who were out of school were in the factories but there is every reason to suppose that in Rhode Island and in the other States many children were at work who should have been at school.

WOMEN WORKERS IN THE EARLY MILLS

Legislation for women came much later than that for children, and indeed was hardly differentiated from legislation for men before the Civil War. In neither field was anything of consequence accomplished during this period. Yet forces were already at work preparing the way for legislation to follow, and it is proper to sketch here an outline of the conditions of labor, especially of women, in the factories and mills, and of the agitation for the legal regulation of the labor of men, especially for the limitation of their hours of labor.

Although the conditions under which the women worked were far from ideal, there is every reason to believe that their entrance into the mills in New England was for most of them an advantage. When Miss Harriet Martineau first came to America in 1836, she pointed out that comparatively few occupations were open to women, and mentioned as a favorable symptom that the mills were now giving them new employment and that they were also working in printing offices.[38] In fact, as shown by Miss Abbott, there seem to have been from 1820 to 1840 more than one hundred industrial occupations in which women worked,[39] but it is altogether probable that they occupied in the aggregate comparatively few individuals.

At any rate the mills, especially the cotton mills, offered an opportunity for earning

[37] Stockwell (ed.), *History of Public Education in Rhode Island from 1636 to 1876* (1876), 84.
[38] Abbott, *Women in Industry* (1910), 65, referring to Martineau, *Society in America* (4th ed., 1837), II, 257.
[39] *Ibid.*, 66.

money which was eagerly sought by well educated girls of good families. Many of them had been school teachers, or had the alternative of teaching school, and did not think it beneath their dignity to enter the mills. Most of them looked on service in the factory as an interesting and profitable experience, preparatory to their marriage or the return to their families. Their social status was not lowered by this service. "Do ladies or gentlemen tend the slashers?" was the question put at a meeting of the New England Cotton Manufacturers' Association so late as 1869.[40] Lucy Larcom said that "for twenty years or more Lowell might have been looked upon as a rather select industrial school for young people. The girls were just such girls as are knocking at the doors of young women's colleges today."[41] These were the girls who edited the *Lowell Offering* during the period 1825 to 1850.[42] A memorandum taken from a book kept by John Clark, agent of the Merrimac mills, May 6, 1841, stated that 124 females at work in the Merrimac mills had taught school, while twenty-five or thirty more had withdrawn in the last thirty days to engage their schools for the summer; two hundred and ninety girls had attended school during the evenings of the preceding winter.[43]

RISE OF A CLASS OF FACTORY WORKERS

When a larger percentage of the population worked in the factories, it was clear that factory work was no longer a merely temporary employment for girls from the farm. The increase of immigration and the increasing percentage of newcomers in the factories who had no such home connections as the daughters of farmers, also made their situation less desirable.

A report on labor conditions made in 1850 stated that formerly the female operatives were nearly all New England girls but that then many of them were foreigners, and stated that it would be found "that, in a few years, an entire modification, and depression of the state of society in and about manufacturing places, will be wrought by this cause."[44] This report, the first of its kind in Massachusetts, showed that conditions existed which not only would be thought bad now but which furthermore were already rousing complaints and protests. There were petitions stating that the signers were confined from thirteen to fourteen hours per day in unhealthy apartments, and similar complaints came not only from Lowell, but also from Fall River and Andover. The specific demand was made in a petition from Lowell that a law should be passed making ten hours a day's work in the absence of specific agreement to the contrary.[45] The special legislation committee held sessions to investigate the matter and ascertained that in the Lowell mills the hours of work per day varied, according to the seasons, from 11 hours, 24 minutes to 12 hours, 45 minutes, the latter in the summer months. There were comparatively few children under fifteen years of age, and the opinion of the committee was that the general health of the operatives in the mills was good. Two Lowell physicians said that there was less sickness among the mill people than

[40] *Ibid.*, 99.
[41] *Ibid.*, 112.
[42] *Ibid.*, 109.
[43] Commons, *Documentary History of American Industrial Society*, VIII, 147.
[44] "The Investigation of 1850" (Massachusetts House Document, No. 152, reprinted, *Ibid.*, VIII, 151–187). See p. 170.
[45] "The First Official Investigation of Labor Conditions, 1845" (Massachusetts House Document, No. 50, reprinted *Ibid.*, VIII, 133–150).

among others in the town. Figures from the Boott mill showed that of 203 girls, 29 reported improved health, 119 as good, and 55 not as good compared with the condition previous to employment.[46] The advice of the committee, given unanimously, was that legislation limiting hours of labor was not necessary at that time; and the committee reported in favor of letting things alone to cure themselves. "Labor is intelligent enough to make its own bargains, and look out for its own interests without interference from us."[47]

AGITATION FOR REFORM

Labor had in fact been carrying on for a number of years an active campaign in favor of reforms, and though comparatively little was accomplished before the Civil War, an account of this movement is necessary to an understanding of the conditions of the time. Commons calls the period from 1820 to 1840 the "Awakening Period of the American Labor Movement."[48] There were only sporadic organizations of labor before that time. In 1827, a mechanics' union or trade association was formed in Philadelphia, and this was the first attempt to create an organization which would unite different unions of workingmen as a class for a common object. The labor press began to be established at this time. *The Mechanics' Free Press* in 1828 said, "This is the first time that the workingmen have attempted in a public meeting to inquire whether they possess as individuals or as a class any right to say by whom they shall be governed."[49] Thus the movement came into existence at about the same time as in England.

The first national trade union to be formed in the United States was organized in 1834, and held conventions in different cities in 1835, 1836, and 1837. The panic of 1837 killed it, but the movement continued.[50] It was largely influenced in this period by socialists and other radicals. Robert Dale Owen and Miss Frances Wright were editing the *Free Inquirer*, in New York. Their idea was a Spartan system of education, under which all children were to be fed, clothed, and lodged at the expense of the state, were to dress alike, and were to eat at common tables. We see here the importance attributed to education.[51]

An organization quite distinct from a trade union or a party met in Boston in the years 1831, 1832, and 1833, and in Northampton in 1834. It was called the New England Association of Farmers, Mechanics, and Other Workingmen. They planned to extend their organization and to agitate for far-reaching reforms both in politics and in social and economic relations. They proposed "the consideration of the ten hour system and whether it is expedient for this convention to make its adoption by their associates indispensable, or to leave it to the discretion of the various associations of New England." They also recommended better education, and a change in the factory system, calculated to bring this about, as already mentioned in connection with child labor.[52] Characteristic is the demand for the ten-hour day, and for better education.

[46] *Ibid.*, 133, 134, 142, 144, 146.
[47] *Ibid.*, 150.
[48] *Ibid.*, V, 20.
[49] *Ibid.*, V, 21.
[50] *Ibid.*, V, 22–23.
[51] Persons, et al., *Labor Laws and Their Enforcement* (1911), 10.
[52] *Ibid.*, 11–12.

Some went even beyond the ten-hour day. In the words of Douglas, the editor of the *New England Artizan*, "We contended that 8 hours a day was time enough to devote to regular productive labor. That this quantity of labor was as much as the human constitution could bear with impunity for any considerable length of time, and that all beyond this was bodily destroying toil."[53] Robinson, one of the leaders, thought that it ought to be made a crime to work more than six hours a day.

A new organization, the Workingman's Party, first mentioned in Massachusetts in 1830 to 1833, included among its principles: "abolition of imprisonment for debt; a mechanic's lien law; banking reform; reduction of the fees of professional men to a fair level with the wages of laboring men; and to make provision by law for the education of all classes."[54] These objects the members expected to accomplish through the ballot box, and in 1833, the Workingman's Party in Lowell nominated a full representative ticket. One of their nominees was returned from Lowell that year, and the General Court is said to have contained seven workingmen.

The absence of a well defined factory class helps to account for the lack of legislation and to a certain extent made legislation unnecessary. In 1841, H. A. Miles, in the *North American Review*, contrasted the hours of labor in England, attention paid to ventilation, and so forth, with conditions prevailing in the United States. In spite of the long hours, the conclusion was, on the whole, favorable to the American factories, on account of other things, such as the smaller proportion of child labor, the boarding house system, and above all, the fact that Massachusetts had no permanent factory population, four-fifths of the operatives being young women from the country, who, after spending four or five years in the factories, returned home.[55]

REFORM MOVEMENT IN MASSACHUSETTS, 1840–1850

The germ of a factory class was, however, already in existence, and in alliance with industrial workers who had not yet entered a factory it kept alive the question of the conditions of labor. In 1842 pressure was brought to bear upon the Massachusetts General Court, by means of petitions.[56] These came particularly from the towns of the southeastern part of the State, where the foreign element was largest, such as Fall River, Mansfield, Taunton, and New Bedford; most of them were headed, "The Ten Hour Republican Association." The petition from Taunton, which was the longest, contained 463 signatures. In most of the petitions, the object aimed at seemed to be simply a uniform rule, established by law, in other words, a standard of measurement. The Lowell petition, however, which was not presented until 1843, and which contained almost 1600 names, asked definitely for a law which would prevent the employment of persons by manufacturing corporations for more than ten hours a day, and based the demand upon the arguments that such a law would serve to lengthen the life of those employed, and give them more leisure for mental and moral cultivation, and more time to attend to their own personal affairs.[57]

The movement for reform in the conditions of labor now took the form of a definite

[53] *Ibid.*, 15.
[54] *Ibid.*, 11.
[55] *Ibid.*, 24.
[56] *Ibid.*, 24–25.
[57] *Ibid.*, 26.

organization.[58] The Mutual Benefit Society of the Journeymen Cordwainers of Lynn proposed a convention of the workers of Massachusetts, which was held at Boston in October 1844, and which gathered together some 200 delegates, mainly from the manufacturing towns. This group, termed The Workingmen's Association, was supported by two periodicals, the Lynn *Awl*, and the *Voice of Industry*, published first at Fitchburg and later at Lowell. The demand for a ten-hour day and for the restriction of child labor was combined with socialistic reasoning ("labor is the only creator of value"), and for a time the new association was in danger of wasting itself in doctrinaire discussion. A representative of Brook Farm was present at the first meeting, and the next year the radical reformers, aiming at national and international regeneration, social and political as well as economic, obtained control. The meeting of 1845 was attended by Charles A. Dana, Albert Brisbane, even by Robert Owen himself, and representatives of Brook Farm were given the important offices. The mass of the members refused, however, to be led into a political crusade for the regeneration of society. They renamed themselves in 1846 the New England Labor Reform League, they advocated specific reforms in laws relating to disposal of the public lands and to mechanics' lien, and they put the ten-hour day at the head of their program.

The new League experimented in different forms of political activity, and discussed, without action, the plan of a general strike. It faded away in 1847, but it had forced upon the legislature a consideration of the proposal of a ten-hour day. Reports on the subject were made by a committee of the Massachusetts House in 1845, and by a committee of the Senate in 1846. In both cases, however, the committees refused to recommend action. The general objection was that the facts did not show abuses sufficiently serious to justify legislative interference. The opponents of reform took the ground, in general, that the effect of the ten-hour law in Massachusetts would "be to close the gate of every mill in the State." They also asserted that an inevitable effect would be a material reduction in wages. Both House and Senate fell back upon the *laissez faire* doctrine. They admitted that abuse existed, but the committee felt that the remedy was not with them. They "look for it in the progressive movement in art and science, in a higher appreciation of man's destiny, in a less love for money, and a more ardent love for social happiness and intellectual superiority."[59]

In spite of this disappointing outcome the movement for the ten-hour day had not been entirely barren of results. It was something to have induced committees of the legislature to discuss the question, and to have forced them to admit the competence of the State to legislate regarding it. Further, the factory workers had obtained a slight practical concession. In 1847 the mills of Lowell, followed by those in New Hampshire, extended the time allowed for meals to 45 minutes throughout the year. The hours set for beginning and for closing the day remained as before but the worker saved 15 minutes a day from labor during eight months, and 30 minutes during the remaining four.[60]

[58] *Ibid.*, 29 *et seq.*
[59] See *Ibid.*, 49, for a detailed synopsis of the committee's argument.
[60] *Ibid.*, 53.

TEN-HOUR MOVEMENT IN MASSACHUSETTS, 1850–1860

In the decade 1850–1860 Massachusetts was still the storm center of the ten-hour movement. Agitation continued, legislative committees discussed the question, the legislature itself was forced to face the issue, while, in the background, individual employers and groups of mills recognized the trend of the times and made practical concessions. Rather than narrate the annals of the movement in their complex detail, it will be convenient here to sketch the main features of progress in different lines.

The agitation, which was persistent from 1850 to 1856, and was at its height in 1852 and 1853, was better organized and more effective. Frequent meetings were held in the industrial towns. Petitions to the legislature included in 1853 nearly 10,000 signatures, with that of John G. Whittier at the head of one. The petitions were no longer rambling, violent, or weak; most of them followed definite forms, demanding a law which should prohibit any corporation chartered by the Commonwealth from employing a person for more than ten hours in any one day. The influence of able leaders was now apparent in the movement. Three members of the legislature contributed, each in his own way, to give it impetus. James M. Stone, who had advocated the ten-hour day since 1842, was the principal public speaker in its behalf; William S. Robinson, who had married a Lowell mill girl, devoted his newspaper, the Lowell *American*, to the cause; Benjamin F. Butler, a demagogue not too scrupulous, gained some support if he also roused a bitter opposition.

The temper of legislative committees showed a change. The majority of a committee of the House, in 1850, did not think it necessary to support by arguments its conclusion, "it is inexpedient to legislate;" another House committee in 1852 followed the same course, but included some members who suggested a feeble compromise. In 1853 the reformers managed to have one of their number made chairman of the committee, and by his efforts brought the measure to the floor against the majority of the committee. At last, in 1855, they obtained the unanimous report of a House committee in favor of a ten-hour law, and in 1856 got favorable action by the majority of a Senate committee.

The bill which formed the subject of discussion in 1850 had been carefully framed to be practicable and effective. It reduced the daily hours of labor of all persons employed by Massachusetts corporations to eleven on September 1 of that year and to ten on July 1 following; it imposed on the corporation itself, not on any particular officials, the responsibility for carrying out its provisions and the penalty for infraction. This bill was defeated in the House, but obtained a "respectable favorable vote." It was introduced again in 1851, without action, and, slightly modified, was again brought to a vote in 1852, when it failed to pass, 48 to 117. By a political combination it passed the House in 1853, but was killed in the Senate; in 1854 it failed to reach a third reading in the House; and in 1855, after a bitter contest, was postponed by the House to the next legislature. A weaker edition of the measure, introduced in the Senate in 1856, apparently died without action. These years were marked by such absorbing interest in the question of slavery that domestic problems were thrust into the background.

Although the ten-hour movement in Massachusetts did not succeed, before the Civil War, in getting its ideals realized in legislation, it did obtain from many employers practical concessions of considerable importance. In September 1852,[61] the hours of work in the machine shops of five important industrial towns were reduced to eleven; the measure was doubtless aimed to influence the votes of the workers in the election of that Fall. Even before then, in scattered towns and in different industries, but particularly in those connected with the machinists' trade, hours had been reduced to ten by many employers. In Worcester,[62] in 1853, the ten-hour system was said to be "all but universal." At the height of the agitation, in 1853, even the great textile factories gave ground. The corporations of Lowell and Lawrence, followed by those of Salem and other cities, reduced the average hours of labor to eleven; as a general rule, from then on, the working day in the textile factories lasted from 7 in the morning to 7 at night, with three-quarters of an hour at noon for dinner and an earlier closing on Saturday.[63]

FAILURE OF THE SHORT-HOUR MOVEMENT IN THIS PERIOD

To explain the failure of the movement for shorter working hours in this period we must take into account not only the distraction of national politics, but also the fact that the ten-hour day was only one plank of a platform of reform. The factory worker put it in the forefront, but the class of factory workers was still restricted and was not sharply differentiated. The reform party comprised not only men and women of this class, but also independent mechanics, working in their own shops in a small way, and even farmers and other small-scale producers. Conditions still persisted such as those sketched by Commons in an earlier period: "the movement at first was not so much the modern alignment of wage-earners against employer, as the alignment of the producing classes against the non producers. It was the poor against the rich, the worker against the owner."[64] Thus, although the shorter working day was discussed freely and petitions presented in its favor, this movement was coupled with many other movements such as the demand for mechanics' lien laws, better education, the extension of the suffrage, reform of banking, abolition of imprisonment for debt, and so forth.

In spite of the failure of Massachusetts to pass the ten-hour bill, the movement was not altogether without effect elsewhere. President Van Buren had already issued an order, March 31, 1840, providing that persons employed on public works, under the immediate authority of the President and the departments, should be required to work only the number of hours set by the ten-hour system.[65] This, of course, had no general force of law, and applied, at best, to a very limited number of persons. As a sop to the agitators, some of the States passed "ten hour acts," but these were of such a sort as betrayed the weakness rather than showed the strength of the labor movement. They were never meant to be enforced. So Pennsylvania, in 1848, bravely proclaimed "That labor performed during a period of ten hours, on any secular day, in all cotton, woolen, silk, paper, bagging and flax factories, shall be considered a legal day's labor; and that hereafter, no minor or adult, engaged in any such factories, shall be holden or required

[61] *Ibid.*, 87.
[62] *Ibid.*, 76.
[63] *Ibid.*, 88.
[64] Commons, *Documentary History of American Industrial Society*, V, 24.
[65] *Ibid.*, VIII, 85.

to work more than ten hours on any secular day, or sixty hours in any secular week; . . . ." and imposed no penalty for infraction![66] New Jersey, likewise, in 1851, defined ten hours of work in certain manufactures as "a legal day's labor," without indicating any result to follow from working an "illegal" time, and Rhode Island and Connecticut were careful to specify that their ten-hour day was "legal" or "lawful" only as an option, "unless otherwise agreed by the parties."[67] In Rhode Island the employers decided that the working day should be 11½ hours, making a week of 69 hours, and the workers had no choice but to accept this decision.[68]

The progress made in this period in the protection of labor was so slight that to us of a later generation it must seem contemptibly small. Whether the object of protection was children, or women, or adult men, the laws demanded of the employer very little, and exacted in fact much less. The result of all the agitation was the formulation of a problem, rather than an approach to its solution.

Yet it is unfair to condemn the legislators of the period without taking into account the difference of the times in which they lived. The economic conditions were hard, and imposed pretty severe toil on all who sought to earn their livelihood, whether on the farm, in the shop, in the factory or on the frontier. The instruments of production and of transportation were undeveloped; steam power was spreading through the country, but had yet to show its strength. The surplus product was not yet so large as to raise seriously the question whether it must all go to profit, whether it might not be appropriated in part, at least, to an amelioration of the conditions of labor. The class of factory workers was still in process of formation. It had become self-conscious, but it had still to convince the voters and the government that it needed not so much a stimulus to industry as protection from over-work. It raised the question, but for an answer to its appeal it had to wait until after the Civil War.

The agitation for shorter hours was unfortunate, moreover, in that it coincided with the various political controversies connected with the slavery question. The Compromise of 1850, the Kansas-Nebraska Bill of 1854, the Kansas War, the Dred Scott Decision of 1857, the re-alignment of parties on the slavery question, and on the land question, were of all-absorbing interest. It was not until the slavery question was out of the way that progress could be made in the field of labor legislation.

[66] *Laws of Pennsylvania, 1848*, chap. 227, p. 278.

[67] *Acts of New Jersey, 1851*, approved March 18, p. 321; *Acts and Resolves of Rhode Island, January 1853*, p. 245; *The Public Acts of Connecticut, 1855*, chap. xlv, 49.

[68] Persons, et al., *Labor Laws and Their Enforcement*, 77.

BIBLIOGRAPHY

BIBLIOGRAPHIC INTRODUCTION

This bibliography, while in no sense claiming to be an exhaustive list of references on social legislation for the period covered, contains more titles than are cited in the footnotes. The great majority of the titles represent books assembled by the author during almost a quarter of a century as working material for this volume. As the long illness which ended with his death in 1933 prevented the accession of the more recent books, a careful review of the works of the past decade was made during the process of editing the book, and titles pertinent were incorporated. The alphabetical list of general references is preceded by a list of well-known and available bibliographies. *Writings on American History* (annual from 1906 on), by Grace Gardner Griffin, has been used more extensively than any other general historical bibliography.

United States Government Publications

The several general lists and catalogues which, taken together, include practically all the Government publications from 1774 to date, and the lists and indexes issued by the various Government departments and bureaus, have been freely consulted in the preparation of the Bibliography.

Colonies and States

For a study of the sources of Colonial and State history, the essential works are Sabin (continued by Eames and completed by Vail), *Dictionary of Books Relating to America from its Discovery to the Present Time*, and Evans, *American Bibliography*. Covering a period from the discovery of America to 1934, they not only list all Americana, but give bibliographical data, as well as the places where the rare editions are to be found.

Adelaide R. Hasse's *Index of Economic Material in the Documents of the States* (Carnegie Institution of Washington, 1907–1923), which was prepared as a preliminary aid for the work of this series, should be consulted for the States covered.

Contemporary Records

Contemporary records cited in this work such as: *Bradford's History of Plimoth Plantations*, of which the Ford edition of 1912 has been used; *Johnson's Wonder Working Providence*, in the Jameson edition; Cotton Mather's *Magnalia;* and Davenport's *Discourse about Civil Government* are all too well known to need further comment. Collections of contemporary material, such as Force's *Tracts*, the Hart series of *American History Told by Contemporaries*, Jameson's *Original Narratives*, and O'Callaghan's *Documents Relative to the Colonial History of New York*, are familiar and convenient reference works.

Among the newer works from which much help was derived, both for the Colonial and for the later period, must be cited Miss Donnan's monumental *Documents Illustrative of the History of the Slave Trade*, and Mrs. Catterall's equally important work, *Judicial Cases Concerning American Slavery*.

Laws

The libraries which are depositories for the great collections of colonial laws have in some instances issued catalogues. The Henry E. Huntington Library's *Check List of American Laws . . . of the Seventeenth and Eighteenth Centuries*, and the *Charlemagne Tower Collection of American Colonial Laws* should be mentioned in this connection.

Other bibliographies of the laws of various colonies and States, such as Bartlett's *Index* and Bongartz's *Check List of Rhode Island Laws*, Bates' *Bibliographical List of Editions of Connecticut Laws . . . to 1836*, the Ford and Mathew's *Bibliography of Laws of Massachusetts Bay, 1641–1776*, and the bibliographies of Theodore C. Cole, are easily available.

The catalogue compiled by Fiennan W. Coar for the sale of the Benedict collection of laws is an especially careful work and a landmark in its field. The Massachusetts State Library's *Hand-list of Legislative Sessions* was of the greatest value in tabulating the slave laws. The *Check-list of Session Laws*, by Grace E. MacDonald (New York, 1936), is the latest issue of this kind, and was available during the latter part of the revision.

As laws are among the first material to be printed, Douglas Crawford McMurtie's *A History of Printing in the United States* has especial significance for the present study. Volume II, dealing with the Middle and Southern Atlantic States, is the only one so far to appear. The work, when completed, will amplify and supplement the various bibliographies and histories already published by Mr. McMurtie, such as *A Bibliography of Kentucky Statute Law, 1792–1830*, and *The Earliest New Jersey Imprints*. As a final check for bibliographies of laws, Lawrence Keitt's *An Annotated Bibliography of Bibliographies of Statutory Materials of the United States* should be consulted.

The *Colonial Records* of the various States are among the most fertile source material for a study of this nature, and laws that were lost before they reached the printed page are here preserved in their matrix. The State historical societies, especially those of Massachusetts and North Carolina, have also preserved invaluable records. References to these publications are given below under the names of individual States.

The statutes are obviously a source of prime importance to a student of social legislation, and for the convenience of scholars an attempt is made in this Bibliography to list in its various forms the material available under this head. Among general collections, the Charlemagne Tower collection in the library of the Historical Society of Pennsylvania at Philadelphia stands preëminent, with over two hundred volumes "composed largely of original copies of the printed provincial laws of the present States of the Union and of other earlier works relating to the settlement and development." It contains the first edition extant of laws issued by each of the original colonies with the exception of Rhode Island, New Jersey, and Maryland; the first edition of Vermont laws; and those of the British and Danish West Indies. The set of Pennsylvania laws is unequalled, and the Massachusetts laws, with the collection of Dr. George H. Moore as a nucleus, contain 407 items. A full description and history of the collection is given in the preface to its catalogue.

Many of the early editions of laws listed in the Tower collection may be found also in the Henry E. Huntington Library at San Marino, Calif., which includes the great E. Dwight Church collection of American literature. Its greatest treasure is the only known copy of the 1648 edition of *The Book of the General Lawes and Liberties of Massachusetts*, of which fac-simile copies have been made.

The American Antiquarian Society Library in Worcester, Massachusetts, founded by Isaiah Thomas, contains good files of the laws of all the New England States, especially Massachusetts and New Hampshire. Although not catalogued, these are arranged alphabetically and chronologically, and are made available to the student.

Yale University, in its Sterling Memorial Library and the library of its Law School, has a large and valuable collection of early colonial laws, especially those of Connecticut and Massachusetts. The books in the Sterling Memorial Library are catalogued and may be obtained in the Rare Book Room. The Law School library has been enriched by the accession of the Cole collection of five thousand volumes and by the gift of the collection of the late Governor Simeon E. Baldwin, formerly Professor of Law. These have not been catalogued and are kept in the vault, but they are accessible on application.

Outside of the rarer items to be found only in collections, various compilations and reprints of colonial and State laws are accessible in nearly all large libraries. Among these, Hening's *Statutes at Large* is the standard reference for the early laws of Virginia and is too well known to need comment. Grimké, *Public Laws of the State of South-Carolina;* the Bioren *Laws of the Commonwealth* (1700–1822) and the Mitchell and Flanders *Statutes at Large, 1682–1801* (in sixteen volumes) for Pennsylvania; O'Callaghan's *Laws and Ordinances of New Netherlands*, the four-volume edition of *Colonial Laws of New York*, and the *East-Hampton Book of Laws*, for New York Colony; and the Leaming and Spicer *Laws*, for New Jersey, should also be mentioned here.

There were no official Delaware laws before the creation of the State in 1776, "Delaware Colony" being a term used for convenience only to embrace the counties of New Castle, Kent, and Sussex during the period 1703 to 1776. The compilation by Allen D. Chandler of the colonial statutes of Georgia, printed in *The Colonial Records of Georgia*, comprises researches made not only in this country, but in the records abroad, and the results, printed in clear type, make this one of the most valuable additions to colonial legal history. The *Records of North Carolina* also contain the *Laws, 1715–1790*, and, as in the case of Georgia, have simplified greatly the task of tracing colonial laws. The famous *Body of Liberties* of Massachusetts was first published in 1843 by the Massachusetts Historical Society in the *Collections*, and has been reprinted since in various editions of colonial laws; the version used in the present study was the familiar one in Whitmore's edition of *The Colonial Laws of Massachusetts. The Acts and Resolves of the Province of Massachusetts Bay* for 1692–1780, edited by Ames and Goodell in twenty-one volumes, is the standard for all references to Massachusetts colonial laws. The early session laws of Rhode Island, covering the period from 1747 to 1800, have been preserved in fac-simile reprints edited by J. Harry Bongartz.

In the national period, wherever possible, the session laws have been examined, but compilations and digests are available for nearly every State, as will be seen in the alphabetical list. In the interpretation of the laws and their history, the following works may be cited as especially valuable: Reinsch, *American Legislatures and Legisla-*

tive Methods, and Stimson, *Popular Law-making, a Study of the Origin, History and Present Tendencies of Law Making by Statute.*

SECONDARY AUTHORITIES

Societies and Universities

The publications of various societies and universities are a rich source of economic material. In this connection should be mentioned the publications of the American Economic Association and the American Historical Association, the *Studies in History, Economics, and Public Law* of Columbia University, the Johns Hopkins University *Studies in Historical and Political Science*, the Harvard *Economic Studies*, and the Harvard *Historical Studies*. Many very helpful articles are to be found in periodicals such as the *American Economic Review*, the *American Historical Review*, *Political Science Quarterly*, *Journal of Political Economy*, the *Quarterly Journal of Economics*, and the *Journal of Negro History*.

General Histories

The reader who desires to extend his studies beyond the lines followed in the text will find helpful bibliographical suggestions in the *Guide* of Channing, Hart and Turner, last published in 1912, in the general histories and in the manuals of general and of economic history. The various collections such as *The American Nation* edited by Albert Bushnell Hart, and the older *Narrative and Critical History of America* edited by Justin Winsor, also contain useful bibliographies. The monographs issued in the Johns Hopkins University *Studies in Historical and Political Science*, and the Columbia University *Studies in History, Economics and Public Law*, as well as the economic histories for particular sections of the country, such as Weeden's *Economic and Social History of New England*, and Bruce's *Economic History of Virginia*, will be found in the list following.

Education and Land Policy

Among the most helpful books on education and the land policy may be cited Dexter's *History of Education in the United States*, Germann's *National Legislation Concerning Education*, and Schafer's *Land Grants for Education*. Sato, *History of the Land Question;* Treat, *The National Land System, 1785–1820;* and Hibbard, *A History of the Public Land Policy*, are useful presentations of this phase of social legislation. For the Spanish legislation, a special monograph was prepared by Reuben McKitrick under the title, *The Public Land System of Texas;* and Sayles' and Gammel's studies of the laws of Texas, and Garrison's and Yoakum's histories of Texas are illuminating. Much valuable material is also contained in White's *A New Collection of Laws*. The study of the exemption laws rests on monographs written especially for this volume by J. Harding Underwood and W. L. Bailey.

Labor Legislation

The Commissioner of Labor's *Report on the Condition of Woman and Child Wage Earners*, in nineteen volumes, is a comprehensive official source of information. Otey's

Beginnings of Child Labor Legislation in Certain States, Volume VI, has been drawn upon freely in the text. The United States Commissioners of Labor have issued three compilations of labor laws (1892, 1904, 1907) which are, of course, valuable only for comparison in the period covered by this book. The series on *Labor Laws of the United States*, and on *Wages and Hours of Labor*, issued by the Bureau of Labor Statistics, as well as the reports and bulletins of the Department of Labor, are also official sources of information.

The following monographs were written under the direction of the author and with financial assistance from the Carnegie Institution, as preliminary studies for this book: Barnard, *Factory Legislation in Pennsylvania*, Downey, *History of Labor Legislation in Iowa*, Eaves, *A History of California Labor Legislation*, Edwards, *The Labor Legislation of Connecticut*, Fairchild, *The Factory Legislation of the State of New York*, Field, *The Child Labor Policy of New Jersey*, Groat, *Trade Unions and the Law in New York*, and Towles, *Factory Legislation of Rhode Island*. These have all been published. Much of the material in these books relates to the period following the Civil War.

The studies of the legislation regarding seamen were based on a still unpublished manuscript, also prepared for this volume, by Dr. Alba M. Edwards. The *Annual Reports* of the Supervising Surgeons-General of the Marine Hospital Service, and reports such as that of Loring and Edwards in the *Senate* and *House Documents*, yield valuable data. Contemporary material can be found in such books as Jewell, *Among Our Sailors*, and Dana, *Two Years Before the Mast*, and in the *Reports* of the American Seamen's Friend Society and the *Sailors' Magazine and Seamen's Friend*.

Slavery and the Negro

The regulation of slavery occupies the greater part of the history of labor legislation before the Civil War, and the bibliography of this subject is the longest. Contemporary literature is abundant.

For the slave codes, the reader is referred to Stroud, *Sketch of the Laws Relating to Slavery* (1856), William Goodell, *The American Slave Code in Theory and Practice* (1853), and Hurd, *The Law of Freedom and Bondage* (1858–1862). Hurd, giving as he does the history of the laws of the States, together with a short analysis of their contents and with decisions and opinions, is invaluable. Many laws cited by him were not available in the revised codes of the States.

The works of the late Ulrich B. Phillips, notably *American Negro Slavery* and *Life and Labor in the Old South*, stand preëminent in the study of slavery. For the particular States, the Johns Hopkins University *Studies* contain a series of useful studies, among them those of Ballagh and Russell for Virginia, Bassett for the Carolinas, Steiner for Connecticut, Brackett and McCormac for Maryland, Cooley for New Jersey, and Trexel for Missouri. Similar monographs, not in this series, are Fowler's *Historical Status of the Negro in Connecticut*, Northrup's *Slavery in New York*, Moore's *Notes on Slavery in Massachusetts*, and Turner's *The Negro in Pennsylvania*.

BIBLIOGRAPHIES

AMES, JOHN GRIFFIN. *Comprehensive Index to the Publications of the United States Government, 1881–1893* (*House Doc.*, 58 Cong., 2 sess., No. 754. 2 vols., 2d ed., Washington, 1905).

ANDREWS, CHARLES MCLEAN. *Guide to the Materials for American History, to 1783, in the Public Record Office of Great Britain* (Carnegie Institution of Washington, Publ. No. 90A. 2 vols., Washington, 1912–1914).

BARTLETT, JOHN RUSSELL. *Bibliography of Rhode Island. A Catalogue of Books and Other Publications Relating to the State of Rhode Island*... Printed by Order of the General Assembly (Providence, 1864).

BATES, ALBERT CARLOS (comp.). *A Bibliographical List of Editions of Connecticut Laws from the Earliest Issues to 1836* (Acorn Club Publication, No. 3. Hartford, 1900).

BENEDICT, HON. RUSSELL. *Acts and Laws of the Thirteen Original Colonies and States Constituting the Collection Made by Hon. Russell Benedict, Justice of the Supreme Court of New York* (Compiled by Fiennan W. Coar for a public sale, Feb. 27, 1922. New York City).

BONGARTZ, J. HARRY. *Check List of Rhode Island Laws. Containing a Complete List of the Public Laws and Acts and Resolves of the State of Rhode Island to Date* (Providence, 1893).

CHANNING, EDWARD; HART, ALBERT BUSHNELL; AND TURNER, FREDERICK JACKSON. *Guide to the Study and Reading of American History* (rev. ed., Boston and London, 1912).

CLARKE, EDITH E. *Guide to the Use of United States Government Publications* (Boston, Mass., 1918).

COAR, FIENNAN W. See Benedict.

A DICTIONARY OF BOOKS RELATING TO AMERICA, *from Its Discovery to the Present Time* (25 vols., Begun by Joseph Sabin, continued by Wilberforce Eames and completed by R. W. G. Vail; for the Bibliographical Society of America, New York, 1868–1934).

DUTCHER, GEORGE MATTHEW; SHIPMAN, HENRY ROBINSON; FAY, SIDNEY BRADSHAW; SHEARER, AUGUSTUS HUNT; AND ALLINSON, WILLIAM HENRY (eds.). *A Guide to Historical Literature* (New York, 1931).

EVANS, CHARLES. *American Bibliography. A Chronological Dictionary of All Books, Pamphlets, and Periodical Publications Printed in the United States of America from the Genesis of Printing in 1639 Down to and Including the Year 1820* (12 vols., Chicago, 1903–1934).

FLAGG, CHARLES A. *Bibliography of New York Colonial History* (New York State Library *Bulletin*, No. 56. Albany, 1901).

———. *A Guide to Massachusetts Local History: being a Bibliographical Index to the Literature of the Towns, Cities and Counties of the State, Including Books, Pamphlets, Articles in Periodicals, and Collected Works*... (Salem, Mass., 1907).

———. *Reference List on Connecticut Local History* (Albany State Library *Bulletin*, No. 53. Albany, 1900).

FORD, WORTHINGTON C., AND MATTHEWS, ALBERT. *Bibliography of the Laws of Massachusetts-Bay, 1641–1776* (In Colonial Society of Massachusetts, *Publications*, IV; *Collections*, II. Boston, 1910).

GREENE, EVARTS B., AND MORRIS, RICHARD B. *A Guide to the Principal Sources for Early American History (1600–1800) in the City of New York* (New York, 1929).

GRIFFIN, APPLETON PRENTISS CLARK. *Bibliography of American Historical Societies, United States and Canada* (2d ed., revised and enlarged. Washington, D. C., 1907).

GRIFFIN, GRACE GARDNER (comp.). *Writings on American History. A Bibliography of Books and Articles on United States and Canadian History. Published During the Years 1906–* (Washington, 1908–). Continues *Writings on American History, 1902* (ed. by Richardson and Morse, Princeton, 1904) and *Writings on American History, 1903* (ed. by McLaughlin, Slade and Lewis, Carnegie Institution of Washington, Washington, 1905).

HASSE, ADELAIDE R. *Index of Economic Material in Documents of the States of the United States* (13 vols. in 16. Carnegie Institution of Washington. Washington, 1907–1922. Vol. I, California; II, Delaware; III, Illinois; IV, Kentucky; V, Maine; VI, Massachusetts; VII, New Hampshire; VIII, New Jersey; IX, New York; X, Ohio, 2 pts.; XI, Pennsylvania, 3 pts.; XII, Rhode Island; XIII, Vermont).

———. "Materials for a Bibliography of the Public Archives of The Thirteen Original States, Covering the Colonial Period and the State Period to 1789," in American Historical Association, *Annual Report*, 1906, II, 239–572, Washington, 1908.

HENRY E. HUNTINGTON LIBRARY (San Marino, Calif.). *Check List of American Laws, Charters and Constitutions of the Seventeenth and Eighteenth Centuries in the Huntington Library* (compiled by Willard O. Waters, San Marino, Calif., 1936).

HUNT, GAILLARD, et al. (eds.). *Handbook of the Manuscripts in the Library of Congress* (Washington, 1918).

JOHN CARTER BROWN LIBRARY (Providence, R. I.). *Rhode Island Imprints ... 1727–1800* (Rhode Island Historical Society, Providence, R. I., 1914).

KEITT, LAWRENCE. *An Annotated Bibliography of Bibliographies of Statutory Materials of the United States* (Cambridge, 1934).

LARNED, J. N. *The Literature of American History. A Bibliographical Guide in Which the Scope, Character, and Comparative Worth of Books in Selected Lists are Set Forth in Brief Notes by Critics of Authority* (ed. for the American Library Association. Boston, 1902).

———. *Supplement for 1900 and 1902* (ed. by Philip P. Wells. Boston, 1902).

LIBRARY OF CONGRESS. *Check List of Collections of Personal Papers in Historical Societies, Universities and Public Libraries and Other Learned Institutions in the United States* (Library of Congress, Washington, 1918).

MACDONALD, GRACE E. (comp.). *Check-List of Session Laws* (Public Document Clearing House Committee, National Association of State Libraries. New York, 1936).

MCMURTIE, DOUGLAS CRAWFORD. *A Bibliography of Kentucky Statute Law* (Louisville, The Filson Club, 1935).

———. *A History of Printing in the United States. The Story of the Introduction of the Press and of Its History and Influence During the Pioneer Period in Each State of the Union* (Vol. II, *Middle and South Atlantic States*. New York, MCMXXXVI).

MASSACHUSETTS STATE LIBRARY. *Hand-list of Legislative Sessions and Session Laws, Statutory Revisions, Compilations, Codes, etc., and Constitutional Conventions of the United States and Its Possessions and of the Several States to May 1812* (Publ. by the Trustees. Prepared by Charles J. Babbitt, 1912).

POORE, BENJAMIN PERLEY. *A Descriptive Catalogue of the Government Publications of the United States, Sept. 5, 1774 to March 4, 1881* (Washington, 1885).

SABIN, JOSEPH. See A Dictionary, etc.

SWANTON, WALTER I. *Guide to United States Government Publications* (Bureau of Education, *Bulletin* No. 2. Washington, 1918).

TOWER, CHARLEMAGNE. *The Charlemagne Tower Collection of American Colonial Laws* (compiled by S. S. R. Hildebrun for the Historical Society of Pennsylvania. Philadelphia, 1890).

UNITED STATES SUPERINTENDENT OF DOCUMENTS. *Checklist of United States Public Documents, 1789–1909* (compl. by Mary A. Hartwell, 2d ed., Washington, 1911).

VAN TYNE, CLAUDE HALSTEAD, AND LELAND, WALDO GRIFFORD (eds.). *Guide to the Archives of the Government of the United States in Washington* (Carnegie Institution of Washington Publ. No. 14. Washington, 1904. 2d rev. ed., Washington, 1907).

GENERAL REFERENCES

ABBOTT, EDITH. "History of the Employment of Women in the American Cotton Mills," in *Journal of Political Economy*, XVI, 602–621, 680–692, Nov.-Dec. 1908.

———. "The History of Industrial Employment of Women in the United States," in *Journal of Political Economy*, XIV, 461–501, Oct. 1906.

———. "Study of the Early History of Child Labor in America," in *American Journal of Sociology*, XIV, 15–37, July 1908.

———. *Women in Industry: A Study in American Economic History*, with an Introductory Note by Sophonisba P. Breckinridge (New York and London, 1910).

AN ABRIDGEMENT *of the Laws in Force and Use in Her Majesty's Plantations* (London, 1704). See COLONIAL LAWS.

ADAMS, CHARLES FRANCIS, JR. *Three Episodes of Massachusetts History* (2d ed., 2 vols. Boston and New York, 1892).

———. *Trans-Atlantic Historical Solidarity*. Lectures Delivered Before the University of Oxford in Easter and Trinity Terms (Oxford, England, 1913).

———. "An Undeveloped Function," in American Historical Association, *Annual Report*, 1901, I, 47–93, 1902.

ADAMS, CHARLES KENDALL. *Washington and the Higher Education, an Address Delivered before Cornell University, February 22, 1888* (Ithaca, 1888).

ADAMS, EPHRAIM DOUGLAS. "The Point of View of the British Traveler in America," in *Political Science Quarterly*, XXIX, 244–264, June, 1914.
——. *The Power of Ideals in American History* (New Haven and London, 1913).
ADAMS, HENRY CARTER. *Taxation in the United States, 1789–1816* (Johns Hopkins University, *Studies in Historical and Political Science*, II, Nos. 5–6. Baltimore, 1884).
ADAMS, HERBERT BAXTER. *Maryland's Influence upon Land Cessions to the United States* (Johns Hopkins University, *Studies in Historical and Political Science*, III, No. 1. Baltimore, 1885).
——. *Village Communities of Cape Ann and Salem* (Johns Hopkins University, *Studies in Historical and Political Science*, I, Nos. 9–10. Baltimore, 1883).
ADAMS, JAMES TRUSLOW. "Disfranchisement of Negroes in New England," in *American Historical Review*, XXX, 543–547, April, 1925.
——. *The Founding of New England* (Boston, 1921).
——. *New England in the Republic* (Boston, 1926).
——. *Provincial Society, 1690–1763* (New York, 1927).
——. *Revolutionary New England, 1691–1776* (Boston, 1923).
ADAMS, NEHEMIAH. *A South-Side View of Slavery* (4th ed., Boston, 1860).
ADDISON, DANIEL DULANEY. *Lucy Larcom. Life, Letters and Diary* (Boston, 1894).
AIMES, HUBERT HILLARY SUFFERN. "Coartación: A Spanish Institution for the Advancement of Slaves into Freedom," in *Yale Review*, XVII, 412–431, Feb., 1909.
AKAGI, ROY HIDEMICHI. *The Town Proprietors of the New England Colonies. A Study of the Development, Organization, Activities and Controversies, 1620–1778* (Philadelphia, 1924).
ALABAMA. Laws, Statutes, etc.:
Digests, Compilations, etc.;
Aikin, John G. (ed.). *A Digest of the Laws of the State of Alabama containing all the Statutes of a Public and General Nature, in Force at the Close of the Session of the General Assembly in January, 1833. To Which are Prefixed, the Declaration of Independence; the Constitution of the United States; the Act to Enable the People of Alabama to Form a Constitution and State Government, etc.* . . . (Tuscaloosa, 1833; 2d ed., Tuscaloosa and Mobile, 1836).
Clay, C. C. (ed.). *A Digest of the Laws of the State of Alabama Containing all the Statutes of a Public and General Nature in Force at the Close of the Session of the General Assembly in February, 1843* (Tuskaloosa, 1843).
Meed, Alexander B. (comp.). *A Supplement to Aikin's Digest of the Laws of the State of Alabama: Containing all the Unrepealed Laws of a Public and General Nature Passed by the General Assembly, Since the Second Edition of the Digest, Up to . . . April, 1841* (Tuscaloosa, 1841).
Toulmin, Harry (ed.). *A Digest of the Laws of the State of Alabama, Containing the Statutes and Resolutions in Force at the End of the General Assembly in January, 1823* (Cahawba, 1823).
Walker, A. J. (ed.). *The Revised Code of Alabama* (Montgomery, 1867).
Session Laws;
Acts of the General Assembly of the State of Alabama Passed at Its First Session, which was Begun and Held at the Town of Huntsville, on Monday, the twenty-fifth day of October, 1819 and ended the seventeenth day of December (Huntsville, 1820). Photo-facsimile reprint, 53 copies (Washington, July, 1912).
Acts Passed at the Called Session of the General Assembly . . . Held at the Town of Cahawba, the first Monday in June 1821 (Cahawba, 1821). Photo-facsimile reprint, 50 copies (Washington, 1913).
Acts Passed at the Annual Sessions of the General Assembly, 1827– (Cahawba, Tuskaloosa, etc., 1827–).
ALBRECHT, ARTHUR EMIL. *International Seamen's Union of America. A Study of Its History and Problems* (U. S. Bureau of Labor Statistics, *Bulletin* No. 342. Miscellaneous Series. Washington, 1923).
ALDRICH, O. "Slavery or Involuntary Servitude in Illinois Prior to and After Its Admission as a State" (Illinois Historical Society, *Transactions*, 1916, pp. 89–99).
AMERICAN ANTI-SLAVERY SOCIETY. *American Slavery As It Is* (T. D. Weld, comp. New York, 1839).
——. *Constitution, December 4, 1833* (New York, London, 1901). Reprinted in MacDonald, William, *Select Documents Illustrative of United States History, 1776–1861*, Doc. No. 63, pp. 304–305.
AMERICAN AND ENGLISH ENCYCLOPAEDIA OF LAW (2d ed., 32 vols., Northport, L. I., 1896–1905).
AMERICAN ANTIQUARIAN SOCIETY. *Proceedings* (75 vols., Oct. 1813–April 1880; new series, vols. 1– , Worcester, 1813–).
——. *Transactions and Collections* (12 vols., Worcester, Mass., 1820–1911). Title varies: I–VII *Archaeologia Americana;* VIII–XII, *Transactions and Collections.*

AMERICAN ECONOMIC ASSOCIATION. *Publications* (vols. 1– , Baltimore and New York, 1886–).
THE AMERICAN ECONOMIC REVIEW (published by the American Economic Association, vols. 1– , Princeton, N. J., Evanston, Ill., etc., 1911–). Supersedes the *Economic Bulletin* and the *Quarterly* (formerly *Publications*).
AMERICAN HISTORICAL ASSOCIATION. *Annual Reports* (Washington, D. C., 1884–).
———. *Papers*. (5 vols., New York & London, 1885–1891).
AMERICAN HISTORICAL REVIEW (vols. 1– , New York & London, 1896–).
AMERICAN NATION: A HISTORY (A. B. Hart, ed. 28 vols., New York & London, 1904–1918).
AMERICAN SEAMEN'S FRIEND SOCIETY. *Notes on Fifty Years' Efforts for the Welfare of Seamen* (New and enlarged edition, 1878).
[ANBUREY, THOMAS.] *Travels through the Interior Parts of America* (2 vols., London, 1791).
ANDREWS, CHARLES MCLEAN. *Colonial Background of the American Revolution. Four Essays in American Colonial History* (New Haven & London, 1924; rev. ed., New Haven & London, 1931).
———. *The Colonial Period of American History* (Vol. I. *The Settlements*. New Haven and London, 1934).
———. "The Connecticut Intestacy Law," in *The Yale Review*, III (O.S.), 261–294, Nov., 1894 (Reprinted in *Select Essays in Anglo-American Legal History*. Boston, 1907).
———. *The Connecticut Intestacy Law* (Committee on Historical Publications, Tercentenary Commission of the State of Connecticut, No. II. New Haven, 1933).
———. *Land System in the American Colonies* (Sir R. H. I. Palgrave, ed., *Dictionary of Political Economy*, II, 556–560, 1900).
——— (ed.). *Reports on the Laws of Connecticut by Francis Fane, K. C., Standing Counsel to the Board of Trade and Plantations* (Acorn Club Publication No. 12. New Haven, 1915).
———. *The River Towns of Connecticut. A Study of Wethersfield, Hartford, and Windsor* (Johns Hopkins University, *Studies in Historical and Political Science*, VII, Nos. 7–9. Baltimore, 1889).
ANDREWS, ETHAN ALLEN. *Slavery and the Domestic Slave Trade in the United States* (Boston, Mass., 1836).
ANTIQUARIAN (comp.). *The Blue Laws of New Haven Colony*. See Hinman, Roy Ralph.
APPLEGARTH, ALBERT CLAYTON. *The Quakers in Pennsylvania* (Johns Hopkins University, *Studies in Historical and Political Science*, X, Nos. 8–9. Baltimore, 1892).
APPLETON'S *Cyclopaedia of American Biography* (ed. by James Grant Wilson and John Fiske. 6 vols., New York, 1886–1889. New and enlarged edition, revised to 1914 under editorial supervision of Hon. Charles Dick and James E. Homans, vols. 7–12, New York, 1918–1931).
ARKANSAS. Laws, Statutes, etc.:
Digests, Compilations, etc.;
Ball, William McK., and Roane, Sam C. (rev.). *Revised Statutes of the State of Arkansas, Adopted at the October Session of the General Assembly of Said State, A. D., 1837* . . . (Boston, 1838).
Steele and McCampbell (eds.). *Laws of Arkansas Territory* (Little Rock, 1835).
Session Laws;
Acts Passed by the General Assembly of Arkansas [*Territory and State*], *1820–* (Little Rock, 1821–).
ARNOLD, SAMUEL GREENE. *History of the State of Rhode Island and Providence Plantations* (2 vols., New York, London, 1859–1860; 4th ed., Providence, R. I., 1894).
ATWATER, EDWARD ELIAS. *History of the Colony of New Haven to Its Absorption into Connecticut.* (Printed for the Author, New Haven, 1881.)
——— (ed.). *History of the City of New Haven to the Present Time*. By an Association of Writers, with Biographies, Portraits and Illustrations (New York, 1887).
AVERY, ELROY MCKENDREE. *A Complete Index to Avery's History of the United States* (vols. I–VII. Tarrytown, N. Y., 1915).
———. *A History of the United States and Its People, from Their Earliest Records to the Present Time* (7 vols. Cleveland, 1904–1910).
AYRES, WILLIAM. "Land Titles in Kentucky," in Kentucky State Bar Association, *Proceedings of the Eighth Annual Meeting*, Paducah, Ky., July 7–8, 1909, pp. 160–191 (Louisville, 1909).
BACON, LEONARD. *The Genesis of the New England Churches* (New York, 1874).
———. *Slavery Discussed in Occasional Essays from 1833 to 1846* (New York, 1846).
———. *Thirteen Historical Discourses on the Completion of Two Hundred Years, from the Beginning of the First Church in New Haven* (New Haven and New York, 1839).
BACON, L. W. *History of American Christianity* (The American Church History Series, XIII. New York, 1897).

BACON, THOMAS (ed.). *Laws of Maryland at Large with Proper Indexes ... With Notes and Other Matters ... To Which is Prefixed the Charter with an English Translation* (Annapolis, 1765). See Maryland.

BAILEY, EBENEZER. "An Early Workingmens' Association of Fitchburg [Mass.], 1844," in Fitchburg Historical Society, *Proceedings*, IV, 242–252. Fitchburg, Mass., 1910.

BAIRD, CHARLES W. *History of Huguenot Emigration to America* (New York, 1885).

BALDWIN, SIMEON EBEN. "American Business Corporations before 1789," in American Historical Association, *Annual Report*, 1902, I, 253–274.

———. *Constitutional Law* (in *Two Centuries' Growth of American Law.* Yale Bi-Centennial Publication, pp. 9–47. New York and London, 1901).

BALL, CHARLES. *Slavery in the United States of America, Narrative of the Life and Adventures of Charles Ball, Black Man* (Petersburg, Va., 1853).

BALLAGH, JAMES CURTIS. *A History of Slavery in Virginia* (Johns Hopkins University, *Studies in Historical and Political Science*, Extra Vol. XXIV. Baltimore, 1902).

———. "Introduction to Southern Economic History—The Land System," in American Historical Association, *Annual Report*, 1897, IX, 99–129.

———. "Southern Economic History—Tariff and Public Lands," in American Historical Association, *Annual Report*, 1898, X, 223–263.

———. *White Servitude in the Colony of Virginia. A Study of the System of Indentured Labor in the American Colonies* (Johns Hopkins University, *Studies in Historical and Political Science*, XIII, Nos. 6–7. Baltimore, 1895).

BANKS, CHARLES E. "A Sketch of the English Prototype and the Development of a Hospital Service for Seamen in the United States," in United States Marine Hospital Service, *Annual Report of Supervising Surgeon-General, 1899*, pp. 266–274.

BANKS, ENOCH MARVIN. *Economics of Land Tenure in Georgia* (Columbia University, *Studies in History, Economics and Public Law*, XXIII, No. 1. New York, 1905).

BARNARD, J. LYNN. *Factory Legislation in Pennsylvania. Its History and Administration* (University of Pennsylvania, *Publications*, Series in Political Economy and Public Law, No. 19. Philadelphia, 1907).

BASSETT, JOHN SPENCER. *The Constitutional Beginnings of North Carolina (1663–1729)* (Johns Hopkins University, *Studies in Historical and Political Science*, XII, No. 3. Baltimore, 1894).

———. *The History of Slavery in the State of North Carolina* (Johns Hopkins University, *Studies in Historical and Political Science*, XVII, Nos. 7–8. Baltimore, 1899).

———. *Landholding in Colonial North Carolina* (Timothy College *Historical Papers*, Series 2, 1898).

———. *Slavery and Servitude in the Colony of North Carolina* (Johns Hopkins University, *Studies in Historical and Political Science*, XIV, Nos. 4–5. Baltimore, 1896).

BATES, ALBERT CARLOS (ed.). See Connecticut.

——— (ed.). *The Wolcott Papers: Correspondence and Documents during Roger Wolcott's Governorship of the Colony of Connecticut, 1750–1754* (Connecticut Historical Society, *Collections*, XVI. Hartford, 1916).

BATES, SAMUEL AUSTIN (ed.). *Records of the Town of Braintree, 1640–1793* (Randolph, Mass., 1886).

BEARD, CHARLES AUSTIN. *An Economic Interpretation of the Constitution of the United States* (rev. ed., New York, 1935).

———. *Economic Origins of Jeffersonian Democracy* (New York, 1915, 1927).

——— AND BAGLEY, WILLIAM C. *A History of the People of the United States* (New York, 1923; 2nd rev. ed., 1934).

——— AND (MRS.) MARY R. *The Rise of American Civilization* (2 vols. Vol. I. *The Agricultural Era;* Vol. II. *The Industrial Era.* New York, 1927).

BEARD, (MRS.) MARY R. *A Short History of the American Labor Movement* (New York, 1925).

BEARDSLEY, AMBROSE. See Orcutt and Beardsley.

BECKER, CARL L. *Declaration of Independence, a Study in the History of Political Ideas* (New York, 1922).

BECKNER, EARL R. *A History of Labor Legislation in Illinois* (Chicago, 1929).

BEER, GEORGE LOUIS. *British Colonial Policy 1754–1765* (New York, 1907. Reprinted, 1933).

———. *Commercial Policy of England Toward the American Colonies.* (Columbia University, *Studies in History, Economics and Public Law*, III, No. 2. New York, 1893).

———. *The Old Colonial System, 1660–1754* (2 vols., New York, 1912).

———. *The Origins of the British Colonial System, 1578–1660* (New York, 1908).

BELKNAP, J(EREMY). *The History of New Hampshire* (3 vols., Boston, 1791–1792).

BEMIS, E. W., et al. *Local Government in the South and Southwest* (Johns Hopkins University, *Studies in Historical and Political Science*, XI, No. 11. Baltimore, 1893).

BENEZET, ANTHONY. *Observations on the Inslaving, Importing and Purchasing of Negroes; With Some Advice Thereon, Extracted from the Epistle of the Yearly Meeting of the People Called Quakers, Held at London in the Year 1748* (2d ed., Germantown, Penn., 1760).

BERNHARD, KARL, DUKE OF SAXE-WEIMAR EISENACH. *Travels through North America, during the Years 1825 and 1826* (2 vols., Philadelphia, 1828).

BETTLE, EDWARD. "Notices of Negro Slavery as Connected with Pennsylvania," in Pennsylvania Historical Society, *Memoirs*, I, Pt. ii, 351–388, Aug., 1826.

BÉYER, (MRS.) CLARA M. *History of Labor Legislation for Women in Three States*, and *Chronological Development of Labor Legislation for Women in the United States* by Florence P. Smith (U. S. Women's Bureau, *Bulletin* No. 66. Washington, D. C., 1929).

BICKNELL, THOMAS WILLIAMS. *Sowams: with Ancient Records of Sowams and Parts Adjacent* (New Haven, Conn., 1908).

BIDWELL, PERCY WELLS (ed.). "The New England Emigrant Aid Company and English Cotton Supply Associates: Letters of Frederick L. Olmsted, 1857," in *American Historical Review*, XXIII, 114–117, October, 1917.

———. and FALCONER, JOHN I. *History of Agriculture in the Northern United States, 1620–1860* (Carnegie Institution of Washington, Publ. No. 358. Washington, 1925).

BISHOP, JAMES LEANDER. *A History of American Manufactures from 1608 to 1860: Exhibiting the Origin and Growth of the Principal Mechanic Arts and Manufactures, from the Earliest Colonial Period to the Adoption of the Constitution; and Comprising Annuals of the Industry of the United States in Machinery, Manufactures, and Useful Arts, with a Notice of the Important Inventions, Tariffs, and the Results of Each Decennial Census* (3 vols., Philadelphia, London, 1864).

BLACKMAR, FRANK W. *The History of Federal and State Aid to Higher Education in the United States* (United States Bureau of Education, *Circular of Information*, No. 1. Washington, 1890).

BLACKSTONE, SIR WILLIAM. *Commentaries on the Laws of England; in Four Books. Together with Such Notes of Enduring Value as Have Been Published in the Several English Editions, and also a Copious Analysis of the Contents*, etc. (2 vols., ed. by Thomas M. Cooley. 2d ed. revised, Chicago, 1873).

BLAKE, WILLIAM O. *History of Slavery and the Slave Trade Ancient and Modern* (Columbus, Ohio, 1861).

BLEDSOE, ALBERT TAYLOR. *An Essay on Liberty and Slavery* (Philadelphia, 1856).

BLISS, WILLIAM ROOT. *Quaint Nantucket* (Boston and New York, 1896).

BOGART, ERNEST LUDLOW. *Economic History of the American People* (New York and London, 1930; 2d ed., 1935).

———. *An Economic History of the United States* (New York, 2d ed., 1913).

———. "Pushing Back the Frontier." Presidential Address Delivered at Forty-Fourth Annual Meeting of the American Economic Association, Washington, D. C., December 29, 1931, in *American Economic Review*, XXII, 1–9, March, 1932.

BOND, BEVERLY W., JR. *The Civilization of the Old Northwest; A Study of Political, Social and Economic Development, 1788–1812* (New York, 1934).

———. *The Quit-Rent System in the American Colonies.* With an Introduction by Charles M. Andrews (New Haven and London, 1919).

BOONE, RICHARD GAUSE. *Education in the United States; Its History from the Earliest Settlements* (International Education Series, XI. New York, 1889).

BOSTON, MASS. *Boston Town Records, 1631–1822* (11 vols. Boston Municipal Printing Office, 1877–1906). Imprint varies. This series down to 1895 has the title *Report of the Record Commissioners of the City of Boston.*

———. *The By-Laws and Orders of the Town of Boston, Passed at a Legal Town-Meeting, May 22, 1801. ... Together with the Rules and Regulations of the Board of Health, also Sundry Laws of the Commonwealth relating to Town Affairs* (Boston, 1801).

———. *The Charter of the City of Boston and Ordinances Made and Established by the Mayor, Aldermen and Common Council, with such Acts of the Legislature of Massachusetts as Relate to the Government of Said City* (Boston, 1827. Collated and revised by Thomas Wetmore and Edward G. Prescott, Commissioners, Boston, 1834).

———. *The Memorial History of Boston, Including Suffolk County, Massachusetts, 1630–1880* (ed. by Justin Winsor. 4 vols. Boston, 1880–1881).

———. RECORD COMMISSIONERS. *Reports of the Record Commissioners of the City of Boston.* See *Boston Town Records.*

———. RECORDS OF BOSTON SELECTMEN. See *Boston Town Records.*

———. *The Votes and Proceedings of the Freeholders and Other Inhabitants of the Town of Boston, in Town Meeting Assembled, According to Law.* Published by Order of the Town. (Boston, [1772]).

BOURINOT, JOHN GEORGE. *Local Government in Canada. An Historical Study* (Johns Hopkins University, *Studies in Historical and Political Science*, V, Nos. 5–6. Baltimore, 1887).

BRACKETT, JEFFREY RICHARDSON. *The Negro in Maryland. A Study of the Institution of Slavery* (Johns Hopkins University, *Studies in Historical and Political Science*, Extra Vol. VI. Baltimore, 1889).

BRADFORD, WILLIAM. *History of Plymouth Plantation* (Massachusetts Historical Society, *Collections*, 4th ser., III. Boston, 1856).

———. *History of Plymouth Plantation, 1620–1647* (2 vols., ed. by W. C. Ford for the Massachusetts Historical Society. Boston, 1912). References in the text are to this edition.

BRAINTREE, MASS. *Records of the Town of Braintree, 1640–1793* (ed. by Samuel A. Bates. Randolph, Mass., 1886).

BRAWLEY, BENJAMIN. *Social History of the American Negro, being a History of the Negro Problem in the United States Including a History and Study of the Republic of Liberia* (New York, 1921).

A BRIEFE DECLARATION OF THE PLANTATION OF VIRGINIA DURINGE THE FIRST TWELVE YEARS, WHEN SIR THOMAS SMITH WAS GOVERNOR OF THE COMPANIE, AND DOWNE TO THIS PRESENT TYME. By the Ancient Planters Nowe Remaining Alive in Virginia. 1624 (reprinted in *Colonial Records of Virginia. State Senate Doc.*, Extra, Richmond, 1874, pp. 67–83).

BRIGHAM, WILLIAM (ed.). *The Compact with the Charter and Laws of the Colony of New Plymouth; together with the Charter of the Council at Plymouth, and an Appendix, containing the Articles of Confederation of the United Colonies of New England, and other Valuable Documents. Published Agreeably to a Resolve, Passed April 5, 1836, under the Supervision of William Brigham* (Boston, 1836).

BRISSOT DE WARVILLE, JACQUES PIERRE. *New Travels in the United States of America Performed in 1788* (translated from the French ed., Dublin, 1792).

BRODHEAD, JOHN ROMEYN. *History of the State of New York* (2 vols., rev. ed., New York, 1872).

BRONSON, E. B. "Notes on Connecticut as a Slave State," in *Journal of Negro History*, II, 79–82, Jan., 1917.

BROOKHAVEN, N. Y. *Records of the Town of Brookhaven, Suffolk County, N. Y.* (3 vols., Patchogue, N. Y., 1880–1893. Also Patchogue, N. Y., 1888).

BROOKLINE [MASS.]. *Muddy River and Brookline Records, 1634–1838* (Boston, 1875).

BROWN, ALEXANDER. *The First Republic in America* (Boston & New York, 1898).

——— (ed.). *The Genesis of the United States* (2 vols., Boston and New York, 1890).

BROWN, ELMER ELLSWORTH. *The Origin of American State Universities* (University of California, *Publications, Education*, III, No. 1. Berkeley, Calif., 1913).

BROWN, WILLIAM GARROTT. *The Lower South in American History* (New York, 1902).

BROWNE, WILLIAM HAND. *Maryland, the History of a Palatinate* (Boston, 1884).

BRUCE, KATHLEEN. "Slave Labor in the Virginian Iron Industry," in *William and Mary College Quarterly*, 2d series, VI, 289–302; VII, 21–31, Oct. 1926–Jan. 1927.

BRUCE, PHILIP ALEXANDER. *The Economic History of Virginia in the Seventeenth Century. An Inquiry into the Material Condition of the People Based upon Original and Contemporaneous Records* (2 vols., New York and London, 1895. Reprinted 1907).

———. *Institutional History of Virginia in the Seventeenth Century, an Inquiry into the Religious, Moral, Educational, Legal, Military, and Political Condition of the People, Based on Original and Contemporaneous Records* (2 vols., New York & London, 1910).

———. *Social Life of Virginia in the Seventeenth Century, an Inquiry into the Origin of the Higher Planting Class, together with an Account of the Habits, Customs & Diversions of the People* (Richmond, Va., 1907; rev. ed. Lynchburg, Va., 1927).

BRYCE, JAMES. The American Commonwealth (2 vols., London, 1888).

BUCK, PAUL H. "The Poor Whites of the Ante-Bellum South," in *American Historical Review*, XXXI, 41–54, Oct., 1925.

BUFFUM, HUGH STRAIGHT. *Federal and State Aid to Education in Iowa* (Reprinted from October, 1906, and January, April and July, 1907, numbers of *The Iowa Journal of History and Politics* for the State University of Iowa. Iowa City, 1907).

BUGBEE, LESTER GLADSTONE. "Slavery in Early Texas," in *Political Science Quarterly*, XIII, 389–412, 648–668, Sept.–Dec., 1898.

———. "Some Difficulties of a Texas Empresario," in Southern History Association, *Publications*, III, 1899, pp. 95–113.

BUNNER, E. *History of Louisiana from Its First Discovery and Settlement to the Present Time* (New York, 1842).

BURKE, EDMUND. *An Account of European Settlements in America* (2 vols., London, 1770).

BURNABY, REV. ANDREW, D.D. *Burnaby's Travels through North America* (Reprinted from the third edition of 1798 with Introduction and Notes by Rufus Rockwell Wilson in *Source Books of American History*. New York, 1904).
BURY, WILLIAM COUTTS KEPPEL, VISCOUNT. *Exodus of the Western Nations* (London, 1865).
CAIRNES, JOHN ELLIOTT. *The Slave Power, Its Character, Career, and Probable Designs* (New York, 1862).
CALDWELL, LOUIS G. "Early Legislation Regulating the Practice of Medicine," in *Lawyer and Banker*, XVII, 12–25, Jan., 1924; also in *Illinois Law Review*, XVIII, 225–244, 1923.
CALHOUN, JOHN C. *Works* (ed. by Richard K. Crallé. 6 vols., New York, 1851–1867).
CALIFORNIA. Laws, Statutes, etc.:
Digests, Compilations, etc.;
Warfield, S., and Snyder, N. A. (eds.). *Compiled Laws of the State of California Containing All the Acts of the Legislature of a Public Nature, Now in Force, Passed at the Sessions of 1850, 1851, 1852, 1853* (Boston, Mass., 1853).
Wood, W. H. R. (ed.). *Digest of the Laws of California, Containing All Laws of a General Character Which Will be in Force on the First Day of January 1858 [1850–1858]* (San Francisco, Calif., 1857).
Session Laws;
Statutes Passed by the Legislature of the State of California, 1849– (San Jose, 1850–).
CALIFORNIA UNIVERSITY. *Publications in History* (vols. 1– , Berkeley, 1911–).
CALLCOTT, M. S., AND WATERMAN, W. C. *Principles of Social Legislation* (New York, 1932).
CALLENDER, GUY STEVENS (ed.). *Selections from the Economic History of the United States, 1765–1860* (Boston, New York, Chicago, London, 1909).
CAMPBELL, DOUGLAS. *The Puritan in Holland, England and America. An Introduction to American History* (2 vols., 3d ed., New York, 1893).
CAREY, HENRY CHARLES. *The Slave Trade, Domestic and Foreign; Why It Exists and How It May Be Extinguished* (Philadelphia, 1853).
CARLTON, FRANK TRACY. *Economic Influences upon Educational Progress in the United States, 1820–1850* (University of Wisconsin, *Bulletin* No. 221, Economics and Political Science Series, IV, No. 1. Madison, Wis., 1908).
———. *The History and Problems of Organized Labor* (Boston, New York, Chicago, 1911; 2d ed., Boston and New York, 1920).
CARMAN, H. J. *Social and Economic History of the United States. I. From Handicraft to Factory, 1600–1820. II. The Rise of Industrialism, 1820–1875* (2 vols., Boston, 1930, 1934).
CARROLL, BARTHOLOMEW R[IVERS] (ed.). *Historical Collections of South Carolina; Embracing Many Rare and Valuable Pamphlets, and Other Documents Relating to the History of that State, from Its Discovery to Its Independence in the Year 1776* (2 vols., New York, 1836).
CATTERALL (MRS.). HELEN HONOR TUNNICLIFF (ed.). *Judicial Cases Concerning American Slavery and the Negro* (3 vols., Carnegie Institution of Washington Publ. No. 374, 1926–1932).
CAULKINS, FRANCES M. *History of New London, Connecticut. From the First Survey of the Coast in 1612, to 1852* (2d ed. continued to 1860, New London, 1860).
———. *History of Norwich, Conn., from Its Possession by the Indians. Also a Brief Sketch of the Life of the Author, to Which is Added an Appendix, Containing Notes and Sketches, Continuing the History to the Close of the Year 1873* (ed. by H. P. Haven, Hartford, 1874).
CHAMBERS, WILLIAM. *American Slavery and Colour* (London & New York, 1857).
CHANNING, EDWARD. *History of the United States* (6 vols., New York and London, 1905–1925).
———. *The Narragansett Planters. A Study of Causes* (Johns Hopkins University, *Studies in Historical and Political Science*, IV, No. 3. Baltimore, March, 1886).
———. *Town and County Government in the English Colonies of North America* (Johns Hopkins University, *Studies in Historical and Political Science*, II, No. 10. Baltimore, 1884).
CHANNING, WILLIAM E. *Emancipation* (Boston, 1840).
———. *Remarks on the Slavery Question, in a Letter to Jonathan Phillips, Esq.* (Boston, 1839).
———. *Slavery* (Boston, 1835).
CHAPIN, ALONZO B. *Glastenbury [sic] for Two Hundred Years: A Centennial Discourse May 18th, A.D. 1853 with an Appendix Containing Historical and Statistical Papers of Interest* (Hartford, 1853).
CHASTELLUX, FRANÇOIS JEAN, MARQUIS DE. *Travels in North America* (2 vols., London, 1787).
CHAYNEY, EDWARD P. *The Anti-Rent Agitation in the State of New York, 1839–1846* (University of Pennsylvania, *Publications in Political Economy and Public Law*, Series No. 2. Philadelphia, Penn., and New York, 1887).

———. "Condition of Labor in Early Pennsylvania," in *The Manufacturer* (Philadelphia), Feb. 2–16, Mar. 16, Apr. 1, 1891.

———. *Early American Land Tenure* (The Wharton School, *Annals of Political Science*, No. 1. March 1885. Bound with University of Pennsylvania, *Publications in Political Economy and Public Law*, Series No. 1. Philadelphia, Penn., 1885).

CHRONICLES *of the Pilgrim Fathers.* With an Introduction by John Masefield (Everyman's Library, ed. by Ernest Rhys. London, New York, 1910).

CLARK, VICTOR S. *History of Manufactures in the United States, 1607–1860; 1860–1914* (Carnegie Institution of Washington Publ. No. 215 B. 2 vols., Washington, D. C., 1916–1928. Also published in 3 vols., New York, 1929).

CLEWS, ELSIE W. [Mrs. Parsons] *Educational Legislation and Administration of the Colonial Governments* (Columbia University, *Contributions to Philosophy, Psychology and Education*, VI, Nos. 1–4. New York, 1899).

COBB, THOMAS READ ROOTES. *An Inquiry into the Law of Negro Slavery in the United States of America: to Which is Prefixed an Historical Sketch of Slavery* (Vol. I, Philadelphia, 1858). Vol. II not published.

CODMAN, JOHN. "Condition and Requirements of the American Mercantile Marine, as Considered in a Letter Addressed to Charles Sumner, U. S. Senate," in *The Sailors' Magazine*, XXXII, 259–265, May, 1860.

COLLINS, EDWARD DAY. "Studies in the Colonial Policy of England, 1672–1680, the Plantations, the Royal African Company, and the Slave Trade," in American Historical Association, *Annual Report*, 1900, I, 139–192.

COLLINS, WINFIELD HAZLITT. *The Domestic Slave-Trade in the Southern States* (New York, 1904).

COLONIAL CHARTERS. *The Charters of the British Colonies in America* (Printed for J. Almon, opposite Burlington-House, in Piccadilly. London, 1775).[1]

———. *Charters of British Colonies in America* (Dublin, 1776).

———. *A List of Copies of Charters from the Commissioners for Trade and Plantations, Presented to the Honourable the House of Commons, in Pursuance of their Address to His Majesty, of the 25th of April, 1740. Viz. Maryland Charter, granted by King Charles I. in the 8th Year of His Reign; Connecticut Charter, granted by King Charles II. in the 14th Year of His Reign; Rhode-Island Charter, granted by King Charles II. in the 15th Year of His Reign; Pennsylvania Charter, granted by King Charles II. in the 33d Year of His Reign. Massachusetts Bay Charter Granted by King William and Queen Mary in the 3d Year of Their Reign. Georgia Charter Granted by His present Majesty, in the 5th Year of His Reign* (London: Printed in the Year M.DCC.XLI).

———. *The Charters of the following Provinces of North America; viz. Virginia, Pennsylvania, Maryland, Massachusetts Bay, Connecticut, and Rhode Island, Georgia. To which is prefixed, A Faithful Narrative of the Proceedings of the North American Colonies. In Consequence of the late Stamp Act* (London: Printed for W. Owen at Temple-Bar; J. Almon, in Piccadilly; and F. Blyth at John's Coffee-House, Royal Exchange. MDCCLXVI. Price Two Shillings and Six Pence).

COLONIAL LAWS. *An Abridgement of the Laws in Force and Use in Her Majesty's Plantations; (viz) Of Virginia, New-England, Jamaica, New-York, Barbadoes, Carolina, &c. Maryland. Digested under Proper Heads in the Method of Mr. Wingate, and Mr. Washington's Abridgements* (London, Printed for John Nicholson, 1704).

———. *Laws of 1721. The Laws of the British Plantations in America, Relating to the Church and the Clergy, Religion and Learning. Collected in One Volume by Nicholas Trott, LL.D.* (London, MDCCXXI).[2]

COLUMBIA UNIVERSITY, FACULTY OF POLITICAL SCIENCE. *Studies in History, Economics, and Public Law* (vols. 1– , New York, 1893–).

COMAN, KATHARINE. *Economic Beginnings of the Far West: How We Won the Land Beyond the Mississippi* (2 vols., New York, 1912).

COMMONS, JOHN ROGERS. "Horace Greeley and the Working Class Origins of the Republican Party," in *Political Science Quarterly*, XXIV, 468–488. Sept., 1909.

———. *Races and Immigration in America* (New York, 1930).

[1] "This edition contains the first and second Charters of Massachusetts Bay, and those granted to Connecticut, Rhode Island, Pennsylvania, Maryland, Virginia, and Georgia." (Tower Catalogue, p. 34).

[2] Only known copy with this imprint in the Benedict Collection. A copy with the date 1725 in New York Public Library.

——— AND ANDREWS, JOHN B. *Principles of Labor Legislation* (Prepared in cooperation with the American Bureau of Industrial Research. Rev. ed. New York and London, 1920).

——— PHILLIPS, ULRICH B.; GILMORE, EUGENE A.; SUMNER, HELEN L.; AND ANDREWS, JOHN B. (eds.). *A Documentary History of American Industrial Society* (10 vols. Prepared under the Auspices of the American Bureau of Industrial Research, with the cooperation of the Carnegie Institution of Washington. Cleveland, 1910–11).

CONNECTICUT (Colony). Laws, Statutes, etc.:

Acts and Laws of His Majesties Colony of Connecticut in New-England (Boston: Printed by Bartholomew Green and John Allen, 1702). Back title *Connecticut Statutes, 1702. Session Laws, 1702–1715.* No title page or index. Probably a reprint of New London, 1715.

Acts and Laws of His Majesties Colony of Connecticut in New-England. Printed in 1702 and Now First Reissued by the Acorn Club (Hartford, 1901).

Acts and Laws of His Majesties Colony of Connecticut in New-England (Reprinted and Sold by Timothy Green, Printer to His Honour the Governour and Council. New-London, 1715). Prefixed by *The Charter Granted by His Majesty King Charles the Second, to the Governour and Company of the English Colony of Connecticut in New-England in America.* Followed by *Session Laws, 1716–1741,* paged continuously and indexed. The acts are not dated before 1702. This is the 1715 edition of the 1702 revision.

Acts and Laws of His Majesty's English Colony of Connecticut in New-England in America (Printed and Sold by Timothy Green, Printer to the Governour and Company of the Abovesaid Colony. New-London, 1750). Prefixed by *The Charter Granted by His Majesty King Charles II to the Governour, & Company of the English Colony of Connecticut in New-England in America* (New-London, 1750).

Acts and Laws of His Majesty's English Colony of Connecticut, in New-England, in America (Reprinted and Sold by Thomas and Samuel Green, in New-Haven, and Timothy Green, in New-London, 1769). Prefixed by *The Charters Granted by His Majesty King Charles the Second, &c.*

A reprint of the second edition of 1750 revision and compiled session acts to 1768, with the session acts of 1769. Has a new index to page 342.

Acts and Laws Passed by the General Court or Assembly of Her Majesties Colony of Connecticut in New-England (New London, Thomas Short, printer, 1709).

Contains *Session Laws,* to 1714 printed by Thomas Short, and those for 1715 printed by Timothy Green.

The Book of the General Laws for the People Within the Jurisdiction of Connecticut: Collected out of the Records of the General Court, Lately Revised, and with Some Emendations and Additions Established and Published by the Authority of the General Court of Connecticut, Holden at Hartford in October, 1672 (Cambridge, Printed by Samuel Green, 1673).[3]

The Charter Granted by His Majesty King Charles II to the Governour & Company of the English Colony of Connecticut in New-England in America (Printed and Sold by Timothy Green, Printer to the Governour and Company to the Colony Abovesaid, New London, 1718). Prefixed to Connecticut, *Acts and Laws,* 1715.

Charter of the Colony of Connecticut, 1662 (Hartford, 1888; Hartford, 1900).

Charter of the Colony of Connecticut, 1662 (Reprinted by Tercentenary Commission of the State of Connecticut. Committee on Historical Publications, 1933). Contains a *Bibliographical Introduction* by A. C. Bates; *Passage of the Charter through the Seals,* by C. M. Andrews.

The Code of Connecticut, compiled by order of the General Court in the year 1650; comprising the Constitution of Civil Government Established by the freemen, and the body of statute laws then in force, arranged under appropriate titles in alphabetical order. Transcribed in pursuance of a resolution of the General Assembly of the State of Connecticut, passed October session 1817, examined by Thomas Day, Secretary of State (Manuscript copy, transcribed from the Original for the American Antiquarian Society, by Order of the General Assembly of Connecticut, passed October Session, 1817). Presented to the American Antiquarian Society by the General Assembly of Connecticut. Received, June 15, 1818.

The Laws of Connecticut. An Exact Reprint of the Original Edition of 1673. With a Prefatory Note by George Brinley (Hartford, 1865).

Session Laws;

Acts and Laws Passed by the General Court or Assembly of His Majesties Colony of Connecticut, in New-England: Begun and Held at Hartford, New Haven (New-London, etc., 1716–).

[3] The first printed edition of Connecticut laws.

——. Records, Papers, etc.;

The Pitkin Papers; Correspondence, and Documents during William Pitkin's Governorship of the Colony of Connecticut, 1766–1769, with Some of Earlier Date (ed. by Albert C. Bates. Connecticut Historical Society, *Collections*, XIX. Hartford, 1921).

The Public Records of the Colony of Connecticut Prior to the Union with New Haven Colony May 1665, 1636–1776. Transcribed and Published in Accordance with a Resolution of the General Assembly (15 vols. Vols. 1–3 ed. by J. Hammond Trumbull; vols. 4–15 ed. by C. J. Hoadley. Hartford, 1850–1890). Binder's title, *Colonial Records of Connecticut.*

Talcott Papers; Correspondence and Documents (chiefly official) During Joseph Talcott's Governorship of The Colony of Connecticut, 1724–41 (ed. by Mary Kingsbury Talcott, Connecticut Historical Society, *Collections*, IV and V).

The Wolcott Papers; Correspondence and Documents During Roger Wolcott's Governorship of the Colony of Connecticut, 1750–1754, with Some of Earlier Date (ed. by Albert C. Bates, Connecticut Historical Society, *Collections*, XVI. Hartford, 1916).

——— (State). Laws, Statutes, etc.:

Acts and Laws of the State of Connecticut, in America (Printed by Timothy Green, Printer to the Governor and State of Connecticut. New-London: MDCCLXXXIV). Prefixed by *The Charter Granted by His Majesty King Charles the Second, &c. Session Laws* from 1784 to 1792 inclusive.

Acts and Laws of the State of Connecticut in America (Hartford, Conn., Printed by Elisha Babcock, MDCCLXXXVI). Prefixed by *The Charter Granted by His Majesty King Charles the Second . . . The Declaration of Independence . . . Articles of Confederation . . . Treaty of Peace between the United States of America and His Britannic Majesty . . .* Indexed through 1785. Followed by *Acts and Laws*, 1786, 1787, 1788, 1789, paged continuously. Reprint of text of 1784.

Acts and Laws of the State of Connecticut, in America (Hartford, Printed by Hudson and Goodwin, 1796). Prefixed by *The Charter, Declaration of Independence, Constitution of the United States.* Indexed through 1795. A revision, followed by *Session Acts* for 1796, 1797, 1798, 1799, 1800, 1801, 1802, 1803, paged continuously.

Acts and Laws of the State of Connecticut, in America (Hartford, 1805). A Revision to 1805, followed by *Session Acts* of 1806.

The General Statutes of Connecticut (Revision of 1886, Hartford, 1887; Revision of 1902, Hartford, 1902; Revision of 1930, Orange and New Haven, 1930).

Public Acts Relating to Common Schools, in Force in the State of Connecticut, in 1846. Arranged and Published in Pursuance of a Resolution Adopted by the General Assembly, May Session, 1846 (New Haven, 1846).

The Public Statute Laws of the State of Connecticut Compiled in Obedience to a Resolve of the General Assembly, Passed May, 1838. To Which is Prefixed The Declaration of Independence, Constitution of the United States, and Constitution of the State of Connecticut (Hartford, 1839).

The Public Statute Laws of the State of Connecticut, as Revised and Enacted by the General Assembly, in May 1821: to Which are Prefixed the Declaration of Independence, the Constitution of the United States, and the Constitution of Connecticut. Arranged and Published under the Authority of the General Assembly (Hartford, 1821).

The Public Statute Laws of the State of Connecticut. Published by the Order of the General Assembly (2 vols., Hartford; Printed by Hudson and Goodwin, Book I, 1808; Book II [1808–1818], 1820).

The Public Statute Laws of the State of Connecticut Passed Subsequently to the Revision of 1821. Published by Authority of the General Assembly, under the Direction and Superintendence of the Secretary of the State (Hartford, 1824).

The Revised Statutes of the State of Connecticut to Which are Prefixed the Declaration of Independence, the Constitution of the United States and the Constitution of the State of Connecticut (Hartford, 1849).

The Statutes of the State of Connecticut to Which are Prefixed the Declaration of Independence, the Constitution of the United States, and the Constitution of the State of Connecticut. Compiled and Published by Authority (New Haven, 1854).

Digests, Compilations, etc.;

Dutton, H.; Waldo, L. P.; Booth, D. B. (eds.). *The General Statutes of the State of Connecticut: to Which are Prefixed the Declaration of Independence, the Constitution of the United States, and the Constitution of the State of Connecticut. Published by authority of the General Assembly* (New Haven, 1866).

Swift, Zephaniah (ed.). *A Digest of the Laws of Connecticut* (2 vols., New Haven, 1822, 1823).
———. *System of the Laws of Connecticut* (6 books in 2 vols. Printed by John Byrne for the Author. Vol. I, 1795, Vol. II, Windham, 1796).
Session Laws;
Acts and Laws Passed by the General Court or Assembly of the State of Connecticut, 1776–1783 (New London, etc., 1776–1783).
Public Acts of the State of Connecticut, 1813, 1842, 1855 (Hartford and New Haven, 1813, 1842, 1855).
—. Records, Commissions, etc.;
The Public Records of the State of Connecticut . . . with the Journal of the Council of Safety . . . and an Appendix. Published in Accordance with a Resolution of the General Assembly (Charles J. Hoadley, Publisher, Hartford, 1894–1895). A continuation of the *Public Records of the Colony of Connecticut.* Cover title, *Records of the State of Connecticut.*
Tercentenary Commission of the State of Connecticut. Committee on Historical Publications. *The Tercentenary Pamphlet Series* (ed. by Charles McLean Andrews, 1933; George M. Dutcher, 1933–1936. New Haven, 1933–1936).
Connecticut Historical Society. *Collections,* 1860– (Hartford, Conn., 1860–).
Conway, Moncure Daniel. *Testimonies Concerning Slavery* (2d ed., London, 1865).
Cooley, Henry Scofield. *A Study of Slavery in New Jersey* (Johns Hopkins University, *Studies in Historical and Political Science,* XIV, Nos. 9–10. Baltimore, 1896).
Cooley, Thomas M. (ed.). *Blackstone's Commentaries on the Laws of England* (2 vols., 2d ed., Chicago, 1873).
Cotterill, Robert Spencer. "The National Land System in the South, 1803–1812," in *Mississippi Valley Historical Review,* XVI, 495–506. Mar., 1930.
Cotton, John. *An Abstract of Laws and Government. Wherein as in a Mirrour may be Seen the wisdome & perfection of the Government of Christs Kingdome. . . . Collected and Digested into the Ensuing Method, by that Godly, Grave and Judicious Divine, Mr. John Cotton, of Boston in New-England, in his Life-time, and presented to the Generall Court of the Massachusetts. And now published after his death, by William Aspinwall* (London, 1655).
Coxe, Tench. *Tabular Statements of the Several Branches of American Manufactures, etc.* (Philadelphia, 1813). Prepared for the Treasury Department.
———. *A View of the United States of America, in a Series of Papers Written at Various Times, between the Years 1787 and 1794* (Philadelphia, 1794).
Craven, Avery Odelle. "Poor Whites and Negroes in the Ante-Bellum South," in *Journal of Negro History,* XV, 14–25, Jan., 1930.
Cushing, Harry A. *History of the Transition from Provincial to Commonwealth Government in Massachusetts* (Columbia University, *Studies in History, Economics and Public Law,* VII, No. 1. New York, 1896).
Cutler, Manasseh. *Life, Journal and Correspondence* (ed. by his Grandchildren, William Parker Cutler and Julia Perkins Cutler. 2 vols., Cincinnati, O., 1888).
Cyclopedia of Law and Procedure (William Mack, LL.D., Editor-in-Chief. See Vols. XXXV and XXXVI. New York, 1910).
Dallas. See Pennsylvania.
Dana, Richard Henry. *Two Years Before the Mast. A Personal Narrative of Life at Sea* (New York, 1840. New Edition, with subsequent matter by the author, Boston, 1869).
Dane, N. *A General Digest and Abridgement of American Law* (9 vols., Boston, 1823–1829).
Dart, Henry Plauché. "Louisiana Land Titles Derived from Indian Tribes," in *Louisiana Historical Quarterly,* IV, 134–144, Jan., 1921.
Davenport, John. *A Discourse about Civil Government in a New Plantation whose Design is Religion. Written many Years Since, By that Reverend and worthy Minister of the Gospel, John Cotton, B.D. and now Published by some Undertakers of a new Plantation for General Direction and Information* (Cambridge [Mass.]. Printed by Samuel Green and Marmaduke Johnson, MDCLXIII). Wrongly credited to John Cotton.
De Bow, James Dunwoody Brownson. *The Industrial Resources, etc. of the Southern and Western States* (3 vols., New York & New Orleans, 1853).
Delaware.
Archives (15 vols., Wilmington, 1911–1916).
———. (Colony: New Castle, Kent and Sussex). Laws, Statutes, etc.:
Anno Regini Georgii II. Regis Magnæ Britanniæ, Franciæ & Hiberniæ, Septimo. At a General Assembly of the Counties of New-Castle, Kent and Sussex upon Delaware, begun and holden at

New-Castle, the Twentieth Day of October, Anno Dom. 1733. In the Seventh Year of the Reign of Our Sovereign Lord George II, by the Grace of God, of Great Britain, France, and Ireland King, Defender of the Faith, &c. And from thence continued by Adjournment to the Seventeenth Day of March, 1733 (Philadelphia, MDCCXXXIV).

Laws of the Government of New Castle, Kent, and Sussex Upon Delaware. Published by Order of the Assembly (Philadelphia, MDCCXLI). Bound with *The Charter of Privileges, Granted by William Penn, Esq., to the Inhabitants and Territories* (Philadelphia. Printed and Sold by B. Franklin, MDCCXLI).

Laws of the Government of New-Castle, Kent and Sussex, upon Delaware. Published by Order of the Assembly (Philadelphia, 1752). Vol. II (Wilmington, 1763).

Votes and Proceedings of the House of Representatives of the Government of the Counties of New Castle, Kent, and Sussex . . . 20th October, 1762 (Wilmington, 1762; reprint, 1930).

Votes and Proceedings of the House of Representatives, etc. . . . 21st October, 1765 (Wilmington, 1770. Photostatic copy; reprint, 1931).

——— (State). Laws, Statutes, etc.:

Acts of the General Assembly 1777–1792 (2 vols., Lancaster and Wilmington, 1776–1792). Vols. III and IV of old series of *Delaware Laws.*

Laws of the State of Delaware (8 vols., New Castle, Wilmington, and Dover, 1797–1837). Continued by *Laws, 1845–1865* (Vols. X–XII. Dover, 1845–1865).

Laws of the State of Delaware. To the Year of Our Lord, One Thousand Eight Hundred and Twenty-Nine Inclusive (rev. ed., rev. by Willard Hall. Wilmington, 1829).

Poor Laws of the State of Delaware (New-Castle, 1796).

Revised Statutes of the State of Delaware. . . . to 1852 (Dover, 1852).

Revised Statutes of the State of Delaware, of 1852. As They Have Been Amended, Together with the Additional Laws . . . Which Have Been Enacted Since the Publication of the Revised Code of 1852 [to 1893] (Wilmington, 1893).

DEVOE, THOMAS F. *The Market Book Containing a Historical Account of the Public Markets in the Cities of New York, Boston, Philadelphia and Brooklyn. With a brief Description of every Article of Human Food Sold therein. The Introduction of Cattle in America and Notices of Many Remarkable Specimens* (2 vols., New York, 1862).

DEXTER, EDWIN GRANT. *A History of Education in the United States* (New York, 1904).

DEXTER, FRANKLIN BOWDITCH. *Estimates of Population in the American Colonies* (American Antiquarian Society, *Report of the Council,* October 21, 1887. Worcester, Mass., 1887).

——— (ed.). *Extracts from the Itineraries and Other Miscellanies of Ezra Stiles, D.D., LL.D., 1755–1794. With a Selection from His Correspondence* (New Haven, Conn., 1916).

——— (ed.). *The Literary Diary of Ezra Stiles, D.D., LL.D., President of Yale College* (edited under the authority of the Corporation of Yale University by Franklin Bowditch Dexter, M. A. Vol. I, Jan. 1, 1769–March 13, 1776; Vol. II, March 14, 1776–Dec. 31, 1781; Vol. III, Jan. 1, 1782–May 6, 1795. New York, 1901).

———. "The Pilgrim Church and Plymouth Colony" (Chap. viii of Winsor's *Narrative and Critical History of America,* III, 257–294. Boston and New York, 1884).

DICKERSON, OLIVER MORTON. *American Colonial Government, 1696–1765. A Study of the British Board of Trade in its Relation to the American Colonies, Political, Industrial, Administrative* (Cleveland, O., 1912).

DICTIONARY OF AMERICAN BIOGRAPHY (Under the Auspices of the American Learned Societies. 20 vols. Vols. I–III ed. by Allen Johnson, vols. IV–VII ed. by Allen Johnson and Dumas Malone, vols. VIII–XX ed. by Dumas Malone. New York, 1928–1936).

DILLON, JOHN BROWN. *Oddities of Colonial Legislation in America, as Applied to the Public Lands, Primitive Education, Religion, Morals, Indians, etc. Embracing also a Condensed History of the States and Territories* (Indianapolis, 1879).

DISTRICT OF COLUMBIA. *Code of Laws of the District of Columbia. Prepared under the Authority of the Act of Congress of the 29th of April, 1816* (Washington, 1819).

———. *The Revised Code of the District of Columbia. Prepared under the Authority of the Act of Congress* (Washington, 1857).

DODD, STEPHEN. *East-Haven Register* (New Haven, 1824. Revised by Sarah E. Hughes. New Haven, 1908).

DONALDSON, THOMAS. *The Public Domain. Its History with Statistics, with References to the National Domain, Colonization, Acquirement of Territory, the Survey and Administration and Several Methods of Sale and Disposition of the Public Domain of the United States, with Sketch of the Legislative History of the Land States and Territories, and References to the Land System of the Colonies, and Also that of Several Foreign Governments* (Prepared by the Public Land Commission, Committee on Codification in Pursuance of the Acts of Congress of March 3, 1879 and June 16, 1880. Revised July 16, 1881. Washington, 1881).

DONNAN, ELIZABETH (ed.). *Documents Illustrative of the History of the Slave Trade of America* (4 vols., Carnegie Institution of Washington, Publ. No. 409, 1930–1935).

DORCHESTER, MASS. *History of the Town of Dorchester, Massachusetts* (By a Committee of the Dorchester Antiquarian and Historical Society. Boston, 1859).

DOUGLAS, PAUL H. *American Apprenticeship and Industrial Education* (Columbia University, *Studies in History, Economics and Public Law*, XCV, No. 2. New York, 1921).

DOWNEY, E. H. *History of Labor Legislation in Iowa* (Iowa Economic History Series. Iowa City, 1910).

DOYLE, JOHN ANDREW. *English Colonies in America* (5 vols., New York, 1882–1907).

DRAKE, DANIEL. "Report on Western Commercial Hospitals," in *House Executive Documents*, 24 Cong., 1 sess., 1835–1836, IV, No. 195.

DRAKE, SAMUEL G. *History and Antiquities of Boston, the Capital of Massachusetts and Metropolis of New England, from Its Settlement in 1630 to the Year 1770. Also an Introductory History of the Discovery and Settlement of New England* (Boston, 1856).

DU BOIS, WILLIAM EDWARD BURGHARDT. "Enforcement of the Slave-trade Laws," in American Historical Association, *Annual Report*, 1892, pp. 163–174.

———. *The Suppression of the African Slave-Trade to the United States of America, 1638–1870* (*Harvard Historical Studies*, I. New York, 1896).

DUTTON, SAMUEL TRAIN, AND SNEDDEN, DAVID. *The Administration of Public Education in the United States*. Introduction by Nicholas Murray Butler (New York, 1908).

DWIGHT, TIMOTHY. *Travels in New-England and New-York by [T. D.] late President of Yale College* (published by Timothy Dwight. 4 vols., New Haven, 1821–1822).

EARLE, (MRS.) ALICE M. *Customs and Fashions in Old New England* (New York, 1893).

EARLY, JUBAL ANDERSON. *The Heritage of the South, a History of the Introduction of Slavery; Its Establishment from Colonial Times and Final Effect Upon the Politics of the United States* (Lynchburg, Va., 1915).

Written at close of Civil War, but not published until 1915.

EAST HAMPTON, N. Y. *Book of Laws, June Ye 24, 1665* (New York Historical Society, *Collections for the Year 1809*, Vol. I, 307–428. New York, 1811).

EATON, JOHN. *National Aid to Education* (United States Bureau of Education, *Circular of Information*, No. 2. Washington, 1879).

EAVES, LUCILE. *A History of California Labor Legislation* (University of California, *Publications in Economics*, II. Berkeley, 1910).

EDWARDS, ALBA M. *The Labor Legislation of Connecticut* (American Economic Association, *Publications*, 3d ser. VIII, No. 3. New York, 1907).

EGLESTON, MELVILLE. *The Land System of the New England Colonies* (Johns Hopkins University, *Studies in Historical and Political Science*, IV, Nos. 11–12. Baltimore, 1886).

ELTING, IRVING. *Dutch Village Communities on the Hudson River* (Johns Hopkins University, *Studies in Historical and Political Science*, IV, No. 1. Baltimore, 1886).

EMERSON, FREDERICK VALENTINE. "Geographic Influences in American Slavery," in American Geographical Society, *Bulletin*, XLIII, *passim*, Jan.–Mar., 1911.

ENCYCLOPAEDIA OF THE SOCIAL SCIENCES (ed. by Edwin R. A. Seligman, editor-in-chief, Alvin Johnson, associate editor, and others. 15 vols., New York, 1931–1935).

ENO, JOEL N. "Liquor Legislation in Connecticut Colony," in *Journal of American History*, VII, 937–945, 1913.

———. "New York Manors, Townships, and Patents: a Study of Types of Settlements," in *Journal of American History*, IX, 207–216, April, 1915.

FAIRCHILD, FRED ROGERS. *The Factory Legislation of the State of New York* (American Economic Association, *Publications*, 3d ser., VI, No. 4. New York, 1905).

FARNAM, HENRY WALCOTT. *The Economic Utilization of History and Other Economic Studies* (New Haven and London, 1913).

———. *Joseph Earl Sheffield, The Father of the Sheffield Scientific School* (The New Haven Colony Historical Society, *Papers*, VII, 65–119. Printed for the Society, New Haven, 1908).

———. *Die innere Französische Gewerbepolitik von Colbert bis Turgot* (Strassburg, 1878).

———. "Labor Legislation and Economic Progress," in American Association for Labor Legislation, *Proceedings of the Third Annual Meeting*, Publication No. 9. New York, 1910.

———. *Shakespeare's Economics* (New Haven, 1931).
FARRAND, MAX. *The Framing of the Constitution of the United States* (New Haven, 1913).
———. *The Legislation of Congress for the Government of Organized Territories of the United States, 1789–1895* (Newark, N. J., 1896).
——— (ed.). *The Records of the Federal Convention of 1787* (3 vols., New Haven and London, 1911).
THE FEDERALIST ON THE NEW CONSTITUTION *By Publicus. Written in 1788. To which is added Pacificus on the Proclamation of Neutrality written in 1793.* . . . . (2 vols., New York, 1802).
FIELD, ARTHUR SARGENT. *The Child Labor Policy of New Jersey* (American Economic Association, *Publications*, 3d ser., XI, No. 3. Cambridge, 1909).
FINE, NATHAN. *Labor and Farmer Parties in the United States, 1828–1928* (Rand School of Social Science. New York, 1928).
FISHER, SIDNEY G. *Men, Women & Manners in Colonial Times* (Philadelphia, 1898).
FISKE, JOHN. *The Beginnings of New England or the Puritan Theocracy in Its Relations to Civil and Religious Liberty* (Boston and New York, 1894).
FLIPPIN, PERCY SCOTT. *The Financial Administration of the Colony of Virginia* (Johns Hopkins University, *Studies in Historical and Political Science*, XXXIII, No. 2. Baltimore, 1915).
———. "The Land System," in *Georgia Historical Quarterly*, X, 1–25, Mar., 1926.
———. *The Royal Government in Georgia, 1752–1776;* V, "The Land System," in *Georgia Historical Quarterly*, X, 1–25, Mar., 1926.
FLORIDA. Laws, Statutes, etc.:
Digests, Compilations, etc.;
McClellan, James F. (comp.). *Digest of the Laws of the State of Florida from the Year 1822 to the Eleventh Day of March, 1881, Inclusive* (Tallahassee, Fla., 1881).
Session Laws;
Acts and Resolutions Passed by the General Assembly of the State of Florida, 1828– (Tallahassee, 1828–).
FLYNN, JOHN STEPHEN. *The Influence of Puritanism on the Political & Religious Thought of the English* (New York, 1920).
FOLZ, STANLEY. "Exemption Laws and Public Policy," in *The American Law Register*, LIII (O.S.), XLIV (N.S.), 722–737, Dec., 1905.
FOOTE, SENATOR HENRY STUART. "Speech," in *Congressional Globe*, XXIII, 713–720.
———. *Texas and the Texans: or Advance of the Anglo-Americans to the South-West* (2 vols., Philadelphia, 1841).
FORBES, R. B. "Protection to American Seamen," in *The Sailors' Magazine*, XXXII, 195–197, March, 1860 (Reprinted from *Boston Commercial Bulletin*).
FORCE, PETER (ed.). *American Colonial Tracts Monthly* (2 vols., Issued by G. P. Humphrey, 1879–1898).
——— (ed.). *Tracts and Other Papers Relating Principally to the Origin, Settlement, and Progress of the Colonies in North America, from the Discovery of the Country to the Year 1776* (4 vols., Washington, 1836–1846).
FORD, AMELIA CLEWLEY. *Colonial Precedents of Our National Land System as It Existed in 1800* (Wisconsin University, *Bulletin*, No. 352, History Series, II, No. 2. Madison, 1910).
FORD, WORTHINGTON CHAUNCEY (ed.). *Washington as an Employer and Importer of Labor* (Privately Printed, Brooklyn, 1889).
FOSTER, ROGER. *Commentaries on the Constitution of the United States, Historical and Juridical with Observations upon the Ordinary Provisions of State Constitutions and a Comparison with the Constitutions of Other Countries* (Boston, 1895).
FOWLER, WILLIAM CHAUNCEY. *Historical Status of the Negro in Connecticut* (Charleston, S. C., 1901).
FOX, EARLY LEE. *The American Colonization Society, 1817–1840* (Baltimore, 1919. Also Johns Hopkins University, *Studies in Historical and Political Science*, XXXVII, No. 3).
FROTHINGHAM, RICHARD. *The Rise of the Republic of the United States* (3d ed., Boston, 1881).
FUESS, C. M. "Manasseh Cutler," in *Dictionary of American Biography*, V, 13.
FULLER, REV. R., AND WAYLAND, REV. F. *Domestic Slavery Considered as a Scriptural Institution, in a Correspondence Between Rev. R. Fuller of Beaufort, S. C., and Rev. F. Wayland, of Providence, R. I.* (New York and Boston, 1845).
GALES AND SEATON. See United States Congress, Publications.
GAMMEL, H. P. N. *The Laws of Texas, 1822–1897.* See Texas.
GARRISON, GEORGE P. *Texas, A Contest of Civilizations* (Boston and New York, 1903).
GEISER, KARL FREDERICK. *Redemptioners and Indentured Servants in the Colony and Commonwealth of Pennsylvania* (Supplement to *Yale Review*, (O.S.), X, No. 2, August, 1901).

GEORGE, JAMES Z. *The Political History of Slavery in the United States* (New York, 1915).
GEORGIA. (Colony). General Assembly:
I *By-Laws and Laws* 1733–1750, and *Journal of the Trustees for Establishing the Colony of Georgia in America*, 1732–1752.
II *Minutes of the Common Council of the Trustees for Establishing the Colony of Georgia in America*, 1732–1752.
VII-XII *Proceedings and Minutes of the Governor and Council*, 1754–1782.
———. Laws, Statutes, etc.:
Digests, Compilations, etc.;
Chandler, Allen D. (comp.). *Statutes Enacted by the Royal Legislature of Georgia from Its First Session in 1754 to 1768; Statutes, Colonial and Revolutionary, 1768 to 1773; Statutes, Colonial and Revolutionary, 1774 to 1805* (in the *Colonial Records of Georgia*, XVIII and XIX, Parts I and II. 3 vols., Atlanta, Ga., 1910, 1911).
De Renne, G. W. J., and C. C. Jones, Jr. (eds.). *Acts Passed by the General Assembly of the Colony of Georgia*, 1755–1774 (Wormsloe, 1881).
———. Records, etc.:
The Colonial Records of the State of Georgia (compiled under the authority of the Legislature by A. D. Chandler, revised and published by L. L. Knight. 27 vols., Atlanta, 1904–1916).
The Revolutionary Records of the State of Georgia (compiled and published under authority of the Legislature by A. D. Chandler. 3 vols., Atlanta, 1908).
——— (State). Laws, Statutes, etc.:
Digests, Compilations, etc.;
Clayton, Augustin Smith (ed.). *A Compilation of the Laws of the State of Georgia, Passed by the Legislature Since the Political Year 1800, to the Year 1810, Inclusive* . . . (Augusta, Ga., 1812).
Cobb, Thomas R. R. (comp.). *A Digest of the Statute Laws of the State of Georgia, in Force Prior to the Session of the General Assembly of 1851* . . . (2 vols., Athens, Ga., 1851).
Dawson, W. C. (ed.). *A Compilation of the Laws of the State of Georgia, Passed by the General Assembly, Since the Year 1819 to the Year 1829, Inclusive. Comprising All the Laws Passed within those Periods, Arranged under Titles with Marginal Notes, and Notes of Reference to the Laws or Parts of Laws Which are Amended or Repealed. To which are Added Such Concurred and Approved Resolutions as are either General, Local or Private in Nature* (Milledgeville, Ga., 1831). Laws and Resolutions separately paged.
Foster, Arthur (comp.). *A Digest of the Laws of the State of Georgia Containing All Statutes, and the Substance of All Resolutions of a General and Public Nature, and Now in Force which Have Been Passed in Said State from the Year 1820 to the Year 1829 Inclusive* . . . (Philadelphia, 1831).
Lamar, Lucius Q. C. (comp.). *A Compilation of the Laws of the State of Georgia, Passed by the Legislature Since the Year 1810 to the Year 1819, Inclusive. Comprising All the Laws Passed Within those Periods, Arranged under Appropriate Heads, with Notes of Reference, to those Laws or Parts of Laws, Which are Amended or Repealed* . . . (Augusta, Ga., 1821).
Marbury, Horatio, and Crawford, William (eds.). *Digest of the Laws of the State of Georgia From Its Settlement as a British Province, in 1755, to the Session of the General Assembly in 1800, Inclusive. Comprehending All the Laws Passed Within the Above Period and Now in Force. . . . Also the State Constitutions of 1777 and 1798* . . . (Savannah, 1802).
Prince, Oliver H. (comp.). *Digest of the Laws of the State of Georgia Containing All Statutes and the Substance of All Resolutions of a General and Public Nature and Now in Force, Which Have Been Passed in this State, Previous to the Session of the General Assembly of December 1837.* (1st ed., 1822; 2d ed., Athens, Ga., 1837).
Watkins, Robert and George (eds.). *A Digest of the Laws of the State of Georgia. From Its First Establishment as a British Province Down to the Year 1798 Inclusive, and the Principal Acts of 1799* . . . (Philadelphia, 1800).
Session Laws;
Acts of the General Assembly of the State of Georgia, Passed at an Annual Session . . . *1816–* (Milledgeville, Macon, etc., 1816–).
GERMANN, GEORGE B. *National Legislation Concerning Education. Its Influence and Effect in the Public Land States East of the Mississippi River, Admitted Prior to 1820* (New York, 1899).
GIDDINGS, JOSHUA REED. *Resolutions on Slavery* (Reprinted in MacDonald, *Select Documents Illustrative of the History of the United States, 1776–1861*, Doc. No. 69, pp. 333–334).
GOODELL, ABNER CHENEY. "John Saffin and His Slave Adam," in Colonial Society of Massachusetts, *Transactions*, I, 84–112, March 1893.

GOODELL, WILLIAM. *The American Slave Code in Theory and Practice: Its Distinctive Features Shown by Its Statutes, Judicial Decisions, and Illustrative Facts* (New York, 1853).
———. *Slavery and Anti-Slavery; a History of the Great Struggle in Both Hemispheres; with a View of the Slavery Question in the United States* (New York, 1853).
GOUGE, WILLIAM M. "Report on Marine Hospitals," in *Senate Executive Documents*, 34 Cong., 1 and 2 sess., 1855–1856, V, No. 53, pp. 244–247.
GOULD, CLARENCE PEMBROKE. *The Land System in Maryland, 1720–1765* (Johns Hopkins University, *Studies in Historical and Political Science*, XXXI, No. 1. Baltimore, 1913).
———. *Money and Transportation in Maryland, 1720–1765* (Johns Hopkins University, *Studies in Historical and Political Science*, XXXIII, No. 1. Baltimore, 1915).
GRAY, LEWIS CECIL. "Southern Agriculture, Plantation System, and the Negro Problem," in *Annals of the American Academy of Political and Social Science*, XL, 90–99, March, 1912.
——— AND THOMPSON, ESTHER KATHERINE. *History of Agriculture in the Southern United States to 1860* (Carnegie Institution of Washington, Publ. No. 430. Washington, 1933).
GREAT BRITAIN, BOARD OF TRADE.
Journal of the Commissioners for Trade and Plantations, 1704– (vols. 1– , London, 1920–).
———. Laws, Statutes, etc.:
Statutes at Large from Magna Charta to . . . 1761 (Continued by D. Pickering and others to 1807 in 46 vols.) and as
Statutes of the United Kingdom (vols. 47 to 109, to 1869. Cambridge and later London, 1762–1869). *Index* up to 1809 in 3 vols. (London, 1814).
The Statutes at Large from Magna Charta to the Thirtieth Year of King George the Second Inclusive [1225–1757]. (Ed. by John Cay, 6 vols., London ... 1758).
GREELEY, NATHAN. "The First Homestead Bill," in *Magazine of American History*, XVII, 163–165, February, 1887.
GREENE, EVARTS BOUTELL. *Provincial America, 1690–1740* (A. B. Hart, ed. *The American Nation: A History*, VI. New York & London, 1905).
GRIFFIS, WILLIAM ELLIOTT. *The Influence of the Netherlands in the Making of the English Commonwealth and the American Republic* (Boston, 1891).
GRIMKÉ, JOHN FAUCHERAUD (ed.). *The Public Laws of the State of South Carolina from Its First Establishment as a British Province Down to the Year 1790 . . . Also the Constitution of the United States with the Amendments Thereto, and Likewise the Newly Adopted Constitution of the State of South Carolina* (Philadelphia, 1790).
GROAT, GEORGE GORHAM. *Attitude of American Courts in Labor Cases. A Study in Social Legislation* (Columbia University, *Studies in History, Economics and Public Law*, XLII, No. 108. New York, 1911).
———. *Trade Unions and the Law in New York* (Columbia University, *Studies in History, Economics and Public Law*, XIX, No. 3. New York, 1905).
HAINES, CHARLES GROVE. *The American Doctrine of Judicial Supremacy* (New York, 1914).
HALL, EDWIN. *Ancient Historical Records of Norwalk, Conn.; with a Plan of the Ancient Settlement, and of the Town in 1847* (Norwalk, Conn., 1847).
HALL, MARSHALL. *Two-Fold Slavery in the United States, with a Project for Self-Emancipation* (London, 1854).
HALL, PRESCOTT FARNSWORTH. *Immigration and Its Effects Upon the United States* (2d ed., New York, 1913).
HALL, S. H. "A Brief Historical Sketch," in Seamen's Friend Society, *Fiftieth Annual Report with the Semi-Centenary Papers* (1878), pp. 67–73.
HALSBURY, EARL OF, ET AL. *The Laws of England, being a Complete Statement of the Whole Law of England* (31 vols., London, 1907–17).
HAMILTON, ALEXANDER. *Report on Manufactures, December, 1791* (Reprinted in *Reports of the Secretary of the Treasury of the United States, Prepared in Obedience to the Act of May 10, 1800. To Which are Prefixed the Reports of Alexander Hamilton on Public Credit, A National Bank, Manufactures and The Establishment of a Mint*, I, 78–132. 2 vols., Washington, 1837). Short title, *Reports on the Finances, 1790–1814*.
———. *Works* (ed. by Henry Cabot Lodge, 9 vols., New York and London, 1885).
———. *The Works of Alexander Hamilton, Comprising His Correspondence, and His Political and Official Writings* (7 vols., ed. by John C. Hamilton, New York, 1850–51).
———. See also *The Federalist*.
HAMILTON, JOHN B. [Supervising Surgeon-General]. "Service, United States Marine Hospital," in Appleton, *The Annual Cyclopædia for 1879*, new series, IV, 778–794, 1880.

HAMILTON, PETER JOSEPH. *Latin Land Laws and Land Systems in the South* (in *The South in the Building of the Nation*, V, 33–67).
HANEY, LEWIS H. (ed.). *The Land Problem in Texas* (By Members of the Texas Applied Economics Club. University of Texas, *Bulletin* No. 39, July 10, 1915).
HART, ALBERT BUSHNELL (ed.). *American History Told by Contemporaries* (4 vols., New York, 1897–1901).
——— (ed.). *The American Nation. A History from Original Sources by Associated Scholars* (27 vols., New York and London, 1904–1908).
———. "The Disposition of Our Public Lands," in *Quarterly Journal of Economics*, I, 169–183, 251–254, January, 1887.
——— (ed.). *Epochs of American History* (3 vols., New York, 1891–1893).
———. *National Ideals Historically Traced, 1607–1907* (A. B. Hart, ed., *The American Nation: A History*, XXVI, New York & London, 1907).
———. *Slavery and Abolition, 1831–1841* (A. B. Hart, ed., *The American Nation: A History*, XVI, New York and London, 1906).
HART, SAMUEL. "The Fundamental Orders and the Charters," in New Haven Colony Historical Society, *Papers*, VIII, 238–254.
HARTFORD, CONN. *Hartford Town Votes, 1635–1716* (Vol. I in Connecticut Historical Society, VI, Hartford, 1897).
———. *The Memorial History of Hartford County, Connecticut, 1633–1884* (ed. by J. Hammond Trumbull. Boston, 1886).
HARVARD ECONOMIC STUDIES (published under the direction of the Department of Economics, vols. 1– , Boston & New York, 1906–).
HARVARD HISTORICAL STUDIES (published under the direction of the Department of History and Government, vols. 1– , New York & London, 1896–).
HASKINS, CHARLES HOMER. "The Yazoo Land Companies," in American Historical Association, *Papers*, V, 395–437, Oct., 1891.
HAWK, E. Q. *Economic History of the South* (Prentice-Hall History Series, 1934).
HAWKS, FRANCIS LISTER. *History of North Carolina* (2 vols., Fayetteville, N. C., 1857–1858).
HAYNES, N. S. "The Disciples of Christ in Illinois and Their Attitude Towards Slavery," in Illinois Historical Society, *Transactions*, 1913, pp. 52–59.
HAYWOOD, JOHN (compl.). *Manual of the Laws of North Carolina* (Raleigh, 1819).
HELPER, HINTON ROWAN. *The Impending Crisis of the South: How to Meet It* (New York, 1857).
HENING, WILLIAM WALLER (ed.). *The Statutes at Large; being a Collection of all the Laws of Virginia, 1619–1792* (13 vols., Richmond, 1809–1823).
HENRY, HOWELL MEADOES. *The Police Control of the Slave in South Carolina* (Emory, Va., 1914).
HERBERT, HILARY A. *The Abolition Crusade and Its Consequences. Four Periods of American History* (New York, 1912).
HERR, DR. JUR. E. *Der Zusammenbruch der Wirtschaftsfreiheit und der Sieg des Staatssocialismus in den Vereinigten Staaten von Amerika* (Jena, 1906).
HERRICK, CHEESMAN A. *White Servitude in Pennsylvania, Indentured and Redemption Labor in Colony and Commonwealth* (Philadelphia, 1926).
HERRICK, S. *Manual of the United States Homestead and Other Public Land Laws* (Seattle, Wash., 1909).
HESTON, ALFRED MILLER. *Story of the Slave; Wherein is Given Some Account of Slavery and Servitude in New Jersey* (Camden, N. J., 1903).
HIBBARD, AUGUSTINE G. *History of the Town of Goshen, Connecticut, with Genealogies and Biographies Based upon the Records of Deacon Lewis Mills Norton . . . 1897* (Hartford, Conn., 1897).
HIBBARD, BENJAMIN HORACE. *A History of the Public Land Policies* (New York, 1924).
HILKEY, CHARLES J. *Legal Development in Colonial Massachusetts, 1630–1686* (Columbia University, *Studies in History, Economics and Public Law*, XXXVII, No. 2. New York, 1910).
[HINMAN, ROY RALPH], ANTIQUARIAN (comp.). *The Blue Laws of New Haven Colony, Usually Called Blue Laws of Connecticut; Quaker Laws of Plymouth and Massachusetts; Blue Laws of New York, Maryland, Virginia, and South Carolina. First Record of Connecticut; Interesting Extracts from Connecticut Records; Cases of Salem Witchcraft; Charges and Banishments of Rev. Roger Williams, &c; and Other Interesting and Instructive Antiquities* (Hartford, 1838).
HISTORICAL MAGAZINE (23 vols., Boston and New York, 1857–1875).
HOLCOMB, WILLIAM P. *Pennsylvania Boroughs* (Johns Hopkins University, *Studies in Historical and Political Science*, IV, No. 4. Baltimore, 1886).
HOLMES, GEORGE KIRBY. *The Rice Crop of the United States, 1712–1911* (U. S. Dept. Agric., Bur. of Statistics, *Circular*, No. 34).

———. "Some Features of Tobacco History," in American Historical Association, *Annual Report*, 1919, I, 385–407.

———. *The Tobacco Crop of the United States, 1612–1911* (U. S. Dept. Agric., Bur. of Statistics, *Circular*, No. 33).

HOLST, HERMANN EDUARD VON. *Constitutional and Political History of the United States* (Translated from the German by John J. Lalor and Alfred B. Mason. 7 vols., Chicago, 1876).

HOPKINS, SAMUEL. "The Slave Trade and Slavery" (By "Crito," Oct. 13, 1787. Reprinted in *Works*, II, Boston, 1852).

HOUGH, FRANKLIN B. *Constitutional Provisions Relating to Education, Literature and Science in the Several States of the American Union* (United States Bureau of Education, *Circular of Information* No. 7. Washington, 1875).

HOUGHTON, WALTER R. *Conspectus of the History of Political Parties and the Federal Government* (Indianapolis, Ind., 1880).

HULBERT, ARCHER BUTLER (ed.). *The Records of the Original Proceedings of the Ohio Company* (2 vols. Marietta, O., 1917).

HUNTINGTON, N. Y. *Huntington Town Records Including Babylon, L. I., 1653–1873.* With Introduction, Notes and Index. Transcribed, Compiled and Published by Authority of the Two Towns (C. R. Street, ed., 3 vols., Huntington, N. Y., 1887–1889).

HURD, JOHN CODMAN. *The Law of Freedom and Bondage in the United States* (2 vols., Boston and New York, 1858–1862).

HUTCHINSON, THOMAS. *A Collection of Original Papers Relative to the History of the Colony of Massachusetts-Bay* (Boston, New-England. Printed by Thomas and John Fleet, 1769).

———. *The History of Massachusetts from the First Settlement Thereof in 1628, until the Year [1774]*. (2 vols., 3d ed., Boston, 1795–1798).

ILLINOIS. Laws, Statutes, etc.:

The Revised Code of Laws [1827] (Cincinnati, 1829).

The Revised Code of Laws of Illinois Containing Those of a General and Permanent Nature Passed by the General Assembly at the Session of December 1828 and Those Prior Thereto. Published under Authority (Shauneetown, 1829).

The Revised Laws of Illinois Containing All Laws of a General and Public Nature Passed by the Session Ending March 1833 and Prior Thereto. Published under Authority (Vandalia, 1833).

Revised Statutes of Illinois Adopted by the General Assembly in 1844–1845. Published under Authority (Springfield, 1845).

Digests, Compilations, etc.;

Purple, N. H. (ed.). *A Compilation of the Statutes of Illinois of a General Nature In Force January 1, 1856* (2 vols., Chicago, 1856).

Session Laws;

Laws Passed by the General Assembly of the State of Illinois, 1819– (Kaskaskia, 1819–).

ILLINOIS UNIVERSITY. *University of Illinois Studies in the Social Sciences* (vols. 1– , Urbana, 1912–).

INDIANA. Laws, Statutes, etc.:

The Laws of Indiana Territory, 1801–1809 (Reprinted by Illinois State Historical Society. Springfield, Ill., 1930).

Laws of the State of Indiana Passed by the General Assembly, 1853 (Indianapolis, 1853).

Laws of the State of Indiana Passed at the First Sessions of the General Assembly, 1816–1819 (Croydon and Jefferson, Ind., 1817–1820). Paged and indexed separately. Bound in 1 vol.

Revised Laws of Indiana Adopted by the General Assembly in 1831 (Indianapolis, 1831).

Revised Statutes of the State of Indiana, 1843 (Indianapolis, 1843).

Revised Statutes of the State of Indiana Passed by the General Assembly in 1852 (2 vols., Indianapolis, 1852).

INGLE, EDWARD. *Local Institutions of Virginia* (Johns Hopkins University, *Studies in Historical and Political Science*, III, Nos. 2–3. Baltimore, 1885).

———. *Parish Institutions of Maryland* (Johns Hopkins University, *Studies in Historical and Political Science*, I, No. 6. Baltimore, 1883).

INGRAM, JOHN KELLS. *A History of Slavery and Serfdom* (London, 1895).

IOWA. Laws, Statutes, etc.:

The Code of Iowa Passed at the Session of the General Assembly of 1850–1 (Iowa City, 1851).

Laws of the Territory of Iowa Enacted at the Session of the Legislature Commencing on the First Monday in November, 1839 (Burlington, Iowa, 1840).

Laws of the Territory of Iowa Passed at the Extra Session of the Legislative Assembly begun on First Monday in July, 1840 (Burlington, Iowa, 1840).

The Statute Laws of the Territory of Iowa [1838–9] (DuBuque, Iowa, 1839).
Session Laws;
Acts and Resolutions Passed by the General Assembly of the State of Iowa, 1846– (Iowa City, 1847–).

IREDELL, JAMES (Publisher). *Laws of the State of North-Carolina. Published according to the Acts of Assembly* (Edenton: M. DCC, XCI).

JAMES, EDMUND J. *The Origin of the Land Grant Act of 1862; The So-called Morrill Act; and Some Account of Its Author, Jonathan B. Turner* (University of Illinois, *Studies*, IV, No. 1. Urbana, Ill., 1910).

J. F. D. "The Homestead Exemption," in *American Law Register*, X, 641–656, 705–716, Sept. and Oct., 1862.

JAMESON, J. FRANKLIN. *The American Revolution Considered as a Social Movement* (Princeton, N. J., 1926).

——— (ed.). *Johnson's Wonder-Working Providence, 1628–1651* (*Original Narratives in Early American History*, IX. New York, 1910).

——— (ed.). *Original Narratives in Early American History* (Reproduced under the Auspices of the American Historical Association. General editor, J. Franklin Jameson, Vols. I– . New York, 1906–).

JEFFERSON, THOMAS. *Correspondence.* Printed from the originals in the collections of W. K. Bixby (W. C. Ford, ed., Boston, 1916).

———. *Notes on the State of Virginia* (P. L. Ford, ed., Brooklyn, 1894).

———. *The Writings of Thomas Jefferson* (P. L. Ford, ed., 10 vols., New York, 1892–1899).

———. *The Writings of Thomas Jefferson. Being His Autobiography, Correspondence, Reports, Messages, Addresses, and Other Writings, Official and Private* (H. A. Washington, ed., 9 vols., Washington, D. C., 1853–1854).

JENNINGS, WALTER W. *History of Economic Progress in the United States* (New York, 1926).

JERNEGAN, MARCUS WILSON. "A Forgotten Slavery of Colonial Days," in *Harpers*, CXXVII, 745–751, October 1913.

———. *Laboring and Dependent Classes in Colonial America, 1607–1783. Studies of the Economic, Educational, and Social Significance of Slaves, Apprentices, and Poor Folk* (Chicago, 1931).

———. "Slavery and Conversion in the American Colonies," in *American Historical Review*, XXI, 504–527, Apr., 1916.

JERVEY, THEODORE DEHON. "The White Indentured Servant of South Carolina," in *South Carolina Historical and Genealogical Magazine*, XII, 163–171, Oct., 1911.

JEWELL, J. GREY. *Among Our Sailors. With an Appendix Containing Extracts from the Laws and Consular Regulations Governing the United States Merchant Marine* (New York, 1874).

JILLSON, WILLARD ROUSE. *The Kentucky Land Grants; A Systematic Index to All of the Land Grants Recorded in the State Land Office at Frankfort, Kentucky, 1782–1924* (*Filson Club Publications*, No. 33. Louisville, 1925).

JOHNS HOPKINS UNIVERSITY. *Studies in Historical and Political Science* (vols. 1– , Baltimore, 1883–).

JOHNSON, ALLEN. "The Constitutionality of the Fugitive Slave Acts," in *Yale Law Journal*, XXI, 161–182, Dec., 1921.

——— (ed.). See *Dictionary of American Biography.*

JOHNSON, E. A. J. *American Economic Thought in the Seventeenth Century* (London, 1932).

JOHNSON, EDWARD. *History of New England, 1628–1652* (Massachusetts Historical Society, *Collections*, ser. 2, II, 49–95; III, 123–161; IV, 1–51; VII, 1–58; VIII, 1–39. Boston, 1814–1819). Better known by the running title: *Wonder-Working Providence of Sions Saviour in New England.* See also Jameson.

JOHNSON, JOHN HEMSLEY. *Old Maryland Manors with the Records of a Court Leet and a Court Baron* (Johns Hopkins University, *Studies in Historical and Political Science*, I, No. 7. Baltimore, 1883).

JOHNSTON, ALEXANDER. *The Genesis of a New England State* (Johns Hopkins University, *Studies in Historical and Political Science*, I, No. 11. Baltimore, 1883).

———. *History of American Politics* (New York, 1880. Revised and enlarged by William M. Sloane, continued by Winthrop More Daniels, New York, 1910).

JONES, RUFUS MATTHEW, ET AL. *The Quaker in the American Colonies* (London, 1911).

JORNS, DR. AUGUSTE. *Studien über die Sozialpolitik der Quäker* (*Volkswirtschaftliche Abhandlungen der Badischen Hochschulen.* Neue Folge, Heft X. Karlsruhe, i. B., 1912).

JOURNAL OF NEGRO HISTORY. (vols. 1– , Lancaster, Penn., & Washington, D. C., 1916–

JUNGE, FRANZ FRICH. *Amerikanische Wirtschaftspolitik, Ihre Ökonomischen Grundlagen, Ihre Sozialen Wirkungen, und Ihre Lehren für die Deutsche Volkswirtschaft* (Berlin, 1910).

KABLUKOW, NIKOLAI. "Die Russische Gesetzgebung betr. die Versorgung des Volkes bei Missernten," in Braun's *Archiv f. Soziale Gesetzgebung u. Statistik*, IV, 290–314, 1891.

KALM, PER. *Travels into North America* (Second edition reprinted in J. Pinkerton, ed., *Voyages*, vol. XIII).

KANSAS TERRITORY. Laws, Statutes, etc.:

General Laws Passed by the Legislative Assembly of the Territory of Kansas. General and Special Sessions of 1860 (Lecompton, Kans., 1860).

General Laws Passed by the Legislative Assembly of the Territory of Kansas for the Year 1861 (Lawrence, Kans., 1861).

Laws of the Territory of Kansas Passed at the Third and Fourth Sessions of the Legislative Assembly, 1857–1858 (Lecompton, Kans., 1858).

Statutes of the Territory of Kansas Passed at the First Session of the Legislative Assembly, 1855 (Shaunee M. L. School, 1855).

KARRAKER, C. H. "Deodands in Colonial Virginia and Maryland," in *American Historical Review*, XXXVII, 712–717, July, 1932.

KENNEDY, EDWIN WEXLER. *Quit-rents and Currency in North Carolina, 1663–1776* (Baltimore, 1902).

KENTUCKY. Laws, Statutes, etc.:

Laws of Kentucky Comprehending Those of a General Nature Now in Force, and Which Have been Acted on by the Legislature thereof. Together with a Copious Index . . . To Which is Prefixed the Constitution of the United States . . . the Act of Separation from the State of Virginia and the Constitution of Kentucky (Lexington, Ky. Printed by John Bradford, 1799).

Digests, Compilations, etc.;

Littell, William (ed.). *The Statute Law of Kentucky to 1816. Comprehending also the Laws of Virginia and Acts of Parliament in Force in This Commonwealth* (5 vols., Frankfort, 1809–1819).

——— and Swigert, Jacob (eds.). *A Digest of the Statute Law of Kentucky. Being a Collection of All the Acts of the General Assembly of a Public and Permanent Nature . . . to the May Session, 1822, also the English and Virginia Statutes Yet in Force* (2 vols., Frankfort, 1822).

Moorehead, C. S., and Brown, Mason (eds.). *A Digest of the Statute Laws of Kentucky of a Public and Permanent Nature* (2 vols., Frankfort, 1834).

Toulmin, Harry (ed.). *A Collection of All the Public and Permanent Acts of the General Assembly of Kentucky Which are Now in Force . . . Together with Acts of Virginia Relating to Land Title, the Recovery of Rents, and the Encouragement of Learning, Never Before Printed in this State; to Which are Prefixed a Table Explanatory of Technical Terms and a Summary of Criminal Law* (Frankfort, Ky. Printed by William Hunter, 1802).

Wickliffe, C. A., Turner S., and Nicholas, S. S. (eds.). *The Revised Statutes of Kentucky* (Frankfort, 1852).

Session Laws;

Acts Passed at the Sessions of the General Assembly for the Commonwealth of Kentucky, 1796– (Frankfort, 1797–).

Acts Passed by the General Assembly of the State of Kentucky, 1792 . . . (Reprint, 5 vols., Frankfort, 1809).

KETTELL, THOMAS PRENTICE. *Southern Wealth and Northern Profits, as Exhibited in Statistical Facts and Official Figures: Showing the Necessity of Union to the Future Prosperity and Welfare of the Republic* (New York, 1860).

KILTY, JOHN. *The Land-Holder's Assistant and Land-Office Guide, Being an Exposition of Original Titles, as Derived from the Proprietary Government, and More Recently from the State of Maryland* (Baltimore, 1808).

KINGSBURY, BENJAMIN (comp.). *The Massachusetts Townsman or Laws for the Regulation of Forms and Judicial Decisions, Adapted to the Statutes of Massachusetts* (Boston, Mass., 1856).

———. *The Maine Townsman, or Laws for the Regulation of Towns with Formes and Judicial Decisions Adapted to the Revised Statutes of Maine* (5th ed., Portland, 1856).

———. *Introduction to the Records of the Virginia Company of London* (Washington, D. C., 1905).

KINGSBURY, FREDERICK J. "Old Connecticut," in New Haven Historical Society, *Papers*, III, 63–84, 1882.

[KINGSLEY, Z.]. *A Treatise on the Patriarchal System of Society, as It Exists in Some Governments and Colonies in America, and in the United States, under the Name of Slavery, with Its Necessity and Advantages.* By an inhabitant of Florida (4th ed., [n.p.], 1834).

KINSMAN, J. BURNHAM. *The Vermont Townsman: a Compilation of the Laws of Vermont in Relation to the Powers, Duties, and Liabilities of Town Officers and Towns, with Forms, Directions, and Legal Decisions Adapted to the Statutes of the State* (Boston, 1857).

KIRK, WILLIAM. *National Labor Federations in the United States* (Johns Hopkins University, *Studies in Historical and Political Science*, XXIV, Nos. 9–10. Baltimore, 1906).

KIRKLAND, EDWARD CHASE. *A History of American Economic Life* (New York, 1932).

KNIGHT, GEORGE W. *History and Management of Land Grants for Education in the Northwest Territory* (American Historical Association, *Papers*, I, No. 3. New York and London, 1885).

KNOTT, H. W. H. *Dane*, in *Dictionary of American Biography*, V, 63.

LAMB, MRS. MARTHA J. "The Van Rensselaer Manor," in *Magazine of American History*, XI, No. 1, pp. 1–32, January, 1884.

LAMBERT, EDWARD R. *History of the Colony of New Haven Before and After the Union with Connecticut* (New Haven, 1838).

LANDON, JUDSON S. *The Constitutional History and Government of the United States. A Series of Lectures* (Boston and New York, 1889).

LA ROCHEFOUCAULD, LIANCOURT, [FRANÇOIS ALEXANDRE FRÉDÉRIC], DUC DE. *Travels through the United States of North America, the Country of the Iroquois, and Upper Canada, in the Years 1795, 1796, and 1797* (H. Neuman, trans. 2d ed., 4 vols., London, 1800).

LAUBER, ALMON WHEELER. *Indian Slavery in Colonial Times* (Columbia University, *Studies in History, Economics and Public Law*, LIV, No. 3, whole No. 143. New York, 1913).

LEA, HENRY CHARLES. "The Indian Policy of Spain," in *Yale Review*, VIII, 119–155, Aug., 1899.

LESCOHIER, DON D.; BRANDEIS, ELIZABETH; PERLMAN, SELIG; AND TAFT, PHILIP. *History of Labor in the United States* (New York, 1935. Vols. III and IV of Commons, et. al. *History of Labor*).

LEVERMORE, CHARLES H. *The Republic of New Haven, a History of Municipal Evolution* (Johns Hopkins University, *Studies in Historical and Political Science*, Extra Vol. I. Baltimore, 1886).

LEVERMORE, GEORGE. *An Historical Research Respecting the Opinions of the Founders of the Republic on Negroes as Slaves, as Citizens, and as Soldiers* (Boston, 1862. 3d ed., Boston, 1863). Read before the Massachusetts Historical Society, Aug. 14, 1862.

LIPPINCOTT, ISAAC. *Economic Development of the United States* (3d ed., New York, 1933).

"LIST OF INDENTURES Recorded in Boston, 1668–1692" in Bostonian Society, *Publications*, XI, 105–107, 1914.

LOCKE, MARY STOUGHTON. *Anti-Slavery in America from the Introduction of African Slaves to the Prohibition of the Slave Trade, 1619–1808* (Radcliffe College Monographs, No. 11. Boston, 1901).

LODGE, HENRY CABOT (ed.). *George Washington* (American Statesmen Series. 2 vols., Boston and New York, 1889).

LORD, ELEANOR LOUISA. *Industrial Experiments in the British Colonies of North America* (Johns Hopkins University, *Studies in Historical and Political Science*, Extra Vol. XVII. Baltimore, 1898).

LORD, JOHN P. *The Maine Townsman or Laws for the Regulation of Towns with Forms and Judicial Decisions, Adapted to the Revised Statutes of Maine* (3d ed., Portland, 1847).

LORING, GEORGE B. AND EDWARDS, TOM O. "Report Upon the Subject of Marine Hospitals" (1849), in *Senate Executive Document*, 31 Cong., 2 sess., III, No. 14, pp. 1–32. (Congressional Commission for Examining Marine Hospitals, Washington, 1851).

LOUGHRAN, MERIAM E. *The Historical Development of Child Labor Legislation in the United States* (Washington, D. C., 1921).

LOUISIANA. Laws, Statutes, etc.:

Louisiana Civil Code (New Orleans, 1825).

The Laws of Las Siete Partidas, Which are Still in Force in the State of Louisiana (Translated from the Spanish by L. Moreau Lislet and Henry Carleton. 2 vols., New Orleans, 1820).

Digests, Compilations, etc.;

Lislet, L. Moreau (ed.). *A General Digest of the Acts of the Legislature of Louisiana: Passed from the Year 1804 to 1827, Inclusive, and in Force at this Last Period* (2 vols., New-Orleans, 1828).

Martin, Francois-Xavier. *A General Digest of the Acts of Legislature of the Late Territory of Orleans and of the State of Louisiana and of the Ordinances of the Governor under the Territorial Government* (3 vols., New Orleans, 1816).

Session Laws;

Acts Passed by the General Assembly of the State of Louisiana, 1812– (New Orleans, 1812–).

LOUISIANA HISTORICAL SOCIETY. *Publications* (10 vols., New Orleans, 1895–1918).

LOW, A. MAURICE. *The American People. A Study in National Psychology* (2 vols., Boston and New York, 1909, 1911).

LUCAS, ELIZA (MRS. E. L. PINCKNEY). *Journal and Letters of Eliza Lucas* (Wormsloe, Ga., 1850).
LUCAS, S. *Charters of Old English Colonies in America* (London, 1850).
MABIE, HAMILTON WRIGHT. *American Ideals, Character and Life* (New York, 1915).
MACARTHUR, W. "The American Seaman under the Law," in *The Forum*, XXVI, 718–731, Feb. 1899.
MCCORMAC, EUGENE IRVING. *White Servitude in Maryland, 1634–1820* (Johns Hopkins University, *Studies in Historical and Political Science*, XXII, Nos. 3–4. Baltimore, 1904).
MACDONALD, WILLIAM (ed.). *Select Charters and Other Documents Illustrative of The History of America, 1606–1775* (New York, 1899).
———. *Select Documents Illustrative of the History of the United States, 1776–1861* (New York, 1898).
———. *Documentary Source Book of American History, 1606–1926* (3d rev. ed., New York, 1929).
MCDOUGLE, IVAN EUGENE. *Slavery in Kentucky, 1792–1865* (Lancaster, Pa., 1918).
MCFARLAND, H. H. "The Sailors' Law," in *Old and New*, IX, 361–373, March, 1874.
MCGEE, W. J. "Relations of Institutions to Environment," in Smithsonian Institution, *Report*, 1895, pp. 701–711.
MCHENRY, GEORGE. *The Cotton Trade: Its Bearing upon the Prosperity of Great Britain and Commerce of the American Republics, Considered in Connection with the System of Negro Slavery in the Confederate States* (London, 1863).
MCKITRICK, REUBEN. *The Public Land System of Texas, 1823–1910* (Wisconsin University, *Bulletin*, No. 905, Economic and Political Science Series, IX, No. 1. Madison, 1918).
MACLEAR, ANNE BUSH. *Early New England Towns* (Columbia University, *Studies in History, Economics and Public Law*, XXIX. New York, 1908).
MACY, JESSE. *Institutional Beginnings in a Western State* (Johns Hopkins University, *Studies in Historical and Political Science*, II, No. 7. Baltimore, 1884).
MADISON, JAMES. *The Federalist on the New Constitution by Publicus to Which is Added Pacificus, on the Proclamation of Neutrality written in 1793. Likewise, The Federal Constitution* (2 vols., revised and corrected, New York, 1802).
———. *Letters and Other Writings of James Madison, 1769–1836.* Published by Order of Congress (4 vols., Philadelphia, 1865).
———. *The Writings of James Madison* (G. Hunt, ed. 9 vols., New York, 1900–1910).
———. *Journal of the Federal Convention* (ed. by E. H. Scott, 2 vols., Chicago, 1893).
MAGAZINE OF AMERICAN HISTORY (30 vols., New York, 1877–1893).
MAGRUDER, W. W. *The Legal Status of Slaves in Mississippi before the War* (Mississippi Historical Society, *Publications*, IV, 133–142, Oxford, Miss., 1901).
MAINE. Laws, Statutes, etc.:
Acts and Resolves Passed by the Legislature of the State of Maine, 1847, 1848, 1849, 1855, 1856, 1859 (Augusta, Maine, 1847, 1848, 1849, 1855, 1856, 1859).
Laws of the State of Maine Passed by the Legislature from 1821 to 1834 (2 vols., Portland, 1834).
Laws of the State of Maine to Which are Prefixed the Constitution of the United States and of Said State (2 vols., Brunswick, 1821).
Laws of the State of Maine [1822–1831] (3 vols., Portland, 1822, 1831).
Public Acts of the State of Maine Passed by the Legislature, [1820–1830] (1 vol., Portland, 1820–1830).
Public Acts of the State of Maine Passed by the Legislature, 1838 (Augusta, 1838).
Revised Statutes of the State of Maine, Passed October 22, 1840 to which are Prefixed the Constitutions of the United States and of the State of Maine and to which are Subjoined the Public Laws of 1840 and 1841 with an Appendix (Augusta, 1841).
Revised Statutes (2 vols., Bangor, 1857).
Resolves of the Legislature of the State of Maine [1820–1835] (2 vols., Portland, 1820–1827, 1835).
MAINE HISTORICAL SOCIETY. *Collections* (1st series, I–X; 2d series, V–X; 3d series, I– . Portland, 1831–19–).
MAITLAND, FREDERICK WILLIAM. *Domesday Book and Beyond. Three Essays in the Early History of England* (Cambridge and Boston, 1897).
MALLARD, ROBERT Q. *Plantation Life before Emancipation* (Richmond, Va., 1892).
MALONE, DUMAS. See *Dictionary of American Biography.*
MARYLAND. *Archives of Maryland* . . . Published by Authority of the State under the Direction of the Maryland Historical Society (W. H. Browne, ed., 1883–1912; C. C. Hall, ed., 1913–1915; B. C. Steiner, ed., 1916–1927; J. H. Pleasants, ed., 1929–).
Acts and Proceedings of the Assembly, 1637–1777.
Journal and Correspondence of the Council of Safety, 1775–1777.
Journal and Correspondence of the State Council, 1777–1781.
Judicial and Testamentary Business and Proceedings of the Provincial Court, 1637–1666.
Proceedings of the Council (Colony), 1636–1770.

Laws, Statutes, etc.:

Acts Passed by the General Assembly of Maryland, Concerning the Territory of Columbia and the City of Washington (reprinted in Kilty, *Laws of Maryland*).

Acts of the Assembly Passed in the Province of Maryland, From 1692 to 1715 (Printed by John Baskett, Printer to the King's Most Excellent Majesty, MDCCXXIII).

A Compleat Collection of the Laws of Maryland with an Index and Marginal Notes, directing to the Several Laws and the Chief Matters Contained in Them. Collected and Printed by Authority (Annapolis, MDCCXXVII).

Laws of Maryland Made Since MDCCLXIII, Consisting of Acts of Assembly under Proprietary Government, Resolves of Convention, the Declaration of Rights, the Constitution and Form of Government, the Articles of Confederation, and Acts of Assembly Since the Revolution (Annapolis, MDCCLXXXVII).

Proceedings and Acts. See *Archives.*

Digests, Compilations, etc.:

Bacon, Thomas (ed.). *Laws of Maryland at Large, with Proper Indexes. Now First Collected into One Compleat Body, and Published from the Original Acts and Records remaining in the Secretary's Office of the Said Province. Together with Notes and Other Matters, Relative to the Constitution Thereof, Extracted from the Provincial Records. To Which is Prefixed the Charter, with an English Translation* (by Thomas Bacon, Rector of All-Saints Parish in Frederick County, etc. Annapolis, MDCCLXV).

Bisset, James. *Abridgment and Collection of the Acts of Assembly of the Province of Maryland, at Present in Force. With a Small Collection of Precedents in Law and Conveyancing Calculated for the Use of the Gentlemen of the Province* (Printed by William Bradford, Printer . . . for the Author. Philadelphia, 1759).

Herty, Thomas (ed.). *A Digest of the Laws of Maryland being an Abridgement Alphabetically Arranged of all the Public Acts of Assembly Now in Force, and of General Use from the first Settlement of the State, to the End of November Session 1797, inclusive, with reference to the Acts at Large* (Baltimore, 1799).

Kilty, William (ed.). *The Laws of Maryland to Which are Prefixed the Original Charter . . . the Bill of Rights and the Constitution of the State . . . with an Index.* Revised and Collected under the Authority of the Legislature (2 vols., Annapolis, 1799–1800. Additional volumes as follows: Vol. III, ed. by Kilty, Harris and Watkins, Annapolis, 1817; Vols. IV, V, VI, VII, n. d. continue from 1799 to 1818; Vol. VI contains Index of Vols. III–VI; Vol. VII contains Appendix, Land Laws, and Resolutions).

—— (comp.). *A Report of all Such English Statutes as Existed at the Time of the First Emigration of the People of Maryland, and Which by Experience have been found Applicable to Their Local and Other Circumstances; and of Such Others as Have Been Introduced, Used, and Practiced, by the Courts of Law or Equity; and Also Such Parts of the Same as May be Proper to be Introduced and Incorporated into the Body of the Statute Law of the State* (Annapolis, 1811).

Maxcy, Virgil (ed.). *The Laws of Maryland with the Charter, Bill of Rights, etc.* (3 vols., Baltimore, 1811).

Session Laws;

Laws Made and Passed by the General Assembly of the [Colony and] State of Maryland, 1727– (Annapolis, 1727–).

MARYLAND HISTORICAL SOCIETY. *Fund Publications* (37 vols., Baltimore, 1867–1901).

———. *Publications* (3 vols., Baltimore, 1844–1868).

MASEFIELD, JOHN. See *Chronicles of the Pilgrim Fathers.*

MASSACHUSETTS (Colony). Laws, Statutes, etc.:

An Abstract or [of] The Lawes of New England, as they are novv Established (London. Printed for F. Coules and W. Ley. . . 1641).

Acts and Laws, of Her Majesties Province of the Massachusetts-Bay in New-England (Printed by G. B. Green, Boston in New England, 1714). Prefixed by *The Charter Granted by Their Majesties King William and Queen Mary,* etc. (Boston in New England, 1714). Session laws to 1719 added. Paged continuously.

Acts and Laws of His Majesties Province of the Massachusetts-Bay, in New England [1692–1710] (Boston. Printed by Bartholomew Green & John Allen, Printers to His Excellency the Governour and Council . . . 1699). Prefixed by the *Charter* of 1699, and with the Acts and Laws of subsequent sessions paged continuously to 1710. Session laws bound in; varies with different copies.

Acts and Laws of His Majesty's Province of the Massachusetts-Bay in New-England (Boston in New

England, 1726). Prefixed by *The Charter Granted by Their Majesties King William and Queen Mary . . .* (Boston in New-England, 1726).

Acts and Laws of His Majesty's Province of the Massachusetts-Bay in New England [1692–1735] (Boston in New England, 1726). Prefixed by *The Charter Granted by Their Majesties King William, and Queen Mary to the Inhabitants of the Province of the Massachusetts-Bay in New England* (Boston, 1726). Continuation Acts and Laws passed to 1735. Paged continuously.

Acts and Laws, of His Majesty's Province of the Massachusetts-Bay in New-England [1692–1751] (Boston in New-England, MDCCXLII). Prefixed by *The Charter Granted by Their Majesties King William and Queen Mary to the Inhabitants of the Massachusetts Bay in New England* (Boston, MDCCXLII). Reprint of *Session Laws*, 1692–1751. Paged continuously.

Acts and Laws of His Majesty's Province of the Massachusetts-Bay in New England [1692–1760] (Boston, in New England. Printed by S. Kneeland, by Order of His Excellency the Governor, Council and House of Representatives, MDCCLIX). Prefixed by *The Charter Granted by Their Majesties King William and Queen Mary, to the Inhabitants of the Province of the Massachusetts-Bay in New-England.* Reprint of *Session Laws*, Oct. 1692 to Dec. 1760, inclusive. Paged continuously. Session laws bound in; varies with different copies.

Acts and Laws Passed by the Great and General Court or Assembly of the Province of the Massachusetts-Bay in New-England, From 1692, to 1719. To Which is Prefix'd The Charter, Granted by Their Late Majesties King William and Queen Mary, to the Inhabitants of the Said Province, A. D. 1691 (Printed by John Baskett, Printer to the King's Most Excellent Majesty. London, MDCCXXIV).

Acts and Resolves. See Digests, Compilations, etc.

The Body of Liberties. The Liberties of the Massachusetts Colonie in New England, 1641 (Old South Leaflets, General Series VII, no. 164, Boston, 1905. Compiled chiefly by Rev. Nathaniel Ward and adopted by the General Court in 1641, it was first published in 1843 in Massachusetts Historical Society, *Collections*, 3d series, VIII).

The Book of the General Lauues and Libertyes concerning the inhabitants of the Massachusetts (Cambridge. Printed according to order of the General Court, 1648).[4]

The Book of the General Lavvs and Libertyes Concerning the Inhabitants of the Massachusetts, Collected out of the Records of the General Court, for the Several Years Wherein They were Made and Established and now Revised by the Same Court, and Disposed into an Alphabetical Order, and Published by the Same Authority in the General Court Holden at Boston, in May 1649 (Cambridge, 1660).

The Charters and General Laws of the Colony and Province of Massachusetts Bay. Carefully Collected from the Publick Records and Ancient Printed Books. To Which is Added an Appendix, tending to explain the Spirit, Progress and History of the Jurisprudence of the State; Especially in a Moral and Political View. Published by Order of the General Court (Boston, 1814).

The Charter of Massachusetts Bay, 1629 (Old South Leaflets, General Series, I, No. 7. Boston, 1896).

The Colonial Laws of Massachusetts. Reprinted from the Edition of 1672. With the Supplement through 1686. Published by Order of the City Council of Boston under the Supervision of William H. Whitmore, Record Commissioner. Containing a new and complete Index (Boston, 1887).
Contains: *The General Laws and Liberties of the Massachusetts Colony: Revised and Reprinted. By Order of the General Court Holden at Boston, May 15, 1672. Edward Rawson, Secr.* (Cambridge. Printed by Samuel Green, for John Usher of Boston, 1672).

The Colonial Laws of Massachusetts. Reprinted from the edition of 1660, with the Supplements to 1672. Containing also *The Body of Liberties* of 1641. Published by Order of the City Council of Boston, under the Supervision of William H. Whitmore, Record Commissioner. With a Complete Index (Boston, 1889).

The General Laws and Liberties of the Massachusetts Colony: revised & reprinted . . . May 15, 1672. Edward Rawson, Secr. (Cambridge. Printed by Samuel Green, for John Vsher of Boston, 1672).

Laws and Liberties of Massachusetts. Reprinted from the Copy of the 1648 edition in the Henry E. Huntington Library. With an Introduction by Max Farrand (Cambridge, 1929).

Temporary Acts and Laws [1736–1753] of His Majesty's Province of the Massachusetts-Bay in New England (Boston, N. E. Printed and Sold by Samuel Kneeland and Timothy Green . . . MDCCXLII). On back of title page: Boston: Aug. 8, 1741.[5]

[4] Only known copy in Henry E. Huntington Library. Eleven photostatic copies made December, 1927.

[5] Stated to be the edition of 1792 and the earliest edition of Temporary Laws.

Temporary Acts and Laws of His Majesty's Province of the Massachusetts-Bay in New England (Boston, N. E. Printed by Order of His Excellency the Governor . . . and Sold by S. Kneeland in Queen St. 1755). Reverse title page: Printed 1754. Contains acts from 1736 to 1757.

Temporary Acts and Laws of His Majesty's Province of the Massachusetts-Bay in New-England (Boston, New-England: Printed by Order of His Excellency the Governor, etc. and sold by Green and Russell in Queen Street, MDCCLXIII).

Digests, Compilations, etc.;

Ames, Ellis, and Goodell, Cheney (eds.). *The Acts and Resolves, Public and Private, of the Province of Massachusetts Bay from 1692–1780, to Which are Prefixed the Charters of the Province with Historical and Explanatory Notes and an Appendix* (21 vols., Boston, 1869–1922).

Haven, S. F. (ed.). *Records of the Company of the Massachusetts Bay, to the Embarkation of Winthrop and His Associates for New England, as Contained in the First Volume of the Archives of the Commonwealth of Massachusetts* (In American Antiquarian Society, *Archæologia Americana, Transactions and Collections*, III, pt. i. Transcribed and Collated by David Pulsifer and J. B. Felt; ed. by S. F. Haven. Cambridge, 1850).

———. Records, etc.;

Shurtleff, Nathan B. (ed.). *Records of the Governor and Company of the Massachusetts Bay in New England* (5 vols. Boston, 1853–4).

——— (State).

"The First Official Investigation of Labor Conditions, 1845" (reprinted in Commons, *Documentary History of American Industrial Society*, VII, 133–150, from Massachusetts House Document No. 50).

"The Investigation of 1850" (reprinted in Commons, *Documentary History of American Industrial Society*, VIII, 151–187, from Massachusetts House Document No. 153).

"Report on Returns of Children Employed in Factories" (reprinted in Commons, *Documentary History of American Industrial Society*, V, 57–59, from Massachusetts Legislative Files, 1825, Senate No. 8074).

———. Laws, Statutes, etc.:

The Laws of the Commonwealth of Massachusetts, from Nov. 28, 1780 to Feb. 28, 1807. (3 vols., Boston, 1807; 4th vol., Boston, 1807).

Laws of the Commonwealth of Massachusetts from February 28, 1807 to December 14, 1816. Including the Political Years 1807, 1808, 1809, 1810, 1811, 1812, 1813, 1814, 1815, and 1816 (Boston, May 1817). Vol. IV to Royal ed., or Vol. V to Demy ed. Beginning where the edition ends which was printed by order of the Legislature in 1807.

Laws of the Commonwealth of Massachusetts passed at the Several Sessions of the General Court beginning May, 1828, and ending March, 1831 (Vol. XI, Boston, 1831).

The Perpetual Laws of the Commonwealth of Massachusetts from the Commencement of the Constitution, in October, 1780, to the Last Wednesday in May, 1789. To Which are Prefixed the Declaration of Independence, the Articles of Confederation, the Constitution of the Commonwealth, the Treaty of Peace, Between Great-Britain and America, and the Constitution of the United States. Published by Order of the General Court (2 vols., Boston, 1789–1796).

The second volume has title *Laws of the Commonwealth.*

Digests, Compilations, etc.;

Metcalf, Theron (ed.). *The General Laws of Massachusetts from the Adoption of the Constitution to February 1822*, with the Constitutions of the United States and of this Commonwealth. . . . Revised and Published by Authority of the Legislature . . . by Asahel Stearns and Samuel Shaw, Commissioners (2 vols. Boston, 1823).

———. *The General Laws of Massachusetts from June 1822 to June 1827* (Vol. III of above. Boston, 1827).

Thomas, Isaiah (ed.). *The Perpetual Laws of the Commonwealth of Massachusetts from the Establishment of the Constitution to the First Session of the General Court, A. D. 1788* (2 vols., Worcester, Mass., MDCCLXXXVIII and MDCCLXXXIX). Vol. II contains the laws from May 1788 to January 1799.

——— and Andrews, Ebenezer (eds.). *The Perpetual Laws of the Commonwealth of Massachusetts from the Establishment of the Constitution in the Year 1780 to the End of the Year 1800;* with the Constitution of the United States of America and of the Commonwealth Prefixed; to Which is Added an Appendix Containing Acts and Clauses of Acts from the Laws of the Late Colony, Province and State of Massachusetts, which Either are Unrevised or Respect the Title of Real Estate (3 vols., Boston, 1801).

Session Laws;
Acts and Resolves Passed by the Legislature of Massachusetts in the Year 1816, 1834, 1836, 1840, 1842, 1843, 1844, 1845, 1852, 1857 (Boston, 1816, 1834, 1836, 1840, 1842, 1843, 1844, 1845, 1852, 1857).
MASSACHUSETTS ANTI-SLAVERY SOCIETY. *Annual Reports* (Boston, 1833–1853).
MASSACHUSETTS HISTORICAL SOCIETY. *Collections*, 1792– (Vol. I —, Cambridge, Mass., 1792–).
MATHER, COTTON. *Magnalia Christi Americana, or Ecclesiastical History of New England, 1620–1698* (2 vols., Hartford, 1855).
———. *Magnalia Christi Americana: or the Ecclesiastical History of New-England, from Its First Planting in the Year 1620 unto the Year of Our LORD, 1698. In Seven Books by the Reverend and Learned Cotton Mather, M.A. and Pastor of the North Church in Boston, New England* (London, MDCCII).
MATHEWS, LOIS K. (Mrs. Rosenberry). *Expansion of New England. A Spread of New England Settlement and Institutions to the Mississippi River, 1620–1865* (Boston and New York, 1909).
MEAD, NELSON P. "Land System of the Connecticut Towns," in *Political Science Quarterly*, XXI, No. 1, pp. 59–76, March 1906.
MECKLIN, JOHN M. "The Black Codes," in *Southern Atlantic Quarterly*, XVI, 248–259, July, 1917.
———. "The Evolution of the Slave Status in American Democracy," in *Journal of Negro History*, II, 105–125, April–July, 1917.
MERENESS, NEWTON DENNISON. *Maryland as a Proprietary Province* (New York and London, 1901).
MERRIAM, GEORGE SPRING. *The Negro and the Nation: a History of American Slavery and Enfranchisement* (New York, 1906).
MEYER, BALTHASAR HENRY; MACGILL, CAROLINE E.; ET AL. *History of Transportation in the United States before 1860* (Carnegie Institution of Washington, Publ. No. 215 C. Washington, 1917).
MEYER, DR. RUDOLF. *Heimstätten und andere Wirthschaftsgesetze der Vereinigten Staaten von Amerika, von Canada, Russland, China, Indien, Rumänien, Serbien und England* (Berlin, 1883).
MICHIGAN. Laws, Statutes, etc.:
Laws of the Territory (4 vols., Lansing, 1871–84).
The Revised Statutes of the State of Michigan, 1846 (Detroit, 1846).
Session Laws;
Acts Passed by the Legislature of the State of Michigan, 1835– (Detroit and Lansing, Mich., 1836–).
MILLER, WILLIAM DAVIS. "The Narraganset Planters," in American Antiquarian Society, *Proceedings*, XLIII (n.s.), 49–115, April 19, 1933.
MINNESOTA. Laws, Statutes, etc.:
The Public Statutes of the State of Minnesota [1849–1858] (Saint Paul, 1859).
Session Laws;
General Laws Passed by the Legislature of the State of Minnesota, 1857– (Saint Paul, 1858 –).
MISSISSIPPI. Laws, Statutes, etc.:
Revised Codes of the Laws of Mississippi in Which are Comprised All Such Acts of the General Assembly of a Public Nature, as Were in Force at the End of the Year 1823, with a General Index (Natchez, Miss., 1824).
Digests, Compilations, etc.;
Howard, V. E. and Hutchinson, A. (compl.). *Statutes of a Public and General Nature; with Constitutions; also Appendix Containing Acts of Congress; and a Manual for Clerk's, Sheriffs, etc.* (New Orleans, 1840).
Hutchinson, A. (compl.). *An analytical compilation of the Public and General Statutes of Territory and State; with Reference to Local and Private Acts from 1798 to 1848, also Constitutions, Cessions by Choctaw and Chicasaw Indians and Acts of Congress* (Jackson, 1848).
Toulmin, Harry (rev.). *Statutes of the Territory, Revised and Digested Under Authority* (Natchez, 1807).
Session Laws;
Laws of the State of Mississippi Passed at the Sessions of the General Assembly, 1801– (Jackson, 1802–).
———. DEPARTMENT OF ARCHIVES AND HISTORY. *The Mississippi Territorial Archives*, 1798–1803 (D. Rowland, ed., vols. 1– , Nashville, Tenn., 1905–).
MISSISSIPPI HISTORICAL SOCIETY. *Publications* (14 vols. in 13, Oxford, 1898–1914).
MISSISSIPPI VALLEY HISTORICAL ASSOCIATION. *Proceedings* (9 vols., Cedar Rapids, Iowa, 1909–1917).
MISSISSIPPI VALLEY HISTORICAL REVIEW (C. W. Alvord, ed., 1914–1924; M. M. Quaife, ed., 1925– . vols. 1– , Cedar Rapids, Iowa, 1914–).

MISSOURI.
Laws, Statutes, etc.:
Laws of Louisiana and Missouri. Laws of a Public and a General Nature (2 vols., Jefferson City, 1842).
Laws Revised and Digested (2 vols., St. Louis, 1825).
Revised Statutes (St. Louis, 1835).
Revised Statutes (St. Louis, 1845).
Revised Statutes (Jefferson City, 1856).
Digests, Compilations, etc.;
Geyer, Henry S. (ed). *Digest of Laws of Territory Comprising Title to Louisiana.... Treaty of Cession, Organic Laws, Laws of Missouri Territory...; Spanish Regulations for Land Allotment; Laws of United States for Adjusting Land Titles; and Forms for Magistrates* (St. Louis, 1818).
Session Laws;
Acts Passed by the General Assembly of the State of Missouri, 1820– (St. Louis, 1820–).

MISSOURI HISTORICAL REVIEW (published by the State Historical Society of Missouri, vols. 1– , Columbia, 1906–).

MISSOURI HISTORICAL SOCIETY. *Collections* (vols. 1– , St. Louis, 1880–).

MITCHELL AND FLANDERS. *Statutes at Large of Pennsylvania.* See Pennsylvania: Digests, Compilations, etc.

MOODY, VERNIE ALTON. "Slavery on Louisiana Sugar Plantations," in *Louisiana Historical Quarterly,* VII, 191–301, Apr., 1924.

MOORE, GEORGE HENRY. *Notes on the History of Slavery in Massachusetts* (New York, 1866).

MORGAN, EDWIN VERNON. "Slavery in New York; The Status of the Slave under the English Colonial Government," in American Historical Association, *Papers,* V, 337–350, 1891.

MORGAN, LAWRENCE N. "Land Tenure in Proprietary North Carolina," in North Carolina University, *James Sprunt Historical Publications,* XII, No. 1, pp. 41–63, 1912.

MORRIS, RICHARD B. "Primogeniture and Entailed Estates in America," in *Columbia Law Review,* XXVII, 24–51, Jan., 1927.

———. *Studies in the History of American Law with Special Reference to the Seventeenth and Eighteenth Centuries* (New York, 1930).

MORSE, JEDIDIAH (comp.). *The American Gazetteer* (Boston & New York, 1797).

———. *The American Geography; or A View of the Present Situation of the United States of America* (Elizabethtown, N. J., MDCCLXXXIX; 2d. ed., London, 1792).

MORTON, NATHANIEL. *New-Englands' Memorial: or, A Brief Relation of the Most Memorable and Remarkable Passages of the Province of God, Manifested to the Planters of New England in America: With Special Reference to the First Colony Thereof, Called New-Plimouth. Published for the Use and Benefit of Present and Future Generations by Nathaniel Morton, Secretary of the Court for the Jurisdiction of New Plymouth,* Cambridge, 1669. (Reprinted in *New England's Memorial,* by Nathaniel Morton; also Governor Bradford's *History of Plymouth Colony....* Congregational Board of Publication, Boston, 1855).

MORTON, R. L. *The Negro in Virginia Politics, 1865–1902* (Charlottesville, Va., 1919).

MOTLEY, J. M. *Apprenticeship in American Trade Unions* (Johns Hopkins University, *Studies in Historical and Political Science,* XXV, Nos. 11–12. Baltimore, 1907).

MUDDY RIVER. *Muddy River and Brookline Records, 1634–1838* (Brookline Inhabitants, in Town Meeting. Brookline, 1875).

MUNRO, WILLIAM BENNETT. *The Seigniorial System in Canada; a Study in French Colonial Policy* (New York, 1907).

NEBRASKA. Laws, Statutes, etc.:
Laws, Joint Resolutions, and Memorials, Passed by the Legislative Assembly of the Territory of Nebraska, 1857, 1858 (Brunswick, 1857; Omaha, 1859).

NEW AMSTERDAM. *Records.* See New York.

NEW CASTLE, KENT, AND SUSSEX UPON DELAWARE. See Delaware.

NEW ENGLAND. *An Abstract of the Laws of New England.*
See Cotton, John.

NEW HAMPSHIRE (Colony). Laws, Statutes, etc.:
Acts and Laws of His Majesty's Province of New-Hampshire... (Portsmouth, Printed by Daniel Fowle, 1761).

Acts and Laws of His Majesty's Province of New-Hampshire In New England, with Sundry Acts of Parliament. . . . To Which is Prefix'd the Commissions of President John Cutts, Esq., and His Excellency John Wentworth, Esq. (Portsmouth, 1771).
Acts and Laws, Passed by the General Court or Assembly . . . August 1699 . . . (Boston, Printed by Bartholomew Green, and John Allen, 1699).
Acts and Laws, Passed by the General Court or Assembly Of His Majesties Province of New-Hampshire in New England (Boston in New-England, 1716).
Acts and Laws, Passed by the General Court or Assembly of His Majesties Province of New-Hampshire in New England [1696–1725]. (Boston in New England: Printed by B. Green in Portsmouth, 1726).[6]
Temporary Acts and Laws of His Majesty's Province of New-Hampshire (Portsmouth, 1766).
Town Charters, including Grants of Territory within the Present Limits of New Hampshire, made by the Government of Massachusetts and a Portion of the Grants and Charters Issued by the Government of New Hampshire . . . (2 vols. ed. by Albert Stillman Batchellor, Concord, 1894–1895).
——— (State). Laws, Statutes, etc.:
Acts and Laws 1776–1780 of the State of New-Hampshire in America. By Order of the General Assembly. To Which is Prefixed the Resolution of the American Congress, for Establishing a Form of Government in New Hampshire and the Resolve of the Provincial Congress, For Taking up Government in Form with the Declaration of Independence (America. Printed at Exeter, in the State of New Hampshire, MDCCLXXX).
Constitution and Laws of the State of New-Hampshire Together with the Constitution of the United States (Dover, 1805).
The Laws of the State of New-Hampshire, Together with the Declaration of Independence: the Definitive Treaty of Peace between United States of America and His Britannic Majesty: the Constitution of New Hampshire and the Constitution of the United States with Its Proposed Amendments (Portsmouth, Printed by John Melcher, 1792).
The Laws of the State of New-Hampshire, the Constitution of the State of New-Hampshire, and the Constitution of the United States, with Its Proposed Amendments (Portsmouth, Printed by John Melcher, 1797).
Laws of the State of New-Hampshire with the Constitutions of the United States and of the States . . . (Exeter, 1815).
The Laws of the State of New Hampshire with the Constitutions of the United States and of the State Prefixed (Hopkinton, 1830).
The Revised Statutes of the State of New Hampshire, Passed December 23, 1842. To Which are Prefixed the Constitutions of the United States and of the State of New Hampshire (Concord, 1843).
Digests, Compilations, etc.;
The Compiled Statutes of the State of New Hampshire . . . (Concord, 1854).
Batchellor, A. S., and Metcalf, H. H. (eds.). *Laws of New Hampshire Including Public and Private Acts, and Resolves, and the Royal Commissions and Instructions.* With Historical and Descriptive Notes and an Appendix (vols. 1–2, ed. by A. S. Batchellor; vols. 3–7, ed. by H. H. Metcalf. 7 vols., Manchester, 1904–1918).
The Perpetual Laws of the State of New Hampshire from the Session of the General-Court in July 1776, to the Session in December 1788, continued into the Present Year 1789. (Compiled and Arranged to the Wishes of the Gentlemen of the Law, and Under the Direction of the General-Court (Portsmouth, Printed by John Melcher, MDCC, LXXXIX).
Session Laws;
Laws of the State of New-Hampshire Passed June Session (Concord, 1846).
New Hampshire Historical Society. *Collections* (Vol. I– , Concord, 1824–).
New Haven, Conn. *The New Haven Minute Book, 1771–1805* (Unpublished Ms.).
———. *Records of the Colony and Plantation of New Haven from 1638 to 1649*, and *Records of the Colony or Jurisdiction of New Haven from May 1653 to the Union. Together with the New Haven Code of 1656.* Transcribed and edited in accordance with a Resolution of the General Assembly of Connecticut. (Ed. by Charles J. Hoadley. 2 vols., Hartford, 1857, 1858).
New Haven Colony Historical Society. *Ancient Town Records* (2 vols., New Haven, 1917–1919).
———. *Collections* (New Haven, 1907).
———. *Papers* (Vol. I–. New Haven, 1865–).

[6] Regarding this item, the Charlemagne Tower *Catalogue* says: "This is a very nicely executed reprint of the edition of 1716, with the session laws down to 1725–26, but it is thrown upon the world without a word of explanation as to by whom, when, or where it was done." (p. 161).

NEW JERSEY (Colony). *Documents Relating to the Colonial History of the State of New Jersey* (ed. by William Adee Whitehead, F. W. Ricord and W. Nelson. 10 vols., Newark, 1880–1886). Half title, *Archives of the State of New Jersey.*

Laws, Statutes, etc.:

The Laws and Acts of the General Assembly of His Majesties Province of Nova Cæsares or New Jersey, as they were Enacted by the Governour, Council and General Assembly . . . in Divers Sessions, the first of which began in November 1703 (New York. Printed and Sold by William Bradford, 1717).

Digests, Compilations, etc.;

Allinson, Samuel (comp.). *Acts of the General Assembly of the Province of New Jersey . . . 17th Day of April, 1702 to 14th Day of January 1776* (Burlington, MDCCLXXVI).

Kinsey, John (ed.). *The Acts of the General Assembly of the Province of New-Jersey from the Time of the Surrender of the Government . . . to the Fourth Year of the Reign of King George the Second* . . . (Philadelphia. Printed and Sold by William and Andrew Bradford, MDCCXXXII).

Leaming, Aaron, and Spicer, Jacob (eds.). *The Grants, Concessions, and Original Constitutions of the Province of New Jersey. The Acts Passed During the Proprietary Governments, and other Material-Transactions before the Surrender thereof to Queen Anne. . . .* (Philadelphia. Printed by William Bradford, 1758).[7]

Nevill, Samuel (ed.). *The Acts of the General Assembly . . . from the Time of the Surrender of the Government . . . to . . . the twenty-fifth year of the reign of King George the Second* (Philadelphia. Printed by William Bradford . . . MDCCLII).

The Acts of the General Assembly . . . from the Year 1753 . . . to the Year 1761 . . . (Vol. II, Woodbridge in New Jersey, Printed by James Parker, MDCCLXI).

——— (State). Laws, Statutes, etc.:

Laws of the State of New-Jersey. Revised and Published under Authority of the Legislature (Trenton, 1821).

Revised Statutes of the State of New Jersey (Trenton, 1847).

Digests, Compilations, etc.;

Compiled Statutes [1709–1910] (5 vols., Newark, 1911).

Hood, John (compl.). *Index to Colonial and State Laws between 1663 and 1877, inclusive* (Trenton, 1877).

Paterson, William (reviser). *Laws of the State of New Jersey Revised and Published under the Authority of the Legislature* (New Brunswick, N. J., MDCCC).

Wilson, Peter (comp.). *Acts of the Council and General Assembly of the State of New-Jersey, from the Establishment of the Present Government . . . to . . . the 24th Day of December, 1783 . . .* (Trenton, M.DCC.LXXXIV).

Sessions Laws;

An Act Respecting Slaves. Passed at Trenton, March 14, 1798 (Trenton, 1798).

Laws [Acts] Passed by the Legislature of the State of New Jersey 1776– (Trenton, 1776–).

NEW JERSEY HISTORICAL SOCIETY. *Proceedings*, 1845– (1st series, I–X, 1845–1866; 2d series, I–XIII, 1867–1895; 3d series, I– . Newark, N. J., 1847–).

NEW MEXICO. Laws, Statutes, etc.:

Laws of the Territory [Kearney Code] (Santa Fe, 1846).

Revised Statutes (Santa Fe, 1856).

Laws of the Territory of New Mexico Passed by the Legislative Assembly, Session of 1858–1859 (Santa Fe, 1859).

NEW NETHERLAND. See New York.

NEW PLYMOUTH. See Brigham and Plymouth Colony.

NEW YORK CITY (Colony. New Amsterdam).

The Charter of the City of New-York. John Montgomery, Esq., Governor (New York, 1801).

The Charter of the City of New-York; Printed by Order of the Mayor, Recorder, Aldermen and Commonalty of the City, Aforesaid. To Which is Annexed, the Act of the General Assembly Confirming the Same (New York, 1735).

The Records of New Amsterdam from 1653 to 1674 Anno Domini. Published under the Authority of the City. (Vol. 1 ed. by Westbrook and Fernow; vols. 2–7 ed. by E. B. O'Callaghan. 7 vols., New York City, 1897.)

——— CITY. *By-Laws and Ordinances of the Mayor, Aldermen, and Commonalty of the City of New York.* Published by the Authority of the Common Council of New York (New York, 1839).

[7] Known as Leaming and Spicer's *Laws*, prepared under authority of an act of the Assembly, passed in 1752, it is the largest work issued from the press of William Bradford. (*Tower Catalogue*, p. 165).

NEW YORK (Colony. New Netherland). Laws, Statutes, etc.:
Acts of Assembly, Passed in the Province of New-York, from 1691, to 1718 (Printed by John Baskett ... and by the Assigns of Thomas Newcomb, and Henry Hills, deceas'd. London, MDCCXIX).
Acts of the Assembly Passed in the Province of New-York, from 1691, to 1725 [really July 1724] ... (Printed and Sold by William Bradford. New York, 1726).
The Colonial Laws of New York from the Year 1664 to the Revolution, Including the Charters to the Duke of York, the Commissions and Instructions to Colonial Governors ... the Charters of Albany and New York and the Acts of the Colonial Legislature from 1691 to 1775 inclusive (5 vols., Albany, 1894).
East-Hampton Book of Laws. June ye 24th 1665 (In New York Historical Society, *Collections*, I, 305–428, 1809. New York, 1811).
The Laws & Acts of the General Assembly for Their Majesties Province of New-York.... As they were Enacted in Divers Sessions.... April 9th, 1691–September 22, 1693 (At New York, Printed and Sold by William Bradford ... 1694). Facsimile reprint (The Grolier Club, New York, 1894).
The Laws, of Her Majesties Colony of New-York, as They were Enacted ... in Divers Sessions... [April the 9th, 1691–12th November 1709] ([New York] Printed by William Bradford ... 1710).
The Laws, of Her Majesties Colony of New-York, as They were Enacted ... in Divers Sessions ... April the 9th ... 1691 [*–November 4, 1713*] (New York. Printed by William Bradford ... 1713).
The Laws of Her Majesties Colony of New-York, as They Were Enacted ... in divers Sessions ... April 9th, 1691 [*–June 1719*] (Printed by William Bradford. New York, 1719). Facsimile edition (The Grolier Club, New York, 1894).
Laws of the Colony of New York, Passed in the Years 1774 and 1775 ... (Albany, 1888).
Laws of New York, from the Year 1691, to 1751, Inclusive ... (Printed by James Parker, New York, MDCCLII).
Laws of New-York, from the 11th Nov. 1752, to 22d May 1762.... (The Second Volume, with a Table Common to both Volumes. Digested by William Livingston, & William Smith, Jun. Printed by William Weyman, New York, MDCCLXII).
Laws of New-York, from the Year 1691, to 1773 Inclusive ... (2 vols., New-York, 1774).
Laws and Ordinances of New Netherland 1638–1674. See O'Callaghan.
———. *Colonial Tracts* (4 vols., Albany, 1866–1872). E. B. O'Callaghan (ed.), vols. 1–3.
———. *Documents Relative to the Colonial History of New York.* See O'Callaghan.
——— (STATE). Laws, Statutes, etc.:
Revised Statutes (3 vols., Albany, 1829).
Digests, Compilations, etc.;
Greenleaf, Thomas (ed.). *Laws of the State of New-York Comprising the Constitution, and the Acts of the Legislature, Since the Revolution* (1st ed., 2 vols., 1792; 2d ed., 3 vols., New York, 1797–1798).
Session Laws;
Laws of the State of New York Passed at the Sessions of the Legislature, 1777 ... 1801 (5 vols. Albany, 1886–1887).
Laws of the State of New York from the First to the Twelfth Session inclusive (2 vols., New York, 1789).
Laws of the State of New York [1802–1812] (vols. III–VI, Albany 1804–1812).
Laws of the State of New York, Commencing with the First Session of the Senate and Assembly, after the Declaration of Independence, and the Organization of the New Government of the State, Anno 1777 [April 1782] (Poughkeepsie, N. Y., MDCCLXXXII).
Laws of the State of New York (2 vols., Albany, 1886).
Laws of the State of New York Passed at the Fifty-Third Session of the Legislature Begun and held at the City of Albany, the Fifth Day of January, 1830 (Albany, 1830).
———. *The Documentary History of the State of New York.* See O'Callaghan.
NEW YORK HISTORICAL SOCIETY. *Collections* (vols. I-III, IV-V, New York, 1809–30; 2nd series, vols. I-IV, New York, 1811–59). Vol. I, series 1, contains *East Hampton Book of Laws.*
NEWTON, ARTHUR PERCIVAL. *The Colonising Activities of the English Puritans; the Last Phases of the Elizabethan Struggle with Spain* (New Haven, 1914. Half title: Yale Historical Publications, Miscellany, I).
NIEBOER, HERMAN JEREMIAS. *Slavery as an Industrial System; Ethnological Researches* (The Hague, 1900).

NORTH CAROLINA (Colony). *The Colonial Records of North Carolina, 1662–1776* (W. L. Saunders, ed., 10 vols., Raleigh, 1886–1890). Continued as *The State Records of North Carolina* (W. Clark, ed., vols. 11–26, Winston or Goldsboro, 1895–1907).

———. Laws, Statutes, etc.:

Laws, 1715–1790. See *The Colonial Records of North Carolina,* Vols. XXIII, XXIV, XXV.

Digests, Compilations, etc.;

Davis, James (ed.). *A Collection of All the Public Acts of Assembly, of the Province of North-Carolina: Now in Force and Use*... (Newbern, M, DCC, LI).

———. *A Complete Revisal of All the Acts of the Assembly of the Province of North-Carolina Now in Force and Use* (Newbern, 1773).

——— (State). Laws, Statutes, etc.:

The Revised Statutes of the State of North Carolina passed by the General Assembly at the Session of 1836–1837)... (revised by Frederick Nash, James Iredell and William H. Battle. 2 vols., Raleigh, 1837).

Digests, Compilations, etc.;

Haywood, John. *Manual of the Laws of North Carolina* (Raleigh, 1819).

Iredell, James (ed.). *Laws of the State of North-Carolina,* [1715–1790] (Edenton, MDCCXCI).

Martin, Francois-Xavier. *A Collection of the Private Acts of the General Assembly of the State of North-Carolina from*... *1715 to*... *1790, Inclusive, Now in Force and Use* (Newbern, 1794).

Potter, Henry; Taylor, J. L.; & Yancey, Bartlett (eds.). *Laws of the State of North-Carolina, Including The Titles of Such Statutes and Parts of Statutes of Great Britain as are in Force in Said State; together with The Second Charter Granted by Charles II to the Proprietors of Carolina; The Great Deed of Grant from the Lords Proprietors; The Grant from George II. to Lord Granville*... (2 vols., Raleigh, 1821).

Session Laws;

Acts Passed by the General Assembly of the State of North Carolina... 1800– (Raleigh, 1801–).

NORTHRUP, ANSEL JUDD. *Slavery in New York* (New York State Library, *Bulletin,* History, No. 4, Albany, 1900).

NORTHUP, SOLOMON. *Twelve Years a Slave. Narrative of Solomon Northup, a Citizen of New-York, Kidnapped in Washington City in 1841, and Rescued in 1853 from a Cotton Plantation near the Red River in Louisiana* (ed. by D. A. Wilson, Buffalo, N. Y., 1853).

NORWALK, CONN. *Ancient Records.* See Hall, Edwin (ed.).

NOTT, SAMUEL. *Slavery and the Remedy, or; Principles and Suggestions for a Remedial Code* (Boston, 1856).

O'CALLAGHAN, EDMUND BAILEY (ed.). *The Documentary History of the State of New York.* Arranged under the Direction of the Hon. Christopher Morgan, Secretary of State (4 vols. quarto. Albany, 1849–1851).

——— (ed.). *Documents Relative to the Colonial History of the State of New York* (14 vols., Albany, 1861).

———. *History of New Netherland; or New York under the Dutch* (2 vols., Philadelphia and New York, 1846–1848).

———. *Laws and Ordinances of New Netherland, 1638 to 1674.* Compiled and Translated from the Original Dutch Records in the Office of the Secretary of State (Albany, 1868).

——— (trans. & ed.). *Voyages of the Slavers St. John and Arms of Amsterdam, 1659–1663, together with Additional Papers Illustrative of the Slave Trade under the Dutch* (New York Colonial Tracts, III. Albany, 1867).

OHIO. Laws, Statutes, etc.:

Revised Acts of a General Nature Passed by the General Assembly, 1831 (Columbus, O., 1831).

Session Laws;

Acts of the State of Ohio Passed by the General Assembly of the State of Ohio, 1803, 1804, 1805, 1806, 1807, 1818 (Chillicothe, O., 1803, 1804, 1805, 1806, 1807, 1818).

Acts of a General Nature Passed by the General Assembly of the State of Ohio, 1831, 1841, 1850 (Columbus, 1831, 1841, 1850).

Acts of a General Nature and Local Laws and Joint Resolutions Passed by the General Assembly of the State of Ohio, 1857, 1858, 1859 (Columbus, 1857, 1858, 1859).

Acts of a Local Nature Passed by the General Assembly of the State of Ohio, 1843 (Columbus, 1843).

OLMSTED, FREDERICK LAW. A *Journey in the Back Country* (New York, 1860).

———. *A Journey in the Seaboard Slave States in the Years 1853–1854. With Remarks on Their Economy.* Originally Issued in 1856. With Biographical Sketch by Frederick Law Olmsted, Jr., and Introduction by William P. Trent (2 vols., New York and London, 1904).

———. A *Journey through Texas; or, A Saddle-Trip on the Southwestern Frontier* (New York & London, 1857).

ORCUTT, REV. SAMUEL. *A History of the Old Town of Stratford and the City of Bridgeport, Connecticut* (2 vols. Published under the Auspices of the Fairfield County Historical Society. New Haven, Conn., 1886).

——— AND BEARDSLEY, AMBROSE. *The History of the Old Town of Derby, Connecticut, 1642–1880, with Biographies and Genealogies* (Springfield, Mass., 1880).

OREGON (State). Laws, Statutes, etc.:

Digests, Compilations, etc.;

Deady, M. P. (comp.). *The Organic and General Laws of Oregon, 1845–1864* (Portland, Oregon, 1866).

Session Laws;

Laws Passed by the Legislative Assembly of the State of Oregon, 1859– (Salem, 1859–).

OREGON (Territory). Laws, Statutes, etc.:

Session Laws;

Statutes of a General Nature Passed by the Legislative Assembly of the Territory of Oregon, 1850, 1855, 1856 (Oregon City, Salem, 1850, 1856).

ORFIELD, MATTHIAS NORDBERG. *Federal Land Grants to the States, with Special Reference to Minnesota* (University of Minnesota, *Studies in the Social Sciences*, No. 2. Minneapolis, 1915).

ORIGINAL NARRATIVES IN EARLY AMERICAN HISTORY (Reproduced under the Auspices of the American Historical Association. General editor, J. Franklin Jameson. Vols. I– . New York, 1906– . See especially: Vol. VI, *Bradford's History of Plymouth Plantations;* Vol. IX, *Johnson's Wonder-Working Providence.*

OSGOOD, HERBERT LEVI. *The American Colonies in the Seventeenth Century* (3 vols., New York and London, 1904–1907).

OTEY, ELIZABETH LEWIS. *The Beginnings of Child Labor Legislation* (vol. VI of *Report on Condition of Woman and Child Wage-Earners in the United States*, Senate Document, 61 Cong., 2 sess., No. 645, Washington, 1910).

PARMELEE, MAURICE FARR. "The Rise of Modern Humanitarianism," in *American Journal of Sociology*, XXI, 345–359, Nov., 1915.

PARSONS, MRS. ELSIE (CLEWS). See Clews.

[PEMBERTON, T.] *A Topographical and Historical Description of Boston, 1794. By the Author of the Historical Journal of the American War* (Massachusetts Historical Society, *Collections for the Year 1794*, 1st series, III, 241–304. Reprint of 1810).

PENNSYLVANIA (Colony). *Colonial Records* (16 vols. Philadelphia, 1852; Harrisburg, 1851–53).

———. Laws, Statutes, etc.:

The Acts of the Assembly of the Province of Pennsylvania. . . . Together with the Royal, Proprietary, City and Borough Charters; . . . (Philadelphia, Printed and Sold by Hall and Sellers, . . . MDCCLXXV).

A Collection of All the Laws of the Province of Pennsylvania Now in Force. Published by Order of the Assembly (Philadelphia; Printed and Sold by B. Franklin. M,DCC,XLII).

A Collection of Charters and Other Public Acts Relating to the Province of Pennsylvania (Philadelphia, 1740).

The Frame of the Government of the Province of Pennsilvania . . . together with certain Laws Agreed Upon in England by the Governour and Divers Free-men of the Aforesaid Province ([London?], 1682).

The Laws of the Province of Pennsilvania Collected into One Volume . . . (Printed and Sold by Andr. Bradford in Philadelphia, 1714).

The Laws of the Province of Pennsilvania, Passed by the Governour and General Assemblies of said Province, held at Philadelphia in the Years 1715, 1717 and 1718 . . . (Philadelphia, Printed and Sold by Andrew Bradford . . . MDCCXVIII).

The Laws of the Province of Pennsylvania: Now in Force, Collected into one Volume . . . (Philadelphia. Printed and Sold by Andrew Bradford, MDCCXXVIII).[8]

Digests, Compilations, etc.;

Dallas, Alexander James (ed.). *Laws of the Commonwealth of Pennsylvania from the fourteenth day of October, 1700 to the [twenty-seventh day of February 1801]*. Republished under the Authority of the Legislature. (4 vols. Vols. 1–3, Philadelphia, 1793–1795; vol. IV, Lancaster, 1801).

Galloway, Joseph (ed.). *The Acts of the Assembly of the Province of Pennsylvania. . . . And an Appendix, Containing such Acts, and Parts of Acts relating to Property, as are Expired, Altered, or Repealed. Together with the Royal, Proprietary, City and Borough Charters; and the Original*

[8] First printed collection of Pennsylvania laws.

Concessions of the Honourable William Penn to the First Settlers of the Province (Philadelphia, MDCCLXXV).

Kinsey, John (ed.). *A Collection of All the Laws of the Province of Pennsylvania: now in Force...* (Philadelphia, Printed and Sold by B. Franklin, MDCC, XLII). Prefixed by *The Charters of the Province of Pensilvania and City of Philadelphia* (Philadelphia, Printed and Sold by B. Franklin, MDCCXLII).

Staughton, George; Mead, Benjamin N.; McCamant, Thomas (eds.). *Charter to William Penn and Laws of the Province of Pennsylvania, Passed between the Years 1682 and 1700, Preceeded by the Duke of York's laws in Force from the Year 1676 to the Year 1682* (Harrisburg, 1879). Cover title, *Duke of York's Book of Laws, 1682–1700.*

Weiss, Lewis, and Brockden, Charles (eds.). *The Charters and Acts of the Assembly of the Province of Pennsylvania. Containing the Charters of the Said Province, and the City, Boroughs and Towns Thereof; The Titles of all the Laws of the Said Province, Since Its First Establishment Down to the Year 1700: The Acts of the Said Assembly from the Year 1700 to 1743, Now in Force; and the Royal Confirmation and Repeals of the Said Acts.* Compared with the Public Records (2 vols. in one folio. Philadelphia, MDCCLXII).

Session Laws;

An Act for Incorporating the Society, for the Relief of Poor, Aged and Infirm Masters of Ships, their Widows and Children in Philadelphia.... Passed Feb. 24, 1770 (Philadelphia, 1770).

The Acts of the General Assembly of the Commonwealth of Pennsylvania.... And an Appendix, containing the Laws now in Force, Passed Between the 30th day of September 1775, and the Revolution ... (Philadelphia, Printed and Sold by Francis Bailey, M,DCC,LXXXII).

Acts Passed by the General Assembly of the Commonwealth of Pennsylvania, 1776 (Philadelphia, 1782). Contains the laws passed between September 30, 1775 and the Revolution.

——— (State). Laws, Statutes, etc.:

Acts of the General Assembly of the Commonwealth of Pennsylvania. Laws of the Commonwealth (publ. by T. Mc K. Thompson and John Bioren. Vols. V, VI, VII, VIII, Lancaster, etc., 1803, 1804, 1806, 1808).

General Index to Laws . . 1700–1812, 1812–1822 (2 vols., printed by John Bioren, Philadelphia, 1812, 1823).

Laws of the Commonwealth of Pennsylvania from ... 1700–1802 ... (6 vols., Printed by M. Carey and J. Bioren. Philadelphia, 1803).

Laws of the Commonwealth of Pennsylvania from ... 1802–1808.... (Vols. VII and VIII. Printed by J. Bioren. Philadelphia, 1806–1808).

Laws of the Commonwealth of Pennsylvania from ... 1700 to 1810 (4 vols., Printed by J. Bioren. Philadelphia, 1810).

Laws of the Commonwealth of Pennsylvania from ... 1700 to 1822 (vols. V, VI, VII. Printed by John Bioren, Philadelphia, 1812–1822).

Digest, Compilations, etc.;

McKean, Chief Justice Thomas (ed.). *The Acts of the General Assembly of the Commonwealth of Pennsylvania Carefully Compared with the Originals. And an Appendix, Containing the Laws Now in Force, Passed between the 30th Day of September 1775, and the Revolution. Together with the Declaration of Independence; the Constitution of the State of Pennsylvania; and the Articles of Confederation of the United States of America....* (Philadelphia, MDCCLXXXII).

Mitchell, James T., and Flanders, Henry (eds.). *The Statutes at Large of Pennsylvania from 1682–1801* (16 vols., Harrisburg, 1896–1911).

Session Laws;

The Acts of the General Assembly, of the Common-Wealth of Pennsylvania, Enacted into Laws, since the Declaration of Independence on the Fourth Day of July A.D. 1776 (Philadelphia, MDCCLXXIX).

Laws of the General Assembly of the Commonwealth of Pennsylvania. Passed at the Session of 1848 in the Seventy-Second Year of Independence (Harrisburg, 1848).

Pennsylvania Historical Society. *Memoirs of the Historical Society of Pennsylvania* (14 vols., Philadelphia, 1826–1895).

A Perfect Description of Virginia, Being a Full and True Relation of the Present State of the Plantation, Their Health, Peace, and Plenty. . . . London, 1649 (reprinted in P. Force (ed.), *Tracts and Other Papers*, II, No. 8).

Persons, Charles E.; Parton, Mabel; Moses, Mabelle; and Three "Fellows". *Labor Laws and Their Enforcement, with Special Reference to Massachusetts* (ed. by Susan M. Kingsbury in the Fellowship Foundation of the Massachusetts State Federation of Women's Clubs, 1905–1909, New York, 1911).

PHILLIPS, SAMUEL L. *A Treatise on the Law of Mechanics' Lien on Real and Personal Property* (Boston, 1874).
PHILLIPS, ULRICH BONNELL. *American Negro Slavery; A Survey of the Supply, Employment and Control of Negro Labor as Determined by the Plantation Régime* (New York & London, 1918).
———. *The Decadence of the Plantation System in the South* (American Academy of Political and Social Science, *Annals*, XXV, No. 589. Philadelphia, 1910).
———. "The Economic Cost of Slaveholding in the Cotton Belt," in *Political Science Quarterly*, XX, 257–275, June, 1905.
———. "The Economics of the Plantation," in *South Atlantic Quarterly*, II, 231–236, July, 1903.
———. *A History of Transportation in the Eastern Cotton Belt to 1860* (New York, 1908).
———. "On the Economics of Slavery, 1815–1860," in American Historical Association, *Report*, 1912, pp. 150–151.
——— (ed.). *Plantation and Frontier, 1649–1863* (*Documentary History of American Industrial Society*, I–II, Cleveland, 1910).
———. "Slave Crime in Virginia," in *American Historical Review*, XX, 336–340, Jan. 1915.
———. "The Slave Labor Problem in the Charleston District," in *Political Science Quarterly*, XXII, 416–439.
PINKERTON, JOHN. *A General Collection of the Best and Most Interesting Voyages of Travel in all Parts of the World; Many of Which are Now First Translated into English* (17 vols., London, 1808–1814).
PLYMOUTH COLONY (Mass.). *The Book of the General Laws of the Inhabitants of the Jurisdiction of New-Plimouth* . . . (Cambridge, Printed by Samuel Green, 1672).
———. *The Book of the General Laws of the Inhabitants of the Jurisdiction of New Plimouth* (Boston, Printed by Samuel Green, 1685).
———. *The Compact with the Charter and Laws of the Colony of New Plymouth; Together with the Charter of the Council at Plymouth, and an Appendix, Containing the Articles of Confederation of the United Colonies of New England, and Other Valuable Documents.* Published Agreeably to a Resolve Passed April 5, 1836 (ed. by William Brigham. Boston, 1836).
———. *A Declaration of the Warrantable Grounds and Proceedings of the First Associates of the Government of New-Plymouth; In Their Laying the First Foundations of this Government, and in their Making Laws, and Disposing of the Lands Within the Same. Together With the General Fundamentals of Their Laws. Enacted, Ordained, and Constituted, by the Authority of the Associates of the Colony of New-Plymouth* (Boston, MDCCLXXIII).
———. *A Patent for Plymouth in New-England, Jan. 16, 1629, To which is Annexed, Extracts from the Records of the Colony*, . . . (Boston, 1751).
———. *Records of the Colony of New Plymouth in New England.* Printed by the Order of the Legislature of the Commonwealth of Massachusetts (vols. 1–8 ed. by Nathaniel B. Shurtleff; vols. 9–12 ed. by David Pulsifer. 12 vols., Boston, 1855–1861).
———. *Records of the Town of Plymouth.* Published by the Order of the Town (ed. by W. T. Davis. 3 vols., Plymouth, 1889–1903).
THE POLITICAL SCIENCE QUARTERLY (published by Columbia University, Faculty of Political Science, vols. 1– , Boston & New York, 1886–).
POOLE, WILLIAM FREDERICK. *Anti-Slavery Opinions before the Year 1800. . . .* (Cincinnati, 1873).
POORE, BEN: PERLEY (compiler). *The Federal and State Constitutions, Colonial Charters, and other Organic Laws of the United States* (2 vols., 2d ed., Washington, 1878).
PRACTICAL RULES FOR THE MANAGEMENT AND MEDICAL TREATMENT OF NEGRO SLAVES, IN THE SUGAR COLONIES. By a Professional Planter (London, 1811).
QUARTERLY JOURNAL OF ECONOMICS (published for Harvard University; vols. 1– , Boston & Cambridge, 1886–).
QUINCY, JOSIAH. *A Municipal History of Boston During Two Centuries from September 17, 1630 to September 17, 1830* (Boston, 1852).
RAPER, CHARLES LEE. *North Carolina. A Study in English Colonial Government* (New York, 1904).
RAYMOND, JAMES. *Prize Essay, on the Comparative Economy of Free and Slave Labour in Agriculture* (Frederick, Md., 1827).
REINSCH, PAUL SAMUEL. *American Legislatures and Legislative Methods* (American State Series, ed. by W. W. Willoughby. New York, 1907).
———. "The English Common Law in the Early American Colonies," in *Select Essays in Anglo-American Legal History*, I, 367–415, 1907. (Also in University of Wisconsin, *Economics, Political Science, and History Series, Bulletin*, II, No. 4, pp. 397–456, Oct., 1899).

RHODE ISLAND (Colony). Laws, Statutes, etc.:
Acts and Laws of the English Colony of Rhode Island and Providence-Plantations in New England, in America (Newport, MDCCLXVII. Printed and Sold by Samuel Hall). Prefixed by *The Charter, Granted by His Majesty, King Charles II. to the Governor and Company of the English Colony of Rhode-Island and Providence-Plantations....* (Newport... MDCCLXVII).
Acts and Laws of the English Colony of Rhode Island in New-England, in America, passed Since the Revision in June 1767. Compared and Corrected by the Secretary. Newport, 1772 (Facsimile reprint, Providence, 1893).
Acts and Laws of His Majesties Colony of Rhode-Island, and Providence-Plantations in America. Boston in New England: Printed by John Allen for Nicholas Boone, 1179 [*sic*]. Bound with *The Charter and the Acts and Laws of His Majesties Colony of Rhode-Island, and Providence-Plantations in America*, 1719. (A Fac-Simile Reprint with a Bibliographical and Historical Introduction by Sidney S. Rider, Providence, R. I., 1895).
Acts and Laws, of His Majesty's Colony of Rhode-Island, and Providence-Plantations,... To which is Prefixed the Charter Granted by His Majesty King Charles the Second, to the Colony of Rhode Island and Providence Plantations... (Newport, R. I., Printed by James Franklin, 1730).
Acts and Laws of His Majesty's Colony of Rhode-Island and Providence Plantations, in America. (Newport, 1730 [-36?]).
Acts and Laws of His Majesty's Colony of Rhode Island, and Providence-Plantations, In America.... (Newport, Rhode-Island. Printed by the Widow Franklin... MDCCXLV). Prefixed by *The Charter Granted by His Majesty King Charles II to the Governor and Company of the English Colony of Rhode Island and Providence Plantations In New England In America....* (Newport, Rhode-Island. Printed by the Widow Franklin... M,DCC,XLIV).
——— (Colony and State). Laws, Statutes, etc.:
Digests, Compilations, etc.;
Bartlett, John Russell (ed.). *Index to the Printed Acts and Resolves of, and of the Petitions and Reports to the General Assembly of the State of Rhode Island and Providence Plantations from the Year 1758 to 1850* (Providence, 1856). Continued as follows:
Index......1850–1862 (Providence, 1863).
Index......1863–1873 (Joshua M. Addeman, Providence, 1875).
Index......1873–1899 (Charles P. Bennett, ed., Providence, 1875).
Session Laws;
Acts and Resolves, Oct. 1747 to Oct. 1800. (Fac-simile reprints published by J. Harry Bongartz. 50 copies printed).
———. *Records of the Colony (and of the State) of Rhode Island, and Providence Plantations, in New England. Printed by Order of the General Assembly* (ed. by J. R. Bartlett. 10 vols. Providence, R. I., 1856–1865).
——— (State). Laws, Statutes, etc.:
The Public Laws of the State of Rhode-Island and Providence Plantation, as Revised by a Committee and Finally Enacted by the Honourable General Assembly, at Their Session in January, 1798. To Which are Prefixed the Charter, Declaration of Independence, Articles of Confederation, Constitution of the United States and President Washington's Address of September, 1796 (Providence, 1798).
Revised Statutes (Providence, 1857).
Session Laws, etc.;
Acts and Resolves of the General Assembly of the State of Rhode Island and Providence Plantations Passed January, A.D., 1853, 1854 (Providence, 1853, 1854).
Public Laws Passed by the General Assembly of the State of Rhode Island, 1798— (Providence, 1798—).
RHODE ISLAND HISTORICAL MAGAZINE. (July 1880–April 1887, Vols. I–VII. Newport, R. I., 1880–1887).
RHODE ISLAND HISTORICAL SOCIETY. *Collections*, 1827– (Providence, 1827–19–). Irregular before 1903. Publication suspended 1903–1917. Quarterly after 1918.
———. *Proceedings*, 1872–1891, 1900–1914 (Providence, R. I., 1872–1892, 1902–1914).
———. *Publications*, 1893–1901 (Providence, 1893–1901). Discontinued Jan. 1901. *Publications* included *Proceedings*, 1893–1900.
RHODES, JAMES FORD. *History of the United States from the Compromise of 1850* (8 vols., New York, 1893–1919).
———. *History of the United States from the Compromise of 1850 to the McKinley-Bryan Campaign of 1896* (new ed., New York, 1920).

RICHARDSON, JAMES D. *A Compilation of the Messages and Papers of the Presidents, 1789–1897* (10 vols. Published by Authority of Congress. Washington, 1896–1899).

RIPLEY, WILLIAM ZEBINA. *The Financial History of Virginia, 1609–1776* (Columbia University, *Studies in History, Economics, and Public Law*, IV, No. 1. New York, 1893).

ROCHEFOUCAULD LIANCOURT. See La Rochefoucauld Liancourt.

ROSENBERRY, MRS. LOIS KIMBALL (MATHEWS). See MATHEWS.

RUFFIN, EDMUND. "Slavery and Free Labor Defined and Compared," in *Southern Planter*, XIX, 723–741, Dec., 1859.

RUHLAND, GUSTAV. *System der Politischen Oekonomie* (3 vols., Berlin, 1903–1908).

RUSSELL, JOHN H. *The Free Negro in Virginia, 1619–1865* (Johns Hopkins University, *Studies in Historical and Political Science*, XXXI, No. 3. Baltimore, 1913).

SAFFIN, JOHN. "A Brief and Candid Answer to a Late Printed Sheet Entituled 'The Selling of Joseph'" (Boston, 1701). See also Colonial Society of Massachusetts, *Transactions*, I, 103 ff.

SAILORS' MAGAZINE. "Shall the United States Shipping Law of 1872 be Sustained?", in *Sailors' Magazine*, XLV, 353–357, Dec., 1873 (Reprinted from the *Christian Union*, Nov. 13).

———. AND SEAMEN'S FRIEND. "The Abolition of Advance Wages to Seamen—Why Urged and Why Opposed. What Follows, if it be Secured?", in *Sailors' Magazine and Seamen's Friend*, LIII, 97–105, April, 1881.

———. See also Vol. XXIX, July 1857, 382–383; August 1857.

SANBORN, JOHN BELL. *Congressional Grants of Land in Aid of Railways* (Wisconsin University, *Bulletin* No. 30, *Economics, Political Science and History Series*, II, No. 3. Madison, 1899).

———. "Some Political Aspects of Homestead Legislation", in *American Historical Review*, VI, 19–37, Oct. 1, 1900.

SARTORIUS VON WALTERSHAUSEN, AUGUST. *Die Arbeits-Verfassung der Englischen Kolonien in Nord-Amerika* (Strassburg, 1894).

SATO, SHOSUKE. *History of the Land Question in the United States* (Johns Hopkins University, *Studies in Historical and Political Science*, IV, Nos. 7–9. Baltimore, 1886).

SAVAGE, EDWARD H. *Police Records and Recollections, or, Boston by Daylight and Gaslight for Two Hundred and Forty Years* (Boston, 1873).

SAYLES, JOHN AND HENRY. See Texas.

SCHAFER, JOSEPH. *The Origin of the System of Land Grants for Education* (University of Wisconsin, *Bulletin* No. 63, *History Series*, I, No. 1. Madison, Wis., 1902).

SCHLÜTER, HERMAN. *Lincoln, Labor and Slavery. A Chapter from the Social History of America* (New York, 1913).

SCOTT, WILLIAM ROBERT. *The Constitution and Finance of English, Scottish, and Irish Joint-Stock Companies to 1720* (3 vols., Cambridge, England, 1910–1912).

[SEABROOK, WHITEMARSH BENJAMIN]. *An Appeal to the People of the Northern and Eastern States on the Subject of Negro Slavery in South Carolina.* By a South Carolinian (New York, 1834).

SEMPLE, ELLEN CHURCHILL. *American History and Its Geographic Conditions* (Boston & New York, 1903).

SEWALL, SAMUEL. *The Selling of Joseph, a Memorial . . . , Boston of the Massachusetts, June 24th, 1790* (Reprinted in Massachusetts Historical Society, *Collections*, 5th ser., VI, 16; *Proceedings*, VII, 161–165, 1863–1864; and in *Historical Magazine*, VIII, 194–197).

SEYBOLT, ROBERT FRANCIS. *Apprenticeship and Apprenticeship Education in Colonial New England and New York* (Teachers College, Columbia University, *Contributions to Education*, No. 85. New York, 1917).

SHELDON, HEZEKIAH SPENCER (ed.). *Documentary History of Suffield in the Colony and Province of Massachusetts Bay in New England, 1660–1749* (3 pts. in 1 vol., Springfield, Mass. 1879–1888).

SHEPHERD, S. See Virginia.

SHERRILL, P. M. "*The Quakers and the North Carolina Manumission Society*," in Trinity College Historical Society, *Papers*, X, 32–51, 1914.

SHERWOOD, HENRY NOBLE. "The Formation of the American Colonization Society," in *Journal of Negro History*, II, 209–228, July 1917.

SHURTLEFF, NATHANIEL B. (ed.). *Records of the Governor and Company of the Massachusetts Bay in New England* (5 vols., Boston, 1853–4).

SIMONS, A. M. *Social Forces in American History* (New York, 1912).

SIOUSSAT, ST. GEORGE LEAKIN. "The Breakdown of the Royal Management of Lands in the Southern Provinces, 1773–1775," in *Agricultural History*, III, 67–98, Apr., 1929.

———. *English Statutes in Maryland* (Johns Hopkins University, *Studies in Historical and Political Science*, XXI, Nos. 11–12. Baltimore, 1903).

SMITH, E. H. *A Discourse Delivered in 1798 . . . before the New York Society for Promoting the Manumission of Slaves* (New York, 1798).
SMITH, FLORENCE P. See Beyer.
SMITH, JOHN. *Works of Captain John Smith, 1608–1631* (Arber ed., Birmingham, Eng., 1884).
SMITH, THEODORE CLARKE. *Parties and Slavery, 1850–1859* (A. B. Hart, ed., *The American Nation: A History*, XVIII. New York and London, 1906).
SMITH, WILLIAM. *History of New-York from the First Discovery to the Year M.DCC.XXXII. To Which is Annexed, A Description of the Country, with a Short Account of the Inhabitants, Their Religious and Political State, and the Constitution of the Courts of Justice in That Colony. With a Continuation from the Year 1732, to the Commencement of the Year 1814* (Albany, 1814).
SMITH, WILLIAM ANDREW. *Lectures on the Philosophy and Practice of Slavery, as Exhibited in the Institution of Domestic Slavery in the United States: With the Duties of Masters to Slaves* (T. O. Summers, ed., Nashville, 1856).
SMITH, WILLIAM ROY. *South Carolina as a Royal Province, 1719–1776* (New York and London, 1903).
SNOW, CALEB H. *History of Boston the Metropolis of Massachusetts from its Origin to the Present Period with Some Account of Its Environs* (Boston, 1825).
SOUTH CAROLINA (Colony). *The Fundamental Constitutions of Carolina* [*Jan. 12, 1681/82*] (London, 1682).
———. Laws, Statutes, etc.:
Digests, Compilations, etc.;
Trott, Nicholas, collector. *The Laws of the Province of South-Carolina, In Two Parts. The First Part Containing all the Perpetual Acts in Force and Use, with the Titles of Such Acts as are Repealed, Expired or Obsolete. . . . The Second Part Containing all the Temporary Acts in Force and Use. To Which is Added the Titles of all the Private Acts, and the Two Charters Granted by King Charles II to the Lords Proprietors of Carolina. And Also the Act of Parliament For Establishing an Agreement with Seven of said Lords Proprietors for the Surrender of their Title and Interest to His Majesty* (2 vols., Charles-Town, MDCCXXXVI).
———. (Colony and State). Laws, Statutes, etc.:
Digests, Compilations, etc.;
Grimké, John Faucheraud (ed.). *The Public Laws of the State of South-Carolina. From Its First Establishment as a British Province Down to the Year 1790, inclusive, in which Is comprehended Such of the Statutes of Great Britain as Were Made of force by the Act of Assembly of 1712. With an Appendix containing such Statutes as have been enacted or declared to be of force . . . the Titles of all the Laws . . . which have been passed in South-Carolina down to the present time. . . . The Constitution of the United States . . . The Newly Adopted Constitution of the State of South-Carolina . . .* (Philadelphia, MDCCXC).
———. (State). Laws, Statutes, etc.:
Digests, Compilations, etc.;
Acts of the General Assembly of the State of South Carolina, from February, 1791, to December, 1794. Both Inclusive. From December, 1795 to December, 1804. Both Inclusive (2 vols. Columbia, 1808).
Cooper, Thomas, and McCord, David J. (eds.). *Statutes at Large of South Carolina* (10 vols., Charleston & Columbia, 1836–1841. Cooper, vols. 1–5; McCord, vols. 6–10).
Session Laws;
Acts and Joint Resolutions, 1784– (Charleston, etc., 1784–).
SOUTH CAROLINA HISTORICAL SOCIETY. *Collections* (5 vols., Charleston, 1857–1897).
SOUTHERN HISTORY ASSOCIATION. *Publications* (11 vols., Washington, D. C., 1897–1907).
SOWERS, DON C. *The Financial History of New York State from 1789 to 1912* (Columbia University, *Studies in History, Economics and Public Law*, LVII, No. 2. New York, 1914).
SPARKS, JARED (ed.). *The Library of American Biography* (25 vols., Boston & London, 1834–1848).
———. *The Writings of Washington; Being His Correspondence, Addresses, Messages, and Other Papers, Official and Private* (12 vols., Boston, 1834–1837).
STEARNS, BERTHA M. "Early Factory Magazines in New England," in *Journal of Economic and Business History*, II, 685–705, August, 1930.
STEINER, BERNARD CHRISTIAN. *History of Education in Connecticut* (Bureau of Education, *Circulars of Information*, No. 2, Washington, 1893).
———. *A History of the Plantation of Menunkatuck and of the Original Town of Guilford, Connecticut, Comprising the Present Towns of Guilford and Madison* (Baltimore, 1897).
———. *History of Slavery in Connecticut* (Johns Hopkins University, *Studies in Historical and Political Science*, XI, Nos. 9–10. Baltimore, 1893).

STEPHEN, SIR JAMES FITZJAMES. *A History of the Criminal Law of England* (3 vols. London, 1883).
STEPHENSON, GEORGE MALCOLM. *The Political History of the Public Lands from 1840–1862, from Pre-emption to Homestead* (Boston, 1917).
STILES, HENRY R. *The History of Ancient Windsor, Connecticut, including East Windsor, South Windsor, and Ellington, Prior to 1768, the Date of their Separation from the Old Town: and Windsor, Bloomfield and Windsor Locks to the Present Time, also the Genealogies and Genealogical Notes of those Families Which Settled Within the Limits of Ancient Windsor, Connecticut, Prior to 1800* (New York, 1859).
STIMSON, FREDERIC JESUP. *The Law of the Federal and State Constitutions of the United States, With an Historical Study of Their Principles, A Chronological Table of English Social Legislation, and A Comparative Digest of the Constitutions of the Forty-Six States* (Boston, 1908).
———. *Popular Law-Making. A Study of the Origin, History, and Present Tendencies of Law-Making by Statute* (New York, 1910).
STOCKWELL, THOMAS B. (ed.). *A History of Public Education in Rhode Island, from 1636 to 1876* (Providence, 1876).
STOKES, ANTHONY. *View of the Constitution of the British Colonies in North America and the West Indies, at the Time the Civil War Broke Out on the Continent of America, in Which Notice is Taken of Such Alterations as Have Happened Since that Time Down to the Present Period* (London, 1783).
STONE, ALFRED HOLT. *The Early Slave Laws of Mississippi* (Mississippi Historical Association, *Publications*, II, 133–145).
———. "Free Contract Labor in the Ante-Bellum South" (in *The South in the Building of the Nation*, V, 134–144).
———. *Mississippi Constitution and Statutes in Reference to Freedmen, and their Alleged Relation to the Reconstruction Acts and War Amendments* (Mississippi Valley Historical Association, *Publications*, IV, 1901).
"The Mulatto Factor in the Race Problem," in *Atlantic Monthly*, XCI, 658–662, May, 1903.
STORRS, RICHARD S. "Manasseh Cutler", in American Historical Association, *Annual Report*, 1896, I, 47–60.
STREET, C. R. (ed.). *Huntington Town Records*. See Huntington, N. Y.
STROUD, GEORGE M. *A Sketch of the Laws Relating to Slavery in the Several States of the United States* (Philadelphia, 1827; 2d ed., Philadelphia, 1856).
SUFFIELD, MASS. *Documentary History of Suffield in the Colony and Province of the Massachusetts Bay in New England, 1660–1749* (Collected, transcribed and published by Hezekiah Spencer Sheldon. Springfield, Mass., 1888).
SUMNER, HELEN L. [MRS. WOODBURY]. *History of Women in Industry in the United States* (Vol. IX of *Report on Condition of Woman and Child-Wage Earners in the United States*, Senate Document, 61 Cong., 2 sess.,No. 645, Washington, 1910).
SWIFT, ZEPHANIAH (ed.). *A Digest of the Laws ... of Connecticut* (2 vols., New Haven, 1822, 1823).
———. *System of the Laws of Connecticut* (6 books in 2 vols. Printed by John Byrne for the Author. Vol. I, 1795; Vol. II, Windham, 1796).
SYDNOR, CHARLES S. "The Free Negro in Mississippi before the Civil War," in *American Historical Review*, XXXII, 769–788, July, 1927.
TAILFER, PATRICK, M. D.; ANDERSON, HUGH, M. D.; AND DOUGLAS, DA. *A True and Historical Narrative of the Colony of Georgia in America from the First Settlement Thereof until this Present Period. ...* (Charles-town, S. C. Printed for the Authors, 1741. Rochester, G. P. Humphrey, 1897. Reprinted in Force, *Tracts*, I, No. 4, Washington, 1835).
TALCOTT, MARY KINGSBURY (ed.). See Connecticut.
TAYLOR, HOWARD CROMWELL. *The Educational Significance of the Early Federal Land Ordinances* (New York, 1922).
TAYLOR, R. H. "Humanizing the Slave Code of North Carolina," in *North Carolina Historical Review*, VII, 323–331, July, 1925.
[TAZEWELL, LITTLETON WALLER]. "Mode of Acquiring Lands in Virginia in Early Times," in *Virginia Historical Register*, II, 190–194, Oct., 1849.
TEICHMUELLER, H. "The Homestead Law," in *American Law Review*, XXXV, 413–418, May-June, 1901.
TEN BROOK, ANDREW. *American State Universities, Their Origin and Progress: a History of Congressional University Land-Grants* (Cincinnati, 1875).
TENNESSEE. Laws, Statutes, etc.:
Digests, Compilations, etc.;
Caruthurs, R. L., and Nicholson, A. O. P. (eds.). *A Compilation of the Statutes of Tennessee of a*

General and Permanent Nature, from the Commencement of the Government to the Present Time (Nashville, 1836).

Scott, Edward (ed.). *Laws of the State of Tennessee, Including those of North Carolina Now in Force in This State, 1715 to the Year, 1820, Inclusive* (2 vols., Knoxville, 1821).

TEXAS. House Committee on Public Lands. *Report* (Published in *Houston Telegraph and Texas Register*, 1839).

———. Laws, Statutes, etc.:

Digests, Compilations, etc.;

Gammel, H. P. N. *The Laws of Texas, 1822–1897. Austin's Colonization Law and Contract; Mexican Constitution of 1824; Federal Colonization Law; Colonization Laws of Coahuila and Texas. . . . Laws and Decrees, with Constitution of Coahuila and Texas . . . etc.* With an Introduction by C. W. Raines (10 vols., Austin, 1898).

Sayles, John and Henry. *Early Laws of Texas, General Laws from 1836–1879 relating to Public Lands, Colonial Contracts, Headrights, Pre-emptions, Grants of Land to Railroads and Other Corporations, Conveyances, Descent, Distribution, Marital Rights, Registration of Wills, Laws relating to the Jurisdiction, Powers and Procedure of Courts, and all Other Laws of General Interest; Also Laws of 1731–1835, as found in the Laws and Decrees of Spain Relating to Land in Mexico, and of Mexico Relating to Colonization: Laws of Coahuila and Texas; Laws of Tamaulipas; Colonial Contracts; Spanish Civil Laws; Orders and Decrees of the Provisional Government of Texas* (3 vols., St. Louis, Mo., 1888).

———. *Sayles' Annotated Civil Statutes of the State of Texas* (2 vols., St. Louis, Mo., 1898).

———. *A Treatise on the Laws of Texas relating to Real Estate, and Actions to Try Title and for Possession of Lands and Tenements* (2 vols., St. Louis, Mo., 1890–1892).

Session Laws;

Laws Passed by the Legislature of the State of Texas, 1846– (Austin, Texas, 1846–).

THOMAS, DAVID YANCEY. "The Free Negro in Florida before 1865," in *South Atlantic Quarterly*, X, 335–345, Oct., 1911.

———. "Southern Non-Slaveholders in the Election of 1860," in *Political Science Quarterly*, XXVI, 222–237, June, 1911.

THOMAS, THADDEUS P. *City Government of Baltimore* (Johns Hopkins University, *Studies in Historical and Political Science*, XIV, No. 2. Baltimore, 1896).

THORPE, FRANCIS NEWTON (ed. and comp.). *The Federal and State Constitutions, Colonial Charters, and Other Organic Laws of the States, Territories, and Colonies, Now or Heretofore Forming The United States of America.* Compiled and Edited under the Act of Congress of June 30, 1906 (7 vols., Washington, Government Printing Office, 1909).

THORPE, SHELDON B. *North Haven Annals. A History of the Town From Its Settlement 1680, to Its First Centennial 1886* (New Haven, Conn., 1892).

TILLINGHAST, JOSEPH ALEXANDER. *The Negro in Africa and America* (American Economic Association, *Publications*, 3d series, III, No. 2, pp. 399–637. New York, 1902).

TORREY, JESSE. *A Portraiture of Domestic Slavery in the United States with Reflections on the Practicability of Restoring the Moral Rights of the Slave, . . .* (Philadelphia, 1817).

TOWLES, JOHN KER. *Factory Legislation of Rhode Island* (American Economic Association, *Quarterly*, 3d series, IX, No. 3, pp. 442–571. New York, 1908).

TREAT, PAYSON JACKSON. *The National Land System, 1785–1820* (New York, 1910).

TREXLER, HARRISON ANTHONY. *Slavery in Missouri, 1804–1865* (Johns Hopkins University, *Studies in Historical and Political Science*, XXXII, No. 2. Baltimore, 1914).

TROTT, NICHOLAS. *The Laws of the British Plantations in America, Relating to the Church, and the Clergy, Religion and Learning.* Collected in One Volume by Nicholas Trott (London. Printed for J. Clarke, 1725).

TRUMBULL, BENJAMIN. *A Complete History of Connecticut, Civil and Ecclesiastical from the Emigration of Its First Planters, from England in the Year 1630, to the Year 1764; and to the Close of the Indian Wars* (2 vols. New London, Conn., 1898).

TRUMBULL, JAMES HAMMOND (ed.). *The True-Blue Laws of Connecticut and New Haven and the False Blue-Laws Invented by the Rev. Samuel Peters to Which are Added Specimens of the Laws and Judicial Proceedings of Other Colonies and Some Blue-Laws of England in the Reign of James I* (Hartford, Conn., 1876).

———. See Hartford, Conn.

TUCKER, ST. GEORGE. *A Dissertation on Slavery: with a Proposal for the Gradual Abolition of It, in the State of Virginia* (Philadelphia, 1796; reprinted New York, 1861).

TURNER, EDWARD RAYMOND. *The Negro in Pennsylvania. Slavery—Servitude—Freedom, 1639–1861* (American Historical Association, Washington, 1911).

TYLER, LYON GARDINER. *England in America, 1580–1652* (A. B. Hart, ed., *The American Nation: A History*. IV. New York & London, 1904).

———. "Land Systems of the Southern Colonies of England and of the South Atlantic States," in *The South in the Building of the Nation*, V, 43–53.

UNITED STATES. *American Archives: Consisting of a Collection of Authentick Records, State Papers, Debates and Letters and Other Notices of Publick Affairs, the Whole Forming a Documentary History of the Origin and Progress of the North American Colonies, of the Causes and Accomplishments of the American Revolution; and of the Constitution of the Government of the United States to the Final Ratification thereof.* In Six Series.... Prepared and Published under the Authority of an Act of Congress (ed. by Peter Force. 4th series, 6 vols., 5th series, 3 vols. Washington, 1837–1853). First, second and third series have never appeared; fifth series left unfinished. Ends with 1776.

———. *American State Papers. Documents, Legislative and Executive of the Congress of the United States* (Selected and edited under the authority of Congress. 38 vols., Washington, 1832–1861):

———. *Annals.* See Congress. Publications.

———. Bureaus, Departments, etc.

Bureau of the Census. See Department of Commerce [and Labor].

Bureau of Education:

Annual Report of the Commissioner, 1867– .

See especially:

Report, June 2, 1868 (2 vols., Washington, 1865): "Educational Land Policy of the United States," pp. 65–78; "Provisions of the Several States Respecting Education in the Constitutions," pp. 83–135.

"Table Showing Area of States and Territories Containing Public Lands and Quantity Devoted to Educational Purposes up to June 30, 1867."

Report, 1888–1889 (2 vols., Washington, 1891): "A General and Comparative Exhibit of Education in the United States and Foreign Countries" I, pt. i, chap. i–x. "Normal Schools, Manual Training Courses of Study, etc., I, pt. ii, chap. xi–xxi.

Report, June 30, 1908 (2 vols., Washington, 1909): "Statistics of Colleges of Agriculture and the Mechanic Arts Endowed by Acts of Congress Approved July 2, 1862, August 30, 1890, and March 4, 1907."

Hough, Franklin B. "*Constitutional Provisions Relating to Education, Literature and Science in the Several States of the American Union* (*Circular of Information* No. 7, Washington, 1875).

See also Eaton.

Department of Commerce and Labor:

Bureau of the Census;

Bulletins;

Cotton Production (No. 107. Washington, 1910).

Census Reports, 1790–1910.

Census of 1820. *Digest of Accounts of Manufacturing Establishments in the United States and of Their Manufactures. Made Under the Direction of the Secretary of State, in Pursuance of a Resolution of Congress, of 30th March, 1822* (Washington, 1823).

Census of 1860. *Population of the United States in 1860 Compiled from the Original Returns of the Eighth Census Under the Direction of the Secretary of the Interior* (Washington, 1864).

Census of 1900. *Occupations at the Twelfth Census* (Special Report, Washington, 1904).

Bureau of Labor. (See Department of Labor, Bureau of Labor Statistics, after 1913).

Annual Reports of the Commissioner of Labor.

Third Annual Report, 1887. Strikes and Lockouts (Washington, 1888).

Bulletins (Vols. I-XXIV, 1895–1912 issued bi-monthly). After 1912, issued irregularly and deal with a number of different topics.

Department of the Interior:

Annual Report of the Secretary, 1849–

See especially:

Report of the Commissioner of the Land Office, I, 1–110, Washington, 1910).

Areas of Acquisitions to the Territories of the United States; Areas of the States, Territories, and Possessions; Diagram Showing the Historical Development of the States (Washington, 1914).

Department of Labor. (See Department of Commerce [and Labor], 1903–1913).
Annual Report of the Secretary, 1913– .
Bureau of Labor Statistics:
Bulletins, 1913– . (Issued irregularly, and deal with various topics).
Wages and Hours of Labor Series:
History of Wages in the United States from Colonial Times to 1928 with List of Published Sources (Bulletin No. 499, Washington, 1929).
See also Albrecht.
Monthly Labor Review, 1915– .
"Wages of Early American Building-Trade Workers", XXX, 5–15, Jan. 1930.
Commissioner of Labor:
Report on Condition of Woman and Child-Wage Earners in the United States (Prepared under the direction of Charles P. Neill, Commissioner of Labor. 19 vols., Washington, 1910–1914).
See especially:
Otey, Elizabeth Lewis. *The Beginnings of Child Labor Legislation in Certain States* (Vol. VI, 1910).
Sumner, Helen L. *History of Women in Industry in the United States* (Vol. IX, 1910).
Women's Bureau (Permanent Bureau in 1920).
Bulletins, 1919– .
History of Labor Legislation for Women in three States, Massachusetts, New York and California . . . and Chronological Development of Labor Legislation for Women in the United States (Bulletin No. 66, Washington, 1929).
Department of the Navy:
Annual Report of the Secretary for the Year 1882 (3 vols., Washington, 1882).
Department of the Treasury:
Report on the Finances. Reports of the Secretary of the Treasury of the United States prepared in Obedience to the Act of May 10, 1800 . . . to Which are Prefixed The Reports of Alexander Hamilton, on Public Credit, A National Bank, Manufactures, and The Establishment of a Mint (2 vols., Washington, 1837).
Land Office:
Reports of the Commissioner, 1817–1848.
Navigation:
Reports of the Commissioner, 1884– .
Public Health (Marine Hospital) Service:
Reports of the Supervising Surgeon-Generals. See Reports for 1873, 1881, 1893, 1899. See also Banks, Drake, Loring and Edwards, House and Senate Documents.
———. Commissions.
Immigration Commission. *Reports of the Immigration Commission* (published as Senate Documents, 42 vols. Washington, 1911). See especially *Abstracts of Reports of the Immigration Commission. Conclusions and Recommendations and View of the Minority* (2 vols., Washington, 1911).
Marine Hospitals. *Report.* See Public Health, Senate Documents.
———. Congress.
House Documents, Reports, etc.:
President's Message [William McKinley] (*House Doc.*, 56 Cong., 1 sess., I, No. 1, pt. 1, 1899).
Report of the Secretary of the Treasury Showing the Application of the Fund for the Relief of Sick and Disabled Seamen and the Description of the Seamen Relieved Thereby, Jan. 4, 1822 (*State Papers, House Doc.*, 17 Cong., 1 sess., II, No. 13, 1822).
Statement of the Cost of Providing for Sick and Disabled Seamen (*State Papers, House Doc.*, 21 Cong., 1 sess., III, No. 68, 1830).
Statement of Expenditures and Receipts of Marine Hospital Fund (*House Doc.*, 35 Cong., 2 sess., I, No. 3, pp. 132–143. In *Finance Report*, 1858).
See Drake, Daniel.
Senate Documents, Reports, etc.;
Letter of Secretary Woodbury (*Senate Doc.*, 24 Cong., 1 sess., IV, No. 297, p. 1, 1835–1836).
The Nation as a Land Owner (*Senate Doc.*, 57 Cong., 1 sess., XVI, No. 183, Feb. 12, 1902). Written by J. D Whepley, and reprinted from *Harper's Weekly*, XLV, 1204–5, 1238, 1283, 1285, Nov. 30, Dec. 7, and Dec. 14, 1901.

Report of Committee on Commerce (*Senate Exec. Doc.*, 24 Cong., 1 sess., IV, No. 332, p. 4, 1836).
Report of Medical Board (*Senate Doc.*, 25 Cong., 2 sess., I, No. 1, pp. 195–211, 1838).
Report on the Foreign Service. "Tabular Statements of Appropriations." (*Senate Misc. Doc.*, 33 Cong., 2 sess., I, No. 16, p. 30, 1854–1855.)
Report on Marine Hospitals (*Senate Exec. Doc.*, 34 Cong., 1 and 2 sess., V, No. 53, pp. 244–247, 1855–1856).
Report on the Subject of Marine Hospitals (Congressional Commission for Examining Marine Hospitals, *Senate Exec. Doc.*, 31 Cong., 2 sess., III, No. 14, pp. 1–48, 1850–1851). See Loring and Edwards.
Reservation, Sale, and Settlement of Certain Lands (*Senate Doc.*, 53 Cong., 2 sess., V, No. 332, 1893–1894).
Publications:
Annals. See *Debates and Proceedings.*
Congressional Globe. (23 Cong. to 42 Cong., Dec. 2, 1833 to March 3, 1873. Washington, 1834–1873).
Congressional Record: Containing the Proceedings and Debates (43d Congress to date. March 4, 1873– . Washington, 1874–19–).
The Debates and Proceedings in the Congress of the United States; with an Appendix containing important State Papers and Public Documents, and all the Laws of a Public Nature; with a copious index. [First to] Eighteenth Congress,—first session: comprising the period from [March 3, 1789] to May 27, 1824, inclusive. Compiled from authentic materials (Gales and Seaton, publishers. 42 vols., Washington, 1834–1856). Running title: *History of Congress;* Half title: *Annals of Congress of the United States.* Commonly known and referred to as *Annals of Congress.* Continued by *Register of Debates in Congress.*
See especially: 1 Cong., 1789–90; 2 Cong., 1791–1793, in Vol. I; 5 Cong., 1797–1799, in Vol. II.
Register of Debates in Congress, Comprising the Leading Debates and Incidents of the Second Session of the Eighteenth Congress [Dec. 6, 1824] to the first Session of the Twenty-fifth Congress, Oct. 16, 1837] together with Appendix containing the most important State Papers and Public Documents to which the Session Has Given Birth; to Which are Added the Laws Enacted During the Session with a copious Index to the Whole (14 vols. in 29. Washington, 1825–1837). A continuation of *The Debates and Proceedings.*
———. Laws, Statutes, etc.:
Abstract of an Act to Provide for the Valuation of Lands and Dwelling-Houses, and the Enumeration of Slaves within the United States . . . (Vergennes [Vt.], 1798).
An Act Authorizing the Grant and Conveyance of Certain Lands to John Cleves Symmes, and Associates [May 5, 1792] (Philadelphia, 1792).
The Federal and State Constitutions, Colonial Charters and Other Organic Laws of the United States (ed. by Ben: Perley Poore. 2 vols. Washington, 1878).
The Federal and State Constitutions, Colonial Charters and Other Organic Laws of the States, Territories, and Colonies Now or Heretofore Forming the United States of America (comp. and ed. under Act of Congress of June 30, 1906 by Francis Newton Thorpe. 7 vols., Washington, 1909. *House Doc.*, 59 Cong., 2 sess., No. 357).
An Ordinance for the Government of the Territory of the United States, North-west of the River Ohio [July 13, 1787] (New York, 1787).
A Supplement to an Ordinance entitled "An Ordinance for Ascertaining the Mode of Disposing of Lands in Western Territory" [March 19, 1788] (New York, 1788).
A Supplement to an Ordinance Entitled "An Ordinance for Ascertaining the Mode of Disposing of Lands in the Western Territory" [July 9, 1788] (New York, 1788).
Statutes at Large (Washington, 1795–):
Officially Recognized Editions:
Folwell (12 vols., 1795–1815).
Bioren (10 vols., 1815–1845).
Little and Brown (17 vols., 1856–1873).
State Department (1874– , including *Revised Statutes*).
For laws relating to Land, see:
Act of 1795, I, 435;
Act of 1812 (General Land Office Act), II, 716;
Act of 1820, II, chap. li;
Act of 1830, IV, chap. ccvii;

Act of 1841 (Pre-emption), V, 453;
Act of 1850 (Swamp Land), IX, 503; (Donation), IX, 496;
Act of 1853 (Donation), X, 158;
Act of 1854 (Donation), X, 305, 574; (Graduation), X, 574;
Act of 1860 (Swamp Land), XII, 3;
Act of 1862 (Homestead), XII, 392; (Morrill, Agricultural Colleges), XII, 503.
For laws quoted relating to seamen, see;
Act of 1790, I, chap. ix, chap. xxix;
Act of 1792, I, chap. xxiv;
Act of 1798, I, chap. lxvii;
Amendment of 1799, I, chap. xxxvi;
Amendment of 1802, II, chap. ii;
Act of 1803, II, chap. ix;
Act of 1811, II, chap. xxvi;
Act of 1813, II, chap. xlii;
Act of 1817, III, chap. xxxi;
Act of 1825, IV, chap. lxv;
Act of 1835, IV, chap. xl;
Act of 1837, V, chap. xliv;
Act of 1840, V, chap. xlviii;
Act of 1843, V, chap. xlix;
Act of 1850, IX, chap. xxvii, chap. lxxx;
Act of 1851, IX, chap. xliii;
Act of 1856, XI, chap. cxxvii;
Act of 1862, XII, chap. xxxiv;
For laws relating to the slave problem, see:
Act of 1800 (Prohibiting Slave Trade from U. S. to Foreign Countries), II, 70–72;
Act of 1807 (Prohibiting Importation), II, 426–430;
Act of 1850 (Fugitive Slave Act), IX, 462–465; (Abolishing Slave Trade in D. C.), IX, 467.

UTAH (Territory). *Acts, Resolutions and Memorials, Passed at the Several Annual Sessions of the Legislative Assembly of the Territory of Utah, To Which is Prefixed: The Declaration of Independence, the Articles of Confederation, the Ordinance of 1787, The Constitution of the United States.... The Naturalization Laws, The Constitution of the Provisional State of Deseret, The Deseret Laws, and the Organic Acts of Utah.* Published by Virtue of an Act Approved Jan. 19, 1855 (Great Salt Lake City, 1855).

VAN LAER, ARNOLD JOHAN FERDINAND (Archivist). *Van Rensselaer Bowier Manuscripts. Being the Letters of Kiliaen Van Rensselaer, 1630–1643, and Other Documents Relating to the Colony of Rensselaerswyck.* Translated and edited by A. J. F. Van Laer, Archivist. With an Introductory Essay by Nicolass de Roever, Late Archivist of the City of Amsterdam. Translated by Mrs. Alan H. Strong (New York State Library, *History Bulletin*, No. 7. Albany, 1908).

VAN METRE, THURMAN W. *Economic History of the United States* (New York, 1921).

VERMONT (State). Laws, Statutes, etc.:
Acts and Laws of the State of Vermont in America (Dresden [now Hanover, N. H.]. Printed by Judah Padock & Alden Spooner, 1799).
Laws of the State of Vermont, Revised and Passed by the Legislature, in the Year of Our Lord Seventeen Hundred and Ninety-Seven. Together with the Declaration of Independence, the Constitution of the United States with its Amendments; and the Constitution of the State of Vermont with an Appendix containing The Several Laws which have hitherto been passed by the Legislature regarding Proprietors' Meetings, Granting General Land Taxes, exclusive privileges to Companies for Locks, Toll Bridges, Turnpike Roads, &c and the Titles of All the Acts which have not been repealed, or become obsolete (Rutland, Printed by Joseph Fay, MDCCXCVIII).
Statutes of the State of Vermont; Revised and Established by Authority, in the Year MDCCLXXXVII, including Those Passed since That Period until the Sessions Holden in January [*and October-November*] *1791* (Printed in Bennington ... MDCCXCI). Actually published in 1792.
Digests, Compilations, etc.;
Compiled Acts and Laws Passed by the Legislature of the State of Vermont, 1797–1816 (3 vols. Vols. I & II, Randolph, Vt., 1808; Vol. III, Rutland, Vt., 1817).
Kinsman, J. Burnham (comp.). *The Vermont Townsman: a Compilation of the Laws of Vermont in Relation to the Powers, Duties, and Liabilities of Town Officers and Towns, with Forms, Directions, and Legal Decisions Adapted to the Statutes of the State* (Boston, 1857).

Session Laws;
Acts Passed by the Legislature of the State of Vermont at Their October Session (Montpelier, Vt., 1837).
Records, etc.;
Vermont State Papers; Being a Collection of Records and Documents (Middlebury, 1823). Contains the Laws from 1779 to 1786 inclusive.
VIOLETTE, E. M. "The Black Code in Missouri," in Mississippi Valley Historical Association, *Proceedings*, VI, 287–316, 1913.
———. *Spanish Land Claims in Missouri* (Washington University, *Studies*, Humanistic Series, VIII, 167–200, Apr., 1921).
VIRGINIA (Colony). *Colonial Records of Virginia* (*State Senate Document*, Extra, Richmond, 1874).
———. Laws, Statutes, etc.:
An Abridgement of the Publick Laws of Virginia, in Force and Use, June 10, 1720 (London, 1722).
The Acts of Assembly, Now in Force, in the Colony of Virginia.... (Williamsburg. Printed by William Hunter, MDCCLII).
Acts of Assembly, Now in Force, in Virginia. Occasioned by the Repeal of Sundry Acts Made in the Year ... 1748 (Williamsburg, 1752).
The Acts of Assembly, Now in Force, in the Colony of Virginia. With an Exact Table to the Whole (Williamsburg, MDCCLXIX).
Acts of Assembly, Passed in the Colony of Virginia, From 1662 to 1715 (Vol. I, London, MDCCXXVII).
A Collection of All the Acts of the Assembly, Now in Force, in the Colony of Virginia (Williamsburg. Printed by William Parks, MDCCXXXIII).
A Complete Collection of All the Lavvs of Virginia Now in Force. Carefully Copied from the Assembly Records. To Which is Annexed an Alphabetical Table (*London* [*1684*]).
For the Colony in Virginia Britannia. Lavves diuine, morall and martiall, &c ... (printed at London for Walter Burre, 1612).
——— (State), Laws, Statutes, etc.:
Digests, Compilations, etc.;
A Collection of All Such Acts of the General Assembly of Virginia of a Public and Permanent Nature as are Now in Force. Published Pursuant to an Act of the General Assembly Passed on the twenty-sixth Day of January, 1802 (Richmond, MDCCCIII).
A Collection of All Such Public Acts of the General Assembly, and Ordinances of the Conventions of Virginia, Passed since the Year 1768, as are now in Force; With a Table of the Principal Matters. ... (Richmond, MDCCLXXXV).
A Collection of All Such Acts of the General Assembly of Virginia, Of a Public and Permanent Nature, as are Now in Force; ... To Which are Prefixed the Declaration of Rights, and Constitution, or Form of Government ... (Richmond, 1794).
Hening, William Waller (ed.). *The Statutes at Large; being A Collection of All the Laws of Virginia, from the First Session of the Legislature, in the Year 1619....* (13 vols. New York and Richmond, 1809–1823).
Mercer, John (ed.). *An Exact Abridgment of All the Public Acts of Assembly of Virginia, in Force and Use....* (Williamsburg. Printed by William Parks, MDCCXXXVII).
———. *An Exact Abridgment of All the Public Acts of Assembly of Virginia, in Force and Use, Jan. 1, 1758* (Glasgow, MDCCLIX).
Morison, Francis (ed.). *The Lawes of Virginia now in Force* ... (London, MDCLXII).
Pleasants and Pace, pubs. *A Collection of All Such Acts of the General Assembly of Virginia of a Public and Permanent Nature as Are Now in Force* (2 vols., Richmond, 1803–1808). Binding title, *Revised Code.* Pleasants & Pace, pubs., vol. i; Pleasants, vol. 2.
Shepherd, S. (ed.). Continuation of Hening; new series, 1792–1806 (3 vols., Richmond, 1835–1836).
Session Laws:
Acts Passed at the General Assembly of the Commonwealth of Virginia, 1722– (Richmond, 1723–).
VIRGINIA HISTORICAL SOCIETY. *Collections* (12 vols. in 11, Richmond, 1833–1892).
———. *Publications* (vols. 1– , Richmond, 1874–).
THE VIRGINIA MAGAZINE OF HISTORY AND BIOGRAPHY (published by the Virginia Historical Society: vols. 1– , Richmond, 1893–).
WALKER, WILLISTON. *A History of the Congregational Churches in the United States* (American Church History Series, III. New York, 1894; 2d ed., New York, 1897).
———. *Ten New England Leaders* (New York, Boston & Chicago, 1901).
———. *Progressivism—and After* (New York, 1914).

WALTERSHAUSEN, A. SARTORIUS FREIHERR VON. *Die Arbeits-Verfassung der Englishschen Kolonien in Nordamerika* (Strassburg, 1894).
WANSEY, HENRY. *The Journal of an Excursion to the United States of North America, in the Summer of 1794* (1st ed., 1796; 2d ed., Salisbury, 1798).
WARVILLE, BRISSOT DE. See Brissot de Warville.
WASHBURN, EMORY. "Extinction of Slavery in Massachusetts", in Massachusetts Historical Society, *Proceedings*, 1855–1858, III, 188–203.
———. "Slavery as it Once Prevailed in Massachusetts", in *Lowell Institute Lectures*, 191–225, Boston, 1869.
WASHINGTON (TERRITORY). *Statutes of the Territory* (Olympia, 1855).
WASHINGTON, GEORGE. *The Diaries of George Washington, from 1789 to 1791, Embracing the Opening of the First Congress, and His Tours through New England, Long Island, and the Southern States. Together with his Journal of a Tour to the Ohio in 1753* (ed. by Benjamin J. Lossing, Pres. of the Historical Society, Richmond, 1861).
———. *The Writings of George Washington* (W. C. Ford, ed., 14 vols., New York, 1889–1893).
———. *The Writings of George Washington; Being His Correspondence, Addresses, and Other Papers, Official and Private* (J. Sparks, ed., 12 vols., New York, 1847–1848).
WATTS, FREDERICK. *Reports of Cases Argued and Determined in the Supreme Court of Pennsylvania, V, . . . May to Oct., 1836.* (Philadelphia, 1837).
WEATHERFORD, W. D. *Negro Life in the South, with Chapters on Economic Condition of the Negro* by G. W. Dyer (New York, 1910).
WEBB, SIDNEY [Baron Passfield] AND BEATRICE. *The History of Trade Unionism* (London and New York, 1902).
WEBSTER, NOAH. *Effects of Slavery on Morals and Industry.* (Hartford, Conn., MDCCXCIII). Enscribed to The Connecticut Society for the Promotion of Freedom and the Relief of Persons Unlawfully Holden in Bondage. Bound with *Miscellaneous Papers on Political and Commercial Subjects* (No. III, New York, 1802).
WEEDEN, WILLIAM B. *Economic and Social History of New England, 1620–1789* (2 vols., Boston, 1890).
WEEKS, STEPHEN BEAUREGARD. *Southern Quakers and Slavery: A Study in Institutional History* (Johns Hopkins University, *Studies in Historical and Political Science*, Extra Vol. XV. Baltimore, 1896).
WELD, RALPH FOSTER. *Slavery in Connecticut* (Committee on Historical Publications, Tercentenary Commission of the State of Connecticut, No. XXXVII, New Haven, 1935).
WELLINGTON, RAYNOR G. *The Political and Sectional Influence of the Public Lands, 1828–1842* (Boston, 1914).
WESLEY, CHARLES H. *Negro Labor in the United States, 1850–1925. A Study in American Economic History* (New York, 1927).
WESTON (Mass.). *Records of the First Precinct, 1746–1754, and of the Town, 1754–1803* (ed. by Mary Frances Peirce. Boston, 1893).
———. *Records of the Town Clerk, 1804–1826* (ed. by Mary Frances Peirce. Boston, 1894).
WESTON, GEORGE MELVILLE. *The Progress of Slavery in the United States* (Washington, D. C., 1857).
WETMORE, THOMAS, AND PRESCOTT, EDWARD G. (eds.). *Charter and Ordinances of the City of Boston Together with the Acts of Legislature Relating to the City* (Boston, Mass., 1834).
WHEELER, BENJAMIN IDE. *Unterricht und Demokratie in Amerika. Die Quellen der öffentlichen Meinung, das College, die Universitäten, Studentenleben, Schule und Kirche in den Vereinigten Staaten. Vorlesungen gehalten an der Berliner Universität* (Strassburg, 1910).
WHEELER, JACOB D. A *Practical Treatise on the Law of Slavery, Being a Compilation of All the Decisions Made on that Subject, in the Several Courts of the United States, and State Courts* (New York & New Orleans, 1837).
WHELPTON, P. K. "Occupational Groups in the United States, 1820–1920," in *Journal of American Statistical Association*, XXI, 335–343, Sept. 1926.
WHITE, JOSEPH M. *A New Collection of Laws, Charters and Local Ordinances of the Governments of Great Britain, France and Spain, Relating to the Concessions of Land in their Respective Colonies; together with the Laws of Mexico and Texas on the same Subject, to Which is Prefixed Judge Johnson's Translation of Azo and Manuel's Institutions of the Civil Law of Spain* (2 vols. Philadelphia, Penna., 1839). Back title reads *Land Laws in California, Oregon, Texas, &c.*
WHITIN, ERNEST STAGG. *Factory Legislation in Maine* (Columbia University, *Studies in History, Economics and Public Law*, XXXIII, No. 1. New York, 1908).
WHITMORE, WILLIAM H. (ed.). *The Colonial Laws of Massachusetts* (Reprinted from the Edition of 1660, with Supplement to 1672. Boston, 1889).

WHITNEY, ELI. "Memorial. Application for the Extension of a Patent Right, April 16, 1812. No. 319," in *American State Papers, Miscellaneous*, II, 183.

WHITTELSEY, SARAH SCOVILL. *Massachusetts Labor Legislation. An Historical and Critical Study with an Introduction by Arthur Twining Hadley* (Supplement to American Academy of Political and Social Science, *Annals*. Philadelphia, 1901).

WILHELM, LEWIS WEBB. *Local Institutions of Maryland* (Johns Hopkins University, *Studies in Historical and Political Science*, III, Nos. 5–7. Baltimore, 1885).

WILSON, HENRY. *History of the Rise and Fall of the Slave Power in America* (3 vols., Boston, 1872–1877).

WILSON, JOSEPH T. *Emancipation: Its Course and Progress, From 1481 B.C. to A.D. 1875, with a Review of President Lincoln's Proclamation, the XIII Amendment, and the Progress of the Freed People since Emancipation with a History of the Emancipation Monument* (Hampton, Va., 1882).

WILSON, SAMUEL MACKAY. *The First Land Court of Kentucky, 1779–1780 . . .* (Lexington, Ky., 1923).

WILSON, WOODROW. "The Law and the Facts." Presidential Address, Seventh Annual Meeting of the American Political Science Association, in *The American Political Science Review*, V, 1–11, Feb. 1911.

WINDSCHEID, DR. BERNHARD. *Lehrbuch des Pandektenrechts* (5th ed., 3 vols., 1882; 9th ed. Frankfurt-a-M., 1906).

WINSOR, JUSTIN (ed.). *The Memorial History of Boston Including Suffolk County, Massachusetts, 1630–1880* (4 vols., Boston, 1880–1881).

——— (ed.). *Narrative and Critical History of America* (8 vols., Boston & New York, 1884–1889).

WINSTON, GEORGE T. "The Relation of the Whites to the Negroes," in American Academy of Political and Social Science, *Annals*, XVIII, 105–118, July, 1901.

WINTHROP, JOHN. *The History of New England from 1630 to 1649* (2 vols., ed. by James Savage, from his original manuscript with notes. New ed., Boston, 1853).

——— *Winthrop's Journal "History of New England," 1630–1649* (ed. by James Kendell Hosmer, in *Original Narratives of Early American History*, VII. 2 vols. New York, 1908).

WISCONSIN. Laws, Statutes, etc.:

Revised Statutes of the State of Wisconsin Passed at the Annual Session of the Legislature Commencing January 13, 1858, and Approved May 17, 1858 (Chicago, 1858).

Session Laws;

Acts and Resolves of the Wisconsin Legislature in 1849 (Madison, 1849).

General Acts of the Wisconsin Legislature in 1857 Together with Memorials and Resolutions (Madison, 1857).

Laws Passed by the Legislature of the State of Wisconsin, 1848– (Madison, 1848–).

Statutes of the Territory of Wisconsin Passed by the Legislative Assembly at a Session Commencing in November 1838, and at an Adjourned Session Commencing in January 1839 (Albany, N. Y., 1839).

WISCONSIN UNIVERSITY. *Bulletins* (vols. 1– , Madison, 1894–). Economics and Political Science Series (9 vols., 1904–1918); Economics, Political Science, and History Series (2 vols., 1894–1899); History Series (4 vols., 1902–1918).

WITTE, EDWIN E. "Early American Labor Cases," in *Yale Law Journal*, XXXV, 825–837, May 1926.

WOLCOTT, ROGER. *The Wolcott Papers.* See Bates, Albert C. (ed.).

WOODBURY, MRS. HELEN L. (SUMNER). See Sumner.

WOODSON, CARTER GODWIN. *The Education of the Negro Prior to 1861. A History of the Education of the Colored People of the United States from the Beginning of Slavery to the Civil War* (New York and London, 1915).

———. *The Negro in Our History* (4th rev. ed., Washington, 1927).

WORCESTER (Mass.). *Records of the Proprietors of Worcester, Mass.* [*1667–1788*] (ed. by Franklin P. Rice. Worcester Society of Antiquity, *Collections*, II, Nos. 6–8; III, Nos. 9–12. Worcester, 1879–1881).

WRIGHT, RICHARDSON. *Hawkers & Walkers in Early America. Strolling Peddlers, Preachers, Lawyers, Doctors, Players, and Others from the Beginning to the Civil War* (Philadelphia, 1927).

YOAKUM, HENDERSON K. *History of Texas from Its First Settlement in 1685 to Its Annexation to the United States in 1846* (2 vols. New York, 1856).

YOUNG, ALEXANDER. *Chronicles of the First Planters of the Colony of Massachusetts Bay, from 1623–1636. Now first collected from original Records and Contemporaneous manuscripts and illustrated with notes* (Boston, 1846).

APPENDIX

SLAVE TABLES

KEY TO ABBREVIATIONS

General abbreviations: endings of words, such as *ing*, *ed*, etc., omitted. Examples: *whip.*, whipping; *import.*, importation, importing; *employ.*, employed.

ab.—above
accord.—according
af.—after
ag.—against
appreh.—apprehend
ascert.—ascertain
assembl.—assembly, assembling
assoc.—association

bef.—before
beg.—beginning
bet.—between

cap.—capital
certf.—certificate
chg.—charge
childr.—children
circl.—circulating
cit.—citizen
c'ld.—could
cohab.—cohabitation
compens.—compensated
compr.—compromise
condit.—condition
Congr.—Congress, Congressional
conspir.—conspiring, conspiracy
cont.—continued
corp.—corporal
cr.—crime
crim.—criminal
cr'l.—cruel
c'rt.—court

decl.—declaring, declaration
dep.—departing
direc.—direction
disc.—discussion
discr.—discretion.

emanc.—emancipated, emancipation
employm.—employment
entert.—entertainment
exec.—execution
export.—exported, exportation
exten.—extension

f'd.—forbidden
F. N.—free Negro
fr.—from
freed.—freedom

guard.—guardian

harb.—harboring
homic.—homicide

immig.—immigrants, immigrate
import.—imported, importation
impr.—imprisonment
inj.—injury
insur.—insurrection
interm.—intermarriage
intro.—introduction

j. of p.—justice of peace
jurisd.—jurisdiction
just.—justice

kidn.—kidnap, kidnapping

l.—large
legis.—legislature
liq.—liquor
lit.—literature

mansl.—manslaughter
manu.—manumitted, manumission
mdse.—merchandise
med.—medicine
meritor.—meritorious
mos.—months

N.—Negro
nec.—necessary

o.—out
off.—offence
ov.—over
own.—owner

pd.—paid
perm.—permitted
petit.—petition
plant.—plantation
poison.—poisoning, poisonous
prop.—property
publ.—publishing
putt.—putting

qualif.—qualification

rec.—receive
reg.—regarding
registr.—registered, registration
regul.—regulating, regulation
reop.—reopening
req.—required
resid.—resident
resol.—resolution
resp.—responsible
rev.—revolt
rr.—railroad
r't.—right
r'y.—runaway, run away

sed.—seditious
serv.—servant, service
sh.—shall
Sl.—slave
Sl'y.—slavery
St.—State
suffic.—sufficient

terr.—territory
testim.—testimony
tr.—trading
transp.—transporting
tr'l.—trial

un.—under
unan.—unanimous

w.—with
Wh.—white
witn.—witness
w. o —without

Slave Codes Southern States

ALABAMA

The area of the State of Alabama was ceded to the United States by Georgia, South Carolina, and Spain. The larger portion was a part of the Mississippi Territory. The Territorial government was established by Congress in 1817, and Alabama was admitted as a State in 1819. Up to that time the laws of Mississippi applied. No laws affecting the status of the slave were passed during the existence of Territorial government.*

*See Hurd, Law of Freedom and Bondage, II, 150; Thorpe, Federal and State Constitutions, Colonial Charters, and Other Organic Laws, I, 89, fn.

Date	Property Rights	Crimes. By	Crimes. Against	Runaway Patrol Laws	Insurrection and Conspiracy	Protection: Slaves and Free Negroes	Teaching and Preaching	Discrimination and Disabilities	Importation and Exportation	Limitation of Slavery	Emancipation and Abolition	Free Negroes	Resolutions and Sundries	Source	Pages in Text
	I	II		III	IV	V	VI	VII	VIII	IX	X	XI	XII		
Feb. 10, 1803								F'd: fire-hunt.; p'n by whip.						Toulmin's Digest (1823), p.369	
March 1803	See 1807 when law was re-enacted													Ibid.	
March 6, 1805		Strik. Wh.:p'n by whip.* Plot. to murder: p'n by death. Trial by Jury in cap. cr. like free citz. except Jury of Sl.own's. For offences within benefit of clergy: brand. instead of death. See IV	See V	Absent 10 days = r'y. See XI	Unlaw. meet.'s, sed. speeches: p'n by whip. Conspir.: p'n by death.	Cr'l & unusual p'n f'd.	Allowed to go to church.	Witn. ag. Sls. only. F'd: absent w.o. pass; arms w.o. permit; tr.; hir. o.; keep. dogs, horses,hogs.				F'd: meet. w. Sls.; harb. Sls.		Ibid., 627-32	187, 191, 192, 193
July 20, 1805	See VII							Emanc. Sls. c'ld be taken for execution to satisfy debts.			For meritorious service only. Bond req. See VII	See VII		Ibid.,632	197
1807								Sls. not to brand cattle except un. direc. of Wh's Re-enacts 1803.						Ibid., 102	
Feb. 6 1807*		Non-cap. cr.: p'n by brand.& corp. p'n.False test.: p'n by mutil. & pillory.	See V			Steal. & sell. F.N.p'n by death						See V		Ibid., 182-3, 207	
1807								Act of 1805 re-enacted. F'd: tr. w. Sls. & Masters not to license them.						Ibid., 849	
March 1, 1808		No criminals to be import.							Import. regulated. Tax.					Ibid., 633	196

Dec. 22, 1809				R'ys unclaimed: sold.										Ibid., 634	186
Dec. 18, 1812				Patrol law.										Ibid., 635-7	
Dec. 21, 1812		Assault. Wh.: death.			Conspir.: death. Aid. insur.: death.							See IV		Ibid., 224, 225	187
Jan. 15,** 1814		Cap. crimes: rape, burn. house or barn, manslaughter. Trial by 3 Just's & Jury. Non-cap. cr.: trial by J. of P.; p'n by whip.												Ibid., 184-5, 506-7	
Dec.8, 1815									Unlawf.import.Sls.: sold.					Ibid., 637	
Dec. 19, 1815											Amends 1805; suits for freed. given to Superior Court.			Ibid., 638	
Nov. 27, 1816								See XI				F'd: Keep. tavern & sell. liq.		Ibid., 638	
1819	Own. to be compens.in X.	Not to be deprived of Jury trial.	Mutil. or kill. of Sl. p'n like that of Wh. See V		Insur.excepted in IIb.	Suffic. food, clothing. Cr'l treat. f'd.		Suffrage: Wh. males.	F'd: import.as mdse. Legis. c'ld not f'd immigrants import. Sls.		Legis. c'ld not pass emanc. laws w. o. consent of own's.			Constitution, vi, Slaves; Toulmin's Digest, 917, 931	180, 181, 182 fn., 190, 195
Dec. 17, 1819				Harb. fined. Patrol law.				At l.w.o.pass, p'n by patrol.						Toulmin's Digest, 185-6; 639-42	186, 193
Dec. 17, 1819		County Courts jurisd. ov.												Ibid., 185-6, 642	
Dec. 17, 1819		Courts of oyer & terminer; Jury, & Counsel for cr's higher than petit larceny.						See II						Ibid., 185-6	

*Originally passed 1802, but re-enacted with amendments. **Repeals sec. of 1805 relating to striking White person.

ALABAMA

Date	I	II		III	IV	V	VI	VII	VIII	IX	X	XI	XII	Source	Pages
Dec. 24, 1822		Cap. cr.: circuit courts. Trial as of Wh. except as to evidence.										See II		*Acts*, *1822*, p. 4	
Dec. 26, 1822								See XI				F'd: Sell. liq.		Toulmin's *Digest*, 642	
Jan. 1, 1823									To carry U.S. Sl. tr. laws into effect.					*Acts*, *1822*, p. 62	
Dec 24, 1824 *	½ value exec. Sl. p'd own.	Counsel provided in cap. cr.		Harb. Sls. guilty of cap. cr.: fine $500.										*Acts*, *1824*, 41-2	186,
Jan. 2, 1826								F'd: tr. w. Sls.						*Acts*, *1825*, p. 8	
Dec. 30, 1826			Marisl. p'n by whip & brand.									See II b		*Acts*, *1826*, p. 42	
Jan. 13, 1827									F'd: import. for sale or hire af. Aug. 1827.					*Ibid.*, 44	195
Jan. 22, 1829									Repeals 1827.					*Acts*, *1828*, p. 63	196
Jan. 13, 1831		Rape: death;										See II		*Acts*, *1831*, p. 13	
Jan. 16, 1832		F.N. giv. pass to Sl. p'n by transp. or sold for 10 yrs. Sl. writ. pass: whip. See IV			Publ. sed. lit. p'n by death. Assembl. of more than 5 Sls. f'd.	Food and clothing,	Teach. f'd. Could attend Church held by Wh. F'd to preach.	Assoc. w. F.N. p'n by whip. See IV, VI, XI	F'd: import., by immig'ts, (except for personal use); for sale or for hire. Registr. req.			F'd.: to settle in St. af. Jan. '33; asso. & tr. w. Sls.; preach. Giv. pass to Sl. p'n by export. See VI		*Ibid.*, pp. 12-18	187, 190, 197, 201, 203
Dec. 4, 1832						Repeals above.			Repeals above.					*Acts*, *1833*, p. 5	190, 196, 197

Jan. 17, 1834											Freed for meritor. service only. Procedure.	To leave St. within 12 mos.		*Ibid.*, p. 29	199, 208
Jan.7, 1835		If death fr. poison, seller = accessory.						F'd: sale of poison to Sls. & F.N.'s.				See VII		Acts, 1834, p. 8	185
Jan.1, 1836				Patrol law										Acts, 1835, pp. 21-23	193
Jan.9, 1836		Arson & burglary, p'n by death. See VII						Free Wh. person's penalty for II = impr. & fine. Sls.witn.ag.F.N.				See II, VII		Aikin's Digest, 616, 617. See also Acts, 1835, p. 50	
Jan. 10, 1839			Assault on Sl. p'n as on Wh.											Acts. 1838, p. 12	
Feb.2, 1839									See XI F.N.coming to St.: seized as Sl.			See VIII F'd: to come aboard vessels. F.N. employed on ship, in custody in port.		*Ibid.*, pp. 134-6	
Feb.1, 1840									Repeals above.					Acts, 1840, p. 16	
Jan.9, 1841	Own.p'd value of exec. Sl.	Cap.crimes = murder, mansl., robbery, assault of Wh's, arson. Counsel provided. Trials by jury of 2/3 Sl.own's. Non-cap.crimes: perjury, petit larceny, p'n by whip.	Sls. guilty of mansl. of Sls. or F.N. p'n by whip. & brand.	Conceal. crim.Sls. p'n. Steal. Sls. to free them p'n by impr.	Insur., conspir.: p'n by death.	Cr'l p'n f'd.		F'd: sale of poison to Sls.; tr.w.Sls.				See II Mansl. of F.N. by Sl. p'n by whip. & brand. Counsel provided in trials.		Acts, 1841, pp.129, 142-9, 188-90	186, 187, 190, 207
1841		Re-enacts 1831 : rape p'n by death.												*Ibid.*, p. 188	
1843 Penal Code				Steal. or entic. Sls. p'n by impr.										Acts, 1842, p. 41	187
Jan.27, 1845								F'd: tr.w.Sls. fr. boats.						Acts, 1844, p. 154	
Jan. 29, 1846.	Non-res. own. not compensated for exec. Sls.	See I												Acts, 1845, p. 27	

*Repeals Dec. 17, 1819.

ALABAMA

Date	I	II		III	IV	V	VI	VII	VIII	IX	X	XI	XII	Source	Pages
Feb. 26, 1848						Treat Sls.w. humanity. Food & cloth.								Acts, 1847, p.103	190
1848	Fund to compens. own. raised by spec-cial tax on Sls.													Acts, 1848, p. 35	
March 6, 1848								F'd:go.at l. & hir.o.	Sl.deal-ers to be li-censed.					Ibid., 28, 107	191, 192
Jan. 12, 1850		Bail permit. for non-cap.cr's.												Acts, 1850, p. 51	
Feb. 12, 1850								F'd: liq.sell.by and to Sls.or F.N.				See VII		Ibid., 49	191, 204
March 11, 1850								Sls.sell.liq.: whip.						Ibid., 50	
Feb.9, 1852								Sell.liq.to F.N.: fine.				See VII Guard's c'ld be appointed by court.		Acts, 1851, pp. 80-81	204, 206
1852 Code	Master's r't es-tabl.by law.		Whip. Sls.to death = murder.			In add.to 1848, cared for in sick-ness & old age. Childr.* un.10 not to be sold fr. Mother.		Witn.only ag. each other. C'ld not own property.				See VII		Acts, 1852, pp. 239, 390, 392, 424, 591	190, 192, 205
Feb. 18, 1854												Childr.over 14 r't to choose guard.		Acts, 1853-4, p.49	206
Feb. 20, 1854	Master compens. when Sl. is witn. See VII							C'ld be subpoen. as witn.						Ibid., 42	
Feb. 5, 1856					See VII			Agent req.for every 6 Sls.						Acts. 1856, p. 18	193

Feb. 2, 1858								Gam. p'n by whip.				See VII		<u>Acts</u>, <u>1858</u>, p. 35	203
Feb. 6, 1858								F'd: to sell liq. to Sls.				See VII		<u>Acts</u>, <u>1858</u>, pp. 285, 291	
Jan. 25, 1860											Manu. by will or deed: void. Laws of emanc. repealed.			<u>Acts</u>, <u>1860</u>, p. 28	
Feb. 25, 1860												Voluntary enslavement provided for.		<u>Ibid</u>., 63	206

*If owner's interest affected, could sell child over 5 from Mother.

ARKANSAS

Arkansas was included in the Territory of Missouri until 1819, when it was organized as a Territory. The laws of Missouri were proclaimed the laws of Arkansas by the Governor and Judges of the newly organized Territory. The Territory became a State in 1836. The laws of Arkansas Territory up to 1835 are taken from Steele and McCampbell's Laws of Arkansas Territory, 1835.

Date	Property Rights	Crimes By	Crimes Against	Runaway Patrol Laws	Insurrection and Conspiracy	Protection: Slaves and Free Negroes	Teaching and Preaching	Discrimination and Disabilities	Importation and Exportation	Limitation of Slavery	Emancipation and Abolition	Free Negroes	Resolutions and Sundries	Source	Pages in Text
	I	II		III	IV	V	VI	VII	VIII	IX	X	XI	XII		
Oct. 1, 1804	Personal estate.	Admin. medicine W. ill intent: death. Strik. Wh.: whip.	Steal. and sell. of Sls. p'n by death.	P'n by whip. for being on stranger's plant. Harb. Sls. f'd. See VIII	Meet's of Sls., F.N.& Wh. f'd. Insur., death.	See X		F'd: arms; meet's; tr. (w.o. own's consent); go. at l. w.o. pass. See XI	Vessels carrying Sls. fined.		Emanc. allowed. Care of minors & old by former own's.	Allowed license for arms. F'd: to meet w. Sls. Must have certif. of freed. when travel. Hir. o. if unable to pay taxes. See II		Laws of Ark. Terr. (1835), pp. 437, 521-6	186, 187, 192, 197, 203, 204, 207
Oct. 20, 1825				Patrol law. See VII				Go. at l. w.o. pass: whip.						Ibid., 530	186, 193
1836		Legis. power to prevent import. of crimin. Sls. Jury trial.				Legis. power to compel own's to treat Sls. w. humanity.			Legis. power to prevent import. as mdse.		Legis. no power to emanc. w.o. own's consent.			Constitution, iv, 23, 25; vii, Emancipation of Slaves.	180, 181, 182 fn.
Dec. 18, 1837			See XI			See XI						Suits for freed. permitted.		Rev. Stat. (1838), p. 416	207
Feb. 19, 1838	Personal estate.										By will or deed.			Ibid., 427	183
March 3, 1838			See XI	Procedure for r'ys. See XI								Claimant pays damages in unjust arrest.		Ibid., 419	193
Jan. 20, 1843								See XI	See XI			F'd: immig. to St. Residents bef. 1/3/1843, must register.		Acts, 1842-3, p. 61	201
Feb. 3, 1843				Inducing Sls. to r'y p'n by impr.										Ibid., 124	186

Jan.9, 1845									See XI			Amends 1843 to permit entry as serv.		<u>Acts</u>, <u>1844-5</u>, p. 99	
Nov. 22, 1850					Circ'l sed.lit., p'n by impr.							See IV		<u>Acts</u>, <u>1850-1</u>, p. 22	188
Jan.6, 1853								F'd: Work. in places where liq. sold.				See VII		<u>Acts</u>, <u>1852-3</u>, p. 71	
Jan. 10, 1853		See VII, XI						F'd: liq.				See VII Impr.for sell. liq.to Sl.		<u>Ibid</u>., 120	204
Dec. 15, 1854*								Wh's.gam.w.Sls. p'n by fine & impr.						<u>Acts</u>, <u>1854-5</u>, p. 38	
Jan. 19, 1855											Condemn. abolition move. of North.		Resol.	<u>Ibid</u>., 278	
Feb. 2, 1858											No further emanc.; wills, deeds,etc. void.			<u>Acts</u>, <u>1858-9</u>, p. 69	200
Dec. 16, 1858						F'd: hir. o.on Sunday								<u>Ibid</u>., 19	
Dec. 21, 1858				Conceal. r'ys p'n by impr.										<u>Ibid</u>., 31	186
Feb. 12, 1859												None to reside in St. af.1/1/1860. May choose Sl'y or exile.		<u>Ibid</u>., 175	
Feb. 21, 1859								See XI				Masters of vessels employ.or permit.to travel: fined.		<u>Ibid</u>., 252	
Feb. 21, 1859		Sls. p'n by stripes instead of impr.												<u>Ibid</u>., 293	
Jan.1, 1861					Incit. insur.p'n by death.			Overseer for every 2 Sls. in Shelby Co.						<u>Acts</u>, <u>1860-1</u>,pp.83, 87	188
Jan. 14, 1861												Time of removal extended to 1/1/63.		<u>Ibid</u>., 206	

*This Act also repealed laws inflicting corporal punishment on White persons.

FLORIDA

Previous to the cession of Florida to the United States by Treaty of February 22, 1819, the private law of the territory was that of the Spanish Government, and, as in all colonies of Spain, Negroes and Indians were lawfully held in unconditional servitude. The laws down to 1828 are taken from Hurd, _Law of Freedom and Bondage_, II, 190, _et seq._

Date	Property Rights	Crimes By	Crimes Against	Runaway Patrol Laws	Insurrection and Conspiracy	Protection: Slaves and Free Negroes	Teaching and Preaching	Discrimination and Disabilities	Importation and Exportation	Limitation of Slavery	Emancipation and Abolition	Free Negroes	Resolutions and Sundries	Source	Pages in Text
	I	II		III	IV	V	VI	VII	VIII	IX	X	XI	XII		
1822 _Penal Code_	Provis. for title in Sls. See III	Cap. cr.:tried & p'n like Wh's. Non-cap.:tried before J.of P.; p'n by whip.		R'ys to be pursued. Sl. steal. p'n by death.	See XI			F'd: tr.; go. at l.; hir. o.	Vessels not to carry Sls.		Lawful un. conditions	Stealing of, p'n by death. Not to travel about.		Hurd, II, 191	187, 189, 191
1825				Patrol Act.										_Ibid._	193
Dec. 1826									Seamen excepted fr. XI.			Immig. of, f'd.		_Ibid._	201
Jan. 10, 1827				Carry. away Sls. p'n by death.										_Ibid._	
Jan. 10, 1827								F'd: tr.						_Ibid._	
Jan. 11, 1827								Suffrage: limited to Wh's.				See VII		_Ibid._	
Jan. 21, 1827		Provisions for p'n of Sls.												_Ibid._	
Nov. 15, 1828	Personal property.													_Acts_, _1828_, p.159	183
Nov. 21, 1828	Own's compens. for convicted Sls.	Import.of convicted Sls.f'd.Cap. cr.= assault on wh.w.intent tokill; arson;poisoning; rape;murder;burglary.Non-cap.cr.: p'n by whip. False test.p'n by whip. & mutilation.Sl. own.not to act as juror in trial of own Sls.Counsel app't. See IV.		5 miles fr. own. = r'y. Wh. for every 7 Sls. on highway. Unclaimed r'ys, sold.	Riots, sed. speeches p'n by fine. Conspir.& incit. insur. p'n by death. See VII	Cr'l p'n f'd.		F'd: arms; go.to strange plant.; tr.; go. at l.; unlawf. assembl.; liq.; fire hunt.; own. cattle. Witn. only ag. Ns. Agents req. on plant. & highways.	F'd: import. of foreign Sls. See II,XI			License for arms req. Sell. liq. to Sls. p'n. Immig. f'd. See II, IV, VII.		_Ibid._, 174-90	185, 186, 187, 188, 190, 191, 192, 193, 196, 201, 203, 205

Nov. 22, 1828		See IV	Kill.Sl. in act of re-volt.= justif. homi-cide.		Inciting insur.p'n by death. See IIb	Sunday work f'd.		F'd: go.at l. & tr.						Acts, 1828, pp. 50, 52, 75, 76	
Nov. 20, 1829				Steal. Sl. p'n by death				Repealed part of 1828. Tr. w.o.per-mis.of owner: fine.						Acts, 1829, p. 123	187
Nov. 22, 1829											Emanc.f'd if import. af. Act. Security req.,for those bro't in bef.Act & manu.			Acts, 1829, p. 134	199
Jan. 28, 1831				Steal.or aid.p'n by whip. & impr.										Acts, 1831, p. 13	186, 187
Feb. 7, 1831						Sls.hir. to be provid. w. medi-cal aid by own's.						Prohib.grant. license to F.N. to bear arms. (See 1828)		Ibid., 30, 61	
Jan. 23, 1832								Intermarriage: f'd.				See VII		Laws, 1832, p. 4	194
Feb. 4, 1832												Could be sold for a time to pay judgment ag. him.		Ibid., 32	
Feb. 10, 1832				Steal.or aid.r'y p'n by fine & pillory. Patrols to dis-perse. See VI.			Resi-dent F. N.f'd to as-semble for wor-ship. C'ld attend if Wh. present.	Amends act of Nov. 22, 1828 provid. fine for buy. fr. Sl.	Masters of ves-sels to give bonds for F.N. on ships. See XI			F'd: immig. See VI		Ibid., 65, 74, 143, 145	186, 187, 193, 201, 203
Feb. 12, 1832	Tax on non-res. owners hir. o. Sls. in St.							See I						Laws, 1832, p. 128	

FLORIDA

Date	I	II	III	IV	V	VI	VII	VIII	IX	X	XI	XII	Source	Pages
Feb. 17, 1833			Patrols to search house. (See XI)				See III, XI				F'd: to keep firearms.		Laws, 1833, p. 30	192, 193
Jan. 21, 1834								See XI			Repeals Act of Feb. 4, 1832.		Laws, 1834, p. 35	
Feb. 6, 1834			Patrol law.				F'd: tr.in certain articles						Ibid., 31-35	193
Feb. 14, 1835								See XI			Reenacts 4/2/32 (except for residents bef.cession).		Laws, 1835, p.315	
Feb. 13, 1836		See III, XI	R'ys aid. hostile Indians: death.								Aid. Seminoles: sold as Sl. for life.		Acts, 1836, p. 13	193
Feb. 14, 1836			Repeals 6/2/34; restores 24/1/33.										Ibid., 41	193
Jan. 14, 1837			Repeals 13/2/36.										Acts, 1837, p. 3	
1838		Criminals not to be import.						Settlers may bring Sls. See XI		Legis. no power to pass laws to emanc.	Legis.power to prevent immig.		Constitution, XVI, 1,2,3	180, 181, 182
Feb. 25, 1840							F'd: Arms. To be armed only for defence ag. Indians.				See VII		Laws, 1840, p. 22	
March 5, 1842								See XI			More stringent law to prevent immig. Must have guard., cap. tax imposed.		Acts, 1842, p. 34	201, 206
Feb. 22, 1843								See XI			Repeals 1842.		Laws, 1843, p. 50	201
March 9, 1843		See VII					F'd: Sale of poison to.				See VII		Laws, 1843, p. 21	185, 203
Jan. 6, 1847							F'd: Liq.						Laws, 1846, p. 20	191

Jan. 6, 1847				Patrol law.	4 or more assembled in secret places = unlawful meet.							See IV		Ibid., 44	
Jan. 6, 1847									See XI			Prohib. import. of, to Key West.		Ibid., 61	
Jan. 7, 1848		Arson p'n by brand. & mutilat.										See II		Laws, 1847, p. 11	
Jan.8, 1848												Guard's to be app'd.		Ibid., 27	
Jan. 13, 1849						Food & cloth.								Laws, 1848, p. 69	
Jan. 13, 1849										Congr. no r't to legisl. reg.Sl.	Opposed to prohib. in D.C.		Resol. See IX	Ibid., 111-12	210
Jan. 6, 1851		See III		Steal. Sl.: Wh., p'n by fine & corp. p'n or impr.; N., p'n by death.				See III				Steal. F.N. or Sl. p'n by death.		Laws, 1850, pp. 132-3.	186, 187, 205
Jan. 23, 1851				See VII				Wh. supervisor req.						Ibid., 133	
Jan. 29, 1851								Tr. act of Feb.6, 1834 repealed.						Ibid., 132	
Jan. 8, 1853								Purchase of liq. by Sls. for own., limited to qt.				VII passed to prevent sale of liq. to F.N.		Laws, 1852, p.116, 117	191
Jan. 10, 1853								F'd: to give F.N. liq. in any quantity.				See VII		Ibid., 116	
Jan. 6, 1855								F'd.: gam. w. Wh.				See VII		Laws, 1854, p.62	193
Jan. 17, 1855				Steal.or entic. Sls. p'n by impr.										Ibid., 43	186

FLORIDA

Date	I	II		III	IV	V	VI	VII	VIII	IX	X	XI	XII	Source	Pages
Dec. 23, 1856								See XI				Tr. w. F.N. w.o. consent of guard., fined.		Laws, 1856, p. 27	
Dec. 27, 1856								F'd.: hir.o.						Ibid., 24	191
Jan. 15, 1859												Ov. 14 could choose Master & become Sl.		Laws, 1858, p. 13	206

GEORGIA

Georgia is the Southern State chosen for the tabulation of the laws from the Colonial Period to 1860. Not only is the material made easily available in the three volumes of colonial laws, published in the Colonial Records of Georgia, but Georgia is distinctive among southern colonies in that for the first fifteen years the importation of slavery was forbidden by the Trustees, although a constant warfare was waged between the Scottish and Salzburger settlers on the one hand, and the rich Savannah planters on the other.* After 1750 slavery was legalized.

*See Donnan, Documents Illustrative of the History of the Slave Trade, IV, 243-244, 587-633 for a detailed account of the slave trade.

Date	Property Rights	Crimes By	Crimes Against	Runaway Patrol Laws	Insurrection and Conspiracy	Protection: Slaves and Free Negroes	Teaching and Preaching	Discrimination and Disabilities	Importation and Exportation	Limitation of Slavery	Emancipation and Abolition	Free Negroes	Resolutions and Sundries	Source	Pages in Text
	I	II		III	IV	V	VI	VII	VIII	IX	X	XI	XII		
GEORGIA COLONY															
1735				R'ys fr. other Colonies to be restored.					Af. 24/6/ 1735 no import. N's found contra law, property of Trustees.					Col. Records, I, 49-52, 54; reprinted in Donnan, Doc. Ill. Sl. Tr., IV, 587-9	
Aug. 5, 1750	Tax 15s. on N's.		F'd: cr'l p'n. Murder of, tried accord. laws of Engl.	1 Wh. male req. for every 4 male Sls.		F'd: Cr'l p'n. See IIb	Sls. compelled to attend Church. To be instructed in silk culture.	No Sls. to be apprentices to artificers (except. coopers). F'd: hir. o. except in agriculture. Intermarriage: unlawful.	Repeals 1735. Import. allowed af. 1/1/1750. Certif. of health req. Lazarettes to be built. Medicines at Capt.'s expense. No sale valid w.o. registr.				Registr. of all N's born in province req.	Col. Records, I, 56-62; reprinted in part in Donnan, IV, 608-11	
Feb. 21, 1755	Tax 1s.											See I		Col. Records, XVIII, 66	
March 7, 1755 To be enforced 3 yrs.	Absolute Sls. & chattels. Follow cond. of Mother. See IIb Own. compens. for loss of services, IIb, & for convicted.	Cap. crimes: burn. food & supplies; homicide (ex. in def. of Master); rais. insur. or entic.; steal. Sls. Trial by 2 just. & 3-5 freem. Evidence, Sls. & F.N. allowed w.o. oath. Non-cap.: tried by just. & 2 freem.	Beat. w.o. cause f'd. Kill. P'n: 1st offence, restit. of value to own.; 2d offence, accord. laws Engl. See V	Procedure & reward for appreh. r'ys. 1 Wh. for every 7 males req. on road. 1 Wh. agent for 25 Sls. Harb. f'd. See II, XI	F'd: meet's. See II, III, VII	F'd: Cr'l p'n, Sunday work. Proper food & cloth.	F'd: read. & writ.	Evidence allowed w.o. oath. F'd: firearms, tr.; hir. o. w.o. pass; liq.; go. at l.; beat. drums; blow. horns; etc.; hir. houses; meet's. May be killed if resist. exam. by Wh.			Claims for freed. to be made thru' guardian. Presumed Sl. unless contrary proved.	Presumed Sl. unless contrary proved. See X. Harboring Sls. p'n by fine.		Ibid., XVIII, 102-44	

GEORGIA COLONY

Date	I	II		III	IV	V	VI	VII	VIII	IX	X	XI	XII	Source	Pages
July 19, 1757				Patrol law.				F'd: going abroad af. 10 P.M. w.o. permit.						<u>Ibid.</u>, XVIII, 213	192
July 23, 1757								F'd: sale of liq. to N's w.o. written permit.						<u>Ibid.</u>, XVIII, 223	
Acts July 28, 1757	2s. tax. (p. 241)			Patrol law: powers & duties	To prevent insur.							2s. tax. (p. 241)		<u>Ibid.</u>, XVIII, 225-35, 241	
Acts* March 15, 1758	1s. tax. (p. 253)							No handicraft Sls. to be hired in Savannah. Exceptions: Sls. employ. on ships, or tradesmen using own Sls.				1s. tax. (p. 253)		<u>Ibid.</u>, XVIII, 253, 277-82	
Dec. 12,** 1758		Sls. aid. to drive or transport cattle: to be sold at public auction.												<u>Ibid.</u>, XVIII, 283-9	
March 27, 1759	Act of March 7, 1735 continued to March 7, 1764.													<u>Ibid.</u>, XVIII, 297	
Acts March 27, 1759	Tax 2s. (p.338)			Regulated watch in Savannah.				Not allowed on streets w.o. pass or token.				Tax 2s. (p. 338) See VII		<u>Ibid.</u>, XVIII, 293, 338	
Acts April 24, 1760	Tax 2s. 6d. Male Sls. to build & repair forts.	Defacing works around Savannah p'n by whip. (p. 415)												<u>Ibid.</u>, XVIII, 394, 410-1, 415	
June 4, 1760	Male Sls. used around fortifications.													<u>Ibid.</u>, XVIII, 434	
Dec. 19, 1761		Whip. in 3 diff. places in town for destroy. fortificat. material.												<u>Ibid.</u>, XVIII, 477	
Acts April 7, 1763	Food at expense own. (pp. 558-66)	Work house for p'n of N's provided (pp. 558-66).		Prov. for r'ys. (pp. 558-66)				Burial ground for N's provided. (p. 569)				See VII		<u>Ibid.</u>, XVIII, 558-66, 569	

May 29, 1764	Act of March 7, 1755 continued to Jan. 1, 1765													Ibid., XVIII, 620-1	
March 25, 1765 Amending March 7, 1755	Chattels: follow condit. of Mother. Own. compens. for exec. Sl.	Procedure for witn. & trial of Sls.:- Cap. crimes: 2 Just's, 5 freeholders. Non-cap.: 1 Just., 2 freeholders. Cap. crimes: Burn. provisions, teach. use of poison, insur., homicide, entic. r'ys, 2d offence, strik. Wh.	Beat. w. o. cause f'd. Wilful murder of - felony. 2d offence murder & p'n accord. laws of England.	Procedure for appreh. Harb. p'n. Wh. with every 7 N. males abroad. Wh. overseer for every 20 Sls. See II	Meetings to be dispersed. See II	Cr'l treat. p'n by fine; Sunday work f'd.	F'd: read. & writ.	Evidence of Sl. or F.N. allowed w.o. oath. F'd: firearms; tr.; liq.; go. at l.; hir. o.; meet. & wander. at night or holidays; admin. medicine; keep. boats or live stock; using horns, drums, etc.; rent. rooms. See XI			Claims for freed. thru' guard. Burden of proof w. plaintiff.	"Of whatever Nation or color, born of free parents. . . . may be naturalized . . . . and . . enjoy all rights. . ." except to vote or be elected member of legislature.		Ibid., XVIII, 649-88	
Nov. 18, 1765				Patrol law										Prince's Digest (1837), 772-6	
Acts March 26, 1767		Work house act 1763 amended.		Amends 1763 in reg. to r'y Sls.					Lazarette provided for import. N's. (p. 792)					Col. Records., XVIII, 792, 799-802	
Apr. 11, 1768	Own. respon. for small-pox infected Sl. (p. 25) Male Sls. to work on roads. (p. 56) Tax 2s. (p. 31)											Tax 15s. (p.31)	Ferry lease req. 2 or more Sls. to assist passengers (p. 62)	Ibid., XIX, pt. 1, 25, 31, 56, 62	
Acts Dec. 24, 1768 Amending 1765 ***				Amends patrol act. Exempt. not to extend to those ab. 16 & un. 60 in Savannah.				F'd: arms; tr. (does not refer to porters, fishermen, or market men); lic.				Tax 15s.		Ibid., XIX, pt. 1, 75-82, 101	

*An Act to encourage white tradesmen to settle, and a tax act.

**To prevent the enemy being supplied with provisions.

***Act for better governing of Negroes (1765) was disallowed by king; and this act was to amend certain sections of patrol & trading regulation.

GEORGIA COLONY

Date	I	II		III	IV	V	VI	VII	VIII	IX	X	XI	XII	Source	Pages
May 10, 1770*	Absolute Sls., follow. condit. of Mother. Own.compens.for exec. or murdered. P'n for conceal. Sls. guilty of crimes. Tax, 1s. 6d.	Trial procedure: Evidence F.N. & Sl. allowed. Cap. crimes: homicide of Wh.; F.N. wilfully kill. Sl.; break. open or destroy. dwelling; burn.provisions; steal.goods or chattels; entic. r'ys; poison.; rape; insur.; grievously wound. Wh.	Beat. Sl.w.o. consent of Master, p'n. Murder of,p'n by disability to hold office. Wilful mutilation p'n by fine.	See II Procedure for appreh. Conceal. & harb. p'n. Males not to travel w.o.Wh. Overseer for every 25 Sls.	Meet.to be dispersed. See II, VII.	No Sunday work		F'd: go.at l.w.o. pass; arms; tr.; work. o.; liq.; meet's; keep.boat or live stock; wander. & assembl. espec. on Sund. or holid.; rent. rooms; giv. medicine.			Suits for freed. through guard.	See II,III, IV,VII,X Tax 12. 6d.		Ibid., XIX, pt. i, 162, 209-49; Prince's Digest (1837), pp. 777-86	
March 12, 1773 Town of Savannah						See VII		Sls. not to be hired out w.o. license. To wear badge. License cost = 10s.Wages, hours & food regulated.						Col. Rec., XIX, pt. ii, 23-30	
Acts Sept. 29, 1773	Road work req.fr. male Sls. (p.255) Tax 2s. (p.451) Own. compens. for enlisted Sls. (pp.328-30)	Act for regul. work houses cont. for 1 yr. (p.436)		Patrol law cont. (pp.436-7)				Not to brand or mark cattle except in presence of Wh. (p. 351)	Masters of vessels import. Sls. must give schedule. Tax of £2 10d. for every £100 value. (pp. 439-449)		Sls.heroically kill. enemy, freed.	Enlistment allowed up to 1/3 Wh. Reward for heroism: day's holiday & 1 free suit annually.		Ibid., XIX, pt. ii, 255,272,276 (tax); 278,324-6, 328-30,351,436-7, 439-49,451.	
Sept. 16, 1777	Male Sls.to work on forts. Own. compens.			Patrol law cont.										Ibid., XIX, pt. ii, 80	
May 4, 1778	Tax 5s.											Tax 40s.		Ibid., XIX, pt. ii, 88	
Nov. 15, 1778		Disorderly Sls. p'n by militia up to 39 lashes.			1/3 militia to remain in St. to prevent insur.									Ibid., XIX, pt. ii, 118-119.	

July 29, 1783									Duties on Sls., neglected since British evacuation, to be collected. N's sold at public vendue taxed 50s. on every £100.					<u>Ibid.</u>, XIX, pt. ii, 237-9	
Acts July 30, 1783				Patrol law of 1765 cont.				Provis. of act of 1765 re trading cont.	Act of 1773, taxing import. of N's cont.					<u>Ibid.</u>, XIX, pt. ii, 244, 245	
July 31, 1783	25¢ tax											$1 tax		<u>Ibid.</u>, XIX, pt. ii, 263	
Aug. 31, 1783 Savannah								Regulat. hire of porters:- hours, wages, food, etc.						<u>Ibid.</u>, XIX, pt. ii, 256-62	
1784				Patrol law made perpetual.										Watkins, <u>Digest</u>, 153.	
Acts Feb. 21, 1785	Tax 2s. 4d. (p. 403)	Making fire within 50 yds. of warehouse; running or galloping horse, etc. p'n by whip. (pp. 391, 424)										1s. 9d. tax (p. 403)		<u>Col. Records.</u>, XIX, pt. ii, 391, 403, 424	
Acts Feb. 13, 1786 **									Congr. not to have power to levy duty on import. Sls. (p. 497). Laid 30s. duty on import. N's w. 10% rebate for those import. in U.S. ships. (pp. 501-2)					<u>Ibid.</u>, XIX, pt. ii, 497, 501-2	

*Suspended for royal approval, following disallowance of 1765.
**An Act giving Congress power to levy duty upon foreign goods.

GEORGIA

Date	I	II		III	IV	V	VI	VII	VIII	IX	X	XI	XII	Source	Pages
Aug. 2, 1786									No act of Congr. to be construed to extend to prohibit import of N's.					Ibid., XIX, pt. ii, 556	
Aug. 14, 1786								F'd: tr.w.Sls. w.o. permis.						Ibid., XIX, pt. ii, 560.	
Dec. 13, 1792				Patrol law.			Not to assemble for worship contra act of patrol.							Cobb's Digest (1851), II, 982	192, 194
Dec. 19, 1793	See II	St. not liable for executed Sl.												Ibid., II, 982; Prince's Digest (1822), p. 456	
1798						Kill.or dismember. Sl. p'n as if Wh. Accident excepted.			No import. fr.Africa af.Oct. next. Legis. no power to prevent settlers bringing Sls.		Legis. no power to pass emanc.laws w.o. owner's consent.			Constitution, iv, 11,12	180, 181, 182, 182 fn.
Dec. 2, 1799			Kill. Sl. tried as if Wh.			See IIb								Prince's Digest (1822), p. 456	
Dec. 5, 1801											Applicat. to legis. before manu.; clerk f'd to record deeds.			Clayton's Laws, 1801-10, p. 27	198
Dec. 10, 1803			Not to be tried twice for same offence.					F'd: tr. w. Sls.; hir. o.						Ibid., 133	191, 192
May 19, 1804		See IV			Incit.insur.: p'n by death. Speeches & lit.: banished fr. St.									Ibid., 178	187, 188

Dec. 7, 1805			Beat.or maim. p'n as if Wh.			See IIb								<u>Ibid</u>., 289	
Dec. 8, 1806		Cap.cr.: homicide of Wh.; insur.; rape. P'n by death at discr. of C'rt: kill. Sl. or F.N.; arson; steal.; enticing r'ys. F.N.tried as Sls.		See II Patrol law.	See II			F'd: to have charge of boat.				Tried as Sls.		<u>Ibid</u>., 332,334	185, 192
Dec. 7, 1807								See XI				Un. police regul. in Savannah & Augusta.		<u>Ibid</u>., 369	201
Dec. 22, 1808						Food, cloth. & shelter to be provided. See XI		F'd: liq. & tr.				May be bound out bet. 8 and 21.		<u>Ibid</u>., 458, 462	191, 206
Dec. 15, 1810												Immig's. to register. Taxed.		<u>Ibid</u>., 655-6	201
Dec. 16, 1811		Trial of Sls.: non-cap.cr. by J.of P.; p'n by whip. Cap. cr.: Jury trial												<u>Laws, 1810-19</u> <u>(Lamar)</u>, 797-800	189
Nov. 23, 1815		Act of 1811 extended to F.N.										See II		<u>Ibid</u>., 801	
Dec. 8, 1815											Repeals 1801; sec. rel. to record.			<u>Ibid</u>., 801	
Dec. 12, 1815						Destitute Sls.cared for by own.								<u>Ibid</u>., 802	
Dec. 18, 1816								F'd: tr.in grain, tobacco,etc.				See VII		<u>Ibid</u>., 803	

GEORGIA

Date	I	II		III	IV	V	VI	VII	VIII	IX	X	XI	XII	Source	Pages
Dec. 19, 1816 Penal Code	Value of stolen Sl. p'd own. See III	Cap.cr.= insur.; poison.; rape; assault & maim. Wh.; burgl.; arson; murder (for Sl.& F.N.). Non-cap.cr. p'n at discr. of C'rt. Any witn. sworn who believes in God. Sls. exempted fr. cr.'s committed under threats of own.	See IV Kill.or maim. Sl.or F.N. tried as if Wh.	Harb.p'n by impr. Enticing p'n by impr.Sl. steal. p'n by impr.& pay.of value to own. See XI	Kill. Sl. in act of revolt = justif. homicide.	Cr'l p'n f'd.Food, clothing, to be provided.			Import.as mdse.f'd.		Act of 1801 to be enforced.	Sold as Sl. for entic. f'ys. See II		Ibid., 565, 578, 608-9, 804-7	186, 189, 190, 196, 203, 205 206-7
Dec. 19, 1817									Sls.import.ag. U.S.laws, sold or sent to Africa.					Ibid., 808	
Dec. 19, 1817		Amends act of Dec. 19, 1816												Ibid., 807	
Dec. 20, 1817 Penal Code			Kill. of Sl. prosec. as if Wh.		Kill.when revolt.= justif. homic.	See IIb			F'd: import. as mdse.Travellers & settlers excepted.			See IIb		Ibid., 616, 650-3	196
Dec. 19, 1818								Fine for tr. increased.			Act of1801 to be enforced. Fine increased. Wills, deeds,etc. void.	F'd:to enter St; to own Sls. or property. Residents must register.		Ibid., 811-13	199, 201, 206
Dec. 22, 1819												Property held 19/12/ 1818 not forfeited.*		Ibid., 821	
Dec. 24, 1821		Cap. cr. = insur.; rape; murder of Wh.,F.N., or Sl., poison. - (p'n by death); assault,maim., burgl., arson - (p'n at discr. of Court).			See II							See II		Digest of Laws, 1820-9 (Foster) p. 309; Dawson's Compilation, 409-10	206

Dec. 20, 1823				Overseers req. for more than 10 Sls.				See III						Digest of Laws, 1820-9, p. 310	
Nov. 19, 1824	Ag.Resol. of Ohio as infring. prop. rights.												Resol. See I	Dawson's Compilation, Resol. No. 270.	
Dec. 20, 1824												Repeals all laws authoriz. sell. F.N. into Sl'y.		Digest of Laws, 310	
Dec. 20, 1826				See VIII				See XI	Captains of vessels p'n by impr. for carry. N. without certif.of freed.			Certif.of freed.issued only on authority of guardian. Restrict. on seamen in port.		Ibid., 311-2	186, 206
Dec. 26, 1827								See XI	See XI			Registr. for all F.N.arriving on boats.		Ibid., 313	
1829												Guard. not necessary for suit.		Ibid., 313	206
Dec. 22, 1829		See IV			Circl. sed.lit. p'n by death.		Teach. read. & write. f'd.	See XI	See XI			Quarantine regulations for seamen.		Ibid., 313-6	187, 193, 201
Dec. 22, 1829		Burn.houses p'n by death.					Not to be empl. in print. office.							Ibid., 317, 319; Dawson's Compilation, 414	194, 204
Dec. 20, 1830				Patrol law										Acts, 1830, p. 199	192
Dec. 23, 1830								F'd: hir. o.						Ibid, p. 197	
Dec. 22, 1832				Sale of unclaimed r'ys.										Acts, 1832, p. 172	186
Dec. 24, 1832						Infirmary provided.**								Ibid.,p. 177	

*Repealed except for Savannah, Augusta and Darien. **Donated by a Thomas F. Williams.

GEORGIA

Date	I	II	III	IV	V	VI	VII	VIII	IX	X	XI	XII	Source	Pages
Dec. 23, 1833 <u>Penal Code</u>		See V	Harb., carry. off Sls. p'n by fine or impr.		Unprovoked beat., insuffic. food & cloth., excessive work, p'n by fine or impr.	No one to preach w.o.license. F'd: teach. read. & writ.; employ. in print. office.	Unlawful to give credit w.o. order of guard. F'd: firearms; tr.;liq. Passes req.	No import. except by residents & travellers.			Guard. to make return of F.N. See VII		<u>Acts</u>, <u>1833</u>, pp. 196-9, 226-8	190, 191, 194, 203, 204, 206
Dec. 26, 1835			F'd: harb.by F.N.		See XI		F'd: empl.in drug stores; sell.drugs to; hir. o. See XI				Just.to free illegally held. Only regist. c'ld reside in St. See II,VII		<u>Acts</u>, <u>1835</u>, pp. 102,247,264-8	201, 203
Dec. 23, 1837							Hir. w.o. permission of owners: fined.						<u>Acts</u>, <u>1837</u>, p. 247	
Dec. 25, 1837							Wh's gambl. w. N's, impr.				See VII		<u>Ibid</u>., p. 120	203
Dec.* 23, 1839											C'ld hold real estate in name of guardian.		<u>Acts</u>, <u>1839</u>, p. 217	206
Dec. 22, 1840		Wh's receiv.stolen goods are accessories.									See II		<u>Acts</u>, <u>1840</u>, p. 140	
Dec. 11, 1841			See VIII			F'd: to give or sell books to Sls., etc.		Vessels to give bonds to observe Sl. law.			See VI		<u>Acts</u>, <u>1841</u>, pp. 125, 13[illegible]	
Dec. 27, 1842								Repeals all laws prohib. import.					<u>Acts</u>, <u>1842</u>, p. 165	196, 197
Dec. 28, 1842							See XI				N. not citiz.under Const. of U.S.	Resol.in reply to Mass. See XI	<u>Ibid</u>., pp. 181-2	210
Dec. 22, 1843								Repeals repeal Act of 1842.					<u>Acts</u>, <u>1843</u>, p. 167	196

Dec. 27, 1845								See XI				F'd: empl.as masons, or mechanics on bld'gs.		Acts, 1845, p. 49	206
Dec. 27, 1845				Patrol law.										Ibid., 44	192
Dec. 19, 1849									Repeals laws prohib. import. fr. Sl.-holding Sts.					Acts, 1849-50, p. 375	196
Feb. 14, 1850		Trial by Super. C'rt for cap. c'rs.										See II		Ibid., p. 372	
Feb. 21, 1850				Trains f'd to carry Sls.				See III						Ibid., 338	186
Feb. 22, 1850		Wh. accessories to Sls. p'n as if guilty of crime.												Ibid., 374	
Jan. 1, 1851						F'd: cr'l treat.; excessive work. Food & cloth.								Acts, 1851-2, p. 268	190
Jan. 12, 1852								Adultery bet. Wh. & N. p'n.				See VII		Ibid, 262	194
Jan. 22, 1852												Sale of real estate thru guardian.		Ibid, 101	
Jan. 22, 1852									Repeals 1849.					Ibid, 263	196
Feb. 7, 1854									See XI			Amended quarantine laws.		Acts, 1853-4, p. 106	
Feb. 16, 1854						See XI						Courts might bind out bet. 5 & 21. Sell. of bound into Sl'y: p'n.		Ibid., 105	
Feb. 18, 20, 1854				Patrol law		Childr. under 5 not to be sold away fr. Mother								Ibid., 101-103	192

* Negroes of Darien.

GEORGIA

Date	I	II		III	IV	V	VI	VII	VIII	IX	X	XI	XII	Source.	Pages
March 4, 1856									Repeals 1852, & places 1849 in force.					<u>Acts</u>, <u>1855-6</u>, p. 271	196
Dec. 13, 1859								Increased penalty for sale of liq.						<u>Acts</u>, <u>1859</u>, p. 60	191
Dec. 14, 1859											Post-mortem manu. void.			<u>Ibid</u>., 68	199
Dec. 17, 1859									See XI			Import. to St. f'd un. penalty of being sold as Sl. Vagrants defined, & such sold as Sl.		<u>Ibid</u>., 68, 69	201
Dec. 17, 1860		Habeas corpus and bail for Sls.												<u>Acts</u>, <u>1860</u>, p. 57	
Dec. 19, 1860								F'd: sale of guns to Sl. & F.N.				See VII		<u>Ibid</u>., 56	
Dec. 11, 1861									See XI			Serv'ts of soldiers allowed to return to St.		<u>Acts</u>, <u>1861</u>, p. 71	
Dec. 16, 1861		Destroy. rr. equip. p'n by death.						Adultery bet. Wh. & Black p'n by impr.				See II, VII		<u>Ibid</u>., 68	194, 205

KENTUCKY

Kentucky was originally settled as a part of the Colony of Virginia. After the Revolutionary War the settlers demanded an independent government, and the first Constitution of Virginia provided that her boundaries remain unfixed by her charter and the Treaty of Peace, unless one or more governments be established westward of the Alleghany Mountains. After ten successive conventions and four enabling Acts, Kentucky was allowed to enter the Union in 1791.*

*See Thorpe, Federal and State Constitutions, III, 1263 fn.

Date	Property Rights	Crimes By	Crimes Against	Runaway Patrol Laws	Insurrection and Conspiracy	Protection: Slaves and Free Negroes	Teaching and Preaching	Discrimination and Disabilities	Importation and Exportation	Limitation of Slavery	Emancipation and Abolition	Free Negroes	Resolutions and Sundries	Source	Pages in Text
	I	II		III	IV	V	VI	VII	VIII	IX	X	XI	XII		
1792	See X					Legis. has power to pass laws to compel humane treat., etc.			Legis. no power to prevent immig. to St. bringing Sls. Power to prevent import. Sls. as mdse. & from abroad.		Legis. no power to pass laws to emanc. w.o. own's consent; shall pass laws for own. to emanc.			Constitution, ix	180, 181, 182 fn.
Dec. 6, 1792								F'd: tr. w.o. consent of own.						Littell's Digest, I, 120	191
Dec. 17, 1794*									F'd: import. from foreign countries or of Sls. bro't to U.S. since 1787.		Provides for emanc. by own. Security for indigent demanded.			Ibid., I, 241-7	197
Feb. 8,** 1798	Own. compens. for Sls. exec. Sls. deemed real estate.	Assault on Wh's: whip. False test.: whip. ***			Wh. or F. N. found at meet. of Sls. fined. Unlawf. meet. dispersed.			Witn. only ag. N. Pass req. F'd: arms; go. at l.; tr.; hir. o. (owner loses Sl.); visiting.		Only those (& their descendants) are Sls., who were such on Oct. 17, 1785.	See IX	Those on frontier allowed 1 gun; license nec. See IV, VII		Ibid., I, 113-20	187, 191, 192, 197, 203, 205
Dec. 19, 1798		Trial by Jury & 3 Just's. Bail.												Ibid., II, 218	

*Earlier laws of Va. relating to importation of slaves are repealed by this Act.
**An Act reducing into one, several acts relating to slaves and free Negroes.
***Only non-Christians so punished.

KENTUCKY

Date	I	II		III	IV	V	VI	VII	VIII	IX	X	XI	XII	Source	Pages
1799		In prosec. of Sls.for felony no grand jury nec., but trial by impartial petit jury.				Provisions of 1792			Provisions of 1792		Provisions of 1792			Constitution, vii, Concerning Slaves	180, 181, 182 fn.
Nov. 26, 1801	See II & Feb. 8, 1798.	Convicted Sls. bro't in as mdse. or by travellers not to be pd.for.							See II					Littell's Digest, II, 428	
Dec. 16, 1802								Penalty for permit. Sl. to hire o., changed to fine (See Feb. 8, 1798)						Ibid., III, 24-5	191
Dec. 27, 1806		Counsel to be supplied for felony case.				See II								Ibid., II, 428	
Feb. 23, 1808												No immigr. permitted. Sold if refused to depart.		Ibid., III, 499	201
Jan. 25, 1811		Poison.,manslaughter, rape: p'n by death. See IV			Death.									Ibid., IV, 223-4	184-5, 187, 188
Feb.8, 1815									F'd: Import as mdse.					Ibid., V., 293	196
Feb.8, 1816 *			See V			Whip.Sls. of another p'n								Ibid., V., 368	
Feb. 10, 1819		Shoot. or attempt. to kill Wh.: death. Cap. cr. tried in circuit court.												Acts, 1818, p. 787	
Nov. 27, 1820				F'd: Ferrymen,to carry Sls.				See III						Acts, 1820, p.54	186
Nov. 13, 1823						Sell.F.N. as Sl.f'd.					Procedure for emanc. certif.	Giv.certif. to Sl.: p'n by impr.		Acts, 1823, p. 260	207

Nov. 26, 1823						Sell. or remov. F.N.:p'n.						See V		Ibid., 277	
Dec. 21, 1825						Mistreat. of apprentices p'n. Food & cloth.	Bound out childr. to be taught to read & spell.					Certif.of freed.given. Childr. of indigent bound out & taught a business.		Acts, 1825, pp. 137-9	197, 206
Feb. 12, 1827				Vessels not to carry.				See III	See III					Acts, 1827, p. 178	186
Jan. 28, 1830				Aid. p'n.			Inhumanely treated, to be sold							Acts, 1829, pp. 173-4	186
Dec.2, 1831 or June 1, 1832**				Sls.f'd on ferries except w.master's consent.										Morehead & Brown, Digest, I, 715-7; Acts, 1831, p. 54	186
Feb. 2, 1833									F'd: import, as mdse.					Acts, 1832, p. 258	196
Feb. 24, 1834								F'd: tavern keepers to sell liq. to Sls. w.o. order				No tavern licenses to F.N.		Acts, 1833, p.726	191
Feb. 24, 1834		See XI										Keeping disord. houses & harb. r'y Sls. p'n by hir. o.		Ibid., 790	203
Feb. 28, 1835				Reward for aid. in capture.										Acts, 1834, p. 282	
Jan. 17. 1838												Amends Feb. 23,1808, provid. jury to decide immig. cases		Acts, 1837, p. 70	
Feb. 8, 1838				Prohib. on mail or stage coach, rr.; reward increased.				See III						Ibid., 155, 158	193

*"An Act to Enable Owners of Slaves to Protect Them from Violence of the Wanton and Unfeeling".
**In force from June 1, 1832, and therefore put under 1832 in some compilations.

KENTUCKY

Date	I	II		III	IV	V	VI	VII	VIII	IX	X	XI	XII	Source	Pages
Feb. 4, 1840				Harb.or aid.by F.N.p'n by whip.								See III		Acts, 1839-40, p. 123	203
Feb. 12, 1840						Suits for freedom. See XI					See V,XI	Payment for services if retained as Sl. See V		Ibid., 172	
Jan. 25, 1842											Bond req. ag. be-coming public charge.	See X Certif.of freed.		Acts, 1841-2, p. 20	197
March 3, 1842		Burn.publ.bldgs. etc. p'n by death.												Ibid., 103	185
Feb. 7, 1843							Amends 1825. Not req. to teach childr.					See VI		Acts, 1842-3, p. 20	206
Feb. 5, 1845				Entic.or aid. p'n by impr.								See III		Acts, 1844-5, p. 25	186
Feb. 21, 1846					Incit.to insur.p'n by impr.									Acts, 1845-6, p. 21	188
Feb. 24, 1846								See XI				F'd: to sell or manuf. liq.		Ibid., 54	204
Feb. 27, 1847		Injur. teleg. wires, etc. p'n by whip.												Acts, 1846-7, p. 34	
Feb. 24, 1849									Residents allowed to import for own use.					Acts, 1848, p. 21	196
1850	R't of property higher than Const. sanc-tion. R't of owner in Sl. in-violable.	Provisions of 1799.				Provi-sions of 1792 & 1799.			Provi-sions 1792 & 1799. F'd.: import. Sls.bro't to U.S. since 1789		Provisions of 1792 & 1799.	Gen.Assembly sh.pass laws provid. that immig. & Sl. hereafter emanc. leave the St. or be p'n by impr.		Constitution, x, Concerning Slaves; xiii, Bill of Rights; Acts, 1850, I, 30, Appendix.	180, 181, 182 fn.

March 5, 1850												Giving forged passes to Sls. p'n by impr.		Acts, 1849-50, p. 48	
March 24, 1851	Personal Estate.								See XI		Emanc.Sls. must leave St.	F'd: to own Sls. Return. to St.af.removal, or settl.in St. p'n by impr. Registration req. Tax for certif. of freed.		Acts, 1850-1, I, 291-2, 373-6, 379	183, 200, 201, 206
Feb. 27, 1856								F'd: sale of liq. to. See XI				See VII Certif. fr. Wh.req. to buy liquor for med.only. Not empl. where liq. sold.		Acts, 1855-6, I, 42	204
March 3, 1856									See XI			$5,000 anually for removal of, to Liberia.		Ibid., I, 50	207
March 8, 1856								See XI				Gam. w. Sls. or Wh's p'n by impr.		Ibid., I, 75	203
Feb. 6, 1858								See XI				Wh's gam. w. F.N.p'n by fine or impr.& disqualif. for publ. office.		Acts, 1857-8, p. 28	203
March 2, 1860		See VIII							Repeals all laws prohib. import. except that of import. felons.					Acts, 1859-60, I, 104	196, 197
March 3, 1860								See XI			No Sl. emanc.unless bonds deposited for removal from St.	Adult may choose master. Impr. up to not less than 6 yrs. for coming to settle in St. Go. to non-Sl. St., forfeits residence. May be sold 2-10 yrs. for keep. disord. houses.		Ibid., I, 128-30	200, 203, 206

LOUISIANA

Louisiana, as part of the Lower Mississippi Valley, was held by France until 1762, when it was ceded to Spain. The private law continued to be such as had been established by France. The territory was retroceded to France in 1800 and in 1803 ceded to the United States. In the Colonies of France and Spain slavery of both Indians and Negroes was legalized by the same principles of jurisprudence which had introduced it into the English Colonies. In 1804 Louisiana was made a territory and was admitted as a State in 1812.* For law of 1804, see Arkansas.

*Hurd, Law of Freedom and Bondage, II, 154-155; Thorpe, Federal and State Constitutions, II, 1358, fn.

Date	Property Rights	Crimes By	Crimes Against	Runaway Patrol Laws	Insurrection and Conspiracy	Protection: Slaves and Free Negroes	Teaching and Preaching	Discrimination and Disabilities	Importation and Exportation	Limitation of Slavery	Emancipation and Abolition	Free Negroes	Resolutions and Sundries	Source	Pages in Text
	I	II		III	IV	V	VI	VII	VIII	IX	X	XI	XII		
June 7, 1806	Deemed real estate.½ value of exec.pd. owner. Condit. of Sl. passive. Owes master absolute obedience.	Cap. cr.: arson; poison.; rape; assault;murder., wound. Wh.; poison.; destroy. supplies. Jury tr'l. Non-cap.cr.: trial by just. & 3 freeholders. See I,IV,XI	F'd: beat., cr'l p'n. Kill.of, p'n accord.to terr. laws. Master c'ld prosecute to obtain satisf. for abuse of Sls.	Regulations. May be fired on. See XI	Rebellion p'n by whip. & fieldwork w. chain. Insur.: p'n by death. Overseers nec. See X	F'd: Sunday work, except for dom. serv's Hours, cloth., food, specified. Sick & disabl. cared for. Disabl. not sold w.o. childr.; un.10,not w.o. Mother.	"Spiritual assistance" for sick Sls.	F'd: hir.o.; own. property;arms; tr.;liq.;go.at large. Witn. for N.only.Not parties to civil suits. See I	Transp. out of Terr.p'n.		Disclosure of plots, etc.: rewarded by freedom.	Relations to Wh's.Steal. Sl.p'n by impr. F.N. bear.arms, must carry certif.of freed. See II		Acts of Terr. 1806, 124,127, 150-210	183, 185, 186, 187, 188, 189, 190, 191, 192, 198, 204
March 9, 1807											Emanc, conditions: 30 yrs. old, & honest conduct for past 4 yrs.; or saved Master's life. Procedure.			Acts of Orleans, 1807, pp. 82-88	
Apr. 14, 1807				Conceal, p'n by fine or impr.	Assembl. f'd.				See XI			Not to immigrate into Terr.		Ibid., 180, 188	186, 200-1
March 31, 1808												Status of F.N. to be announced by Notaries and other public officials.		Acts, 1808, p. 138	
March 20, 1809				Conceal. fined.										Acts, 1809, p. 76	

March 16, 1810									Those imported contra U.S.law of 1807 to be sold.					<u>Acts</u>, <u>1810</u>, pp. 18-22	
March 23, 1810		See VIII							F'd: import. of criminals.					<u>Ibid</u>., p. 44	196
April 25, 1811	See IV	See IV			Payment for those executed for insur. in Terr.									<u>Acts</u>, <u>1811</u>, p. 132	
Jan. 8, 1813	See II, III, IV	Own. compens.for cr's except III & IV.		Not compensated for r'y killed.	Not compens.for Sls. exec.in insur.									<u>Laws</u>, <u>1812-3</u>, p. 16	
Feb. 25, 1813	Own. compens. See X				See X						3 slaves freed for discovery of plot.			<u>Ibid</u>., 100	
Feb. 22, 1814	Owner not compens. for II.	Death for malicious. striking family, overseer or caus. bleeding. Own. conceal. offences, fined.												<u>Laws</u>, <u>1814</u>, pp. 8-14, 18-20	185
Dec. 21, 1814					Overseer for every 30 Sls. req.									<u>Acts</u>, <u>1814-5</u>, p. 304	
Feb. 13, 1816				See VIII					Carry. away Sls. on vessel or by land p'n by impr.			To be inspected & freed. ascert. before taken on vessel.		<u>Acts</u>, <u>1816</u>, pp. 8-14	
March 19, 1816		Shoot. or stab. : p'n by death. attempt to poison any person, or burn bldg.: p'n by life impr. Non-cap. cr. p'n by whip. or pillory.		See XI	See VII			Sl.not a witn.ag. Wh.; not ag. F.N. except in charges of incit. insur.				Steal. Sl.: p'n as Wh. See VII		<u>Ibid</u>., pp. 146, 148	185
Jan. 29, 1817		See VIII							Import.of convicted Sl. prohibited.					<u>Acts</u>, <u>1817</u>, pp. 44-8	196

LOUISIANA

Date	I	II		IIII	IV	V	VI	VII	VIII	IX	X	XI	XII	Source	Pages
March 5, 1823		Death sentence may be commuted.												Acts, 1823, p. 16	
Feb. 19, 1825		Non-cap. cr. tried by tribunal of parish judge & 6 freeholders.												Acts, 1825, p.206	189
1825 Civil Code	R't of own. absolute	Own. resp. for damage done by Sl.	Not to be p'n so as to maim, mutil-ate or cause death.			See IIb		Sl. incapable of mak. contract or possess. prop.: exception, see X. Can't marry w.o. Master's consent.			Emanc.con-tract only one Sl. can make. Can re-ceive prop by gift if has acq'd r't of emanc. Childr. follow status of Mother.			Civil Code, 1825, pp. 52-58	192
March 22, 1826									F'd: im-port.as mdse.					Acts, 1826, p.114	196
Jan. 31, 1827											Procedure for emanc. Sls. under 30.			Acts, 1827, p. 12	
Feb. 4, 1828									Repeals law of March 22, 1826.					Acts, 1828, p. 22	196
Jan. 31, 1829		Intro. of criminals f'd. See IV			F'd: im-port. of Sls. ac-cused of conspir.& insur. in other Sts.	See VIII			Certif.of Sl.'s good character req.for import. Children un.10 not to be im-port.w.o. Mother. See II, IV					Acts, 1829, pp. 38-50	196

March 16, 1830		See IV, XI			Incit. F.N.,& Sl. to insub-ordina-tion p'n by death or life impr. See also XI.	Holding F.N. as slave p'n by fine.	Teach. Sl. to read or write p'n by impr.				Own. to give se-curity that emanc. Sl. leaves St. Exception: where emanc. for meritor-ious serv. to State or own.	Those enter. St. since 1/1/25 in violation of Act of 14/4/07, deported. Those leav. not to re-turn. Fine for holding F.N. as Sl. Incit. in-sur. p'n by impr., deport. Those enter. State, 1812-1825, must register.		<u>Acts</u>, <u>1830</u>, pp. 90, 92, 94, 96	188, 193, 201, 203, 207
March 24, 1831									Repeals certif. of character for im-port. Sl.					<u>Acts</u>, <u>1831</u>, p. 78	
March 25, 1831											Amends 16/3/30: permit. Sls. emanc. for meritor. serv. to remain in St.	Allowed to leave St. & return on business.		<u>Ibid</u>., 98	201
Nov. 19, 1831									Residents may im-port for own use except fr. Ala., Miss., Ark., or Fla. Not to be sold un. 5 yrs. Register.					<u>Ibid</u>., 4-10	196
Apr. 2, 1832								F'd: liq.						<u>Acts</u>, <u>1832</u>, p. 162	191
Jan. 2, 1834									Repeals Act of 1831.					<u>Acts</u>, <u>1834</u>, p. 6	196
March 26, 1835				See VIII					Amends Feb. 13, 1816. Own. c'ld sue if Sl. lost.					<u>Acts</u>, <u>1835</u>, p. 152	

LOUISIANA

Date	I	II	III	IV	V	VI	VII	VIII	IX	X	XI	XII	Source	Pages
April 1, 1835												Provided for purchase of N's by St. for public works.	Ibid., 195	
March 19, 1839.			See VIII					Masters of vessels to give securities for Sls. unlawfully shipped.					Acts, 1839, p.118	
March 25, 1840			See VIII					Sl. not allowed on vessels w.o. permit.					Acts, 1840, p. 89	
March 16, 1842							See XI	Sls. not to be carried by masters to non-sl. St. Sls. entitled to freed. not to be import. See X, XI		Sls. statu liberi, in St. to be export. when free.	C'ld not come on board any vessel either as employee or passenger. Return. after export., p'n by impr.		Acts, 1842, 308-314, 316.	196, 201
March 26, 1842		Non-cap. cr. not to be p'n by impr.											Acts, 1842, p.520	
March 22, 1843								See XI			Act of 1842 amended. Those who entered prior to 1838 c'ld remain if registered & bonded.		Acts, 1843, p. 45	
April 6, 1843		See IV Attempt. murder p'n by death. Amends Act of 1825. 6 freeholders - jury. Unan. verdict nec. conviction. Cap. cr. p'n at discretion of Cr't.	Incit. or particip. in rev. p'n by death.										Ibid, 92	187, 189

May 30, 1846	See X										Residence in non-Sl. St. does not entitle Sl. to freed.	See X		Acts, 1846, p.163	199, 200
June 1, 1846		Tribunal for cap. cr., of 2 Just. & 10 Sl. own's. Unan. verdict nec.												Ibid., 144	189
Dec. 20, 1848								F'd: liq. Seller forfeits license.						Acts, 1848 (extra sess.), p. 64	
Feb. 12, 1852								See XI				Wh's gambl. w. N. or Sls. fined & impr.		Acts, 1852, p. 16	203
March 18, 1852								Tr. f'd.	See X		Emanc. permitted if Sl. sent to Africa & bonds given.			Ibid., 214, 225	200
March 16, 1854	Own. comp. exec. Sl. 2/3 value.	See I												Acts, 1854, p.149	
March 15, 1855 **		Takes up p'n for murder, arson, rape, etc. Trials		Conceal. r'ys p'n	Insur. or encouragement of, p'n by death or life impr. Attempt to produce discontent p'n by death or impr. at hard labor.	F'd: cr'l. treatm.; whip.; lack of cloth. & food, etc. Court power to sell such Sl.		F'd: Gambl. w. Sls.; tr.; arms. Pass req.	No childr. un. 10 to be import. w.o. Mother. See XI		Sls. not entitled to freed. by stay. in non-Sl. St.	Sls. witn. ag. F.N. Deported fr. St.		Acts, 1855, pp. 379-91 See Hurd, II, 165	185, 188, 190
March 6, 1857											F'd: emanc.			Acts, 1857, p. 55	

*See Act of 1840.
**Long act digested from previous laws. Repeals all conflicting laws.

LOUISIANA

Date	I	II		III	IV	V	VI	VII	VIII	IX	X	XI	XII	Source	Pages
March 19, 1857		Cap.cr. - murder; wound.;shoot.;arson; poison.;rape;insur.;3d offence strik.wh.or family;robbery;burglary.P'n at discretion of Court: destroy.food,revolt ag.overseer, larceny.P'n by whip: cutting down trees or timber.		Procedure for r'ys. General depot established.	See II			F'd: tr.w.o.permis. of owner.						Ibid., 172, 183, 229-31	
March 17, 1859												Permits F.N. to choose master & become Sl. Childr.un. 10 to follow status of Mother.		Ibid., 214	206

MARYLAND

As one of the original thirteen colonies, Maryland carried over into the Federal Period the body of laws under which it has operated as a colony.

Date	Property Rights	Crimes By	Crimes Against	Runaway Patrol Laws	Insurrection and Conspiracy	Protection: Slaves and Free Negroes	Teaching and Preaching	Discrimination and Disabilities	Importation and Exportation	Limitation of Slavery	Emancipation and Abolition	Free Negroes	Resolutions and Sundries	Source	Pages in Text
	I	II		III	IV	V	VI	VII	VIII	IX	X	XI	XII		
1776	Not to be deprived of property except by judgm. of peers.							Suffrage: property qualif.						Constitution, Bill of Rights, v, xvii	
1783									Temp. act to prohib. import.					Hurd, II, 19	
April 1787*								F'd: hir. o. except as pilot & at harvest.						Maxcy, Laws, II 26	191
1790											Amends 1752 reg. "petitions for freed."			Hurd, II, 19	
Nov. 1796						Childr. not to suffer for parents' offences. Repeals 1715, 1728.		No F.N. to vote or hold office, or give evidence ag. Wh. Sls. not allowed at l. F'd: sell. liq.; keep. horse grounds; races, etc.	Not to be import. as mdse. Instantly freed. Settlers & travellers excepted.		Repeals 1752 (to prevent emanc. of disabled & superann. Sls.). Un. 45, manu. by will & deed. Petitions of freed., deeds, etc.	Provides penalty for export. & sell. F.N. & for import. F.N. into St. Not to sell certif. of freed. to Sls. Idle may be exported. See VII		Maxcy, Laws, II, 351	192, 196, 197, 205
Dec. 31, 1801		See VII						Sls. witn. ag. F.N. accused of steal.				See VII		Laws, 1692-1818, III, 59 (1801), ch. 109.	192
Jan. 8, 1803	Own. p'd value of slaves sold for crime to foreign country.	See I		Unclaimed r'ys sold					Import. from D.C. permitted					Ibid., III (1802), ch. 68, ch. 92, ch. 96.	186
Jan. 19, 1805				R'y N. servants p'n: time of service extended.								See III		Ibid., III (1804), ch. 90	

*An old (1812) edition of Maryland laws, says: "Continued by 1794, Chap. 71, to 30th Jan. 1798, when it expired. Revived and continued 1798 Ch. 10 to end of session."

MARYLAND

Date	I	II		III	IV	V	VI	VII	VIII	IX	X	XI	XII	Source	Pages
Jan. 25, 1806								See XI			Certif. of freed. regulated.	F'd: to sell corn, wheat, tobacco w.o. certif.		*Ibid.*, III (1805), ch. 66, 80	
Jan. 3, 1807								F'd: hir. immig. F.N.	See XI			F'd: to immigrate to St. See VII		*Ibid.*, III (1806), ch. 56	201
Jan. 4, 1807								See XI				F'd: to own dogs or guns w.o. certif.		*Ibid.*, ch. 81.	192, 204
Dec. 24, 1808		Any N. may be witn. ag. F.N. or Sl.						See II				See II		*Ibid.*, IV (1808), ch. 81	192
Jan. 6, 1810								Suffrage: limited to Wh.				See VII		*Laws*, IV (1809), ch. 83 Constitution, Amendment XIV	
Jan. 6, 1810	Own. pd. value of impr. Sl.	See I, IV			Insur. p'n by death; conspir. by impr.							See IV		*Laws*., IV (1809), ch. 138	188
Jan. 7, 1810											Childr. of future emanc. Sls. may be free before actual emanc.			*Ibid.*, ch. 171	198
Dec. 23, 1810		P'n for putting quicklime in streams.		Amends 1803. R'ys to be bro't before Just.							Sls. to be emanc., not to be sold out of St.			*Ibid.*, IV (1810), ch. 15, 36 & 63	186
Dec. 16, 1812	Own. permitted to hire o. Sls.							See I						*Ibid.*, IV (1812), ch. 76	
Dec. 31, 1813											Sls. tempor. taken to D.C. not freed thereby.			*Ibid.*, V (1813), ch. 56	
Feb. 3, 1818											P'n for sell. Sls. about to be emanc. o. of St.			*Ibid.*, V (1817), ch. 12	

Feb. 4, 1818								F'd: go. at l.						Ibid., V (1817), ch. 104	
Feb. 16, 1818								F'd: Sls. in retail stores at night.						Ibid., ch. 227	
Feb. 10, 1819				Entic. Sls. to r'y p'n by impr.										Ibid., VI (1818), ch. 157	186
Feb. 17, 1819							Bound childr. to be taught to read & write.					Childr. c'ld be bound out to learn trade.		Ibid., ch. 189	206
Feb. 18, 1819		Non-cap.cr. p'n by whip. or banishment.							Citizens c'ld import Sls. resident in U.S. since 1783, for employm.					Ibid., ch. 197, 201	
Feb. 3, 1820		F.N. or Sls. guilty of cap. cr. p'n by hang. or banishment.										See II		Laws, 1819-20, ch. 159	
Feb. 23, 1822		Repeals 1723; substitutes whip. for cropping ears.												Law, 1821-2, ch. 240	
Feb. 4, 1825				Masters of vessels f'd to transp. Sls.w.o. certif. of freed. Register of passeng. req.					See III			See III		Laws, 1824-5, ch. 85	
Feb. 10, 1825						Old & infirm Sls. belong. to insolvent estates provided for.								Ibid., ch. 100	

MARYLAND

Date	I	II	III	IV	V	VI	VII	VIII	IX	X	XI	XII	Source	Pages
March 2, 1826											Arrest of vagrant F.N. Childr. to be bound out.		Laws, 1825-6, ch. 161	206
March 8, 1826							See XI				Certif.req. to sell to-bacco. Buy-er p'n by fine.		Ibid., ch. 199	
March 12, 1827		See XI									Imprisoned F.N. to be banished or sold.		Laws, 1826-7, ch. 229	
Jan. 18, 1828			Sls. entic. others to r'y p'n by whip. Amends 1819.										Laws, 1827-8, ch. 15	186
Jan. 31, 1828							Sell. liq. near camp meetings p'n by whip.						Ibid., ch. 29	191
March 12, 1832								See XI			Board app'td to aid colon-ization in Liberia.		Laws, 1831-2, ch. 281	
March 14, 1832		Non-cap. cr.: F.N. p'n by banish.		See XI		C'ld as-semble for re-ligious services only w. Wh.min-ister.	Hir. immig. F.N. p'n by fine. Buy. fr. Sls. or F.N. w.o. certif.: p'n by fine. F'd: tr. w.o. certif. See VI	F'd: im-port. as mdse. Sls. so import., free on removal to Liberia. See XI			F'd.immig., p'n by fine & sale. Re-main. o. of St.30 days consid. aliens,sail-ors, etc., excepted. Asso. w. Sls. at un-lawful meet-ings: p'n like Sls. F'd.: tr. w.o.certif., sell. liq. & gunpowder to: fined. See VI, VII		Ibid., ch. 323	196, 201, 204
March 23, 1833								Amends 1832, providing except's.					Laws, 1832-3, ch. 317	

Feb. 26, 1834				Reward for r'ys increased.										<u>Laws</u>, <u>1833-4</u>, ch. 111	
March 24, 1836		F.N. on 2nd convict. to be sold o. of St.										See II		<u>Laws</u>, <u>1835-6</u>, ch. 200	
March 30, 1836									Import. & export.to & fr. Va. permitted.					<u>Ibid</u>., ch. 329	
April 2, 1836					Print. & circulat. inflam. lit. = a felony.									<u>Ibid</u>., ch. 325	
March 2, 1837								Vessels not to be navigated by N's.					See VII	<u>Laws</u>, <u>1836-7</u>, ch. 150	
March 10, 1837	Own. to be compens.										Sl'y not to be abol. unless by unanimous vote,etc.			<u>Constitutional Amendment</u>, xvii, 26	181, 199
March 14, 1837													Am.Coloniz. Society incorp.	<u>Laws</u>, <u>1836-7</u>, ch. 274	
Feb. 15, 1839		See III		Sl. r'ys to another St. = felons.										<u>Laws</u>, <u>1838-9</u>, ch. 63	
Apr. 4, 1839				F'd: to transp. Sls. on rrs. & steamboats w.o.consent of own.										<u>Ibid</u>., ch. 375	187
March 7, 1842					Spread.of inflam. lit. thru Post Office to be watched. See XI						Receiv. abol.lit. p'n. See XI	Knowingly receiv.inflam. lit.p'n by impr. 10-20 yrs.		<u>Laws</u>, <u>1841-2</u>, ch. 272	
March 3, 1843											See XI	Search ordered of houses suspected of having abolit.papers.		<u>Laws</u>, <u>1842-3</u>, ch. 163	

MARYLAND

Date	I	II		III	IV	V	VI	VII	VIII	IX	X	XI	XII	Source	Pages
March 9, 1843		See XI						See XI			See XI	Belong. to secret society: 1st offence, fine; 2nd offence, sold as Sl. for life.		Ibid., ch. 281	206
March 1, 1844				Asking Congr. to pass law p'n w. impr. rescuers of r'y Sls.									Resol. See III	Laws, 1843-4, Res. No. 28	
March 9, 1844	See XII												Resol.: St. alone has r't to legisl. reg. sl'y	Ibid., Res. No. 57	210
March 10, 1845								Travel regulat. See XI				Allow. to leave St., May to Nov. for 30 days w. permit.		Laws, 1844-5, ch. 283	
Feb. 18, 1846							Camp meet's prohibited, but worship in regular places allowed. Amends 1832.							Laws, 1845-6, ch. 94	
March 9, 1846						See XI						F.N. of good character c'ld form charitable societies under police inspection. Amends 1843.		Ibid., ch. 284	206
March 10, 1846	Own. compens.	As banishment insufficient: Sls. guilty of murder, rape, arson, etc. to be p'n as other persons.												Ibid., ch. 340	184

Jan. 26, 1847		See VII						Not witn. ag. Wh.				See II		<u>Laws</u>, <u>1846-7</u>, ch.27	192, 205
Feb. 9, 1850										In regard Vermont's resol; condemn. Sl'y.			Resol. See IX	<u>Laws</u>, <u>1849-50</u>, Res. No. 28	210
Feb. 26, 1850		Convicted Sls. excepted. See VIII							Repeals tax on import. Sls.					<u>Ibid</u>., ch. 165	
Feb. 26, 1850											Ag. attempt of Congr. to abolish Sl'y.		Resol. See XI	<u>Ibid</u>., Res. No. 37	210
Feb. 27, 1850				Entic. r'ys p'n by impr.										<u>Ibid</u>., ch. 296	186
1851								Suffrage: Wh. males only.						<u>Constitution</u>, 1, 1.	
March 10, 1854				See XI				See XI				Leav. before expir. of term: to be returned to employer.		<u>Laws</u>, <u>1854</u>, ch. 273	
March 6, 1856						See XI						Parents to be paid for childr. bound out.		<u>Laws</u>, <u>1856</u>, ch. 87	
March 8, 1858											Leaving St. condition of emanc. No Sl. un. 10 or ov. 45, or unable to care for self to be emanc.	See X		<u>Laws</u>, <u>1858</u>, ch. 307	199, 208
March 9, 1858								F'd: to use boats on Potomac w.o. license.				See VII		<u>Ibid</u>., ch. 356	

MARYLAND

Date	I	II		III	IV	V	VI	VII	VIII	IX	X	XI	XII	Source	Pages
March 10, 1858		F.N.convicted of single larceny value $5, sold as Sl.2-5 yrs.Robbery,10 yrs.Steal. or kill.horse, mule:2-14 yrs. Steal, Sl.:3-12 yrs. Steal. less than $5: 2-5 yrs. Arson: death or life impr.		F.N.enticing Sl.to r'y: 5 yrs. or life. See II								See II		Ibid., ch. 324	204
March 7, 1860								See XI				App't Board of Managers to control F.N.'s in certain counties.		Laws, 1860, ch. 232	
March 10, 1860											F'd:emanc. by deed or will.	Over 18, c'ld petition court to choose Master & become Sl. Childr. un. 5 follow status of Mother.		Ibid., ch. 322	199, 206
March 10, 1860				Ask. Congr. to work for treaty w.Great Britain in reg. r'ys.									Resol. See III	Ibid., Res. 2	210

MISSISSIPPI

Part of the area of what is now Mississippi was originally under the laws of Great Britain, Spain and France. It came into the possession of the United States in 1798, and Georgia, who claimed jurisdiction over Alabama and Mississippi, ceded her claims in exchange for part of the proceeds of the sale of public land. Mississippi was admitted as a State in 1817.

Date	Property Rights	Crimes By	Crimes Against	Runaway Patrol Laws	Insurrection and Conspiracy	Protection: Slaves and Free Negroes	Teaching and Preaching	Discrimination and Disabilities	Importation and Exportation	Limitation of Slavery	Emancipation and Abolition	Free Negroes	Resolutions and Sundries	Source	Pages in Text
	I	II		III	IV	V	VI	VII	VIII	IX	X	XI	XII		
Apr. 7, 1798									F'd: import. after establ. of Terr.					Act establishing Terr. Gov. of Miss. 1798, sec. 7	
March 6, 1805		See Ala.												Toulmin's Ala. Digest, 627-632; Toulmin's Miss. Digest (1807), p. 378	
July 20, 1805		See Ala.									See Ala.			Toulmin's Ala. Digest, 632	197
Feb. 10, 1807		Counsel provided at trial of Sls. No own. on jury. Non-cap. cr. p'n by brand. False testim. p'n by pillory & whip.				Counsel provided.		Testim. allowed in Sl. trial.				See VII		Statutes, 1816, p. 223	185
March 1, 1808 see also Ala.		No criminals to be imported.							Regulat. for import. & sale tax.					Toulmin's Ala. Digest, 633	196
Dec. 22, 1809 See also Ala.				R'ys unclaimed to be sold.										Ibid., 634-5	
Dec. 18, 1812 See Ala.				Patrol Law.										Ibid., 635-7	192, 193
Dec. 21, 1812		Trial of Sls. charged w. treason.												Ibid., 183-4	

MISSISSIPPI

Date	I	II	III	IV	V	VI	VII	VIII	IX	X	XI	XII	Source	Pages
Jan. 15, 1814 See Ala.		Amends 1812. Trial of Sls. for cap. cr.: Assault, arson, rape, etc.											Ibid., 184-5	185
Nov. 27, 1816 See Ala.											Not to be licensed to run taverns.		Ibid., 638	203
1817		No crim. Sls. to be bro't to St. In cap. cr., Gen. Assemb. no power to deprive Sl. of trial by petit jury.			Humane treat-ment req.			Gen.As-semb.no power to prevent immigr. bring. Sls.Power to pre-vent Sls. import. as mdse.		Gen.Assemb. no power to emanc. Sls.w.o. consent of Master. Exception: meritori-ous ser-vice to St.			Constitution, vi, Slaves, secs. 1 & 2	180, 181, 182, 182 fn.
1818							Separate burial grounds provided.						Rev. Code (1824), p. 319	
1819		Proof req., Sls. import. not crim-inals. Amends March 1808.						See II Tax of $20 on Sls. import.as mdse. Amends March 1808.			Not to im-migrate or become resident.		Hurd, II, 145-6 (quoting Hut-chinson's Digest, 524).	
Dec.17, 1819 See Ala.			Patrol law & r'y Sls.				At l. w. o. pass, p'n by patrol.						Toulmin's Digest, 639	192, 193
Dec. 17, 1819		Court laws. See Ala.											Ibid., 185-6, 642	
1822			Patrol law, r'ys.				P'n Sls. w.o. passes. Dogs kept by N.killed. F'd: to keep stock.						Howard & Hutchin-son, Statutes (1840), p. 171	192, 193
June 13, 1822							Hunt. w. fire p'n by whip.						Rev. Code (1824), p. 319	
June 14, 1822			Steal. Sl. p'n. by death.										Ibid., 297	

June 18, 1822*	Personal estate. Carry. Sl.w.o. own's permis. to another St.p'n by fine & impr.	No criminals to be import.Fighting p'n by stripes. Cap.cr. = arson, murder, rape, assault. (See 1829), poison. Jury trial for cap. cr. Non-cap. p'n by branding, corporal p'n. & pillory. See I,VII,XI.		Procedure for r'ys. Keepers of toll bridges & ferries not to allow Sls. to cross w. o. pass. Harb.p'n by fine. See XI	Assembl's, riots & sed. speeches p'n by stripes. Conspir. to rebel p'n by deach.	No cruel p'n.		F'd: cultiv. of cotton for own use; weapons, w.o. permit; liq.; tr.; hir. o.;visit.; keep. animals.	Sls.born in U.S. import.w. certif. See II,XI		Emanc. by will in writ. & proof of meritorious serv. Procedure for claim. freed.	Not to immigrate to St. F'd.: weapons w.o. license; tr. on Sundays; supply.Sls. w. liq.; harb.Sls. Must register.Assist. rebel. of Sls. p'n by death. See IV,X		<u>Ibid</u>., 368-88	183, 185, 186, 187, 188, 190, 191, 192, 193, 196, 197, 199, 201, 203, 204, 207
June 28, 1822		See VII						Witn. only ag. each other.						<u>Ibid</u>., 130	192
June 29, 1822								Fine for sell.liq., to Sl. F'd: enter't, at inn.						<u>Ibid</u>., 367	191
Jan. 16, 1823	Own. to pay for counsel.	Counsel provided in cap. cr.		F'd: harb.	F'd:meetings of ov. 5;remain. on strange plant. over 4 hrs.	See II	Permits given for worship w. Wh. minister.	See IV,VI				See IV		<u>Ibid</u>., 389-91	186, 189
Feb. 1, 1825								F'd: keep. stock.						<u>Laws</u>, <u>1824-38</u>, p. 63	
Feb. 10, 1825	Declar. mdse.							See I						<u>Ibid</u>., 83	
Jan. 25, 1826		Whip. for sell. liq. near churches.						Free persons p'n by fine. See II				See II & VII		<u>Ibid</u>., 90	
1829		Assault: death penalty on proof of malice, if kill.does not occur.												<u>Ibid</u>., 201	185
Dec. 16, 1830		See IV			Circl.of sed.lit. p'n: Wh. by fine; N. by death.		See VII	F'd:employ. on print.presses; or keep.tavern.				See VII		<u>Ibid</u>., 328-30	188

*An Act to Reduce into One the Several Acts Concerning Slaves, Free Negroes and Mulattoes.

MISSISSIPPI

Date	I	II	III	IV	V	VI	VII	VIII	IX	X	XI	XII	Source	Pages
Dec. 20, 1831						F'd: to preach.	See VI, XI F'd: to trade.				Bet.16 & 50, to leave St., or be considered r'y Sls. Courts c'ld issue license to stay. See VI,VII		Ibid., 349, 352	203
1832		As 1817, except no jury trial nec			As 1817			F'd: import. as mdse. af. 1/5/1833. Settler may bring in purchased Sls. until 1845.		As 1817.			Constitution, Slaves, vii, 1, 2,3	180, 181
March 2, 1833		Tried like Wh. in cap. cases.											Laws, 1824-38, p. 408	184
March 2, 1833								Provided for amend. to Constit. reg. import.					Ibid., 478	196
Dec. 23, 1833								Tax on Sls. import. for sale.					Ibid., 524	196
May 13, 1837								F'd: import. as mdse.					Ibid., 758-9	196
Feb. 16, 1839		See III	Harb. r'ys p'n by fine & impr. for Wh. & F.N., whip. for Sls.				See III				See III		Laws, 1839, pp. 95-6	186
1839 "New criminal code"		F.N. triable & p'n as Wh's.	Steal. Sls. p'n by 10 yrs. impr.	Aid. insur.; circl. lit. p'n by impr.							See II		Hurd, II, 148 (quot. Hutchinson's Digest, 970, 978, 994). See also, Statutes (1840), p. 720	188

Feb. 7, 1840									Legis. may pass laws regul. or prohib. import.					Amendment 1 to <u>Constitution</u>.	
Feb. 26, 1842									F'd: ex-port. in order to emanc.		F'd: emanc. by will. See VIII	Security for good behav. may be de-manded. Pro-hibited fr. com. into St.		<u>Laws</u>, <u>1842</u>, pp. 65-70	199
Feb. 16, 1846	½ value exec. Sl. pd. own.	See I												<u>Laws</u>, <u>1846</u>, p. 193	
Feb. 23, 1846									Repeals 1837 f'ding import. Code of 1822 to be en-forced.					<u>Ibid.</u>, 234, 243	196, 197
Feb. 29, 1848	Law of 1846 re-pealed.	See I												Hutchinson's <u>Code</u> (1848), p. 542	
March 6, 1850								F'd: tr. w. Sls.						<u>Laws</u>, <u>1850</u>, p. 100	
1852				Incit. r'ys p'n by fine.										<u>Laws</u>, <u>1852</u>, p. 137	
Feb. 27, 1854		Trial of non-cap. cr's before 2 just. & 5 Sl. holders.												<u>Laws</u>, <u>1854</u>, p. 126	
Aug. 6, 1861					Wh's incit. Sls. p'n by impr.									Laws, 1861, p. 67	188

MISSOURI

Missouri became a Territory in 1812. Before that date the Acts of Louisiana Territory were in force. It became a State in 1820.

Date	Property Rights	Crimes By	Crimes Against	Runaway Patrol Laws	Insurrection and Conspiracy	Protection: Slaves and Free Negroes	Teaching and Preaching	Discrimination and Disabilities	Importation and Exportation	Limitation of Slavery	Emancipation and Abolition	Free Negroes	Resolutions and Sundries	Source	Pages in Text
	I	II		III	IV	V	VI	VII	VIII	IX	X	XI	XII		
Oct. 1, 1804*	Personal Estate.	F.N.assault. Wh., p'n by whip	Steal. & sell. as Sls. p'n.by death.	Patrol law.	Death	See IIb		Fd: tr.,arms,go.at l.entert.			Minors and aged to be cared for.	See IIb		Laws, Ark. Terr. (1835), pp.521,525	See Ark.
1820	See X Own's to be fully compens.	Gen. Assembly, power to prevent import. of criminals. Sls. not to be deprived of impartial trial by jury. P'n like Wh. for cap. cr. Counsel assigned.	Kill. Sls. p'n as if wh.			Gen. Assembly, power to oblige own's to treat Sls. w. humanity.			Gen. Assembly,no power to prevent settlers from import.Sls. Power to prev. import. of Sls. as mdse. & those fr. foreign countries.		Gen.Assemb., no power to pass laws for emanc. of Sls. w. o. consent of owners. Power to permit owners to emanc.Sls., giving security.	Gen. Assemb., power to prevent F.N. settling in St.		Constitution, iii, 26,28	180, 181, 182 fn.
Dec. 9, 1822								F'd: tr. w.o. consent of Master.						Laws, 1821-3, p. 26.	191
Dec. 30, 1824												Suits for freedom.		Rev. Laws, 1825, p. 404; Hurd, II, 169.	198
1825				Appreh. r'ys.										Rev. Laws, 1825, p. 747; Hurd, II, 169.	
Jan. 18, 1831									Own's w. limited no. of Sls. r'd to take them out of St.					Laws, 1830-1, p. 95	
Jan. 26, 1833					See XI		See XI	See XI				Not permitted to assemble w. Sls. in taverns. P'n for disturb. relig. meeting.		Laws, 1832-3, p. 64.	206

Feb. 1, 1837					Publish.& distrib. lit.or speak. to incite insur.: fine & impr.									Laws, 1836-7, p. 3	188
Feb. 12, 1839													Resol. R't of St. to deal w. sl'y.	Laws, 1838-9, p. 337	209
Feb. 13, 1841				Masters of ships not to transp. Sls.				See III	See III					Laws, 1840-1, p. 146	193
Feb. 15, 1841								F'd: hir. o.						Ibid., 147	191
Feb. 16, 1841				Declar. N.Y. law in reg. to r'ys viola- tion of Consti- tution.									Resol. See III	Ibid., 337	209
Jan. 4, 1843				Entic. Sl. to r'y p'n by impr.										Laws, 1842-3, p. 102	186
Feb. 17, 1843		See VII						F'd:to sell poison. drugs to Sls. w.o. consent of own.						Ibid., 102	185
Feb. 23, 1843								See XI				Immig.to St. by,f'd.Nat- ives allowed to go back & forth if no domicile in a free St. Residents must have license to remain. Mas- ters of ves- sels to re- port if F. N. on board.		Ibid., 66	201-2

* See Arkansas for fuller details.

MISSOURI

Date	I	II	III	IV	V	VI	VII	VIII	IX	X	XI	XII	Source	Pages
Feb. 16, 1847						Teach. N's to read p'n by impr. Relig-ious meet's under N. preach-er f'd unless Wh's pre-sent.	See VI,XI				Bond req.for removal fr. one county to another. F'd: to mig-rate into St.		Laws, 1846-7, pp. 103,104	193, 202
Dec. 13, 1855								See XI			$3000 annu-ally for 10 yrs.approp. to transport F.N.to Liberia.		Laws, 1855, p. 367	196
March 3, 1857											Go.to free St.& return. p'n by fine $500 & impr.		Laws, 1856-7, p. 82	202
Dec. 1, 1859								Repeals Act of 1855 wh. provided fines for import.of Sls. not belong.to resi-dents.					Laws, 1859-60, p. 90	196, 197

NORTH CAROLINA

As one of the original thirteen colonies, North Carolina carried over into the Federal Period the body of laws under which it had operated as a Colony.

Date	Property Rights	Crimes By	Crimes Against	Runaway Patrol Laws	Insurrection and Conspiracy	Protection: Slaves and Free Negroes	Teaching and Preaching	Discrimination and Disabilities	Importation and Exportation	Limitation of Slavery	Emancipation and Abolition	Free Negroes	Resolutions and Sundries	Source	Pages in Text
	I	II		III	IV	V	VI	VII	VIII	IX	X	XI	XII		
1776								Suffrage: no dist. of color.						Constitution, VII, VIII, IX	
1777								Witn. only ag. each other.			Emanc. for meritorious serv. only.	See VII		Potter, Taylor & Yancy, Laws (1821), I, 270-1, 300	192, 197, 198-9, 205
1777								F'd: to Sls., to cultivate tobacco for own use in certain counties.						Ibid., I, 343	
1778								F'd: hir. o.			Illegally freed Sls. sold.			N.C., Colonial Records, XXIV, 227	
1778				F'd: entic. & harb.		See 1779		F'd: tr.				See 1779, V		Ibid., XXIV, 220	
1779*			See V			Steal. F. N. & sell. as Sl. p'n by death.						See V		Laws (1821), I, 375-6	
1779	Own. compens. for exec. Sl.	See I												Colonial Records, XXIV, 282-3	
March 27, 1779				Patrol exempt fr. road duty. Amends 1753.										Ibid., XXIV, 276-7	
May 10, 1779								F'd: to raise live stock.						Ibid., XXIV, 260-1	192
1781	Own. rec. ½ value of exec. Sl.	See I												Ibid., XXIV, 382-3	
1783		In minor cr's. 1 just. may p'n.						F'd: tr. w. N's.				See VII		Ibid., XXIV, 496-7	

*Date 1778 in Colonial Records, XXIV, 220.

NORTH CAROLINA

Date	I	II		III	IV	V	VI	VII	VIII	IX	X	XI	XII	Source	Pages
1784				Masters of vessels not to carry off Sls.					See III					_Ibid._, XXIV, 591	
Dec. 29, 1785 *	No compens. for exec. Sl.	F.N. fined for assisting Sl. in cr., harb.		See II				Own. to pay fee of 1s. for Sls. hir. o. No Sl. to have tr. or occupat. w.o. permission of own. See XI				To wear badge or cloth with word FREE. Buying fr., or selling to Sl. p'n. Entertain. Sls. p'n. by fine & whip. See II		_Ibid._, XXIV, 725-31	
Jan. 6, 1786 **									Prohibitive duty on import. Sls. Returns to be made to clerk.					_Ibid._, XXIV, 792-4; Laws (1821), I, 541	195
1787		To prevent steal. See VII		See VII				F'd: to board vessels bet. sunrise & sunset on Sunday. F'd: intermarriage bet. F.N. and Sl. w.o. master's consent.				F'd: to entertain Sls. bet. sunrise & sunset on Sunday. See VII		_Laws_ (1821), I, 562; _Colonial Records_, XXIV, 890	194, 202-3
1791			Kill. Sl. same as kill. Wh. except. when under moderate correction.	F'd: harbor. by merchants or traders on Sabbath.		See IIb		Travel. w. forged certif. p'n by whip. See III						_Laws_ (1821), I, 653	188-9
1791		Kill. cattle not belong. to Master p'n by whip.												_Ibid._, I, 678	

1792				Death penalty for Master allow. Sls.on board w. intent to es-cape. Amends 1787.				See III						Ibid., I, 684-5	186
1793		Trial by Jury, offenses affect. life,& limb. Own's to defend & pay expenses.				See II								Ibid., I, 706	189
1794				Patrols may p'n wander. Sls. by whip. Exempt fr. jury duty.	See VII, XI			Sls. must have permit to meet at houses or planta-tions. Fd: hir.o.				F'd: to meet in houses or plantations for danc. or drink.		Ibid., I, 740-2	191, 192, 193, 203
1795					Militia to sup-press disorder of Sls. & F.N.				F'd: im-port. of Sls. over 15.		Emanc.Sls. give bonds for good behavior.	F.N.coming to St.give bond for good behav-ior. See IV		Ibid., I, 787-8	199
1796											Emanc.for meritori-ous serv. only.			Ibid., I, 801	197
1796	Own.com-pens.2/3 value Exec.Sl.	See I										Funds for I raised by poll on N's.		Ibid., II, 828-9	
1798						Aged & infirm Sl. to be pro-vided w. proper food & clothing.								Ibid., II, *863	190
1800						Steal. & sell.F.N. as Sl.p'n by fine & impr. Amends 1779						See V		Ibid., II, 927	

*Applies to town of Wilmington.
**Donnan (Slave Trade, IV, 240) says the demand for this law came from the western part of the State and that it was repealed in 1790 (Statutes, 1794, ch. 2); and for four years Negroes could be imported. The date is 1787 in Colonial Records.

NORTH CAROLINA

Date	I	II		III	IV	V	VI	VII	VIII	IX	X	XI	XII	Source	Pages
1801						See XI					Bonds to £100 for Sl.emanc., as security.	Bonds of £250 to secure ag. free orphan children's removal fr. St. and their sale.		_Ibid._, II, 946-8	199
1802					Aid.conspir.p'n by death or banishment.							See IV		_Ibid._, II, 977-9	187, 186
1805								F'd: tr. w. masters of vessels.						_Ibid._, II, 1048	
1806	Gifts of Sls.valid only when in writ.													_Ibid._, II, 1068-9	
1810												R'ts & privileges of insolv. debtors extended to F.N.		_Ibid._, II, 1196-7	207
1812								C'ld be enlisted in militia only as musicians.				See VII		_Ibid._, II, 1218	206
1812								F'd: to act as pilots.				See VII		_Ibid._, II, 1235	
1816		Trials involv. life, before Superior Court & like trials of Wh's.							Sls. import. contra Act of Congr. to be sold for benefit of St.					_Ibid._, II, 1350-4	189, 195
1817			Kill. Sl. = homicide.											_Ibid._, II, 1407	
1818		In cap. cr's, Sls. r't to challenge jurors.		Unclaimed r'ys sold at auction.		See II					Power to emanc. rests w. Superior Court.			_Ibid._, II, 1446-7, 1452	186, 199
1819								F'd: tr.						Ibid., II, 1484	191

1821				Fd: harb., aid.										Laws, 1821, p. 40	186
1822	Poll tax on Sls.								Tax on import. Sls.			Poll Tax		Laws, 1822, ch.1, p. 6	
1823		Rape p'n by death.												Laws, 1823, p. 42	185
1825				Cap. p'n for Masters of ships aid. r'ys. Harb.p'n by fine.										Laws, 1825, p. 13	186
1826								F'd: tr. w.o. own's permis.				Tr. w. Sl., p'n by whip.		Laws, 1826, p. 7	
1826		F.N., r't of trial by jury in cases under this act.				Duty of person to whom F.N. is bound to provide food & cloth.	Bound F.N. to be taught mechan. tr.	See XI	$500 fine for import. F.N.			F'd: to immigr. into St. Idle bound over to Court, authorized to hire them out, childr. bound out. See II,V,VI		Ibid., 13-15	201, 202, 206
1828-9								F'd: tr. in fire arms & powder.				F'd: to sell fire arms to Sls.		Laws, 1828-9, p. 19	
1830-1 chaps. iv-x				Harb. r'ys p'n by fine of $100. (ch.viii) Patrol to disperse Sls.gam. (ch. x)	Circl. of sed. lit. = felony. (ch. v)		F'd: teach. Sls.to read, write & figure. (ch.vi)	F'd: gam. with Sl. (ch. x) See XI F'd: Intermarriage bet. F.N. & Sl. & bet. F.N. & Wh. (ch. iv)			Petition filed bef. emanc. Bond of $1000 for good behav.while in St. To leave St. forever in 90 days. May emanc.by will. Emanc.for meritorious serv. of Sls. ov. 50; bond of $500 req. (ch. ix)	F'd: to peddle outside own county (ch. vii); Gam.with Sls.(ch. x)		Laws, 1830-1, pp. 9-15	188, 193, 194, 199, 208
1830-1 Amends 1826												If absent from St.90 days c'ld not return. (ch. xiv)		Ibid., 16	

NORTH CAROLINA

Date	I	II	III	IV	V	VI	VII	VIII	IX	X	XI	XII	Source	Pages
1830-1								See XI			Vessels fr. another St. with F.N. aboard, subject to quarantine 30 days. N. not to go on shore or communicate w. shore. (ch.xxx)		Ibid., 29-31	
1830-1				Wh. overseers for over 15 Sls. (ch. cxxxix)									Ibid., 119	
1830-1				No Sls. to assemble or muster on election days. (ch.clvi)			See IV						Ibid., 130-1	
1831-2		Cutt. off of ears abolished as p'n. (ch.xii)				F'd: preach. (ch.iv)	F'd: to go at l. or keep house as free man. (ch.iv) See XI				Unable to pay fine under criminal law, to be hir. o. (ch.xiii) See VI		Laws, 1831-2, pp. 7, 10-11	194, 205
1831-2											Amends Act of 1830 (ch.vii). Unlawful to peddle without license. (ch.xxviii)		Ibid., 24	
1831-2							Act of 1741 permitting carrying of gun repealed. (ch.xliv)						Ibid., 34	192
1832-3			F'd: aid. escape or steal. Sls., un. penalty of death										Laws, 1832-3, p. 12	186
1835							Suffrage: N. barred to 4th generation.						Amendment to Constitution, Art. 1, sec. 3, nos. 2 & 3.	

1838-9								F'd: Inter-marriage bet. F.N. & Wh.				See VII		*Laws*, *1838-9*, p. 33	
Jan. 11, 1841								See XI				F'd: to carry arms.		*Laws*, *1840-1*, p. 61	
Jan. 12, 1841				F'd: transp. of Sls. on rrs, steamboats, stage coaches.				See III						*Ibid.*, 99	193
Jan. 8, 1845								See XI				F'd: to sell liq.		*Laws*, *1844-5*, p. 123	203
Dec. 24, 1852				Law of 1832-3 re-enacted.										*Laws*, *1852*, p. 160	186
Feb. 16, 1859		Court has power to fine F.N. in addition to other p'n.						See XI				F'd: to buy or sell liq. except for medicine. Fines (see II) may be used to maintain bastard childr.		*Laws*, *1858-9*, pp. 70-71	203-4
Feb. 23, 1861					Import. & circl..of incend. lit.f'd under p'n of death. Incit. Sl. or F. N. to rebel p'n by death.			See XI				F'd: to carry arms; to buy, hire, or have control over Sls. See IV		*Laws*, *1860-1*, pp. 39, 68-70	204, 206

SOUTH CAROLINA

As one of the original thirteen colonies, South Carolina carried over into the Federal Period the body of laws under which it had operated as a Colony.

Date	Property Rights	Crimes By	Crimes Against	Runaway Patrol Laws	Insurrection and Conspiracy	Protection: Slaves and Free Negroes	Teaching and Preaching	Discrimination and Disabilities	Importation and Exportation	Limitation of Slavery	Emancipation and Abolition	Free Negroes	Resolutions and Sundries	Source	Pages in Text
	I	II		III	IV	V	VI	VII	VIII	IX	X	XI	XII		
Oct. 9, 1776	Own's p'd 10s. a day for XII.												Sls. to be conscripted for publ. works.	McCord, Stat. at L.(1840), VII, 428-9	
March 28, 1787	Sheriff to sell every other part of personal prop. bef.N's.								Forfeiture of Sl. & fine of £100 for every Sl. import. contra Installment Act.					Ibid., VII, 430: Grimké, Public Laws, 420	
Feb. 27, 1788				R'ys to be taken to jail. Fine for detaining.										Grimké, Public Laws, 441-2	
Nov. 4, 1788									No Sl. except prop. of U.S.citizens to be import. before 1/1/1793. Penalty as above.					Ibid., 466-8	195
Acts March 13, 1789								F'd: to brand cattle in absence of Wh.; to hunt w. fire.						Ibid., 486,497	193
Dec. 21, 1792									F'd: import.from Africa,W. I.etc.for 2 yrs.; Sls.fr. other Sts. (except. by settlers & travellers).					Acts, 1791-4, I, 215-8; Stat. at L., VII, 431-2	

May 10, 1794								See XI				Bet. 18 & 45, obliged to serve in Militia.		Acts, 1791-4, I, 328	
Dec. 20, 1794									Extends act of 21/12/92 to 1/1/97.					Ibid., I, 391; Stat. at L., VII, 433	
Dec. 19, 1796									Extends acts of 1792 & 1794 to 1/1/99.					Acts, 1795-1804, II, 90; Stat. at L., VII, 434.	
Dec. 20, 1796								F'd: tr.,p'n by fine.						Acts, 1795-1804, II, 91; Stat. at L., VII, 434-5	191
Dec. 21, 1798									Acts of 1792, 1794, 1796 extended to 1/1/01.					Acts, 1795-1804, II, 215; Stat. at L., VII, 435	
Dec. 20, 1800									Act of 19/12/96 extended to 1803.					Stat. at L., VII, 436	
Dec. 20, 1800									F'd: import.as mdse. Import.of 10 Sls. allowed. Ferrymen fined for import.N.			F'd: to enter St.		Ibid., VII, 436-40	
Dec. 20, 1800				Patrol to disperse assembl's. (See VI)	See VII	See VII	No meet. for mental instruction bef. sunrise or af. sunset.	Unlawful Assemb. of Sls. & F.N. to be dispersed. Own's to empl. overseers for 10 or more.			Procedure for emanc. Certif. req. as to ability for self support.	See VI,VII		Ibid., VII, 440-3	192, 193, 198, 203

SOUTH CAROLINA

Date	I	II		III	IV	V	VI	VII	VIII	IX	X	XI	XII	Source	Pages
Dec. 19, 1801				Harb.N., illegally import.: fined.					Suppl. to import. act. N. to be sold; procedure, etc. Travellers may have 2 N. attendants.					_Ibid._, VII, 444-6	
Dec. 17, 1803							Law of 20/12/ 1800 amended. No religious assemb. w. majority of Whs. present shall be disturbed before 9 P.M.							_Ibid._, VII, 448-9	
Dec. 17, 1803									Repeals acts prohib. foreign import., of: 1792, 1794, 1796, 1798, 1800, 1802. N's import. contra. act, forfeited. Act of 1801 in force.					_Ibid._, VII, 449-50	
Dec. 19, 1816									F'd: import. of Sls. & F.N. 2nd offence p'n by death.			See VIII		_Acts_, _1816_, p. 22	
Dec. 18, 1817								Penalty for tr. increased.						_Stat. at L._, VII, 454-5	191

Dec. 18, 1817									Import. permitted of Sls. owned by residents before 19/12/16.					Ibid., 455-8	
Dec. 16, 1818									Act of 1816, 1817 repealed.					Acts, 1818, p. 57; Stat. at L., VII, 458	197
Dec. 18, 1819				Patrol to whip r'ys or those bear. arms.				F'd: to carry arms w.o. certif.				See III, VII		Acts, 1819, p. 29	
Dec. 20, 1820		See IV			Circl. of lit. f'd. F.N. whipped & banished for 2nd offence. See XI	Bring. in F.N. & hold. as Sls.: fined.			See XI		F'd: Emanc. except by act of legis.	F'd: to enter St. Masters of vessels fined for bring. in F.N. See IV, V		Acts, 1820, p. 22; Stat. at L., VII, 459-60	188, 197, 201, 202, 204
Dec. 20, 1821			See V			Death for malic. kill. Sl. Kill. in sudden passion: fine.								Acts, 1821, p. 12	
Dec. 20, 1821				Harb. p'n				See III, XI				P'n for III by whip.		Ibid., 20; Stat. at L., VII, 460-1	186, 205
Dec. 21, 1822					Aid. rebell. or insur. p'n by death.			F'd: hir. o.. on own time. See XI	See XI			Leav. St., f'd to return. Tax on residents. Seaman f'd to land. Over 15 must have guard.		Acts, 1822, p. 11, 13; Stat. at L., VII, 461-2	188, 191, 206
Dec. 21, 1822	Own. compens. for Sls. exec. as result of insur. in Charleston.				See I									Acts, 1822, p. 38	

SOUTH CAROLINA

Date	I	II		III	IV	V	VI	VII	VIII	IX	X	XI	XIII	Source	Pages
Dec. 20, 1823								See XI	Sls. from W.I., Mexico, S.A., Europe or north of Washington not to be import. Not lawful to buy back Sl. who has been in any of these places.			F'd.: to migrate to St. even as employees on vessel; employment as pioneer; carry. arms. No Capt. to bring into St.; leaving, not to return.		Acts, 1823, p.59; Stat. at L., VII, 463-6	
Dec. 17, 1831	See II	Own. or guard. has r't. of challenge in cap. cr.				See II		F'd: to sell liq.				F'd: to distill or sell liq. See II		Acts, 1831, p.13; Stat. at L., VII, 467-8	204
Dec. 19, 1833		P'n by brand. abolished: Sls. & F.N. p'n by whip. for non-cap.; hang. for cap. In cap. cases may have new trial.										See II		Acts, 1833, p. 40	205
Dec. 17, 1834							F'd: teach. Sls. to read or write. See VII	Sls. & F.N. not to be employed as clerks, or salesmen. F'd: to sell liq. to Sls.; gaming p'n by whip.				F.N. guilty of VI, whipped. See VII		Acts, 1834, pp. 13-15; Stat. at L., VII, 468-70	191, 193
Dec. 19, 1835								See XI	See Ded. 20, 1823.		Repeals 20/12/1820.	See Act 20/12/23. F'd: carry. firearms w. o. consent of guard.		Acts, 1835, p.34; Stat. at L., VII, 470-4	
Dec. 21, 1836								Giv. fraud. permits to Sls. p'n.						Acts, 1836-7, p.83	
Dec. 20, 1837			See V			Kidn. F.N. to deprive him of liberty p'n by fines & impr.						See V		Acts, 1837, p. 58	207
Dec. 21, 1839		Trial of Sl. or F.N. before magistrate & 5 freeholders.		Patrol law								See II		Acts, 1839-40, p. 22 Hurd, II, 98.	192

Dec. 17, 1841						Persons fined for beat. Sl. not under their charge.		Gifts to Sl. to be void.			A deed of emanc., bequest, etc. to take effect after death of own., to be void.			Acts, 1841, pp. 154, 155	199
Dec. 19, 1843	Own. compens. for Sl. exec. for cr.	Conceal. Sl. guilty of cap. cr. p'n by fine & impr. Death for attempted rape.										See II		Acts, 1843, pp. 257,258,269	185
Dec. 18, 1844					Foreigners disturb. peace of St. in rel. to Sls. to be fined, impr. & banished. Residents: fined & impr.							See IV		Acts, 1844, p.292	
Dec. 18, 1844		See XI			Disturb. peace of St. p'n by fine. See XI			See XI				Right of writ of Habeas Corpus taken from F.N.		Ibid., p. 292	
Dec. 19, 1849								Act of 21/12/22 amended by providing fine of $50.						Acts, 1849, p. 578	
Dec. 21, 1857								Act of 20/12/96 amended by providing whip. in add. to fines for tr. w. Sl.						Acts, 1857, p. 615	191
Dec. 21, 1858	Value of exec.Sl. to be apprais-ed at not more than ½ of real value; amending Act of 1843.						Own's inflict. cr'l p'n on Sl. p'n by impr.* and fine.							Acts, 1858, pp. 738, 742	190

*Owners could inflict such punishment as "may be necessary for the good government of the same".

TENNESSEE

The laws of North Carolina, of which Tennessee was a part, applied to the latter until changed by its cession in 1790. Tennessee was admitted to the Union in 1796. See the laws of North Carolina from 1776 to 1796.

Date	Property Rights	Crimes: By	Crimes: Against	Runaway Patrol Laws	Insurrection and Conspiracy	Protection: Slaves and Free Negroes	Teaching and Preaching	Discrimination and Disabilities	Importation and Exportation	Limitation of Slavery	Emancipation and Abolition	Free Negroes	Resolutions and Sundries	Source	Pages in Text
	I	II		III	IV	V	VI	VII	VIII	IX	X	XI	XII		
1790											No regulat. made or to be made by Cong. shall tend to emanc. Sls.			Act of Cession of Tenn. to the U.S., in Thorpe, Am. Charters, VI, 3412	
1794								Witn. only ag. each other.						Acts, Terr. Assembly, 1794, ch. 1, sec. 32, in Scott's Laws, 1715-1820, I, 470-1	192, 205
1796								Suffrage: freemen.				See VII		Constitution, iii, 1	
Oct. 23, 1799			See V	Power to patrols to arrest Sls. & search for arms.		P'n for wilfully kill. Sl. except in case of moderate correction: death.		Seizure & sale of stocks belong. to Sls.						Scott's Laws, I, 640; Hurd, II, 90	
Oct. 26, 1799				Entic.or harb.p'n by fine.				F'd: tr.w.Sls. w.o. consent of own,						Scott's Laws, I, 650	186, 191
Nov. 13, 1801											Emanc. thru Court w. security ag. becom. publ. chg.			Ibid., I, 714	198
Nov. 3, 1803					P'n for using words of inflam. nature before Sl.			F'd: tr. w. Sls. (fine); assembl. of Sls. in house.						Ibid., I, 777-8	191, 193

Sep. 13, 1806				Police powers given patrols. Meet. & harb. Sls. p'n.	Sed.lang., riots,unlawful. assembl., p'n by stripes.			See III & IV				To be registered. Travel. w.o. regist.,imprisoned until identified. See III		Ibid., I, 959	186, 192, 193, 202
Nov. 30, 1807												Repeals section of law of 1806, provid. fine for impr.		Ibid., I, 1079	
Oct. 21, 1812									F'd: import. as mdse. for 5 yrs.					Ibid., II, 101	196
Oct. 28, 1813								F'd: tr. w. & sell. liq. to Sls.; hir.o.						Ibid., II, 182, 183	191
Nov. 1, 1813			Beat. Sl. of others p'n like abuse of Wh's.			See IIb								Ibid., II, 131	
Nov. 9, 1815		Trial by 3 just. & jury of 9 freeholders.												Ibid., II, 246	189
Nov. 17 1817											In suits for freed., defend. to give bond; plaint. to be in custody.			Ibid., II, 372	
1822								F'd: Inter-marriage to 3d generat.						Caruthers & Nicholson's Statutes (1836), p. 451	194
Nov. 28, 1823								F'd: hir. o.						Acts, 1823, p. 76	
Nov. 9, 1825		Trial by jury of Sl. holders only. Own. c'ld give bail & defend, except in cap. cases.												Acts, 1825, p. 20	
Dec. 6, 1825				Unclaimed r'ys sold.								Registrat. of, req.		Ibid., 128	186

TENNESSEE

Date	I	II	III	IV	V	VI	VII	VIII	IX	X	XI	XII	Source	Pages
Dec. 6, 1826		See VII, XI						F'd: import. as mdse. & of criminals.			F'd: import. of F.N. convicted of cr.		Acts, 1826, p. 31	196
Dec. 1829 Penal Laws.					Kidn. & sell.F.N. as Sl.p'n by impr.						See V		Acts, 1829, p. 30	207
Dec. 7, 1829										In emanc. by will Court req. to give decl. of freed.	See X		Acts, 1829, p. 49	
Jan. 9, 1830							Liq.sell.by Sl. p'n by whip.;sale to, by fine.						Ibid., 102	191
Dec. 16, 1831										Prohib. emanc.except on cond. of removal from St.	F'd to come to St.		Acts, 1831, p. 121	199, 201, 202, 208
Dec. 21, 1831		Act of 1825 amended so that non-Sl. holders c'ld serve on jury. See V		Assembl. in large nos. f'd. Conspir. p'n by death.	P'n by pillory & cutting off ears abolished.		F'd: to practice medicine.				See V		Ibid., 121-4	185, 187
Oct. 15, 1832							No license issued to sell liq. unless oath taken not to sell to Sls.						Acts, 1832, p. 47	191
Sep. 25, 1833			See VII				F'd: masters of vessels,stage coaches, etc. carry.Sls. or F.N. w.o. pass or certif. of freed.				See VII		Acts, 1833, p. 2	187, 193
Nov. 23, 1833										Exempt.fr. Act of 1831, Sls. who had contracted for freed. before 1831.	See X		Ibid., 99	199

Nov. 26, 1833		Rape p'n by death.										Payment of $10 fr. St. treasury for each F.N. transported to Africa. See II		Ibid., 76,94	207
1834								Suffrage: Wh's only.			Legis. no power to emanc.Sls. w.o. consent of own.			Constitution, 11, 31; iv, 1	
Feb. 10, 1836				Forged passes & harb. p'n.										Acts, 1835-6, p. 174	
Feb. 13, 1836					Print. or writ.sed-it.lit., incit. by word,etc., p'n by impr.		Sermons calculated to incite rebel. p'n. See IV							Ibid., 145-6	188
Feb. 19, 1836				Harb. or conceal, aid.r'ys p'n by impr.										Ibid., 168	186
Feb. 20, 1836		Circuit Courts jurisdiction in cap. cases. Tried as Wh's Counsel provided. Assault, rape, battery = cap. cr.						See XI				F'd: to keep grocery or tippling shop.		Ibid., 92, 167	185, 203
Dec. 29, 1839								F'd: own.live stock; hir.o.;tr. in liq.						Acts, 1839-40, p. 82	
Feb. 4, 1842											See XI	In St. prior to 1836 may petit.to reside in county. Bonds for good behav. req.		Acts, 1841-2, p. 229	202
Dec. 31, 1849											See XI	Repeals 1842, & puts law of 1831 in force.		Acts, 1849-50, p. 300	202

TENNESSEE

Date	I	II		III	IV	V	VI	VII	VIII	IX	X	XI	XII	Source	Pages
Feb. 9, 1850		F.N. guilty of rape to hang. F. N. aid. Sls. access. to murder, p'n by death.										See II		Ibid., 304	
Feb. 16, 1852												Childr. of indigent to be bound o.		Acts, 1851-2, p. 235	206
Feb. 23, 1852												Natives do not req.bond for good behav.		Ibid., 237	
Feb. 28, 1852		Admin.poison p'n by death.										See II		Ibid., 251	185
Nov. 18, 1853		Mansl. p'n at discr. of Court.												Acts, 1853-4, p. 157	
Feb. 24, 1854									See X		Emanc.Sl. to be transported to Africa.	See X		Ibid., 121	199
Dec. 19, 1855									Repeals 1826 prohibit. import. as mdse					Acts, 1855-6, p. 71	196, 197
Feb. 28, 1856								See XI				F'd: to buy & sell market stuff.		Ibid., 77	204
March 3, 1858												Ov. 18 may choose Masters & become Sls.		Acts, 1857-8, p. 55	206
March 15, 1858								See XI				To work on roads as other hands.		Ibid., 331	
March 20, 1858		See IV			Incit.insur. or kill.Masters p'n by death.							See IV		Ibid., 94	188
March 23, 1860		Putt.obstruction on rrs.or injur. same p'n by death.										See II		Acts, 1859-60, p. 108	205

TEXAS

The area of what is now the State of Texas was part of the Republic of Mexico. In 1827 it became the State of Coahuila and Texas. The Texas Declaration of Independence was signed in 1835, and the Constitution of the Republic of Texas in 1836. Texas was annexed by the United States in 1845.

Date	Property Rights	Crimes By	Crimes Against	Runaway Patrol Laws	Insurrection and Conspiracy	Protection: Slaves and Free Negroes	Teaching and Preaching	Discrimination and Disabilities	Importation and Exportation	Limitation of Slavery	Emancipation and Abolition	Free Negroes	Resolutions and Sundries	Source	Pages in Text
	I	II		III	IV	V	VI	VII	VIII	IX	X	XI	XII		
March 11, 1827									No import. after Constit. is publ.		None born Sl. after publ. of Constit.			Constitution of Coahuila and Texas, Preliminary Dispositions, 13.	180, 199
Sept. 15, 1827							F.N. childr. born of Sls. to rec. best educat. in publ. schools	Lists of Sls., births & deaths to be registered.			Sls. of own. with no heirs, freed on own's death.	See VI		Congressional Decrees, in Laws, 1822-97 (Gammel), I, 188-9	198
Nov. 24, 1827						May change Masters. Former own. to be indemn.								Ibid., I, 202	
March 17, 1836								No descentants of Africans to be citizens.	Congr. to pass no laws to prohibit immig. fr. bring. Sls. Import. except fr. U.S. f'd, declared piracy.		Sls. to remain Sls. Congr. no power to emanc. No Sl. own. to emanc. w.o. consent of Congr. unless Sl. leaves country.	Not to reside permanently w.o. consent of Cong.		Republic of Texas, Constitution, General Provisions, 9,10; in Laws, 1822-97, I, 1079	180, 196, 199
Dec. 21, 1836				Death p'n for steal. or entic. Sl.		Sell.F.N. as Sl.p'n by death.			Death: p'n for import. Sls. in violation of Constit. of 1836.			See III,V		Ibid., I, 1247, 1251, 1257	

TEXAS

Date	I	II		III	IV	V	VI	VII	VIII	IX	X	XI	XII	Source	Pages
June 5, 1837								F'd: Intermarriage bet descend. of Europeans & descend. of Africans. (1294)				Residents at time of decl. of indep. (1836) & their natural issue c'ld remain in St. (1292)	Resol. See XI	<u>Ibid.</u>, I, 1292, 1294	194, 202
Dec. 14, 1837		Cap. cr's, F.N. & Sls.: insur.; poison. rape & assault on Wh.; maim. Wh.; arson; murder; burglary. Non-cap. cr's.: using abusive lang. or threaten. Wh.; p'n by whip. County Court w. jury of 12. See III		Aid. & entic. r'ys p'n by fine = to value of Sl. or sold to sl'y for life. Harb. p'n by fine of $500-$1000 & impr.	See II							See II, III		<u>Ibid.</u>, I, 1385-6	185, 188, 189, 203
Jan. 15, 1839				Harb. r'ys : $500-$1000 & impr. 6 mos. to yr.										<u>Ibid.</u>, II, 46	186
Feb. 5, 1840			Murd. of Sl. or treat. so cruelly as to cause death, p'n as in case of Wh. See V			Unreasonable cruelty p'n by fine. See IIb		F'd: tr. & liq.; arms.				F'd: to immig. to St. Penalty, bonded or sold for 1 yr. 2 yrs. time allowed to move out of St. All to leave by 1/1/42.	President's Proclamation. see XI	<u>Ibid.</u>, II, 325, 326, 345, 346	190, 191, 192, 201, 202
Nov. 16, 1840									For suppression of African Sl. Tr.				Treaty bet. G.B. & Texas. See VIII	<u>Ibid.</u>, II, 889-98	
Feb. 5, 1841				Advert. & sale of unclaimed r'ys.										<u>Ibid.</u>, II, 649	186

Dec. 21, 1842												Time for removal extended 2 yrs. C'ld apply Courts to stay, giving bond.	President's Proclamation. See XI	Ibid., II, 879	202
Oct. 13, 1845	See X	No criminal Sls. to be brought in.	Dismembering or kill. Sl. p'n as if Wh.		Insur. excepted under IIb.	Legis. r't to pass laws compell. own. to treat w. humanity & provide cloth. & food.		Census of free Wh. inhab. only. Suffrage: Africans excepted	Legis. no power to prevent immig. bring. Sls. (criminals excepted). R't to prevent import. Sls. as mdse.		Legis. no power to emanc. Sls. w.o. consent of & pay. to own's. To permit own's to emanc.	See VII		Constitution, iii, 1, 2; viii, Slaves	180, 181, 182 fn., 199
May 11, 1846								F'd: hir. o. for more than 1 day a week.						Ibid., II, 1501	191
May 13, 1846								N's to 3d generat. witn. only ag. each other.				See VII		Ibid., II, 1685	192, 205
Feb. 2, 1848									Protesting, as insult to Southern people, ag. attempt of Federal Gov. to prevent citizens emigrat. & settl. in Terr's w. Sls.	See VIII			Resol. See VIII	Ibid., III, 20	210
Feb. 14, 1848						Amends Act of 1840, decreasing fine.								Ibid., III, 29	190

TEXAS

Date	I	II	III	IV	V	VI	VII	VIII	IX	X	XI	XII	Source	Pages
March 18, 1848									St. will not submit to law prohib. cit-izens tak. Sls.to any terr. ac-quired fr. Mexico.	See IX		Resol. See IX	*Ibid.*, III, 132	
Jan. 30, 1850									On ex-tens. of Sl'y.			Resol. See IX	*Ibid.*, III, 531	210
Dec. 3, 1850		Own. assist. criminal Sls. to escape, p'n by fine.	Patrol. See VII.				Sls. at l. af. 10 P.M. and on Sunday appreh. by patrol & p'n by whip. F'd: arms, tr. (w.o. consent of owner). Amends 1840.						*Ibid.*, III, 870-2	191, 192
Jan. 24, 1852	Own. p'd ½ value exec. Sl.	See I											*Ibid.*, III, 912	
Feb. 3, 1853		See XI for F.N. Conspir. & all cap. cr's. listed under F.N., p'n by Death. Non-cap. cr's p'n by 50 stripes instead of by impr. as in case of F.N. N's tried in Dist. C'rt in cap. cr's with Jury trial of 12 free-holders; counsel.		See II			See XI				Cap. cr.: murder or wound. w. intent to kill; rape. Non-cap. cr. p'n like Wh., ex-cept:- using abusive lang. to Wh.; carry. fire arms; punish. Sls. w.o. permis. of owner; riot; unlaw-ful assembl.; administer. medicine:- p'n by whip.		*Ibid.*, III, 1298-9	187, 189, 205

Feb. 9, 1854			Murd. Sl. p'n as if Wh.			Kidn. & sell. F. N. as Sls. p'n by fine & impr.						See V		Ibid., III, 1503	207
Nov. 20, 1855										Compromise of 1850.			Resol. See IX	Ibid., IV, 263	210
July 1856	Right of Master in Sl. absolute.	Masters may correct Sl. to perfect obedience. Wh. may p'n for: insolence; on premises w.o. permis.; unbecom. conduct in presence of Wh. female; insult. lang.; drunkenness; caus. disturb. (Art. 802) Cap. cr's: murder; insur.; arson; rape; robbery; assault, and aid. same (Arts. 812,824) Other offences p'n by whip.		Masters of vessels receiv. r'ys p'n by impr. 10-30 yrs. (Art.654) Steal. or entic. Sls., p'n by impr. 5-15 yrs. (Art 656) Aid. or help. r'ys, 3-10 yrs. (Art.661)	Aid. insur. p'n by fine & impr. not less than 10 yrs. (Art.650) Caus. discontent, p'n by impr. 5-15 yrs. (Art.653) See II			Giv. liq. to Sls. p'n by fine. (Art. 668, 669) Wh's marry. N's to 3d gener. p'n by impr. 2-5 yrs. (Art. 386) See IIa	Masters of vessels carry. away Sls.: p'n 10-30 yrs. impr (Art.654)			P'n by death for same offences as Sl. (See II); Also for aid. insur. & kidn. Wh. female. Other offences p'n by whip. & public work. (Art. 824)		Ibid., IV, 1036, 1046, 1047, 1048, 1049, 1059-60, 1061	185
Aug. 25, 1856									See XI			Amendm. to 1840. Masters of vessels import. F.N. fined $100-$1000.		Ibid., IV, 466	202
Aug. 30, 1856								Sls. f'd to carry gun w.o. permit fr. own. Wh. overseer must accompany Sls. bear. arms.						Ibid., IV, 499	192
Jan. 27, 1858												Ov. 14 c'ld choose Masters & become Sls.		Ibid., IV, 947	206
Feb. 13, 1858				Reward of 1/3 value to captor of r'y Sl.										Ibid., IV, 1074	

TEXAS

Date	I	II	III	IV	V	VI	VII	VIII	IX	X	XI	XII	Source	Pages
Feb. 16, 1858									Endors. Con-vent. of Sl. Sts.to answer quest. of Sl'y.			Resol. See IX	_Ibid._, IV, 1155	210
Aug. 28, 1858		Amends Penal Code 1856. Master aid. Sl. in cr. may be prosecuted as principal. Cap.crimes increased to 8.	Advis. Sl. to r'y; harb. : 3-10 yrs.	Insur.: death. Incit. insur.: impr.	Amends Penal Code 1856. Fine for cr'l. treatm. of Sls. (Art. 670)	Amends Penal Code 1856. Finc for cr'l. treatm. of Sls. (Art. 670)	F'd: tr. Intermarriage bet. N. & Wh.or person of mixed blood, p'n by impr.				See VII Crime by, p'n like those of Sl.		_Ibid._, IV, 1029, 1036,1048-1061	185, 186, 187, 188, 190, 194

VIRGINIA

As one of the original thirteen colonies, Virginia carried over into the Federal Period the body of laws under which it had operated as a Colony.

Date	Property Rights	Crimes: By	Crimes: Against	Runaway Patrol Laws	Insurrection and Conspiracy	Protection: Slaves and Free Negroes	Teaching and Preaching	Discrimination and Disabilities	Importation and Exportation	Limitation of Slavery	Emancipation and Abolition	Free Negroes	Resolutions and Sundries	Source	Pages in Text
	I	II		III	IV	V	VI	VII	VIII	IX	X	XI	XII		
June 29, 1776					See XII				See XII		See XII		"By prompting our Negroes to rise in arms against us, these very negroes whom by an inhuman use of his (George III) negative, he hath refused us permission to exclude by law."	Preamble, Thorpe, Am. Charters & Constitutions, VII, 3815.	
1776				See VIII					Masters of vessels req. not to carry away Sls.					Hening, Stat. at L. (1821), IX, 187	187
1777								Only witn. ag. each other.				See VII		Ibid., IX, 411	192
1778									F'd: to import Sl.; declared free. Not apply to settlers.	See VIII				Ibid., IX, 471-2	195, 197
1779	Tax on property provides that it sh. not extend to N. Sl. or serv.							"Citizen" limited to free Wh.					Poll tax on Sl. capable of work.	Ibid., X, 12, 166	

VIRGINIA

Date	I	II		III	IV	V	VI	VII	VIII	IX	X	XI	XII	Source	Pages
1782				See VII				Wander. Sl. to be impr. or hir. o.						Ibid., XI, 24	191
1782						See X					Emanc. permitted; certif. fr. Master. Aged & infirm to be supported.			Ibid., XI, 39-40	
1782								F'd: to hir. o. Wander. Sl. to be arrest. & sold.						Ibid., XI, 59	193
1783											Provided for emanc. of Sl. who served in army dur. Revolution			Ibid., XI, 308-9	
1784				Patrol law.				Not more than 1/3 of those employed on river craft sh'd be Sls.						Ibid., XI, 404,489	192
1785				See VII	Riots, unlawful assembly, sed. speeches, p'n by. flog.			Wander. w.o. permit p'n by stripes. F'd: arms & tr.			Emanc. those who had entered St. since beg. of session & who had lived in St. 1 yr.			Ibid., XII, 182-3	191, 192
1786	Value of condemned Sl. to be pd. own.	Unan. decision nec. in trial for treason or felony. No person having interest in Sl. to sit upon trial.				See II, X					Suits for freed. prosecuted as for freeman.	See X		Ibid., XII, 345	
Jan. 5, 1788			See V			Steal. & sell. F.N. p'n by death.						See V		Ibid., XII, 531	207
Nov. 21, 1788			Repeals Act 1723 decl. kill. of Sl. mansl. only.			See IIb								Ibid., XII, 381	

Dec. 26, 1788									Modifies law reg. import. of Sls. & extends privl. to those immig.w. Sls. to Ky. district.					<u>Ibid</u>., XII, 713-4	
Dec. 17, 1792	Sl. considered personal estate.	Lift. hand ag. Wh. p'n by 30 lashes. Castration of Sl. convicted of attack on Wh.woman. Conspir. & steal. Sl. p'n by death. False testim. p'n by ear nailed to pillory, etc. & flog.		See VIII Steal. Sl.p'n by death.	Conspir. a felony p'n by death.			F'd: Meeting of Sls.	Masters of vessels not to carry Sls. out of St. w. o.permis. of own.		Emanc.Sls. may be taken to satisfy debt.contracted bef. emanc.	See II, X		Shepherd, <u>Stat. at L</u>. (1835), I, 122-130.	185, 187, 188, 193
Dec. 22, 1792				Patrol law.										<u>Collection of Acts</u> (1803), pp. 287-8	192
Dec. 12, 1793									Sls. bro't. fr. Africa or West Ind. to be export. at importer's expense. See XI			Prohibited F.N. fr. immig. to St.		Shepherd, <u>Stat. at L</u>., I, 239	200, 202
Dec. 25, 1795											Amends Act of 1792, penaliz. for aid given in unsuccessful suits for freed.			<u>Ibid</u>., I, 363-5	207
Dec. 23, 1796									Land own's permitted to carry Sls. in & out of St.					<u>Ibid</u>., II, 19	
Jan. 18, 1798								F'd: peddling				See VII		<u>Ibid</u>., II, 94	204

VIRGINIA

Date	I	II	III	IV	V	VI	VII	VIII	IX	X	XI	XII	Source	Pages
Jan. 25, 1798			Harb.: p'n. Wh's by fine; F.N., by whip.	Death for free persons incit. Sl. to insur.			See III			Members of abol.socs. disqual. fr. serv. on juries in suits for freed.	See III,IV		Ibid., II, 77	186, 187
Jan. 15, 1801		See IV		Sls. guilty of conspir.c'ld be sold out of U.S.									Ibid., II, 279-80	
Jan. 21, 1801		See VII					Sls. permitted to testify ag. F.N.				See VII		Ibid., II, 300	
Jan. 20, 1802			See VII				Masters of vessels not to allow Sls. on board.						Ibid., II, 326	187
Jan. 21, 1804								Sl. c'ld be brought back fr. D.C.					Ibid., III, 76	
Jan. 24, 1804				See VII			Meet's of Sls. at night unlawful.						Ibid., III, 108	193
Jan. 31, 1805						Bound orphans to be taught read., writ. and arith.					See VI		Ibid., III, 124	193
Jan. 25, 1806								Sale by St. of Sl. brought into St. & kept for 1 yr.		Emanc. Sl. remain. in St. 1 yr. forfeited freed.	See X		Ibid., III, 251, 252	200, 208
Feb. 4, 1806							See XI				F'd: carrying arms without license.		Ibid., III, 274	204
Feb. 10, 1808		Death pen. for burn. barns. Brand. for burn. stacks of wheat.											Ibid., III, 377	

Jan. 17, 1811									Citizens may import. Sls. held by marriage, inheritance, etc., from U.S.					Acts, 1810-11, pp. 15-16	195
Jan. 22, 1811		Cutt. down trees at Old Point Comfort p'n by whip.										P'n for II by fine.		Ibid., 80	
Feb. 9, 1811								F'd: carry. firearms aboard boat.				See VII		Ibid., 57	204
Feb. 14, 1812									Citizens & others c'ld bring Sls. not for sale provided equal no. of female Sls. exported.					Acts, 1811-12, p.34	195
Jan. 24, 1816											Sls. emanc. since 1806 c'ld apply to live in county.	See X		Acts, 1815-16, pp. 51-2	
Feb. 20, 1817		See IV			Incit. to insur. p'n by death.							See IV		Acts, 1817, p. 22	187, 188
Jan. 17, 1818											Proced. for persons suing for freedom.	See X		Acts, 1817-18, pp. 71-2	
March 2, 1819		See VIII							Permitted import. non-criminal Sls. born in U.S.A.					Acts, 1818-9, p. 37	195, 197
Feb. 16, 1820												Hir. o. for not less than 8¢ a day for payment of taxes.		Ibid., p. 26	206

VIRGINIA

Date	I	II		III	IV	V	VI	VII	VIII	IX	X	XI	XII	Source	Pages
Feb. 5, 1822				R'ys sold only on order of Court.										Acts, 1821, p. 23	186
Feb. 12, 1823				R'ys in jail to receive cloth.										Acts, 1823, p. 34	
Feb. 14, 1823		Trespass or destruction of property by Sls. p'n by whip. Rape p'n by death.										See II		Ibid., 36-37	185
Feb. 21, 1823		F.N. or Sls. attempt. to kill Wh. p'n by whip. & banished fr. U.S. forever. See XI						See XII				Convicted of offences usually p'n by impr. of more than 2 yrs., p'n by stripes & sold as Sls. at discr. of Jury. See II		Ibid. 35-36	205
Feb. 25, 1824				Entic. to r'y or harb. p'n by fine or whip.										Acts, 1824, p. 37	186
Jan. 6, 1825		F.N.: p'n by death for rape on Wh. woman.										See II		Acts, 1825, p. 22	205
Feb. 18, 1825		F.N.: petit larceny p'n as if Wh.; grand larceny by whip.& banishment.										See II		Ibid., 37	205
Feb. 24, 1827											Repeals act provid. for sale of emanc. Sls. remain. in St. ov. 12 mos. (see 1806)	See X		Acts, 1826, p. 25	200, 208

Feb. 12, 1828		Sls. convicted of petit larceny p'n by whip.										P'n by impr. instead of flog. See II		Acts, 1827, pp. 29, 30	
Jan. 27, 1829				Assist. r'ys p'n by fine or impr.										Acts, 1828, p. 25	186
April 7, 1831							Unlaw- ful for F.N. to meet to be taught read. & writ.					Remain. in St. contrary to law, to be sold. See VI		Acts, 1830-1, p. 107	193, 200, 202, 208
April 13, 1831								F'd: tr. w. Sls. w. o. consent of own.						Ibid., 130	
Feb. 27, 1832								F'd: to sell. liq. to Sls.						Acts, 1832, p. 24	191
March 15, 1832		P'n by death for kill. Wh. See XI			Writ., print., or circl. lit. advis. insur. p'n: 1st offence,- corp. p'n; 2nd, death.		F.N.& Sls. f'd to preach or hold meet's. Wh.min- ister c'ld give relig. instr.	F'd: to sell liq. near publ. assem- bly.				F'd: to own Sls.; carry arms w. o. permit; sell liq. (see VII). P'n like Sls. for petit lar- ceny (see 1828) See II, IV		Acts, 1831-2, pp. 20-23	187, 188, 191, 194, 204, 205, 206
Marth 4, 1833									See XI			$18,000 approp. annually for 5 yrs. to trans- port F.N. to Liberia.		Acts, 1832-3, p. 14	202
March 11, 1834				Aiding r'ys p'n.					See XI			Prohibited immig. to St. from U.S. Masters of vessels p'n for import.		Acts, 1833-4, pp. 77, 79-80.	186
Feb. 7, 1835		Trespass.& driv. ov. bridge faster than walk p'n by whip.										P'n for II by fine.		Acts, 1834-5, p. 52	

VIRGINIA

Date	I	II		III	IV	V	VI	VII	VIII	IX	X	XI	XII	Source	Pages
Feb. 12, 1835		Bail for non-cap. cr.												<u>Ibid</u>., p. 45	
March 6, 1835		Burn. woods, fields, grain: felony.						See II, XI				Cr's. in II considered misdemeanor.		<u>Ibid</u>., p. 46	
March 10, 1835				Va. Sl. Insurance Co. incorp. to insure ag. r'ys.										<u>Acts</u>, <u>1834-5</u>, p. 161	
Feb. 16, 1836											Va. alone r't to control Sl'y in St.		Resol. See X	<u>Acts</u>, <u>1835-6</u>, pp. 395-6	209
March 23, 1836		P'n by death for obstruct. rrs.			Circl. & print. incend. lit. p'n.			Others than Sl. p'n by impr. for obstruct. rrs. See II			Persons advocat. abolit. guilty of high misdemeanor.	Transported outside U.S. for IV		<u>Ibid</u>., 44-8	187
March 22, 1837											Emanc. Sls. may apply for permis. to remain in St.	See X		<u>Ibid</u>., <u>1836-7</u>, pp. 47-9	201
March 25, 1837				F'd: rrs. transport Sl. w.o. authority.										<u>Ibid</u>., 101	187
Feb. 5, 1838		Destroy. oyster beds p'n.						See II F. persons p'n by fine. Sl. by whip.				See II, VII		<u>Acts</u>, <u>1838</u>, p. 87	
Apr. 7, 1838							See XI					F'd: to return to St. hav. left it to be educated.		<u>Ibid</u>., 76	

March 11, 1839				F'd: keepers of ferries, to carry Sls.				See III						Acts, 1839, p. 47	187
April 9, 1839				Patrol may force open Sl. & F.N. houses to searcn for arms.				See III				See III		Ibid., 24	192
March 14, 1840	Own.p'd for Sls. exec.	See I												Acts, 1839-40, p. 51	
March 17, 1840				Relative to demand of Gov of Va. for surrender of 3 r'ys by N.Y.									Resol. Discus. of Sts. r'ts, Sl'y, etc. See III	Ibid., 155-69	209
March 13, 1841				Vessels dep. for N.Y. must have certif. that no Sls. on board. Aid. Sl. to escape p'n.				See III				F'd: to come to St.		Acts, 1840-41, pp. 79-82, 83	187
March 27, 1843		Inj. or destroy. rrs. p'n: free person by impr.; Sl. by death. F.N. & Sls. admin. poison with intent to kill to suffer death.						Admin. or sell. med. p'n by lashes. See II, XI				C'ld not sell agricult. products in Richmond & Accomack Cos. w.o. certif. See II, VII		Acts, 1842-43, pp. 59, 69	185, 204

VIRGINIA

Date	I	II		III	IV	V	VI	VII	VIII	IX	X	XI	XII	Source	Pages
Feb. 15, 1844													Resol. condemn. Resol. of Mass.reg. tax.& re-presenta-tion ac-cord. to no.of free persons.	Acts. 1843-44, p.115	210
March 14, 1848*	Steal. Sls.p'n by impr. Persons deny. property r'ts. in Sls. p'n by impr.	See IV Sl. p'n. w. death where free person p'n.3 yrs. impr. Less than 3 yrs.,corp. p'n. Using provok. lang. p'n. by whip.		Harb. r'ys.on vessel p'n. 2-5 yrs.impr. See I	Circl. incend. lit. p'n. 1-5 yrs. impr.			See II				See, II, IV		Acts, 1847-8, pp. 101, 102, 117-120, 125, 126, 161-4	185, 186, 187
Jan. 20, 1849										Denied r't of gov.to control Sl'y			Resol. re Wilmot Proviso. See IX	Acts, 1848-9, pp. 257-8	210
Feb. 7, 1849 *r (1850)				Relat. to legis. in Congr. re fug. Sls.									Resol. See III	Acts, 1849-50, pp. 240-54	210
1850											Emanc.Sls. forfeit freedom by remain. more than 12 mos. in St. Gen.Assem. may pass laws impos. re-stric. & conditions on emanc. Gen.Assem. not to emanc. any Sl. or de-scend. bef. or af. birth of descend.	Gen.Assem. may pass laws for relief of St. fr. F.N. pop-ulation.		Constitution, iv, 19,20, 21 (Slaves)	181, 200

March 29, 1851													Resol. re action S.C. reg. South. Congr.	Acts, 1850-51, p. 201	
March 30, 1852								Richmond may prohibit rais. hogs & dogs by N's.				See VII		Acts, 1852, p.263	
April 12, 1852								F'd: gambl. or betting.				See VII		Ibid., 84	193
May 7, 1852								See XI				Alexandria authorized to sell F.N. for non-pay. of taxes.		Ibid., 241	
May 17, 1852								Fredericksburg may prohibit rais. hogs & dogs by N's				See VII		Ibid., 285	
May 22, 1852								Staunton may prohibit rais. hogs by N's.				See VII		Ibid., 304	
April 6, 1853								See XI	See XI			$30,000 ann. ap-prop. for 5 yrs. to remove F.N. to Africa. Coloniza-tion B'd estab. Tax levied on all F.N. males 21-55 yrs. old.		Acts, 1852-3, p. 58	202
Feb. 18, 1856												C'ld choose Masters & become Sls.		Acts, 1855-6, pp. 37-8	206
March 5, 1856								F'd: hir. Sls. in D.C.						Ibid., 45	
March 15, 1856								F'd: sale of poison. drugs to Sls. & F.N.				See VII		Ibid., 45	
March 17, 1856				All but govt. and foreign vessels inspect. for r'ys.										Ibid., 38	187

*The act codified laws relating to the punishment of free Negroes and slaves.
**Date given.

VIRGINIA

Date	I	II		III	IV	V	VI	VII	VIII	IX	X	XI	XII	Source	Pages
March 31, 1858								See XI				Incap. of acquir. Sl. except by descent.		Acts, 1857-8, p. 46	206
April 1, 1858								See XI				Liq. sold to F.N. only on certif. of 3 J. of P. that F.N is sober, orderly & of good character.		Ibid., 51	204
April 7, 1858		Convicts to be employed on publ. works.												Ibid., 39	
March 29, 1860		See XI										Convicted of cr. p'n by impr. C'ld be sold into absolute Sl'y.		Acts, 1859-60 pp. 163-4	205

Slave Codes Northern States

CALIFORNIA

Prior to its admission to the Union, citizens of what is now the State of California were under the civil law of Mexico. An independent government was established by Americans and other inhabitants in 1846; the Treaty of Guadalupe Hidalgo in 1848 brought it within the limits of the United States, and it was under a provisional military government until its admission to the Union in 1850.* The Mexican law operated as a personal law in determining the individual right of Mexicans. "It may be doubted, therefore, whether the Mexican law prohibiting slavery could, by continuing as the local law, have presented such an universal attribution of liberty as should have prevented the judicial recognition of the relation of master and slave, when coming from some State in which they had been in that relation."

*Thorpe, American Charters, Constitutions and Organic Laws, I, 377, 391; Hurd, Law of Freedom and Bondage, II, 200-202.

Date	Property Rights	Crimes		Runaway Patrol Laws	Insurrection and Conspiracy	Protection: Slaves and Free Negroes	Teaching and Preaching	Discrimination and Disabilities	Importation and Exportation	Limitation of Slavery	Emancipation and Abolition	Free Negroes	Resolutions and Sundries	Source	Pages in Text
		By	Against												
	I	II		III	IV	V	VI	VII	VIII	IX	X	XI	XII		
Nov. 13, Dec. 20, 1849								Suffrage: Wh. only			Sl'y abolished.	See VII		Constitution, 1, 18; 11, 1. Statutes, 1850-58, p. 29.	214, 220
Apr. 16, 1850			See V			Kidn., sell.as Sl.: impr.						See V		Statutes, 1850-58, p. 335.	217
Apr. 22, 1850								Intermarriage: void.						Compiled Laws, 1850-53, p. 175.	217
Apr. 29, 1851								See XI				50% or more N. blood disqual. as witn. ag. Wh.		Ibid., 591; Statutes, 114.	216
Apr. 15, 1852				Procedure in case of r'ys; Sls. bro't in prior to Admis. to Union, held fugitives.										Compiled laws, 1850-53, p. 231.	222
1854				1852 amended.										Hurd, Law of Freedom and Bondage, II, 204	222
1854								See XI				Indians and N. with $\frac{1}{2}$ N. blood disqual. as witn. ag. Wh.		Ibid., II, 204.	216

CONNECTICUT

As one of the original thirteen colonies, Connecticut carried over into the Federal Period the body of laws under which it had operated as a Colony.

Date	Property Rights	Crimes By	Crimes Against	Runaway Patrol Laws	Insurrection and Conspiracy	Protection: Slaves and Free Negroes	Teaching and Preaching	Discrimination and Disabilities	Importation and Exportation	Limitation of Slavery	Emancipation and Abolition	Free Negroes	Resolutions and Sundries	Source	Pages in Text
	I	II		III	IV	V	VI	VII	VIII	IX	X	XI	XII		
1774									Import. f'd. £100 penalty.					Statutes (1808), I, 624; Session Laws, 1773–83, p. 403	218
1777											Certif. of good health fr. selectmen for Sls. bet. 25 & 45 to be secured by own., who is then not respons. for support of emanc. Sl.			Statutes (1808), I, 624; Session Laws, 1773–83, p. 479	
1784*		Steal. p'n by whip.		See VII				F'd to travel w.o. pass; Ferrymen f'd to transport. Vagrants taken up. Tr. f'd; abroad af. 9 P.M., p'n by whip.	As above		As above. Unless certif. obtained, own. liable. All born af. 1/3/84 to be free at 25.	F.N. not to travel w.o. pass.		Statutes (revision of 1784), pp. 233–5; Statutes (1808), I, 623–5.	212, 213, 218
Oct. 1788			See V			Kidn. & remov. F. N. or one entitled to freed. at 25, p'n by fine of £100 w. damages.			No inhabit. of St. to take N's on board his vessel as mdse. £500 penalty for every vessel. Insurance void. Ships clearing for Africa to give bond.		See V	See V Childr. born af. 1/3/84 must be registered.		Acts & Laws, 1788 bound with Statutes (rev. of 1784), pp. 368–9; Statutes (1808), I, 626–8.	213, 217, 218

*The revision of 1784 gives the law in force at that date, including some statutes carried down from Colonial times. The only new provision is that given under emancipation.

CONNECTICUT

Date	I	II		III	IV	V	VI	VII	VIII	IX	X	XI	XII	Source	Pages
1789*									Act to prevent Sl. tr. strength-ened.					Acts & Laws, 1789 bound with Statutes (rev. of 1784), p. 388	
May 1792									£100 fine for trans. Sls. out of St. Contracts for sale of Sls. void.					Acts & Laws, 1792 bound with Statutes (rev. of 1784), pp. 412-3	
1792											As acts of 1777 & 1784. Emanc. to be record-ed.			Ibid., 413	
Feb. 1797		Repeals Act of 1708 p'n. Sls. by whip. for defamation.												Ibid., 229-30	
May 1797											Additional Act to 1792: Childr. born af. 1/8/97 free at 21.			Statutes (1808), I, 625-6	213
Oct. 1797								Repeals colonial regulations reg. travel, etc. See 1784.						Ibid., I, 626	217
Oct. 1802								Suffrage: property qual. Colonial act retained				See VII		Ibid., I, 355-8	220
1814								Suffrage: free Wh. males only.				See VII		Ibid. (1808-1818), II, 162	221
1818								As above.						Constitution, vi, 2	221

1821 **						Kidn. & remov. F. N. fr. St. p'n. by $400 fine.			Travel-lers al-lowed Sls. Those re-moving fr. St. may take Sls. Im-port.& Sl. tr. f'd. See 1784 & 1788.		Emanc. Sls. in want sup-ported by own. un-less cer-tif. ob-tained.	See V		Public Statutes (rev. of 1821), pp. 152, 428-83	217
1833							F'd: To establ. schools for N. childr. w.o. consent of ma-jority of civil autho-rities.					See VI		Public Statute Laws (1835), pp. 321-2	221
May 31, 1838							1833 repeal-ed.							Public Acts, 1838, p. 30	221, 222
June 1838				Proced-ure & trial of r'ys fr. other Sts.										Ibid., 32	222
June 6, 1844				Repeals above because of deci-sion of Supreme Court.										Public Acts, 1844, p. 33	223
June 12, 1848						Masters to sup-port for-mer Sls. unable to care for them-selves.			Import. f'd. Fine $350.		No person to be held in Sl'y. Masters to support former Sls. ex-cept where exempted by law.	See V,X		Statutes (comp. 1854), p. 798; Public Acts, 1848, p. 70	213
1854			See V			$500 fine for kidn. F.N.& sell as Sl.						See V		Statutes (1854), pp. 798-9	217, 223

*See also Donnan, Documents Illustrative of the Slave Trade, III, 3.
**The revision of 1821 gives the then existing law, and in a footnote states, "Slavery was never directly established by statute; but has been indirectly mentioned by several statutes, and frequently recognized by courts, so that it may be said to have been established by law."

DELAWARE

As one of the original thirteen colonies, Delaware carried over into the Federal Period the body of laws under which it had operated as a Colony.

Date	Property Rights	Crimes By	Crimes Against	Runaway Patrol Laws	Insurrection and Conspiracy	Protection: Slaves and Free Negroes	Teaching and Preaching	Discrimination and Disabilities	Importation and Exportation	Limitation of Slavery	Emancipation and Abolition	Free Negroes	Resolutions and Sundries	Source	Pages in Text
	I	II		III	IV	V	VI	VII	VIII	IX	X	XI	XII		
1721	2/3 value exec. Sl. pd. own.	Trial by 2 Just's. P'n.: rape - pillory and cutting off ears; Steal. - whip.; Fire-arms - 21 lashes.			Assembl. of ov. 6 in no. p'n by whip.			F'd: firearms See IV				Childr. of Wh. woman and N., servants until 31.		Laws, 1700-97, I, 102-5, 108	
1760						See X,XI					Court may free childr. of Wh. woman and N.	Penalty on sell. F.N., £100 See X		Ibid., I, 380-4	
Oct. 3, 1767		Assault on Sl. or F.N.: 39 lashes.										See IIa		Ibid., I, 436-7	215
Sept. 21, 1776									No Sl. to be import. as mdse. See X.		No person import. fr. Africa to be held as Sl.			Constitution, 1, xxvi	213
1787		F.N. horse-steal.: sold to West Ind.				See XI		F.N. f'd to vote or hold office; not witn. ag. Wh.	Export. f'd. w.o. permit. Import.: £20 fine & Sl. free.		Former manu. ratified; securities not necessary for old and infirm Sls.	Cannot vote or hold office. May hold property. See IIa		Laws, I, 884; See also Hurd, II, 74-81	213, 216, 219
1789		Cap. cr., tried by jury; repeals older laws.							Sls. devised or inherited may be import. Forfeiture of vessels equipped for Sl. tr.					Hurd, II, 74-81	215, 219
1792								Suffrage: Wh. only				See VII		Constitution, iv	220

1793						Kidn.F.N. p'n. by whip. & pillory.			Sl. ex-port. w. o. permit free.			See V		Rev. Code, 1093, from Hurd, II, 74-81	217
1795						See XI						Repeals act of 1721 as unjust (Childr. of Wh. woman & N. father, serv. until 31).		Laws, I, 1201	213-4
1797		Sl. beat..a Sl. or F.N.: whipped. Rape: whip. & pillory.							Attempt to ex-port = freedom of Sl.		Verbal contracts, void. Pro-cedure. Emanc. by will.	See II		Laws, I, 1321	214, 215
1798								Regulations at elections, liq. sales.				See VII		Hurd, II, 74-81; Laws, III, 7	
1799		See VII						Testimony allowed when no Wh's present, except in bastardy ag. Wh. man.						Hurd, II, 80; Laws, III, 80	216
1807		Larceny by F.N.: may be sold.						Intermarriage: void; Minister p'n.	See XI			May be sold to make re-stitution in II. Non-re-sident, pro-hib. fr. en-tering, ex-cept with certif. of good charac-ter.		Laws, IV, 108	215, 216, 219
1810											Manu. at future time, Sls. until time of manu. Issue,-Sls. un-til 25 & 21.			Ibid., IV, 337	
1811		Re-enacts law of 1807.							See XI			Immigr. to St. f'd. Re-sident F.N. remaining out of St. 6 mos. becomes non-resident. See II.		Ibid., IV, 400,408	215, 219

DELAWARE

Date	I	II	III	IV	V	VI	VII	VIII	IX	X	XI	XII	Source	Pages
1816			Taken before J. of P., deliver-ed only on proof. Harb. f'd. Did not af-fect travel. or those under Act of Cong. of 1793.					See III					Rev. Stat. (1829), p. 413; Hurd, II, 74-81	222
1819					See X					Sl. may be freed w.o. bond but own. lia-ble for care.			Rev. Stat. (1829), p. 412 ff	
1826		New cr. law. Sls. charged with cap. cr. tried as freemen.											Hurd, II, 74-81; Laws, VI, 740	215
1826			Proced-ure.										Rev. Stat. (1829), 291.	222
1827		Gen. criminal code of 1826 ap-plicable to Sls.						Re-enacts provi-sions ag. import. and ex-port.					Ibid., 149-56	219
1829								Licenses to import and ex-port Sls.					Hurd, II, 80	219
1831							Suffrage: Wh. only				See VII		Constitution, vi, 1.	220
1832						Non-res. f'd. to preach.	F'd.: firearms; meet's af. 10 P.M. See VI, XI.	See XI			Provisions to enforce law of 1811 ag. immig.		Hurd, II, 80; Rev. Code, ch. 52	216
1833							Written consent of master for mar-riage of serv. or Sl.				License for marriage not required, but certif. of freed.		Rev. Code, 237; Hurd, II, 80	

1835												License to use guns.		Hurd, II, 80	
Jan. 16, 1837		For assault, F.N. may be sold as serv. to pay fine.						See II				See II		Laws, 1837, p. 64	
Feb. 21, 1837				Entic. Sl.: fine.										Ibid., 184	213
Feb. 15, 1839		F.N.: larceny, Court may graduate p'n.										See II		Laws, 1839, pp. 256-7	
1841		See VII						Distinction bet. Black & White insolvents.				See VII		Hurd, II, 80	216
Feb. 22, 1843								Act of 1841 revived.						Laws, 1843, pp. 524-5	
1849				Entic.: must leave St.										Hurd, II, 80	
1849												Absence fr. St. limited to 60 days to keep residence.		Rev. Code, ch. 52, sec. 1; see Hurd, II, 80	
1849												Idle to be hired out to compulsory service.		Hurd, II, 80	216
1851									Emigration f'd.			See VIII		Ibid., 81	219
1852		J. of P. jurisdiction ov. Sls. See XI						F'd.: F.N. hold. office, voting. Hold. property only r'ts allowed. Suffrage: Wh. only.			Procedure, suits for freed.	Competent witnesses in criminal cases. See VII, X		Rev. Code, ch. 52, sec. 12; Hurd, II, 81	216, 220
1855								F.N.: barred fr. political & camp meet's.	Fine for import. F.N.			See VII, VIII		Laws, 1855, ch. 257; Rev. Code, ch. 52; Hurd, II, 81	216, 219
1857				Fine on capt. of ship or conductor of train, carry. Sl. out of St.					See III					Laws, 1857, p. 436	213

ILLINOIS

Illinois was originally part of the Northwest Territory ceded by Virginia in 1783 and 1784. In 1800, together with Indiana, it was separated as Indiana Territory. It was organized as a separate territory in 1809 and the pre-existing laws of the old Indiana Territory continued on the mere principle of continuation of laws. In 1812 it was enacted that "all laws passed by the legislature of Indiana Territory which were in force on the first day of March, 1809, in that Territory, that are of a general nature and not local to Indiana Territory, and which are not repealed by the governor and judges of the Illinois Territory, are hereby declared to be in full force in this Territory."*

Hurd makes the following comment regarding the status of slavery in Illinois: In 1778, a law of Virginia provided for the government of a county named Illinois, in which Negroes had been held in slavery by the French settlers. It had been claimed, therefore, that the slavery of the "French Negroes" and their descendants could not be abolished, either by Congress or the State, in view of the fact that Virginia in her Act of Cession had stipulated that "the French and Canadian inhabitants . . . who have professed themselves citizens of Virginia, shall have their possessions and titles confirmed to them."**

*Hurd, Law of Freedom and Bondage, II, 132, quoting from Hays v. Borders, 1 Gilman 46.
**Hurd, Ibid., 132, fn. 2. See Virginia Act of Cession, 1783, in Thorpe, Federal and State Constitutions, II, 956.

Date	Property Rights	Crimes By	Crimes Against	Runaway Patrol Laws	Insurrection and Conspiracy	Protection: Slaves and Free Negroes	Teaching and Preaching	Discrimination and Disabilities	Importation and Exportation	Limitation of Slavery	Emancipation and Abolition	Free Negroes	Resolutions and Sundries	Source	Pages in Text
	I	II		III	IV	V	VI	VII	VIII	IX	X	XI	XII		
1818								N.& Ind., Mul. excepted fr. militia. Suffrage: Wh. only.			Sl'y prohib.			Constitution, ii, 27; v, 1; vi, 1 See also Compiled Statutes (1856), I, 39	214, 216, 220
1819*		See VII						Witn. only ag. each other.				See VII		Laws, 1819, p. 143	216
March 30, 1819		Disord. & lazy: stripes. Absent 10 mi. fr. home: 35 lashes. Serv. p'n. by whip., free men by fine.	Appeal to Court allowed injured.	Harb. p'n. as theft. Carry. away Sl's: fine.	Riots,unlaw. assemb., sed. speeches: whip.	Suitable food, cloth., lodg., new & complete suit at end of serv. Kidn. F.N.p'n by fine.		No. N.to purchase serv.other than own color. F'd: hir. o. w.o. master's consent; tr. Pass.req.	See XI		Bonds nec. for Sls. bro't in to be freed.**	Certif. of freed. at end of service. Certif. of freed. req. for black settlers. Residents must register. May acquire property dur. service. See V	Contracts made during serv., void.	Laws, 1819, pp. 354-61	214, 215, 216, 217-8, 219, 222
Jan. 6,* 1827	Send. serv.of another out of St. p'n.			Harb. f'd.		See I		F'd: liq.						Rev. Code (1827), pp. 156-7; Hurd, II, 134-5	214, 216, 222
Feb. 2, 1827	As above.	See VII						Not a witn.ag. Wh. 1/4 N. blood= Mul.						Hurd, II, 135	

Jan. 17,* 1829		Increases penal character of law.		N. w.o. certif., arrested as r'y.				Intermarriage f'd.			Non-res. Sls. hir.o. in St. in order to instit. suits of freed.: arrested.	Bond of $1000 security req.of N.coming to reside. See III		Rev. Code (1829), pp. 109, 111; Hurd, II, 135	216, 219
Feb. 1, 1831									See X		Fine for import.N's to free them.	Bonds req. before coming to St. See X		Laws, 1831, p. 101; Hurd, II,135	219
1841	See XI											Certif. of freed.to be provided F. N. Not conclus. ag. claim of ownership.		Hurd, II, 135	
1845								Re-enacts 1827.						Rev. Stat. (1845), p. 154	
March 3, 1845	Laws of 1819 and 1829 re-enacted.													Rev. Stat. (1850), pp. 776-84	222
March 5, 1845			See V			Remov.w. o.establ. claim = Kidn.						See V		Rev. Stat. (1856), pp. 366-7.	217
March 5, 1848								Re-enacts 1818.	F.N.not to immig. & settle in St.		Sls. not to be bro't. to St. in order to free them.	See VIII		Constitution, vi, 1; viii, 1; xiv, Persons of Color	219-20
Feb. 12, 1853				Provides for claim. r'ys.				1/4 N.blood= Mul. See XI	Fine for any but travellers import. N.		No Sl. to be bro't. to St. to be freed.	Misdem. to come to St. to reside.		Laws, 1853, pp. 57-9	220, 222
1855							School funds= to Taxes fr, N's to be used for schools	See VI				See VI		Laws, 1855, p. 85	217, 221
Feb. 15, 1855			See V			Agents to reclaim kidn. F.N.						See V		Ibid., 1855, p. 186	

*Acts of 1819, 1827 and 1829 appear in revisions of 1845, 1850, 1858.
**Hurd states that this part of the law was amended in 1825 (Acts, 50) and 1833 (Rev. Stat.,466); "relieving from some penalties." (Hurd II, 134).

INDIAN TERRITORY

Indian Territory, successively a part of Louisiana, Missouri, and Arkansas, differs from the other territories in that it was established by Act of 1834 to provide a home for Indian nations, with a recognized power of self-government. According to Hurd, it might be questioned whether any law derived from colonizing Europeans could have any territorial extent in this district. Involuntary servitude appears to have been recognized among the Indians, however, and the tribes who formerly occupied lands within the southernmost States had held Negro slaves, under their customary law, before their removal to Indian Territory.*

*Hurd, Law of Freedom and Bondage, II, 189-90.

Date	Property Rights	Crimes		Runaway Patrol Laws	Insurrection and Conspiracy	Protection: Slaves and Free Negroes	Teaching and Preaching	Discrimination and Disabilities	Importation and Exportation	Limitation of Slavery	Emancipation and Abolition	Free Negroes	Resolutions and Sundries	Source	Pages in Text
		By	Against												
	I	II		III	IV	V	VI	VII	VIII	IX	X	XI	XII		
1857											Gen. Council no power to pass laws for emancipation.			Hurd, II, 190 (Laws of Choctaw Nation, Jan. 1857, Art. vii, Slaves)	

INDIANA

Indiana as well as Illinois and Ohio were parts of the Northwest Territory. In 1800 Indiana Territory, containing Illinois and Indiana, was designated at the time of the separate organization of Ohio Territory, and the law of the former Northwest Territory continued, with the guarantee in the Ordinance of 1787. The Territorial government was established in 1814, and in 1816 the Enabling Act was passed to form a Constitution and for the admission of the Territory to the Union.

Date	Property Rights	Crimes By	Crimes Against	Runaway Patrol Laws	Insurrection and Conspiracy	Protection: Slaves and Free Negroes	Teaching and Preaching	Discrimination and Disabilities	Importation and Exportation	Limitation of Slavery	Emancipation and Abolition	Free Negroes	Resolutions and Sundries	Source	Pages in Text
	I	II		III	IV	V	VI	VII	VIII	IX	X	XI	XII		
Sept. 22,* 1803	A law concerning servants.													Hurd, II, 123	
1806	Serv. decl. personal property in cases of execution ag. Master for term of serv.													Hurd, II, 123 (1st Assembly, 2d Sess., ch. 10)	
1806				Harb. f'd.				Passes req. Wander. f'd.						Ibid., II, 123-4	
Sept. 17, 1807	See VIII, XI								Own's. may bring Sls. ov. 15 to Terr.; record of service bef. clerk of court. C'ld. hold males to 35, females to 32.			Childr. of indentured to serve Master until 30 (males), 28 (females)		Ibid., II, 124-6 (Terr. Laws, 1807-8, p. 423.)	220
Sept. 17, 1807	Extends Act of 1806.													Ibid., II, 126 (Rev. Code (1807), p. 188)	
Dec. 14.** 1810						Penalty of $1000 for remov. N. fr. St. w.o. certif. fr. court.			See V			See V		Ibid., II, 126 (3d Assembly, 1st Sess., ch. 28)	217, 220
1816								Exempted fr. St. Militia.			Sl'y abolished.			Constitution, VII, 1; XI, 7	214

*Title only given by Hurd.
**Repeals Act of 1807

INDIANA

Date	I	II		III	IV	V	VI	VII	VIII	IX	X	XI	XII	Source	Pages
1816				Procedure for claim. r'ys; penalties for harb.		Penalty for remov. N. w.o. proper certif.						See V		Hurd, II, 127-8	222
1817 *								F'd: cohab. & intermar.						*Ibid.*, II, 128	216
1817		See VII						Not witn. ag. Wh's.				See VII		*Ibid.*, II, 128	216
1818				Amends 1816, increas. penalty.										*Ibid.*, II, 128	
March 22, 1819 & Feb. 17, 1823	Time of service may be sold as personal estate.											See I		*Ibid.*, II, 128-9	
Jan. 22, ** 1824			Trial before jury of fugitives claim. freed.	Procedure for claim. r'ys.		See IIb						See IIb		Hurd, II, 129; *Rev. Laws* (1831), p. 278	222
Feb. 10, 1831		Convict. on cr. ch'g. causes bond forfeiture.				Remov. w.o. claim on services = kidn.: p'n. by fine & impr.		See VIII	N. immig. to give bonds. See II. Travellers allowed Sls.			See V, VIII		*Rev. Laws, 1831*, pp. 183, 375	217, 220
Feb. 10, 1851								Limits militia to Wh. males. Suffrage: limited to Wh. See XI	See XI		Sl'y abolished.	No N. to settle in St. Contracts void. Fines to go to coloniz. of N. willing to emigr.		*Constitution, Bill of Rights*, 37; ii, 5; xii, 1; xiii	216, 220
March 5, 1852								Intermarriage void bet. Wh. & those w. 1/8 or more N. blood.						Hurd, II, 131	216

Apr. 28, 1852									See XI			Indiana Colony to be bo't in Africa. $5,000 approp. for coloniz. fund.	See XI	Rev. Stat. (1852), I, 222	220
June 18, 1852												Unlawful for N. to settle or become inhabitant. Enforces Constit., 1851, xiii.		Hurd, II, 131; Rev. Stat. (1852), I, 67	
Feb. 14, 1853								Right of evidence denied those w. 1/8 or more N. blood.						Laws, 1853, p. 60	216
March 3, 1853									See XI			Further approp. for coloniz. fund.	See XI	Acts, 1853, p. 23	220
March 1, 1855									See XI			Further approp. for coloniz. fund.	See XI	Acts, 1855, p. 87	220

*Re-enacted 1831.
**Held unconstitut. 1849-50 (Hurd II, 129, Note).

IOWA

Iowa was part of the Louisiana Territory in which the colonial law of France prevailed. It was thus within the district of Louisiana in 1804, and within the Territory of Missouri in 1812. As such it was within the terms of the Act of Congress of March 6, 1820, by which in section 8 it was enacted "that in all territory ceded by France to the United States under the name of Louisiana, . . . not included within the limits of the State contemplated by this act (Missouri), slavery and involuntary servitude otherwise than in the punishment of crimes whereof the parties shall have been duly convicted, shall be, and is hereby forever prohibited."*

On the admission of Missouri as a separate Territory in 1821, the area which later became Iowa appears to have had no local legislative authority until June 28, 1834, when it was made part of Michigan Territory, and, by Act of April 30, 1836, of Wisconsin Territory. In 1838 the Territorial Government of Iowa was established; and Iowa was admitted as a State in 1846.

The act of establishing the territory secured to the inhabitants all the rights and privileges of the Territory of Wisconsin, and thus slavery is prohibited by this act as well as by the act of 1820.

*Thorpe, Federal and State Constitutions, IV, 2148.

Date	Property Rights	Crimes By	Crimes Against	Runaway Patrol Laws	Insurrection and Conspiracy	Protection: Slaves and Free Negroes	Teaching and Preaching	Discrimination and Disabilities	Importation and Exportation	Limitation of Slavery	Emancipation and Abolition	Free Negroes	Resolutions and Sundries	Source	Pages in Text
	I	II		III	IV	V	VI	VII	VIII	IX	X	XI	XII		
Jan. 21, 1839				Procedure for claiming r'ys.				See XI	Permitted to travellers thru St. w. servants.			Not allowed to settle w. o. certif. of freed. & security of $500.		Terr. Iowa, Statutes, 1838-9, pp. 65-7	220, 222
Jan. 6,* 1840								Intermarriage void and illegal.						Laws, 1839-40, p. 42	216
May 18, 1846								Suffrage: limited to Wh. males.			Sl'y prohibited.			Constitution, 1, 23; 11, 1	214, 220
Feb. 5, 1851		See VII						Not competent witn. ag. Wh.	See XI			F'd. to settle. Resident F.N. not affected.		Laws, 1850, pp. 172, 322	216, 220

*Code of 1851 does not have this provision among marriage laws.

KANSAS TERRITORY

Prior to the Act of 1854 organizing the Territories of Nebraska and Kansas, the land now included in Kansas was under the jurisdiction, first of Louisiana (1804), then of Missouri (1812). Although it was not finally admitted to the Union until 1861, it is of peculiar interest because of the dramatic controversy regarding slavery, shown in the various Constitutions submitted, which raged there during the years just before the Civil War.

Date	Property Rights	Crimes: By	Crimes: Against	Runaway Patrol Laws	Insurrection and Conspiracy	Protection: Slaves and Free Negroes	Teaching and Preaching	Discrimination and Disabilities	Importation and Exportation	Limitation of Slavery	Emancipation and Abolition	Free Negroes	Resolutions and Sundries	Source	Pages in Text
	I	II		III	IV	V	VI	VII	VIII	IX	X	XI	XII		
1855		Rape of Wh.: castration.				Kidn.free person & sell. as Sl.: impr. 10 yrs.		See II, Wh. p'n. by impr. 5 yrs.						Kan. Terr. Statutes, 1855, pp. 242-4.	217
1855						See X					Procedure for suits of freed.			Ibid., 381	
1855				Procedure in case of fugitives.										Ibid., 386	222
1855								Intermarriage illegal and void.						Ibid., 488	217
Sept. 15, 1855	Circl. lit.deny. r't. in Sls.: 2 yrs. impr.*	Abolitionists not to sit on jury in cases arising under this Act. See IV		Aid.escape: death or impr. 10 yrs.Prevent. arrest of r'ys.: 2 yrs. impr.	Rebell.: death. Rais. or aid. insur., advocat. rebell. thru speech or writ., circl. lit.: death. Circl. lit. to cause disob. & dissat.: impr. 5 yrs.							See IV		Ibid., 715-7	215, 216
Feb. 9, 1858	Repeals Act of Sept.15, 1855**	See I		See I	See I									Laws, 1857-8, p. 345	

*Section repealed Feb. 5, 1857 (Laws, 1857, p. 77).
**Passed over Governor's veto.

KANSAS TERRITORY

Date	I	II	III	IV	V	VI	VII	VIII	IX	X	XI	XII	Source	Pages
July 29. 1859 *							Suffrage: limited to Wh.			Sl'y abolished.			Constitution, Bill of Rights, 1, 6: Kan. Terr., Laws, 1861, p. 48, 57	214, 220
Feb. 23, 1860										Sl'y prohibited.**			Laws, 1860, p. 200	214

*Thorpe gives date of 1855.
**Passed over Governor's veto.

MAINE

Maine was separated from Massachusetts and admitted to the Union as a separate State in 1820.

Date	Property Rights	Crimes By	Crimes Against	Runaway Patrol Laws	Insurrection and Conspiracy	Protection: Slaves and Free Negroes	Teaching and Preaching	Discrimination and Disabilities	Importation and Exportation	Limitation of Slavery	Emancipation and Abolition	Free Negroes	Resolutions and Sundries	Source	Pages in Text
	I	II		III	IV	V	VI	VII	VIII	IX	X	XI	XII		
1819								Suffrage extended to all males.						Constitution, ii, 1; Public Acts, 1820-1830, p. x; Laws, 1821-34, I, 22	220
Feb. 19, 1821								Intermarriage f'd.						Laws, 1821-34, I, 420	216
March 15, 1838						Kidn. F.N.: impr. 5 yrs. or $1000 fine.						See V		Publ. Acts, 1838, p. 470	217
July 27, 1849										Ag. exten. of Sl'y. to new Terr's.			Resol. See IX	Acts & Resolves, 1849, p. 192	224
March 17,* 1855				Judges not to take cogniz. of claims for fugitives arrested under Act of Cong. of 1850.										Ibid., 1855, p. 207	223
March 17, 1855				Repeal of Fugitive Sl. law.							Abolition of Sl'y. in D.C.		Resol. See III, X	Ibid., 1855, p. 261	224
Apr. 10, 1856										Ag. exten. of Sl'y. Kan.-Neb. controversy.			Resol. See X	Ibid., 1856, p. 366	224

*Rev. Stat. of 1857, p. 491, ch. 80, sec. 53 has only provision of Apr. 14, 1857, and not that of March 17, 1855. The latter is, however, in Rev. Stat., 1855, ch. 182, §2.3.

MAINE

Date	I	II		III	IV	V	VI	VII	VIII	IX	X	XI	XII	Source	Pages
Apr. 14,* 1857				County attor-neys to give le-gal aid to fugi-tives.										Ibid., 1857, p. 28	224
Apr. 15, 1857										Kan.-Neb. con-tro-versy.			Resol. See IX	Ibid., 1857, p. 58	224
Apr. 15, 1857						Attempts to exer-cise au-thority over Sls. imported: p'n. by fine & impr.					Frees all Sls. bro't. into St.			Ibid., 1857, p. 38	217
Apr. 4, 1859											Ag. Sl'y.		Resol. See X, and con-demning U.S. Su-preme Ct. for Dred Scott de-cision.	Ibid., 1859, p. 286	224

*Rev. Stat. of 1857, p. 491, ch. 80, sec. 53 has only provision of Apr. 14, 1857, and not that of March 17, 1855. The latter is, however, in Rev. Stat., 1855, ch. 182, §2,3.

MASSACHUSETTS

Massachusetts is the oldest of the New England colonies and its laws have been preserved from the first compact. It is also one of the two New England States in which the slave trade reached importance. As Miss Donnan states, this traffic began at a surprisingly early date, before that of Rhode Island, and continued throughout the colonial period.* It was also here that the abolition sentiment found its most fertile soil. For these reasons Massachusetts was chosen as the New England State in which to trace the slave laws from the early colonial records.

*See Donnan, Documents Illustrative of the History of the Slave Trade, III, 1.

Date	Property Rights	Crimes: By	Crimes: Against	Runaway Patrol Laws	Insurrection and Conspiracy	Protection: Slaves and Free Negroes	Teaching and Preaching	Discrimination and Disabilities	Importation and Exportation	Limitation of Slavery	Emancipation and Abolition	Free Negroes	Resolutions and Sundries	Source	Pages in Text
	I	II		III	IV	V	VI	VII	VIII	IX	X	XI	XII		
MASSACHUSETTS COLONY															
1641						Such (See X) sh. have liberties & Christian usage of Law of Israel.					Ordered: "That there shall never be any Bond-slaverie." War captives & those sell. themselves excepted.			Liberty No.91, in the following editions: Colonial Laws, Whitmore ed. of 1887, p. 10; 1889, p. 10; also facsimile ed. of 1648, p.4	65
Nov. 4,* 1646						Steal. N's. in Africa condemned.			N's. unlawfully import. to be sent back.					Col. Rec., II, 136,168; III,84 (slightly different spelling)	
May 27, 1652								See XI				N.** servants, 16-60, enlisted & trained w. militia.		Ibid., III, 268; IV, pt. 1, 86	
May 1656								See XI				No N's. to be armed or trained		Ibid., III, 397; IV, pt. 1, under "Military Orders"	
1692/3	Sls. assessed at £20 estate.													Acts & Resolves, I, 92	
March 2, 1693/4								Tavern keepers not to allow N. servants to drink w. o. perm. fr. Master.				See VII		Ibid., I, 154	

*This order of the General Court followed the stealing of some Negroes in Guinea by a Captain Smith and a Mr. Keyser. Documents connected with the case and the Order are reprinted in Donnan, Doc. III, of Hist. of Slave Trade, III, 4-8. Miss Donnan says regarding this Order, "Though Massachusetts' protests against the slave trade began at an early date it is hardly possible to ascribe them to this episode, as do some writers. The burden of the objection to the importation of 1646 was not against the trade but against the violence by which the slaves have been acquired" (Ibid., p. 8 fn.).

**Law reads "Scotsmen, Negers, & Indians inhabiting with or servants to the English."

MASSACHUSETTS COLONY

Date	I	II		III	IV	V	VI	VII	VIII	IX	X	XI	XII	Source	Pages
March 2, 1693/4		N. servants p'n. by whip. for steal. goods.						Penalty for buy. goods fr. N. or Ind. servants = restoration, or, if sold, double value & fine.				See II, VII		Ibid., I, 156	
Nov. 22, 1693/4								Exempts N's. from militia.				See VII		Ibid., I, 130	
May 30, 1694											Discouragement to christening Sls. may be removed by a law taking away pretext that baptism releases them fr. servitude.		Memorial fr. ministers to Gov.'r & Gen. Assembly.	Ibid., I, 537; Archives, XI, 79	
March 15, 1694/5	Sls. taxed 1s. as personal estate.											N. servants' poll tax 1s.		Acts & Resolves, I, 199	
June 18, 1694/5	Sls. taxed 1s.											N. servants ov. 16, poll tax 1s.		Ibid., I, 167	
Sept. 14, 1694/5	Sls. taxed 2s.											N. servants, poll tax 2s.		Ibid., I, 179	
Oct. 27, 1694/5	Tax cont.											Tax cont.		Ibid., I, 187	
1695/6*	N. Sls. assessed: males ov. 14 at £20 estate; females at £14.											N. servants tax cont.		Ibid., I, 214	
June 17,** 1696	Taxed as personal estate.											Tax cont.		Ibid., I, 240	
Dec. 19, 1696	As above.											Tax cont.		Ibid., I, 258	

June 19, 1697	As above.													Ibid., I, 278	
Oct. 29, 1697	As above.													Ibid., I, 302	
June 13, 1698		Whip. not ov. 20 stripes for stealing.						Buy.or sell,stolen goods fr. N.'s. p'n.: restoration or forfeiture of double value of goods.				See II		Ibid., I,325; Acts & Laws (1698)*** ch. vi; Acts & Laws (1742),p. 92 Acts & Laws (1759),p. 82;	
June 21, 1698								Drink.in taverns f'd.				See VII		A & R. I,327,ch. 10;(1699),p.122 (1726),ch.viii, p. 101 (1742), p. 94 (1759) ch. viii, p. 84	
March 23, 1699/1700	As above.													A & R., I, 413	
June 30, 1701/2	As above.													Ibid., I, 483	
June 25, 1702	As above.													Ibid., I, 495	
July 28, 1703											No emanc. unless ₤50 security ag. becoming publ. charge.			A & R.,I,519 (1699), p. 245 (1726), p. 176 (1742), p. 157 (1759), p. 144	
Dec. 1, 1703		See VII						Not to be abroad af. 9 P.M. unless on errand of Master. Sent to House of Correction.				See VII		A & R., I,535-6 (1699), p. 256 (1726), p. 177 (1742), pp.158-9 (1759), p. 145	
July 27, 1703/4	As above.													A & R., I, 521	
June 24, 1704/5	As above.													Ibid., I, 551	

*This assessment value for taxation purposes continues year after year.
**In "An Act for Granting unto His Majesty a Tax Upon Polls & Estates", Art. 1: "All Indian, mulatto and negro servants to be estimated as personal estate." This classification occurs in all the revenue bills and is but briefly noted chronologically in the table.
***Date of ed. only will be given after this entry.

MASSACHUSETTS COLONY

Date	I	II		III	IV	V	VI	VII	VIII	IX	X	XI	XII	Source	Pages
June 30, 1705/6	As above.													Ibid., I, 569	
Dec. 5, 1705/6		Impr. & sold out of colony for VII. Strik. Christian p'n. by whip.				No Master to reasonably deny marriage to one of same race.		Fornication & Intermarriage w. Wh's f'd, p'n.: see II. No authorized person to perform marriage. See V.	£4 duty on all import. af. 1/5/06. Drawback allowed for export. or death.			See V, VII		Ibid., I, 578 (1699), pp. 288-9 (1705), ch. vi (1726), pp. 187-8 (1759), p. 152	
June 12, 1707		See XI		Harb. f'd.				F.N.'s not to harb. w.o. Master's consent. Fine 5s. See XI				Civic duties on roads in place of military duties of Wh's. Sent to House of Correction if unwill. to work. In case of alarm, to attend parade of militia. See VII		A & R., I, 606 (1699), pp. 309-10 (1726), p. 191 (1742), p. 171 (1759), p. 157	
June 13, 1707	As above.													A & R., I, 610	
Nov. 29, * 1707	Sls. estimated as other personal property @ 1 penny on £1 Males, 14 & over @ £20 value; females 14 & over, at £15 value.											Servants rated as poll (12 pence) and not as personal property.		A & R., I, 615	

Feb. 26,** 1708/9									Af.1/5/09 duty on Ind. Sls. = that on African. No Ind.to be import. af. 29/8/09. Bounty to those import. Wh. servants					A & R., I, 634	
Aug. 3, 1712									An Act to prohibit import.of Ind. servants or Sls.			See VIII		A & R., I, 698 (1742), ch. v, p. 188	
Sept. 14, *** 1728/9									As duty on N's often evaded, entry must be made w. clerk. £8 penalty. To continue 7 yrs.					Ibid., II, 517 (1726),ch. xiv, p. 414	
Jan. 26, 1738/9									Masters to give lists of N's.Those bro't. by land,entered & duty p'd. Drawback allowed. To continue 10 yrs.					Ibid., II,981-2	
Feb. 2, 1744/5								No lottery tickets to be delivered N's. N's. not entitled to benefit of lottery.				See VII		Ibid., XIII,p. 431	
Jan. 31, **** 1745/6								F'd: sell. liq. to Sls.						Ibid., III, 257	

*"An Act for better Inquiry into the Ratable Estate of the Respective Towns of this Province." This rating continued practically every year, and other references to the acts will be omitted from this table.
**An Act to encourage the Importation of white servants.
***This law does not appear in 1759 edition.
****Excise Act.

MASSACHUSETTS COLONY

Date	I	II	III	IV	V	VI	VII	VIII	IX	X	XI	XII	Source	Pages
Feb. 10, 1746/7		Swear. or curs. p'n by fine or public whip.									See II		*Ibid.*, III, 319	
June 23, * 1748/9							F'd.: Sell. liq. to Sl. Penalty £3.						*Ibid.*, III, 414	
June 18, 1751/2							As above, penalty £2.						*Ibid.*, III, 571	
June 4, 1752/3							As above.						*Ibid.*, III, 613	
Jan. 5, 1752/3		Break. & exting. lamps, p'n. by whip., 10 lashes. See VII					Wh's. for same offence p'n. by fine or impr.				See II, VII		*Ibid.*, III, 646	
Jan. 5, 1752/3	Masters respon-sible for ser-vants.	Parad., assembl., bonfires, carry. pageants, mas-quer. at night p'n by whip. In force 3 yrs.					See II				See II		*Ibid.*, III, 648	
June 15, 1753/4							F'd.: sell. liq. to Sls.						*Ibid.*, III, 676	
Dec. 19, 1754/5							As above. Penalty increased to £4.						*Ibid.*, III, 785	
March 4, 1756							As above.						*Ibid.*, III, 906	
Oct. 15, 1756/7		Act of Jan. 5, 1752/3, reenacted for 5 yrs.											*Ibid.*, III, 997-8	
Feb. 5, 1757							As above.						*Ibid.*, III, 1013	
Jan. 26, 1758							As above.						*Ibid.*, IV, 59	

March 20, 1758/9								As above.						Ibid., IV, 204	
Feb. 13, 1759/60								As above.						Ibid., IV, 308	
Jan. 30, 1761/2								As above.						Ibid., IV, 497	
Sept. 16, 1776/7									F'd to sell N's. captured on high seas. To be treat. as pris. of war.					Ibid., XIX, 568	
June 8, 1779/80								Exempt fr. draft.				See VII		Ibid., XXI, 30, 397	
MASSACHUSETTS															
1780								Suffrage: to male citizens with freehold estate.						Constitution, ch. i, sec. ii, art. ii; ch. i, sec. iii, art. iv.	220
June 22, 1786								Intermarriage f'd. bet. Wh's., N's & Indians.						Acts & Resolves, 1786-7, p. 10; Perp. Laws (1801), I, 323-4	216, 217
March 26, 1788						See XI			Import. fr. Africa f'd. Fine: £50 for each Sl. £200 for vessel - Insurance void.			Friend of kidn. Negroes may bring action.		Acts & Resolves, 1786-7, pp. 615-7; Perp. Laws (1801), I, 407-9	218
March 26, 1788												Only those who are subjects of U.S. or Morocco allowed to stay in St. ov. 2 mos.		Acts & Resolves, 1786-7, p. 626; Perp. Laws (1801), I, 413	218

*Excise Act.

MASSACHUSETTS

Date	I	II		III	IV	V	VI	VII	VIII	IX	X	XI	XII	Source	Pages
Feb., 24, 1820										Ag. exten-sion			Resol. See IX.	Resolves, Jan. 1820, p. 151	224
Apr. 1, 1834								Repeals Act of 1786 as regards Indians						Laws, 1834-6, XIII, p. 256	217
Apr. 12, 1837													Resol. condemn. Congr. Act to lay Sl'y pe-tit. etc. on table.	Resolves, 1835-8, p. 559	224
Apr. 23, 1838											Abolish Sl'y in D.C.		Resol. See X	Ibid., 742	224
Apr. 23, 1838										Ag. ad-mit. new Sl. Sts.			Resol. See IX	Ibid., 743	
March 21, 1839									Cong. to enforce laws to f'd. Sl. tr.				Resol. See VIII	A & R., 1839, p. 97	224
March 21,* 23, 1840									Cong. sh'd. suppress Sl. tr. in D.C. & bet. Sts.	No new Sl. Sts. to be ad-mitted			Resol.'s ag. H. of Rep's. resol. to deny r't. to Sl'y. petitions. See VIII, IX	Ibid., 1840, pp. 262-4	
March 3, 1842									Cong. to use every effort to suppress Sl. tr.				Resol. See VIII.	Ibid., 1842, p. 563	210
Feb. 25, 1843								Acts f'd. inter-marriage repealed.						Laws & Resolves, 1843-5, p. 4	217
March 24, 1843				No judge to take cogni-zance of cases un. Act of Cong. of Feb. 12, 1793										Ibid., 33	223

Feb. 27, 1847										Ag.exten.to new Terr's. See XII			Resol. See IX	Laws, 1847-50, p. 506	224
Apr. 26, 1847										Con-demn. Annex. of Texas as ex-tend. Sl. terr.			Resol. See IX	Ibid., 541	
Feb. 27, 1849									To abo-lish Sl. tr.in D.C.	Ag. Sl'y in N. Mex.& Cal.	Abolish Sl'y in D.C.		Resol. See VIII, IX,X	Laws, 1847-50 (1849), p. 200	224
May 1, 1850										Ag.ex-ten. & admis. of new Sl. Sts.			Resol. See IX	Laws, 1850, pp. 518-20	
Apr. 6, 1855				Fugitive Sl. Act of Cong. declared uncon-stitu-tional.									Resol. See III	Laws, 1854-5 (1855), p. 946	224
May 21,** 1855				Extended Act of 1843 to apply to Fugitive Sl. Act of 1850; prohi-bited arrest of r'ys; disqua-lified atty's acting for claim-ants: prohib. St.Mili-tia fr. aid.in appreh.										Laws, 1854-5 (1855), pp. 924-9	223

*By governor's direction, according to request of legislature, copies of these resolutions were transmitted. In his message the governor deplores the Congressional measure denying the right to petition against slavery as tending "to inflame" and as "inexpedient and unjust".

**Passed over Governor's veto.

MASSACHUSETTS

Date	I	II		III	IV	V	VI	VII	VIII	IX	X	XI	XII	Source	Pages
March 27, 1858				Sec. of Act of 1855 disqual. att'ys. repeal-ed.										*Ibid.*, 1858, p. 151	223

MICHIGAN

The French established a colony in what is now Michigan in 1702. It was ceded with other French territory to Great Britain in 1763, and annexed to Quebec. Under the treaties of 1782-1783, it became a part of the United States. Its first territorial government was established in 1805 by the act dividing Indiana Territory into two separate governments; and in 1837 it was admitted to the Union.

Date	Property Rights	Crimes By	Crimes Against	Runaway Patrol Laws	Insurrection and Conspiracy	Protection: Slaves and Free Negroes	Teaching and Preaching	Discrimination and Disabilities	Importation and Exportation	Limitation of Slavery	Emancipation and Abolition	Free Negroes	Resolutions and Sundries	Source	Pages in Text
	I	II		III	IV	V	VI	VII	VIII	IX	X	XI	XII		
1816*			See V.			Kidn.F.N. : impr. 5 yrs.						See V.		Terr. Laws (1871), I, 127	217
1816		Corp.p'n.for all but cap.cr's.												Ibid., I, 133	215
Apr. 13, 1827 **				Conceal, p'n.by fine. Proceed's for r'ys.		Kidn.F.N. : impr. 1-10 yrs.			Immig.N. req. to give security for good behavior & self support. See XI			Certif. of freed.req. before settlement. Registration req. See V,VIII		Ibid., II, 634-6	217, 220, 222
Nov. 2, 1835								Limits suff. to Wh. males.			Sl'y abolished.			Constitution, ii, 1; xi; Rev. Stat. (1846), pp. 19, 25	214, 220
1846 ***								Intermarriage f'd.						Rev. Stat. (1846), p. 330	217
Feb. 13, 1855				R'ys protected; defended; entitled to habeas corpus; trial by jury. Sheriffs not to impr. See V		Decl.F.N. a fugitive to secure removal: p'n by impr. 3-5 yrs. Kidn. : fine or impr. See III						See V		Laws, 1855, pp. 413-16	217, 223
Feb. 15, 1859						Forcibly impris. or transport.fr. St. or claim.any person import.as Sl.: fine or impr.			See V			See V		Laws, 1859, p. 526	217

*Hurd gives date as 1815. **Hurd gives as 2 Acts. ***Hurd gives 1838.

NEBRASKA

Nebraska had the same territorial history as Kansas until it was made a Territory in 1854. It was not admitted to the Union as a State until 1864.

Date	Property Rights	Crimes By	Crimes Against	Runaway Patrol Laws	Insurrection and Conspiracy	Protection: Slaves and Free Negroes	Teaching and Preaching	Discrimination and Disabilities	Importation and Exportation	Limitation of Slavery	Emancipation and Abolition	Free Negroes	Resolutions and Sundries	Source	Pages in Text
	I	II		III	IV	V	VI	VII	VIII	IX	X	XI	XII		
1857		See VII						F'd: to give testimony in any cause.				See VII		_Laws_, _1857_, p. 107	216
1858			See V	Kidn. f'd.		Entic. F. N. to sell as Sl. p'n by impr. 1-7 yrs.						See V		_Laws_, _1858_, p. 49	217, 224
Jan. 15,* 1861											Sl'y Abolished.			_Laws_, _1861_, p. 43	214

*Passed over Governor's veto.

NEW HAMPSHIRE

As one of the original thirteen colonies, New Hampshire carried over into the Federal Period the body of laws under which it had operated as a Colony.

Date	Property Rights	Crimes By	Crimes Against	Runaway Patrol Laws	Insurrection and Conspiracy	Protection: Slaves and Free Negroes	Teaching and Preaching	Discrimination and Disabilities	Importation and Exportation	Limitation of Slavery	Emancipation and Abolition	Free Negroes	Resolutions and Sundries	Source	Pages in Text
	I	II		III	IV	V	VI	VII	VIII	IX	X	XI	XII		
June 2, 1784											Sl'y.abolished thru Bill of Rights.			Constitution, Bill of Rights; Laws (1792), p. 22	212
Dec. 28, 1792								Enrollment in militia limited to Wh.			As above.			Laws (1805), p. 251	216
1843 and 1847								Gives suffrage to every male citizen except paupers.						Rev. Stat. (1843), p.81; Laws, 1847, ch.492 and Compiled Stat. (1854), p. 85	220
June 30, 1847										Ag.exten.to new Terr's.	Ag.Sl'y.		Resol. See IX, X	Laws, 1847, p. 488	224
Dec. 29 & 30, 1848, Jan. 4, 1849										Ag.exten.to new Terr's.	Ag.Sl'y.		Resol. See IX, X	Laws, 1848, pp. 710-12	224
July 7, 1849										Ag.exten.to new Terr's.	Ag.Sl'y.		Resol. See IX, X	Laws, 1849, pp. 874-6	224
July 14, 1855										Ag.exten.			Resol. On Mo. Compr. & Kan.-Neb. bill. See IX	Laws, 1855, pp. 1613-5	224
July 12, 1856										Ag.encroachment of Sl. power of the South.			Resol. See IX	Laws, 1856, p. 1781.	224

NEW HAMPSHIRE

Date	I	II	III	IV	V	VI	VII	VIII	IX	X	XI	XII	Source	Pages
June 26, 1857					Color or previous cond. of serv't. no bar to citizenship. Holding as Sl. any N! = felony.		Gives suffrage to all N's equal w. Wh's See V			Sls. bro't. in: free. See V	See V, VII	See V	Laws, 1857, p.1876	218, 220
June 27, 1857									See XII			On Dred Scott decision.	Laws, 1857, p. 1925	224
July 26, 1858									Ag. exten. to new Sts.			Resol. See IX	Laws, 1858, p. 2031	224
June 28, 1859										Ag. Sl'y.		Resol. See X	Laws, 1859, p. 2140	224

NEW JERSEY

As one of the original thirteen colonies, New Jersey carried over into the Federal Period the body of laws under which it had operated as a Colony.

Date	Property Rights	Crimes By	Crimes Against	Runaway Patrol Laws	Insurrection and Conspiracy	Protection: Slaves and Free Negroes	Teaching and Preaching	Discrimination and Disabilities	Importation and Exportation	Limitation of Slavery	Emancipation and Abolition	Free Negroes	Resolutions and Sundries	Source	Pages in Text
	I	II		III	IV	V	VI	VII	VIII	IX	X	XI	XII		
1781								Enlist. in Continent. Army f'd.						Wilson's Acts, 1776-83, p. 209	216
1786									F'd.		Emanc.authorized.			Rev. Laws (1821), p. 377	212, 218
Nov. 24, 1788									Suppl. Act.		Suppl.Act.			Ibid., 376	
March 18, 1796		Corp. p'n. for non-cap. cr's.												Ibid., 262	215
March 14,* 1798		Begging: own. fined.	Habeas corpus granted.	Harb. f'd. R'ys. arrested.	Disord. assembl's, dispersed, p'n.: whip.	Sell. to persons unable to maintain: fine. Cruel treat. f'd. Own.resp. for maintenance.	Born af. 26/11/ 1788: taught to read.	Witn. only ag.Sls. F'd.: tr., empl't. w.o. permit, at l.af. 10 P.M., hunt. on Sunday. F. N. f'd. to travel or work w.o. certif. of freed.	Sl. tr. f'd. Vessels confi sc. No import. except by settlers. Prov.made for export. by own's.		Emanc.bet. 21 & 40 by writing or will. Certif. of health req. Un. 21 & ov.40 bonds req.	Non-resident not to travel,reside or work w.o. certif. See VII		Ibid., 369-79	212, 215, 216, 217, 218, 221, 222
Feb. 20, 1799		Disord. & disob. Sls. sent to work house.												Patterson's Laws (1800),p.379;Rev. Laws (1821),p.444	215
1804 **											Childr. born af. 1804: free, serv's.until 21 & 25.			Hurd, II, 65	212
1812						See VIII			F'ds.removal of Sls. except w. their consent.		See VIII			Rev. Laws (1821), p. 373	219

*Repeals 1713/14 (regulations), 1755/6 (regulations), 1768 (crime), 1769 (duty), 1786 (manumission), 1788 (supplement to 1786).
**Hurd says this law is to be found in Laws, 251, and that it was amended in 1806 (Laws, 668), and supplemented in 1808 (Laws, 112), in 1809 (Laws, 200), in 1811 (Laws, 313), and reenacted in 1820. Unfortunately the Session Laws for these years were not available.

NEW JERSEY

Date	I	II		III	IV	V	VI	VII	VIII	IX	X	XI	XII	Source	Pages
Feb. 24, 1820		Criminals c'ld be export.				Consent of Sl. nec. for export. w. own.			Export. f'd: Sl. freed. Sl. tr. vessels forfeited. Exceptions: resid. own. Sl. 5 yrs., remov. fr. St.: criminals. See V		Certify.of childr. & serv's.un. law of 1804. Deeds of manu. recorded.			Rev. Laws (1821), pp. 679-85	219
May 31, 1820		Arson, burgl., rape, assault p'n. accord. to law or by exportation.						See II	See II					Ibid., 736	215
June 1, 1820								Suffrage: Wh. males only. *						Ibid., 741	220
June 10, 1820												Childr.freed un. Act of 1804 to settle where born, or may choose residence.	See XI	Ibid., 765	212
Nov. 3, 1820		Own's. to give bond for transp. criminals.							See II					Ibid., 793	
Dec. 26, 1826				Procedure for r'ys Seizing w.o. leave, fine & impr.										Laws, 1826, p. 90	222
Feb. 15, 1837				Jury tr'l. in r'y. cases.										Laws, 1836-7, p. 134	222

1844								Suffrage: Wh. males only. **						<u>Rev. Stat.</u> (1847), p. xxiii	220
April 18, 1846							Support of former Sls. & childr. provided for.		Export. of apprentices f'd.		Prohib. Sl'y. Former Sls. apprentices until able to support themselves			<u>Rev. Stat.</u> (1847), p. 382	213
Feb. 16, 1847										Ag. exten. to new terr.			Resol. See IX	<u>Laws</u>, <u>1847</u>, p. 188	224
March 2, 1849										Ag. exten. to new terr.			Resol. See IX	<u>Laws</u>, <u>1849</u>, p. 334	224

*Constitution of July 2, 1776 granted suffrage to "all inhabitants . . . . , of full age, who are worth fifty pounds" and who have lived 12 months in the Colony.
**Thorpe's reprint says "every male citizen".

NEW MEXICO

New Mexico was originally included within the boundaries of the Republic of Texas. It became a Territory in 1850, although the final cession by Mexico did not take place until 1853.

Date	Property Rights	Crimes By	Crimes Against	Runaway Patrol Laws	Insurrection and Conspiracy	Protection: Slaves and Free Negroes	Teaching and Preaching	Discrimination and Disabilities	Importation and Exportation	Limitation of Slavery	Emancipation and Abolition	Free Negroes	Resolutions and Sundries	Source	Pages in Text
	I	II		III	IV	V	VI	VII	VIII	IX	X	XI	XII		
Feb. 3, 1859	Act to provide for protection of property in Sls.	Forg. papers of freed.: impr. Disord. cond.: corp. p'n. Rape: death. Fines commuted to whip. at discr. of Court.	Murd. of Sl. = Murd. of Wh.	R'y Sl.: procedure. Steal. or aid. escape: fine.	Incit. insur.; furnish. arms to Sls.: p'n.	Own. bonded to provide food, cloth., shelter. Inhum. treat. f'd. Hold. F.N. as Sl.: impr. See IIb		F'd.: tr.; gam.; go. at l., w.o. pass; hir. o.; witn. ag. Wh.; intermarriage. Slave applies only to African race.			Emanc. f'd.	See IIa, V		Laws, 1858-9, pp. 64-80	214, 215-6, 217, 218

NEW YORK

As one of the original thirteen colonies, New York carried over into the Federal Period the body of laws under which it had operated as a Colony.

Date	Property Rights	Crimes By	Crimes Against	Runaway Patrol Laws	Insurrection and Conspiracy	Protection: Slaves and Free Negroes	Teaching and Preaching	Discrimination and Disabilities	Importation and Exportation	Limitation of Slavery	Emancipation and Abolition	Free Negroes	Resolutions and Sundries	Source	Pages in Text
	I	II		III	IV	V	VI	VII	VIII	IX	X	XI	XII		
1781	Land granted owner as compen.										Manu. of Sls. serv. in regiments.			Laws (1886-7), I, 351	212
Apr. 12, 1785		Jury tr., in cap. cr's.							Import. as mdse. f'd. Sl. freed.		Proceeding. No bonds needed where Sls. un. 50, or able to provide for themselves.			Ibid., II, 121-22	217
May 1, 1786						Destitute cared for by St.					Sls. forfited to St.: freed.			Ibid., II, 316; Greenleaf's Laws (1792), I, 278	212
Feb. 22, 1788*	See II, X	Tresp. & begg.: Own. liable.		Harb. f'd.		Own. to maintain destitute; sale of aged & infirm f'd to those unable to care for them.		F'd: employ., tr., & liq., w.o. consent of own. Witn. only ag. each other.	Buy., & sell. Sls. to another St. f'd. Sls. free.		Sls. to be Sls. until emanc. Childr. follow status of Mother. No emanc. thru baptism.	Own. liable, support of freed.		Laws (1886-7), II, 675-9; Greenleaf's Laws (1792), II, 85-8.	216, 219, 222
March 22, 1790		Criminals may be transp. fr. St.							See IIa		Certif. of emanc.: how issued.			Greenleaf's Laws (1792), II, 312	215
March 9, 1798											Quaker emanc. legalized.			Laws (1886-7), IV, 168	
March 29, 1799											Childr. born af. 4/7/1799: free. Serv. until 28 & 25. Registered.	Own's. may abandon childr. to care of St. See X		Ibid., IV, 388	212
April 8, 1801									No Sls. import. except by settlers.		No emanc. thru baptism.			Ibid., V, 548; Hurd, II, 53-4	219
1802											Amends acts 1799 & 1801.			Hurd, II, 54	

* An act revising all slave laws, and combining them into one act.

NEW YORK

Date	I	II		III	IV	V	VI	VII	VIII	IX	X	XI	XII	Source	Pages
March 31, 1807									10 yr.residents permit.to remove fr. St. Sls.owned 10 yrs.					Laws (1809),V,92	219
Feb. 19, 1808						See X,XI					Act to incorporate Soc. to manu. Sls. and to protect freed.			Ibid., V, 256	
Apr. 1, 1808			See V			Sell.F.N. p'n by impr. to 14 yrs.; 2d off. life.						See V		Ibid., V, 300	217
Feb. 17, 1809						R't to recover property in courts. See XI		Intermarriage bet. Sls. and free: valid; childr. legitimate.			Childr. c'ld be emanc. if parents able to support.	C'ld hold & inherit estates,as if free born. See V, VII, X		Ibid., V, 450	217
March 30, 1810							Childr. of Sl. Mother, taught to read.							Laws (1812), VI, 33	221
April 5, 1810						Own. liable for support. See VIII			Emigrants fr.Va.& Md. See X		In certain counties, Sls. c'ld be hired out 7 yrs, then freed. See VIII			Ibid., VI, 81	
April 9, 1811								Certif.of freed. req.bef.voting.				See VII		Ibid., VI, 288	220
1813			See V			Fine added to p'n un. 1808.						See V		Laws, 1813, II, 209	217
1813									Amends Act 1801					Hurd, II, 54-55	
Oct. 24, 1814	See X										Freedom on discharge fr. colored regiments.			Laws, 1814 (38 sess.), 23	

1816						See XI						An act for maintenance of F. N.		Hurd, II, 55	
March 31, 1817							Childr. of Sls. to be taught to read. bef.18, & rec.4 quarters schooling.		Travel. perm. to bring in Sls.for 9 mos.; residents perm. to remove fr. St. for 6 mos. Sls. import. af. 4/7/99 to serve till 28 & 25.		Freed all born bef. 4/7/99,af. 4/7/1827.			Laws, 1817, pp. 140-4	213, 219, 221
April 9, 1819									Export.of Sls.: fine & impr.		Sls. sold to non-residents freed.			Laws, 1819-21, V, 172	219
1821								Suffrage: 3 yrs. cit., & freehold of $250.				See VII		Constitution, II, 1	220, 221
Sept. 1826								Suffrage disability kept.				See VII		Constitutional Amendments, II	
1828				Procedure for return of r'ys.		Kidn. & sell. as Sl. p'n.			Immig.may bring Sls. born af.4/7/96 and bef. 4/7/1827. Import. af.1817:- serve until 28 & 25. Import. af. 1828:- serve until 21.		Frees all Sls. born or bro't to St. No person to be sold as Sl. See VIII			Rev. Stat. (1829),I,659; Hurd,II,57-8	213
1829									Term of service changed to 21.		See VIII			Rev. Stat. (1829),I,657	219
1834				Amends 1828.										Hurd, II, 58	
May 19, 1836													Resol.St. r't to settle Sl.quest.	Laws, 1836, p.811	

NEW YORK

Date	I	II		III	IV	V	VI	VII	VIII	IX	X	XI	XII	Source	Pages
Feb. 12, 1840													Resol.ag. Cong. action on Sl. petitions, etc.	Laws, 1840, p. 349	224
May 6, 1840				Claims for r'ys settled by Jury.										Ibid. (63 sess.), 174	209, 222
May 14, 1840						Agents app't. to claim kidn.F.N.						See V		Ibid., 319	217
May 25, 1841									Repeals, 1801, 1817, & 1819; term of serv., 1829.			Repeals 1817.		Laws, 1841, p. 227	219
April 11, 1842				Concern. fugitive Sls. fr. Va.									Resol. See III	Laws, 1842 (65 sess.), 419	224
May 14, 1845							Schools for N. childr.					See VI		Laws, 1845 (68 sess.), 327	221
Jan. 27, 1847										Ag.extension to Mex. terr.			Resol. See IX	Laws, 1847 (70 sess.), 377	224
Jan. 10, 1848										As above.			Resol. See IX	Laws, 1848 (71 sess.), 578	224
Jan. 16, 1852													Resol. Census, Wh.& colored.	Laws, 1852 (75 sess.), 729	
April 14, 1852							Colored schools, Canandaigua.	To attend colored schools only.				See VI, VII		Ibid., 430	

April 16-18, 1857											See XII No Sl'y in St.		Resol. See X. Also Supreme Ct. has impaired confidence of people.	Laws, 1857, II, 797	224
April 8, 1859								For amend. to abol. property qualif. (See 1821)				See VII	Resol. See VII	Laws, 1859, p. 1209	224
April 12-18, 1859									Condemning re-opening of Sl. tr.				Resol. See VIII	Ibid., 1210	224
April 13, 1860								Property qualif. of N. voters abolished.				See VII		Amend. to Const.; in Laws, 1860, p. 597	

OHIO

Massachusetts, Connecticut and Virginia claimed the whole or parts of the lands from which the present State of Ohio was taken. These claims were ceded to the Federal Government, and Ohio became a State in 1803.

Date	Property Rights	Crimes By	Crimes Against	Runaway Patrol Laws	Insurrection and Conspiracy	Protection: Slaves and Free Negroes	Teaching and Preaching	Discrimination and Disabilities	Importation and Exportation	Limitation of Slavery	Emancipation and Abolition	Free Negroes	Resolutions and Sundries	Source	Pages in Text
	I	II		III	IV	V	VI	VII	VIII	IX	X	XI	XII		
1795								Selling liq. to Sls. f'd.						Hurd, II, 115	216
1802											Sl'y abolished.			Constitution, VIII, 2	214
Jan. 5, 1804				Harb. f'd. Procedure for claiming r'ys.				F'd to hire N. w.o. certif.				No N. to settle w.o. certif. of freed. Residents to regist. & secure certif.		Acts, 1804, pp. 356, 357	220, 223
Jan. 25, 1807								Not a witn. ag. Wh's.				Immig. N's to provide bonds for good behav.		Laws, 1806, p. 53	216, 220
Jan. 25, 1819						Kidn. & transp. F. N. out of St. p'n by impr. 1-10 yrs.						See V		Laws, 1818, p. 56	217
Feb. 15, 1831						Repeals 1819 & provides impr. of 3-7 yrs.								Statutes, 1831, p. 442	217
Feb. 26, 1839				Procedure for r'ys in accordance w. U.S. Constit.										Statutes, 1841, p. 595	222, 223
Jan. 19, 1843				Repeals 1839.										Acts, 1843, p. 13	222, 223
Feb. 10, 1849							Separate schools, where not admitted to white schools.	Repeals 1807.				Repeals 1807.		Acts, 1849, pp. 17, 18	216, 221

Apr. 16, 1857				Prohib. impr. of fugitives.										Laws, 1857, p. 170	224
Apr. 17, 1857				Fine & impr. for arresting fugitives.		Provides ag. kidn. F.N. See VIII			Import. of Sls.= false impr.: p'n by fine & impr. Slaves free.			See V		Ibid., 1857, pp. 186, 221	217, 220, 224
Feb. 23, 1858				Repeals 1857.										Laws, 1858, p. 10	220, 224
March 27, 1858									Repeals 1858.					Ibid., p. 19	
Apr. 2, 1859								Election judges to reject persons of African blood claiming to be Wh.						Acts, 1859, p. 120	220
Apr. 4, 1859				Authorizes jailors to receive r'ys by auth. of U.S. officials.										Ibid., 1859. p. 158	224

OREGON TERRITORY

Oregon became a part of the United States by the treaty with Great Britain of 1846. The territorial government was organized in 1848, and it was admitted as a State in 1859.

Date	Property Rights	Crimes By	Crimes Against	Runaway Patrol Laws	Insurrection and Conspiracy	Protection: Slaves and Free Negroes	Teaching and Preaching	Discrimination and Disabilities	Importation and Exportation	Limitation of Slavery	Emancipation and Abolition	Free Negroes	Resolutions and Sundries	Source	Pages in Text
	I	II		III	IV	V	VI	VII	VIII	IX	X	XI	XII		
July 5, 1845*											Sl'y prohibited.			Art's of Compact, in Hurd, II, 215; citing Statutes, 39	
Aug. 14, 1848								Suffrage: to Wh. males.						Act of Congress, sec. 5, in Laws of Oregon, 1845-64, p. 69	220
Sept. 26, 1849 **									Immig. of F.N. f'd. Capts. transp. N's: fined.			See VIII		Laws, 1850, p. 181	
Jan. 30, 1854									Repeals Act of 1849.					Statutes, 1855, p. 551	
1855								Not witness ag. Wh.						Ibid., 130	216
Sept. 18, 1857								Suffrage f'd.: Negro, Chinaman & Mulatto. See XI	Import. of F.N. f'd.		No Sl'y in St.	F.N. not residing in St. at time of Const. f'd to enter, hold real estate, or make contracts, etc.		Constitution, 1, 35,36; 11, 6	214, 220

*Hurd states that this is "earliest act of local legislation."

**The reason for this act is stated, as follows: "Whereas, situated as the people of Oregon are, in the midst of an Indian population, it would be highly dangerous to allow free Negroes and mulattoes to reside in the Territory, or to intermix with the Indians, instilling into their minds feelings of hostility against the white race."

PENNSYLVANIA

The first State to adopt the principle of gradual emancipation, and the seat of the Quaker abolition movement, Pennsylvania has been selected as the best representative of the Middle Colonies in which to trace slave legislation through the Colonial Period and down into the Civil War.

Date	Property Rights	Crimes By	Crimes Against	Runaway Patrol Laws	Insurrection and Conspiracy	Protection: Slaves and Free Negroes	Teaching and Preaching	Discrimination and Disabilities	Importation and Exportation	Limitation of Slavery	Emancipation and Abolition	Free Negroes	Resolutions and Sundries	Source	Pages in Text
	I	II		III	IV	V	VI	VII	VIII	IX	X	XI	XII		
PENNSYLVANIA COLONY *															
Sept. 22, 1676											No Christian to be kept in bond sl'y, except indentured servants. A record of service kept.			Duke of York, Laws, 13	
April 25, 1682								Suffrage limited to free men.						Frame of Government, II, in Thorpe, Am. Charters, V, 3055	
1700		An Act for trial of N's.										See II		Noted in Dallas, Laws, I, 21	
1705 **		Repeals 1700. 2 Just's & 6 freeholders to try N's charged w. murder, burgl., manslaughter, rape. Duties & powers of court. Steal. over $5: branded w. T; attempt. rape: branded w. R.			See VII			Not allowed to carry guns or to assemble (4 or more).	No Indian Sl. to be import. af. 25/3/06					Ibid., I, 62-3. Collection of all Laws, 83-6; Laws of Province, 69-72.	
1710									An Act for laying a duty on N's.					Dallas, Laws, I, 87; Collection, 116, ch. clxxii	
1711									Act to provont import. of N's & Indians.					Laws of the Province, 113; Collection, 127, ch. clxxxiii	

*As the compilations and digests give in full only those laws in force at the time of publication, it is possible here to list only the titles of those laws which had expired, together with such meager information as is given in footnotes.
**Repealed by the Act of 1780.

PENNSYLVANIA COLONY

Date	I	II		III	IV	V	VI	VII	VIII	IX	X	XI	XII	Source	Pages
June 7, 1712									Suppl. Act to prevent import. & Act laying an import duty.					Dallas, Laws, I, 93, 94.	
Feb. 20, 1713									Repeals 1710.					Ibid., I, 87	
1714									Act laying duty on N's imported.					Collection, 154, ch. ccix	
May 28, 1715									Act for laying duty on N's imported.					Dallas, Laws, I, 116; Laws of Province, 145	
1717									Continuing duty on N's.					Laws of Province, 169; Collection, 180.	
Feb. 22, 1718									Continuing duty on N's.					Dallas, Laws, I, 124	
July 21, 1719									Repeals Act of May 28, 1715.					Ibid., I, 148	
1720									Duty on import. of N's.					Laws of Province, 178	
Feb. 24, 1721									Act laying duty on N's cont. until 14/5/22.					Dallas, Laws, I, 151	
Aug. 26, 1721								Giving Sls. liq. or entertain. them w.o. consent of Master p'n by fine.						Laws of Province, 187; Collection, 195; Dallas, Laws, I, 157	
May 12, 1722									Act for laying duty on N's imported.					Laws of Province, 203; Collection, 209; Dallas, Laws, I, 168	

1725									As above.					Collections, 333	
March 5, 1725/6									As above.					Dallas, Laws, I, 230	
March 5, 1725/6	Own.compens.for exec. Sls.	£5 above import. duty to be paid for N's convicted of crime. Cohab. of Wh. & N. p'n by fine of £30 or sold as serv. for 7 yrs.		F.N. herb. or entic. fined 5s. 1st hr., 1s. thereafter. Reward for apreh.N. 10 miles fr. home w.o. leave. Harb.or conceal. except in bad weather p'n by 30s. every 24 hrs.				F'd: tr. w. Sls., hir. o., tippl. in tavern: p'n by whip. Absent w.o. leave after 9 P. M. p'n by whip. Intermarriage: penalty of £100 for marrying Wh. & N.; N. marrying Wh. to be Sl. for life. See also III	Import duty £5. See II		Security to be given for emanc. N's.	Those neglecting to work to be bound out 1 yr. Childr.& those un.21, to be bound out to 24 & 21. See III,VII Sold if unable to pay fine.		Laws of Province, 321-5; Collection, 335-40; Dallas, Laws, I, 230	
1728									40s. duty on all N's import.Settlers to pay no duty.					Collection, 354,359	
May 10, 1729									£2 duty on N's import. for sale; none, for personal use. Drawbacks allowed.					Laws of Province, 357-61; Dallas, Laws, I, 241	
March 14, 1761									Duty on N's import.					Dallas, Laws, I, 416	
April 22, 1761									Suppl.to above.					Ibid., I, 406	
Feb. 26, 1773									Act for making perpetual,duty on N's import.					Ibid., I, 671	

PENNSYLVANIA COLONY

Date	I	II	III	IV	V	VI	VII	VIII	IX	X	XI	XII	Source	Pages
Sept. 7, 1778								Act to collect duties on N's, due 1776.					Ibid., I, 782	
PENNSYLVANIA														
March 1, 1780	Own.com-pens.for exec.	Tried like other inhab. Repeals 1705/6,1725/6.	R'ys fr. other St's.not to bene-fit fr. act. Proce-dure.		Own. re-spons.for support unless emanc. bef. 28.		Sl. not witn. ag. freeman	Repeals 1705, 1725, 1761, 1773, 1778 (duty on import.). Sls.im-port. as mdse.: free.		Sl'y abol. Childr. born af. act serv. until 28; then free. Sls.to be regis-ter-ed.	No contract to hold N. longer than 7 years or until 28. See II,VII		Stat. at L., 1682-1801 (1904), X, 67-73	212, 216, 217, 222
1780												Captured N. at sea, del'v'd to cap-tors	Ibid., 101	
Oct. 1, 1781										War refu-gees al-lowed to keep Sls. until 6 mos. af. end of war.			Ibid., 367-8	
March 29, 1788					Removal & sell. of Sls. fr. St.:fine. Separat. of fami-lies f'd for ov.10 miles.			Sls.bro't in by settlers: free. Sl. tr. f'd; vessels forfeit-ed. F'd: export. w.o.con-sent.		See VIII	Childr.lia-ble for serv. until 28 - must be registered. Serv.for 7 yrs.not to be export. w.o. consent.		Ibid., XIII, 52-6	217, 218

Dec. 8, 1789											Incorp. Penn.Soc. for Abol.& for the Relief of F.N.	See X	See X	<u>Ibid.</u>, 424	
Dec. 22, 1819										Ag.ad-mis-sion of Mo. as Sl. St.			Resol. See IX.	<u>Acts</u>, <u>1819-20</u>, p. 198	224
March 27, 1820						Kidn. de-fined. Sell. kidn. F. N.: fine $500-$2000, & 7-21 yrs. impr.						See V		<u>Ibid.</u>, 104-6	217
Apr. 2, 1821						Those im-port. in-digent.N. serv's ov.28 li-able for their support.								<u>Acts</u>, <u>1820-21</u>, p. 254	
March 25, 1826				Proceed-ings for r'ys.		Re-enacts 1820. Knowingly tr. in kidn.Sls. p'n. Pen-alties of 1780 & 1788 re-pealed & 1820 sub-stit.								<u>Acts</u>, <u>1825-6</u>, pp. 150-5	217, 222, 223
April 17, 1827				All sales of r'ys void.Re-moval of Sl.fr. St.as mdse. fined.					See III					<u>Acts</u>, <u>1826-7</u>, p. 485	222
Jan. 23, 1829											Abol. of Sl'y in D.C.		Resol. See X	<u>Acts</u>, <u>1828-9</u>, p. 371	224
1838								Suffrage: Wh. free-men.						<u>Constitution</u>, iii, 1.	220

PENNSYLVANIA

Date	I	II	III	IV	V	VI	VII	VIII	IX	X	XI	XII	Source	Pages
March 3, 1847			Seiz. r'ys unlawfully: fined. Writ of habeas corpus allowed. Fugitive law amended, increasing difficulty of claimant.		P'n. for kidn. increased.		Provisions of 1780 re incompetence as witness repealed.			Repeals 1781.			Acts, 1847, pp. 206-8	216, 217
March 31, 1860					Kidn. penalty: fine up to $2000 & impr. hard labor up to 12 yrs.								Acts, 1860, p. 406	217

RHODE ISLAND

As one of the original thirteen colonies, Rhode Island carried over into the Federal Period the body of laws under which it had operated as a Colony.

Date	Property Rights	Crimes By	Crimes Against	Runaway Patrol Laws	Insurrection and Conspiracy	Protection: Slaves and Free Negroes	Teaching and Preaching	Discrimination and Disabilities	Importation and Exportation	Limitation of Slavery	Emancipation and Abolition	Free Negroes	Resolutions and Sundries	Source	Pages in Text
	I	II		III	IV	V	VI	VII	VIII	IX	X	XI	XII		
1750								F'd.: liq. & entert.: go. at l. af. 9 P.M.; tr. w.o. consent.						Publ. Laws (1798), 611-12	
1770								F'd.: liq. & entert.: go. at l. af. 9 P.M.; tr. w.o. consent.				Disord. houses kept by, to be broken up and keeper bonded.		Ibid., 611-12	
1774) 1776) 1779) 1784) 1785) 1798)		Criminal Sl's may be transported.		Conceal. & harb. f'd.		Remov. w. o. consent of Sl. = loss of r't in Sl. Own. respon. for emanc. Sl. See XI			No import. Sl. freed. & to enjoy personal property. Travellers excepted.		Certif. of emanc. to be issued in V, VIII. Born af. 1/3/1784 to serve for life. Childr. freed. Gradual emanc. law.	Childr. freed un. X to be supported by own. of Mother or Town until 21. F.N. supported as other paupers.		Ibid., 607-11	218, 222
Feb. 14, 17; Mar. 8, May 5, Oct. 25, 1778	Value estim. & own. compens.												Sls. allowed to enlist.	Bartlett's Index, 1758-1850 (1856), p. 327	
Oct. 5, 1779						Sls. not to be sold o. of St. w.o. their consent.								Ibid., 329	
Dec. 3, 1782											For abolit.		Petition of Quakers. See X.	Ibid., 331	
Feb. 6, May 18, 1784									Import. & sale f'd.		Grad. abol. of Sls. Childr. born af. 1/3/1784: free.			Ibid., 332; Hurd, II, 49	213

RHODE ISLAND

Date	I	II		III	IV	V	VI	VII	VIII	IX	X	XI	XII	Source	Pages
1785											Repeals part of Act of 1784.			Bartlett's Index, 333; Hurd, II, 49	
1787									To prevent Sl. tr.		Encourage abolit.			Bartlett's Index, 333	218
June 5, 1790											Additional Act to charter abol. Soc.			Ibid., 334	
Nov. 5, 1842								Suffrage: no discrimination as to color; a property qual.			Sl'y f'd.			Constitution, 1, 4; 11, 1.	213, 220
1844								Intermarriage f'd: minister fined.						Rev. of Publ. Laws of R.I. (1844), pp. 268-9	217
1844						Provides for support of indigent Sls. See XI						F.N. emanc. before 30, supported by Masters, or Town.		Ibid., 342	
Jan. 1848				F'ds sheriffs, etc., recog. Cong. Act of Feb. 12, 1793.										Publ. Laws, 1846-8, p. 714	223
1848											Abol. of Sl'y in D.C. or removal of govern. to free St.		Resol. See X	Acts, 1848 (May), 11.	224
1849										Ag. extens. of Sl'y in new Terr's.			Resol. See IX	Acts, 1849 (Jan.), p. 35	224
1850													Resol. ag. Sl'y	Acts, 1850 (May), p. 6	224
1854				Prov. of 1848 ex-extended to Act of Sept. 18, 1850.										Rev. Stat. (1857), pp. 532-76	223

UTAH*

Utah, like California, was part of the Mexican organization until after the Treaty of Guadalupe Hidalgo of 1848. It became a Territory in 1850.

Date	Property Rights	Crimes By	Crimes Against	Runaway Patrol Laws	Insurrection and Conspiracy	Protection: Slaves and Free Negroes	Teaching and Preaching	Discrimination and Disabilities	Importation and Exportation	Limitation of Slavery	Emancipation and Abolition	Free Negroes	Resolutions and Sundries	Source	Pages in Text
	I	II		III	IV	V	VI	VII	VIII	IX	X	XI	XII		
March 18, 1849								Suffrage & military service: white males.						<u>Const. for State of Deseret</u>**	214-5, 220
1852 Servant law	Own. entitled to services after satisfac. evidence is filed. May p'n serv.					Duties toward serv. Forfeit serv. when guilty of abuse.	Serv's to be sent to school.	Duties of serv. to Master outlined. Intermarriage, sexual intercourse w. serv's of African race: f'd.				See I, V, VII.		<u>Laws of 1855</u>, ch.17	215, 217, 221

*See Hurd, II, 211-215 for all references to Utah given here.
**Hurd states that this Constitution is printed with the <u>Acts of the Assemblies of the Territory of Utah</u> (Salt Lake City, 1855).

VERMONT

The State of Vermont was originally claimed by Massachusetts, New Hampshire and New York. Massachusetts and New Hampshire gave their consent to its independence in 1782, but New York did not agree to its admission as a State until 1790.

Date	Property Rights	Crimes By	Crimes Against	Runaway Patrol Laws	Insurrection and Conspiracy	Protection: Slaves and Free Negroes	Teaching and Preaching	Discrimination and Disabilities	Importation and Exportation	Limitation of Slavery	Emancipation and Abolition	Free Negroes	Resolutions and Sundries	Source	Pages in Text
	I	II		III	IV	V	VI	VII	VIII	IX	X	XI	XII		
July 2, 1777								Suffrage: free men.			No male af.21, no female af. 18 held as Sls.			<u>Constitution</u>, ch. I, secs. 1,8	212
Oct. 30, 1780* (Hurd, 1786)						Transp. or sell. as Sl.: fine.			See V		See V	See V		<u>Statutes</u>, <u>1787</u>, p. 117 Hurd, II, 37-38, quotes <u>Laws, 1787</u>, qto., p. 105	
Oct. 22, 1825											Abol. Sl'y in U.S.		Resol. See X	<u>Laws</u>, <u>1825</u>, p. 146	224
Nov. 16, 1836									Claimed Cong. r't to abol. Sl. tr.				Resol. See VIII	<u>Laws</u>, <u>1836</u>, p. 44	224
1837										Ag.annex.of Texas, or any Sl.St.			Resol. See IX	<u>Laws</u>, <u>1837</u>, p. 60	224
1838										As above.			Resol. See IX, & ag.Cong. Act to table Sl. resols. etc.	<u>Laws</u>, <u>1838</u>, p. 23	224
1839										As above			Resol. as above.	<u>Laws</u>, <u>1839</u>, p. 20	224
Oct. 29, 1840			See III	R'ys: tr'l by Jury; aid by St. at-t'y. Removal af. adverse decis.= kidn.		See III								<u>Laws</u>, <u>1840</u>, p. 13	223
1841											Abol.Sl'y in D.C.		Resol. See X	<u>Laws</u>, <u>1841</u>, p. 33	224

1842									Abol. of Sl. tr.		Abol. of Sl'y in D. C.& Terr's.		Resol. See VIII, X	Laws, 1842, p. 97	224
1843									As above.		As above.		Resol. See VIII, X	Laws, 1843, p. 32	224
Nov. 1, 1843				Courts, sheriffs, etc.f'd to re-cog. cases un. Con-gr.Act of Feb. 12,1793. 1840 re-pealed.										Laws, 1843, p. 11	223
1846										Ag.ad-mit. Sl. Sts.			Resol. See IX	Laws, 1846, p. 48	224
1847										As above.			Resol. See IX	Laws, 1847, p. 47	224
1848									Abol. of Sl. tr.		Abol.of Sl'y tr. in D.C. and Terr's.		Resol. See VIII, X	Laws, 1848, p. 40	224
1849									Abol. of Sl.tr.on high seas.		Abol. of Sl'y in D.C.		Resol. See VIII, X	Laws, 1849, p. 48	224
Nov. 13, 1850				R'ys: habeas corpus; aid by St.at-t'ys: tr'd by Jury.		See III								Laws, 1850, p. 9	223
Nov. 13, 1850										Ag.ad-mit. any Sl.St.			Resol. See IX	Ibid., 53	224
1851									Ag.Sl.tr. on high seas un. Am.flag				Resol. See VIII	Laws, 1851, p. 71	224
Nov. 14, 1854						Remov.or sell.F.N. : fine & impr.						See V		Laws, 1854, p. 51	217

*Hurd gives date as 1786. He states that the law does not appear in the Compilations of 1808, and suggests that it may have been repealed with the revision of the laws at the admission of the State in 1791, as conflicting with the fugitive slave provision.

VERMONT

Date	I	II	III	IV	V	VI	VII	VIII	IX	X	XI	XII	Source	Pages
1855									Kans.-Neb. con-trov.			Resol. See IX	Laws, 1855, p. 87	224
Nov. 15, 1855			Fug.Sl. law a viol. of U.S. Const.									Resol. See III	Ibid., p. 91	224
Nov. 25, 1858			Trial by Jury permit-ted both sides.		Hold. as Sl.: fine & impr. Repeals cont'ry Acts.		See XI	No inhab. consid. mdse.	See XI	No inhab. consid. property. Sls. free when brought to St.	Color no bar to r'ts and privileges of citizen-ship.		Laws, 1858, p. 42	213
1858										See XII		Resol. Dred Scott decision.	Laws, 1858, p. 66	224

WASHINGTON TERRITORY

Washington became a part of the United States through the treaty with Great Britain of 1846. Its territorial government was established in 1853.

Date	Property Rights	Crimes By	Crimes Against	Runaway Patrol Laws	Insurrection and Conspiracy	Protection: Slaves and Free Negroes	Teaching and Preaching	Discrimination and Disabilities	Importation and Exportation	Limitation of Slavery	Emancipation and Abolition	Free Negroes	Resolutions and Sundries	Source	Pages in Text
	I	II		III	IV	V	VI	VII	VIII	IX	X	XI	XII		
Jan. 29, 1855								Intermarriage f'd.						Laws, 1854-5, p. 33	217

WISCONSIN

See Illinois for earlier organization of Wisconsin. The territorial government was established in 1836, and it was admitted as a State in 1848.

Date	Property Rights	Crimes By	Crimes Against	Runaway Patrol Laws	Insurrection and Conspiracy	Protection: Slaves and Free Negroes	Teaching and Preaching	Discrimination and Disabilities	Importation and Exportation	Limitation of Slavery	Emancipation and Abolition	Free Negroes	Resolutions and Sundries	Source	Pages in Text
	I	II		III	IV	V	VI	VII	VIII	IX	X	XI	XII		
Apr. 20, 1836								Suffrage: Wh. males only.						Act of Cong. Estab. Terr. Gov., Statutes, 1839, p. 24	
1839						Kidn. & sell. as Sl.: p'n. by fine.						See V		Ibid., 1839, p. 349	217
Feb. 1, 1848								Suffrage: Wh. & Ind. male citiz. of U.S.				Sl'y abolished.		Constitution., 1, 2; iii.	214, 220
March 22, 1849*								Suffrage granted N's.				See VII		Acts & Resol., 1849, p. 85	220
May 27, 1857*								As above.						Ibid., 1857, p. 45	
1858				Dist. Att'y to protect fugitives. 2 witn. req. to prove Sl.		See III								Rev. Stat., 1858, p. 912	224

*The Acts of March 22, 1849 and May 27, 1857 were submitted to the people for ratification as amendments. It was claimed that the Act of 1849 was not ratified, as a smaller vote was cast for the Amendment than for the election of officers. But the Supreme Court of Wisconsin decided that it was unnecessary to have a majority only on this particular act, and that the suffrage was granted Negroes in 1849. See 20 Wis., 571 ff.

INDEX